MUSEUM REGISTRATION METHODS

MUSEUM REGISTRATION METHODS

THIRD EDITION, REVISED

Dorothy H. Dudley, Irma Bezold Wilkinson, and Others

AMERICAN ASSOCIATION OF MUSEUMS
Washington, D.C.
1979

Copyright © 1958, 1968, 1979 by the American Association of Museums, Washington, D.C.

All rights reserved.

Library of Congress Catalogue Card Number: 79-52058

Printed in the United States of America

COVER:

The Artist in His Museum, by Charles Willson Peale
Courtesy of the Pennsylvania Academy of the Fine Arts, Philadelphia

Composed in Linotype Palatino by Monotype Composition Company, Inc., Baltimore, Md.

Printed by Maple Press Company, York, Pa.

Designed by Gerard Valerio, Bookmark Studio

Published 1979, Second printing 1981, Third printing 1989.

CONTENTS

FOREWORD vii

PART 1: BASIC PROCEDURES 1

1: THE REGISTRATION DEPARTMENT 3

2: INCOMING AND OUTGOING MATERIAL 11

3: THE REGISTRATION OF OBJECTS 21

4: MEASURING AND MARKING OBJECTS 41
    Supplement I: Supplies for Marking 56
    Supplement II: Marking Specific Kinds of Objects 57

5: STORAGE AND CARE OF OBJECTS 65
    Supplement: Storage Requirements and Methods 73

6: LOANS FROM MUSEUM COLLECTIONS 89

7: PACKING AND SHIPPING 95

8: IMPORTING AND EXPORTING 115
    Supplement I: Provisions and Documents Required for Duty-Free Entry into the United States 127
    Supplement II: Additional Information and Addresses 134

9: INSURANCE 139
    Supplement: Concise Glossary of Insurance Terms 151

BIBLIOGRAPHY 155

FORMS AND RECORDS 167

PART 2: SPECIFIC APPLICATIONS 199

A: A PROCEDURE FOR ACQUIRING OBJECTS, INCLUDING PARTIAL GIFTS, AT THE MUSEUM OF MODERN ART 201
    BETSY B. JONES

B: A CLASSIFICATION SYSTEM FOR ART OBJECTS 205
    WINIFRED KENNEDY

C: Classifying Paintings, Drawings, and Prints by Media, with a Note on Classifying Constructions   208
   LAWRENCE J. MAJEWSKI

D: Cataloguing in the Metropolitan Museum of Art, with a Note on Adaptations for Small Museums   219
   MARCIA COTTIS HARTY, MARICA VILCEK, AND BRICE RHYNE

E: Cataloguing Prints in the Museum of Modern Art   228
   DOROTHY L. LYTLE AND RIVA CASTLEMAN

F: Inspecting and Describing the Condition of Art Objects   237
   RICHARD D. BUCK

G: Registration Records in a History Museum   245
   MARGOT PAGE PEARSALL AND HOLLY B. ULSETH

H: Registration in a Historic House Museum   253
   DIANE GREENE TAYLOR

I: A Standard Terminology for Describing Objects in a Museum of Anthropology   267
   GERALDINE BRUCKNER

J: A Registrar's Role in a Natural History Museum   281
   ANITA MANNING

K: Accessioning, Marking, and Storing Scientific Collections   301
   WILLIAM A. BURNS AND JEROME G. ROZEN, JR.

L: Registration Methods in a Museum of Science and Industry   307
   STERLING H. RUSTON

M: Computers and Registration: A Definition of Terms   311
   DAVID VANCE

N: Computers and Registration: Principles of Information Management   319
   CAROLE E. RUSH AND ROBERT G. CHENHALL

O: Computers and Registration: A Case Study   335
   HOLLY M. CHAFFEE AND JEFFREY M. NEFF

P: Computers and Registration: Practical Applications   340
   THERESE VARVERIS

Q: Rules for Handling Works of Art   355
   ERIC B. ROWLISON

R: Preparing Art Exhibitions for Travel   367
   VIRGINIA PEARSON AND ELIZABETH L. BURNHAM

S: The Ideal Container for Travel of Humidity-Sensitive Collections   389
   NATHAN STOLOW

T: Planning Ahead: The Registrar's Role in a Building Program   395
   DAVID VANCE

Glossary   409
   PATRICIA NAUERT

Contributors   417

Acknowledgments   421

Index   425

FOREWORD

Museum Registration Methods had its origins in discussions among registrars at annual meetings of the American Association of Museums. While some registrars had had long experience in registering museum accessions and loans, there was little written information available for those who were new to the museum field or whose museums were beginning new loan activities. The need for a manual to describe procedures for registering and cataloguing museum accessions and loans became amplified in the years following the Second World War, as large collections of European art were brought to the United States for exhibition while their museums were being repaired. More art was traveling than ever before, and the people responsible for arranging the exhibitions and registering and handling the works of art keenly felt the lack of a basic text on museum procedures. In 1952 those attending the Registrars Section at the annual meeting of the American Association of Museums voted to support a manual treating these subjects. Dorothy H. Dudley, then registrar at the Museum of Modern Art, and Irma Bezold Wilkinson, then registrar at the Metropolitan Museum of Art, were asked to undertake the project.

The work of these two remarkable women culminated in the publication of *Museum Registration Methods* in 1958. Since that time the role of the museum registrar has become increasingly professional, a tribute to the standards and influence of the book's two authors. Their manual of registration procedures is recognized and well established as the most important reference on the subject. A second edition of the book, published in 1968, was quickly sold out, and work was begun on an expanded edition. Now, on the twentieth anniversary of the first publication of this museum classic, a greatly enlarged and thoroughly updated edition begins a new stage in the long and honorable history of *Museum Registration Methods*.

The basic procedures for the registration of objects set forth in the first edition of *Museum Registration Methods* have not changed; they have proved their effectiveness through time and their adaptability to the requirements of many kinds of museums. One book, however, cannot be comprehensive in the treatment of procedures for all institutions. *Museum Registration Methods* continues to be directed primarily to art museums, but in this edition significant efforts have been made to address the needs of registrars in history and science museums and to demonstrate an understanding of the special requirements of small museums. This edition also acknowledges improvements in methods and materials that have occurred in the museum field in the past ten to twenty years. It incorporates new information on the marking and storage of museum collections and the packing and shipping of objects, changes in tariff laws and regulations governing importing and exporting, and new developments in museum insurance. In addition, authors of articles in part 2 have revised their contributions, and new articles have been added on rules for handling works of art, on registration in a historic house museum and a natural history museum, and on the use of computer technology for museum registration. Portions of the book have been revised specifically for the benefit of students who may be using this as a textbook in the many museum training programs that have become available in recent years. All bibliographies, illustrations, and sample forms and records have been updated, and a glossary of registration terms has been added.

As with the two earlier editions, this third edition of *Museum Registration Methods* would not have been possible without the enthusiastic support of a great many people. Authors of articles and others who have helped in essential ways are featured in the section on contributors. Cooperating museums are listed there as well. In addition, the special assistance and advice of Douglas J. Robinson, registrar at the Hirshhorn Museum and Sculpture Garden, Smithsonian Institution, and Maryell Semal, assistant director of the Japan House Gallery, are acknowledged with warmest appreciation. We also are grateful to editorial consultants Paula A. Degen and Ann Hofstra Grogg for the care with which they guided this revision from its earliest stages to its completion. Finally, the longstanding commitment of the American Association of Museums to the importance of this publication, the generous support of the National Endowment for the Arts, and additional assistance from the Shell Companies Foundation made this book a reality.

The third edition of *Museum Registration Methods* is indeed a product of the collective wisdom and experience of many individuals and institutions. It is chiefly, however, a monument to the work and inspiration of its original authors, whom we recognize here with highest regards and deepest thanks.

KENNETH STARR
President
American Association of Museums

November 1978

DOROTHY H. DUDLEY, 1902–79

*"A teacher affects eternity;
he can never tell where his influence stops."*

The Education of Henry Adams

Museum Registration Methods was in galley proofs when word came of the death January 26, 1979, of its coauthor Dorothy H. Dudley. Only a few days before, she had completed her review of those proofs, culminating nearly a quarter century of researching and writing for three editions of this monumental work. Through this book, through her work as registrar at the Museum of Modern Art from 1936 to 1968, and through her active involvement in the American Association of Museums, she played an instrumental role in defining museum registration and setting standards for professional practices. For all who knew Dorothy Dudley, and especially for those involved with her in this project, the loss of her unfailing good judgment, dedication, and friendship is sorely felt.

PART 1 BASIC PROCEDURES

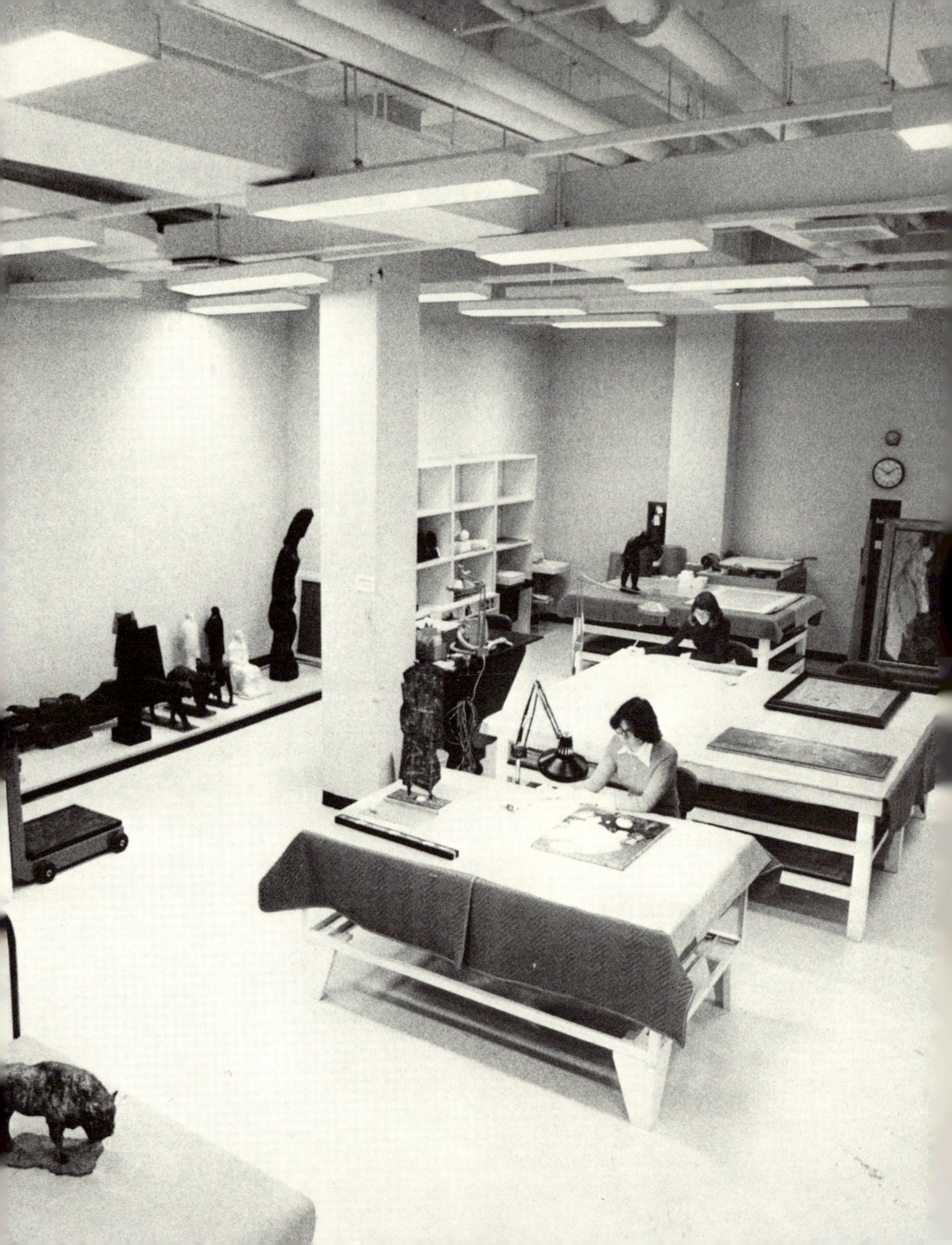

1 THE REGISTRATION DEPARTMENT

Whenever any work of art, or scientific specimen, or historical object enters a museum, it must be identified immediately by some clear and ready means and its entry and subsequent disposition must be accurately and permanently recorded. By whom and how this record is to be maintained are determined by the administrative head of the museum, who may appoint a registrar to be responsible for the records of all the collections in the museum or may make each curator responsible for those of his or her own department. In either case, a sound basic registration system must be established.

The registration and the physical handling of objects as they move in and out of art and history museums are generally responsibilities assigned to a registrar. In science museums, particularly in large museums of natural history, where the handling of different types of specimens requires specialized knowledge and techniques that vary from field to field, this work is frequently a curatorial responsibility. Even in these museums, however, there may be a central office of records where a registrar, or other staff member, maintains a file of accessions, and donors, lenders, and other sources of acquisition, based on information supplied by curators. In small museums of art, science, and history, where no separate registration department exists, the director or curator may be responsible for the registration of all objects.

The procedures outlined in this manual presume the existence of a central registration department where the registrar makes and keeps records and performs other duties closely related to the entry, exit, and safekeeping of museum material. These procedures are the result of the experience of many museums and are methods that have been found to be the most efficient and least burdensome to the museum staff. While the details may vary from one institution to another, the fundamental records and procedures are basically the same. Each museum must decide, after analyzing its needs, how much of this detail to retain.

Fig. 1.1. Work space and equipment to be used in the registration functions of a museum should facilitate the safe handling of museum objects and the processing of all necessary records.

Function

The basic responsibility of a registration department is the recording of all objects that enter or leave the museum. From this follows the responsibility for their safe handling and storage while they are being recorded, for their unpacking, packing, and transportation, and for keeping track of their movement at all times.

Since the first records made should identify an object and serve as a basis for later documentation or cataloguing, it is most important that the entry records be accurate and clear. These entry records are later expanded in various ways and filed under whatever categories—by donors, cultures, materials, and so forth—that will make the information they contain most accessible and useful for the ongoing activities of the museum.

Staff

Although the work done in the registration department does not necessarily require that the registrar and registration staff have expert knowledge of the subjects covered by the museum, they must have sufficient general background in these subjects, and familiarity with the related vocabulary, literature, and documentary sources, to be responsive to the needs of the museum's curatorial departments. Essential prerequisites for registration work include a sound formal education at an accredited college or university and specialized study or experience through internship or in-service training, leading to a knowledge of museum methods and techniques. Some familiarity with business procedures, records management, and data processing is also useful. The staff should read professional publications, attend professional meetings and training programs, and otherwise keep abreast of new techniques in museum registration and record keeping in general in order to realize when equipment and established procedures should be changed or modified.

Above all, the registrar must have a genuine appreciation for the objects that pass through the department and maintain a sense of responsibility for their safety. Registrars may sometimes be required to work on many tasks simultaneously, and so the ability to remain composed and clear thinking is important. The registrar must also have an eye for detail and be able to maintain complete, clear, and accurate records, understanding, however, that such records are not an end in themselves but rather a tool essential to all activities of the museum.

Whether the registrar works alone or with assistants depends not so much on the size of the museum as on the extent of its activities: for instance, whether a large amount of loan material is normally received for special exhibitions, or whether there are a great number of yearly acquisitions. When a large registration staff is required, the registrar should know how to allocate responsibilities. An efficient registration department might consist of a registrar as supervisor; assistants for record keeping, condition reports, and routine processing of forms; cataloguers; secretaries; and persons trained to handle, pack, and unpack the objects. In museums where automatic data processing is in use, the registration staff might also include a computer technician or a cataloguer

Figs. 1.2–3.
The shipping and receiving area of the museum should be designed for safe, efficient handling of all types and sizes of shipments and vehicles. The shipping and receiving area at the Philadelphia Museum of Art, for example, is 80 by 52 feet. In accordance with state codes, it is equipped with ionization detectors and exhaust fans to detect and expel fumes. The parking area is 64 feet long and has a height clearance of 14 feet, 1 inch. Along two sides is an L-shaped dock 48 feet long and 32 feet wide at its base. Built into the dock is a hydraulic lift platform with a capacity of 15,000 pounds. The lift has a vertical travel of 44 inches and is surrounded on two sides by guard rails. The concrete dock is edged with rubber bumpers to protect the hydraulic lift from damage. Wheel chocks on 6-foot chains are kept handy.

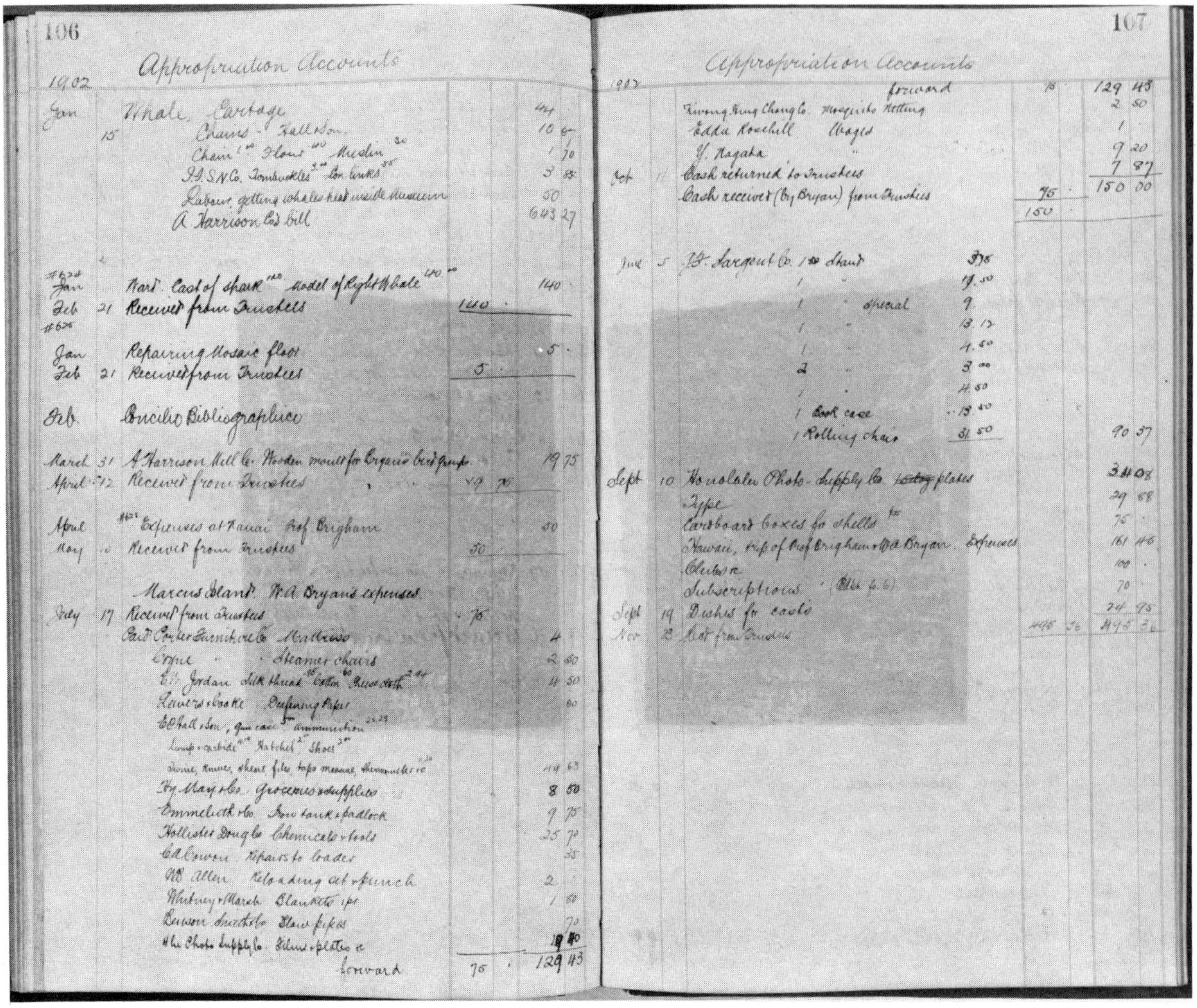

Fig. 1.4.
Archival quality supplies should be used for permanent registration records. The results of acid migration are evident in the darkened areas of these pages in a curator's account book, where a note was inserted. Use of buffered, acid-free paper, cards, and folders can prevent such damage in files.

trained to code and type information directly into the computer. (For a general discussion of computers and registration work, see articles M–P.)

Work Space and Equipment

A registration department should have enough space and equipment to ensure the safe handling and storage of all objects and to enable all necessary records to be made, maintained, and protected. Those who are planning new work space should keep in mind the succession of steps necessary to process objects. The design of new space should accommodate not only the needs of the registration department but also all other departments concerned with the security and safety of museum collections. In addition to the registration office, where the final records are made and kept, there should be adequate space for receiving and unpacking, examining and recording, photographing, storing, and packing and shipping. To ensure minimum handling of the objects, the areas provided for each of these activities should be near to each other and accessible to the service entrance. The registration office and its files may be located either near these working areas or near curatorial departments, depending on the needs of the museum and the physical limitations of the building. (For a general discussion of registration work space, see article T.)

The registration department should be equipped with racks and padded shelves in an area that can be locked for temporary storage of objects awaiting examination. In addition, there should be fireproof file cabinets fitted with locks, a safe or vault for very valuable objects, and a large worktable. Various registration functions will require pads to be placed on the table when fragile objects are examined, and such tools as a magnifying glass, measuring tapes, calipers, triangles, and scales; marking equipment such as tags, labels, ink, and paint;

Fig. 1.5.
A painting cart with upright racks is used for moving paintings and other framed works. Small paintings are stacked across the cart against the racks, as shown here; large paintings are stacked along the length of the cart. The floor of the cart is padded with indoor/outdoor carpeting that has no pile which might snag delicate frames.

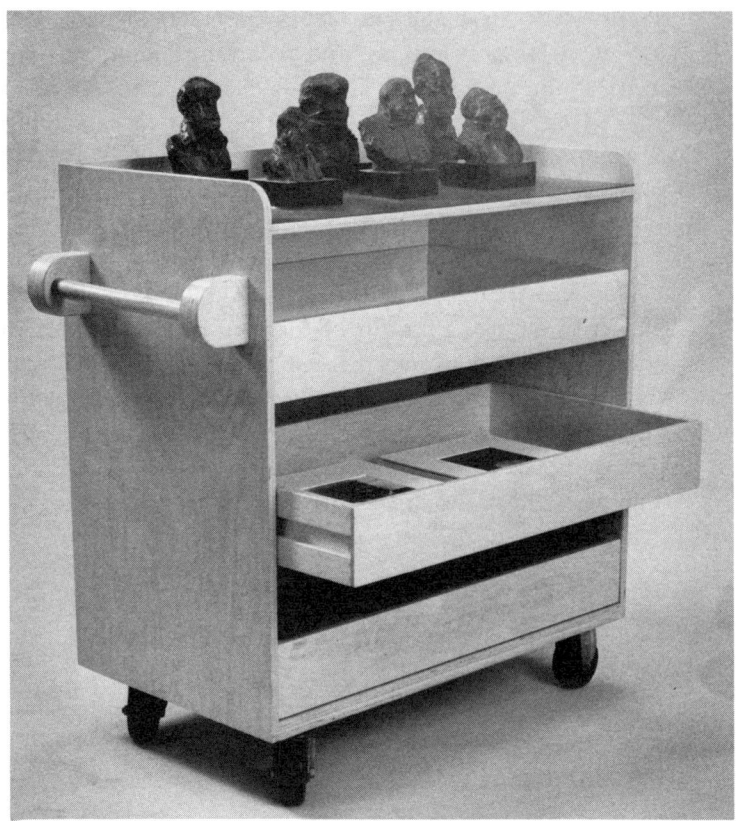

Fig. 1.6.
Trucks with padded, removable trays are used for moving small objects.

and supplies such as acid-free glassine and tissue paper, and Japanese mending tissue for protecting paintings, textiles, unframed prints and drawings, and other objects when necessary. Other useful equipment includes hygrothermographs or sling psychrometers for recording temperature and humidity in storerooms; a camera for making photographs of the objects; and, if the budget permits, some kind of duplicating or photocopying machine for making multiple copies of cards or other records. Where automatic data processing is in use, direct or indirect access to input and output devices, such as a typewriter terminal, will also be needed.

All work surfaces must have good lighting. Worktables should be set under an overhead light for general illumination, and portable lights should be available to give greater illumination on objects being examined. Any fluorescent lights should be fitted with filters to screen out ultraviolet rays, which are harmful to some kinds of museum objects. For moving objects within the building the registrar should have trucks or dollies equipped with racks and padded trays, platform trucks and a forklift for large or heavy objects, and padded trays for small fragile objects to be carried by hand.

See Forms and Records, pages 167–98.

The registrar will need cards and forms for the agreements and receipts that are issued to lenders, donors, or vendors. Other forms may also be useful,

Fig. 1.7.
The registrar's work space should be clean and well lit, with uncrowded areas for examining and recording objects as well as for temporary storage. The safety of objects is of primary concern, as evidenced by the padding of worktables and carts and the use of Fome-Cor separators in bins in the registrar's work area at the Hirshhorn Museum and Sculpture Garden, Smithsonian Institution.

depending on the amount of detailed information required by various departments and the extent of the museum's activities. All permanent records should be kept on a card or paper stock that is buffered and acid free. Additional items to help the registration department perform its functions include an unabridged English-language dictionary, foreign-language dictionaries as needed, a good atlas, a handbook of the department's office procedures, and reference books related to the museum's collections.

2 INCOMING AND OUTGOING MATERIAL

In all museums where a registrar is responsible for checking and recording the movement of material into and out of the museum, it is essential (1) that he or she be notified in writing as far in advance as possible of anticipated arrivals and departures, and (2) that objects be routed through the registration department or recording room. If it is necessary to have objects taken directly to curatorial departments or placed immediately in a gallery or some other location, the registrar should see that they are delivered to that location and examine and record them there. If the receiving and shipping room is not directly under the registrar's control, a close cooperation between the two offices should be maintained to ensure the immediate reporting of all arrivals.

In some museums, the director or curators use forms to notify the registrar to expect, collect, release, or deliver material, and to explain the purpose for which it is being received or released. Other forms are sometimes used by the shipping custodian or building superintendent to report incoming and outgoing material.

See forms I.A, I.B, I.C, and III.A and figures J.2 and K.1.

Incoming Material

In general, objects are received in a museum for study or examination; as purchases, gifts, or bequests for the permanent collection; as loans for special exhibitions; or as extended loans to the museum for long-term, sometimes indefinite, use. For whatever reason an object comes to a museum, the registrar has several responsibilities in receiving the new material.

COLLECTING

For incoming local material, the registrar may be concerned only with arranging pickup by van or station wagon. If the museum owns a van, the registrar can send trained museum personnel to make these collections. If commercial movers must be employed, the registrar must see that they are trained in the careful handling of all material they collect. For this purpose, the museum's trained handlers may assist in moving the objects. Or one commercial mover may be employed regularly, and, if possible, arrangements made to have the same driver and helpers on the truck each time. Through proper supervision

Fig. 2.1.
The registrar's role in recording incoming material may actually begin in the field.

and tactful suggestion, these persons will shortly become experienced in the moving of museum objects.[1]

For domestic shipments from greater distances, the registrar must issue instructions for the collecting, packing, and forwarding of the objects unless these arrangements are made by the lenders, donors, or vendors. For material shipped to the museum from foreign countries, the registrar issues these instructions to the museum's forwarding agents or customs brokers, unless the arrangements are made by the senders. Customs brokers are usually employed to act as freight-forwarding agents, to clear the shipments through customs upon arrival in the United States, and to deliver them to the museum for examination by customs officials. (For a general discussion of packing and shipping, see chapter 7; for a general discussion of importing and exporting, see chapter 8.)

RECEIVING AND UNPACKING

Depending on the size and staff or the policy of the museum, the unpacking of shipments is supervised by the director, curator, registrar, or building superintendent, although this is usually the responsibility of the registrar. In any case, the registrar should be well informed about the techniques of safe packing and handling of museum material. (See, in addition to chapter 7, articles Q–S.)

If upon delivery there is a possibility that the temperature and humidity inside a box differ greatly from the atmosphere of the unpacking area, it may be desirable to wait before opening the box until the contents have had a chance to acclimatize gradually. Both the box and its contents should be carefully examined for signs of insect infestation and, if necessary, isolated for fumigation. For efficiency and for the safety of the objects, only one box should be opened at a time and each object inspected carefully as the wrappings are removed.

All loose wrapping and packing material should be removed from the box and inspected to ensure that no objects or parts of objects are inadvertently left inside. If the packing methods are complex, careful diagrams and/or photographs should be made so that boxes may be repacked in the same manner as received. A radical departure from the original packing procedure is justified only when objects are received in damaged condition because of faulty packing, or when it is obviously not safe to repack them in the same fashion.

Unless the objects are permanent acquisitions, all packing and wrapping materials should be saved and placed back in the boxes, which are then closed, marked or numbered to identify them with the objects, and stored for reuse. If the boxes are to be discarded, lids and boxes should be discarded separately to ensure that no objects are inside and thrown away by mistake.

---

1. Robert P. Sugden, *Safeguarding Works of Art: Storage, Packing, Transportation and Insurance* (New York: Metropolitan Museum of Art, 1948), p. 51.

2: INCOMING AND OUTGOING MATERIAL

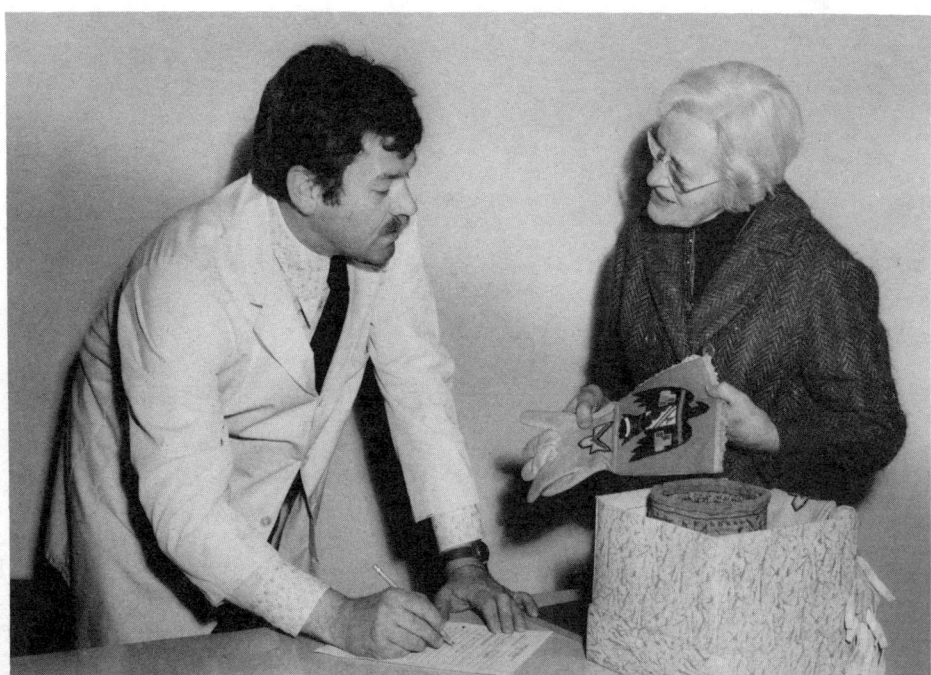

Fig. 2.2.
As soon as an object arrives at a museum, the registrar makes an immediate record of pertinent information and provides the depositor, donor, lender, or vendor with a receipt.

See forms II.A, III.D, and III.H.3 and figures G.6 and L.1.

RECORDS OF ENTRY

Objects enter a museum for a wide variety of purposes, and their final disposition may not be known at the time of entry. Nevertheless, a receipt acknowledging the arrival of the object must be issued and the entry of the object recorded. The receipt documents the deposit of the object and should set forth the conditions whereby the museum accepts responsibility for it. Many museums require the presentation and surrender of this receipt when the object is returned to its depositor or lender.

The first records for all incoming material should include the following information:

IDENTIFYING NUMBER (the temporary deposit number, explained below, except if the object is received on loan for a special exhibition, in which case the loan number may be assigned immediately)

SOURCE (name and address of owner or representative of owner)

DATE OF ENTRY

DESCRIPTION

RECORD OF CONDITION

PURPOSE FOR WHICH RECEIVED (i.e., for study or examination; as gift, bequest, purchase, or loan)

VALUE OR PRICE (if known)

LOCATION IN THE MUSEUM

DISPOSITION (to be completed later, i.e., when accepted for the permanent collection, returned to depositor, etc.)

BASIC PROCEDURES

See form II.A.1.

See form II.A.2 and figure L.1.

See figure 3.9.

For objects placed on temporary deposit, whose final disposition is not known, many museums use the receipt itself as the record of entry. One copy is issued to the depositor, one attached to the object, and one filed as the record of entry. Some museums file the receipt as record of entry under the name of depositor or source. In other museums, where an identifying number is assigned to the object upon entry, the receipt is filed by number. This initial identifying number is here called the temporary deposit number, although a variety of terms are used by museums. It appears on the receipt and on any identifying tags or labels attached to the object. (For a general discussion of labeling objects on temporary deposit, see chapter 4.)

Temporary deposit numbers are usually assigned in simple sequence upon order of arrival—1, 2, 3, 4, etc.—and are often prefixed with an identifying code such as "TD." The numbers may be recorded consecutively in a central log book in order to avoid the skipping or repeating of a number. If a group of objects arrives at the same time from a single source, a separate temporary deposit number need not be assigned to each object. Rather the next available temporary deposit number (e.g., TD 283) is assigned to the collection as a whole and, if necessary, compound numbers (e.g., TD 283.1, TD 283.2, TD 283.3, etc.) can be assigned to each individual object in the collection either immediately or when convenient. Once final disposition of the object is made and it either leaves the museum or is retained as a permanent accession, the temporary deposit number becomes inactive. Many registrars periodically review the temporary deposits currently in the museum's possession and report these to the curators and the director so that objects are not retained on temporary deposit unnecessarily.

In contrast to objects brought into the museum on approval, for examination and study, or for similar purposes for which disposition is not known and adequate documentation cannot take place, the ultimate purpose and disposition of objects received as temporary loans for special exhibitions are known from the beginning. Museums may assign these objects loan numbers immediately upon arrival, bypassing temporary deposit numbers if they are used. Loan numbers are permanent, unique numbers, and are explained in detail, as are loan records, in chapter 3. The registrar will be advised in advance, of course, to expect the loans, so registration can be expedited at the time of entry and the objects will be ready for installation in galleries as quickly as possible.

It is important that the registrar be allowed adequate time to unpack all objects with care, issue the proper receipt, make the required records of entry, tag or label the objects, and, where it is the registration department's responsibility, examine the objects for condition. In order to protect museum objects, pencil rather than pen and ink should be used for recording information or, in fact, for any work in the immediate vicinity of the objects. Later, or in another area, records can be filled in more permanently with ink.

Fig. 2.3.
On-site registration of underwater archaeological recoveries may pose unusual problems. A Revolutionary War shipwreck, directly beneath this Maine State Museum registrar's worktable, yielded thousands of artifacts ranging widely in size, weight, composition, fragility, and significance. In order to prevent rapid deterioration by exposure to air, objects had to be examined, recorded, and numbered while still wet. Special marking materials and techniques were employed to ensure that identifying numbers remained attached and legible through lengthy conservation treatments.

EXAMINING FOR CONDITION

The examination of objects for condition is an important duty of the registrar in many museums. In others, this examination is made by the director, curator, or conservator. (For a general discussion of condition, see article F.) Ideally, objects should be photographed when first received. If the object shows any damage, distortion, or disintegration, these photographs, known as condition photographs, should clearly show every detail of this condition, both as a record and as a guide for the conservator. Photographs of three-dimensional objects should be taken from four vantage points so that, if the object is later damaged, conservators will have an accurate idea of its original shape. The date of the photograph is an important part of the record and should appear on all negatives and prints, along with the object's identifying number. (Photograph records are discussed in greater detail in chapter 3.)

Damage that has occurred in transit must be reported at once to the carrier, the insurance company covering the shipment, and the owner of the object. In such cases, the photographic record of condition must be made for the museum's protection. A self-developing camera is useful for making these photographs if the museum has no photographer on staff. The damaged object, the shipping box, and the packing materials should be preserved for inspection by the representatives of the carrier and the insurance company. No repairs should be made to the damaged object without written permission from the owner. Similarly, if damage has occurred to museum objects being returned from an outgoing loan, the director or curator should authorize any repairs. If the registrar handles insurance on such shipments, he or she must make the claim for damage as soon as the cost of repairs and the extent of depreciation have been determined.

It should be noted that kinetic art objects and working models powered by electricity may present some special condition problems. Such objects should be inspected for safety by a qualified person as soon as they are received to see that wiring complies with the electrical Underwriters' Laboratories standards, that weak or faulty plugs and wires are replaced, and that fuses are installed as needed to prevent overloaded circuits.

STORING

See form I.B.2.

Objects in the custody of the registrar must be safely stored. The space assigned to the registration department for temporary storage during unpacking, packing, inspection, and processing should be under the control of the registrar. There should be a separate area, preferably climate controlled, for the storage of packing boxes and packing materials if they are to be used for future shipments, and the registrar's records should show the location of these boxes. (For a general discussion of the storage and care of collections, see chapter 5.)

2: INCOMING AND OUTGOING MATERIAL

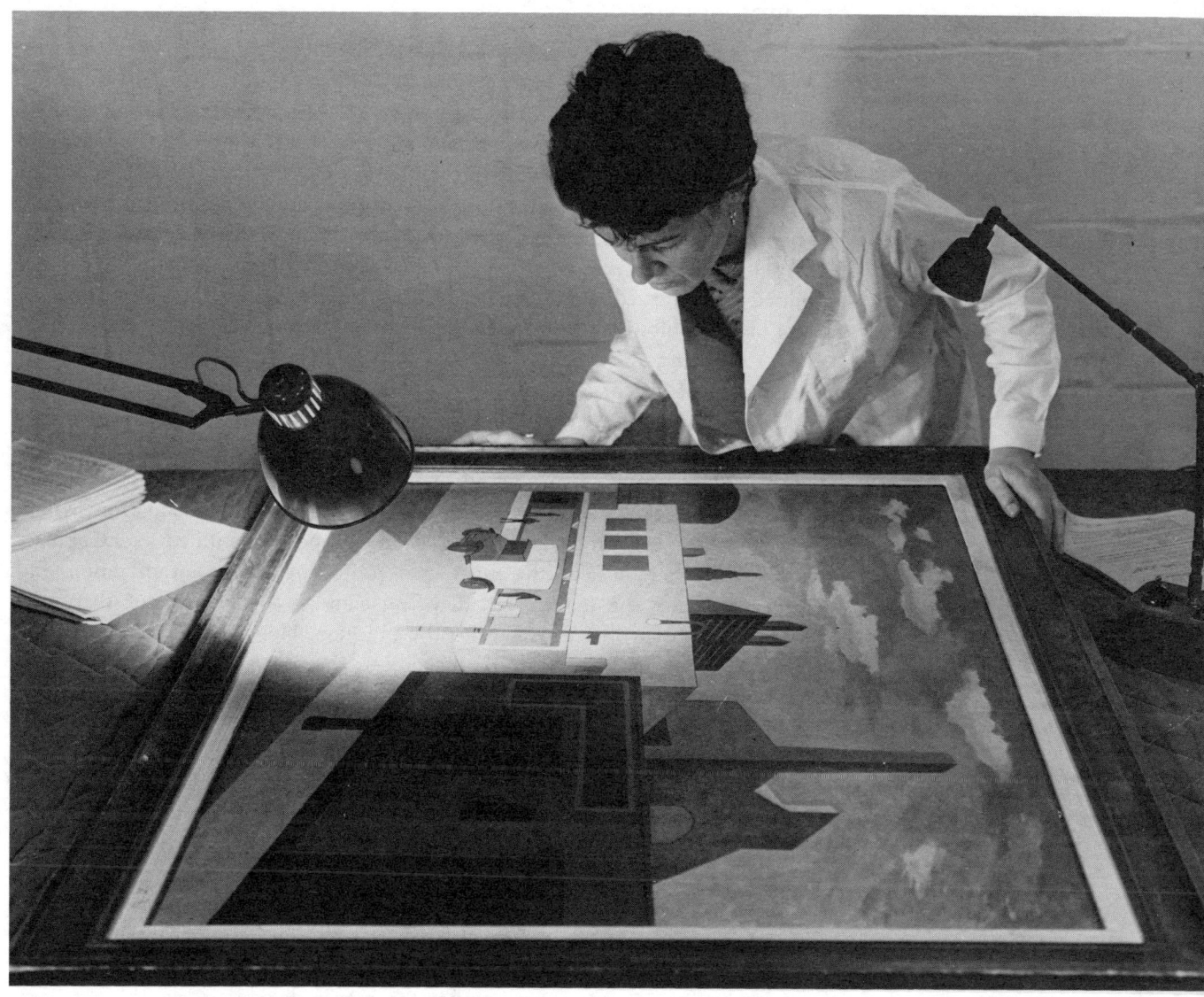

Fig. 2.4.
Incoming objects are carefully examined for condition. Scrutiny under the intense illumination of portable extension lights will reveal flaws and damages in the surface of a painting. All flaws and damages are noted in the object's condition record.

Outgoing Material

See forms I.C, also I.A and III.A.

See form III.E.1.

See forms II.A.2, II.B, III.E, III.G, III.H.1, and III.H.3 and figure J.3.

RECORDS OF EXIT

Complete records of all outgoing shipments of museum material must also be kept by the registrar. Before such shipments are permitted to leave the building, they should be covered by a written order or release signed by the registrar or other responsible staff member. Shipments that consist of objects from the permanent collections or of objects on temporary deposit must first be approved by the director or curator, who notifies the registrar and supplies the necessary information for the records and receipts. (For a general discussion of outgoing loans, see chapter 6.) Loans received for special exhibitions, however, are usually automatically returned to the lenders by the registrar unless the director or the curator of the exhibition or the lender gives other instructions.

Before releasing any object, the registrar should check the records to see that no conditions of gift or loan and no regulations of the museum are violated by shipping it. The registrar must also see that the museum's insurance will cover the object when it leaves the museum, or ascertain that adequate insurance is being otherwise provided. Above all, it is the registrar's duty to make certain that the object is released only into the hands of the bailor (person from whom it was received) or a properly authorized and properly identified agent or successor of that person. For the museum's protection, such authorization and identification must be in writing. The museum, as bailee, cannot deny the bailor's rights to an object on loan to the museum. However, in the event that a third person claims ownership of the object, the museum must not deliver it to either party until checking with its attorneys. Laws governing such matters differ from state to state.[2]

If the owner of the object has died while it is in the museum's possession, the executor or administrator of the estate must ordinarily provide, at minimum, a court certificate of recent date showing his or her appointment and, in states where applicable, a waiver by the state inheritance tax authorities. The museum must have these papers in hand before it surrenders any property of an owner who has died. Local law may also impose additional restrictions or requirements, and it is advisable in every case for the museum to consult with its attorneys. Finally, the museum should require written authorization from the duly certified executor or administrator before delivering the object to any other person, and in no case should the museum fail to secure an official museum receipt signed by the recipient.

EXAMINING, PACKING, AND SHIPPING

Before outgoing material leaves the museum, its condition should be checked by the registrar or curator or conservator, as the institution's policy may dictate. If condition photographs exist, this inspection should include the comparison of object and photographs. New photographs should be taken if any significant

---

2. David B. Little, "The Registrar, Taxes and the Burden of Proof," paper presented at the annual meeting of the American Association of Museums, Charleston, S.C., June 1958.

changes have occurred. The registrar should call to the attention of the curator any condition that might, in his or her opinion, impair the safety of the object in transit. The advice of a conservator, if available, should be obtained. However, the final decision as to whether shipment should be made is the responsibility of the curator.

The registration department generally makes arrangements for the packing of all objects leaving the museum. This will include issuing instructions to packers for rebuilding old boxes or making new ones, supervising the packing of the objects, and inspecting the boxes to see that they are properly marked and labeled with the addresses of the shipper and consignee. The registrar also makes transportation arrangements, or hires freight-forwarding agents to do so, and should see that the carrier or agent selected receives carefully prepared handling and shipping instructions. In the case of foreign shipments, the registrar also sees that all special papers required by the U.S. Customs Service and other government agencies, by transportation companies, and by the countries of destination are properly prepared. Usually, customs brokers will be hired to serve as the museum's forwarding agents for foreign shipments. (See chapters 7 and 8.)

See forms VIII and IX.

Insurance and Reports

Arrangements for adequate insurance coverage of incoming and outgoing material in transit and during its stay in the museum or in a borrowing institution are normally the registrar's responsibility. The amount of coverage is based on valuations established by the curatorial department or, in the case of a loan, by the lender. In addition, nominal insurance may be placed with the carrier as a precaution for careful handling. If changes in values are to be reported to insurance companies, it is more efficient to report periodically the total amount added to or canceled from the museum's policy than to report individual changes with each arrival or departure. (For a general discussion of insurance, see chapter 9.)

The director may require from the registrar periodic reports of material received and released during the calendar or fiscal year. The information in these reports varies according to the museum's requirements, but it usually includes the following data:

Number of objects acquired for the permanent collection
Number of objects lent from the permanent collection to other institutions
Number of objects acquired as extended loans
Number of objects borrowed for special exhibitions
Lists of donors, lenders, and borrowers

Such reports are part of the registrar's responsibility for keeping track of objects coming into or going out of the museum. In addition, the registrar has the responsibility for keeping records of all objects as long as they are in the custody of the museum—whether on a temporary or permanent basis. This major aspect of the registration process is described in the chapter that follows.

3
THE REGISTRATION OF OBJECTS

Fig. 3.1. Throughout the registration process primary consideration must be given to the welfare and safe handling of the museum objects.

A "register," by definition, is an official written record, and it is the museum registrar's responsibility to provide an immediate, brief, and permanent means of identifying each object in the permanent or temporary custody of the museum and to record its source, status, and disposition. To this end the registrar maintains an accumulation of many types of records, which vary among museums of different sizes, specialties, and activities. The function of the records, however, remains essentially the same: to document and account for the objects for which the museum has assumed responsibility.

The registration process, then, involves the activities of compiling and maintaining a cumulative inventory of all objects in the museum's custody. These include objects on loan to the museum for special exhibitions; objects on temporary deposit with the museum for study, consideration for possible acquisition, or any other purpose; and objects that have been accepted as accessions or extended loans to the museum's collections.

Registration differs from cataloguing, which is the function of classifying objects methodically and usually with descriptive detail. Cataloguing objects in a museum, or arranging them in proper classifications, requires specialized knowledge and is a curatorial responsibility. However, in many museums, catalogue information is recorded by the registrar in consultation with curators, and catalogue files are maintained in the registrar's office. In this chapter, cataloguing is considered only to the extent that it influences registration. (For discussions of cataloguing in greater detail, see articles B–E, I, and K.)

This chapter describes the registration procedures and the basic records needed for objects accepted as accessions to the permanent collections or as extended loans or received as temporary loans for special exhibitions.

The Numbering System

The first step in planning a registration procedure is to determine a numbering system for identifying the museum's objects. Actually, several series of numbers, assigned according to the status of the object, can be used. The most satisfactory numbering system shows when an object entered the museum's custody and whether as a permanent accession, extended loan, temporary loan for exhibition, or temporary deposit. Temporary deposit numbers are discussed in

22　　　　　BASIC PROCEDURES

*Fig. 3.2.
In the following series of photographs from the Arizona Historical Society, various steps of one museum's registration procedure are illustrated. Here the registrar assists the curator by filling out a temporary deposit receipt in the presence of the donor.*

chapter 2. Accession numbers assigned to objects in the permanent collection and loan numbers assigned to objects borrowed for special exhibitions and to extended loans are discussed in the following pages.

ACCESSION NUMBERS

To accession is to record an increase or augmentation. As soon as an object is accepted as part of the museum's permanent collections, the registrar accessions it by assigning it a controlling number, referred to here as the accession number.

It is not likely that a sequence of simple numbers (1, 2, 3, 4) will be adequate for museum accessions, except perhaps in the case of a small, homogeneous collection under the care of one person. Such a system would be inadequate for dealing with accessions of single objects and large groups of objects simultaneously. The exact number of objects to be accessioned cannot be quickly determined when a large collection is received at one time from a single source, such as an expedition, a bequest, or a gift. For example, when a large group of objects is acquired from an archaeological expedition, it is almost impossible to

Fig. 3.3.
Recent donations are placed in a specially designed room for pest control treatment. The staff pays particular attention to organic materials.

Fig. 3.4.
The registrar prepares a work sheet on each museum acquisition. Completion of the work sheet often requires research in published and unpublished literature and consultation with curators and other specialists.

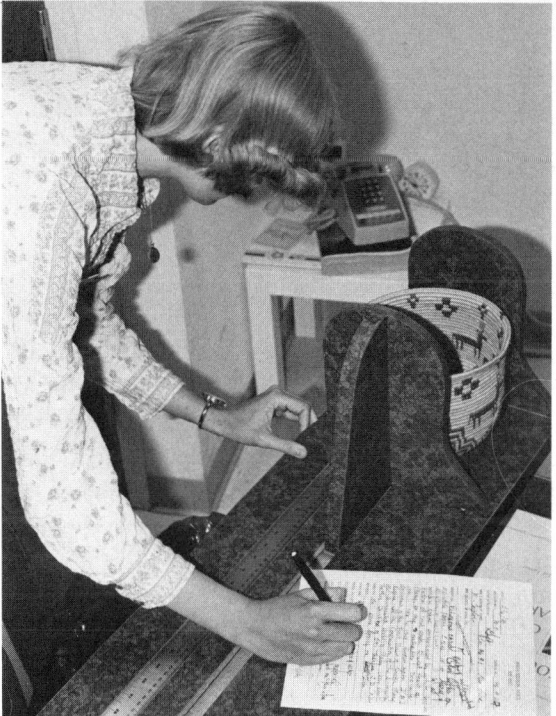

Fig. 3.5 (left).
Each object is carefully measured, and the measurements are recorded on the work sheet. Here an osteometric board is used to measure a basket in both inches and centimeters.

Fig. 3.6 (above).
After the work sheet has been completed, the permanent record is prepared. Here the registrar types the catalogue card from the information that has been gathered.

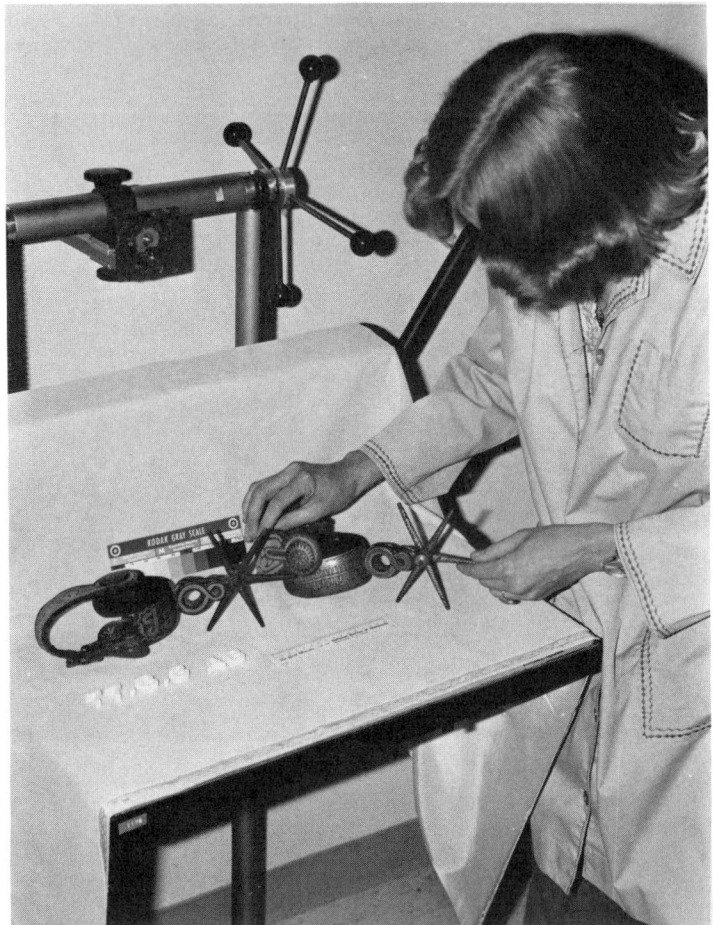

Fig. 3.7.
To complete the registration procedure, a descriptive or catalogue photograph is made of the object. The accession number is photographed along with the object. Note the use of a scale for size in inches and centimeters. A gray scale is used for black and white photographs, a standard color scale for color slides or prints.

know how many numbers will need to be assigned, for many fragments will eventually be rejoined; several potsherds may ultimately constitute a single vessel. Pending this determination, the accessioning of objects that subsequently enter the collection would have to be delayed.

The use of alphabetical prefixes to the numbers to designate material or function (P, painting; C, ceramics; F, furniture) or geographical area (NA, North America; A, Asia; AF, Africa) makes it possible for each group to be numbered independently. However, such a system requires that an object be identified before it is given a number, and this, again, may cause accessioning to be delayed in cases where the material, use, or provenance is not easily determined. Another disadvantage of such a system is that a later change in the original attribution (a rare but not impossible occurrence) would necessitate changing the accession number of that object.

The difficulties encountered in a sequence of simple numbers or of numbers preceded by designating letters are avoided by the use of compound numbers consisting of two or more parts separated by a decimal point or a hyphen, each

3: THE REGISTRATION OF OBJECTS

Fig. 3.8.
When registration has been completed, the registrar places the object in storage.

part following its own sequence. This system is both more uniform and more flexible than the others. Of several variations, the simplest one, and the one in most general use today, is composed of the year in which the object was officially accepted as a permanent accession and a second part composed of a number assigned sequentially within that year.

The first part of the number is the year; this, of course, changes annually. The second part of the number begins with "1" each year and runs consecutively through the number given to the final accession for that year. For example, in the year 1978, the number assigned to the first object accepted as part of the permanent collection would be 78.1; the accession number for the second object would be 78.2. Some museums include a century digit for the year, or even the full year number, to avoid possible confusion, e.g., 978.1 or 1978.1.

This numbering system is generally satisfactory both for museums where accessions are for the most part single items and for museums where accessions frequently consist of groups of objects. The advantage of the compound system for the latter is that the accession number may be extended as required by additional decimal points followed by further numbers or letters. Delay in accessioning a large collection received at one time from a single source can be avoided by using a number composed of three parts: the year of acquisition; the number assigned within that year to the collection; and the serial number of the individual item within that collection. For example, in the year 1978, the numbers 78.1 through 78.5 inclusive would be assigned to the first through fifth accession, each consisting of a single object. The sixth accession, consisting of a group of objects, would receive the number 78.6, and the twenty-second object in that group would be assigned the number 78.6.22. The first two parts (i.e., 78.6) can be assigned and placed on all objects in the group immediately upon acceptance; the third part may be assigned and attached either at the same time or after the exact number of objects has been determined, but without delaying the accessioning of subsequent acquisitions.

Similarly, when an accession consists of a group of objects that belong together as a set or series, or when a single object is composed of several parts, the accession number may be extended by adding a decimal point followed by numbers or letters. Customarily, numbers are used for subparts that can be exhibited individually, apart from other subparts, and letters for subparts that are normally exhibited together and not individually. For example, for a portfolio of six prints, the two- or three-part number would be followed by a decimal point and a number for each print (e.g., 78.7.1 through 78.7.6). The number for a teapot and lid would be followed by "a" for the teapot and "b" for the lid (78.8a and 78.8b). A portfolio of twelve prints that is the eighteenth item in a large bequest would be assigned 78.9.18.1 through 78.9.18.12; a teapot and lid that constitute the nineteenth item in the same bequest would be 78.9.19a and 78.9.19b. If the next accession were a set of china, with place settings for eight and occasional serving dishes and platters, the entire set would be assigned the accession number 78.10. The dinner plates, for example, would then be assigned 78.10.1, with numbers for the individual plates following another decimal point—78.10.1.1 through 78.10.1.8. The luncheon plates would be assigned 78.10.2.1 through 78.10.2.8, the dessert plates 78.10.3.1 through 78.10.3.8, and so on. The component parts of syllabub cups with covers would be identified by number plus letter—78.10.4.1a and 78.10.4.1b through 78.10.4.8a and 78.10.4.8b. Thus, accession numbers composed of compound numbers offer great flexibility for identifying not only parts of large accessions but also sets and pairs within accessions.

In many museums the compound numbers assigned by the registrar at the time of accession and marked on the objects are also called catalogue numbers. All recorded information can be traced through them, so other numbers are not considered necessary. However, in some museums, particularly in the science field, special catalogue numbers based on classification are assigned by the curators of various departments to the items in their collections. In such cases, if a registrar or other staff member keeps a central file of accessions, these "curatorial" numbers should be included for purposes of cross-referencing. These numbers do not in any way reduce the importance of a unique and permanent accession number, which serves as the basic controlling number for the object.

LOAN NUMBERS

Objects that are received by the museum either as temporary loans for special exhibitions or as extended loans are assigned loan numbers. Objects on temporary loan can be assigned loan numbers immediately upon entry. Objects on extended loan are also assigned loan numbers upon entry in some museums; in others, where extended loans must be accepted by action of the board of trustees, they are treated as temporary deposits until they are either accepted or returned.

Loan numbers are a different series from accession numbers. They should indicate that the objects to which they are assigned are loans and not permanent accessions. Many museums accomplish this by reversing the permanent accession system just described. Loans are numbered consecutively within the year they are received. The loan number assigned to the object or group of objects borrowed at one time from one source is placed first, followed by the year in which the loan is received, and, finally, if for a group of objects, the serial number of the individual object within the loan. For example, in the year 1978 the number assigned to the first object received on loan would be 1.78; the second number, for the second object, would be 2.78. If the third loan consisted of a group of objects, its number would be 3.78, with the first object of the group being 3.78.1, the second object 3.78.2, and so forth.

There is, however, the possibility of confusion between a loan number and a permanent accession number. For example, 78.36.1 may be the first object in permanent accession 36 of the year 1978, or it may be the first object in loan 78 of the year 1936. Museums that assign century digits or full year numbers

TEMPORARY RECEIPTS

Receipt Number	Date	Depositor	Artist	Purpose	Disposal
237	10/30/78	Martin	Denning	possible acquisition	acc. m.c. 11/16/78
238.1-3	11/2/78	Harding	Norwood	"	acc. m.c. 11/16/78
239	11/2/78	Ballard	Sheppard	"	ret'd 12/12/78
240	11/2/78	Wheeler gallery	Goodman	"	acc. m.c. 11/16/78
241.1-2	11/6/78	Kelly	Collins	"	.1 acc m.c. 11/16/78 .2 ret'd 12/15/78
242	11/17/78	Burton	Hayes	study	ret'd 1/12/79
243.1-5	1/5/79	Locke gallery	Misc.	possible acquisition	
244	1/10/79	Jordan	Morgan	conservation	
245.1-4	1/31/79	Thomas	Thomas	possible acquisition	
246	2/6/79	Hall Gallery	Frost	"	
247	2/9/79	Borden	Merriman	study	ret'd 2/14/79
248.1-2	2/12/79	Greene	.1 Owens .2 Rogers	possible acquisition	.2 ret'd 2/26/79
249	2/20/79	Fuller	Read	"	
251	2/22/79	Kerry	Johnson	"	

Fig. 3.9.
A list or log of consecutive numbers assigned for each numbering series a museum uses will help prevent the repeating or skipping of a number, especially in large registration departments where several people may be assigning numbers to temporary deposits, accessions, and loans. Information recorded in these lists or logs is minimal. The log for temporary deposit numbers at the Hirshhorn Museum and Sculpture Garden, Smithsonian Institution, is filled in by hand and includes the receipt number, date the object enters the museum, name of depositor, name of artist, purpose of entry into the museum, and, when it has been determined, final disposition of the object, with date.

avoid this problem—1978.36.1 could not be confused with 78.1936.1, unless, of course, the museum's accessions and loans number into the thousands every year. For museums that do not include century digits or full year numbers, the confusion can be avoided by writing the year in full for loans only, or by preceding the year with an apostrophe (e.g., 36.1978.1 or 36.'78.1).

Some museums use prefix letters to distinguish loans. Instead of reversing the order of the year and the number within the year, they precede the series for loans with the letter "L." Thus the first loan received for 1978 would be numbered L 1978.1; the second, L 1978.2. If desired, this numbering system for loans may be further refined by distinguishing between extended loans ("EL") and temporary loans received for special exhibitions ("TL"). Museums whose loan numbers are the reversal of the permanent accession numbering system, as described above, may also distinguish between extended loans and temporary loans by the prefix "EL." Thus, if the thirtieth loan number assigned for the year were to an object accepted by the museum as an extended loan, the number would be EL 30.78.

RECORDING THE NUMBER

It is important, no matter which numbering system is used, to be certain that no number is assigned to more than one object and that no number in a series is ever skipped. This problem can be avoided by maintaining a central list of the consecutive numbers in each series. For instance, a museum using temporary deposit numbers, permanent accession numbers, and loan numbers would maintain three separate lists. Since the purpose of these lists is merely to prevent the repeated use or the skipping of a number, entries need contain only minimal information, such as date received and source of acquisition and, if desired, artist, maker, or a brief description. (See figure 3.9.)

All objects should be marked with permanent accession or extended loan numbers as soon as possible after they have been officially accepted, and any preliminary tags attached at the time of entry should be removed. The numbers for temporary loans, like those for objects on temporary deposit, are never painted on, but are usually typed on labels or tags that can be attached where they can be easily removed before objects are returned to lenders. (For a general discussion of the marking of museum objects, see chapter 4.)

Permanent Accessions and Extended Loans

Assigning the appropriate number to an object is only one part of the registration process. In addition, the registrar must maintain the various records that provide a functional inventory of the collections.

Similar types of records will be needed for permanent accessions and for extended loans. Some museums prefer to stipulate a renewable time limit when accepting extended loans, but, for the most part, these loans are treated as adjuncts to the permanent collections. Records for these objects may be on cards and filed either with the permanent collection cards or separately, whichever method the museum finds most useful. Their identifying number will distinguish the objects from permanent accessions in some way, as explained earlier in this chapter. When the museum returns an extended loan, a notation must be made on all records, and a receipt of delivery obtained from the lender and filed by the registrar. If, on the other hand, an extended loan becomes part of the permanent collection, all records, of course, must be changed accordingly, although a record of its former status should be retained in appropriate files.

See forms III.E and III.G.

For the purposes of this chapter, the records described for permanent accessions are also applicable to extended loans and no further distinctions will be made.

ACCESSIONS FILE

Once the decision is made to accession an object, the registrar begins to prepare the formal records. (Preliminary records made at time of entry are described in chapter 2.) The first accession records should include the following information:

ACCESSION NUMBER
DATE RECEIVED
DATE ACCEPTED
SOURCE OF ACQUISITION (purchase; gift; bequest; expedition, including field number; etc.)
ARTIST, MAKER, CULTURAL GROUP, SPECIES (if known)
TITLE AND/OR DESCRIPTION
DATE OR PERIOD (if known)
EXACT MEASUREMENTS (in both inches and centimeters)
CONDITION
PURCHASE PRICE (if applicable; or reference made to department where purchase records kept)
INSURANCE VALUE (optional)
DATE RECORDED AND INITIALS OF RECORDER

These records for each object are listed or filed in the order of acquisition as shown by the accession number. When a compound numbering system showing the year of acquisition is used, the accession file becomes a cumulative year-by-year record of the objects acquired for the permanent collection.

See forms V.A and figures B.1–2, E.1, G.1, and L.2.

Accession records may be kept in a ledger or on cards, or both. The disadvantage of the ledger book is that it becomes more and more cumbersome and inflexible as new accessions are listed or as more space is needed for changes or additional information concerning previous entries. Many registrars consider it simpler to keep accession records on cards, and, if earlier records have been kept in books, to have them remade onto cards for the new file. Cards have uniformity, space for additional information, and maneuverability, and they may be duplicated to form other files.

Accession cards should be filed in numerical order. The possibility that a card may be mislaid or lost is minimized if the cards are held in drawers by rods, or if drawers are locked. In museums where automatic data processing is in use,

3: THE REGISTRATION OF OBJECTS

computer-printed accession lists as well as cards can be provided, if both are considered necessary.

The registrar's accession records are the key to the museum's collections. It is a good idea to have accession records and other important registration files microfilmed or placed on microfiche cards, not only to reduce storage space for noncurrent records but so that all records can be easily removed from the museum in case of emergency. Better protection, of course, is provided if the microfilmed records are stored outside the museum. Records made under computer control, stored in magnetic form, should be maintained in multiple copies at different locations. The regular procedure for altering or adding to such records should include, as the final step, the production of new duplicate tapes to minimize the danger of losing the only copy of the museum's records.

THE CATALOGUE

See forms V.C and figures D.3–6, E.4, G.5, I.1, J.4, K.2–4, P.5, and P.7.

As mentioned earlier, cataloguing is a curatorial function, but catalogue cards are frequently prepared in the registration department on the basis of information supplied or approved by curators. Under this arrangement, the following and possibly other information pertinent to the particular collection being registered and catalogued is recorded on the catalogue card:

ACCESSION NUMBER
CATALOGUE NUMBER (if different from accession number)
ARTIST, MAKER, CULTURAL GROUP, SPECIES
PROVENANCE
MARKS (labels, seals, etc.)
DATE OR PERIOD
TITLE AND/OR DESCRIPTION
MEDIUM OR MATERIAL
SOURCE OF ACQUISITION (purchase; gift; bequest; expedition, including field number; etc.)
DATE RECEIVED
DATE ACCEPTED
INSURANCE VALUE (optional)
PURCHASE PRICE (if applicable; or reference made to department where purchase records kept)
PHOTOGRAPH AND/OR NEGATIVE NUMBER OR SKETCH OF OBJECT
LOCATION AND DESCRIPTION OF SIGNATURE (copyright mark if it occurs)
EXACT MEASUREMENTS (in inches and centimeters)
CONDITION
PUBLICATIONS OR REFERENCES
HISTORY (ex-collections, exhibitions, etc.)
DATE CATALOGUED AND INITIALS OF CATALOGUER

See forms V.B and figures E.2–3, N.4, and P.2.

In assembling information for these records, museum staff members generally find it convenient to use a work sheet, a prepared form with headings designating the data to be filled in. The terminology used in recording the data should be uniform and clear, and items should always appear in the same order. When the information has been reviewed by the curator, it is transferred to the catalogue card. All data should also appear in the same location on each card.

FILES MADE FROM DUPLICATE CARDS

The information assembled for the accession and/or catalogue cards will serve the registrar in a variety of ways as well as be of use to other departments in the museum. Thoughtful planning should be given to the extent and arrangement of the information and the number and kinds of files that are developed from the basic registration records.

See forms V.C.2 and V.C.3.

The assembled information may be typed on one card and exact duplicates made to form the various files in the registrar's office, or one master card may be prepared with complete information and other cards with skeletal information filed under whatever categories are necessary. In some museums, the registrar makes duplicate cards for the curatorial offices.

The production of duplicate records by mechanical methods saves a great deal of time and reduces the possibility of typographical errors. Several duplicating methods are now in use. In some museums, the original record is made on a master sheet and duplicates reproduced by an offset lithography process; in others, carbon copies are made of the original card at the time it is first typed. "Automatic" typewriters, which program magnetic tapes or cards to retype the data rapidly, have been put to good use in some registration departments, as have photocopying machines. In a few museums the required cards are now produced under computer control.

See figures P.5 and P.7.

It is best to record only basic information on the master sheet or card so that the duplicate cards will be suitable for use by the general public as well as by the museum staff. Confidential information, such as names of anonymous donors and records of condition, can then be recorded on additional cards and kept with the basic records in a file that is not used by the public.

Duplicate cards might be filed under such headings as:

SOURCE OF ACQUISITION
LOCATION
MEDIUM OR MATERIAL
COUNTRY, CULTURE, OR SPECIES
ARTIST OR MAKER
SUBJECT

Source-of-Acquisition Records. Source-of-acquisition records are important in every museum. One method for producing this file is to duplicate either the accession or catalogue card for each object and file the cards under the name of each donor, bequest, expedition, vendor, purchase fund, or lender. However, if the source file is made by this method, duplicate filing cabinets, plus space in which to house them, must be provided. A more practical alternative is to make a card for each donor, vendor, or other source of acquisition, on which gifts, purchases, or loans can be listed chronologically, with accession or loan numbers. These cards are then arranged alphabetically in a central source-of-acquisition file.

Location Records. Location records are also important, for they show the exact location—in museum exhibition galleries, in storage, out on loan, or elsewhere—of every object in the museum's collection. The location records also constitute a record of an object's exhibition history.

In some museums, these records are maintained in curatorial departments; in others, they are the responsibility of the registration department. Under the latter arrangement, the registrar must be advised of changes in location so that records can be kept up to date.

Location information may be included with the accession or catalogue files. A second card may be filed behind the first for this purpose, or the cards may be flagged with tabs that indicate, by color, whether an object is on exhibition in the museum, in storage, on loan, or elsewhere. Or separate files of duplicate cards may be maintained for each gallery or other location, and the cards shifted from one file to another as objects are moved. If the storage of permanent collections is one of the duties of the registrar, a separate file can be kept showing storage location, date removed, where sent, and date returned.

Other Records. A separate registration file is sometimes kept for gifts in which a museum has only a remainder (future) or fractional interest. Cards in this file include as much of the information mentioned above as possible and also show the percentage of the museum's equity at the date of acquisition. It is customary to assign accession numbers to these gifts even though the museum's interest in them may be small or entirely in the future. (For a discussion of remainder and fractional interest gifts, see article A.) Similarly, some museums keep a separate file on extended loans, as described earlier, rather than filing these cards with the accession cards for the permanent collection. Another card file kept by some museums is a deaccessions file, made up of cards pulled from the accessions file when an object is officially removed from the collection, as described later in this chapter. Still another type of file indexes the collection by subject. (See articles D, E, G, H, and N). The number and kinds of records maintained by the registration department will vary with the scope of the registrar's functions at a given institution, the extent of the institution's programs, and the staff available.

RELATED FILES

In addition to the records made from duplicates of the accession or catalogue cards, the registrar is usually responsible for maintaining other files documenting the permanent accessions, temporary loans, and other objects in the museum's custody.

Acknowledgments, Receipts, and Related Documents. A receipt should be issued to donor, vendors, and lenders for objects offered as gifts, purchases, or extended loans. The number on this receipt is usually the temporary deposit number or the loan number assigned on entry. (See chapter 2.) One copy of the receipt is filed by the registrar, and additional copies are sent as required to curatorial and other offices. Formal acknowledgments of gifts and extended loans and also letters declining objects not accepted are usually issued by curatorial or administrative offices after official action has been taken by the trustees of the museum.

> See forms II.A, III.D, and III.H.3 and figures G.6 and L.1.

The registrar's files should contain information on any special conditions or restrictions pertaining to gifts, loans, or bequests. If possible, registration files should contain all the original documentation on collections and loans, including statements from donors (deeds of gift) that the objects are offered as gifts to the permanent collection. If these documents must be filed in other museum offices, the registrar should be informed of them and have access to them, or should obtain photocopies for the registration department files.

> See forms IV.A and figure G.3.

Photograph Records. Photograph records should be kept of all objects in the museum's collections. In larger museums, photographing collections, maintaining photo files, and responding to requests for photographs are often handled by separate photographic services and rights and reproductions departments; in smaller museums these duties are sometimes the responsibility of the registrar. In any event, the registrar should be familiar with the kinds of photographs needed and have access to them and record the negative numbers in the appropriate files.

> See forms IV.B and figures A.1, A.4, and G.4.

Several types of photographs are necessary. The condition photographs, described in chapter 2, should clearly show all defects, flaws, or changes in the object. They should be maintained in a file of condition photographs that supplements the record of condition reported on accession and catalogue cards. They may be filed first by the size of the negative, then by accession number, by artist or maker, or by title. The accession number and the date of the photograph should appear on the negative, and the negative number should appear on all prints. Condition photographs should be made at time of entry if possible, and, if the museum budget permits, each time a valuable object leaves the museum, returns again, or when any change has taken place.

Descriptive or catalogue photographs are made to be attached directly to the accession and catalogue cards. These photographs are for identification only and do not need to be as detailed as condition photographs. There are various methods for making descriptive photographs. For instance, 35-mm photographs can be made from existing 8-by-10-inch prints or from the objects themselves. The negatives can be printed as contact sheets, and the individual frames clipped and pasted on the appropriate cards. Some museums photograph the objects and make prints on sensitized paper, which is cut to the size of the cards and filed directly behind the appropriate accession or catalogue card. Whatever the method, it is important that the negative number of the photograph be included on the cards.

> See forms V.C.2–3 and figures E.4, P.5, and P.7.

Insurance and Valuation Records. If the permanent collection is insured under a scheduled policy based on the individual values of each object, a record of valuation is kept in the curatorial, business, or registration departments, and changes in value are reported to the insurers as required. The registrar will probably be the person to report changes in valuation or to process claims, so it is important that valuation records in the registration department are up to date. The procedures for making insurance reports vary with the type of insurance coverage and are described in chapter 9.

DEACCESSION RECORDS

When an object is removed permanently from the collection, it is deaccessioned or canceled. The object may be retired or withdrawn for a variety of reasons, such as deterioration, loss, or transfer by gift, sale, or exchange. Before canceling any records, the registrar must receive written authorization from the director or other responsible person that official action has been taken to deaccession an object. In some museums, copies of the minutes of meetings showing formal action of the board of trustees are sent to the registrar. The registration records are then marked "Deaccessioned by authority of the trustees," with the date the action was taken.

The disposition of the object is noted in red on the accession card, which can be either refiled in its original place or filed with cards of other deaccessioned objects. If it is removed from the accessions file, a substitute card bearing the accession number and a reference to the original card is filed in its place. A

FIG. 3.10 REGISTRATION RECORDS

PERMANENT COLLECTION AND EXTENDED LOANS	LOANS FOR SPECIAL EXHIBITIONS
Preliminary record: *work sheet*	Preliminary record: *loan agreement, work sheet, or checklist*
Accession record	Numerical record of loan numbers assigned
Receipt: *to donor* / *to vendor* / *to lender for extended loan*	Receipt: *to lender*
Insurance: *as museum system specifies*	Insurance: *as lender specifies*
Photographic condition file	Photographic condition file
Gift acknowledgment when gift accepted; receipt for extended loan returned	Receipt of delivery
Source-of-acquisition card	Lender's card
Location record	
Final record: *catalogue card*	Final record: *loan card (optional)*

record of disposition must also be noted on source-of-acquisition cards. All other cards and records should be removed from the active files and destroyed if not needed, or the disposition of the object should be noted on them and the cards placed in a special file for deaccessioned objects. All numbers assigned to an object while it was the property of the museum are retired with the object and not reassigned.

Loans for Special Exhibitions

The registration of loans for special exhibitions is, in some ways, more complex than the accessioning of objects acquired for permanent collections or as extended loans. Although the numbering system and the records made are basically the same (see figure 3.10), the work is complicated by the number of objects involved and by the fact that they must be collected from and returned to lenders. This involves making arrangements for packing, transportation, and insurance; issuing receipts when objects arrive; and, later, sending receipts of delivery for lenders to sign to acknowledge the return of their objects. Furthermore, the work preceding the exhibition must be done quickly in order to allow sufficient time for the objects to be installed in the galleries.

INFORMATION TO BE RECORDED

See forms I.A and III.A.

The director or the curator of the exhibition should notify the registrar of incoming domestic and foreign shipments or of any loans that are to be collected. This may be done by simply forwarding to the registration department copies of letters requesting loans and subsequent correspondence. In any case, the director or the curator of the exhibition usually furnishes the registrar with lists showing the names and addresses of lenders, descriptions of the objects to be borrowed, insurance valuations, and any other information needed for registration department receipts and records. Later, the loan numbers assigned as the objects are received by the museum are added to these lists.

See forms III.B and III.C.3 and figure J.1.

Most borrowing museums send loan agreement forms to lenders to be completed, signed, and returned. Loan agreement forms are contracts between lenders and borrowers, and, in some cases, the borrowing museum signs the form as well. The director or the curator of the exhibition uses copies of these forms for compiling the published exhibition catalogue, and the registrar uses them in checking, numbering, and recording the loans as they arrive.

Loan agreement forms generally include the following information, as applicable:

NAME OF EXHIBITION AND DATES
NAME AND ADDRESS OF LENDER
CREDIT LINE (i.e., form in which lender wishes acknowledgment to appear in published catalogue and on label)
NAME OF ARTIST OR MAKER
EXACT TITLE OF WORK OR NAME OF OBJECT
MEDIUM OR MATERIALS
DATE EXECUTED

SIGNATURE OF ARTIST OR MAKER
EXACT MEASUREMENTS (if three-dimensional object, also weight) in both inches and centimeters (and pounds and kilograms)
INSURANCE VALUE (if the borrowing museum is to insure)
NAME OF INSURER (if lender is to insure)
SELLING PRICE (when applicable)
PACKING AND SHIPPING INSTRUCTIONS
LOCATION AND NEGATIVE NUMBER OF PHOTOGRAPH
CONDITION OF OBJECT
DATE AND METHOD OF ARRIVAL AND RETURN
PERMISSIONS (from copyright holder, to display and photograph the loan and reproduce it in the exhibition catalogue, for publicity, or for educational purposes; from owner, to remove frames and glass if necessary and to reframe or remat if desirable)
SPECIAL INSTRUCTIONS
LEGAL CONDITIONS OF THE LOAN AGREEMENT (usually printed on the back of the loan agreement form)

Special forms following this general outline may be devised for specific types of exhibition material. While there may be variations in the content of the loan agreements, they are devised for the same purpose—to obtain sufficient information to identify, describe, acknowledge, and protect the borrowed object.

Some of this information is supplied by the director or the curator of the exhibition and some by the lenders. When the object is checked by the registration department, the loan number assigned to the object is recorded on the loan agreement form. If a collection of several objects is borrowed from a single source and the terms of agreement are identical for all of them, the objects may be listed on the same form.

The condition of the loan should be recorded as soon as it is received, and, especially if there is damage, a condition photograph should be made. It may be advisable to compare the condition of the loan as received with its condition before shipment, and in such cases lenders must be asked to supply their condition photographs. If the curatorial or conservation department makes the condition record, a copy should be sent to the registrar. All necessary information is recorded on work sheets, which the registrar uses in preparing receipts to send to lenders and in making whatever other records are needed in the registration department.

See form VI.A.1.

RECEIPTS TO LENDERS

See forms III.D and figure G.6.

Incoming loan receipts should be issued to lenders as soon as possible after loans have been registered. Copies are filed by the registrar and sent as needed to the director or the curator of the exhibition and other departments. Some museums have found it efficient to make an additional copy as a receipt of delivery to be signed by the lender when the loan is returned. The following information should appear on the incoming loan receipt:

Name and address of lender
Titles and dates of exhibition
Description of loan
Loan number
Date received by museum
Mode of shipment
Insurance value (or statement to the effect that the lender is insuring the loan)
Condition of object (optional)
Legal conditions of the loan agreement

Fig. 3.11.
This visible record location file serves the Department of Painting and Sculpture at the Baltimore Museum of Art. The accession number, short title, artist, abbreviated medium, dimensions, and permanent location are typed on cardstock strips, which are inserted alphabetically into the metal panels. If location is temporarily changed, a tiny label is applied to the strip, then removed when the object is returned. The file is also convenient for quick answers to questions such as, How many Rembrandts do you have?

See forms VI.B.1 and figures G.7, J.2, and K.1.

See form VI.C.1.

Reports on the condition of loans are sometimes omitted from incoming loan receipts unless parts of the object or collection appear to be missing or there are damages that are obviously new. This may be a difficult judgment, especially if no outgoing condition reports or photographs were made by the lender. Legal conditions of the loan agreement are usually printed on the back of the incoming loan receipt, just as they are on the loan agreement form itself.

The registrar's copy of the incoming loan receipt may be filed under the title of the special exhibition, or, if receipts are numbered, it may be filed numerically and reference to the receipt number made in the lenders' file. (See below.) After incoming loan receipts for several exhibitions have accumulated, they are usually bound and retained as part of the permanent records kept in the registration department. Some museums prefer to file these receipts together with loan agreements and correspondence pertaining to the loan.

LENDERS' FILE AND LOAN FILE

A record of lenders with reference to the objects borrowed from them is usually made on cards for a source or lenders' file. Each loan may be recorded on these cards with dates received and returned, or reference made to the loan receipt where this information appears.

Sometimes a permanent card record is made for each loan. However, copies of incoming loan receipts and a file of lenders are frequently the only permanent records kept in the registration department for loans to special exhibitions.

INSURANCE

If loans to special exhibitions are insured by the borrowing museum, values must be recorded and reported to the insurers as required. These reports, as well as any claims for damages, are frequently made by the registrar, although in some museums they are handled by the treasurer or business manager. If another department does handle insurance claims, the registrar must report damages to that department as soon as they have been noted. If the lender is insuring the loan, it is important for the borrowing museum to request a certificate of insurance naming the borrower as an additional insured or waiving rights of subrogation against the borrower. (For a general discussion of insurance, see chapter 9.)

See forms II.B.1, III.D.1, III.E, III.G, III.H.1, and III.H.3 and figure J.3.

RECEIPTS OF DELIVERY

When an object on loan is returned, the borrowing museum requests a signed receipt from the lender acknowledging the return of the loan. In some museums, lenders are asked to surrender the original incoming loan receipts issued when the loans were received. In others, separate receipts of delivery or copies of the original incoming loan receipts are sent to lenders to sign and return to the museum. These receipts are filed in the registrar's office.

4

MEASURING AND MARKING OBJECTS

As part of the process of registration, the registrar must take and record the measurements of the object and mark it with an identifying label or number so that it will be distinguished from all other objects in the museum's custody. Explicit and routine procedures are necessary if the registration department is to perform these tasks efficiently and safely. This chapter describes some of the methods for measuring and marking that registrars have developed for dealing with a variety of museum objects.

Measuring

Measuring museum objects is important both for identification and for calculating storage and exhibition space requirements. Every registration department should have as standard equipment calipers, transparent triangles, folding rules, and steel and cloth tape measures showing both English and metric measurements. For the safety of the objects, steel tape measures should be used with caution and measurements should be initially recorded in pencil, not pen, on work sheets and later transferred to the permanent record.

In general, the dimensions (height, length, width, depth, diameter) are all taken at the greatest point. If this is not done, a notation should explain the point of measurement. It is convenient to give the dimensions in the same order, for example, height, width, depth; height, length, depth; height, diameter; or any other combination of these. Height usually precedes width in recording the measurement of paintings, drawings, and prints. Overall measurements are given for objects with separable parts, such as a teapot with a cover. Whether separate measurements will be recorded for component parts depends on the type of object. Measurements should be made and recorded in both English and metric units.

PROCEDURES FOR MEASURING COLLECTIONS

Paintings are measured on the reverse along the outer edges of the stretcher or panel. Measurements are taken along the lower edge and along the left or right side, whichever is standard procedure in the museum. If the frame prevents this, "sight" measurements, indicating the measurements of what can be seen,

Fig. 4.1.
Curators in natural history museums make and record detailed measurements of the specimens in their collections.

are taken from the front until the painting can be unframed. Measurements of watercolors, gouaches, drawings, and prints are taken at the right and lower edges of the composition and of the sheet of paper upon which the composition appears. (For measuring prints, see, in addition, article E.) If it is impossible to remove the mat, the opening of the mat is measured and sight measurements noted on the record. If the composition is very irregular, it is squared off by enclosing the outermost points within imaginary lines by means of transparent triangles or strips of transparent material; the dimensions of the resulting rectangle are then taken. For sculpture, measurements are taken of the greatest height and width (or length) and depth. If the base is an integral part of the sculpture, it should be included in the height. If not, its height, width, and depth may be noted separately. Whenever possible, sculpture should be weighed for future reference in shipping and exhibit installation.

In general, for other three-dimensional objects, such as glassware, tools, and firearms, the principal dimensions are taken with notes indicating whether handles, bases, or other component parts are included. If a potsherd must be measured, dimensions are taken as it touches a flat surface. The more delicate calculations of curvatures and indentations are left to the archaeologist.

In many science museums detailed measurements of natural history specimens are made and kept only by curators. If a registrar makes a preliminary record, it may be necessary only to note whether a specimen is immature or adult, unless there is something unusual about the size. Registrars responsible for recording detailed measurements of natural history specimens should follow procedures prescribed by the museum's scientific staff or others experienced in this area. For example, to measure an animal it may be necessary to record the length of the body and tail, the length of the hind leg, the width of the skull, and so forth.

GUIDELINES FOR MEASURING COLLECTIONS

Registrars generally find it convenient to draw up a set of measuring rules applicable to the specific collections in their museums.[1] For example, a registrar might establish guidelines for measuring works of art—paintings, watercolors, drawings, prints, and sculpture—such as those listed below:

1. Measures in both English and metric units. English measurements are expressed in inches (not feet) and metric measurements in centimeters. The metric measurements include one digit to the right of the decimal point, even if it is zero.
2. Take measurements to the next larger unit, not the nearest unit. Paintings, watercolors, drawings, and sculpture are measured to the next larger eighth of an inch and to the next larger millimeter. Prints are measured to the next larger sixteenth of an inch and to the next larger millimeter.
3. Record height first, then width, then depth if needed, or diameter. If more than one dimension is given for sculpture, record height first, then greater horizontal

---

1. The sample guidelines provided in this section are adapted from those of the Museum of Modern Art; the Hirshhorn Museum and Sculpture Garden, Smithsonian Institution; and the Colorado Historical Society.

Fig. 4.2.
All accessions must be carefully measured in English and metric units. Paintings are measured face down.

dimension, then lesser horizontal dimension. If a work is circular or irregular in shape, the abbreviations "(diam.)" or "(irreg.)" follow the inch measurements in parentheses.

PAINTINGS: Measure the rigid support, on the reverse if possible.

Rectangular painting: measure on the reverse along the right and the lower edges. Ex.: 14 x 20" (35.6 x 50.8 cm.).

Circular painting: measure the diameter. Ex.: 63⅞" (diam.) (162.3 cm.).

Oval painting: measure the major and minor axes. Ex.: 42½ x 28" (oval) (108.0 x 71.1 cm.).

Lozenge-shaped painting: measure the major and minor axes. Ex.: 27¾ x 27¾" (diagonal) (70.5 x 70.5 cm.).

Irregular painting: measure the maximum height and width with reference to the position in which the painting would be hung, and whatever else is necessary (describe shape). Ex.: 37¼ x 45⅞" (irreg. pentagon) (94.7 x 116.6 cm.).

DRAWINGS, PRINTS, AND WATERCOLORS (works on paper or similar nonrigid material, including oil on paper if not mounted on a rigid support): Measure the sheet and, where appropriate, the composition.

a. Always give sheet measurements first, preceded by the word "sheet."

b. If it is impossible to measure the sheet, measure the mat opening and record this measurement first, preceded by the word "sight."

c. If the artist has made a line around the composition, list the measurement, preceded by the abbreviation "comp."

d. In cases where the artist has not made a line around the composition, but where the composition is limited to a relatively distinct section of the sheet, measure the composition or decorated area and list this measurement, preceded by the abbreviation "comp."

EXAMPLES:

Watercolor: Sheet 21¾ x 36" (55.2 x 91.5 cm.).
            Comp. 20 x 34½" (irreg.) (50.8 x 87.7 cm.).
Drawing: Sight 9 x 12½" (22.9 x 31.8 cm.).

SCULPTURE: Include base in height measure if it is an integral part of the sculpture. Otherwise record height, width, and depth of base separately. If the greater horizontal dimension of a sculpture is larger than the height, measurements should be recorded as height, length, and depth rather than height, width, and depth. The weight of the sculpture should also be recorded in pounds and kilograms of the whole and of each separate piece.

EXAMPLES:

Bronze sculpture: 29⅛" h. (74.0 cm.) including bronze base 6 h. x 5 w. x 4½" d. (15.3 x 12.7 x 11.4 cm.). Wt. 56 lbs. (26 kg.) including base.

Wood sculpture with separate stone base by the artist: 73" h. (185.3 cm.). Stone base 8 h. x 14¼" diam. (20.3 x 36.2 cm.). Wt. 124 lbs. (a. 56 lbs., b. 68 lbs.) (57 kg. [26 kg., 31 kg.]).

Stone sculpture without base: 22" h. (55.9 cm.). At base 6 w. x 5¾" d. (15.3 x 14.6 cm.). Wt. 24 lbs. (11 kg.).

Plaster relief: 34 h. x 23¼ w. x 2½" d. (86.4 x 59.0 x 6.4 cm.). Wt. 17 lbs. (8 kg.).

Steel sculpture: 47 h. x 93 l. x 26" d. (119.4 x 236.3 x 66.0 cm.). Wt. 378 lbs. (172 kg.).

Mobile (it is often impossible to measure a mobile as precisely as other sculpture; it should be measured in its most extended natural position): 23 h. x 52" (approx.) max. diam. (58.4 x 132.1 cm.). Wt. 10½ lbs. (5 kg.).

4: MEASURING AND MARKING OBJECTS

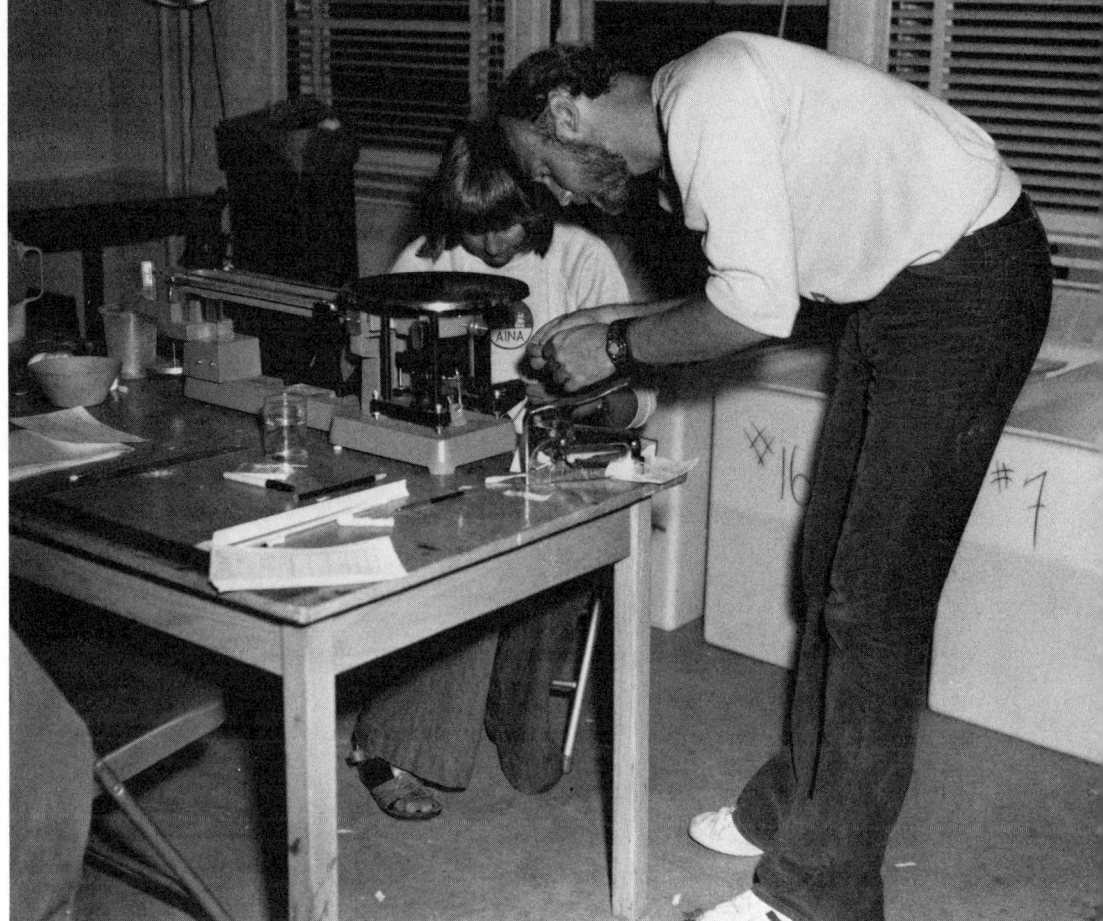

Fig. 4.3. Weighing of artifacts may be part of the registration procedure, as in this facility established by the Maine State Museum to process artifacts from an underwater archaeological site. The weight of objects recovered from the water is important both for description and for subsequent conservation treatment.

A registrar at a history museum might establish guidelines for measuring artifacts as follows:

Record all measurements in both metric and English units. Use maximum outside dimensions that apply except in the cases of clothing and weapons. (See below.) Choose the dimensions that apply to the particular object being measured: the *length* is the largest dimension (exclusive of height), along the front or back; the *width* is the measurement perpendicular to the length, between the front and back; the *height* is the distance from top to bottom of objects that stand (in their normal positions); the *diameter* applies essentially to circular objects. Under "Other Measurements," record clothing (unless standard clothing size is marked in garment), weapons, and anything else to which the standard designations of length, width, height, and diameter do not apply.

CLOTHING:
1. *Men's clothing:*
    a. *Trousers:* Give the waist measurement, with the waistband closed and buttoned, and the inseam length. Ex.: Waist: 90 cm. (35½ in.); inseam: 73.7 cm. (29 in.).

b. *Shirts:* Give the chest circumference under the armpits when buttoned, the circumference of the neck with the collar buttoned, the length of the sleeve from the middle of the back to the end of the cuff, and the length at the center back. Ex.: Chest: 90.0 cm. (35½ in.); neck: 45.7 cm. (18 in.); sleeve length: 17.8 cm. (7 in.); center back: 77.5 cm. (30½ in.). Size: Medium, 38–40.

c. *Coats and vests:* Give the chest circumference under the armpits when buttoned and the length at the center back. Ex.: Chest: 102 cm. (40⅛ in.); length: 54.6 cm. (21½ in.).

2. *Women's clothing:* Give skirt length and bust and waist measurements, when fastened. Ex.: Skirt: 99.0 cm. (39 in.); bust: 90.0 cm. (35½ in.); waist: 65.5 cm. (25¾ in.).

3. *Shoes:* Give foot measurements—length and width of sole, plus height from bottom of heel to top of shoe at center back. Ex.: Length: 29.2 cm. (11½ in.); width: 7.6 cm. (3 in.); heels: 6 cm. (2⅜ in.) high. Women's size: 9B.

WEAPONS:

1. *Firearms:* Give the barrel length and total length. Ex.: Barrel length: 68.0 cm. (26¾ in.); total length: 114.3 cm. (45 in.).

2. *Swords and knives:* Give length of the blade and total length. Ex.: Saber blade: 83.8 cm. (33 in.); total length: 97.8 cm. (38½ in.); scabbard: 90.5 cm. (35⅝ in.).

Marking

Every object in a museum—whether it is part of the permanent collection, on loan for a special exhibition, or on temporary deposit—must be identified by a number, tag, or copy of its receipt. Marking or labeling museum objects so that they may be immediately identified and linked to their documentation is an important part of the registrar's responsibilities.

TEMPORARY DEPOSITS

When an object is placed on temporary deposit with the museum, it must be identified by a label showing its temporary deposit number or by a copy of the receipt showing the source, date received, and purpose of entry. The temporary deposit number should not be applied directly to the object. The kinds of labels and the methods used for attaching them to the objects must be chosen with care; the labels should do no harm to the object and should be easy to remove when the object is returned to the depositor or is made a part of the permanent collection.

LOANS

Objects received on temporary loan for a special exhibition are marked with the loan number as soon as they arrive. The marks on loans for special exhibitions should not be permanent but should be clear and readily accessible. Loan numbers are usually typed on labels or tags, which are attached to the objects. In some museums only the lender's name appears with the loan number. In others, a label with lender's name and address, title or description of loan, artist or maker's name, and other information is attached to each loan object. Except for paintings, drawings, prints, and other framed works, where this label is frequently left on the reverse of the frame or protective backing as a record of

4: MEASURING AND MARKING OBJECTS

Fig. 4.4.
Objects exhibited in this historic house setting are marked on the bottom or in another inconspicuous place.

exhibition history, the borrower's marks on objects are removed before they are returned to the lenders. Extended loans may be marked in a more permanent way, as described below, if permission is granted by the lender.

ACCESSIONS

Marks on objects in the permanent collection should be long lasting, clear, and readily accessible. The marks themselves consist of the object's accession number and, occasionally, the museum's name. The numbers should be as small and legible as possible. They should be located in an inconspicuous place, so that they will not interfere with the design, decoration, or maker's mark or be visible when the object is on exhibition. They should not be placed in an area that receives wear, friction, or pressure from the object's own weight, or on a piece that can be separated from the object. If possible, the number should, at the same time, be clearly visible or accessible when the object is in storage or placed in a reference collection. For this purpose some museums attach an auxiliary label or tag, which is removed before the object is placed on exhibition. All marks should be ultimately removable, should this ever be desired, with a method of removal entailing no injury to the object. Often, however, objects come into the collection with numbers given by previous owners affixed. Where possible, these should be preserved, as they contribute to the object's provenance and unique identity.

The materials and locations of marks vary from object to object: condition, size, weight, and surface finish should all be considered in selecting the materials and the location of marks. The advice of a conservator should be sought when necessary. In general, museums have found artist's oils, acrylic paints, and inks suitable for marking objects of glass, metal, ceramics, bone, and wood; oils or inks are used for objects made of plastic, as formulations which themselves contain plastic may dissolve the surface of the object on contact; a medium lead pencil is used for marking books, works of art on paper, and other paper products; cotton or linen tapes bearing the number are carefully sewn on textiles; and acid-free paper tags or tags of 100 percent rag content are attached to hides, skins, and some leather objects. When these procedures are not suitable, other methods are used. For example, hand-stamped metal tags might identify armor and large animal specimens. Very small objects may be marked by the attachment of jeweler's tags or linen or cotton loops, or the objects may be placed in boxes or vials marked with the accession number. In natural history collections, tags are placed under insect pins, and fluid-resistant paper or fiber labels marked with permanent inks are inserted inside jars with the fluid-preserved specimens.

The oil paint generally used is vermilion or cadmium red, or Venetian red, which is permanent under the widest range of conditions. Oil paints are slightly thinned with turpentine. For smooth surfaces, a compatible lacquer may be used instead of turpentine to improve the paint's adherence qualities. White or black paint is used where red would not be discernible, or a small band of paint is applied in one color and the number painted on in a contrasting color. Some museums today prefer acrylics to oils, because acrylics dry much faster, but as they are thought not to last as long as oils, the numbers should be sealed with a protective overcoat. Acrylics are thinned slightly with water. Other museums use white or black inks instead of paints.

Whether oils, acrylics, or inks are used, the surface to be marked should first be dusted and, if necessary, cleaned according to the advice of a conservator. It is often a good idea, especially with porous materials, to prepare the surface with a primer—museums use varnish, lacquer, liquid plastic, liquid silicone, or clear nail polish. Acrylic formulations are often recommended but must not be used on plastic surfaces. After the primer is dry, the numbers are painted on with a sable or camel's hair watercolor brush, which is flattened for bold numbers and reduced to a fine point for small ones. For very small objects, such as rings, the brush is reduced to three or four hairs. Inks are applied with a fine-point or crow quill pen. When the numbers are thoroughly dry (approximately one hour for acrylics and inks, up to three days for oils unless a dryer is applied or air blower used), the number may be sealed with another layer of primer.

The use of undercoats and overcoats protects both the object and the number. An overcoat is especially important for china, silver, glassware, and other objects that will be cleaned or polished frequently. Such objects should be checked periodically and renumbered if necessary. Undercoats not only provide a smooth surface on which to place the number; they also prevent the mark from being absorbed, thereby facilitating its removal with solvents should that ever become necessary. Alcohol is the solvent for oil paint; acetone is the solvent for lacquer. For removing the number on lacquered objects, the advice of a conservator should be sought.

Medium lead pencils are used in marking paper objects, since a hard lead might crease or dent the paper and a soft lead might smudge. Ink, which has a tendency to spread, and indelible pencils should never be used. In the past many museums stamped the museum's name on the reverse of prints to indicate ownership, but this practice has been largely discontinued because the ink itself may bleed through the paper, the stamping is irreversible, and the stamps are considered by some to be a defacement of the work of art. For books and for prints bound in books, a bookplate is often pasted inside the front cover, but a selected page further on in the book may also be marked, usually with the museum's monogram and the accession number repeated in pencil. Documents are stamped with a special ink recommended by the Library of Congress.[2]

Linen or cotton twill bias tape or unbleached, prewashed linen labels are used for marking costumes, rugs, tapestries, and other fibrous objects. Some museums specially order cloth labels for this purpose, which show the museum's name and leave space for the object's accession number. The number itself is

---

2. Library of Congress, *Marking Manuscripts*, Preservation Leaflet 4 (Washington, D.C., 1977), available without charge from the Assistant Director for Preservation, Library of Congress, Washington, D.C. 20540.

Fig. 4.5. The marking of museum objects is a detailed task that requires patience and a steady hand.

written in with permanent ink; some museums prefer to use a ball-point pen for this procedure, as liquid ink tends to spread. Or the number may be typed on the label by taping the label to a piece of paper, which is then inserted into a typewriter. After the number has been applied, the label is gently stitched to the reverse of the textile with a single cotton or silk thread. Only a few stitches are needed at each end or corner of the label; it does not have to be tacked down all the way around. Care should be taken to make the stitches as invisible as possible from the outside. For fragile textiles and laces, the label can be attached by a single loop of thread. Mountings, containers, and supports for textiles are also marked with the accession number.

For all objects of the same class, the number should be placed in the same location so that it can be readily found. All separable parts, accessory pieces, and containers of the object, for example, a snuff box and its cover, or a knife and its sheath, should be numbered (e.g., 78.120a and 78.120b). Heavy objects should never be numbered on the bottom, but at the back, near the base, so the mark can be read without danger or difficulty. Rugs and large textiles that will be rolled are often labeled on the reverse diagonal corners so that the number can be easily located when the rug is stored. For the same reasons, some museums find it useful to mark paintings on the reverse of two diagonal corners of the stretcher and the frame, so that when the work is hanging in a gallery, the lower number can be seen without removing it from the wall; and if the work is stacked in the storeroom, the upper number can be seen. Numbers are marked on frames of works of art on paper in a similar manner, as well as marked on the reverse lower corner of the work itself and on the mat, backing board, and other separable parts of the frame.

GUIDELINES FOR MARKING COLLECTIONS

Registrars sometimes find it convenient to draw up a set of rules for marking the various objects in their museums' collections, together with recommended supplies that are regularly stocked. The following comprehensive set of guidelines might be useful, for example, in a museum with a wide variety of works of art and historical artifacts.[3]

IDENTIFICATION NUMBERING PROCEDURES

The following paragraphs describe procedures for marking temporary, semipermanent, and permanent identification numbers on all objects within the museum. It should be recognized that materials acceptable for industrial or domestic labeling are not necessarily acceptable for museum work, both because of the special value of museum artifacts and because of the duration of the contact between material and artifact.

I. TEMPORARY MARKING METHODS:

The following methods are considered safe for marking objects for short periods of time. They should be used only where semipermanent identification is not immediately possible. Temporary labeling should be restricted to field use, to identify objects that will undergo immediate and extensive restoration during which more permanent numbers would be obliterated, and to identify objects on loan or left in the temporary custody of the museum. The following tags may be used safely:

Unbleached linen tape: The tape should be stiffened and sized with flexible acrylic latex before applying identification numbers in India ink or with a typewriter. The numbers should be applied to unsized tape with laundry marking ink or waterproof, permanent India ink. Tape marked with laundry ink should be washed in water to remove acid before application to the object. The tape should be pierced at one end for attachment to the object by cord. Metal eyelets should *not* be installed.

Permalife Bristol Board: 0.010 inch thickness or Permalife catalogue card or cut-up Permalife file folders.

Cardboard tags: These tags, attached with cord, should be used only on the outside of mailing tubes, crates, and so forth, as cardboard slowly deteriorates, discoloring and

---

3. The sample guidelines provided here are adapted from those of the National Museum of History and Technology, Smithsonian Institution, which were developed for the museum's use by the Conservation Analytical Laboratory, Smithsonian Institution.

becoming brittle in the process, and can actually accelerate the deterioration of materials with which it is in contact.

Self-stick embossing tape (e.g., Dymo): This material may be used if cut double length after embossing and folded back on itself around a piece of cord and stuck to itself. No adhesive should remain uncovered; if adhesive is accidentally left exposed, talcum powder should be rubbed onto the surface. Only the cord should be attached to the object.

Metal tags: Impressed or embossed zinc or aluminum or tinplate strips may be useful for iron or steel objects. For objects of copper or copper alloys, including bronze, brass, or tinplate items, zinc or aluminum tags attached at *both* ends may be used. A metal tag attached at only one end can hammer, abrade, or smear itself against the object when the object is moved. Metal tags made of noble metals such as copper (or silver or gold!) should not be used as they are likely to cause corrosion of the metals they touch. Always handle bare metal with clean white gloves.

These tags should be attached with the following:

Cord: Soft cotton cord may be used. The larger the cross-sectional area of the cord, the less chance of chafing and damage to the object being tagged.

Wire: Copper and aluminum wire with a covering of polyvinyl chloride (PVC), polyethylene, or nylon may be used *temporarily*—contact with PVC over several months may cause corrosion. This covered wire is often referred to as "hook-up" wire. If available, covered solid copper telephone or communications wire may also be used. Wire should not be wrapped or twisted snugly around museum objects but should be twisted around itself at the label end, leaving a loose loop around the object. The twisted wire must be clipped off square as a final operation in order to minimize the risk of a protruding conductor that might scratch the object.

II. SEMIPERMANENT MARKING METHODS:

Semipermanent labels will be found on the majority of museum objects. The following suggested methods are for marks that can be applied directly to the museum object, will not cause deterioration, and can be safely removed at any time in the future.

A. *Impervious materials:* glass, stoneware, glazed pottery, brass, steel, etc.

1. Clean the surface thoroughly but gently using ethanol on a clean cotton swab or sodium bicarbonate powder on a swab moistened with distilled water. It is not necessary to remove lacquer or other permanent protective coatings if they are in good condition.

2. Write the numbers onto the surface using a Rapidograph or quill pen and Higgins or other nonwaterproof black India ink. This ink does not solidify quickly in the pens and can be washed out with water; it writes well over varnish and will not be redissolved by an overcoat of varnish. Users should be cautioned that metal-nib pens can scratch if applied forcefully. Oil paint may be used in place of ink, applied with a fine brush and diluted, if necessary, with odorless paint thinner (e.g., VMP naphtha). Watercolors may be applied if they will adhere to the surface, but are not generally recommended. Acceptable colors—that are durable, not especially poisonous, and unlikely to react chemically with surfaces to which they have been applied—are Venetian red oil (ferric oxide), blue black oil (bone black and ultramarine), zinc white oil (zinc oxide), yellow ochre oil or watercolor (hydrated ferric oxide), ivory black watercolor (bone black), Chinese white watercolor (zinc oxide), and oil painting primer (titanium oxide and zinc oxide). Winsor & Newton brand color names are specified because their composition is known.

3. Allow 5 minutes for ink to dry and 24 hours for oil paint. Drying may be hastened by an air blower.

4. Apply a small rectangular patch of varnish (Acryloid B–72) over the numbers.

5. Permit the varnish to dry thoroughly (about 15 minutes), using the air blower if necessary.

6. Clean brushes used with oil paint in Varsol. Clean pens used with Higgins or other nonwaterproof India ink in a 10% borax solution. Store brushes used with varnish in the varnish or clean in toluene. As toluene is moderately toxic, the usual precautions of good ventilation during use and hand-washing afterwards should be employed. Make certain the rim of the container of varnish is absolutely clean so that the lid may be tightly closed without sticking.

B. *Porous materials*: wood, gilt on gesso, unglazed pottery, terra-cotta, etc.

1. Clean the surface thoroughly using ethanol on a clean cotton swab.

2. Seal the surface of a small rectangular area using one or more coats of varnish (Acryloid B–72). Allow each coat to dry, and continue to apply until the final coat does not disappear into the material.

3. Inscribe the numbers, following the procedures outlined above for impervious materials.

4. Apply a covering coat of varnish.

C. *Other objects*:

Leather and flexible materials: Use a sealer before numbering. Seal only an area of sufficient size to contain the numbers.

Textiles, fabrics, and costumes: Sew onto the material a tag made of unbleached linen that has been prenumbered with marking ink and washed. The washing will remove acid liberated by some kinds of marking inks. Use ball-point needles and thread that is compatible with the fabric.

Paper products: Use a 2–H pencil, which will mark the paper with graphite but will not smudge, and press gently to avoid indentation. Works of art on paper should be marked on the reverse side at the lower *margin*. This is especially important for coated paper, such as glazed photographic prints, on which the pressure of the pencil on the back can be seen from the front.

Plastics: It is safest to use the suggested oil paints, and no sealers, for marking objects made of plastic, as some types of plastics are dissolved by toluene, the solvent used in sealers.

III. Permanent Marking Methods:

Metal surfaces can be permanently marked with a scriber or engraving tool. Works of art on paper can be stamped in ink, or a sharp, 2–H or harder, pencil may be used for writing the number, and pressed firmly, so as to indent the paper. Such labeling, which can never be removed from the object, should be undertaken only by specific arrangement with the responsible curator. This type of labeling is discouraged if a semipermanent method can be applied successfully.

IV. Unacceptable Marking Methods:

The following materials and methods are *not* to be used:

Pressure-sensitive tape (including cellophane, masking, and adhesive tape): Pressure-sensitive tape should *never* be used on museum objects. The adhesive sticks more and more tightly to the object as time passes. Many museum objects have been permanently marred with this material.

Self-stick labels: The adhesive of many self-stick labels can deteriorate within several months to an ooze that will penetrate paper products. Some adhesives can cause corrosion to metals around the periphery of the label. After removal these labels leave irreparably dark areas on finished wood, especially wood exposed to excessive illumination.

Rubber cement: This substance behaves somewhat like self-stick labels and should be avoided. It can cause staining of organic materials and tarnishing of metals.

Self-stick embossing tape: This tape has an adhesive backing that, like many self-stick labels, can deteriorate within a few months to an ooze that can penetrate paper and is difficult to remove from most surfaces even though the tape itself can be removed. These labels, although attractive in appearance, should not be used directly *on* museum objects.

V. LOCATION OF LABELS:

The number assigned to an object should be clearly visible when the object is placed in storage or in a reference collection. It should not be essential to move the object in order to see the number, for the unnecessary touching and moving of museum objects is known to be the greatest single source of damage to them. Positioning numbers for storage purposes, however, should be secondary to placement for display purposes. If the semipermanent number will not be seen in storage, an auxiliary label or tag should be used. It should be removed prior to placing the object on display and left in storage to represent the displaced object. Numbers should also be affixed to storage boxes, cases, and containers in which the object is normally placed. Again, the number should be clearly visible when the object is in storage; at the same time, the object's appearance when placed on exhibit must be considered.

The number should never be positioned in an area that is subject to abrasion—the bottoms of objects, for example, or positions likely to be touched by neighboring objects. The number should never be affixed solely to a bracket, arm, or trim piece that could become separated from the object. Nor should the number be placed on a loose or flaking surface that is likely to undergo restoration or preservation treatment to the extent that the number would be obliterated in the process. If this is in doubt, the number should be affixed in more than one place.

On objects of the same class or type, the number should appear consistently in the same location(s). For graphics, prints, and illustrations, the number should be placed on the reverse side at *two* diagonally opposite corners. If the object is hinged in a mount, it should be marked on the unhinged end. If the object is mounted in such a manner that its reverse side is not accessible, the number should be placed on the reverse side of the mount.

The number should be unobtrusive but clearly visible at the normal viewing distance from the object when in storage. A numeral height of 1/16 inch for every two feet of viewing distance (e.g., 3/16 inch at six feet) will prove satisfactory if the numbers are well formed and the recommended materials used. The use of an auxiliary tag, with larger numbers in ink, is suggested when the object in storage must be viewed at some distance (e.g., the top of a rack of shelves). Extreme care should be taken to ensure that the numbers will be legible and clearly distinguishable (e.g., 3 from 8, and 1 from 7).

Numbers should exhibit maximum contrast against the base color of the object. The following colors are recommended as guidelines:

BACKGROUND	SUGGESTED MARKING COLOR
white and off-white	black or red
black	white
dark blue, green, and blue green	white or yellow
pale blue, green, and blue green	black
gray	red or black
yellow	black
brown	white or yellow

Numbers punched or embossed in relief without a contrasting color are scarcely legible under fluorescent lighting. When used on tags, such numbers should be of greater height—3/16 inch for each two feet of viewing distance.

Supplements

This chapter was prepared with the assistance of thirty-three institutions, which generously shared their experience in marking collections. They are listed below, together with the identifying initials used in these supplements.

American Museum of Natural History, New York	AMNH
American Swedish Historical Museum, Philadelphia	ASHM
Art Institute of Chicago	AIC
Baltimore Museum of Art	BMA
Buffalo Museum of Science	BMS
California Academy of Sciences, San Francisco	CAS
Chicago Historical Society	CHHS
Children's Museum, Indianapolis	CM
Colorado Historical Society, Denver	COHS
Corning Museum of Glass, Corning, N.Y.	CMG
Field Museum of Natural History, Chicago	FMNH
Fort Worth Museum of Science and History	FWMSH
Idaho State Historical Society, Boise	ISHS
Kansas State Historical Society, Topeka	KSHS
Metropolitan Museum of Art, New York	MMA
Museum of the American Indian, New York	MAI
Museum of Fine Arts, Boston	MFA
Museum of Modern Art, New York	MOMA
National Gallery of Art, Washington, D.C.	NGA
National Trust for Historic Preservation, Washington, D.C.	NTHP
New Jersey Historical Society, Newark	NJHS
New York State Historical Association, Cooperstown	NYSHA
Newark Museum	NM
Oakland Museum	OM
Oregon Historical Society, Portland	OHS
Peabody Museum of Archaeology and Ethnology, Cambridge, Mass.	PMAE
Rochester Museum and Science Center	RMSC
Smithsonian Institution	
Conservation Analytical Laboratory, Washington, D.C.	SI-CAL

Cooper-Hewitt Museum, The Smithsonian Institution's National Museum of Design, New York	SI-CHM
Hirshhorn Museum and Sculpture Garden, Washington, D.C.	SI-HMSG
National Museum of History and Technology, Washington, D.C.	SI-NMHT
Textile Museum, Washington, D.C.	TM
University Museum, University of Pennsylvania, Philadelphia	UM

SUPPLEMENT I: SUPPLIES FOR MARKING

The following materials were mentioned by the contributing museums as regularly used for marking objects in their collections. Where possible, brand names have been specified.

PAINTS: Museums use both oils and acrylics. Specifically mentioned were:

Aqua-Tec Acrylic Polymer Emulsion, in toluidine red and titanium white (BMA)

Testors Model Enamel, in red, white, and black (BMA)

Winsor & Newton oils in Venetian red, blue black, zinc white, and yellow ochre; watercolors (where they will adhere to the surface) in ivory black, Chinese white, and yellow ochre; also oil painting primer (SI-CAL)

INKS: Museums use primarily India ink and drawing ink, in both black and white, generally permanent or waterproof. CAS notes that in all cases where numbers are written in ink, a varnish is used as a primer. India or permanent ink applied by ballpoint pen is used by NTHP and RMSC for applying numbers to cloth labels sewn on textiles, as liquid ink tends to spread. For the same reason, COHS and SI-CAL suggest using laundry markers to mark cloth labels. SI-CAL cautions that inked labels must be washed before they are attached to the object in order to remove acids liberated by some inks. Permanent felt-tip pens are used by FWMSH and MOMA to mark stretchers and frames. A permanent, waterproof, and alcohol-proof ink must be used for labeling fluid-preserved specimens, as the label is placed inside the jar with the specimen. Inks specifically mentioned for marking museum objects were:

Higgins Engrossing Ink (a waterproof, black carbon writing ink) (FWMSH, KSHS)

Higgins Non-waterproof India Ink (SI-CAL recommends this ink because it writes well over varnish, will not be redissolved by the application of an upper layer of varnish, and does not solidify in pens)

Pelikan Waterproof Drawing Ink (CAS, OHS)

Sheaffer Skrip Ink, in permanent jet black (BMA)

For labels filled in on the typewriter, both fabric and carbon film ribbons are used.

BRUSHES: Museums use sable and camel's hair watercolor brushes for applying paints, inks, primers, and protective coats.

PENS: Museums use crow quill pens and fine steel-nib pens; SI-CAL cautions that steel pens, especially Rapidograph pens, can scratch if applied too forcefully. Specifically mentioned were:

Castell pen (CM)

Koh-I-Nor Rapidograph pen (FMNH, FWMSH, SI-CAL)

BASE COATS OR PRIMERS: Some museums use clear varnishes as primers; others prime with a coat of color, generally white or gray but ultimately depending, of course, on the color of the object and the paint or ink selected for marking it. Clear nail polish has also been used successfully. Specifically mentioned were:

Acryloid B–72, a liquid plastic (PMAE, SI-CAL)

DuPont 305 series, high-speed lacquer-type primer-surfacer, in platinum gray (RMSC)

Flexbond Liquid Adhesive (SI-CAL suggests as a primer and overcoat for leather and flexible materials)

Gaylord Magic Mend Liquid Paper Adhesive (SI-CAL suggests as a primer and overcoat for leather and flexible materials)

Liquitex Polymer Medium, a gloss base coat (SI-CAL)

Pactra 'namel (airplane paint), in chrome silver (FWMSH)

Pactra XF–2 Quick Drying Enamel, in white (KSHS)

PROTECTIVE COATS: Clear base coats can also be used as protective coats. Specifically mentioned were:

Acryloid B–72, a liquid plastic (PMAE, SI-CAL)

Dow 803 Silicone (KSHS)

Flexbond Liquid Adhesive (SI-CAL suggests as a primer and overcoat for leather and flexible materials)

Gaylord Magic Mend Liquid Paper Adhesive (SI-CAL suggests as a primer and overcoat for leather and flexible materials)

Krylon No. 1303 Crystal Clear Spray Coating (RMSC applies with a brush)

PAPER TAGS: Museums use tags of acid-free paper or of 100 percent rag content. Fluid-resistant tags and tags of parchment or fiber are used for labeling fluid-preserved specimens.

CLOTH LABELS: Museums use labels of cotton, cotton twill, linen, linen twill, and unbleached linen. These labels can be sized in order to receive the number in ink by treatment with clear nail polish, liquid silicone, or flexible acrylic latex. KSHS cautions that tape so treated must be cut long enough so that the untreated ends can be tucked under the treated middle and prevent the coating from touching the fabric. SI-CAL cautions that the label should be washed after the ink has been applied to remove acids liberated by some kinds of marking inks.

THREAD: Museums use heavy linen, cotton, or nylon thread or cord for attaching tags to objects and specimens. For sewing labels on textiles, cotton or silk thread is used. SI-CAL suggests that the thread be compatible with the fabric; SI-NMHT, Division of Textiles, cautions that some threads of synthetic fibers like polyester and nylon may cut fragile yarns.

NEEDLES: Museums use small-size and ball-point needles for sewing labels on fabric objects. The needles must be in perfect condition—straight and rust free.

SUPPLEMENT II: MARKING SPECIFIC KINDS OF OBJECTS

The following additional information on marking specific kinds of objects, pertaining primarily to the location of marks, was supplied by the contributing museums.

AMPHIBIANS: See REPTILES AND AMPHIBIANS.

ARMS AND ARMOR: Metal tags stamped or engraved with the number are attached with loops of wire (CAS, MMA).

BASKETS: The number is applied in paint or ink, often over a base coat, if the reeds of the basket are long and wide enough; if not, a tag or label is tied or sewn to the basket (BMA, CAS, COHS, ISHS, KSHS, OHS, PMAE, RMSC, UM).

BIRDS: Eggs are marked in pencil or ink, usually above or below the opening (CAS, FMNH, FWMSH, NM, RMSC). Mounted birds are numbered on the bill with ink (BMS, NM), or on the leg or toe (RMSC); or the base is numbered in ink (FMNH, FWMSH); or a label is pasted to the bottom of the stand or perch (AMNH). Nests are marked by a tag attached to the inside (FMNH, NM); or the tray holding the nest is marked (FWMSH). Skeletons are tagged (FWMSH). Bones are numbered in ink, often with a primer and overcoat, in the center or largest part (AMNH, CAS, FMNH); a label is also pasted to the box in which the skeleton is kept (AMNH). Skins are identified by a tag attached to the feet (AMNH, BMS, CAS, FMNH, FWMSH); or they are numbered on the reverse, in ink (RMSC). Specimens preserved in alcohol are identified by a label inside the jar (AMNH, FMNH, FWMSH).

BOOKS (INCLUDING MANUSCRIPT ALBUMS, PORTFOLIOS, SCRAPBOOKS, AND SKETCHBOOKS): For books of moderate value, a bookplate bearing the number is attached inside the front cover. All loose pages, and portfolios or containers, are numbered in pencil (MMA, NTHP, OM). Books are numbered on the verso of the title page in pencil, and spines are numbered in ink or paint or with tape labels (SI-CHM). If the inner covers are marbelized or decorated, the number is marked in pencil on the first plain page, where it will not deface (BMA, NTHP). For rare books, or books that are works of art in which every page is precious, an acid-free paper marker bearing the number in pencil is inserted (BMA, OHS, SI-CHM). Scrapbooks and sketchbooks are numbered in several places as they are often cheaply bound or in weakened condition from use and the pages are liable to separate from the binding (KSHS). See also MANUSCRIPTS AND DOCUMENTS.

BOTANICAL SPECIMENS: Labels are attached to herbarium sheets (BMS, FMNH, FWMSH, NM) or to the vial or box containing the specimen (FMNH, FWMSH, RMSC). When type photographs are made, a small scale with the number of the print is fastened to the herbarium sheet and photographed along with the herbarium labels of the institution to which the original specimen belongs (FMNH).

BRONZES: See METAL OBJECTS.

CERAMIC OBJECTS (INCLUDING CHINA, ENAMELS, IVORIES, PORCELAIN, POTSHERDS, POTTERY, AND OTHER GLAZED, IMPERVIOUS SURFACES): The number is applied in paint or ink, with a protective overcoat, in an inconspicuous place not likely to be worn by handling and not obscuring any marks (AIC, BMA, CAS, CHHS, CM, COHS, FWMSH, KSHS, MAI, MMA, MOMA, NTHP, NYSHA, OHS, OM, PMAE, RMSC, SI-CAL, SI-CHM, SI-NMHT). The number is placed on the bottom, inside the lip, or near the bottom on the outside (ISHS). Or the number is placed under the base, inside the rim of the foot. Care must be taken to place the number where it will not be scraped as the piece is set down or moved. If necessary, the number can be placed near the lower edge of the back (KSHS). Potsherds are marked on the side without decoration (ISHS, KSHS). Pottery pipes are marked on the bottom of the bowl or, if broken, on the inside surface or on the pipestem end (RMSC).

CHINA: See CERAMIC OBJECTS.

COINS: The number is applied with paint or ink on the rim if possible; if not, the number is marked on the box, envelope, or coin holder in which the coin is kept (BMA, COHS, FWMSH, MAI, NTHP). One museum has an ongoing photographic project for record documentation, which is particularly important for artifacts like jewelry and coins that cannot be marked (OHS).

COSTUMES: A cloth label with the number applied in ink is sewn to the fabric; for details on preparing and attaching the label, see supplement I (CAS, CM, COHS, FWMSH, KSHS, MAI, MMA, NM, NTHP, NYSHA, OHS, PMAE, RMSC, SI-CAL, SI-NMHT, UM). Or a jeweler's tag with the number is attached (FWMSH). The label should not obscure any maker's labels. For dresses, coats, shirts, and blouses, the label is sewn on the back neckband; for skirts and trousers, on the back waistband; for hats, inside the band; for gloves, inside; for scarves, on the reverse in a corner (NTHP). Or, for garments with sleeves, the tag is sewn inside the left sleeve opposite the underarm seam; this is invisible when displayed, yet easy to get to if the garment is stored with the left side toward the outside of the closet. For vests and other sleeveless garments, the label is sewn inside the left armhole at the side seam. For hats, the label is sewn on the center back hatband or on the reverse of the maker's label; if the hat has no maker's label, the label is sewn inside the lower edge of the center back of the crown (KSHS). Or the label is sewn on seams inside sleeves, armholes, and/or pants legs (RMSC). The number is painted on the bottom of shoes (NTHP). On shoes with heels, the number is written in ink on the heel breast parallel to the bottom of the sole; on shoes without heels, the number is placed on the heel at the back of the shoe. For belts, the number is written in ink inside near the buckle; if the belt has no buckle, the number is placed inside near the end (RMSC).

DOLLS: Jeweler's tags bearing the number are attached (FWMSH). Or the number is applied in ink to the back of the head at the nape of the neck or, if this is not possible, to the foot. Lacquer is used as a base coat except on vinyl or plastic surfaces, which it damages. An acid-free tag is attached to dolls in storage so that the number may be seen without having to touch or move the doll (CM).

DRAWINGS (INCLUDING WATERCOLORS): The number is marked in pencil on the reverse of the work and on the mat; if framed, the frame is marked as for paintings (AIC, BMA, CAS, COHS, KSHS, MMA, MOMA, NGA, NYSHA, PMAE, RMSC, SI-CHM).

EMBROIDERIES: See TEXTILES.

ENAMELS: See CERAMIC OBJECTS.

FANS: The number is applied in paint or ink on the back end of the stick (SI-CHM), on the back of the handle (KSHS), or on the back side of one rib (ISHS).

FEATHERS: The number is applied in ink on the shaft (CAS), or on the bottom of the quill (COHS, MAI); or an acid-free paper tag or jeweler's tag is attached (ISHS, RMSC).

FIREARMS: The number is applied in paint or ink on the handle or stock (MAI) or near the trigger on the floor plate (ISHS). For long arms, the number is placed on the left side of the barrel at the breach end; for revolving firearms, numbers placed on cylinders can be turned away from sight when the object is on exhibit (KSHS). Powder horns are numbered on the back edge near the opening; powder flasks are numbered on the back side on the metal edge near the opening (RMSC).

FISHES: Specimens preserved in alcohol are marked with labels placed inside the jars or by a tag tied through the mouth or gill opening or around the caudal peduncle (CAS, FMNH). For skeletal material, the number is applied in ink, often with a primer and an overcoat, directly on the bone. Bones too small to number are placed in containers affixed with typed labels (CAS, FMNH). Duplicate labels are placed on top of and inside the container (FMNH).

FOSSILS: The number is applied in ink, often with a primer (generally white) and an overcoat, on a flat or interior surface where it will not rub off or obscure any important feature (AMNH, BMS, CAS, FMNH, FWMSH). In the case of specimens consisting of several pieces, such as disarticulated fossil vertebrates, the number is marked on each fragment (CAS, FMNH). A label is placed in the bottom of the box in which the vial is stored (RMSC). Microscopic invertebrates are mounted in standard slide mounts and labeled (FWMSH).

FURNITURE: The number is applied in paint or ink, with a primer and an overcoat, especially if the wood is porous or dark. Commodes and chests are marked on the bottom left corner of the back; chairs, at the back of the back left leg; tables, underneath a leaf, on the apron, or at the base of a leg. Heavy or fragile pieces should be marked so that numbers are visible without having to move the object (AIC, CHHS, MOMA, NGA, NM, OM, SI-CHM). If a piece is completely upholstered, a label is sewn near the right back leg. For beds, the number is painted on the outer side of both legs at the head of the bed. For tables, the number is painted on the underside of the top if possible, otherwise on the right-hand side near the back on the edge of the top as inconspicuously as possible. For lamps, the number is painted on the lower right-hand side near the back, or on the base if there is one. For mirrors and sconces, the number is painted on the reverse of the lower right and upper left corners of the frame; this allows the number to be seen easily while the object is either hanging on the wall or stacked in storage. If the object is extremely heavy, the number is placed on the edge of the frame along the lower left side (NTHP). All parts such as drawers, keys, removable shelves, etc., are numbered (KSHS).

GEMS: See MINERALS.

GLASS (INCLUDING GLASSWARE): The number is applied in paint or ink, protected with an overcoat. The number should be as small and legible as possible; it should not be seen when the piece is on exhibition (CAS, CHHS, CMG, COHS, ISHS, MMA, MOMA, NTHP, OM, PMAE, RMSC, SI-CAL, SI-CHM, SI-NMHT). The number is placed on the back edge of a rim or foot, if wide enough, otherwise at the center of the bottom of a foot beneath the stem or on a lower back edge that will not be very visible to a viewer of an exhibit (KSHS). White paint is used on clear glass to minimize the visibility of the number when the object is on display (BMA, MFA).

GOLD: See METAL OBJECTS.

GOURDS: The number is applied in ink, on a primer if necessary, with an overcoat (CAS, MAI, PMAE, RMSC). The number is placed at the bottom or at the lower back edge (COHS, KSHS).

INSECTS: Specimens pinned dry are marked with standard labels, of 100 percent rag, that are pinned directly below the specimen. The position on the pin, which is kept uniform by the use of a pinning block, is parallel to the insect's longitudinal axis and readable from the left side (AMNH, BMS, FMNH, FWMSH). Specimens preserved in alcohol are marked with labels inserted inside the jar (AMNH, FMNH, FWMSH). Specimens preserved on microscopic slides are marked with standard adhesive labels attached directly to the slide (FMNH, FWMSH).

IVORIES: See CERAMIC OBJECTS.

JEWELRY: If possible, the number is applied in paint or ink in an inconspicuous place not likely to be worn by handling. If the piece is very small, a jeweler's tag bearing the number is attached (BMA, CAS, COHS, FWMSH, KSHS, MMA, NGA, OHS, OM, RMSC, SI-CHM), or a cloth tag marked with a carbon ribbon typewriter is sewn around the piece (PMAE). Numbers usually go on the back of pendants, watchcases, charms, and fobs (KSHS).

LACE: A linen label bearing the number is sewn on a corner or near the end of the piece with a small loop of thread or with one or two stitches on the reverse (MMA, NM, SI-CHM).

LEATHER: The number is applied in paint or ink on a smooth, inconspicuous surface (CAS, COHS, FWMSH, NTHP, PMAE, RMSC, SI-CAL, SI-NMHT). It can be placed on the back side or on the front, under a flap (ISHS). Unless the leather is rawhide, however, or an extremely stiff, nonporous leather as was used for fire buckets, it may be damaged by solvents should numbers marked in paint or ink ever have to be removed (KSHS). For buckskin and rawhide, a laundry marker may be used (COHS). For flexible leathers, a cloth label may be attached by stitches passed carefully around and underneath the thread with which the leather object has been constructed, provided that the existing stitching is strong enough to withstand such manipulation. Cloth labels can also be attached to linings or to the underside of maker's labels (KSHS). Or they may be looped by sewing their ends together around an appendage such as a strap or belt loop. Or the number may be placed on metal decoration or hardware (KSHS, NTHP).

LINENS: See TEXTILES.

LOWER INVERTEBRATES: Dried crustaceans are marked by typed labels or metal tags affixed with wire to the specimen (FMNH). Fluid-preserved specimens are marked with standard labels placed inside the jar (FMNH, FWMSH).

MAMMALS: Bones are marked in ink, over a primer, in the center of the largest part of the bone, or near the proximal end of long bones, at the lower back center of the skull, or on the right ramus of the jaw (AMNH, CAS, COHS, FMNH, FWMSH, UM). The numbering of skeletal material is done on the most completely ossified portion, as ink will spread in porous bones, particularly from immature mammals (FMNH). Small bones are kept in numbered boxes (FMNH, UM). Or the number is written on the outside of the container mount if the container is large enough to hold the entire skeleton (FWMSH). Small skins are numbered in ink on the reverse (COHS), sometimes on the inner part of the neck, sometimes near the leg (MAI); or they are identified by a label tied to a hind foot (AMNH, BMS, CAS, FMNH, FWMSH). Large skins are also numbered on the reverse or identified by a label attached through a natural opening, like the eyes or nose, that is unlikely to tear (FMNH). Large skins may also be perforated with a three-cornered awl in the middle of the lower back (AMNH, CAS, FMNH). Skulls are marked in ink on the cranium and mandible (AMNH, CAS, FMNH, FWMSH, RMSC), or a tag is attached (FWMSH). A label is also placed in the vial or on the box where the specimen is stored (FMNH). Specimens preserved in alcohol are identified by a label placed inside the jar (FMNH, FWMSH) or attached to a hind foot of the specimen (AMNH).

MANUSCRIPT ALBUMS: See BOOKS.

MANUSCRIPTS AND DOCUMENTS: The number and an ink-stamped identifying symbol are generally placed on the written or blank side of the document. For complete information, see the Library of Congress's Preservation Leaflet 4, *Marking Manuscripts*, cited in note 2 and in the general bibliography.

MASKS: The number is applied in ink, inside, near the bottom (CAS, COHS, ISHS, MAI, PMAE, UM). For fabric masks, a cloth label is sewn inside the center at the top. For paper masks, the number is written in pencil at the bottom center on the reverse (KSHS).

METAL OBJECTS (INCLUDING BRONZES, GOLD, AND SILVER): The number is applied in paint or ink in an inconspicuous place and protected with an overcoat (AIC, ASHM, BMA, CAS, COHS, FWMSH, KSHS, MFA, MMA, MOMA, NTHP, OM, PMAE, RMSC, SI-CAL, SI-NMHT). The number is painted on the bottom so as not to obscure any marks. If silver flatware is to be exhibited with the hallmarks up, the number may be placed on the other side (NTHP). If the piece is too small for numbering, a cotton tag bearing the number is attached, and the object placed in a plastic bag (PMAE).

MINERALS (INCLUDING GEMS AND ROCKS): The number is applied in white or black ink, depending on the color of the specimen, placed so as not to obscure any important feature or on a small rectangle of primer in a contrasting color in the lower right-hand corner (BMS, CAS, COHS, FMNH, NM, PMAE). If the specimen is too small to number directly, it is placed in a vial on which the number is marked (PMAE). Gems are stored in boxes, with a label placed in the bottom of the box (RMSC), or in gem papers, marked with the number (BMS).

PAINTINGS: The number is applied in paint or ink on reverse diagonal corners of the stretcher and frame. For loans, a gummed sticker is pasted on the protective backing (AIC, CHHS, COHS, KSHS, MAI, MMA, MOMA, NJHS, NTHP, OHS, OM, PMAE, RMSC).

PAPER AND CARDBOARD OBJECTS: The number is marked in pencil in an unobtrusive place (FWMSH, OHS).

PHOTOGRAPHS: The number is marked in pencil, lightly, on the reverse, preferably in a corner of the lower margin. If the photograph is hinged in a mount, the number is placed on the unhinged end. The mount, or mat, is also numbered and, if framed, the frame is marked as for paintings (BMA, CHHS, COHS, ISHS, KSHS, MOMA, NTHP, NYSHA, OM, RMSC, SI-CAL, SI-NMHT). For cased tintypes, ambrotypes, and daguerreotypes, the number is applied in ink, with a primer and overcoat, on the top back flap of the preserver and picture unit and on the lower back of the case by the hinge. Uncased tintypes, ambrotypes, and daguerreotypes are marked in the same way, with the number on the top back flap of the preserver, if there is one, or on the top back center (KSHS).

PORCELAIN: See CERAMIC OBJECTS.

PORTFOLIOS: See BOOKS.

POTSHERDS: See CERAMIC OBJECTS.

POTTERY: See CERAMIC OBJECTS.

PRINTS: The number is marked in pencil, lightly, on the reverse, preferably on a lower corner in the margin. If the print is hinged in a mount, the number is placed on the unhinged end. The mount, or mat, is also numbered and, if framed, the frame is marked as for paintings (AIC, BMA, CHHS, COHS, KSHS, MMA, MOMA, NGA, NYSHA, OM, RMSC, SI-CAL, SI-NMHT).

REPTILES AND AMPHIBIANS: Eggs are marked in ink above and below the opening (FMNH). Skeletal specimens are marked with tags attached to the larger parts, and/or the numbers are written in ink, over a primer, directly on each bone (AMNH, FMNH, FWMSH). Skins and skulls are marked with standard identification tags (FMNH, FWMSH). Specimens preserved in alcohol are marked with a metal or resistant paper tag tied to a leg or around the neck (FMNH, FWMSH).

ROCKS: See MINERALS.

RUGS (INCLUDING TAPESTRIES): A cloth label with the number applied in ink is sewn to reverse diagonal corners so the number is easily found when the rug or tapestry is rolled. For details on preparing and attaching the label, see supplement I (CAS, COHS, KSHS, MAI, MMA, NGA, NM, NTHP, OM, PMAE, RMSC, TM).

SCIENTIFIC INSTRUMENTS: The number is applied in ink, with a protective coat, in an inconspicuous place (COHS, KSHS, OHS, RMSC). All removable parts are numbered. Instruments that have revolving parts can be numbered and the part then revolved to the far side when exhibited (KSHS).

SCRAPBOOKS: See BOOKS.

SCROLL PAINTINGS: The number is applied in paint or ink on the knob of the scroll (BMA, MFA, MMA). It is also painted on the box (BMA). Or a jeweler's tag bearing the number is attached to the cord at the opening end of the scroll (MFA, MMA).

SCULPTURE: The number is applied in paint or ink, with a protective overcoat, at the lower rear base, where it can be seen without having to lift or move the sculpture, or, if there is no base, in an inconspicuous place not likely to be worn by handling (AIC, BMA, KSHS, MAI, MFA, MMA, MOMA, NGA, NM, OM, SI-HMSG).

SHELLS: The number is applied in ink, with a primer and a protective overcoat, in an inconspicuous place not likely to be worn by handling (BMS, CAS, NM, PMAE).

SILVER: See METAL OBJECTS.

SKETCHBOOKS: See BOOKS.

STAMPS: The number is written in pencil on the back (KSHS). Mounted stamps are numbered on the back of the mount and on the hinge beneath the stamp (ISHS, KSHS). The envelopes in which the stamps are stored are also marked (ISHS).

TAPESTRIES: See RUGS.

TERRA-COTTAS: The number is applied in paint or ink, with a primer and a protective overcoat (CAS, KSHS, MMA, RMSC, SI-CAL, SI-NMHT). The number is placed where it will not be scraped as the piece is set down or moved. It may be under the base, inside the rim of the foot; if necessary, it may be put near the lower edge of the back (KSHS).

TEXTILES (INCLUDING EMBROIDERIES AND LINENS): Two cloth labels, with the number applied in ink, are sewn on with the grain of the fabric to reverse diagonal corners, so the number is easily found when the textile is rolled. For details on preparing and attaching the label, see supplement I (AIC, BMA, BMS, CM, COHS, FMNH, FWMSH, KSHS, MMA, MOMA, NM, NTHP, PMAE, SI-CAL, SI-CHM, SI-NMHT). For fragile textiles, jeweler's tags are sometimes attached in a position that does not obscure the design and is strong enough to hold the tag; the tag should not have to be removed when the piece is on exhibit (AIC, BMS, FMNH, MMA, NM). The tag is sewn on the lower left back corner of the piece, preferably along a hem or selvage (KSHS). Archaeological textiles (fragments) supported between two layers of prewashed nylon tulle have a label of cotton twill, onto which the number has been typed and sealed with varnish, sewn into the tulle next to them (CAS). When textiles are wrapped on tubes, or mounted on boards, the support is marked (BMA, MOMA, SI-CHM). For draperies and curtains, the label is sewn on the reverse lower left corner of each panel; if very sheer, the label is sewn on the reverse but on the outside corners where it will be less conspicuous. For pillow cases, the label is sewn inside the left corner of the bottom half, near the hem. For decorative pillows, the label is sewn on the reverse lower left corner (NTHP).

WATERCOLORS: See DRAWINGS.

WEAPONS (INCLUDING THOSE WITH LONG SHAFTS—ARROWS, CLUBS, HARPOONS, KNIVES, ETC.): The number is applied in ink, generally with a primer and a protective overcoat (CAS, COHS, ISHS, KSHS, MAI, OHS, PMAE, RMSC). The number is placed near the butt end, writing from the end toward the point (PMAE, UM). The number is placed on the handle of clubs and tomahawks, on the shaft of arrows, and on the inside end of bows (MAI). Swords and knives are numbered under the hilt (KSHS).

WOOD: The number is applied in paint or ink, with a primer and a protective overcoat, in an inconspicuous place not likely to be worn by handling (CAS, CM, COHS, FWMSH, KSHS, MMA, NYSHA, OM, PMAE, RMSC, SI-NMHT).

ZOOLOGICAL MATERIAL: Each category of animal is generally marked in a standard way. See "Survey of Marking Techniques for Identifying Wild Animals in Captivity," volume 8 of the *International Zoo Yearbook,* cited in the general bibliography.

5

STORAGE AND CARE OF OBJECTS

*Fig. 5.1.
At the Hirshhorn Museum and Sculpture Garden, Smithsonian Institution, small pieces of sculpture are stored on padded shelves. Large and heavy pieces are stored off the floor, on skids that can be transported by the museum's hydraulic lift truck. A movable staircase and large paper tags make accession numbers easy to read, eliminating the need for touching or lifting objects. Note that worktables in the storage area are padded.*

The storage and care of museum collections are essentially the province of curators and conservators. However, since the registrar is responsible for the temporary storage of objects while they are being unpacked, packed, examined, and registered, and since in some museums the registration department oversees the storage of permanent collections for the curators, the registrar must be well informed about safe handling techniques and must have a basic knowledge of approved storage methods. This chapter is intended to guide the registrar in the physical handling and temporary storage of incoming and outgoing material and to help the registration staff work intelligently with curators in caring for the museum's collections.

The material presented here is based partly on the work of Robert P. Sugden, formerly registrar at the Metropolitan Museum of Art, and on responses from museums of art, history, and science in various sections of the country to a request for information about storage methods. (These museums are listed in the supplement.) Information on the storage of natural history specimens has also been included for registrars in small museums who are sometimes called upon to handle mounted birds and animals, shells, minerals, and other specimens that in the larger museums are handled only by specialists, with special equipment, in the scientific departments.

Storage Areas

CONTROL OF STOREROOMS

Ideally, a separate area should be assigned to the registration department for the processing and temporary storage of objects moving in and out of the museum. This area should be maintained at the same relative humidity as the display or storage areas to which the objects will proceed next. Time should be allowed for the objects to equilibrate. A safe or vault in the registrar's office or in a storeroom should be available for the safekeeping of some of the more valuable objects that are being processed.

For storage, objects are generally separated into categories according to composition or material (ceramics, textiles, wood, and so forth). When possible, each material is stored in a separate area, with the proper temperature and

humidity conditions. Within categories, objects of a similar class (costumes, rugs, laces) are stored together, sometimes arranged by size, sometimes by geographic origin or culture area, sometimes by accession number. Scientific collections are stored phylogenetically or according to standard classification systems in each field. If possible, accession numbers should be clearly visible; an object should not have to be lifted or moved for its number to be seen. The contents

*Fig. 5.2.
Storerooms and the work areas within them must be kept neat and clean. In this storeroom for drawings and prints at the Hirshhorn Museum and Sculpture Garden, Smithsonian Institution, a worktable provides well-lit work/study space, yet the stored drawings and prints are protected from illumination. Framed works are kept in bins, and matted works in Solander boxes. Unmatted and oversize works are stored flat in sliding trays fixed inside closed cabinets.*

of storage units, drawers, and closets should be marked on the outside to prevent unnecessary opening.

Large museums often have elaborate, specially designed storage areas; small museums must sometimes store all collections in one room. In any case, access to storage areas must be controlled by the departments responsible for the objects stored within them, and records must be kept of storage locations. Pass keys to these areas should be restricted, not only because of the possibility of loss or damage to objects but also because material may be disarranged by people not familiar with the storage system.

Periodic checks or inventories of collections may be the responsibility of the registration department. How frequently these are made and whether the collection as a whole is examined, or only "spot" inventories taken, depend on the size of the museum's collections and staff and the kinds of records that are kept. The inventory serves several purposes. It is a systematic check to see that all objects can be accounted for and that they are stored properly. It brings objects that may require conservation treatment to the attention of the registrar or curator. It is also a check on the adequacy of the museum's location records.

SAFETY WITHIN STOREROOMS

Storage areas should be fireproof as far as possible and should be equipped with fire security devices such as smoke detectors and heat sensors. They should also be cleaned on a regular basis. Dust and dirt should be filtered out, and doors kept closed at all times. A neat and orderly arrangement of both storage and work areas within the storerooms will help prevent accidents and damage to museum objects. Packing, marking, conservation, and design and installation materials—plastic foams, wood, nails, cardboard boxes, paints, alcohol, paint thinners, and cleaning agents—constitute a danger to museum objects and a fire hazard and should never be kept in collection storerooms. Likewise all pens, inks, and sharp tools should be excluded, and not even carried on the person; only pencils should be used when working in storerooms. Because of the damaging effects of light on museum objects, all storerooms should be kept dark when not in use. Windows should be sealed and covered, and fluorescent lights fitted with ultraviolet filters. Textiles used as dust covers should be periodically cleaned and fireproofed. (For more detailed information on the design and equipment of storerooms, see article T.)

Dollies, picture trucks, tray trucks, and ladders should be provided for safety in moving objects from one location to another and should be kept at hand. Objects should be moved only by personnel trained in the physical handling of works of art or other museum objects. Handlers should know, for instance, that ceramic and glass vessels and sculpture should never be picked up by the handle, rim, or an arm but should be held in the hand and, if large, be supported by the other hand; that furniture should be lifted, never pushed, as the legs are frequently fragile; that the faces of paintings should never be touched and that paintings are best held by placing one's hands against the opposite edges, or, if two people are handling a large painting, by each placing one hand beneath and the other on the side; that in handling silver and other metals, gloves or a soft cloth should be used to prevent contact with the skin and consequent tarnishing. (For more detailed information on the handling of museum objects, see article Q.)

ATMOSPHERIC CONDITIONS IN STOREROOMS

The atmosphere in storerooms must be controlled. Most museums try to maintain the temperature in storerooms at 65–70° F., with a relative humidity of 40–60 percent, depending on the materials of objects stored there. The importance of maintaining a constant relative humidity in storerooms cannot be overemphasized. The effects of humidity and temperature on museum objects are ably explained by Murray Pease, a former conservator at the Metropolitan Museum of Art.

> RELATIVE HUMIDITY. Definition: *Relative humidity is the proportion of actual moisture to the maximum possible amount of moisture in the air at a specified temperature.* It is expressed in percentages.
>
> All air contains some water vapor, mixed with the air gases. The amount varies, but at a given temperature there is a maximum limit to the amount the air will hold. This limit is low at low temperatures, high at high temperatures.
>
> When air holds its limit of moisture, it is at 100% relative humidity. If the temperature of that air is then raised, its capacity for moisture will increase but its moisture will be the same, therefore its relative humidity will go down. If the temperature is reduced instead of raised, its capacity will be unequal to the amount of moisture present, and condensation will occur.
>
> MEASUREMENT: The simplest and one of the most accurate instruments for measuring relative humidity is the sling psychrometer. It consists of two ordinary thermometers, one having a sleeve of wet cloth over its bulb. When a rapid current of air is passed over it, evaporation from this sleeve cools the bulb, and the wet-bulb thermometer registers lower than the dry. The amount of evaporation, and therefore the wet-bulb temperature, is controlled by the relative humidity of the air. Prepared tables, known as psychrometric tables, give the relative humidity figures for all wet- and dry-bulb thermometer readings.
>
> SIGNIFICANCE: Fibrous materials such as paper, wood and cloth absorb moisture from the air at high relative humidities and give it off at low relative humidities. Their fibres expand when moisture is absorbed, contract when it is given off. Therefore all changes in relative humidity of the surrounding air will affect the shape and condition of works of art made from these materials. The forces involved are great, and the effects may be serious.
>
> IDEAL CONDITIONS: Paintings on paper, wood, cloth, and other hygroscopic materials are safest in an atmosphere of uniform, moderate temperature and humidity (40–60%). High or low extremes, and repeated fluctuations of humidity are equally to be avoided. The same is true of temperature, not because of the temperature itself, but because of its effect on relative humidity.[1]

A continuous record of temperature and humidity levels in a given area can be obtained with a hygrothermograph, an instrument that uses a bimetallic plate to measure temperature changes and a band of human hairs to measure humidity changes. Both these devices are connected to pens that record the

---

1. Quoted in Robert P. Sugden, *Safeguarding Works of Art: Storage, Packing, Transportation and Insurance* (New York: Metropolitan Museum of Art, 1948), pp. 32–33. This book is a classic text for museum conservation.

fluctuation on a sheet of graph paper attached to a revolving drum. Typically, this chart records a week's readings. The accuracy of the hygrothermograph should be checked regularly against a good mercury thermometer and a sling psychrometer, operated by a trained user, and recalibrated as necessary.

The air in museum storerooms should be circulated continuously to ensure that conditions are uniform throughout the area and to provide the ventilation required for good care of textiles, leather, and other organic materials, but strong drafts of air should be avoided. The museum's air circulation system should contain filters to help remove dust and atmospheric pollutants. The registrar should work closely with the museum's building services manager and/or engineers, as well as conservators, in monitoring the climatic conditions within the building.

Storage Equipment

STORAGE UNITS

The design and composition of storage cabinets, shelving, worktables, and other materials and supports used in storerooms are important in protecting museum objects.[2] Shelves should be adjustable so that they can accommodate objects of various sizes. They should be neither too high nor too deep to afford easy access to the objects and must, of course, be strong enough to bear their weight. Storage units with interchangeable parts are useful in some cases. For the protection of objects, shelves and worktables are often padded with a soft material like felt, a heavy-grade linoleum, or an indoor-outdoor carpet with no pile, bonded to a thin layer of rubber. The latter should be avoided in unventilated spaces. Worktables are often covered with the kinds of quilted pads used by moving companies.

Cabinets, shelving, worktables, and other storeroom fixtures and cases are generally made of wood or metal, or a combination of the two; occasionally they are made of plastic. The properties of each material must be considered in selecting them.

Wood. Wood is almost certain to be acidic, and it can exude harmful resins. Wood sealing treatments can, in addition, damage textiles, as can splinters and rough or warped wood surfaces. Wood blocks out light; it is more resilient than metal and therefore affords more protection against chipping and breaking should an object accidentally be dropped. It will not buckle, like metal, under the weight of heavy objects, but it may warp. It is subject to water and insect damage, and is less likely to be airtight than denser materials like plastic. Wood can be completely consumed by fire, but, in the case of a fire brought quickly under control, it can afford better protection than a positive conductor of heat, like metal.

2. The following information on the qualities of materials used for storage units and materials is from Sugden, *Safeguarding Works of Art: Storage, Packing, Transportation and Insurance*, pp. 15–17; David B. Little, *Safeguarding Works of Art: Transportation, Records, and Insurance*, AASLH Technical Leaflet 9, from *History News*, 18:5 (May 1963); the Metropolitan Museum of Art; and the Conservation Analytical Laboratory, Smithsonian Institution, and the Division of Textiles, National Museum of History and Technology, Smithsonian Institution.

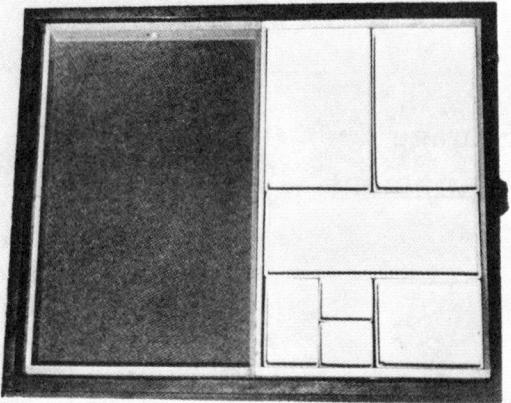

Figs. 5.3–4. Drawers with interchangeable wooden trays of various sizes are useful for storing small objects.

Metal. Metal is likely to be more costly, for its volume, than other materials, but is often lighter. It can rust, may have sharp corners or protrusions, and may encourage the condensation of moisture on its surfaces. When enameled, metal is less likely to be reactive than wood, but some enamels cause paper in contact to yellow. Metal blocks out light, is not subject to insect damage, and can be made both rustproof and waterproof. Metal is so positive a heat conductor that it provides little protection from fire, though it may retain some semblance of its outer form. Aluminum, however, can reflect radiant heat and retard rise in temperature beyond the metal.

Plastic. Plastic can be expensive or inexpensive, depending on the type. It is waterproof. If sealed, it may permit moisture condensation when there are changes in temperature, thus encouraging the growth of mold and mildew and producing water stains. It is transparent and can develop a static charge. Under fire conditions most types melt; some types soften in the presence of moth crystals; some types are chemically reactive in other ways.

STORAGE MATERIALS

Many small objects are stored in specially divided and lined drawers or trays. Coins, gems, and stamps are protected in envelopes. Prints and works of art on paper are mounted and stored in Solander boxes. Ceramic pieces are some-

5: STORAGE AND CARE OF OBJECTS

times placed in fitted casings. Textiles stored flat are protected by layers of tissue paper. Costumes are stored in bags or boxes with plastic windows through which the contents may be seen. Furniture and other objects are protected by dust covers. The properties of the materials selected for such support and protection must be considered as carefully as the storage units themselves, for they, too, come into direct contact with museum objects. These materials should be chemically inert, flexible, and resilient, and have a high buffering action on the relative humidity.

Cloth. Of all the fabrics available, undyed, unsized cotton cloth is recommended. Flexibility and cost depend on weight, density, and finish. Most such cloth is flexible enough not to be too space consuming, and most blocks out light. But, untreated, cloth is not waterproof and cannot be sealed; it is subject to insect damage; and, although nonacidic, it can become acidic after contact with acidic materials and so should be changed periodically.

*Fig. 5.5.
Unframed works of art on paper are stored in acid-free Solander boxes to protect them from light and dust.*

Paper. Ordinary paper—including brown wrapping paper, white and blue tissue, and newspaper—is acidic and should not be placed where it will come into contact with museum objects, for the acid may migrate and cause damage, especially to papers and textiles. Special papers described as nonacidic or acid free are more desirable, but some papers can become acidic after contact with acidic materials and so should be changed periodically. Nonacidic paper that contains an acid neutralizer, or buffer, is most desirable, because it will neutralize any acid that might start to change its pH. It is available as tissue and in various weights of heavier papers and envelopes. Waterproof papers containing tar should not be used in conjunction with materials that have been exposed to moth crystals, because the tar becomes liquid when exposed to moth-proofing chemicals.

Plastic. Some weights of plastic are fairly inexpensive. Plastic sheeting is flexible enough not to be too space consuming; it covers, yet is transparent; but it attracts dust if it develops a static charge. It is waterproof. If sealed, it may permit moisture condensation when there are changes in temperature, thus encouraging the growth of mold and mildew and producing water stains. Under fire conditions, most types of plastic melt. Some types may be chemically reactive; polypropylene, polyethylene, and polyester are considered the least reactive.

Fumigation of Storage Areas

Rugs and textiles containing wool or silk, fur garments, ethnological specimens with wool or feather decoration, mounted animals and birds as well as animal and bird skins, pinned insects, and some botanical specimens require constant protection against moths and other pests. In some museums, refrigerated vaults or gas chamber storerooms are used for the protection of these objects in storage. Gas chamber storerooms are sealed periodically, and gas is injected into the room from cylinders. This method of fumigating must be done only by experienced personnel, as it is harmful to humans if used incorrectly.

Various insecticides can also be used in protecting collections. Paradichlorobenzene (PDB) is probably the most effective protective agent that can be used with some safety. It is used with objects that can be stored in airtight cabinets. The dosage should be carefully controlled so that it is strong enough to be effective but not above the allowable exposure for humans. The surrounding space should be well ventilated. Vapona is more effective, but it must not be allowed to come into contact with human skin. Naphthalene and camphor flakes are used as moth repellents in a similar way; although they vaporize less quickly than paradichlorobenzene and are therefore less effective, they last longer. Some museums no longer use insect repellents in closed cabinets because of the health hazard and resort to periodic fumigation instead.

Materials for which the closed-area vapor treatment is impractical may be protected with a good commercial insecticide spray. The spray is applied to the surroundings, not to the objects, to leave one gram of insecticide to each square meter of wall. For direct application to textiles and ethnographic materials, some museums use Edolan-U. Information on insecticides considered safe for use where there will be some human contact can be obtained from local agents of the federal Occupational Safety and Health Administration.

Before any newly acquired object is stored, it should be examined carefully for possible infestation. This may be difficult to detect. For instance, the larval stage is the feeding stage in the moth cycle, so there can be danger even when no moths are visible. A soiled object is much more susceptible to insect damage than a clean one, so anything that can be cleaned safely should be cleaned. For cleaning museum objects, as for fumigating them, the advice of curators and conservators should be sought.

Works of art on paper and other museum objects of paper may be fumigated periodically with thymol to help prevent mold and foxing stains.

Supplement

STORAGE REQUIREMENTS AND METHODS

This chapter was prepared with the assistance of thirty institutions, which generously shared their experience in storing and caring for collections. They are listed below, together with the identifying initials used in this supplement.

Alaska State Museum, Juneau	ASM
American Museum of Natural History, New York	AMNH
Arizona Historical Society, Tucson	AHS
Art Institute of Chicago	AIC
Buffalo Museum of Science	BMS
California Academy of Sciences, San Francisco	CAS
Children's Museum, Indianapolis	CM
Cleveland Museum of Natural History	CMNH
Corning Museum of Glass, Corning, N.Y.	CMG
Field Museum of Natural History, Chicago	FMNH
Guggenheim Museum, New York	GM
Merrimack Valley Textile Museum, North Andover, Mass.	MVTM
Metropolitan Museum of Art, New York	MMA
Museum of Fine Arts, Boston	MFA
Museum of International Folk Art, Santa Fe	MIFA
Museum of Modern Art, New York	MOMA
National Gallery of Art, Washington, D.C.	NGA
New Jersey Historical Society, Newark	NJHS
New York State Historical Association, Cooperstown	NYSHA
New York State Museum, Albany	NYSM
Newark Museum	NM
Oakland Museum	OM
Peabody Museum of Archaeology and Ethnology, Cambridge, Mass.	PMAE
Rochester Museum and Science Center	RMSC
Smithsonian Institution	
Conservation Analytical Laboratory	SI-CAL
Cooper-Hewitt Museum, The Smithsonian Institution's National Museum of Design, New York	SI-CHM
Hirshhorn Museum and Sculpture Garden, Washington, D.C.	SI-HMSG
National Museum of History and Technology, Washington, D.C.	SI-NMHT
Textile Museum, Washington, D.C.	TM
University Museum, University of Pennsylvania, Philadelphia	UM

The relative humidity figures are generally those recommended by Murray Pease; they are approximate and need not be adhered to absolutely. It is more important that fluctuation in relative humidity be reduced to a minimum, and that the relative humidity to which an object has been equilibrated be continued, as fluctuation is the most common cause of deterioration. In addition, there are objects that do not fall neatly into any one of the categories used, such as a leather belt ornamented with silver disks, a steel knife with an ivory grip and a painted wooden sheath, or one of the new materials or combinations of materials used by artists. Then, too, considerations other than the purely physical enter into the planning of storage, as it is sometimes desirable to store together groups of quite different objects—for example, in an ethnological collection, everything from a particular tribe or village, or in a historical collection, everything associated with one person.

The information included here is very general and is not intended as instruction in the use of the materials mentioned. Curators, conservators, and references such as those listed in the general bibliography should be consulted for information about the protection of collections.

AMPHIBIANS: See REPTILES AND AMPHIBIANS.

ANATOMY: Embalmed material is stored in Monel Metal tanks or in glass jars, depending on the size of the specimen, and is protected from light (FMNH). Skeletons, depending on their size, are stored loose, in cardboard boxes, in wooden trays, or on shelves in cabinets (FMNH). Skulls are separated from postcranial material; skulls are stored in padded cardboard boxes, postcranial material in wooden boxes (CMNH) or in wooden or metal trays inside wooden or metal storage cabinets (AMNH).

ARCHAEOLOGICAL SPECIMENS: Large objects, including whole stone and pottery vessels, are stored on open shelving and in covered cartons. Small objects (stone, bone, potsherds) are stored in trays or cardboard boxes in cabinets (AHS, AMNH, ASM, CAS, CMNH, PMAE, UM). Stone specimens, particularly soft stone like limestone, should be stored in a relative humidity of less than 50 percent (CAS, MMA, UM). Lithic material is stored in unsealed plastic bags (CAS). Archaeological bronzes should be checked periodically for "bronze disease," a rapidly spreading and very destructive corrosion, and affected pieces should be promptly removed and treated by a conservator (MMA, UM). Very fragile archaeological textiles are supported (sewn) between two pieces of prewashed nylon tulle; the actual textile is not touched by the thread but is given support by the stitching; it is also visible and so direct handling of the textile is avoided (CAS). Perishable objects should be given the same care as other materials of the same fragility (see CERAMICS; GLASS; JEWELRY; METALS; STONE; TEXTILES).

ARMS AND ARMOR: Metal armor should be stored in a reasonably dry room (see METALS); accessories and shields, in a moisture-controlled room (see WOOD); and lacquered Japanese objects, in a room with some humidity (see LACQUER). Ideal storage methods for various types of armor are: suits of armor in fiberboard cartons or on their mannequins (custom built for each suit), covered loosely with a plastic sheet; large parts of armor (helmets, breastplates, etc.) on open shelves, covered with plastic sheets; objects of great importance or fragility, in specially made plywood boxes with one side of plastic to enable examination without handling; shields, in plastic bags, hung on the wall; banners, rolled in tubes (see RUGS); pole arms, standing in racks; swords, in cabinets provided with vertical panels of a large-mesh wire through which blades are passed so that the hilts are visible at a glance; delicate eighteenth-century court swords and Japanese mounted swords, in cabinets with shallow trays; elements and accessories of armor, in drawers in metal or wooden cabinets; Japanese sword fittings, in cabinets with shallow drawers, individual spaces allocated for each piece (MMA). See also FIREARMS; WEAPONS.

5: STORAGE AND CARE OF OBJECTS

BARK CLOTH AND BARK CONTAINERS (INCLUDING BIRCHBARK AND ELM BARK AS WELL AS THE SO-CALLED TAPA CLOTH OF THE PACIFIC ISLANDS): A rather high relative humidity, about 55 percent, is best. Tapa and the less fragile bark cloth are wrapped around a core support, which is itself wrapped with aluminum foil or acid-free tissue paper to prevent acid leakage (CAS, MIFA). The rolled cloth is wrapped in muslin and stored on a Unistrut metal framing system (CAS). Or the cloth can be stored flat in cabinets or on open shelves (MIFA, UM). Birchbark containers are stored on open shelves (CMNH, PMAE). They are kept in unsealed plastic bags (CAS).

BASKETS: The relative humidity should be at least as high as for wood, that is, about 55 percent. Baskets are stored on open shelves (AHS, ASM, CMNH, MIFA, NYSM, UM). Shelves are lined with closed-cell polyethylene for padding; baskets are placed along an exterior wall for coolness (ASM). Baskets should be protected against dust; they are stored in unsealed plastic (polyethylene) bags. Brittle and flexible baskets are stuffed with acid-free tissue (CAS, PMAE). Baskets should not be stacked in or on one another (AHS, CMNH). If ornamented with feathers or wool, they must be protected against moths (UM).

BIRDS: Eggs are stored in padded, divided drawers or trays or in cotton-lined cardboard boxes protected from dust in cabinets (ASM, CAS, FMNH). Mounted specimens are stored on shelves in cabinets with naphthalene flakes or in a fumigation vault (CAS, FMNH), or in metal cabinets, with plastic-bottomed trays, and protected with insect repellents (AMNH). Nests and skins are stored in wooden or plastic-bottomed trays or in drawers, in dustproof cabinets that are fumigated periodically (AMNH, CAS, FMNH). Or eggs, nests, and skins may all be stored in metal cabinets containing PDB (CMNH). Skeletons are stored in boxes in a dust-free area. Fluid-preserved specimens are stored in jars or crocks in metal cabinets (AMNH).

BOATS: Large sailboats and power launches are stored on specially constructed cradles. Canoes, guide boats, etc., are laid on their keels directly on the floor. Refinished decks are covered with polyethylene as dust covers. All boats are checked periodically for sagging or hogging (NYSM).

BOOKS: Relative humidity should be constant, at about 40–50 percent (SI-CAL, from the Library of Congress). Books are stored on wooden library shelving or in shallow wooden drawers that are lined (AHS, ASM, MIFA). Rare books, and manuscript and map materials, are stored under controlled temperature and humidity (CMNH), including the use of air-particle filtration and fire-prevention heat sensors (MVTM). They are housed on shelves (CMNH) or are wrapped in glassine and placed in Solander boxes stored in the main storage vault or in a secure cabinet in the library (GM).

BOTANICAL SPECIMENS: Dry seeds, fruits, fibers, gums, and resins are stored in containers of various sizes, in boxes in cabinets or in trays in drawers (CMNH, FMNH). Pickled specimens are kept in glass bottles (FMNH). Herbarium specimens are stored flat, in folders, in metal cabinets or cases, and protected against insect pests (ASM, CMNH, FMNH). PDB is used for fumigation (CMNH).

BRONZES: See METALS.

CERAMICS (INCLUDING PORCELAIN, POTSHERDS, AND POTTERY): Both relative humidity and the degree of protection against dust required depend on the degree of firing and the type of surface. Poorly fired pieces and those with a fugitive paint surface should not be exposed to a high relative humidity. They are stored in drawers, or on shelves in cabinets, or on open shelves; shelves are usually covered with a resilient material (AHS, ASM, CAS, CMNH, MMA, MOMA, NYSM, OM, UM), such as Fisher Scientific polyethylene bench and drawer liner (SI-CAL). Those pieces that do not stand by themselves are either inverted or stabilized with foam collars (CAS). Small items are stored in separate

Figs. 5.6–7. These modular storage units at the Costume Institute of the Metropolitan Museum of Art were designed both to preserve costumes and accessories and to make them readily available for study. Note the venetian blinds, which, when raised, allow easy access to the costumes and, when lowered, shield them from light while permitting circulation of air. The units are covered inside and out with an inert plastic paint to protect them from rust and acid.

padded boxes, placed in wooden drawers in metal cabinets. Paper padding is used inside vessels (CMNH). The pieces are covered with DuPont microfoam sheeting, and plates and similar pieces are interleaved with microfoam (AHS). Potsherds are stored in trays or cardboard boxes in cabinets (AHS, ASM, CMNH, PMAE, UM).

COINS: A low relative humidity, under 40 percent, is desirable. Coins are stored in individual boxes or in small individual envelopes in trays, boxes, or shallow drawers (ASM, MFA, MMA, NJHS). Or they are stored in coin frames and placed in photographic slide storage pages (AHS).

COSTUMES: A cool, dry atmosphere is best (see FURS; TEXTILES). Filtered air is desirable, and for some materials periodic mothproofing is essential. The storeroom should be dark when not in use. Garments are generally hung on padded or wide-shoulder hangers in cabinets or wardrobes (AHS, ASM, CAS, MIFA, MMA, NYSM, PMAE, UM). Hangers are wide, made of plastic, and covered with acid-free tissue (AHS). Some varieties of plastic, however, will soften in the presence of PDB moth crystals (SI-CAL). The costumes are protected from dust with plastic bags (MIFA, MOMA), open at the

bottom (NYSM), or with individual muslin garment bags (AHS). Fragile pieces or pieces with heavy applied ornamentation are stored flat in boxes or in shallow drawers, or loosely folded (AHS, CAS, CMNH, MIFA, MMA, PMAE, UM). Acid-free glassine, e.g., Promatco Reflex Matte #85 (SI-CAL), is used underneath folded garments and between folds (CMNH, NYSM). Robes are sometimes rolled or stored flat in boxes or shallow drawers instead of being hung or folded. Accessories such as shoes, hats, and gloves may be kept in cabinets or drawers (CAS, MMA, PMAE, UM). Hats are stored on a top shelf of the wardrobe, on plastic wig heads if necessary, and shoes along the floor of the case. On occasion accessories are suspended from the hanger in a small muslin bag. An inventory list on each door and a card tied to the hook of the hanger make locating items fast and easy. The hangers of coat and trousers are tied together with string (NYSM).

DOLLS: Dolls are stored on commercial doll stands that have been padded with fiber-fill and covered with muslin (CM). They are placed in closed cabinets (NYSM), on open shelves covered with microfoam sheeting in a light-tight textile room (AHS), or on open shelves protected from contact by means of acid-free paper. Dolls are covered lightly with plastic open at the bottom and perforated to allow movement of air. Clothing is sometimes supported from underneath with acid-free tissue. China legs, hands, and arms (if uncovered) are protected with acid-free tissue or an inert polyethylene foam. "Sleep-eyes" dolls are sometimes stored face down (and never on their backs) to protect the delicate weight mechanisms in their heads (CM).

DRAWINGS: See PAPER.

EGGS: See BIRDS; REPTILES AND AMPHIBIANS.

EMBROIDERIES: See TEXTILES.

ENAMELS: The relative humidity should be less than 50 percent and constant (SI-CAL). Enamels are stored on wooden shelves in closed closets; small pieces are stored in padded drawers (MMA).

ETHNOLOGICAL SPECIMENS: Nonperishable objects are kept on open shelves or hung on walls or on wire screens. Perishable objects are stored in trays or drawers in mothproof cabinets. Objects with easily damaged surfaces are kept in dustproof cabinets or wrapped in soft paper. For many ethnological specimens, protection against moths and other insect pests is essential (AHS, AMNH, ASM, CMNH, FMNH). All specimens are stored in unsealed plastic bags so that insect activity may be readily assessed. Regular checks are made for insect damage, and the specimens are fumigated if necessary (CAS). Objects that can be damaged by routine handling have mounts made for them (PMAE). Perishable objects should be given the same care as other materials of the same fragility (see BASKETS; CERAMICS; COSTUMES; FURS; LEATHER; MASKS; MATTING; METALS; SHIELDS; STONE; TEXTILES; WEAPONS; WOOD).

FANS: Fans are stored on open shelves in a light-tight textile room or in dust-free cases or in wooden drawers in metal cabinets (AHS, CMNH, MIFA, NYSM). Or they are stored in specially designed cases of cloth-covered cardboard, with slots shaped to fit the fans and designed to fit into standard storage boxes (SI-CHM). Fans are stored folded (NYSM).

FILM: Black-and-white film should be stored in a relative humidity of 40–50 percent, flat color film in a relative humidity of 15–25 percent (SI-CAL, from Kodak). Glass-plate negatives are placed in acid-neutralizing Permalife envelopes and stored on open wooden shelving (NYSM).

FIREARMS: Long firearms are stored in a specially constructed wooden cabinet (metal cabinets are not likely to be sturdy enough for these heavy pieces, nor are metal cabinets in special sizes likely to be available), one to three pieces to a drawer; pistols are stored in metal or wooden cabinets (MMA). One museum stores firearms and swords in airtight, roll-around plywood cases (NYSM); another in vertical racks (SI-NMHT).

FISHES: Skeletal material is stored in wooden or cardboard boxes in cabinets. Specimens preserved in alcohol are stored in drums, crocks, tanks, or glass jars, depending on the size. All specimens are protected from light (AMNH, CAS, FMNH).

FOSSILS: Large fossils are placed on shelves or open racks; small fossils, in steel storage cans or in cardboard, plastic, or wooden trays or boxes, or on shelves, in dustproof cabinets; tiny fossils, in gelatine capsules or glass vials; microscopic specimens, in cardboard slides with a central depression covered by a glass slide; thin sections are covered by glass cover slips that protect the specimens (AMNH, BMS, CAS, CMNH, FMNH).

FURNITURE: A constant relative humidity of about 55 percent is best; for composite pieces of which one or more elements are wood, it is absolutely essential. Furniture is stored on arm racks, platforms, or decks in ventilated rooms and is protected from dust with muslin or plastic (polyethylene) (AHS, MIFA, MMA, MOMA, NGA, NM, NYSM, OM). Objects should not be stacked on one another (AHS). See also WOOD.

FURS: Cold storage is best; if cold storage is impossible, furs should be kept in a cool, dry atmosphere and fumigated periodically. Furs are stored flat on open wooden shelving or in wooden drawers in closed metal cabinets (AHS, CMNH, NYSM). Furs are covered with glassine, and PDB is used as a fumigant (CMNH). Some kinds of furs and skins that have not had certain tanning treatments are subjected to an Edolan-U treatment; others are periodically fumigated (CAS).

GEMS: See MINERALS.

GLASS: A constant relative humidity of 40–50 percent is best. Glass is stored on wooden or metal shelves, preferably felt covered or otherwise padded, so as to be shock proof, and shallow enough for all pieces to be seen (AHS, ASM, CAS, CMG, OM). The shelves have sliding doors with screens or glass windows (CMG, NYSM). Or the glass is covered with DuPont microfoam sheeting; plates and other similar pieces are interleaved with microfoam sheeting or padding (AHS, NYSM). Very delicate pieces are wrapped in tissue, placed in well-fitting boxes, and stored in closed metal cabinets (CAS). Glass objects should not touch each other and should be protected from dust and moisture. Objects with painted decoration or having fragile weathering crusts should not be subjected to strong spotlights (CMG).

ILLUMINATIONS: See PAPER.

INSECTS: Dry pinned specimens are stored in trays lined with cork or foam (Ethafoam, polyurethane) and placed in standard entomological cases or trays (glass-topped) in insect-proof cabinets (AMNH, CAS, CMNH, FMNH). Unmounted specimens are stored on sheets of Cellucotton in covered, shallow cardboard boxes in insect-proof cabinets (CAS, FMNH). Low humidity is desirable; light should be excluded as far as possible; and fumigation should be done periodically (AMNH, CAS, CMNH, FMNH). Naphthalene and Vapona are used as fumigants (CMNH). Specimens preserved on microscopic slides are stored in standard slide boxes, in cardboard trays on open shelves (CAS), or in Lab-Aid flat filing units with removable slide trays (FMNH). Fluid-preserved specimens are stored in standard metal cabinets and inspected periodically to make sure the alcohol has not evaporated (AMNH).

IVORIES: A rather high humidity, at least 55 percent, is best, and it is important that it be constant. Old ivory is particularly susceptible to sudden changes in temperature. Ivories are protected from dirt and dust with cloth covers or unsealed plastic bags and stored on open shelves, in lined wooden drawers, or in trays in cabinets (ASM, CAS, CMNH, MIFA, MMA). Scrimshaw is wrapped in acid-free tissue and stored in dust-free cabinets with foam-lined drawers (NYSM).

*Fig. 5.8.
Entomological collections are pinned in cork- or foam-lined trays and stored in glass-topped cases, like these at the Denver Museum of Natural History. When not in use, the cases fit like drawers into wall units.*

JEWELRY: A relative humidity of 40 percent is best for fine metal jewelry, as a high humidity fosters tarnish, although even a very low relative humidity will not prevent it. Jewelry is stored in individual boxes or divided drawers, both lined, in secure cabinets (AHS, ASM, CMNH, NYSM, SI-CHM). Or each piece is individually wrapped in soft cotton or tarnish-preventive cloth (CAS) or in neutral pH paper (OM) and stored in individual boxes in cabinets. Decorative jewelry is mounted on silk- or velvet-lined trays that fit in drawers in cabinets (SI-CHM). Ornaments of shell, teeth, feathers, and so forth, may be stored under the same conditions as costumes (UM).

LACES: See TEXTILES.

LACQUER (ORIENTAL): If dry and in good condition, lacquer should be kept in a relative humidity of about 55 percent unless it has equilibrated to some other level safely. Fluctuation of heat or humidity is very destructive, as is low humidity (SI-CAL). Lacquer is stored on open shelving (MIFA).

LEATHER: A relative humidity of 55 percent, with moderate light air and no draft, is best. Leather is stored flat on wooden drawers in metal cabinets, with glassine underneath (CMNH), on Mylar-covered wooden shelving (AHS), or in acid-free cardboard boxes or on open shelves, care being taken to avoid contact with brass such as buckles, spurs, buttons, etc., which corrode when in contact with tannic acid (NYSM). Tack and harnesses are hung by the metal bits or heavier parts on a pegboard. Saddles are stored on single or multiple saddle storage racks, some covered with nylon carpeting. Saddle bags are stored separately on shelving. A number of special pieces have specially constructed supportive and protective cases (AHS). Large shields are hung on pegboards in an air-conditioned room (CMNH). Tlingit Indian armor is stored on mannequins on wooden shelves (ASM).

LOWER INVERTEBRATES: Dried crustaceans are stored in individual trays in drawers in steel cabinets; fluid-preserved specimens are stored in individual vials or in jars on shelves in steel cabinets (FMNH).

MAMMALS: Skeletons are stored in boxes or trays and protected from radical changes in humidity and temperature. Large skulls, with antlers, are hung from metal racks; others are placed on shelves in cabinets, in boxes, or in trays in slide-tight cases; small skulls are stored in vials or in pasteboard boxes with skins or in special skull boxes (AMNH, FMNH). Skins are hung by the head from racks or bars or stored in boxes or trays in cabinets; they should be fumigated periodically (AMNH, CMNH, FMNH). PDB is used as a fumigant (CMNH). Prepared skins are stored on shelves in cabinets with insect repellent or on open shelves in fumigation vaults. Specimens preserved in alcohol are kept in jars on shelves or in cabinets. Large fluid-preserved specimens are kept in concrete, stainless steel, or plastic tanks or drums (FMNH).

MASKS: The relative humidity and the degree of protection against dust and insects required depend on the material of which the mask is made. Masks are stored in cases on large shelves, in wooden trays in metal cabinets (CMNH, PMAE, UM), or they are hung on wire racks, pegboards, or heavy wire mesh screens by hooks inserted into screw eyes on the reverse (ASM, FMNH, MIFA, PMAE, UM). Flat storage is preferred, as occasionally the attachments for hanging will loosen or break and the mask will fall. In addition, some museums refrain from inserting screw eyes into valuable specimens (ASM, FMNH).

MATTING: The same high relative humidity as for baskets, about 55 percent, is best. Mats should be stored flat or loosely rolled, never folded (CMNH, UM).

METALS (INCLUDING BRONZES, COPPER, GOLD, IRON, SILVER, STEEL, AND TIN): A low relative humidity, below 40 percent, is best. Metals are stored on open shelves or in a closed cabinet with wooden trays or shelves, often padded to prevent scratching (AHS, ASM, CMNH, MIFA, MMA, UM). Metals are stored with silica gel to maintain low humidity (CAS). Archaeological bronzes should be checked periodically for a destructive corrosion known as "bronze disease," and affected pieces should be promptly removed and treated by a conservator (MMA, UM). Arrow points are stored in drawers partitioned and lined with acid-free tissue (CMNH). Silver is polished and wrapped in antitarnish tissue paper (AHS) or placed in a plastic bag that is tied to prevent access of air, which causes tarnishing, and stored in a locked metal case (NYSM). Or silver is stored in cabinets lined with tarnish-preventive cloth; camphor may be used for added protection against tarnishing (MMA, UM). Delicate tin toys are placed in dust-free, glass-fronted cabinets so that they are easy to locate when needed; this arrangement decreases the possibility of painted surfaces being scratched when individual items are wrapped or unwrapped (NYSM).

MINERALS (INCLUDING GEMS AND ROCKS): Minerals and rocks are stored in trays, drawers, or boxes, in dustproof and light-tight cabinets (ASM, CAS, CMNH, FMNH, RMSC). Large specimens are stored on open shelves (CAS, FMNH, RMSC). Deliquescent minerals are coated with Vinylseal diluted with acetone and stored in wooden drawers in dustproof cabinets. Light-sensitive minerals are stored in black boxes in light-tight cabinets (BMS, FMNH). Gems are stored in gem papers (BMS).

MINIATURES: See PAINTINGS.

MUSIC BOXES AND NOVELTIES: Music boxes and novelties are stored on open shelves and covered by individual glass domes or polyethylene to keep dust and dirt off. Ship models are stored inside display vitrine, housed in custom-built wooden shipping cases, and placed on open shelves. Toys are stored in cabinets or wrapped in acid-free paper and stored in Paige or Hollinger boxes on open shelving; large toys are placed on open shelving and covered with plastic (NYSM).

MUSICAL INSTRUMENTS: The chief characteristic of musical instruments is that they are "live" objects—their vibrating strings, membranes, and reeds, their bone plectra and ivory keys, are all means of making sound. Many are composed of several different materials, e.g., wood, metal, and leather, and even instruments of a single material, such as wood, may have several varieties, each with individual reactions and problems of care. Thus the basic requirement for storage is that all instruments be kept in an area with controlled humidity and temperature; sharp or sudden changes in either can cause opposite and destructive effects in a single instrument. Instruments constructed of plant fibers (e.g., bamboo) or that have been lacquered or varnished require a fairly high humidity; keyboard instruments, a moderate humidity; brasses, which are less susceptible to changes, a dryer air. Instruments can be stored on wooden shelves by kind and size; wood is preferable to metal because it will not buckle with weight and will not scratch. Small instruments, e.g., pottery whistles, clappers, bells, etc., can be stored in partitioned wooden boxes or narrow drawers. Accessories are stored with the instruments to which they belong; additional collections, such as mouthpieces, bows, reeds, etc., can be stored in the same manner as small instruments. Lacquered and varnished instruments should be wrapped for protection. Musical instruments require continuous care to keep them "alive" and so must be within reach (MMA). Instruments are stored in wooden drawers or on shelves (AHS, ASM, CMNH, NYSM). Each musical instrument is individually placed in an unsealed plastic bag and stored on Aircap (bubble plastic) in closed metal cabinets, with no instrument touching another (CAS). Pianos and large musical instruments are stored on the floor and covered with polyethylene (NYSM).

5: STORAGE AND CARE OF OBJECTS

Fig. 5.9. Paintings are best stored hung on sliding screens. The screens used for painting storage at the Smith College Museum of Art are made of aluminum.

PAINTINGS (INCLUDING MINIATURES): A constant relative humidity of about 55 percent should be maintained, with moderate air circulation. The sliding screen method of storage is preferred. Paintings are hung with S-hooks, which fit the regular installation screw eyes or picture hangers, on screens of aluminum panels or heavy diagonal mesh on a rigid framework. Protective coverings of plywood, cardboard, or fiberboard are attached to the backs of the stretchers (AIC, CAS, GM, MFA, MIFA, MMA, MOMA, NGA, NJHS, NM, NYSHA, NYSM, OM). One museum has found that these sliding screens could be built and installed by a local fence-and-gate contractor at a much lower price than that charged by the specialists in museum storage (NJHS). Or paintings can be hung on metal hardware mesh attached to walls (AHS). If possible, paintings are stored in shadow box frames with ultraviolet filter Plexiglas (GM). Paintings can also be stored in wooden or metal bins, or cabinets, with separation sheets of corrugated cardboard between them (MIFA). Stacking should be avoided if possible; however, if paintings must be stacked, they should be separated by sheets of corrugated cardboard and should rest on pads; composition or fiberboard separation sheets are satisfactory but corrugated cardboard, though not permanent, is best, as it gives under pressure. It is better not to use covering pads and blankets as they become dirty and can do considerable damage if allowed to come into contact with the painted surface. Miniature paintings are stored in shallow drawers in closed cabinets (AIC, MFA, MMA, MOMA, NGA, NM, NYSHA, NYSM, OM). Miniatures are placed on a layer of acid-free tissue to prevent sliding when the drawer is pulled open (NYSM). Thymol is used for mold fumigation (CAS).

PANEL PAINTINGS: As with all complex pieces of which wood is one of the elements, a constant relative humidity of about 55 percent is absolutely essential; circulation of air is desirable to provide uniform conditions in the storage area, but direct drafts should be avoided. The surface should be protected against dust and scuffing (MMA). See also WOOD.

PAPER (INCLUDING DRAWINGS, ILLUMINATIONS, PHOTOGRAPHS, PRINTS, WATERCOLORS, AND OTHER WORKS OF ART ON PAPER): A constant relative humidity of not more than 50 percent must be maintained for the preservation of paper objects. They should not be exposed to direct light, should be completely sealed against dust, and are best stored in Solander boxes on wooden shelves. Since paper with woodpulp or processed with certain chemicals is dangerous, only rag-stock, acid-free paper or mat board, preferably buffered, should be used in direct contact with such works. Acid will migrate from papers with higher acid content to papers with lower acid content, and the acid causes paper to yellow, become brittle and weak, and eventually deteriorate beyond repair. Unframed works of art such as drawings, watercolors, and prints, should be covered with chalk-filled tissue paper, acid-free glassine paper, or Japanese mending tissue and placed in hinged mats with window fronts. They are hinged to the mats with Japan paper and a small amount of starch paste along one edge only. Two or three standard-size mats should be used, and storage boxes (usually Solander boxes) made to fit these sizes so the material will not shift around in the box and cause damage by abrasion. Oversize material may be stored in portfolios. Cabinets with shelves designed to accommodate the standard-size Solander boxes and portfolios are usually used for storage. Shelves that pull out facilitate the handling of the boxes; in particular, a pull-out shelf on which to rest one box at a time as it is taken out is very helpful. Framed works of art on paper are stored in bins (some carpeted) or on screens (AIC, CAS, GM, MFA, MOMA, NGA, NJHS, NM, UM). Some unframed works are wrapped in glassine and stored flat in portfolios or acid-free folders or metal map cases or cabinets (AHS, ASM, CMNH, MIFA, MVTM, NYSM). Documents are stored in acid-free boxes (AHS). Very large works that are matted may be stored on shelves. Unframed works are covered with acid-free glassine, except for photographs, which are hinged in double mats (not dry mounted) (MOMA). All works, except those done in a friable media (e.g., pastels), are framed under ultraviolet Plexiglas (GM, MOMA). Large and awkward posters are mounted on Fome-Cor with an acid-free covering and protected with clear Mylar (a polyester) (NYSM). Thymol is used for mold fumigation and to prevent foxing stains (AIC, CAS).

PAPYRUS (INSCRIBED): A very slightly higher relative humidity than for paper is desirable. Papyrus documents are stored flat or mounted between glass (MMA).

PARCHMENT: Parchment is stored like leather, in a relative humidity of 50–60 percent (SI-CAL, from the Library of Congress).

PHOTOGRAPHS: See PAPER.

PLASTER OBJECTS: The relative humidity should be less than 50 percent; but below 35 percent plaster can lose water, and "dusting" of surfaces has been observed in dry conditions (SI-CAL). Plaster objects are stored on open shelves and protected with dust covers (AHS, CMNH, MMA). Gessoed frames are hung on a hardware mesh (AHS).

PORCELAIN: See CERAMICS.

POTSHERDS: See ARCHAEOLOGICAL SPECIMENS; CERAMICS.

POTTERY: See CERAMICS.

PRINTS: See PAPER.

REPTILES AND AMPHIBIANS: Hard-shell eggs are stored in cardboard trays in mothproof cabinets; skins are stored on wooden racks in a closed, ventilated, dark room; skeletal specimens are stored in wooden boxes (CAS). The storage area is air-conditioned, and the specimens protected from heat and light (AMNH). Skulls are stored unboxed on shelves; specimens preserved in alcohol are stored in tanks or jars, depending on the size, in an open room but protected from light (FMNH). Or specimens preserved in alcohol are stored in wooden trays that fit movable shelves in metal cases (AMNH).

ROCKS: See MINERALS.

RUGS: A relative humidity of 40 percent is best. When exhibited, rugs are almost always hung, and they may also be hung (unrolled) when in storage, but it should be remembered that they need a periodic rest period. They should not be folded but may be rolled and wrapped, using moth crystals. A satisfactory method is to roll against the pile, with the right side inward, on poles, three inches or more in diameter, of thoroughly seasoned wood. Or the cores can be made of cardboard, but cardboard tends to sag. In either case, the poles or cores must be wrapped in aluminum foil or acid-free tissue to protect the rug against the acidity of wood or cardboard and possible sap leakage from wood. The pole or core should extend beyond the rug on each side, and then itself be suspended at these ends. This suspension avoids undesirable pressure from the weight of the pole, and from the rug itself, on the rug. Rolls should not be stacked on shelves, as this exerts undesirable pressure on the lower rugs. A roll more than twelve feet long, however, unless reinforced with steel, will sag in the middle if suspended, and so must be laid on a shelf; its position should be changed periodically. Periodic fumigation is required (AHS, AIC, CAS, MIFA, MMA, MOMA, NGA, NYSM, TM). To protect against dust, each rug is loosely wrapped with plastic (polyethylene), which is open at each end (CAS, MIFA, MOMA). Or the rugs are covered with Mylar (AHS) or other polyester (SI-CAL) held in place with linen tape. They are kept in a light-tight textile room (AHS).

SCIENTIFIC INSTRUMENTS: Nautical instruments are stored in Paige boxes on open shelves (NYSM).

SCREENS (ORIENTAL): Because of their complicated construction and the high relative humidity in Japan, screens require a higher relative humidity than other paper products: 55 percent is best. Screens may be stored as they are in Japan: folded and wrapped separately in cloth covers (traditionally silk, but also unbleached cotton muslin) and placed, usually in pairs, inside wooden storage boxes with removable covers, or in cabinets with padded grooves at the top and bottom to hold them in place (MFA, MMA).

SCROLL PAINTINGS: In general, the same rules apply to scrolls as to paper items, but the relative humidity should be slightly higher: about 55–60 percent is best. Scroll paintings are wrapped in cloth (silk or unbleached cotton muslin) and stored in individual boxes or kept in drawers, or on shelves (MFA, MMA).

SCULPTURE: Small pieces are stored on open shelves, in bins, or in cabinets; large pieces are stored on platforms with the weight evenly distributed and the object held in place with wedges. Bronze reliefs may be hung on sliding screens (AIC, ASM, MIFA, MOMA, NGA, NM, NYSM, SI-HMSG). Soapstone pieces are stored on padded shelves; small items are placed in special trays (CMNH). As far as possible, it is a good idea to wrap and box pieces individually (GM). Heavy pieces are stored on individual skids that are built to fit the platform of the lift truck; this allows easy transport (NM). See also CERAMICS; METALS; PLASTER OBJECTS; STONE; WOOD.

SHELLS: Shells are stored in trays or drawers, divided and lined, in dustproof cabinets (ASM, CAS, FMNH, RMSC).

Fig. 5.10. The Oriental and Ancient storage area at the Cleveland Museum of Art has a central statuary storage dock with cupboards for additional storage underneath. Small objects are housed on shelves.

SHIELDS: Shields are stored flat on shelves or hung on walls or on heavy wire mesh screens or pegboards. If they are carved or painted, care should be taken to protect the surface; if of skin with the hair on, or if decorated with feathers, they should be protected against insect pests (CAS, CMNH, UM). Shields should be given the same care as other objects of the same material (see LEATHER; METALS).

SILVER: See METALS.

SKELETONS: See ANATOMY; BIRDS; FISHES; MAMMALS; REPTILES AND AMPHIBIANS.

STAMPS: Stamps are mounted with stamp hinges or in plastic mounts on acid-free pages in albums; duplicates are stored in stock cards or sheets and then in Mylar or glassine envelopes (AHS).

STONE: For archaeological specimens, which may contain salts, and for ancient soft stone generally, like limestone, in which dampness can produce serious deterioration, the relative humidity should be kept below 50 percent and constant. For harder stone in good condition the relative humidity is not particularly important, but it should remain constant (CAS, MMA, UM). Stone objects are stored on open shelving (AHS, ASM, NYSM); small items are stored in padded boxes (CMNH). Lithic material is stored in unsealed plastic bags (CAS).

TAPESTRIES: A relative humidity of 40 percent is best. Small pieces are stored flat in acid-free boxes; larger pieces may be hung or rolled and stored as described for RUGS (AIC, MFA, MMA, NGA, NYSM). Folding is not recommended, but if it must be done the first fold should be parallel to the warp threads so that when the tapestry is hung these folds will be horizontal and the weight of the tapestry will help hang them out; vertical folds will never come out through hanging. Glassine paper should be placed over and between folds (CMNH, MFA).

TERRA-COTTAS: Stable relative humidity is most important, preferably 45–55 percent (SI-CAL). Small terra-cotta pieces are stored in padded, individual boxes, in wooden drawers in closed metal cabinets (CMNH).

TEXTILES (INCLUDING EMBROIDERIES AND LACES): A relative humidity of 40–50 percent and a temperature of 65–70° F. are best, but the most important thing is stability and the avoidance of sudden changes in either. Textiles should be stored in a ventilated room and protected from light when not being used, and against insects and dirt. Small pieces are stored flat between sheets of buffered, acid-free tissue, on trays or shelves (AHS, CMNH, MOMA, MVTM, NYSM, SI-NMHT, TM). Or they can be mounted on mat boards (MOMA) or on uniform stretchers that fit in study-room cases where they are placed horizontally (MFA), or they can be framed behind, but not touching, glass (CAS). Large pieces can be rolled and covered following the same procedure as described for RUGS. Textiles must be rolled carefully, to avoid creasing (MFA, SI-NMHT), and should not be rolled too tightly (SI-NMHT). Folding should be avoided if at all possible; if not, sharp folds should be avoided by padding the folds with strips of washed, unsized cotton cloth (SI-NMHT) or acid-free glassine paper (AHS, CAS, CMNH, MFA). The textile should not be refolded along the original fold lines, and should be refolded periodically. Textiles should be removed from storage periodically and aired (SI-NMHT). Samplers, small textiles, and needlepoint are removed from old mounts or frames and sewn down on unbleached muslin backed with a four-ply rag board and stored in a metal map case lined with acid-free paper (NM). Very fragile textiles are supported (sewn) between two pieces of prewashed nylon tulle; the actual textile is not touched by the thread but is given support by the stitching; it is also visible and so direct handling is avoided (CAS). PDB crystals will protect against mildew and mold as well as against insects; blue tissue paper has traditionally been believed to help prevent the discoloration of lace and linen; only an acid-free variety should be used. Tar-lined paper should never be used in wrapping textiles as high temperature and PDB vapor will soften the tar and can cause serious damage to fabrics. Kraft-type paper over tissue will serve as dust protection (FMNH, MFA, PMAE, TM).

WATERCOLORS: See PAPER.

WEAPONS (INCLUDING THOSE WITH LONG SHAFTS—ARROWS, HARPOONS, LANCES, SPEARS): Weapons with long shafts are placed horizontally on long, well-supported, plastic-covered hooks, which in turn hang from a pegboard. They are protected from dust by a plastic sheet (CAS). Or they may be hung vertically, head end up, on a heavy wire mesh screen, by attaching a hook to a wire wrapped around the shaft behind the head (UM). Or they are stored in special weapons cabinets or weapons racks (AHS, CMNH). Or they may be stored flat on shelves (ASM, UM). Bows should be unstrung and stored flat or on special holders (UM). See also ARMS AND ARMOR.

WOOD: A constant relative humidity of about 55 percent is best for all wooden objects; for composite pieces of which one or more elements are wood (furniture or painted panels, for example), it is absolutely essential. Circulation of air is desirable to provide uniform conditions in storage areas, but direct drafts on wooden objects should be avoided. All fine wooden pieces should be protected against dust; this is particularly important for painted pieces, which should be provided with dust covers or wrapped in soft paper. Small items are stored in drawers in cabinets or on shelves; large pieces are stored on platforms (ASM, CMNH, MIFA, NM, PMAE). Each piece is protected from other pieces and from dust by unsealed plastic bags and placed on Aircap (bubble plastic) in closed metal cabinets (CAS). See also FURNITURE; PANEL PAINTINGS.

6

LOANS FROM MUSEUM COLLECTIONS

Fig. 6.1. International loan exhibitions draw large crowds to the public areas at museums and, behind the scenes, mean special responsibilities for the registrars of both the lending and the borrowing institutions.

See forms III.A.

Loans from the collections of a museum must be authorized. The person responsible for authorizing loans varies from museum to museum, depending on the size, staff, type of collections, and value of the individual loans. It is the practice of many museums, large and small, to have all loans approved by the board of trustees. Some museums refer only very important long-term, or very valuable, loans from the collections to the trustees for approval, leaving less important loans to be approved at the discretion of the director. In some museums, the director is responsible for approving all loans; or, in museums with varied collections, the curator of each department or collection may be responsible for approving a loan from the material in his or her care.

Before a loan is approved by the director or curator or referred by the director to the trustees for approval, the object and its record must be checked for any detail that would prevent its being loaned. The records of the curator and the registrar should disclose whether there is any previous commitment for the object for the dates requested; whether it is an integral part of the museum's gallery installations; whether it is in good enough condition to travel; whether there is any stipulation from the donor, if a gift or bequest, stating that it is not to be loaned; or whether it has been imported under permanent exhibition bond and requires permission from U.S. Customs before it can be removed from the museum. (For an explanation of permanent exhibition bond, and restrictions on material under bond, see chapter 8.)

The following procedure is suggested for handling outgoing loans after they have been approved by the director, curator, or board of trustees. It has proved satisfactory in several museums where the movement of museum objects is handled by the registrar and can, of course, be modified to suit the requirements of other museums.

Notice to Registrar

When a loan has been approved, the borrowing museum will send its loan agreement form, or a letter to that purpose, to the lending museum. In some museums it is the registrar's responsibility to review the conditions of the loan and sign the form. In others, this responsibility belongs to the director or the

See forms III.B and III.C.3 and figure J.1.

See forms III.C and III.H.1–2 and figure G.8.

curator. At this point some lending museums also issue their own outgoing loan agreement to the borrower to verify the conditions under which the loan is being granted.

After the loan agreement is signed, the registrar should be authorized to release the object and provided with the following additional information: the name and address of the borrower, the purpose for which the object is being borrowed, the period of the loan (the exhibition title and dates, if for an exhibition), and the date it should arrive at its destination or the date it is to be shipped. The registrar should also be advised of any special packing, shipping, or insurance arrangements. The director or curator may notify the registrar of outgoing loans by sending to the registration department the original or a copy of the initial request and a copy of the reply to the borrower. If the full information needed by the registrar is not available at the time of the first correspondence, it should be forwarded as soon as received. The originals or copies of subsequent correspondence concerning the loan should also be sent to the registrar so that he or she may be kept up to date as to the status of the loan and any changes in the arrangements. The registrar may of course be notified by memorandum or by a form detailing the necessary information instead of by copies of correspondence.

Often the registrar is responsible for reserving all loans. This is easily noted by the use of colored flags on the cards of the objects committed for loan. If there should be a group of objects offered from which the borrower is to select, all items should be reserved until the final selection is made.

Arrangements for Packing, Insurance, and Transportation

The lending museum is responsible for packing the objects in such a way as to ensure their safe arrival at the borrowing institution. If the loan involves a particularly fragile item, the lender should not only pack it accordingly but should provide the borrower with special packing instructions for its return. At that time, the borrower is responsible for repacking the object or objects in exactly the same way as received, using the same boxes, packages, pads, and other furnishings when possible, unless a change is specifically authorized by the lending institution. Or the lending museum may request that the borrower engage a commercial packer, experienced in the handling of fragile objects and fine arts, to collect, pack, and ship the loan. The packer must be given the special packing, handling, and shipping instructions, which the lender may specify. In either case, the borrowing institution is generally responsible for the cost of packing the objects at both ends. If the lending museum is to bill the borrower for the packing, the registrar at the lending museum must see to it that accurate records of packing costs are kept.

Insurance coverage for loans from museum collections may be arranged by the borrowing institution in accordance with the lender's instructions. In such cases, the borrowing institution normally furnishes the lending museum with a certificate of insurance. Or the lending museum may prefer to maintain its own insurance and bill the borrower for the premium from the time the objects

Fig. 6.2.
A loan exhibition of architectural drawings and photographs is mounted in a small gallery.

are removed from their normal places of exhibition or storage until they are returned in satisfactory condition. In either case, the lending museum is responsible for determining the valuation of the objects to be loaned and also whether a valuation is to be declared to the shipper. Many standard fine arts policies do not provide coverage for insured material outside the continental United States and Canada or on fairgrounds. In these cases, it must be agreed upon in advance whether the borrower or the lender is to be responsible for providing proper coverage.

The borrowing museum generally makes arrangements for transporting the loans, subject to the approval of the lender, and is responsible for the costs. The selection of the type of transportation depends on such factors as distance, size, weight, and cost, as well as the type, value, and nature of the material to be shipped. (For more detailed discussions of packing, shipping, and insurance, see chapters 7 and 9.)

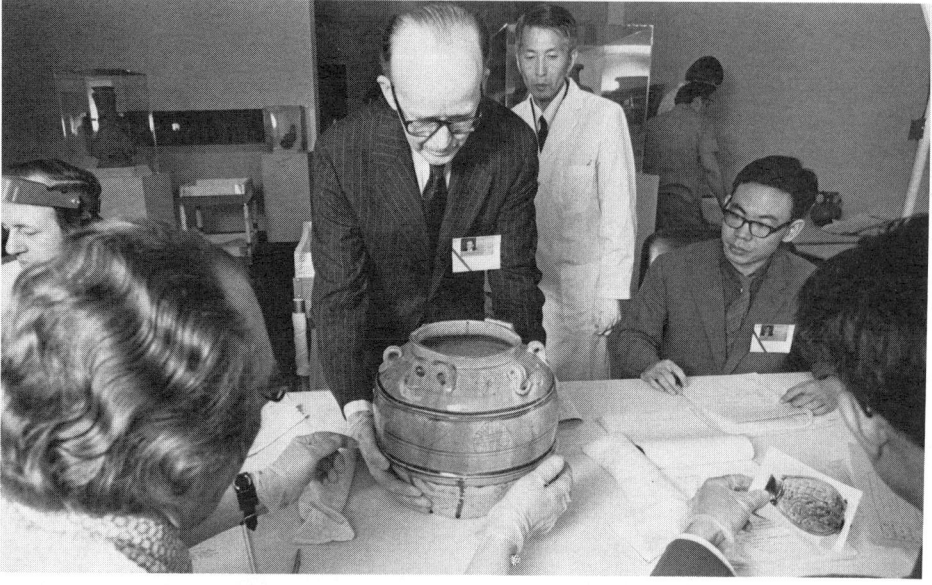

Fig. 6.3.
An object from the internationally significant loan exhibition "Archaeological Finds of the People's Republic of China" is carefully examined for condition by representatives from Chinese museums and the National Gallery of Art.

Releasing Material after Authorization

See forms I.C.2–3.

Once the registrar has been authorized to release objects for loan and has made the necessary arrangements for packing, insurance, and transportation, the next step is to prepare the objects for shipment. If the outgoing loan is to be packed by the museum staff, a work or production order or memorandum should be sent to the packer as far in advance as possible. It should state when the work is to be done and, if the packer does not have the responsibility for storing boxes, whether boxes are available for the loan or whether they will have to be made. The memorandum should also include any special packing instructions. The staff in charge of the handling and moving of objects within the building should be informed at this time of the location of the reserved loans so that the objects can be removed from storage and exhibition areas to be packed. It is often the registrar who gives the order to the shipping room and personally oversees the packing and shipping.

Many institutions use a printed release form for outgoing material. This form, signed by the registrar, lists the objects, the name and address of the borrower, the exhibition title and dates, the carrier, and the date when the loan is to be shipped. It should be sent to the shipping room well in advance of the shipment date, and may also be used to notify the responsible staff to remove the objects from storage or exhibition.

Before packing begins, the registrar must again check the condition of each object against its condition as recorded in the registration department files and its condition photographs, especially if considerable time has elapsed since the approval of the loan. Any changes should be noted, and new condition photographs taken, if necessary. The objects themselves should then be made as secure as possible to avoid damage in handling and transit. Paintings, for example, should sit securely in their frames. Simpler frames are sometimes provided for

6: LOANS FROM MUSEUM COLLECTIONS

traveling, and the glass on glazed paintings replaced with Plexiglas. (For a full description of packing and shipping museum objects, see, in addition to chapter 7, articles R and S.)

Receipts from Borrowers

See forms III.F and III.H and figure J.3.

To assure notification of the arrival and provide for a signed acknowledgment of the loan, the lending museum sends a receipt to the borrower. Usually, two copies of an outgoing loan receipt are sent on the same date that the loan is shipped, one copy to be returned with signature and date when the loan is received, and the other to be retained by the borrower. Outgoing loan receipts should include the following information:

NAME AND ADDRESS OF BORROWER
TITLE AND DATES OF THE EXHIBITION (or purpose for which the loan is being made)
ACCESSION NUMBER
DESCRIPTION
VALUE

The outgoing loan receipt should also list the conditions under which the loan has been granted.

Returned Loans

See forms II.B.1, III.D.1, III.E, III.G, III.H.1, and III.H.3 and figure J.3.

The registrar must devise a system for keeping track of outgoing loans and their approximate return dates. When a loan is returned to the lending museum, the borrower is notified by a signed receipt. In addition, the registrar should immediately notify the director or appropriate curator of the loan's return and check the object for any damage or change in condition. Minor changes not requiring attention may be merely noted in the condition record, but more serious changes or damages should be brought to the attention of the curator or director, who makes the decisions concerning repairs and insurance claims. The date returned should be noted on the registrar's copy of the outgoing loan receipt and on the card recording location or exhibition history. Insurance should be reinstated if it was canceled at the beginning of the loan period. The objects themselves are then ready to be returned to exhibition galleries or to storage.

Bills to Borrowers

See forms I.C.1 and III.F.2.

Although in many institutions billing the borrower for the charges involved in the loan is handled by the business office, this may also be a responsibility of the registrar. Packing charges can be based either on an exact record of the hours worked and the cost of materials used or on a system of flat rates to cover different size boxes and special packing jobs. Commercial packers very often bill the borrower directly. If the lending institution maintains its own insurance, the charges to the borrowing institution can be figured on the basis of the rate of the policy. Billing for transportation charges can often be avoided by having the loans shipped "collect" and returned "prepaid." However, if this is not possible, the charges for transportation can be added to the bill for packing and insurance.

7 PACKING AND SHIPPING

The safety of museum collections must be the first consideration in preparing them for shipment and in selecting a method of transportation. The type of material involved, its fragility, size, weight, and value, the date it is needed at its destination, the climate or climates through which it is to travel, and the cost must all be considered in determining how it is to be packed and shipped. The registrar and other staff members concerned with the packing and shipping of collections must know about safe packing techniques and the services offered by various carriers. The purpose of this chapter is to provide a basic introduction to these responsibilities.

Packing

Before arrangements are made for packing and shipping, curators or conservators should determine that the objects to be transported are inherently sound. Detailed condition reports, including photographs, are made. The registrar must then see to it that protective materials for works of art, such as frames, mounts, and backing boards, and all parts and pieces of three-dimensional objects are strong and secure. Nothing should be subjected to the strain of travel until these conditions have been met.

Museum shipments must be packed by experienced personnel in accordance with both museum standards of safety and the requirements of the carriers that will be transporting the shipments. Packing contracted to a commercial firm should be closely supervised by the registrar or other responsible museum staff member. The variety of hazards that may befall shipments must be kept in mind, as well as the task of those who will receive and unpack the shipment, and perhaps repack it for return. Complex packing arrangements should be explained by photographs and/or simple diagrams, which accompany the shipment. An extra copy of the instructions on the inside of the box is helpful to unpackers. If the object must be taken apart before packing, photographs and/or diagrams should be made at several stages to assist in reassembling it for exhibition and in repacking it for return shipment. Such photographs can also be an aid in settling damage claims.

Three basic rules should be followed in packing museum objects: (1) provide a strong, closed, waterproof box; (2) protect the objects within the box against

Fig. 7.1. A registrar's responsibility for outgoing objects calls for the careful supervision of packing for shipment.

movement, vibration, and shock; and (3) plan the packing with unpacking and repacking in mind, making it as uncomplicated as possible. Methods of protecting objects within the box differ for each kind of material and should be approved by the various museum personnel responsible for their safety. Individual objects may need to be brought to the attention of the packer and conservator and special methods devised for protecting them during handling and transportation. A conservator or other specialist should also be consulted when insulation against temperature and humidity changes is required.

Application of these basic rules has resulted in the development of relatively standard packing methods for certain types of exhibition material. Current methods are, of course, subject to improvement as new materials are discovered, tested, and approved. Although many of the procedures for packing objects described below were developed primarily at art museums, they are used and recommended by the staffs of history and science museums as well. (For additional information on packing museum objects, see articles R and S.)

GENERAL RULES FOR PACKING MUSEUM OBJECTS

The Box

Boxes must be closed on all sides, strong enough to hold the objects packed within them, and capable of withstanding handling and transit hazards such as dropping or crushing by contact with other boxes. (See figure 7.2.) Open crates should never be used for packing paintings and other fragile objects.

1. Boxes should be constructed of one of the following materials. The choice depends on the size, weight, and fragility of the objects being packed, the destination of shipment, and the method of transportation. For shipments by air, ocean, or motor freight, boxes are always made of wood.

   a. Seasoned wood, such as no. 2 Ponderosa pine shelving, at least ¾ to 1 inch thick.

   b. Fir plywood up to ½ inch thick or, for unusually heavy objects, ¾ inch thick. Grade A-D (grade A for the exterior of the box) and, for some boxes, the waterproof variety of plywood (i.e., marine grade) are recommended. Plywood boxes whose measurements exceed 3 by 3½ feet should be reinforced with strips of solid wood on all edges.

   c. Sturdy corrugated cardboard or fiberboard for ordinary long distance shipments of small, lightweight, nonfragile objects and for long or short distance shipments of unique or fragile objects, if transported in a motor van owned and/or operated by the museum or a commercial moving van hired exclusively for each shipment.

2. Interior measurements of the box should be at least 2¼ inches greater than the largest objects to be packed. To allow heavy pieces to be removed with ease, the interior measurements may need to be even larger.

7: PACKING AND SHIPPING

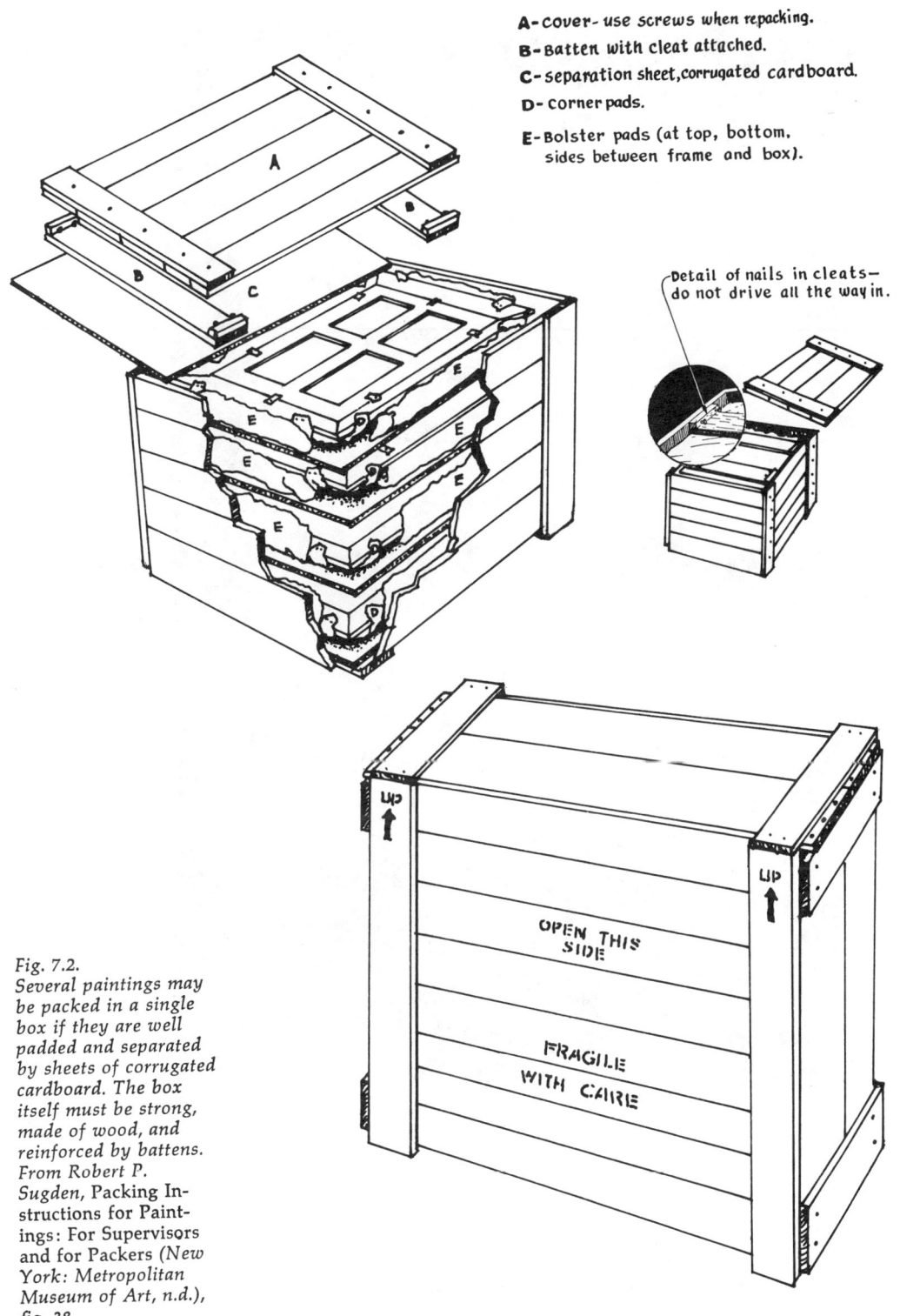

A- Cover- use screws when repacking.
B- Batten with cleat attached.
C- separation sheet, corrugated cardboard.
D- corner pads.
E- Bolster pads (at top, bottom, sides between frame and box).

Detail of nails in cleats—
do not drive all the way in.

Fig. 7.2.
Several paintings may be packed in a single box if they are well padded and separated by sheets of corrugated cardboard. The box itself must be strong, made of wood, and reinforced by battens. From Robert P. Sugden, Packing Instructions for Paintings: For Supervisors and for Packers (New York: Metropolitan Museum of Art, n.d.), fig. 38.

Fig. 7.3.
Handling instructions and symbols must be clearly stenciled on boxes ready for shipment. Note, too, the weight and size stenciled on this box, as well as the box number.

3. All exterior edges should be protected and reinforced with riding battens. Oversize boxes may require diagonal battens as well in order to provide additional structural rigidity and ease in handling. Boxes that are apt to be carried by forklifts because of their weight should have 2-by-4s nailed to the bottom battens to permit the forklift blades to slide under the box easily. Large or heavy boxes to be lifted by cranes should have lifting eyes solidly bolted to the top four corners.

4. Covers should be fastened with screws or bolts, never with nails. Nailing lids closed requires hammering the box after the object is inside, unnecessarily causing dangerous vibrations. In addition, a lid that has endured nails being pounded in and removed can rarely be reused.

5. Boxes should be lined with waterproof paper stapled or glued, never tacked, to the inside walls. Some waterproof paper contains tar that becomes liquid when exposed to mothproofing chemicals; this variety should not be used in boxes containing textiles or other objects that have been mothproofed.[1] Floors of boxes for heavy pieces of sculpture should be covered with Masonite so that the sculpture can slide in and out with ease.

6. Boxes for shipments that may be subjected to extreme heat, cold, humidity, or dryness should provide protection, through interior insulation, against the stress of sudden change and excessive moisture. During prolonged exposure to high humidity, moisture may penetrate a box or may condense out of the enclosed air if the box cools rapidly. Porous materials such as wood or fiberboard (Homasote) provide some insulation against sudden changes in temperature. When properly preconditioned (held at the same humidity level as objects for several days prior to packing), these materials help to stabilize internal humidity by absorbing water vapor from wet air and releasing it when conditions are drier. It is important, therefore, that any waterproofing be near the outer surface of the packing, enclosing as much as possible of these stabilizing materials together with the object to be protected. The object should never be wrapped airtight in plastic or other vaporproof material alone if there is any chance of its being cooled before the box is opened. Such cooling would result in condensation on the inner surface of the wrapping and therefore damage to the object.[2]

7. Insofar as possible, the gross weight of a packing box should not exceed weights that can be safely handled by two people. Both the carrier's and recipient's ability to handle, receive, and store heavy or oversize boxes should be taken into consideration.

8. Boxes ready for shipment should be clearly marked with their weights and sizes and the names and addresses of consignors and consignees. If old boxes are being reused, the old markings, especially the names and addresses, should be removed. Cautionary instructions for handling, or their symbols, such as "Fragile" (broken wine glass) and "This End Up" (arrows), should also be stenciled on the box. (See figure 7.3.) The box should be marked to indicate if an off-balance piece is being shipped (e.g., "Heavy End") in order to facilitate

---

1. David B. Little, *Safeguarding Works of Art: Transportation, Records, and Insurance*, AASLH Technical Leaflet 9, from *History News*, 18:5 (May 1963).

2. For further information about insulating shipments, registrars should consult conservators. See also article 5 and its bibliography.

handling. For security reasons, neither the value nor the nature of the contents should be indicated. Large boxes and all boxes being shipped to foreign countries should be strapped with metal banding for added protection. (For marking boxes to be shipped to foreign countries, see chapter 8.)

PROTECTION WITHIN THE BOX

Objects within the box must be protected from contact with other objects, from contact with the walls of the box, and from the transmission of external shock or vibration during transit.

1. Depending on their fragility, size, and weight, objects should be floated in or cushioned with resilient material or held in place by padded braces. For example, paintings for shipments to and from a single destination are often packed with pads fitted around the corners of their frames and are placed face down in the box between sheets of corrugated cardboard, Fome-Cor board, or fiberboard (e.g., Masonite), or packed in boxes with built-in corner pads. Sculpture and other three-dimensional objects are protected against movement by padded braces and/or by loose-fill packing materials. (See figures 7.4, 7.6–8.) Braces should also be screwed to the box to help prevent shocks to objects. Braces can be covered with resilient or soft materials, such as cloth-covered Ethafoam or hard rubber, rubberized hair, plastic foams, or felt and canton flannel; loose-fill packing materials include, among others, plastic foams in the form of pellets. The cushioning material used within the box should be both moisture resistant and shock absorbent. To protect fragile objects against abrasion or possible harmful effects of some of the artificial foams, it is advisable to make the cushioning material into cloth- or paper-covered pads, unless objects are already wrapped or packed in an inner container.

2. Surfaces of objects should be protected with materials such as acid-free tissue, glassine or mulberry paper, soft cloth, cotton, or mineral wool. Fragile objects of glass, ceramic, or metal should be protected by several layers of cotton or other soft material, provided surfaces will not be snagged in the process.

3. Glass on paintings, drawings, and prints should be taped or replaced with Plexiglas. (See figure R.3 and article Q.) Plexiglas should not be used, however, on works done in a friable media, as the static electricity of Plexiglas can lift and damage the surface of such works. If the work is large and replacement with Plexiglas is not feasible, the glass should be removed, taped, and packed in a separate compartment in the bottom of the box or in a separate box. Clear, unpainted glass components of machinery or furniture should be taped or padded or, if possible, removed and packed separately.

4. Extremely fragile objects should be double boxed. The objects should be packed first in an inner container, which is then floated in polyurethane foam, expanded polystyrene pellets, or other resilient material in an outer box.

Fig. 7.4.
Small sculpture will be protected in shipment if braced in a box and surrounded by strands of expanded polystyrene.

BASIC PROCEDURES

Fig. 7.5.
Double boxing provides added protection to the works of art packed in the boxes above. Note the handle attached to one of the inner boxes, which will aid in pulling the box out for unpacking.

Figs. 7.6–8.
Padded braces secure sculpture and other three-dimensional objects in their boxes. Note the details of a box with its contents removed, shown on the opposite page: braces, which will be screwed into position to protect the objects against shocks, are clearly identified to show their proper location for repacking; double boxing is provided for especially fragile objects.

7: PACKING AND SHIPPING

5. Heavy and light objects should not be packed in the same box. However, if this is unavoidable, partitions should be made to form separate compartments for the different objects, and weight should be distributed evenly.

PACKING MATERIALS

Packing materials of plastics such as polyurethane, polyethylene, and polystyrene have been used for some time for cushioning commercial shipments. Some of these materials are used by museums; for example, polyurethane foam has been made into corner pads for paintings and is used to line boxes for small fragile objects; expanded polystyrene in the form of pellets is used for loose-fill packing. New materials and changes in older materials are frequently developed. However, before new materials used successfully for commercial shipments can be recommended for general use in packing museum shipments, conservators and scientifically trained consultants should be asked to test them to see whether they are flammable or combustible, contain substances that give off vapors, or have properties such as excessive static electricity that might be harmful to museum objects.

SIMPLIFIED PACKING FOR MOTOR VAN SHIPMENTS

Museum shipments carried long distances by motor van, especially when combined with cargo from other shippers, should be packed in the seasoned wood or fir plywood boxes recommended for sea and air transportation. However, these boxes may not always be necessary for short trips by motor van, such as local collections and deliveries, or for longer trips when objects are forwarded in vans hired exclusively for the museum's shipment or in vans owned and/or operated by the museum for the movement of collections. In determining the type and amount of packing that should be used for a particular van shipment, cost as well as safety should be considered. For instance, sometimes it is less expensive to pack in a strong, closed container that can be stacked and so conserve space in the van than to have the shipment travel unpacked or lightly packed so that top loading is not possible.

Small, fragile objects should always be packed in corrugated cardboard, fiberboard, or wooden boxes. For local collections and deliveries, however, paintings, furniture, and nonfragile objects may be carried unpacked—but not unwrapped. They still must be protected by pads and corrugated cardboard separation sheets and braced against movement. Extremely large paintings can be protected by placing resilient pads around the corners of frames and by covering, but not sealing, with polyethylene sheeting, glassine paper, or Kimpac. If polyethylene is used on paintings done with acrylic paint, an initial wrapping of glassine paper must separate the paint surface from the polyethylene, since polyethylene tends to fuse with acrylic paint when the two come into contact. When a frame is not strong, or in the absence of a frame, carrying handles may be screwed to the back of the stretcher for easy handling and for protection during loading and unloading. These handles, however, should be attached by a skilled person

Fig. 7.9. Paintings and other framed works need not be boxed for local collections and deliveries if the shipments will be made in vans owned by the museum or hired exclusively for its use. The works should be padded and wrapped, however. Then sheets of Masonite tied securely around the works to make a "sandwich" will provide adequate protection during shipment.

who understands the problems of handling and the structure of the stretcher. Large, heavy pieces of sculpture or other heavy, bulky objects, whether boxed, crated, or unboxed, should travel on pallets or skids constructed to permit handling with forklift trucks.

For longer trips and even for some local trips, it is advisable to provide additional protection. Solid wood boxes will always be essential for valuable and fragile works, but if exclusive use of a van is obtained, simplified packing methods may be used for many shipments and thus reduce their cost. Paintings and other framed works no larger than 46 by 94 inches can be protected by sandwich-type packing. First, the frame is cushioned by corner pads and unglazed works are covered with glassine paper or polyethylene. Then, sheets of Masonite, at least one inch larger on all sides than the frame, are placed on the front and back. The "sandwich" is then securely tied with rope or heavy twine. (See figure 7.9.) The size limitation of 46 by 94 inches is determined by the maximum dimensions of standard order sheets of Masonite (4 by 8 feet).

Shipping

See forms VIII.

Registrars and other staff members concerned with museum shipments should understand thoroughly the conditions and liabilities under which carriers accept shipments as well as their packing specifications and their rates. These are published by most carriers and can be easily obtained upon request. Receipts, bills of lading, and airwaybills (airbills) are contracts between shippers and carriers as well as receipts for the material accepted for shipment. The registrar must make sure that written instructions to carriers are clear and precise.

The registrar must also see to it that museum shipments are properly insured. Carriers assume only a limited liability for goods entrusted to them unless a value in excess of the customary or statutory liability is declared by the shipper. In this case, however, there are additional charges based on the value declared. A shipper making such a declaration is, in effect, purchasing insurance coverage through the carrier, and this should not be necessary when a shipment is fully covered under another policy. Shippers of valuable material, however, often declare a nominal value as a safe-handling precaution. (For a general discussion of insurance, see chapter 9.)

In some cases, the value of a shipment may determine the method of transportation selected. For an exhibition consisting of several boxes, door-to-door containerization (see page 111) might be best, or the shipments could be staggered for protection against total loss. It is always a good idea to stagger the shipments of an exhibition consisting of the work of a single artist or an entire unique collection. Insurance policies may set limitations to the total value that may be shipped by any one conveyance.

In other cases the size, weight, and number of boxes to be shipped may determine the method of transportation. For instance, wide-bodied jet freighters may be necessary for some air shipments, or containerization may be desirable. Sample weights and measurements of small, medium, and large packing boxes are tabulated in figure 7.10 as a guide to registrars planning the method and estimating the cost of packing and transportation.

7: PACKING AND SHIPPING

FIG. 7.10 TABLE OF MEASUREMENTS AND WEIGHTS OF PACKING BOXES
FOR ESTIMATING THE COST OF PACKING AND TRANSPORTATION

This table is for solid wood boxes only; allowance should be made for use of plywood, which is lighter in weight. The dimensions below are in the following order: height, width, depth. The paintings are oil on canvas with lightweight protective backings and "L" frames approximately ¾ inch in width (weight will vary according to the type of support and the size of the frame). A flat-pack box is built for the painting to be packed flat, or horizontally, to the plane of the lid; a slide-pack box is built for the painting to be slid in vertically, perpendicular to the lid. (See article R.) Both boxes travel vertically. The sculptures are bronze (weight will vary according to the medium of the sculpture—marble, wood, bronze, etc.—and the extent to which this medium occupies the volume of the sculpture's overall dimensions). Very large and heavy sculpture should be packed in a box with a pallet or skid constructed to permit handling with a forklift truck.

OIL PAINTING	FRAMED	Box	GROSS WEIGHT
Small	30 x 42 x 1½"	35½ x 47½ x 7" (Flat Pack)	70 lbs.
Medium	48 x 72 x 2"	53½ x 77½ x 7½" (Flat Pack)	140 lbs.
Large	96 x 144 x 3"	101½ x 149½ x 8½" (Flat Pack)	230 lbs.
Small	30 x 42 x 1½"	36⅝ x 50½ x 6¾" (Slide Pack)	90 lbs.
Medium	48 x 72 x 2"	54⅝ x 80½ x 7¼" (Slide Pack)	170 lbs.
Large	96 x 144 x 3"	102⅝ x 152½ x 8¼" (Slide Pack)	270 lbs.
WATERCOLOR, DRAWING, OR PRINT	FRAMED AND GLAZED	Box	GROSS WEIGHT
	24 x 30 x 1½"	29½ x 35½ x 7¼" (Flat Pack)	60 lbs.
	24 x 30 x 1½"	30⅝ x 38½ x 6¾" (Slide Pack)	80 lbs.
SCULPTURE	OVERALL	Box	GROSS WEIGHT
Small	11 x 8½ x 8½"	18½ x 16 x 16"	65 lbs.
Medium	46 x 56 x 28"	53½ x 67½ x 39½"	400 lbs.
Large	74 x 69 x 30"	70 x 93 x 57" (With Skid)	2,260 lbs.

Various methods of transportation and some precautions to be taken to ensure the safety of shipments are described below. These services change from time to time, and registrars should consult the carriers and their publications for information on current policies when arranging for shipment.

Freight-forwarding agents are well informed on the policies, requirements, and schedules of all kinds of carriers, and museums frequently find it convenient to engage their services. Freight-forwarding agents will arrange for the transportation, including pickup and delivery, of museum shipments, and, if desired, some agents will arrange for the packing as well. These agents are technically indirect carriers; they issue their own invoices, receipts, bills of lading, and airwaybills, even though the shipments will travel on ships or planes owned and operated by independent commercial carriers. For international shipments, museums generally engage customs brokers, who are foreign freight forwarders and cargo agents specially trained and licensed in importing and exporting. Customs brokers not only arrange for international transportation but make certain that shipments comply with all importing and exporting regulations. They prepare the documents required by the U.S. Customs Service and the customs offices of other countries and will actually see the shipments through customs. (For a discussion of importing and exporting, see chapter 8.)

AIR TRANSPORTATION

Airlines offer the most rapid means of transportation for long distance domestic and foreign shipments. Airline companies are required by law to file their services, classifications, rates, charges, rules, and regulations with the Civil Aeronautics Board and to make them available for inspection by shippers on request. Shippers can therefore easily obtain information about the standard amount of liability assumed by the airlines and all other terms and conditions under which shipments are accepted. Airbills and airwaybills issued for domestic and foreign shipments are contracts between shippers and carriers.

See forms VIII.A.

Air freight rates are filed with the Civil Aeronautics Board and are subject to its regulations. Museum shippers should check with forwarding agents to see if regulations in the rate schedules of airlines exclude shipments of works of art or other valuable objects if the declared value exceeds $500. Additional charges are made if higher value declarations are permitted. Museum insurance policies should also be checked in case value declarations in specified amounts are required for shipments forwarded by air freight.

Air freight rates apply from airport to airport. Delivery to and from airport terminals can be arranged by the airlines at additional cost, but works of art and other shipments of extraordinary value are sometimes excluded from the normal pickup and delivery services offered by the airlines. Special services, such as delivery in armored cars, may be provided by the airlines on request, but at much higher rates. Shippers and consignees can, however, make their own pickup and delivery arrangements, or have door-to-door transportation arranged by reliable agents.

Ideally, all arrangements for the air shipment of valuable and fragile museum objects should be handled by museum personnel or by reliable agents who can supervise all movements: (1) from shippers to airports; (2) through terminals into the planes; (3) from the planes to and through terminals; and (4) from terminals to final destinations. Supervision at terminals is especially advisable in airports where security and assembly areas and loading and unloading equipment are inadequate or outdated.

The all-cargo planes of the scheduled airlines, which operate over regular routes and according to regular schedules, are recommended for museum shipments. They provide both the greatest security and ease of handling and are generally available between major cities both within the country and abroad. Cargo destined for shipment on cargo planes is placed in containers or on pallets, which are loaded and unloaded at cargo terminals.

The need for special stowage conditions and the size of boxes may determine the type of cargo plane on which a shipment is forwarded. For example, valuable and fragile objects may require shipment on a plane with pressurized and temperature-controlled cargo compartments for protection against changes in atmospheric pressure and temperature; shipments containing boxes of great size will be limited to planes with door openings large enough to accommodate them. Airline cargo managers can provide information about the availability and schedules of planes that will meet the requirements of shippers. They should be told the sizes and weights of the boxes when asked to reserve space on the desired flights.

Where all-cargo flights are not available, museum shipments must sometimes be transported on passenger planes. Wide-bodied passenger planes, such as Boeing 747s, Lockheed L 1011s, and Douglas DC 10s, are best, as their cargo space is large enough to permit the loading of containers and pallets. Containers and pallets are filled at the cargo terminal but loaded onto the plane at the passenger terminal with other baggage. At the destination they are unloaded at the passenger terminal and taken, once again, to the cargo terminal. Thus, there is added handling at airports beyond that for all-cargo flights. Smaller passenger planes, such as Boeing 707s and 727s and Douglas DC 8s and 9s, cannot accommodate containers and pallets, so there is still more handling and risk of mishap. Cargo for these planes must first be taken to the cargo terminal in individual boxes. Then, since container units cannot be used, the individual boxes are moved to the passenger terminal for loading. Because of increased handling and exposure, the shipment of museum objects by passenger plane should be avoided whenever possible and used only when there is no other means of transportation available, or when the shipment is small enough to be carried on the plane by a courier.

HIGHWAY TRANSPORTATION

Commercial carriers offer a door-to-door delivery service for domestic shipments. A delivery service without stops to collect and deliver other cargo can be arranged by hiring the exclusive use of a van, and, if desirable, arrangements can be made for special guards or museum couriers to accompany the van.

Registrars should attempt to find a carrier experienced in transporting works of art and other museum collections. If none is available, however, moving companies that specialize in carrying household goods can be engaged. Or, for long-distance shipments, vans with air-suspension systems designed for transporting delicate electronic equipment may be even more suitable. Climate-controlled vans are also available, at additional cost. Motor freight is not generally used for shipments of fragile material or high value, but for heavy or bulky shipments of moderate value, this may be an economical method.

Companies offering interstate transport are governed by the regulations of the Interstate Commerce Commission and by state regulatory bodies. Classifications, rules and regulations, rates, mileage guides, and the services offered by interstate moving companies are published in the tariff circulars issued by the Household Goods Carrier's Bureau (2425 Wilson Boulevard, Arlington, Va. 22201). Companies operating motor vans or trucks within a city or state are not governed by the Interstate Commerce Commission, but their rates, regulations, and services are generally subject to the approval of regulatory bodies in each city and state. The conditions under which shipments are accepted by these carriers appear on the bills of lading issued to shippers.

See forms VIII.B.

OCEAN TRANSPORTATION

Steamship lines once offered transportation service for shipments on both the fast passenger liners and the slower cargo ships or freighters. Passenger liners are best for museum shipments as the time in transit is shorter, but they are now rarely, if ever, available. Many freighters, however, moving between specified ports on a fixed schedule, provide efficient transportation. Museum shippers or their agents should request special stowage for valuable and fragile shipments, in security areas and areas that are well ventilated or air conditioned to prevent damage from extreme changes in temperature and humidity and from other hazards. A statement requesting special stowage should appear on dock receipts.

Freight rates are usually determined by steamship conferences, which are voluntary associations of steamship lines. Steamship lines and conferences serving United States foreign trade as common carriers are required by law to file their transportation rates and charges with the Federal Maritime Commission and to make them available to shippers for inspection on request. The obligations, liabilities, and rights of both carriers and shippers are defined in the clauses of bills of lading issued when goods are received for shipment. Bills of lading serve both as receipts for goods to be shipped and as contracts to deliver them.

Information about the scheduled sailing and arrival dates of ocean carriers, and available cargo space and rates, may be obtained from the inward and outward freight departments of the steamship lines or from customs brokers and foreign freight forwarders. Ocean transportation is complicated by the fact that many documents are required both by the carriers and by the governments of the United States and foreign countries, and museums generally engage customs brokers to handle these shipments.

RAIL TRANSPORTATION

Freight services offered by the railroads are not generally used for museum shipments. However, for unusually heavy or bulky shipments of moderate value rail freight may be desirable. Shippers or their agents usually arrange delivery to and from the rail terminals. Local railroad agents should be consulted about this method of transportation.

MAIL SERVICE

The shipment of museum objects by mail is not recommended for highly valuable and fragile pieces because of transit and handling hazards, the Postal Service's limitations on the size and weight of packages, and the limited value for which underwriters are willing to insure mail shipments. It is common practice, however, to send some natural history specimens by mail, and for small shipments of replaceable and nonfragile objects of little value, parcel post may prove economical and convenient. If mail shipment is used, special care should be taken to see that containers are strong enough to ensure protection from the weight of other parcels, from pressure and friction, and from climate changes and repeated handlings.

Packages shipped as first-class mail or by priority rate parcel post will go by air if air transportation is available; otherwise they will travel by surface transportation. Domestic parcel post packages are limited to 70 pounds and a combined length and girth of 100 inches. The weight and size limitations on international packages, and the customs documents and declarations required, are determined by the country of destination. (See chapter 8.) More valuable objects may be shipped by registered mail, return receipt requested. Packages must be sealed with paper, not plastic, tape and clearly addressed on one side only, including name and address of sender. The addressee and sender should also be identified inside the package, in case the outer labels or wrappings are torn or disappear.

Registry provides the shipper with person-to-person signature service and shipment in guarded mail pouches equipped with special locks. Also, registered mail usually receives more careful handling. Some foreign countries, however, do not accept all registered mail. Regulations, rates, and services are published in the *Postal Service Manual* and in *International Mail* (publication 42), which can be purchased from the Superintendent of Documents (Government Printing Office, Washington, D.C. 20402), or obtained from local postmasters.

CONTAINERIZATION

In recent years the containerization of shipments has increased steadily. Carriers have designed large receptacles, called containers, in sizes and shapes suited to the transport of cargo by rail, truck, ship, and airplane. The registrar should learn about the various types of containers and the services offered by carriers in order to select those safest and most suitable for museum shipments.

Many carriers offer door-to-door containerization. With this service, a container is delivered to a museum, packed with the sealed boxes prepared by the museum staff, and taken to the carrier. With access to more than one method of transportation and with the services of freight-forwarding agents, the container can move directly as a single unit to the premises of the consignee for unloading and unpacking. Shipments thus receive greater physical protection and security than individual boxes shipped separately.

If the volume of a shipment from any one institution does not justify the

Fig. 7.11.
Containers are specially designed to fit securely into the holds of airplanes as well as the cargo areas of other carriers. The containerization of museum shipments ensures greater protection than can be provided to individual boxes shipped separately.

exclusive use of a container, the box or boxes are delivered to the carrier for loading in a container or on a pallet with other shipments. Arrangements can be made for customs brokers and forwarding agents to supervise the loading and unloading of the museum's boxes at the points of departure and arrival in international air shipments, but this is not always possible for domestic air shipments. Nor is it always possible for brokers to supervise the loading and unloading of containers used in ocean transport, as loading schedules at the docks are often uncertain. For this reason, ocean shipment of valuable pieces in less than full containers is not recommended.

Regardless of the type of service selected, museum objects to be shipped in containers should be carefully packed in closed, waterproof wooden boxes.

As with other carrier services, rates and regulations for containerization are subject to change, and registrars should consult carriers and the museum's customs brokers and forwarding agents for detailed, up-to-date information.

COURIER-ACCOMPANIED SHIPMENTS

The high value or fragile quality of some objects may justify the use of a courier, often someone on the museum's staff, to accompany the shipment. The chief responsibility of the courier is to ensure the safety and security of the museum shipment. He or she must stay with the shipment at all times and, in particular, supervise its loading and unloading. The courier should know how each box is packed and its special handling and stowage requirements. He or she should also be familiar with all routine procedures at ports of departure and arrival, including customs clearance. (Information on the customs entry of courier-accompanied shipments is included in chapter 8; see also chapter 8, supplement II.C.) When the shipment has arrived safely, or if there is any change of itinerary, the courier notifies the museums involved and the shipping agents, if any.

As with unaccompanied shipments, forwarding on all-cargo aircraft is preferred. The courier arrives at the port of departure in advance of the shipment and witnesses the boxes being placed into containers, the sealing of each container, and the loading of the aircraft. The courier must know the identification number and seal number of each container and its position on the aircraft. During the flight, the courier usually rides in the cockpit. At all stops he or she must watch the unloading and reloading of cargo to make sure that the museum's shipment is not misplaced or mishandled. If the museum's shipment is unloaded for repositioning in the cargo hold, the courier is responsible for seeing that it is not left in adverse or dangerous conditions—rain, snow, or extreme cold or heat—before being reloaded. All shipping papers must travel directly with the shipment, but copies are held by the courier and airmailed to the agents handling the shipments.

Courier-accompanied shipments on passenger flights should be avoided if at all possible. If a passenger flight is the only alternative, the museum or its agent is advised to provide the courier with an assistant at the port of departure and to prearrange clearance with airline officials. While the courier is checking in at the passenger terminal, the assistant can be present at the cargo terminal to make certain that the shipment is carefully handled and indeed taken to the passenger terminal for loading. If possible, this assistant should accompany the cargo to the plane, witness the loading, and send a confirming message to the courier aboard the plane. A local shipping agent should be engaged at each intermediate stop to ensure that the museum's shipment is not unloaded. In case of an unscheduled stop, the courier must do everything possible to obtain permission to go to the plane's side and observe any movement of cargo. The shipping papers and a copy of the airwaybill will assist in establishing the courier's identity to the airline crew. At the port of arrival the courier should be met by another agent, who will make sure that the cargo is carefully unloaded from the plane and delivered to the cargo area.

8 IMPORTING AND EXPORTING

Every country has a series of customs laws and regulations designed to protect and promote the general well-being of its peoples. These laws are usually detailed and complex; in the United States the U.S. Customs Service enforces over four hundred statutes that regulate the entry and exit of everything that crosses our borders. Penalties for violation of customs laws and regulations are severe and may result in fines, criminal charges, and confiscation of goods. It is therefore imperative that museums participating in international shipments of art objects, other cultural material, and scientific specimens, whether for examination and study, temporary exhibition, or acquisition, comply with the laws and regulations of all the countries involved.

The responsibility for arranging and supervising museum shipments is usually a duty of the registrar. Although registrars should be as well informed as possible of the regulations pertaining to international shipping, they cannot be expected to be conversant with customs laws and regulations the world over. It is therefore strongly recommended that museums anticipating import and export shipments engage customs brokers, for whom knowledge of customs laws and procedures is a profession. In many countries customs brokers are government licensed; in the United States they are licensed by the U.S. Treasury Department and the Federal Maritime Commission and approved by the International Air Transport Association.

Customs brokers will make certain that shipments are handled in conformity with all regulations and that the required forms, documents, and permits are properly completed and filed. They will actually clear the shipment through customs. In addition, as forwarding agents, they will arrange for transportation and, if desired, for packing the shipment as well. Their knowledge and experience will expedite the shipment, and their fees are usually reasonable when compared to the time required should a museum attempt to handle shipping

Fig. 8.1.
The proper documents must be presented to U.S. Customs officials at the time of inspection. Here a customs inspector (left) and two customs import specialists examine a containerized shipment of imported merchandise entering the United States.

This chapter was prepared with the assistance of Percy S. Royals, chairman of the board; Albert J. Sorrentino, president; William J. Augerot, vice-president, imports; David B. Epstein, vice-president, exports, all of W. R. Keating and Co., New York, customs brokers specializing in the handling of works of art in this country and abroad. Their valuable, professional advice is gratefully acknowledged.

116 BASIC PROCEDURES

8: IMPORTING AND EXPORTING

and customs details on its own. To speed this work, many museums grant their customs brokers "customs power of attorney," or authorization to sign shipping and customs documents on behalf of the museum. This power of attorney, which usually requires special action by the board of the institution, authorizes the customs broker to act on behalf of the importing museum only in matters dealing with U.S. Customs.

The customs brokers who specialize in fine arts and other museum shipping are, of course, of the greatest assistance. Institutions engaging a broker for the first time should ask for recommendations from other museums and make every effort to locate a firm that is sensitive to their particular requirements.

The purpose of this chapter is to outline briefly some of the regulations and procedures that pertain to museum shipments so that museums, as importers and exporters, can work effectively with their agents. Many details of international shipping and customs clearance are rightly the business of customs brokers and need not be treated at length here. Yet registrars, in particular, need to be familiar with these regulations and procedures, not only to facilitate their own work and that of their agents but to be able to apprise curators and other museum staff involved in importing and exporting of requirements and responsibilities. The general information on procedures and regulations in this chapter is outlined in greater detail in supplements, which summarize the regulations and documents required for importing and exporting and some restrictions on materials that can be imported.

Imports

ARRANGEMENTS FOR PACKING AND FORWARDING TO THE UNITED STATES

Countries all over the world are tightening restrictions on the export of their art, cultural objects, and natural history specimens to limit the loss of material that rightfully belongs to their own people. Most countries require an export license or permit. The government of Japan, for example, requires a contract of loan in order to obtain the export license for any exhibition to be sent outside that country. All Latin American countries now prohibit the export of pre-Columbian monumental or architectural sculpture and murals without an export license, and this restriction is supported by U.S. law. Museums importing objects and specimens—whether for possible acquisition or for temporary loan—must be very careful to comply with all export laws and regulations of the countries from which these materials are removed. The museum's shipping agent in the exporting country should be consulted prior to each shipment. In addition, it is important that works of art borrowed temporarily be properly registered with the customs service of the country of export before shipment takes place. Otherwise, the borrowing museum may have to pay foreign import duties and/or taxes when these works are returned to their lenders or owners.

The importing museum should be certain that its foreign forwarding agents have all packing and shipping instructions well in advance of the desired shipping date, particularly when a large loan exhibition is being assembled. These

Fig. 8.2.
Museum objects to be shipped for loan exhibitions overseas must be packed with special care and are often unpacked by representatives of both the lending and the borrowing institutions.

agents will need time to collect and pack each object, make the export arrangements in accordance with the regulations of their government, and prepare the invoices and other documents required by U.S. Customs for entry. They should also be advised of the insurance arrangements, the transportation method desired, the dates by which the shipment must arrive, and whether freight charges are to be prepaid or payable at destination. If this is the first time the museum has employed a particular foreign agent, it may be a good idea to include, in addition, a list of the documents required by U.S. Customs. (See supplement I.A–C.)

The value of a particular shipment or its sensitivity to temperature and humidity change may necessitate the use of a courier. (See supplement II.C.) Such shipments should be forwarded on all-cargo aircraft rather than on passenger flights, if possible. All-cargo flights allow the courier direct access to loading and unloading and provide for better security and protection from the environment during these procedures. (For additional information, see chapter 7.) If, however, a passenger flight must be used, it will be the courier's responsibility to check before the time of departure that the vendor or lender has complied with all export requirements. Shipments traveling as accompanied baggage on these flights are, of course, subject to security examinations at the airport of departure. These examinations may create problems, particularly in the case of delicate, specially packed art objects that should not be unpacked and repacked by inexperienced people in crowded passenger terminals and in areas where temperature and humidity are not controlled.

U.S. ENTRY PROVISIONS

In the early years of this century, import regulations frequently tended to obstruct rather than encourage the movement of cultural material from one country to another, despite the intentions of lawmakers. New forms and media of art were frequently denied duty-free entry because there were no provisions for them in customs tariff schedules. In the 1920s, for example, Brancusi's abstract sculpture, *Bird in Space,* was classified by customs officials as a "manufactured metal implement" and subject to a duty of 40 percent. The 1927 court ruling in this important case was more friendly to the new art form, but the definition of sculpture as "imitations of natural objects" was broadened only to include natural forms not represented in their exact proportions.

Not until 1959 were the regulations governing the importation of works of art significantly liberalized. In that year, a ten-year effort on the part of the American Association of Museums Committee on Customs and many people in museums throughout the country helped secure the passage of an amendment to the Tariff Act of 1930. That amendment clarified the wording of the law, eliminating many of the obstacles to the free importation of original works of art and preparing the way for dealing with inevitable innovations in style and material. Free entry was granted, for example, to certain tapestries and ethnographic objects, to all prints made by hand-transfer processes, and, for the first time, to collages, mosaics, abstract sculpture, and other new forms and media of art. (See supplement I.B.)

Since the passage of this amendment, the trend has been toward increasing liberalization. For example, an antique has been redefined as an object produced at least one hundred years prior to the date of entry (instead of made before 1830), and antique furniture can now be entered at any port of entry instead of at previously designated ports. This was a very important liberalization for museums. The provision concerning the entry of works of art not specifically described in other provisions has been liberally interpreted, and in recent years assemblages, musical sculptures, and works of kinetic art have been allowed duty-free entry. The Tariff Classification Act of 1962, which further amended the basic Tariff Act of 1930, incorporated in its new schedule the liberalization of customs regulations granted by the 1959 amendment and reaffirmed to museums and educational institutions the privilege of importing dutiable items under exhibition bond.

Still further progress was made in 1966 by the important Educational, Scientific, and Cultural Materials Importation Act, commonly known as the Florence Agreement. Sponsored by UNESCO, this agreement was designed to facilitate the international circulation of visual and auditory materials of an educational, scientific, and cultural character, and it guaranteed duty-free treatment to many items not already permitted free entry under existing provisions.

Under current tariff laws and with the special provisions for cultural, scientific, and educational institutions, it is now possible for museums to import free of duty practically any object or specimen, not otherwise restricted, that is intended for the permanent collection, for special exhibition, or for examination and study. The museums and the objects themselves, however, must meet certain criteria to qualify for duty-free entry under these laws, and the museums must see to it that the proper documents are submitted to U.S. Customs. Documents required for all import shipments, regardless of kind or purpose of material being imported, are listed in supplement I.A. Following this list (supplement I.B–D), provisions that govern the importing of museum objects are outlined, together with information on the additional special documents that must be filed for certain kinds of material and certain kinds of entry. Restrictions are listed where applicable, and discussed in greater detail on pages 120–22 and in supplement II.A.

Current Tariff Laws

Current tariff laws generally permit duty-free entry to antiques, ethnographic objects, paintings, pastels, drawings, sketches, prints, sculptures, mosaics, other works of art, tapestries, science material, and printed matter. These items, however, must meet certain specifications. In addition, for antiques and works of art certifications of antiquity, originality, and authenticity may be required. These requirements and the documents necessary to obtain free entry for these items are listed in supplement I.B.

SPECIAL PROVISIONS FOR CULTURAL, SCIENTIFIC, AND EDUCATIONAL INSTITUTIONS

Under current laws, cultural, scientific, and educational institutions are exempted from paying duty on articles normally subject to duty if the articles are imported for permanent use or for exhibition purposes.

The following articles may be imported by such institutions for their permanent use: audiovisual material, sculptures and statuary, patterns and models, scientific instruments and apparatus, and scientific specimens. U.S. Customs may require evidence of the character of the institutions using this provision. The articles themselves must be imported exclusively for the permanent use of the institution and are subject to certain restrictions by U.S. Customs for a period of five years after importation, during which time they may not be offered for distribution, sale, or other commercial use. Regulations and documents pertaining to the permanent use provision are listed in supplement I.C.1.

Articles not allowed free entry under current tariff laws or special provisions may be imported duty free by qualifying institutions if they are intended for exhibition purposes only and are entered under permanent exhibition bond. To qualify, the museum must make an application, by letter, to U.S. Customs. Articles under bond must be kept on the premises of the museum and be available for customs inspection for a period of five years after entry. They may not be offered for sale and may be transferred to other institutions or galleries only with the permission of customs. If the articles are exported before the end of the five-year period, they must be packed and shipped under customs supervision in order that the museum's liability under the bond will be canceled. At the end of five years the bond expires, and restrictions on the use of the articles are terminated.

The registrar must keep a record of all the objects in the museum that are under permanent exhibition bond. This record should indicate the location of the objects and the date when the bond will expire and the museum's liability be canceled. If an object under permanent exhibition bond is disposed of at any time during the five-year period, the record must indicate what this disposition was and that it was approved by U.S. Customs, so that this information can be furnished to customs if requested. When material under bond is insured, the amount of insurance should be increased to cover the duty that would become due if an article should be destroyed, lost, or stolen. The regulations and documents pertaining to permanent exhibition bond are listed in supplement I.C.2.

IMPORT RESTRICTIONS

Customs inspectors enforce the laws, requirements, and restrictions of over two dozen government agencies that regulate the entry of articles considered injurious or detrimental to the general public welfare. Many of the restrictions and regulations pertain to the kinds of materials that museums may, on occasion, import. For example, the Department of Agriculture's restriction on raw plant material may apply to baskets made of certain kinds of straw and grasses.

Fig. 8.3.
A New York customs import specialist examines an ivory carving.

The Department of the Interior regulates federal restrictions on the importation of endangered species and of articles made from them—horn, bone, feathers, skins, ivory, and so forth—regardless of when they were produced. Further, museums importing exhibition catalogues or other publications from abroad should be aware that, while books and catalogues may often be imported duty free, the provisions of the Trade-Mark Act of 1946 must be complied with. These provisions require that the name of the country in which the book or catalogue was printed appear on the title page or elsewhere as specified; books that show the city only, or no place of publication at all, will be denied entry. Import restrictions are especially severe on items produced in certain countries. For instance, at the time of this writing, articles produced in Cambodia, Cuba, North Korea, Rhodesia, and Vietnam are strictly regulated and cannot be brought into the country without an import license issued by the Department of the Treasury. In addition, importing pre-Columbian monumental or architectural sculpture or murals from Mexico, Central America, or South America without an export license from the country of origin is illegal, and failure to comply can invoke the U.S. National Stolen Properties Act.

Regulations and restrictions on materials such as these change frequently. The list provided in supplement II.A may serve as a guide to the kinds of materials that are often restricted and to the agencies that regulate them.

PROVISION FOR DUTY-FREE RETURN OF EXPORTED MATERIAL

Current tariff regulations allow for the duty-free return of all United States products. In addition, other articles, regardless of country of origin, may be returned to the United States duty free if they were exported solely for exhibition, examination, or experimentation, or for scientific or educational purposes, and are re-entered by or for the account of the person who exported them. Documents required to qualify for the duty-free re-entry of these materials are listed in supplement I.D.

U.S. CUSTOMS CLEARANCE

A customs entry must be made by the importing museum or its customs broker within five days after the arrival of the shipment in the United States. This is essential for the safety and security of the shipment. Otherwise, the shipment will be sent to a government-bonded warehouse, and the importer will have to pay an additional charge to withdraw it. Airlines may request that entry be made within forty-eight hours after arrival, and charge the museum for storage after that time.

If the importing museum has granted its customs broker customs power of attorney, it may consign shipments directly to its customs broker for clearance through U.S. Customs and delivery to the museum. (See page 117.) To assure that the customs broker meets the shipment and to avoid delays in clearance, the foreign forwarding agents should transmit all instructions in advance of the shipment's arrival. For air shipments, this usually means attaching two copies of all shipping documents to the airwaybill accompanying the shipment and sending the airwaybill number and all other flight information to the importing customs broker by Teletype. For ocean shipments, bills of lading, invoices, and other required documents must be mailed to the customs broker in time to arrive in advance of the shipment. The registrar should request copies of all shipping papers and, in general, should have on file copies of all documents relating to a particular shipment.

For entry clearance, the importing museum or its customs broker must, of course, present the proper documents to U.S. Customs at the time of inspection. These include the bill of lading or airwaybill, the appropriate invoice, and any special documents required by customs either for the kind of object being entered or by the kind of entry being made. For example, to import a Queen Anne highboy under the provisions of the tariff governing antiques, the importing museum or its customs broker must present proof of age and origin on the shipper's invoice. To import a group of baskets under permanent exhibition bond, the museum must first obtain the approval of customs to enter objects under permanent exhibition bond and then, at the time of entry, complete Customs Forms 3325 and 7565. If the baskets are made of grasses or plant material currently quarantined by the U.S. Department of Agriculture, again a permit must have been applied for in advance, and arrangements made for fumigation at the point of entry. (See supplements I and II.) Busy registrars and museum staff

8: IMPORTING AND EXPORTING

Fig. 8.4.
Customs inspectors complete paper work following inspection of a truckload of imported goods.

members are often only too happy to let customs brokers handle these details.

Customs examination and clearance may be arranged at the place of first arrival or may take place at one of the over three hundred designated port-of-entry cities in the United States and its territories. If desired, however, the importing museum or its customs broker may apply by letter to U.S. Customs for permission to have shipments delivered to the museum, or, if necessary, to a warehouse approved by U.S. Customs, for unpacking and customs examination. Under this arrangement, the shipment will be placed under customs seal at the port of arrival. The customs official there will affix on each box a customs seal, or warning label, as a guarantee to the examining officer that the box has not been opened. The customs broker or the museum will arrange for the transport of the shipment directly to the museum or approved warehouse, where it will be opened in the presence of a customs official. For security reasons this procedure is strongly recommended for shipments of great value and fragility.

For shipments destined for a city other than the port of arrival, the importing museum or its customs broker should arrange for a through airwaybill. Under this type of airwaybill, the airline will prepare the required "immediate transportation entry" form (Customs Form 7512) and forward the shipment in bond on an approved common carrier to the customs office nearest the city of destination. The museum, or its shipping agent or customs broker, should arrange supervision at all transfer points to assure the safety of the shipment and should see to it that the shipment is on the scheduled flight to the final destination. If the shipment is not traveling on a through airwaybill, a customs broker in the city of arrival must prepare the transportation entry form, arrange for further in-bond transportation, and mail all documents to the designated customs office, where they will be needed for final examination and clearance.

Copies of all entries and documents should also be sent to the importing museum.

Courier-accompanied shipments must also be entered in accordance with U.S. Customs. If the shipment is carried as hand baggage (not freight), the courier must list the shipment and its value on his or her personal customs declaration, stating that it is carried for the institution, and must comply with the usual customs regulations. On arrival, the courier must be met by the importing museum's customs broker, who will take the shipment under customs seal, or warning label, at the arrival building and make the official customs entry. The broker must, of course, be given the name of the courier and the pertinent flight information in advance and must have, as well, the signed commercial invoice in duplicate. If the courier is not met, the shipment cannot be released upon arrival and will be taken to the airline cargo area; the courier will be given a post-entry certificate, which will be needed for formal customs entry. As security measures for the transportation of the shipment from the passenger terminal to the cargo area are always difficult, and often impossible, to arrange, it is strongly recommended that the importing museum plan for a customs broker to meet the courier. Otherwise, the courier's services are inoperative at the most crucial point in the voyage.

For shipments imported by mail, a customs declaration showing contents and value must be attached to the package. One set of invoices and other documents required by customs should be enclosed in the package and duplicates mailed, by airmail, to the addressee. Packages from the same sender to the same addressee, arriving on the same ship or aircraft, are considered as one shipment. If the aggregate value of the shipment is under $250, an informal entry is made by customs officials. The packages are then delivered to the addressee, and the duty, if any, is collected by the Postal Service. If the aggregate value exceeds $250, a formal customs entry must be made.

Exports

PREPARING EXPORT SHIPMENTS

Objects scheduled for export shipments must be packed with great care and be well cushioned against shock. The boxes should be strong, waterproof, and clearly marked, for they must provide protection during various stages of transit, loading and unloading from carriers, and exposure to a variety of climates. In general, the packing methods described in chapter 7 and in articles R and S apply to foreign as well as domestic shipments.

However, boxes destined for foreign ports are marked differently from domestic shipments. The names and addresses of consignor and consignee, which must appear on boxes shipped within the United States or between the United States and Canada, are not required for foreign shipments. Instead, the consignor, the destination, and the box numbers are identified on the boxes by abbreviations, or identifying marks, that refer to the documents accompanying the shipment. Each box is also marked as "Packed in U.S.A."

An abbreviation of the exporting museum's name identifies the consignor. For example, the Museum of Modern Art is identified as MOMA. Directly under these initials appear the city and port of destination and, under them, the number of the individual box. For example:

>
> MOMA
> SAO PAULO
> VIA SANTOS
> NO. 2

Care should be taken to see that the same number is not duplicated in a shipment consisting of several boxes.

In addition, each box is marked with its gross weight and measurements, in both English and metric designations. For exports to certain countries the net weight (weight of actual material), legal weight (weight of actual material plus the inner container or wrapper), and tare weight (weight of packing case) must be shown along with gross weight, preferably in both pounds and kilograms.

Finally, special handling instructions are marked on each box, with cautions in English and the appropriate foreign language or languages. For shipments that will travel through several foreign countries, these instructions are often in the form of symbols. Frequently used cautions include "Use No Hooks," arrows indicating "This End Up," broken wine glasses or bottles indicating "Fragile," and an umbrella indicating that protection from the elements is required. For security reasons, neither the value nor the nature of the contents should be indicated. Box markings should be as simple as possible to be easily seen and understood. They should be stenciled with waterproof ink on two sides of the box.

The bills of lading or airwaybills accompanying the shipment must include, first of all, the museum's identifying mark and the city and port of destination as stenciled on the exterior of the box. The invoices for the shipment, which are typed on the exporting museum's letterhead, show the same information and include, in addition, the full name and address of the consignor and consignee, a description of each item with its valuation, the marks and number of the box in which it is packed, the gross weight (again in pounds and kilograms) and measurement of each box, and other weights as required. When loans from abroad are being returned, the values that were shown on the invoice covering the import shipment should be repeated on the invoice for the export shipment. Copies of the invoices should be sent to all the customs brokers and forwarding agents who will handle the shipment as well as to the consignee.

U.S. EXPORT PROVISIONS

Export shipments are subject to U.S. Customs inspection and export regulations as well as to inspection and import regulations in the country of destination. To prepare the proper documents and secure an export license, if necessary, the museum's customs broker will need to know the nature of the material being exported, whether it is of domestic or foreign origin, whether it is being returned to owners after exhibition in the United States, and whether it is currently under permanent exhibition bond. Export licenses are not usually required for the types of material exported by museums; but when they are, the museum's customs broker will advise the shipper so that application can be made without delay.

Loans from abroad being exported for return to lenders should be consigned to the same agents who forwarded them to the United States. If material is being exported temporarily for a special exhibition abroad, this should be noted on the invoice and on the export declaration to help establish the proof of export required for duty-free re-entry. Paintings and other works of art on paper should be specified as framed or unframed, so no question will arise at the time of re-entry concerning duty on frames. In addition, the ultimate consignee or professional agent should be advised that a declaration stating that the objects were imported from the United States for special exhibition will be required on the invoice for the return shipment. An outline of the documents required for export shipments appears in supplement I.E.

FORWARDING TO FOREIGN CONSIGNEES

The registrar should notify the museum's customs broker or shipping agent as far in advance as possible of the shipment to be exported, the transportation method desired, the name of the consignee, the date the shipment is needed at its destination, and the insurance arrangements. The customs broker or shipping agent should be given, in addition, an estimate of the number of boxes, total weight, and measurements of each box in the shipment so that cargo space can be booked in advance. The broker or agent should also be given specific instructions as to how the charges are to be paid—whether to deliver to the ultimate consignee free of all charges, to prepay charges to port of entry or airport only, or to make all charges payable at destination.

When the shipment is packed and all customs and shipping papers prepared, the customs broker or shipping agent will arrange to have the boxes collected and delivered to the carrier. A shipment from a city in the interior of the country is forwarded to agents at an airport or port of exit, where arrangements are made for delivering it to the carrier. If insurance is not arranged by the exporting museum, the registrar should notify the consignee, or whoever is responsible for insuring the shipment, of the date of departure and the name of the ship, airline, or other carrier on which it is to be forwarded.

Consignees or their agents abroad clear shipments through the customs of their countries and arrange ultimate delivery. However, if the exporting museum employs the agents abroad, these agents must be instructed as to the ultimate delivery of the shipment. When returning loans to lenders, the museum may be liable for heavy duties and/or taxes on works of art if these works were not properly registered with the customs service of the lender's country at the time they were borrowed. The burden of the responsibility lies with the party who erroneously effected exportation or removal without proper documentation. In addition, if the loans are not being returned directly to the lenders, and are entered through the customs of a third country, the exporting museum will likely be liable for these duties and taxes, and museums should be aware of this liability in considering loan agreements that call for export from one country and return to another.

Supplements

SUPPLEMENT I: PROVISIONS AND DOCUMENTS REQUIRED FOR DUTY-FREE ENTRY INTO THE UNITED STATES

The following sections present a summary of the provisions and documents required for the duty-free entry of items frequently imported or exported by museums. This information is presented as a guide only; it is not intended to substitute for the services of a reliable customs broker. In addition to the forms described, there are numerous other required forms, export licenses, consular documents, shipping permits, and dock receipts. Furthermore, customs regulations are constantly changing; so, too, are the restrictions imposed by government agencies. For the most current information, the museum should contact its customs broker; the U.S. Customs Service (Department of the Treasury, Washington, D.C. 20229); or the district director or regional commissioner of customs in a nearby city. (See supplement II.B.)

The section numbers of *Customs Regulations of the United States (CRUS)* and the section numbers of the Tariff Act of 1930, as amended, are given, where applicable, in parentheses. For the tariff schedules, see *Tariff Schedules of the United States (Annotated)*, published annually.

The contents of Supplement I are as follows:

A. General Documents Required for Import Shipments
B. Provisions for Duty-Free Entry
C. Special Provisions for Cultural, Scientific, and Educational Institutions
D. Provisions for Duty-Free Return of Exported Material
E. General Documents Required for Export Shipments

A. GENERAL DOCUMENTS REQUIRED FOR IMPORT SHIPMENTS

1. BILL OF LADING OR AIRWAYBILL AND CARRIER'S CERTIFICATE: Bills of lading and airwaybills are contracts of carriage between shipper and carrier and receipts for the shipment. Airlines or agents issue airwaybills, and ocean and other carriers issue bills of lading. These, or carrier's certificates, certifying the name of the owner or consignee of the articles being imported, serve as evidence of the right to make entry.

2. INVOICE: on purchased articles, the bill of sale; if not purchased, a statement from the exporter showing the name and address of consignor and consignee, an itemized description of the contents and value of each item, the identifying marks and numbers

of packages, and, for some shipments, other information as required by U.S. Customs. It is filed with customs when entry is made (sections 141.81 through 141.92, *CRUS*, and sections 481 through 484, Tariff Act of 1930).

a. COMMERCIAL INVOICE: a statement prepared by the exporter giving the information mentioned above for shipments for which a SPECIAL CUSTOMS INVOICE is not required; also called a shipper's invoice.

b. CUSTOMS FORM 5515—SPECIAL CUSTOMS INVOICE: required for shipments when the purchase price exceeds $500 and rate of duty is based upon, or regulated in any manner on, the value of the goods; also required for nonpurchased goods when value exceeds $500. A COMMERCIAL INVOICE may be attached to this form. A SPECIAL CUSTOMS INVOICE is not required for shipments of articles that are not for sale, e.g., duty-free art shipments, exhibition material entered under bond, and other material entered for cultural, educational, scientific, or exhibition purposes (section 141.83, *CRUS*).

c. PRO-FORMA INVOICE: prepared by the importer to describe the contents of a shipment when the COMMERCIAL INVOICE or the SPECIAL CUSTOMS INVOICE is not available. Bond must be given by the importer to produce the required invoice within six months from the date of entry.

3. PACKING LIST: a list giving measurements, weights, identifying marks, numbers, and contents of each packing box. This list is sent to the consignee unless this information appears on the invoice.

4. CUSTOMS DECLARATION FOR PARCEL POST SHIPMENT: a declaration showing the contents and value of a shipment. It is prepared by the exporter on a form provided by the postal administration of the country of export and must be attached to the package. An invoice or statement of value and any other documents required by U.S. Customs should be enclosed in the package and copies sent separately to the addressee (section 145, *CRUS*).

B. PROVISIONS FOR DUTY-FREE ENTRY

The following materials are permitted free entry under current tariff laws. They are listed together with the specifications and documents (in addition to those listed above) required to secure free entry in each case. Some restrictions are noted where applicable; for further information, see supplement II.A.

1. ANTIQUES AND ETHNOGRAPHIC OBJECTS

a. Antiques made prior to 100 years before their date of entry (766.2520 [silverware], 766.2540 [furniture], and 766.2560 [all other antiques]).

b. Ethnographic objects in traditional aboriginal styles made at least 50 years before their date of entry (766.2560).

Document required:

PROOF OF ANTIQUITY: declaration (on invoice) by the seller, owner, or other person having competent knowledge of the facts, stating the place and approximate date of production and, in addition, for articles subject to Foreign Assets Control regulations (see supplement II.A), the name and address of the person from whom they were acquired and the date acquired. If the declaration is not available, the district director or regional commissioner of customs may, at his or her discretion, accept a statement from the owner or borrower in this country giving all the known facts to show how long the articles have been in existence and where they were produced (section 10.53(a), *CRUS*, as amended).

NOTE: Imports of articles made from endangered species (e.g., horn, bone, feathers, skins, ivory, etc.), regardless of when they were made, are generally prohibited by the Department of the Interior. Imports of articles made of certain raw plant material (e.g., straw, certain grasses, etc., used for making baskets), are generally restricted by the Department of Agriculture. Pre-Columbian monumental or architectural sculpture and murals may be imported only if the country of origin certifies the exportation. (See supplement II.A.)

2. WORKS OF ART

   a. Paintings, pastels, drawings, and sketches, whether originals or not, executed wholly by hand (765.0300).

   Documents required: none.

   b. Prints, sculpture, mosaics, and other works of art.

   i. Engravings, etchings, lithographs, woodcuts, and other prints printed by hand from hand-produced plates, blocks, or stones (765.1000).

   ii. Original sculptures "made in any form from any material . . . , whether in round or in relief, and whether cut, carved or otherwise wrought by hand, or cast" and the first ten "castings, replicas, or reproductions made from the sculptor's original model," including those finished after the sculptor's death (765.1500).

   iii. Original mosaics (765.2000).

   iv. Original collages and other "original works of the free fine arts (and copies if signed and the name of the artist is known) in any media including, but not limited to, applied paper or other materials, manufactured or otherwise, such as are used on collages" (765.2500).

   Document required:

   DECLARATION OF ORIGINALITY: a declaration in the following form by the artist (or by foreign shipper if it is shown on the declaration why it is impossible to obtain the signature of the artist) attached to the invoice for the shipment:

   I, _____, do hereby declare that I am the producer of certain works of art, namely _____, covered by the annexed invoice dated _____; that any mosaics included in that invoice are originals; that any sculptures or statuary included in that invoice are the original works or models or one of the first ten castings, replicas, or reproductions made from the sculptor's replicas, or reproductions made from the sculptor's original work or model; and that any etchings, engravings, woodcuts, lithographs, or prints made by other hand-transfer processes included in that invoice were printed by hand from hand-etched, hand-drawn, or hand-engraved plates, stones, or blocks.

   (date and place)   (signature of artist, seller, or shipper)

   The declaration of the artist, or the declaration of the seller or shipper (formerly CUSTOMS FORM 253), may be waived upon a satisfactory showing that it is impossible to produce (section 10.48, *CRUS*).

   NOTE: Picture frames, if not antique (produced 100 years prior to date of entry), whether on or removed from paintings, prints, etc., are dutiable at the rate of 6 percent (206.6000).

   c. Tapestries: Gobelin and other hand-woven tapestries fit only for use as wall hangings and valued over $20 per square foot (364.0500).

Document required:

CERTIFICATE OF AUTHENTICITY: a certificate executed by the manager or other responsible employee of the factory producing the tapestries. If the absence of this certificate is satisfactorily explained, other evidence establishing the authenticity may be accepted (section 10.54, *CRUS*).

3. SCIENCE MATERIAL

   a. Skeletons and other "preparations of anatomy" (870.2700).
   b. Fossils (870.2700).

Documents required: none.

4. PRINTED MATTER

   a. Books, tourist and other literature.
      i. Books not specially provided for (270.2580).
      ii. Printed matter not specially provided for, suitable for use in the production of such books as would themselves be free of duty (274.7300).
      iii. Tourist and other literature, including posters (270.7000).
   b. Printed matter produced more than 20 years prior to importation.
      i. Architectural, engineering, industrial, or commercial drawings and plans printed on sensitized materials by any photographic process (273.4500).
      ii. Photographs, engravings, etchings, lithographs, and woodcuts, and pictorial matter produced by relief or stencil printing processes not specially provided for (274.5000).

Documents required: none.

NOTE: Imports of books and catalogues must comply with the importing provisions of the copyright law and Trade-Mark Act of 1946. (See supplement II.A.)

C. SPECIAL PROVISIONS FOR CULTURAL, SCIENTIFIC, AND EDUCATIONAL INSTITUTIONS

Under current laws, cultural, scientific, and educational institutions are exempted from tariffs on dutiable articles that are imported for permanent use or for exhibition.

1. PERMANENT USE

The following articles are permitted free entry for the permanent use of any public library, any public institution, or any nonprofit institution established for educational, scientific, literary, or philosophical purposes, or for the encouragement of the fine arts. U.S. Customs may require evidence of the character of the institutions using these provisions. Articles covered by these provisions are entered duty free by declaration. Except where otherwise stated, they must be imported exclusively for the institutions involved and not for distribution, sale, or other commercial use within five years after being entered. They may be transferred to another institution or exported or destroyed under customs supervision within this five-year period without duty liability being incurred. If otherwise transferred, or used for commercial purposes within five years after being entered, it is the obligation of the importing institution to report the violation to customs and to pay the appropriate duty.

   a. Audiovisual material: drawings and plans, reproductions thereof, engravings, etchings, lithographs, woodcuts, globes, sound recordings, recorded video tapes, and photographs and other prints (851.1000).

Document required:

CUSTOMS FORM 3321—DECLARATION FOR FREE ENTRY OF ARTICLES FOR COLLEGES, RELIGIOUS INSTITUTIONS, ETC. (section 10.43, *CRUS*).

NOTE: Other audiovisual material, such as developed photographic film, including motion picture film, is permitted free entry under 870.3000 when certified by the U.S. Information Agency (section 10.121, *CRUS*).

b. Sculptures and statuary (851.2000).

Document required:

CUSTOMS FORM 3321—DECLARATION FOR FREE ENTRY OF ARTICLES FOR COLLEGES, RELIGIOUS INSTITUTIONS, ETC. (section 10.43, *CRUS*).

c. Patterns and models exclusively for exhibition or educational use (851.5000).

Document required:

CUSTOMS FORM 3321—DECLARATION FOR FREE ENTRY OF ARTICLES FOR COLLEGES, RELIGIOUS INSTITUTIONS, ETC. (section 10.43, *CRUS*).

NOTE: Models of the inventions and other improvements in the arts, to be used exclusively as models, are also permitted free entry under 737.0500 (section 10.43, *CRUS*).

d. Scientific instruments and apparatus.

  i. Scientific instruments and apparatus, provided no articles of equivalent scientific value for the purposes intended are being manufactured in the United States (851.6000).

  ii. Repair components (851.6500).

Documents required: none.

NOTE: Nonprofit scientific or educational institutions, whether public or private, wishing to import instruments and apparatus under these provisions must apply by letter to the Secretary of the Treasury in accordance with regulations specified in sections 10.114 through 10.118, *CRUS*.

e. Scientific specimens.

  i. Wild animals (including birds and fish) for use, or for sale for use, in any scientific public collection for exhibition for scientific or educational purposes (852.2000).

Document required:

CUSTOMS FORM 3321—DECLARATION FOR FREE ENTRY OF ARTICLES FOR COLLEGES, RELIGIOUS INSTITUTIONS, ETC.: declaration of the ultimate consignee showing that animals or birds were "specially imported pursuant to negotiations conducted prior to importation for the delivery of animals or birds of a named species meeting agreed specifications of reasonable particularity and that they are intended at the time of importation for public exhibition in a collection maintained for scientific or educational purposes and not for sale or for use in connection with any enterprise conducted for profit" (section 10.75, *CRUS*).

  ii. Specimens of archaeology, mineralogy, or natural history (including specimens of botany or zoology other than live zoological specimens) imported for any public or private scientific collection for exhibition or other educational or scientific use, and not for sale or other commercial use (870.2700).

Document required:

DECLARATION OF IMPORTER: a declaration stating that articles entered under 870.2700 are imported for public or private scientific collection for exhibition or other educational or scientific use and are not for sale or other commercial use (section 10.47, *CRUS*). Customs Form 3321, while not specifically required, is acceptable evidence of the status of the importing institution.

NOTE: Importation of plants and plant products is subject to special regulations of the Department of Agriculture (sections 12.10 through 12.15, *CRUS*). (See supplement II.A.)

2. PERMANENT EXHIBITION BOND

Works of art, photographs, artistic antiquities and copies, collections in illustration of the progress of the arts and sciences, decorative or applied art objects, and other dutiable material not allowed free entry under existing tariff provisions may be imported, duty free, by qualifying cultural, scientific, and educational institutions if imported for exhibition purposes only and entered under permanent exhibition bond. To obtain permanent exhibition bond status, the museum must submit a letter of application, together with its charter and bylaws and proof of its tax-exempt status, to the U.S. Customs Service (Department of the Treasury, Washington, D.C. 20229). If the application is approved, U.S. Customs will address a letter of authorization to the museum and to the U.S. Customs district office nearest to the museum. The museum's copy of the letter will serve from that date on to authorize the use of permanent exhibition bond; no further applications are necessary.

Articles imported under permanent exhibition bond are subject to customs auditing and control for five years from the date of importation. They must be kept on the premises of the museum during this period and be available for customs examination at all times. They may be transferred to similar institutions or even to a commercial gallery for noncommercial use if a proper application is made to and approved by U.S. Customs. They may not be sold or offered for sale. If the importing museum should decide, however, to sell or offer the articles for sale, or to use them contrary to the bond provisions, it should advise U.S. Customs and pay the appropriate duty; no penalty is imposed. If the articles are to be returned to the owner within the five-year period, U.S. Customs must supervise the packing, transfer to, and loading into the export carrier in order that the museum's liability under the bond will be canceled. At the end of the five-year period the bond is liquidated and the articles are no longer under customs control. The importing institution then has unrestricted use of them.

Documents required:

AUTHORIZATION (IN LETTER FORM) FROM U.S. CUSTOMS

See form IX.B.1.

CUSTOMS FORM 3325—DECLARATION ON ENTRY OF THEATRICAL EFFECTS FOR TEMPORARY USE OR OF WORKS OF ART, ETC., FOR TEMPORARY OR PERMANENT EXHIBITION (section 10.49, *CRUS*).

See form IX.C.1.

CUSTOMS FORM 7565—EXHIBITION BOND (sections 10.49 and 113.14(c), *CRUS*).

D. PROVISIONS FOR DUTY-FREE RETURN OF EXPORTED MATERIAL

The following articles are permitted duty-free re-entry.

1. PRODUCTS OF THE UNITED STATES RETURNED AFTER EXPORTATION WITHOUT HAVING BEEN ADVANCED IN VALUE OR IMPROVED IN CONDITION (800.0000).

Documents required:

CUSTOMS FORM 3311—DECLARATION FOR FREE ENTRY OF RETURNED AMERICAN PRODUCTS AND/OR CERTIFICATE OF EXPORTATION (section 10.1, *CRUS*).

FOREIGN SHIPPER'S DECLARATION: invoice of returned American goods, and declaration of foreign exporter if value exceeds $500, stating that the articles are products of the United States and that they have not been advanced in value or improved in condition and naming the port from which they were exported and the date of export. For example:

I, _____, declare that the articles herein specified are to the best of my knowledge and belief, the growth, produce, or manufacture of the United States; that they were exported from the United States from the port of _____ on or about _____, 19____; that they are returned without having been advanced in value or improved in condition by any process of manufacture or other means.

(date and place of signing)   (signature of exporter or authorized agent)
(section 10.1, *CRUS*).

2. MISCELLANEOUS ARTICLES: articles returned after temporary exportation solely for exhibition, examination, or experimentation, for scientific or educational purposes, if imported by or for the account of the person who exported them:

a. For exhibition, examination, or experimentation, for scientific or educational purposes (802.1000).

b. For exhibition in a circus or menagerie (802.2000).

c. For exhibition or use at any public exposition, fair, or conference (802.3000).

Documents required:

CUSTOMS FORM 3311—DECLARATION FOR FREE ENTRY OF RETURNED AMERICAN PRODUCTS AND/OR CERTIFICATE OF EXPORTATION (sections 10.66 and 10.67, *CRUS*).

FOREIGN SHIPPER'S DECLARATION: declaration made by the foreign shipper on or attached to the invoice for articles returned and entered under 802.1000, 802.2000, and 802.3000, stating that the articles described therein were imported from the United States for temporary use in an exhibition or for temporary educational or scientific use and describing the specific use to which they were put while abroad. For example:

I, _____, do hereby declare that the merchandise herein described was imported from the United States, and that it was sent to _____ for temporary use at the exhibition entitled _____, held at _____ on _____, 19____.

(date and place of signing)   (signature of exporter or authorized agent)
(sections 10.66 and 10.67, *CRUS*).

DECLARATION BY ULTIMATE CONSIGNEE: statement that articles returned and entered under 802.1000 are those which were exported and that they have not been changed in condition (section 10.67, *CRUS*).

CUSTOMS FORM 4455—CERTIFICATE OF REGISTRATION: declaration of the importer for articles (of either domestic or foreign origin) returned and entered under 802.2000 or 802.3000 (section 10.66, *CRUS*).

E. GENERAL DOCUMENTS REQUIRED FOR EXPORT SHIPMENTS

1. BILL OF LADING OR AIRWAYBILL: same as for imports (supplement I.A, above).

Original ocean bills of lading are sent to the consignees. Airwaybills are not needed by consignees in order to take possession of shipments.

2. INVOICE: same as for imports. In addition, consular documents and/or a CERTIFICATE OF ORIGIN may be required by some countries of destination.

3. PACKING LIST: same as for imports.

4. COMMERCE FORM 7525-V—SHIPPER'S EXPORT DECLARATION: a declaration showing name and address of consignor and of consignee, marks and number of packages, description of the material being shipped, values, commodity numbers, etc. The declaration must be filed by the exporter or the exporter's agent with U.S. Customs. Export declarations are not required for shipments of less than $50 in value.

5. EXPORT LICENSE: An export license is not usually required for the types of material exported by museums. If a license is not required, the SHIPPER'S EXPORT DECLARATION (above) should show that the material is being exported under a GENERAL LICENSE. If a VALIDATED EXPORT LICENSE is required, application on COMMERCE FORMS FC 419 and FC 420 must be made to the U.S. Department of Commerce. The license numbers will be assigned on these forms and returned to the applicant.

6. DECLARATIONS FOR PARCEL POST SHIPMENTS:

a. POSTAL SERVICE FORM 2966—CUSTOMS DECLARATION: a statement showing contents and value of the shipment, name and address of sender and of addressee, description of the parcel (box, package, bag, etc.), and alternate disposition instructions. It is prepared by the sender and tied to the outside of the parcel.

b. POSTAL SERVICE FORM 2922—INTERNATIONAL PARCEL POST STICKER: instructions as to alternate disposition, or forwarding address. It is signed by the sender and pasted on each parcel.

c. POSTAL SERVICE FORM 2972—DISPATCH NOTE: similar to POSTAL SERVICE FORM 2966 but with space provided for a receipt to be signed by the addressee. It is prepared by the sender and attached to the parcel, as required by countries of destination.

NOTE: Regulations for international parcel post shipments can be found in current issues of the *Postal Service Manual* and *International Mail* (publication 42), which can be purchased from the Superintendent of Documents (Government Printing Office, Washington, D.C. 20402).

7. CUSTOMS FORM 3495—APPLICATION FOR EXPORTATION OF ARTICLES UNDER SPECIAL BOND: Permission to export under customs supervision must be requested by the exporter or the exporter's agent whenever articles under permanent exhibition bond (862.1000) are to be exported. The form is filed with U.S. Customs.

8. IMPORT LICENSE: as required by some countries of destination. The consignee in the country of destination applies for the license when required.

SUPPLEMENT II: ADDITIONAL INFORMATION AND ADDRESSES

A. IMPORT RESTRICTIONS

This information on import restrictions that may pertain to museum shipments has been compiled on the basis of explanations given in various federal government publications available from the Superintendent of Documents (Government Printing Office, Washington, D.C. 20402). It is by no means all-inclusive. More detailed, current information can be obtained from the agencies listed below; the U.S. Customs Service

(Department of the Treasury, Washington, D.C. 20229); the district director or regional commissioner of customs in a nearby city (see supplement II.B); and customs brokers.

ANIMALS (INCLUDING WILDLIFE, PETS, FISH, BIRDS, ETC.): Many animals are subject to prohibitions, restrictions, and permit and quarantine requirements, and may be entered only through designated ports of entry. Included are all birds, mammals, reptiles, crustaceans, fish, mollusks, protected marine mammals, and endangered species of wildlife as listed by the Department of the Interior. Parts or products of these animals —fur skins, whalebone articles, bird feathers and eggs, and so forth—are similarly prohibited and restricted. Write to the U.S. Fish and Wildlife Service, Department of the Interior, Washington, D.C. 20240; Foreign Quarantine Program, Public Health Service, Center for Disease Control, Atlanta, Ga. 30333; Bureau of Epidemiology, Veterinary Public Health Service, Center for Disease Control, Atlanta, Ga. 30333; Veterinary Services, Animal and Plant Health Inspection Service, Department of Agriculture, Federal Center Building, Hyattsville, Md. 20782; National Marine Fisheries Service, Department of Commerce, Washington, D.C. 20235.

BIOLOGICAL MATERIALS: Disease organisms and vectors for research and educational purposes require import permits. Write to Foreign Quarantine Program, Public Health Service, Center for Disease Control, Atlanta, Ga. 30333.

BOOKS AND CATALOGUES: Unauthorized foreign reprints of books protected by American copyright, books falsely claiming copyright in the United States, and books in which the country of origin is not properly printed are prohibited entry. In addition, foreign-made editions of some books by American authors and of some books first published in the United States are restricted unless entered as accompanied baggage for personal use. Write to Copyright Office, Library of Congress, Washington, D.C. 20540; and U.S. Customs Service, Department of the Treasury, Washington, D.C. 20229.

FIREARMS AND AMMUNITION: Firearms and ammunition are subject to restrictions and import permits, and all weapons, ammunition, and other devices prohibited by the National Firearms Act are denied entry unless specifically authorized. Write to Bureau of Alcohol, Tobacco and Firearms, Department of the Treasury, Washington, D.C. 20226.

MEATS, LIVESTOCK, POULTRY: Meats, livestock, poultry, and their by-products are restricted or entirely prohibited. Write to Animal and Plant Health Inspection Service, Department of Agriculture, Federal Center Building, Hyattsville, Md. 20782.

MERCHANDISE ORIGINATING IN CAMBODIA, CUBA, NORTH KOREA, RHODESIA, AND VIETNAM: Articles produced in these countries can be imported only with a special license. Write to Office of Foreign Assets Control, Department of the Treasury, Washington, D.C. 20220.

NARCOTICS AND DANGEROUS DRUGS: Narcotics and dangerous drugs are prohibited entry by law.

PLANTS (INCLUDING VEGETABLES, FRUITS, PLANT PRODUCTS, ETC.): All cuttings, seeds, and unprocessed plant products are either prohibited from entering the country or require an import permit. Write to Quarantines, Department of Agriculture, Federal Center Building, Hyattsville, Md. 20782.

TEXTILES (INCLUDING WOOL, FUR, AND FABRIC PRODUCTS): Importations of fur and fiber products are restricted by various labeling acts. Write to Federal Trade Commission, Washington, D.C. 20580.

TRADEMARKED ARTICLES: Trademarked foreign-made articles often cannot be imported without consent of the trademark owner if the trademark is recorded with the Department of the Treasury. Write to U.S. Customs Service, Department of the Treasury, Washington, D.C. 20229.

OTHER: Prohibited articles include absinthe, lottery tickets, obscene articles and publications, seditious and treasonable materials, hazardous articles (e.g., fireworks, dangerous toys, toxic or poisonous substances), and switchblade knives. Write to U.S. Customs Service, Department of the Treasury, Washington, D.C. 20229.

B. CUSTOMS OFFICES

District directors of customs are located in the following cities. They can be contacted for current information on importing and exporting regulations and requirements.

ALABAMA
  Mobile 36602
ALASKA
  Anchorage 99501
ARIZONA
  Nogales 85621
CALIFORNIA
  San Diego 92188
  San Francisco 94126
  San Pedro 90731
CONNECTICUT
  Bridgeport 06609
DISTRICT OF COLUMBIA
  Washington 20018
FLORIDA
  Miami 33131
  Tampa 33602
GEORGIA
  Savannah 31401
HAWAII
  Honolulu 96806
ILLINOIS
  Chicago 60607
LOUISIANA
  New Orleans 70130
MAINE
  Portland 04111

MARYLAND
  Baltimore 21202
MASSACHUSETTS
  Boston 02109
MICHIGAN
  Detroit 48226
MINNESOTA
  Duluth 55802
  Minneapolis 55401
MISSOURI
  St. Louis 63105
MONTANA
  Great Falls 59401
NEW YORK
  Buffalo 14202
  New York 10048*
  Ogdensburg 13669
NORTH CAROLINA
  Wilmington 28401
NORTH DAKOTA
  Pembina 58271
OHIO
  Cleveland 44114
OREGON
  Portland 97209
PENNSYLVANIA
  Philadelphia 19106

PUERTO RICO
  San Juan 00903
RHODE ISLAND
  Providence 02903
SOUTH CAROLINA
  Charleston 29402
TEXAS
  El Paso 79985
  Galveston 77550
  Houston 77052
  Laredo 78040
  Port Arthur 77640
VERMONT
  St. Albans 05478
VIRGIN ISLANDS
  St. Thomas 00801
VIRGINIA
  Norfolk 23510
WASHINGTON
  Seattle 98104
WISCONSIN
  Milwaukee 53202

* Write to the regional commissioner of customs.

C. THE RESPONSIBILITIES OF COURIERS AND PROCEDURES FOR COURIER-ACCOMPANIED INTERNATIONAL SHIPMENTS

Courier service is a serious and special responsibility, appropriate whenever museum objects need accompaniment for reasons of value or sensitivity to temperature and humidity change. Like a groom traveling with a skittish racehorse, the chief responsibility of the courier is to ensure the safety and security of the shipment. Constant supervision is essential. The responsibilities of the courier are to:

1. be well informed, through careful preflight briefing, of names and phone numbers of responsible agents in countries of departure and destination, of customs

procedures at points of departure and arrival, and of the way in which each box is packed;

2. stay with the shipment at all times;

3. supervise loading and unloading;

4. check conditions and procedures at scheduled stops and/or at airports to which the flight is diverted;

5. notify shipping agents and the exporting museum of safe arrival and any change in itinerary.

International shipments require a formal customs entry. The courier should determine before the time of shipment that all export requirements of the country of export are complied with. All shipping papers travel directly with the shipment, but copies are carried by the courier and airmailed to the customs broker in the country of destination.

It is strongly recommended that courier-accompanied shipments be made on all-cargo rather than passenger aircraft. All-cargo flights permit the courier greater access to loading and unloading procedures and allow for closer supervision than do passenger flights, and they provide better security on the ground and in the air. In addition, shipments traveling as accompanied baggage on passenger flights are subject to X-ray and other security examinations at the airport of departure. Security examinations may create problems, particularly in the case of delicate, specially packed objects that should not be unpacked and repacked without the assistance of professional packers and especially not in passenger terminal areas with fluctuating or unfavorable temperature and humidity conditions. In the case of small objects in fitted boxes, the packing and repacking may not be a problem.

The courier accompanying a shipment on an all-cargo flight must arrive at the point of departure in advance of or with the museum's shipment and remain with it. The courier must witness the museum's boxes being loaded onto pallets or placed in containers. If containers are used, the courier must witness the sealing of the containers and know the seal and identification numbers. The courier must then witness the loading of the aircraft and know the position on the aircraft of the pallets or containers that hold the museum's shipment. At all stops the courier must watch the unloading and loading of any cargo, making sure that the museum's shipment is not misplaced or mishandled. If the museum's shipment is taken off for repositioning on the plane, the courier must see that it is not left in adverse or dangerous conditions—such as rain, snow, extreme cold, or extreme heat—before being reloaded.

The courier accompanying a shipment on a passenger flight must list the shipment and its value on his or her personal customs declaration and comply with the usual customs regulations. It is imperative that at the port of entry the courier be met by the customs broker; otherwise customs release cannot take place at the time of arrival. In order to meet the courier, the customs broker must have in advance the signed commercial invoice in duplicate, the name of the courier, and exact information on the flight number and time of arrival. If possible, it should be arranged for the courier to arrive on a business day and not later in the day than early afternoon; otherwise the museum may have to pay overtime charges to customs officials and brokers. If the prior arrangements for customs release have not been made, the museum's shipment will not be released upon arrival and the courier will be issued a post-entry certificate, which will be needed by the customs broker to make the customs entry. As security measures for transportation from the passenger terminal to the cargo area are always difficult, and often impossible, to arrange, the courier's services are consequently void at the most crucial point of the voyage.

9 INSURANCE

This chapter is directed to registrars and others who may be responsible for administering insurance policies covering loans and permanent collections. It is intended as a basic guide to help them work with museum insurance representatives, and with conservators, curators, and other members of the staff who are involved in protecting the museum against damage or loss of objects in its custody. Because a registrar's role includes record keeping and arranging for packing, shipping, and handling of the objects, the registrar is often the best able of all the museum staff to know what an institution's insurance needs really are. Also, the registrar will most often be involved in working with an insurance representative in settling losses that do occur. It is important, therefore, that the registrar be familiar with all the various precautions taken by the museum to prevent loss or damage and to maintain its collections in good condition. The registrar's files must identify each object for which the museum is responsible, whether in the permanent collection or borrowed, show its disposition, and show its condition and value. It is important, too, that the registrar read and understand the insurance policies covering the museum's collections, including all endorsements and policy modifications, and discuss with the insurance representative anything that is not clear.

This chapter suggests procedures for handling insurance reports and claims for damage. References are also made to words that are defined in the supplement to this chapter. However, this information should not take the place of careful study of a museum's insurance policy and consultations with its insurance representative.

Fig. 9.1. A museum fire is especially tragic, for it endangers not only life and property but also cultural patrimony that can never be replaced.

This chapter was prepared with the assistance of HUNTINGTON T. BLOCK and JOHN B. LAWTON of Huntington T. Block Insurance of Washington, D.C., specialists in fine arts insurance. Their valuable, professional assistance in preparing this chapter and the glossary supplement is gratefully acknowledged.

Fine Arts Insurance

Insurance is not a substitute for the precautions taken by museums in safeguarding their collections, but it is a means of compensating them financially if loss or damage occurs. It is a truism that a museum should put its money into safety and security before insurance. Despite the best preventive and protective measures, however, occasional losses or damages do occur, owing to a variety of causes, such as bursting steam and water pipes, vandalism in the galleries, fire, theft, or—the number one cause—accidents while objects are being handled or transported.

Insurance offers financial protection against such fortuitous (accidental or unexpected) losses. When damages can be repaired, insurance will cover the cost of both restoration and the important factor of depreciation. In the case of total loss, museum objects that are unique cannot, of course, be replaced; but the payment of the insured value makes it possible for the museum to purchase new acquisitions that may to some extent substitute for the lost item in the collection. (See DEPRECIATION; FORTUITOUS; INSURABLE INTEREST; INSURABLE LOSS; INSURANCE.)

Fine arts insurance is normally handled as so-called inland marine or inland transportation insurance, which came into use after the liberalization and extension of coverage in ocean marine policies. Unlike underwriters for other forms of insurance, marine and inland marine underwriters are not restricted to narrow lines of coverage. They can make it possible for property to be insured against "all risks" under one policy instead of under several separate policies. (See ALL RISK POLICY; INLAND MARINE INSURANCE; MARINE INSURANCE.)

The fine arts policy was first written in answer to the need for a broad coverage for art collections. No longer limited to the fine arts, it is now used by all types of museums and historical societies to insure a variety of museum quality objects. It may cover permanent collections as well as the property of others that is on loan to exhibitions or held for study and possible acquisition. It may be written on either an all risk or named peril basis. It may be used to insure objects: (1) only while on the premises; (2) only while in transit; or (3) while on the premises, in transit, and at other locations. (See ALL RISK POLICY; NAMED PERIL POLICY.)

When insurance covers objects only while on the premises, it is possible to arrange individual trip transit insurance if occasional shipments are made. However, when frequent shipments are made from the permanent collections, or if objects are being continually borrowed for exhibition, floater coverage is preferable. Fine arts floater policies cover insured objects against all risks, or certain specified risks, from the time they leave the hands of the owners until they are returned, whether during packing and unpacking, storage, exhibition, transit, or at other locations. The term "floater" means that objects are covered anywhere within the territorial limits of the policy. The protection "floats" with the property. This coverage, often referred to as "wall-to-wall," or in Europe as "nail-to-nail," is essential protection for any institution with an active outgoing loan program. (See FLOATER POLICY; NAMED PERIL POLICY; WALL-TO-WALL.)

Floater policies do not normally cover property outside the continental United States and Canada, although many insurance policies are now being endorsed to include Hawaii and Alaska. Most floater policies do not cover property on the premises of national or international expositions unless special arrangements are made and the policies endorsed accordingly. Also, such policies may specify limits of liability in any one conveyance or in any one location or for any one object. These limits should be carefully checked before arrangements are made to ship museum objects. In order for these policies to cover transoceanic shipments, specific extra arrangements must sometimes be made, although many policies now automatically provide limits for foreign shipments as well. (See ENDORSEMENT; RIDER.)

The amount and kind of insurance protection purchased by museums varies, as does the rate, which is expressed in "X" cents per hundred dollars of value per month, per year, per trip, or often expressed as a flat annual dollar amount of premium. Some museums do not insure their own collections unless they leave the premises. The decision not to insure is usually made when it is felt that a sound, fireproof building, fire watches, gallery guards, night watchmen, alarm systems, carefully trained and supervised handlers, and conservation facilities provide sufficient protection. However, the apparent increase in thefts and acts of violence in museums and in the holding of valuable museum objects for ransom has led more and more museums to insure at least a portion of their permanent collections.

When collections on the premises are insured, policies are generally written for one or both of the following types of coverage:

Coverage based on a stated or flat amount (i.e., a fixed amount of loss that can be claimed in any one occurrence): Museums calculate the amount for which they wish to be protected, based upon their considered judgment of their probable maximum loss, and buy insurance accordingly. With a loss limit of $1 million, for example, claims for loss or damage to one or several objects in a given incident would be covered up to the stipulated amount of $1 million. Policies with this type of coverage have proved feasible in museums with large and extremely valuable permanent collections, especially when the cost of full coverage would be prohibitive. However, it should be pointed out that under such an arrangement, the valuation clause of the policy becomes extremely important. Buyers of this type of museum insurance generally insist upon a valuation clause that will pay on the basis of current market value of the object or objects as of the day they are damaged or destroyed. Museum administrators who approve this type of loss limit policy must, of course, accept the risk for any losses beyond the limits specified in the policy.

Coverage based on the value of individual objects: Policies with this type of coverage are called scheduled policies because they are based on a list maintained in the museum's records giving a specified value for each object or on a list or schedule furnished to the insurance company. Sometimes such policies refer simply to the books and records of the insured. Scheduled policies are used by some museums for insuring both permanent collections and borrowed objects. If the insured values of objects in the permanent collection are to be based on current market values, these values must be kept up to date, and increases and decreases of value reflected in amounts reported to the insurance company or maintained in the museum's books or records. Since this record keeping can be a formidable task for even a well-staffed museum, the valuation clause described above is generally preferred. Scheduled policies are, however, essential for insuring objects borrowed for special exhibitions, because the amount of insurance purchased is based on the insurance values set forth in the loan agreement for each object borrowed.

If the objects in the permanent collection are insured only when on the premises or are not covered at all while on the premises, outgoing loans can, of course, be insured either under a floater policy arranged by the lender or by the borrower, or individual trip transit insurance can be arranged as mentioned previously. (For a discussion of insurance coverage for loans from permanent collections, see chapter 6.)

Policies are often written with deductible or franchise clauses. Deductibles are agreed amounts that are deducted from the total loss claimed; therefore if the amount of a loss is less than the deductible, no claim at all is made. Franchises are similar to deductibles except that the insurance company pays the entire amount if a claim equals or exceeds the amount of the franchise. Both clauses reduce the number of small claims and the paper work necessary in processing them and therefore can be influential in reducing premiums. If deductibles or franchises are included in their policies, museums should remember to budget funds to cover the cost of losses or repairs not amounting to a claim. (See DEDUCTIBLE; FRANCHISE CLAUSE; LIMIT OF LIABILITY; LOSS LIMIT; SCHEDULED INSURANCE POLICIES; VALUED INSURANCE POLICIES.)

PURCHASING INSURANCE

It is customary for brokers or broker-agents, who are experts in fine arts insurance, to be selected to advise museums on their insurance problems and to act for them in placing their insurance with reliable companies. Selecting the appropriate amount of insurance requires the guidance of someone trained and experienced in this specialized field who can intelligently estimate the probable maximum loss the museum might suffer, given the safety and security measures in effect. The amount and kind of coverage to be purchased are usually determined by the administrator or business manager of the museum with the advice of the trustees and of outside insurance experts and also in consultation with members of the staff who are familiar with the number and variety of risks that should be covered. The registrar may be called upon to help determine the coverage needed, and should, in fact, participate in all discussions leading to the purchase of insurance. (See INSURANCE AGENT; INSURANCE BROKER; INSURANCE BROKER-AGENT.)

Fig. 9.2.
Insurance should never be a substitute for security precautions. Some large museums have a central security station where closed-circuit television monitors will show any disturbances in exhibit or storage areas.

A registrar with the responsibilities described in previous chapters becomes familiar with the hazards to which objects are subjected and is in a good position to work with the insurance representative in administering the permanent collection and loan policies. The registrar's responsibilities include control of the entry and exit of objects, and their safe handling and safe keeping while in the custody of the museum. In fact, the records of the condition of each object and the files identifying and recording the location of each object are an essential part of that responsibility.

The registrar should make certain that the insurance companies maintaining the coverage are informed not only of the curatorial and registration procedures but also of all the museum's security regulations and protective measures, such as guarding and alarm systems, packing and shipping methods, conservation procedures, and overall claim experience. This information as well as the physical condition and location of the building, and its published fire insurance rate, will influence the underwriter in determining the amount of risk acceptable and the rates to be charged. In the last analysis, it is the underwriter who determines the premium the museum must pay, so no safety or security information should be considered too insignificant to mention. (See FIRE RATING; INSURANCE UNDERWRITER; LOSS EXPERIENCE OR LOSS RATIO.)

There is no one form of policy or established rate for insuring a museum's permanent collection or loans. Standard fine arts policies should be adapted to fit the requirements of each museum. Museums may decide to purchase more than one type of fine arts coverage to provide varying amounts and kinds of protection for permanent collections, loans to special exhibitions, and extended loans. Some may decide to purchase separate policies to cover each loan exhibition. All policies, however, should provide coverage against all risks, or certain specified risks, of physical loss or damage from external cause.

While a policy will usually state that it insures against risks "of physical loss or damage from any external cause," there are important exceptions and limitations that will be spelled out. These should be studied and understood. Normally the exclusions are:

> Wear and tear, gradual deterioration, insects, vermin, inherent defects, or damage sustained due to and resulting from any repairing, restoration, or retouching process
>
> War, insurrection, rebellion, revolution, or civil war (note that riot is not an exclusion)
>
> Nuclear damage
>
> Shipments by mail unless registered first class or insured parcel post and less than the value that is specified

(See INHERENT VICE; WAR RISK.)

Before a final decision on coverage is made, the policy or policies being considered should be checked carefully and the insurance representative asked to explain all of the provisions, particularly any other exclusions that appear. It is important that the museum request the removal of any additional exclusions that are not to its advantage, for example, clauses excluding breakage of fragile objects, and fidelity exclusions concerning the possible dishonesty of museum personnel. If the fidelity exclusion cannot be removed, employee bonds should be checked to see if they are adequate and—so as to avoid conflict in the event of a loss—issued by the same company that is covering the collections. (See BOND; FIDELITY EXCLUSION.)

Policies should also be checked to see if provisions that would be to the advantage of the museum may be added, for example: the payment of the current market value of objects at the time of loss; the insurance of the museum's interest in remainder gifts and jointly owned property; the automatic insurance of transoceanic shipments (ocean and air transit coverage); coverage during strikes, riots, and civil disturbances; and bailee or legal liability (protection in case lenders' insurers subrogate against borrowing museums). It may also be desirable to include deductibles or franchises to reduce both the premium and the number of small claims. (See BAILEE; BAILEE'S LIABILITY; LEGAL LIABILITY; STRIKES, RIOTS, AND CIVIL COMMOTION; SUBROGATION; VALUATION CLAUSE.)

It should be made clear in policies that the museum, at its discretion, can release insured objects to its packing, forwarding, and carrying agents either without value declarations or with nominal value declarations to guarantee the safest handling. A limited amount of liability is assumed by these agents, and insurance companies can subrogate against them and collect a percentage of a claim if damages have been caused by their negligence. If a warranty on the use of competent packers is included in the policy, as is generally the case, it should be phrased so that the museum, "to the best of its ability," will provide for insured objects to be packed and unpacked by competent packers. Any seemingly restrictive clauses in the policy should be reworded if possible. For example, the museum should not be required to report a loss or damage "immediately after it occurs," but to report it "as soon as practicable" or "immediately after its discovery."

When a large amount of insurance protection is purchased, policies are written by several insurance companies to distribute the risk. The museum deals with one company through the insurance representative, and that company, known as the lead company, shares the risk with one or more other companies. The lead company establishes the rate and services the account. It may sometimes be advisable to arrange a special and separate policy for a traveling exhibition having an extremely high value instead of covering it under the museum's existing policy. Rates for this special coverage can sometimes be negotiated on a more favorable basis than those available on the museum's own policy. (See LAYERING; LEAD COMPANY; REINSURANCE.)

Objects in transoceanic shipments forwarded by either ship or airplane are covered by marine insurance. This special insurance can normally be arranged as automatic coverage under a floater policy, and the value of each shipment reported periodically. Separate rates are charged for overseas shipments, and these rates should be discussed with the insurance representative. Rates by air are usually lower than by ship. The insurance representative can explain certain clauses, such as delay, deviation, general average, and particular average, that appear in marine insurance policies. (See MARINE EXTENSION CLAUSE; MARINE INSURANCE.)

Once the insurance coverage has been agreed upon and a policy or policies issued, the registrar and other staff members concerned should meet with the insurance representative periodically to discuss problems in the policy, the claims adjustment service, the possible revision of rates, future plans, and other matters relating to the museum's insurance program.

INSURANCE REPORTS

Policies based on a stated or flat amount of coverage (a loss limit) do not require a report of individual values, for the objects are covered up to the fixed limit for any loss or damage in a given incident. They may, however, require periodic re-evaluation. With this kind of coverage it is imperative that the valuations of objects in case of loss or damage be responsive to market conditions at the time of loss or damage. These loss limit, nonreporting policies eliminate the necessity of frequent revision and detailed reporting as values increase or decrease.

Scheduled policies based on the specified values of individual objects require the periodic reporting of amounts at risk. Reports, however, may be made with a minimum of detail. For example, it may be possible for reports of total amounts at risk, instead of itemized values, to be made for periods varying from every month to every three years, with adjustments to premiums after each report. When lists with itemized values are not made, museums permit the insurance company to have access, if necessary, to their records of insurance values. For reporting additions and cancellations for special exhibitions, it may be advantageous to report each month the total amount at risk as of the last day of the preceding month and pay a monthly premium. If, for budgetary purposes, it is desirable to break down the total amount at risk, the total value of additions and cancellations for each loan exhibition may be shown. For example:

MUSEUM OF ART   DATE_____

INSURANCE REPORT   POLICY NO._____

Exhibitions	Previous Report	Added	Canceled	Balance This Report
Eight American Sculptors	$150,000		$100,000	$ 50,000
Landscape Paintings	60,000	$ 50,000		110,000
Twentieth-Century Drawings		75,000		75,000
	$210,000	$125,000	$100,000	$235,000
Other Museum Exhibitions at Risk	$200,000			$200,000
	$410,000			$435,000

The total value of new acquisitions to the permanent collections or of objects canceled, if any, may also be shown on this report if they are covered on the same scheduled policy.

It should be pointed out that in recent years the trend has been away from the necessity of filing monthly reports, even for special exhibitions. Modern policies covering permanent collections are generally being written to include substantial automatic protection for loans so that reports are only required when policy limits are exceeded. Whether or not to report is a matter to be determined by the museum's insurance carrier and the registrar.

INSURANCE CERTIFICATES

Occasionally a packing agent, freight forwarder, or a lender requires a certificate of insurance stating that the object or objects being packed, forwarded, or loaned are fully insured by the museum. In some instances the agent, forwarder, or lender may ask to be named as an additional insured. Normally, this certificate, signed by the insurance company or its agent, is written evidence of insurance in force. It is sometimes possible, however, for the insurance representative to supply a form that can be filled in and signed by the registrar for this purpose. (See ADDITIONAL INSURED CLAUSE; CERTIFICATE OF INSURANCE; COVER NOTE.)

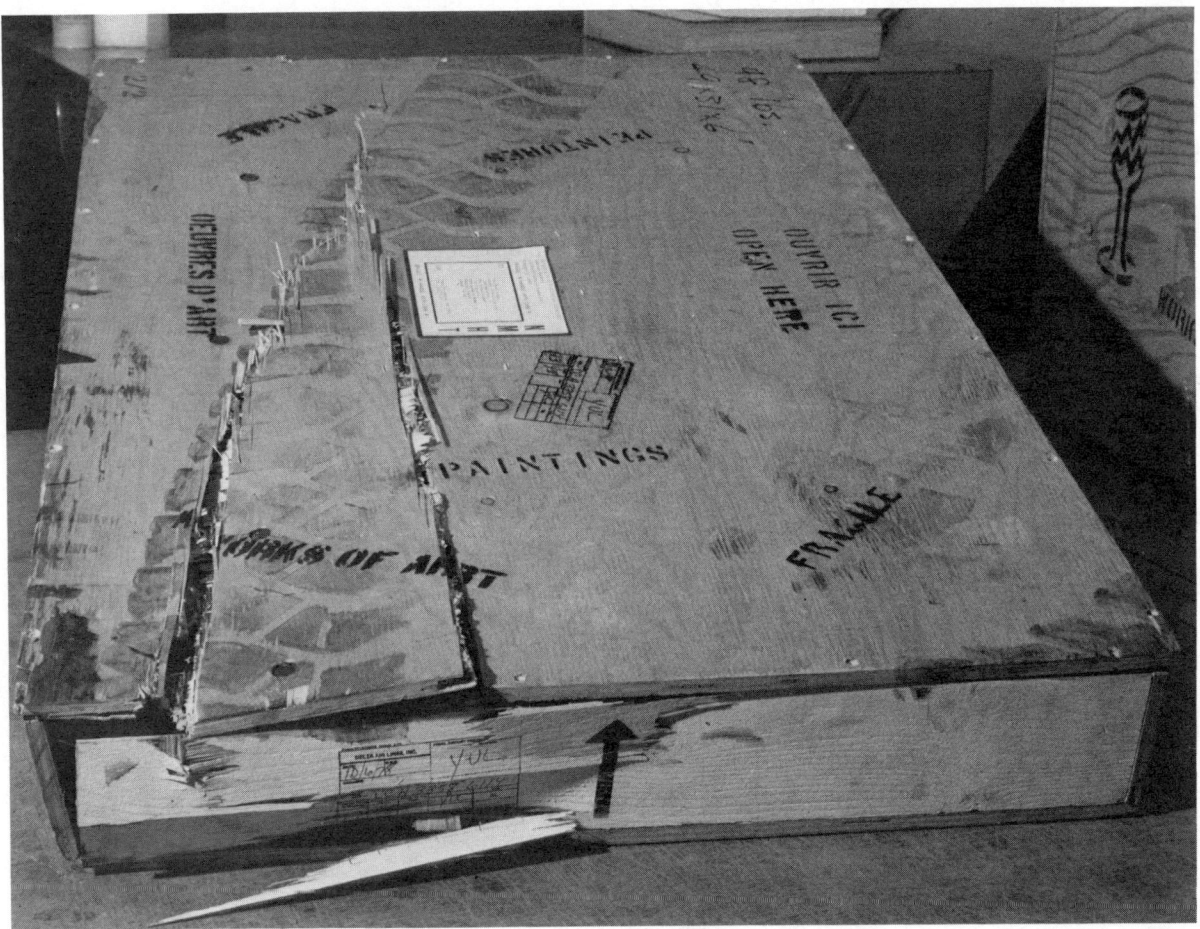

Fig. 9.3.
Even with careful packing precautions, damage can occur during transit, as in the destruction of this crate containing an oil painting owned by the Montreal Museum of Fine Arts.

SUBROGATION AND WAIVER OF SUBROGATION

The subrogation clause in a policy allows the insurance company to assume the rights of the insured to collect from a third party if a loss or damage is caused by the negligence of the third party and not by an "Act of God" (i.e., an event over which man has no control). A waiver of subrogation is an agreement whereby the insurance company waives this right to subrogate against a third party. A waiver should be requested by borrowing museums when lenders wish to maintain their own insurance. The museum's packing and carrying agents who are legally liable to certain extents, usually specified by Interstate Commerce Commission regulations, may also request that subrogation against them be waived. When this latter request is granted, the insurance company usually agrees to waive subrogation only beyond the carrier's common law or statutory liability. Most museums carry a fixed amount of bailee or legal liability insurance to cover those instances when objects are in their custody but for which no subrogation waiver has been forthcoming. (See Act of God; Subrogation; Waiver of Subrogation.)

Insurance Claims

It is customary for an insurance adjuster to be appointed by the insurance company to settle claims for loss or damage. The registrar should request that the company choose in advance an adjuster who has some understanding of fine arts or other objects covered by the museum's policy. (See INSURANCE ADJUSTER.)

Before reporting a loss or damage, the registrar must understand the following conditions under which a claim can be made:

- The object lost or damaged must have been covered by the policy at the time of loss
- The loss or damage must have resulted from a peril insured against
- The total loss or amount of repairs plus depreciation, if any, must exceed the amount of the museum's deductible or equal or exceed the amount of a franchise if included in the policy

The registrar must also understand and will want to explain to the museum's staff or lenders concerned that if total loss is claimed and paid, the insurance company owns what is left of the object. There may be instances when even a damaged object is better than not having it at all. In cases where a total loss is claimed and the insurance company takes the salvage, arrangements can usually be made for the damaged or destroyed object to be "bought back" at a reasonable price. (See DEPRECIATION; INSURABLE LOSS; SALVAGE.)

REPORTING A LOSS OR DAMAGE

If an insurance claim is justifiable, the insurance representative must be notified in writing of the loss or damage as soon as practicable after it is discovered. The report of loss or damage, which should provide a description of its extent and the circumstances surrounding it, does not itself constitute a claim. It is simply a notification that conditions have been recorded that may lead to a claim. Damage that has occurred in transit should also be reported to the carrier, and whenever possible, inspected by the carrying agency's representative. As mentioned previously, carriers normally have a very limited liability, and insurance companies will subrogate against them and collect a percentage of the claim if damages have been caused by their negligence. (For a discussion of the liability of carriers and value declarations made by shippers, see chapter 7.)

If an object has disappeared and theft is suspected, a report should be made immediately to the local police and, if the value is over $5,000 or involves interstate commerce, also to the Federal Bureau of Investigation, as well as to the insurance representative. Other agencies interested and helpful in recovering stolen art are the Art Dealers Association of America (575 Madison Avenue, New York, N.Y. 10022) and the Art Theft Archive (46 East 70th Street, New York, N.Y. 10021). It is important that a photograph and complete description of a stolen object be supplied to the investigators as soon as possible.

If an object has been damaged, a condition photograph should be made as soon as possible and a conservator consulted and asked to estimate the cost of repairs. Serious damage should be immediately reported to the insurance ad-

9: INSURANCE

Fig. 9.4.
Risks to museum objects are also risks to registration records. In the event of total loss, as by fire, duplicates of essential registration records stored outside the museum will provide the documentation necessary for determining the extent of loss.

juster and inspected by him in consultation with the conservator and any others concerned. It is usually not possible to determine the amount of depreciation until restoration has been completed.

Insofar as is practicable, damaged objects should be kept in their damaged state until the adjuster has made an examination. This does not preclude, however, whatever action may be necessary to prevent further loss. First-aid treatment should be made only by a trained conservator. No repairs should be made without the specific consent of the owner or before the insurance adjuster has approved the conservator's estimate of the cost of final restorative repairs.

THE ACTUAL CLAIM

When final costs of restoration are known and the amount of depreciation, if any, has been agreed upon by all concerned, the total amount is reported to the insurance company. When an adjuster has been employed, he or she prepares a proof of loss, a document which must be signed and notarized to substantiate the claim. Settlement is made either with the lender, if the damaged object is a loan, or with the museum, as either owner or borrower. If there is disagreement between the museum or lender and the insurer as to the amount claimed, settlement is based on a standard procedure as specified in the policy. (See APPRAISAL CLAUSE; PROOF OF LOSS.)

When processing claims the registrar should understand that provision is made under the sue-and-labor clause in the policy for the insurance company to reimburse the museum for expenses incurred while attempting to recover lost or damaged property. This clause requires the insured "to sue, labor and travel" when necessary in order to assist the insurance company in recovering a loss.

A good insurance program is the product of careful negotiation both by the museum purchasing the insurance and by the insurance representative acting on the insurance company's behalf. The Insurance Committee of the Association of Art Museum Directors made an extensive study of insurance for museums and determined that the record of loss in the museum field has been favorable. That study and a more aggressive posture by insurance buyers has resulted in substantial premium savings to museums across the country. However, perhaps the most significant insurance saving was brought about by the Congress of the United States, when on December 20, 1975, it enacted into law Public Law 94–158, known as the Arts and Artifacts Indemnity Act.

Arts and Artifacts Indemnity Act

This legislation provides an opportunity for individuals, nonprofit agencies, institutions, and governments to indemnify eligible items borrowed from abroad on exhibition in the United States and eligible items for exhibition abroad when there is an exchange exhibition from a foreign country. Indemnity is another word for insurance, and in this case the indemnity agreement is backed by the full faith and credit of the United States. Furthermore, the museum pays no premium for this protection.

Exhibitions of works of art as defined in the legislation that have educational, cultural, historical, or scientific value will be considered eligible so long as they are certified by the Secretary of State as being in the national interest. Any institution may arrange indemnification up to $50 million for a single exhibition. A loss deductible of $15,000 applies only per exhibition and not per loss. In other words, $15,000 is the most a museum could lose in an indemnified exhibition.

Very specific rules and regulations govern application for indemnification, but the substantial insurance savings available make it almost mandatory for any museum contemplating an international exhibition to acquaint itself with the guidelines. Questions regarding the legislation and administrative guidelines may be addressed to the Executive Secretary of the Federal Council on the Arts and the Humanities (National Foundation on the Arts and the Humanities, Washington, D.C. 20506).

Supplement

CONCISE GLOSSARY OF INSURANCE TERMS

ACT OF GOD: a happening, such as a tornado, a hailstorm, etc., over which man normally has no control.

ADDITIONAL INSURED CLAUSE: an agreement, often limited as to term, whereby a third party, with a valid insurable interest, is made an insured under the policy. A borrowing museum often requests a CERTIFICATE OF INSURANCE furnishing evidence of the existence of the lender's policy when the lender elects to maintain its own insurance.

ALL RISK POLICY: covers against "all risks of physical loss or damage from any external cause except as herein excluded." The exceptions or exclusions are specifically listed. Most fine arts policies are on an "all risk" basis.

APPRAISAL CLAUSE: provides for the selection of a competent and disinterested appraiser to establish actual loss in the mutual interest of both parties in event of disagreement between the insured and the insurer as to the amount of loss.

ASSURED: synonymous with "insured."

BAILEE: a person to whom goods, the property of others, are entrusted for a special purpose and for a limited period.

BAILEE'S LIABILITY: liability, normally for a loss due to the bailee's own negligence. (NOTE: a so-called ACT OF GOD could not be construed as due to the negligence of a BAILEE.)

BINDER: a memorandum or temporary contract of insurance issued in anticipation of the issuance of the policy itself. A binder, either oral or written, is a valid contract. A binder must be specific as to the risk to the insured, the time the protection commences, the name of the insured, and the amount.

BOND: a written agreement of obligation between the insurance company and the insured indemnifying for dishonest acts of all officers and employees of the named insured. It is a two-party contract conditioned for an employer-employee relationship.

CERTIFICATE OF INSURANCE: written evidence of insurance in force signed by the insurance company or its agent. Museums or lenders often require certificates of insurance from one another before releasing works of art on loan.

COINSURANCE CLAUSE: a provision in a policy whereby the insurance company's liability or payment is limited to that proportionate part of the loss that the total insurance purchased bears to the total value at risk or to an agreed percentage of the total value at risk. A clause to be avoided in dealing with fine arts.

COVER NOTE: a document issued by a representative of the insurance company confirming that insurance has been effected. A cover note is similar to a BINDER, but is a term particularly identified with insurance arranged at LLOYD'S of London.

DEDUCTIBLE: an agreed amount of loss that an insured must suffer before the policy will pay. A deductible often serves as a device to lower the overall premium.

DEPRECIATION: the difference between the value now and a lower value at a subsequent time. In fine arts insurance, depreciation is an important factor. It represents the difference in value, if any, before damage and after restoration.

ENDORSEMENT: a modification of an insurance policy by means of a written, typed, or printed addition, either to the policy itself or on a piece of paper which should be attached to it. An endorsement is sometimes referred to as a RIDER.

EXCESS INSURANCE: a term used to identify insurance that is not operative until a loss exceeds a stated amount. In fine arts insurance, it is sometimes possible, particularly when dealing with very substantial values, to reduce premiums by arranging layers of excess insurance over basic or primary insurance.

FIDELITY EXCLUSION: a clause sometimes found in fine arts policies that normally excludes protection for losses caused by the infidelity or dishonesty of the insured's employees or persons to whom the property is entrusted.

FIRE RATING: a term used to identify the established annual cost per $100 of fire and lightning insurance on a building or its contents. This rate is normally promulgated by a local rating bureau and is used by all insurance companies as a basis for establishing the all risk fine arts rate.

FLOATER POLICY: covers property anywhere including in transit, in storage, or at any location. The protection "floats" with the property.

FORTUITOUS: accidental, unexpected, or occurring by chance.

FRANCHISE CLAUSE: similar to a DEDUCTIBLE except that once a loss equals or exceeds the amount of the franchise, the insurance company must pay the entire loss. This clause is rarely used in actual practice.

INHERENT VICE: the quality that an object has to deteriorate or damage itself without external help. Inherent vice normally is excluded in fine arts insurance policies.

INLAND MARINE INSURANCE: generally refers to the protection of property that is subject to movement and not limited to one location. Buildings would not be a subject for inland marine insurance. The protection of fine arts, on the other hand, is normally handled as inland marine insurace.

INSURABLE INTEREST: the interest in something that the buyer seeks to insure. In order to make a valid contract of insurance, the buyer (insured) must have something to lose.

INSURABLE LOSS: a loss that is of a FORTUITOUS nature.

INSURANCE: a promise by an insurance company to indemnify or make whole a financial loss.

INSURANCE ADJUSTER: the representative appointed by the insurance company to settle claims in a manner satisfactory to the insured and in accordance with the protection afforded by the insurance contract.

INSURANCE AGENT: the agent of the insurance company. As such, his or her acts, omissions, and knowledge are those of the principal. The agent's authority, rights, and obligations are defined by agency contract and by law. Normally the agent has the authority to bind (attach protection on behalf of his or her principal), within certain limitations.

INSURANCE BROKER: normally defined as the representative of the insured; the broker advises on and negotiates for the best insurance contracts on behalf of his or her principal. Normally the broker does not have the authority to bind.

INSURANCE BROKER-AGENT: an individual who is an AGENT for some companies and a BROKER for others. (NOTE: It is most important that a museum's insurance representative have the authority to bind.)

INSURANCE UNDERWRITER: an employee of the insurance company charged with the responsibility of accepting or rejecting risks presented to the company by BROKERS or AGENTS and establishing on what terms acceptable risks will be insured.

LAYERING: the practice of buying insurance in layers (primary, first excess, second excess, etc.) rather than in a lump sum—a device often used to reduce premiums when large amounts of insurance are purchased and to obtain broader participation of insurance companies.

9: INSURANCE

Lead Company: a term used in connection with subscription policies (those in which several insurance companies participate for a specified percentage). The lead company normally establishes the rate and, with the Broker-Agent, services the account; the other companies normally follow the lead for their percentage of participation.

Legal Liability: similar to Bailee Liability but, whereas bailee liability is a contractual liability, legal liability is only that determined or established in a court of law or imposed by law.

Limit of Liability: the most the insured may collect under various circumstances as specifically outlined in the policy. In fine arts insurance, there might be one limit for objects being transported, another while they are on the museum premises, and still another while at someone else's premises. It is extremely important to know what these limits are, so that they are never exceeded without prior notification to the Broker-Agent.

Lloyd's: world famous as a source for unusual or hard-to-place insurance. Lloyd's is a place of doing business rather than an insurance company. Insurance may be arranged only by approved Brokers through Underwriters representing syndicates of private investors. An insurance arrangement at Lloyd's may require several days, as each underwriter (or syndicate) usually commits only for a small proportion of the total risk, and many underwriters must be seen before coverage of a risk is 100 percent "complete."

Loss Experience or Loss Ratio: usually expressed as a percentage showing the amount of losses compared to the amount of premiums in a given time period. A consistently low loss ratio should result in lower premiums.

Loss Limit: the same as Limit of Liability and is often something less than actual total values.

Marine Extension Clause: certain special insurance provisions that normally apply when property is undergoing overseas transport by vessel or air. These provisions contain standard wording (established in admiralty law) giving important extra protection.

Marine Insurance: insurance having to do primarily with property in transit. Originally confined to coverage of risks of ocean transportation, marine insurance now covers transportation over inland waterways and on land generally—thus, ocean marine and Inland Marine.

Named Peril Policy: the perils insured against which are so stated in the policy. Any perils not stated, whether by intent or otherwise, are not insured. This type of policy is normally to be avoided in arranging fine arts insurance.

Probable Maximum Loss: the largest loss that can be expected if all loss prevention systems are operating properly. Many museums employ the probable maximum loss concept to establish the amount of insurance, or Loss Limit, they will buy to cover their permanent collections.

Proof of Loss: the burden of proof on the insured to demonstrate that a loss has occurred. The policy usually specifies the manner in which this must be accomplished, including the time by which notice of loss must be filed. In practice, the proof of loss is prepared by the Adjuster and states the total amount to be claimed; it must be signed, notarized, and returned to the adjuster.

Reinsurance: a device used by the original insurer to spread, or reinsure, among other insurance companies the risk that the insurer has accepted. This is common in fine arts insurance because of the high values involved.

Rider: the same as Endorsement.

SALVAGE: property "salvaged" from a loss. If an insurance company pays a total loss, it has in fact "purchased" the salvage.

SCHEDULED INSURANCE POLICIES: policies based on a list or schedule giving a specified value for each object insured.

STRIKES, RIOTS, AND CIVIL COMMOTION: coverage for all manner of civil disturbances short of war or act of war. It is important protection to purchase, particularly for traveling exhibitions.

SUBROGATION: entitles the insurance company to any rights of the insured to collect its loss from a third party under the rules of LEGAL LIABILITY, to the extent, of course, of the indemnification afforded by the contract of insurance. Subrogation is important in fine arts insurance; for example, insurance companies will subrogate against carriers in the amount for which they will be liable.

VALUATION CLAUSE: the clause that tells exactly what the insured will be paid in the event of a claim, or how the amount of the claim will be determined. This is the most important clause in a fine arts policy.

VALUED INSURANCE POLICIES: policies in which specific values of the property insured are made a part of the policy and the amounts so stated are payable by the insurance company in case of total loss. Many fine arts policies are written on a valued basis, but normal fluctuation of values calls for institutions so insured to re-examine declared values frequently.

WAIVER OF SUBROGATION: an agreement whereby the insurance company or the insured waives right of subrogation against a third party. This is often required by a borrowing museum when a lender maintains its own insurance, or vice versa.

WALL-TO-WALL: a clause in a fine arts policy that extends protection from the wall (or normal repository) where the shipment originates until it is returned; an important concept because the period of packing and unpacking is automatically insured. The British prefer the term "nail-to-nail."

WAR RISK: protection normally available only during an overseas shipment and virtually unobtainable while property is on land.

WAREHOUSE-TO-WAREHOUSE: the same concept as WALL-TO-WALL, but applies only during course of overseas shipment from point of origin to point of destination.

BIBLIOGRAPHY

This bibliography is intended primarily for registrars, but, as registrars must be familiar with the work of curators, cataloguers, and other members of the museum staff, it includes basic references in many areas of museum work. It is necessarily selective, and, by and large, limited to a few classic studies and recent works of substance. In addition, bibliographies on specialized subjects appear in articles C, D, E, F, H, I, J, M, Q, R, and S.

The Profession

Items listed below amplify the information in chapter 1. Included are standard references for the museum field in general and for the training of museum professionals. Also included are the names and addresses of professional organizations whose journals and other publications should be referred to regularly for current approaches, research activities, and updated information. The General section lists several comprehensive books on museum procedures that are relevant to many other categories in this bibliography, but, because of space limitations, the citations could not be repeated.

GENERAL

American Association for State and Local History. *Directory of Historical Societies and Agencies in the United States and Canada.* 11th ed. Nashville: AASLH, 1978.

American Association of Museums. *America's Museums: The Belmont Report.* Washington, D.C.: AAM, 1969.

———. *Museum Ethics: A Report to the American Association of Museums by Its Committee on Ethics.* Washington, D.C.: AAM, 1978.

———. *Museums, Their New Audience: A Report to the Department of Housing and Urban Development by a Special Committee of the American Association of Museums.* Washington, D.C.: AAM, 1972.

———. *The Official Museum Directory, 1978/79.* Skokie, Ill.: AAM and National Register Publishing Company, 1978.

Canadian Museums Association. *Directory of Canadian Museums.* Ottawa: CMA, 1978.

Coleman, Laurence Vail. *Manual for Small Museums.* New York: G. P. Putnam's Sons, 1927.

———. *The Museum in America: A Critical Study.* 3 vols. Washington, D.C.: AAM, 1939.

A Guide to Museum-Related Resource Organizations. Reprint from *Museum News,* 57:2 (Nov./Dec. 1978).

Guthe, Carl E. *The Management of Small History Museums.* 2d ed. Nashville: AASLH, 1964.

———. *So You Want a Good Museum: A Guide to the Management of Small Museums.* Washington, D.C.: AAM, 1973.

Hudson, Kenneth, and Ann Nicholls, eds. *The Directory of World Museums.* New York: Columbia University Press, 1975.

Lewis, Ralph H. *Manual for Museums.* Washington, D.C.: Department of the Interior, 1976.

MacBeath, George, and S. James Gooding, eds. *Basic Museum Management.* Ottawa: CMA, 1969.

Museums of the World. 2d ed. New York: R. R. Bowker, 1975.

National Endowment for the Arts. *Museums USA: Art, History, Science, and Other Museums.* Washington, D.C.: NEA, 1974.

Noble, Joseph V. "Museum Manifesto." *Museum News,* 48:8 (Apr. 1970), 16–20.

Rath, Frederick L., Jr., and Merrilyn Rogers O'Connell, eds. *A Bibliography on Historical Organization Practices.* 3 vols. Nashville: AASLH, 1975, 1977, 1978.

Roy Choudhury, Anil. *Art Museum Documentation and Practical Handling.* Hyderabad, India: Choudhury & Choudhury, 1963.

United Nations Educational, Scientific and Cultural Organization. *The Organization of Museums: Practical Advice.* Museums and Monuments 9. Paris: UNESCO, 1960.

——— and International Council of Museums, Museum Documentation Centre. *International Museological Bibliography.* Annual.

University of Michigan Graduate Program in Museum Practice. *Selective Bibliography on Museums and Museum Practice: Museums of Art and History in the United States.* Ann Arbor: University of Michigan Graduate Program in Museum Practice, 1974.

PROFESSIONAL TRAINING

American Association of Museums. *Museum Studies, A Curriculum Guide for Universities and Museums: A Report of the Museum Studies Curriculum Committee of the American Association of Museums.* Washington, D.C.: AAM, 1973.

Burcaw, G. Ellis. *Introduction to Museum Work.* Nashville: AASLH, 1975.

International Council of Museums. *Training of Museum Personnel.* Reports and Papers on Museums 5. London: Hugh Evelyn, for ICOM, 1970.

"The Museum and the University." *Museum News,* 47:8 (Apr. 1969), entire issue.

"Museum Studies." *Museum News,* 57:2 (Nov./Dec. 1978), entire issue, includes report of the AAM Museum Studies Committee.

Reimann, Irving G. "Preparation for Professional Museum Careers." *Curator,* 3:3 (1960), 279–85.

"The Role of the Registrar." *Registrars' Report,* 1:1 (May 1977), entire issue.

Shine, Carolyn R. "The Registrar: Curator-without-Portfolio." *Museum News,* 42:6 (Feb. 1964), 33–35.

Smithsonian Institution, Office of Museum Programs. *Museum Studies Programs in the United States and Abroad.* Apr. 1976. Addendum, Oct. 1977. Order from Museum Reference Center.

Waller, Bret. "Museum Training: Who Needs It?" *Museum News,* 52:8 (May 1974), 26–28.

PROFESSIONAL ASSOCIATIONS, JOURNALS, AND REFERENCE CENTERS

American Association for State and Local History (AASLH), 1400 Eighth Ave. So., Nashville, Tenn. 37203. Publications include *History News,* monthly to members; technical leaflets; books; directories.

American Association of Museums (AAM), 1055 Thomas Jefferson St., NW, Suite 428, Washington, D.C. 20007. Publications include *Museum News*, bimonthly to members or by subscription; *Aviso*, monthly to members or by subscription; reprints from *Museum News*; books and pamphlets; committee reports; directories.

American Institute for Conservation of Historic and Artistic Works, Inc. (AIC) (formerly International Institute for Conservation of Historic and Artistic Works—American Group), 1522 K St., NW, Suite 804, Washington, D.C. 20005. Publications include *Journal of the American Institute for Conservation of Historic and Artistic Works* (formerly *Bulletin of the American Group—IIC* and *Bulletin of the AIC*), semiannually to members or by subscription.

American Library Association (ALA), 50 E. Huron St., Chicago, Ill. 60611. Publications include journals; books.

Association of Systematics Collections (ASC), Museum of Natural History, University of Kansas, Lawrence, Kans. 66045. Publications include *ASC Newsletter*, bimonthly by subscription; manuals; books; seminar proceedings.

Canadian Conservation Institute (CCI), National Museums of Canada, Ottawa, K1A OM8, Canada. Publications include *Canadian Conservation Institute Newsletter*, quarterly to members.

Canadian Museums Association, P.O. Box 1328, Station B, Ottawa, K1P 5R4, Canada. Publications include *Gazette*, quarterly to members or by subscription; *Museogramme*, monthly to members; books; directories.

Conservation Center of the Institute of Fine Arts, New York University, 1 E. 78th St., New York, N.Y. 10021.

Curator, quarterly by subscription, American Museum of Natural History, Central Park West at 79th St., New York, N.Y. 10024.

Intermuseum Conservation Association (ICA), Allen Art Bldg., Oberlin, Ohio 44074.

International Centre for the Study of the Preservation and the Restoration of Cultural Property, 13 Via di San Michele, 00153, Rome, Italy.

International Council of Museums (ICOM), Maison de l'Unesco, 1 rue Miollis, 75015, Paris, France. Publications include *ICOM News*, quarterly to members or by subscription; conference papers.

ICOM Committee of the American Association of Museums, 1055 Thomas Jefferson St., NW, Suite 428, Washington, D.C. 20007. Publications include *AAM/ICOM Newsletter*, quarterly to members.

International Institute for Conservation of Historic and Artistic Works (IIC), 6 Buckingham St., London, WC2N 6BA, England. Publications include *Art and Archaeology Technical Abstracts*, semiannually to members or by subscription; *Studies in Conservation*, quarterly to members or by subscription; conference papers.

Museum Reference Center, Office of Museum Programs, A & I Bldg., Rm. 2235, Smithsonian Institution, Washington, D.C. 20560.

Museums Association, 87 Charlotte St., London, W1P 2BX, England. Publications include *Museums Journal*, quarterly by subscription; *Museums Bulletin*, monthly by subscription; annual directory; information sheets; handbooks for museum curators.

National Trust for Historic Preservation, 740 Jackson Pl., NW, Washington, D.C. 20006. Publications include *Historic Preservation*, bimonthly to members; *Preservation News*, monthly to members; books.

Registrars' Report, monthly by subscription, Box 112, Bicentennial Station, Los Angeles, Calif. 90048.

United Nations Educational, Scientific and Cultural Organization (UNESCO), 7 Place de Fontenoy, 75700, Paris, France. Publications include *Museum*, quarterly by subscription; books.

Registration and Catalogue Records

Items below amplify the discussions of records of objects in chapters 2, 3, 4, and 6. For classification of man-made objects, see Robert G. Chenhall's recent *Nomenclature for Museum Cataloging*. Adoption of the nomenclature suggested in this book may help to standardize the classification of man-made objects in the way that the classification of scientific specimens has long been standardized. The book also contains a comprehensive bibliography, which the reader desiring more detailed information on classification is advised to consult. See also the bibliographies in Lewis, *Manual for Museums*. Some museums have found early and reprinted editions of Sears, Roebuck and Montgomery Ward catalogues helpful in identifying historical objects.

RECORDS FOR ACCESSIONS AND LOANS

Ball, Laurel. "Recording Agricultural Collections." *Museums Journal*, 72:2 (Sept. 1972), 55–57.

Boardman, Edward T. "Simplified Records for Small Science and History Museums." *Museum News*, 25:17 (Mar. 1, 1948), 6–8.

Borhegyi, Stephan de. *Curatorial Neglect of Collections*. Reprint from *Museum News*, 43:5 (Jan. 1965).

―――, and Alice Marriott. "Proposals for a Standardized Museum Accessioning and Classification System." *Curator*, 1:2 (1958), 77–86.

Bowditch, George. *Cataloging Photographs: A Procedure for Small Museums*. AASLH Technical Leaflet 57. From *History News*, 26:11 (Nov. 1971).

Cannon-Brookes, Peter. "The Loan of Works of Art for Exhibition." *Museums Journal*, 71:3 (Dec. 1971), 105–07.

Chenhall, Robert G. *Museum Cataloging in the Computer Age*. Nashville: AASLH, 1975.

Cox, Janson L. *Photographing Historical Collections: Equipment, Methods, and Bibliography*. AASLH Technical Leaflet 63. From *History News*, 28:5 (May 1973).

Dunn, Walter S., Jr. *Cataloging Ephemera: A Procedure for Small Libraries*. AASLH Technical Leaflet 58. From *History News*, 27:1 (Jan. 1972).

Feldman, Franklin, and Stephen E. Weil, eds. *Art Works: Law, Policy, Practice*. New York: Practising Law Institute, 1974.

Freundlich, A. L. "Museum Registration by Computer." *Museum News*, 44:6 (Feb. 1966), 18–20.

Gifford, Philip C., Jr. "The Elephant and the Tortoise." *Curator*, 9:2 (1966), 125–33.

Graham, John M., II. *A Method of Museum Registration*. Reprint from *Museum News*, 42:8 (Apr. 1964).

Guthe, Carl E. *Documenting Collections: Museum Registration and Records*. AASLH Technical Leaflet 11. From *History News*, 18:7 (July 1963). Rev. ed. 1970.

Hilliard, David Craig. "Museums and the New Copyright Law." *Museum News*, 56:6 (July/Aug. 1978), 49–51.

Humphrey, Philip S., and Ann C. Clausen. *Automated Cataloging for Museum Collections: A Model for Decision and a Guide to Implementation*. Lawrence, Kans.: ASC, 1977.

Hurst, Richard M. "Putting a Collection on Film." *Curator*, 13:3 (1970), 199–203.

"ICOM Guidelines for Loans." *ICOM News*, 27:3/4 (1974), 78–79.

MacDonald, Robert R. "Toward a More Accessible Collection: Cataloguing at the Mercer Museum." *Museum News*, 48:6 (Feb. 1969), 22–26.

Manning, Anita. *Converting Loans to Gifts: One Solution to "Permanent" Loans*. AASLH Technical Leaflet 94. From *History News*, 32:4 (Apr. 1977).

Manning, Raymond B. "A Computer-Generated Catalog of Types: A By-Product of Data Processing in Museums." *Curator*, 12:2 (1969), 134–38.
Metropolitan Museum of Art. *Computers and Their Potential Applications in Museums*. New York: Arno Press, for the Metropolitan Museum of Art, 1968.
Morita, Tsuneyuki. "Preparations for the Fine Arts Exhibition" and "The Fine Arts Museum at Expo' 70, Osaka: Memorandum of Agreement." *Museum*, 24:2 (1972), 89–101.
"Museums and Computers." *Museum*, 23:1 (1970–71), entire issue.
Nauert, Patricia, ed. *Reg Tech*. Los Angeles: Los Angeles County Museum of Art, Museum Associates, 1975.
Neff, Jeffrey M., and Holly M. Chaffee. "REGIS—A Computerized Museum Registration System." *Curator*, 20:1 (1977), 32–41.
Oddon, Yvonne. "The Documentation of Collections in General Museums." *ICOM News*, 23:3 (Sept. 1970), 55–60.
Peters, James A. "The Computer and the Collection-at-Large." *Curator*, 13:4 (1970), 263–66.
Reibel, Daniel B. *Registration Methods for the Small Museum: A Guide for Historical Collections*. Nashville: AASLH, 1978.
Rensberger, John M., and William B. N. Berry. "An Automated System for Retrieval of Museum Data." *Curator*, 10:4 (1967), 297–317.
Ricciardelli, Alex F. "A Model for Inventorying Ethnological Collections." *Curator*, 10:4 (1967), 330–36.
Riefstahl, Rudolf M. "Museum Photography." *Museum News*, 44:2 (Oct. 1965), 20–23.
Roads, C. H. "Data Recording, Retrieval and Presentation in the Imperial War Museum." *Museums Journal*, 67:4 (Mar. 1968), 277–83.
Schneider, Mary Jane. *Cataloging and Care of Collections for Small Museums*. Columbia, Mo.: University of Missouri, Museum of Anthropology, 1971.
Shapiro, Harry L. "Borrowing and Lending." *Curator*, 3:3 (1960), 197–203.
Spalding, C. Sumner. *Anglo-American Cataloging Rules*. 2d ed. Chicago: ALA, 1978.
Squires, Donald F. "An Information Storage and Retrieval System for Biological and Geological Data." *Curator*, 13:1 (1970), 43–62.
Sturtevant, William C. "Ethnological Collections and Curatorial Records." *Museum News*, 44:7 (Mar. 1966), 16–19.
Theime, Mary. *Registration of Museum Objects*. Slide/Tape Training Kit 4. Nashville: AASLH, 1974.
Thompson, Enid T. *Local History Collections: A Manual for Librarians*. Nashville: AASLH, 1978.
United States, Department of the Treasury, Internal Revenue Service. *Income Tax Deduction for Contributions*. Publication 526. Washington, D.C.: GPO, annual.
———. *Valuation of Donated Property*. Publication 561. Washington, D.C.: GPO, annual.
———, General Services Administration, National Archives and Records Service, Office of Records Management. *Forms Analysis*. Washington, D.C.: GPO, 1960. Rpt. 1974.
———. *Forms Design*. Washington, D.C.: GPO, 1960. Rpt. 1975.

Van Gelder, Richard G., and Sydney Anderson. "An Information Retrieval System for Collections of Mammals." *Curator*, 10:1 (1967), 32–42.
Vanderbilt, Paul. *Filing Your Photographs: Some Basic Procedures*. AASLH Technical Leaflet 36. From *History News*, 21:6 (June 1966).
Whiting, Alfred F. "Catalogues: Damn 'Em—An Inter-Museum Office Memo." *Curator*, 9:1 (1966), 85–87.

CLASSIFICATION OF OBJECTS

Chenhall, Robert G. *Nomenclature for Museum Cataloging: A System for Classifying Man-Made Objects.* Nashville: AASLH, 1978.

———, and Peter Homulos. "Museum Data Standards." *Museum News,* 56:6 (July/Aug. 1978), 43–48.

Cutbill, J. L., ed. *Data Processing in Biology and Geology.* Proceedings of a Symposium held at the Department of Geology, University of Cambridge, 24–26 September, 1969. New York: Academic Press, for the Systematics Association, 1971.

Darbee, Herbert C. *A Glossary of Old Lamps and Lighting Devices.* AASLH Technical Leaflet 30. From *History News,* 20:8 (Aug. 1965).

Eaches, Albert R. *Scales and Weighing Devices: An Aid to Identification.* AASLH Technical Leaflet 59. From *History News,* 27:3 (Mar. 1972).

Emery, Irene. *The Primary Structures of Fabrics: An Illustrated Classification.* Washington, D.C.: Textile Museum, 1966.

Gettens, Rutherford J., and George L. Stout. *Painting Materials: A Short Encyclopedia.* 1942. Rpt. New York: Dover Publications, 1966.

Gill, Arthur T. *Photographic Processes: A Glossary and Chart for Recognition.* Information Sheet 21. London: Museums Association, 1978.

Glass, Elizabeth, comp. *A Subject Index for the Visual Arts.* London: Her Majesty's Stationery Office, 1969.

Hall, Eugene Raymond. *Collecting and Preparing Study Specimens of Vertebrates.* University of Kansas, Museum of Natural History Miscellaneous Publication 30. Lawrence, Kans.: University of Kansas, 1962.

Hodges, Henry W. *Artifacts: An Introduction to Primitive Technology.* New York: F. A. Praeger, 1964.

Hodgkinson, Ralph. *Tools of the Woodworker: Axes, Adzes, and Hatchets.* AASLH Technical Leaflet 28. From *History News,* 20:5 (May 1965).

Kelly, Kenneth L., and Christian Rohlfing. *A Universal Color Language.* Reprint from *Museum News,* 43:10 (June 1965).

Mayer, Ralph. *The Artist's Handbook of Materials and Techniques.* 3d ed. New York: Viking Press, 1970.

Mitchell, C. M. *Applied Science and Technology before the Industrial Revolution.* Handbook for Museum Curators E 7. London: Museums Association, 1961.

Munsell Color Company. *Munsell Book of Color: Matte Finish Collection* and *Munsell Book of Color: Glossy Finish Collection.* 2 pts. Baltimore: Munsell Color Company, 1967, 1966.

Murdock, George P., et al. *Outlines of Cultural Materials.* 4th ed. New Haven: Human Relations Area Files, 1961.

Rempel, John L. *Tools of the Woodworker: Hand Planes.* AASLH Technical Leaflet 24. From *History News,* 26:9 (Sept. 1971). Rev. ed.

MEASURING AND MARKING OBJECTS

Anderson, Sydney. "Two Semiautomatic Systems for Linear Measurement." *Curator,* 15:3 (1972), 220–28.

Marking Manuscripts. Library of Congress Preservation Leaflet 4. Washington, D.C.: Library of Congress, 1977.

Richards, Charles M. "Formulae for Museum Measurements." *Museum News,* 25:19 (Apr. 1, 1948), 7–8.

"Survey of Marking Techniques for Identifying Wild Animals in Captivity." *International Zoo Yearbook,* 8 (1968), 384–408.

Fig. D.1.
Subject index cards for Gauguin's Ia Orana Maria
(7.5 by 12.5 cm.), Metropolitan Museum of Art.

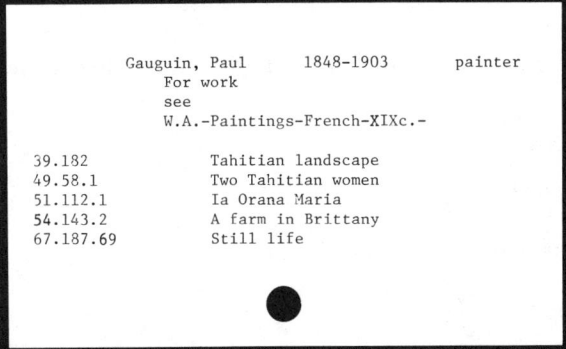

Artist entry.

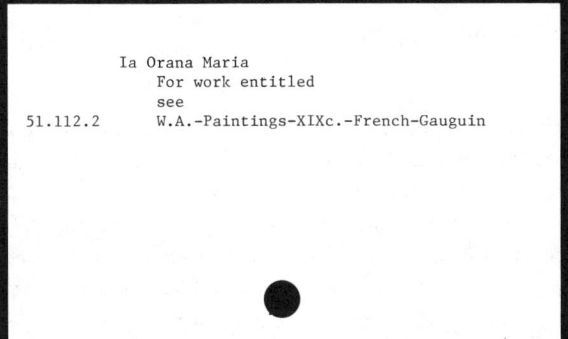

Title entry.

Cross-reference.

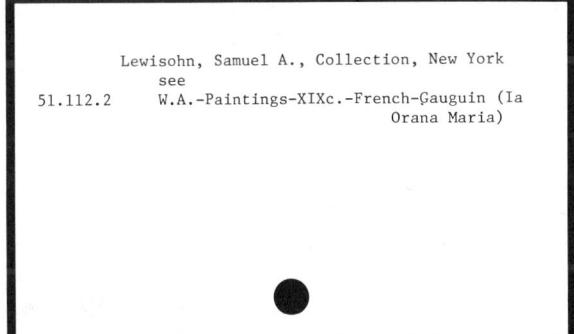

Ex-collection.

Fig. D.2.
Subject index cards for Jacob Hurd's silver loving cup
(7.5 by 12.5 cm.), Metropolitan Museum of Art.

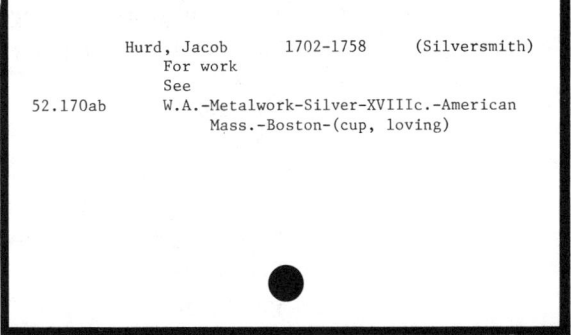

Maker entry.

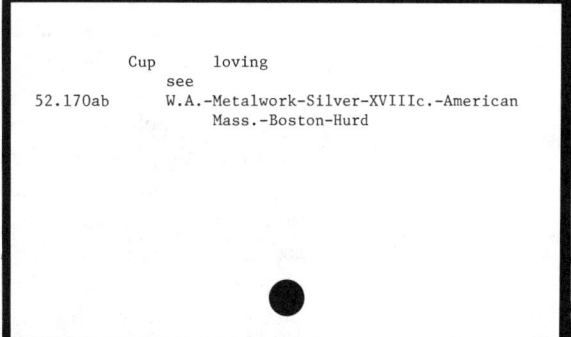

Subject entry.

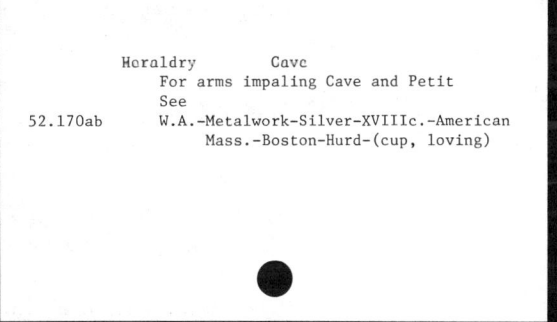

Subject entry.

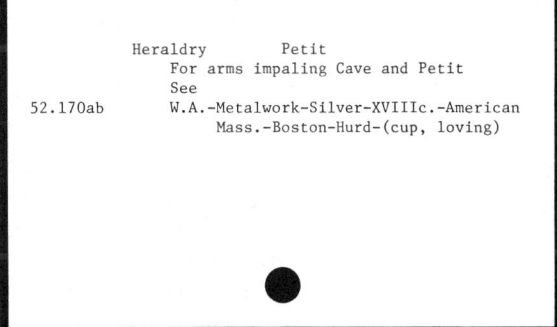

Subject entry.

century, and country. The appropriate items are placed in the following order:

    ACCESSION NUMBER (in upper left corner)
    HEADING (artist and title, or descriptive heading, followed by a short descriptive text)
    HERALDRY
    INSCRIPTION
    SIGNATURE AND DATE (or maker's mark)
    MATERIAL AND MEASUREMENTS
    NAME OF DONOR OR VENDOR (latter with price and name of appropriate fund)
    EX-COLLECTIONS
    PROVENANCE
    PERIOD
    DESIGNER OR DECORATOR, etc. (name and dates)
    CITY OR PLACE (maker and dates, for ceramics, silver, etc.)
    CLASSIFICATION, CENTURY, COUNTRY

A photograph of the object is printed on special stock of the same size and weight as the catalogue card. The accession number and negative number are typed in the upper left-hand corner, and the photograph is filed immediately behind the first catalogue card. Additional cards, each with the accession number typed at the top left corner and bearing further description, notes, exhibitions, and references, are placed in correct order behind the photograph. All the cards for the object are tied together through the bottom hole with string, which can be cut and retied when new material is added.

Examples of various types of catalogue cards are shown in figures D.3 and D.4. For Gauguin's painting *Ia Orana Maria*, the complete set of cards totals twenty.

Deaccessioning Procedures

When the trustees authorize the disposal of an object, all records for it are removed from the active files. The accession card and photograph from the registrar's accession file are placed in a numerical file of deaccessioned objects, which forms a cumulative record of all objects ever disposed of from the collections. A cross-reference card is placed in the registrar's accession file in order to maintain the numerical sequence. The duplicate of the accession card filed in the alphabetical donor-vendor file is stamped "Deaccessioned" and returned to keep that file up to date. The card from the central catalogue is also stamped and is put in a separate file, arranged by classification, for deaccessioned objects, and cross-reference cards are inserted in the catalogue itself and in the Catalogue Department's numerical file. The subject index entries for the artist or maker and title of the object are stamped "Deaccessioned" and left in the subject index, but all other entries are removed. All pictures of the object are withdrawn from the Photo Sales Department.

Simplified Records for Small Institutions

For an institution as large as the Metropolitan Museum of Art, it is essential that one complete set of records be reserved for curatorial use and two other sets for the central catalogue, which is open to the public as a general information service. However, for a smaller institution, such extensive records may be too expensive to maintain or otherwise unnecessary. In such cases, a system based on one set of simplified records may be employed.

Care of Collections

Items listed below amplify the information in chapter 5. Because of the vast number of sources on the care and conservation of objects, because of the difficulty of representing fairly all the kinds of materials that might appear in museum collections, and because of the availability of excellent bibliographies on these subjects, the section on Care and Storage is very selective. Very brief and specialized treatments have not been included, as access to the extensive literature on conservation is provided by the aids listed in the General section. The technical publications of the AAM, AASLH, and Museums Association are particularly useful. Citations listed under The Museum Environment include references on museum climate, security, and design.

GENERAL

American Association for State and Local History. Current Technical Leaflets include discussions of storage and the care and handling of antique silver, clocks, costumes, leather, leather book bindings, local archival materials, metals, rare books and paper, and textiles. Slide/tape training kits are available on such subjects as handling museum objects and matting and framing paper objects.

American Association of Museums. Current *Museum News* Reprints include discussions of storage, the examination of works of art, and the care and handling of decorative arts objects, enameled objects, glass, linen, paintings, photographic collections, polychromed wood sculpture, rugs, textiles, and works of art on paper; as well as collections of essays from the magazine's column on conservation; and rules for handling works of art.

"Conservation." *Museum News*, 50:3 (Nov. 1971) to the present. Regular column on conservation; authors have included conservators Caroline Keck, Lawrence J. Majewski, and Richard Buck; some columns available as *Museum News* Reprints.

"A Conservation Bibliography." *Registrars' Report*, 1:4 (Nov. 1977), entire issue.

Curator. Cumulative Index to Volumes 1 through 20. 20:4 (Dec. 1977).

International Centre for the Study of the Preservation and the Restoration of Cultural Property. See especially *Climatology and Conservation in Museums* (1960) and *Synthetic Materials Used in the Conservation of Cultural Property* (1963).

International Council of Museums. See especially *Problems of Conservation in Museums* (1969).

International Institute for Conservation of Historic and Artistic Works. See especially *Conservation of Paintings and the Graphic Arts* (1972); *Conservation of Stone and Wooden Objects* (1970); *IIC—American Group Technical Papers from 1968 through 1970* (1970); *1964 Delft Conference on the Conservation of Textiles* (1965); *Recent Advances in Conservation* (1963).

Majewski, Lawrence J. "Every Museum Library Should Have . . . ." *Museum News*, 52:3 (Nov. 1973), 27–30.

Museums Association. Current Information Sheets and Handbooks for Curators include discussions of storage and the care and handling of costumes, pictures, prints and drawings, and textiles, and a guide to herbarium practice.

Phillimore, Elizabeth. *A Glossary of Terms Useful in Conservation: With a Supplement on Reporting the Condition of Antiquities.* Ottawa: CMA, 1976.

Rath, Frederick L., Jr., and Merrilyn Rogers O'Connell, eds. *A Bibliography on Historical Organization Practices.* Vol. 2: *Care and Conservation of Collections.* Compiled by Rosemary S. Reese. Nashville: AASLH, 1977.

Smithsonian Institution. A slide/lecture series dealing with conservation and taped lectures on topics such as paper and textile conservation are available from the Museum Reference Center.

Studies in Conservation. Cumulative Index, Volumes 1–12, 1952–1967. Compiled by Garry Thomson. London: IIC, 1969.

Technical Studies in the Field of the Fine Arts. Subject Index. Compiled by Bertha M. Usilton. Pittsburgh: Tamworth Press, 1964.

United Nations Educational, Scientific and Cultural Organization. See especially *The Conservation of Cultural Property* (1968).

United States, Department of Agriculture. Current publications relating to conservation include discussions of the treatment of clothes moths and carpet beetles, mildew, silverfish and firebrats, stains, wood decay, and wood-destroying beetles.

CARE AND STORAGE

"An Approach to Stone." *Registrars' Report*, 1:2 (Sept. 1977), entire issue.

Barrow, William J. *Manuscripts and Documents: Their Deterioration and Restoration.* 2d ed. Charlottesville: University Press of Virginia, 1972.

Burnham, Elizabeth L., and Eric B. Rowlison. *Handling Works of Art.* Film, 20 minutes, 16 mm; videotape, ¾ in. New York: Downtown Community Television Center, 1975. Order from the Museum of Modern Art.

Clapp, Anne F. *Curatorial Care of Works of Art on Paper.* 2d ed. rev. Oberlin, Ohio: Intermuseum Laboratory, 1974.

Cunha, George Martin, and Dorothy Grant Cunha. *Conservation of Library Materials: A Manual and Bibliography on the Care, Repair, and Restoration of Library Materials.* 2d ed. 2 vols. Metuchen, N.J.: Scarecrow Press, 1971–72.

Dolloff, Francis W., and Roy L. Perkinson. *How to Care for Works of Art on Paper.* Boston: Museum of Fine Arts, 1971.

Duckett, Kenneth W. *Modern Manuscripts: A Practical Manual for Their Management, Care, and Use.* Nashville: AASLH, 1975.

Fall, Frieda Kay. *Art Objects, Their Care and Preservation: A Handbook for Museums and Collectors.* La Jolla, Calif.: Lawrence McGilvery, 1973.

Feller, Robert L., Elizabeth H. Jones, and Nathan Stolow. *On Picture Varnishes and Their Solvents.* Rev. ed. Cleveland: Press of Case Western Reserve University, 1971.

Greathouse, Glenn A., and Carl John Wessel, eds. *Deterioration of Materials: Causes and Preventive Techniques.* National Research Council, Prevention of Deterioration Center. New York: Reinhold, 1954.

Guldbeck, Per E. *The Care of Historical Collections: A Conservation Handbook for the Nonspecialist.* Nashville: AASLH, 1972.

Horton, Carolyn. *Cleaning and Preserving Bindings and Related Materials.* 2d ed. rev. Chicago: ALA, Library Technology Program, 1969.

Kane, Lucile M. *A Guide to the Care and Administration of Manuscripts.* 2d ed. Nashville: AASLH, 1966.

Keck, Caroline K. *A Handbook on the Care of Paintings, for Historical Agencies and Small Museums.* Nashville: AASLH, 1965.

Leene, Jentina E., ed. *Textile Conservation.* Washington, D.C.: Smithsonian Institution, 1972.

Organ, R. M. *Design for Scientific Conservation of Antiquities.* Washington, D.C.: Smithsonian Institution Press, 1968.

Parsons, Claudia S. M., and F. H. Curl. *China Mending and Restoration.* London: Faber and Faber, 1963.

Plenderleith, H. J., and A. E. A. Werner. *The Conservation of Antiquities and Works of Art: Treatment, Repair, and Restoration.* 2d ed. New York: Oxford University Press, 1971.

Pomerantz, Louis. *Is Your Contemporary Painting More Temporary Than You Think? Vital Information for the Present-Day Artist.* Chicago: Chicago Chapter Artists Equity, 1962.

Preservation and Conservation: Principles and Practices. Edited by Sharon Timmons. Washington, D.C.: Preservation Press, 1976.

Ruhemann, Helmut. *The Cleaning of Paintings: Problems and Potentialities.* New York: Praeger, 1968.

Savage, George. *The Art and Antique Restorer's Handbook: A Dictionary of Materials and Processes Used in the Restoration & Preservation of All Kinds of Works of Art.* Rev. ed. London: Barrie and Jenkins, 1976.

Stout, George L. *The Care of Pictures.* 1948. Rpt. New York: Dover, 1975.

Sugden, Robert P. *Care and Handling of Art Objects.* New York: Metropolitan Museum of Art, 1946.

———. *Safeguarding Works of Art: Storage, Packing, Transportation and Insurance.* New York: Metropolitan Museum of Art, 1948.

Waterer, John W. *A Guide to the Conservation and Restoration of Objects Made Wholly or in Part of Leather.* New York: Drake Publishers, 1972.

Weinstein, Robert A., and Larry Booth. *Collection, Use, and Care of Historical Photographs.* Nashville: AASLH, 1977.

Winger, Howard W., and Richard Daniel Smith, eds. *Deterioration and Preservation of Library Materials: The Thirty-Fourth Annual Conference of the Graduate Library School, August 4–6, 1969.* Chicago: University of Chicago Press, 1970.

Zigrosser, Carl, and Christa M. Gaehde. *A Guide to the Collecting and Care of Original Prints.* Sponsored by the Print Council of America. New York: Crown Publishers, 1965. Rpt. 1973.

THE MUSEUM ENVIRONMENT

American Library Association, Library Technology Program. *Protecting the Library and Its Resources: A Guide to Physical Protection and Insurance.* Chicago: ALA, 1963.

Cameron, Duncan. "Environmental Control: A Theoretical Solution." *Museum News,* 46:9 (May 1968), 17–21.

Douglas, R. Alan. "A Commonsense Approach to Environmental Control." *Curator,* 15:2 (1972), 139–44.

Feller, Robert L. *Control of Deteriorating Effects of Light on Museum Objects: Heating Effects of Illumination by Incandescent Lamps.* Reprint from *Museum News,* 46:9 (May 1968).

———. *The Deteriorating Effect of Light on Museum Objects: Principles of Photochemistry, the Effect on Varnishes and Paint Vehicles and on Paper.* Reprint from *Museum News,* 42:10 (June 1964).

Hanlan, J. F. *The Effect of Electronic Photographic Lamps on the Materials of Works of Art.* Reprint from *Museum News,* 48:10 (June 1970).

Harrison, Raymond O. "Planning for Action and Growth." *Museum News,* 51:3 (Nov. 1972), 21–24.

———. *The Technical Requirements of Small Museums.* Technical Paper 1. Ottawa: CMA, 1966.

Harvey, John. "Air-Conditioning for Museums." *Museums Journal,* 73:1 (1973), 11–16.

Hunter, John E. *Security for Museums and Historic Houses: An Annotated Bibliography.* AASLH Technical Leaflet 83. From *History News,* 30:5 (May 1975).

International Council of Museums. *Museum Security.* Paris: ICOM, with the assistance of AAM, 1978.

International Institute for Conservation of Historic and Artistic Works. *Contributions to the London Conference on Museum Climatology, 18–23 September 1967.* Edited by Garry Thomson. Rev. ed. London: IIC, 1968.

Keck, Caroline K., et al. *A Primer on Museum Security.* Cooperstown: New York State Historical Association, 1966.

Lusk, Carroll B. "The Invisible Danger of Visible Light." *Museum News,* 53:7 (Apr. 1975), 22–23.

———. "Museum Lighting III." *Museum News,* 49:6 (Feb. 1971), 18–22.

Museum News, 44:3 (Nov. 1965), and 50:5 (Jan. 1972), entire issues.

"Museums and the Theft of Works of Art." *Museum,* 26:1 (1974), entire issue.

National Fire Protection Association. *Protecting Our Heritage: A Discourse on Fire Protection and Prevention in Historic Buildings and Landmarks.* Edited by Joseph Jenkins. 2d ed. Boston: NFPA, with the assistance of AASLH, 1970.

———. *Recommended Practice for the Protection of Museum Collections from Fire.* NFPA 911. Rev. ed. Boston: NFPA, 1974.

Santen, Vernon, and Howard Crocker. *Historical Society Records: Guidelines for a Protection Program.* AASLH Technical Leaflet 18. From *History News,* 27:9 (Sept. 1972).

Stolow, Nathan. "The Action of Environment on Museum Objects, Part I: Humidity, Temperature, Atmospheric Pollution." *Curator,* 9:3 (1966), 175–86.

———. "The Action of Environment on Museum Objects, Part II: Light." *Curator,* 9:4 (1966), 298–306.

———. "The Microclimate: A Localized Solution." *Museum News,* 56:2 (Nov./Dec. 1977), 52–63.

Thomson, Garry. *Conservation and Museum Lighting.* Information Sheet 6. 3d ed. London: Museums Association, 1978.

———. "Planning the Preservation of Our Cultural Heritage." *Museum,* 25:1/2 (1973), 15–25.

Packing and Shipping

Items listed below amplify the information in chapter 7. See also the publications of IIC listed under Care of Collections and the bibliographies for articles R and S.

"Air Transport." *Registrars' Report,* 1:3 (Oct. 1977), entire issue.

"Circulating Exhibitions." *Registrars' Report,* 1:7 (1979), entire issue.

Buchanan, John. "The Movement of Art: Questions and Answers." *Art Gallery,* 16:9 (June 1973), 8–9, 82.

Fall, Frieda Kay. *New Industrial Packing Materials: Their Possible Uses for Museums.* Reprint from *Museum News,* 44:4 (Dec. 1965).

Gordon, James B. "Packing of Michelangelo's 'Pieta.'" *Studies in Conservation,* 12:2 (May 1967), 57–69.

Gould, D. A. *Crate Specifications.* Washington, D.C.: Smithsonian Institution Traveling Exhibition Service, 1975.

Household Goods Carrier's Bureau. *Mileage Guide* and *Tariff on Household Goods,* both with supplements. Issued and sold by the Household Goods Carrier's Bureau, 2425 Wilson Blvd., Arlington, Va. 22201.

Keck, Caroline K. *Safeguarding Your Collection in Travel.* Nashville: AASLH, 1970.

Marriner, Paul C. "Criteria for Packing Works of Art for Travelling Exhibitions." *Canadian Conservation Institute Newsletter,* no. 5 (Nov. 1974), 3–5.

Ruggles, Mervyn. "Transportation and Conservation of Twenty-Three Mural Paintings: An Exercise in Logistics and Preservation." *Bulletin of the AIC* [now *Journal of the AIC*], 13:2 (1973), 17–29.

Stolow, Nathan. *Controlled Environment for Works of Art in Transit*. London: Butterworths, for the International Centre for the Study of the Preservation and the Restoration of Cultural Property, 1966.

———. *Fundamental Case Design for Humidity Sensitive Museum Collections*. Reprint from *Museum News*, 44:6 (Feb. 1966).

———. "The Technical Organization of an International Art Exhibition." *Museum*, 21:3 (1968), 182–240.

"Suggestions to Persons Selecting Traveling Exhibitions." *American Federation of Arts Quarterly*, 1:4 (1963), 12–20.

United Nations Educational, Scientific and Cultural Organization. *Temporary and Travelling Exhibitions*. Museums and Monuments 10. Paris: UNESCO, 1963.

United States, Department of Commerce, Interstate Commerce Commission. *Summary of Information for Shippers of Household Goods*. Washington, D.C.: GPO, 1974.

———, Postal Service. *Domestic Postage Rates, Fees, and Information*. Notice 59. Washington, D.C.: GPO, 1978.

———. *International Mail*. Publication 42. Washington, D.C.: GPO. Sold by subscription.

———. *Postal Service Manual*. Washington, D.C.: GPO. Sold by subscription.

"Van Transport." *Registrars' Report*, 1:5 (Dec. 1977), entire issue.

Wakefield, Hugh. "Travelling Exhibitions." *Museum*, 23:2 (1970–71), 146–53.

Importing and Exporting

Items listed below amplify the information in chapter 8. Sources on state laws pertaining to the collection and transportation of specimens are also included.

Bavin, Clark R., and Alan Levitt. "A Hank of Hair and a Bag of Bones." *Museum News*, 52:8 (May 1974), 39–41.

Berger, Thomas J., and John D. Phillips. *Index to U.S. Federal Wildlife Regulations*, with quarterly updates. Lawrence, Kans.: ASC, 1977. Sold by subscription.

Custom House Guide. Edited by Edward H. Kiernan et al. Philadelphia: Arthur S. Binns, annual. Sold by subscription from North American Publishing Company, with *American Import and Export Bulletin*, monthly.

Denson, Eley P., Jr. "Endangered Species and Public Law 91–135." *Museum News*, 48:9 (May 1970), 22–23.

Genoways, Hugh H., and Jerry R. Choate. "Federal Regulations Pertaining to the Collection, Import, Export, and Transport of Scientific Specimens of Mammals." *Journal of Mammalogy*, 57:2 (1976), supp.

Hart, C. W., Jr. "The Burden of Regulation." *Museum News*, 56:3 (Jan./Feb. 1978), 22–25.

"Imports and Exports." *Registrars' Report*, 1:6 (1978), entire issue.

International Council of Museums. *The Protection of Cultural Property: Handbook of National Legislations*. Compiled by Bonnie Burnham. Tunisia: Ceres Productions, for ICOM, 1974.

McGaugh, M. Houston, and Hugh H. Genoways. *State Laws As They Pertain to Scientific Collecting Permits*. Museology 2. Lubbock: Texas Tech Press, 1976.

Pegden, Norman. "A Comparison of National Laws Protecting Cultural Property." *Museum*, 26:1 (1974), 53–60.

Serr, Harold. "Museums and the 1968 Gun Control Act." *Museum News*, 48:3 (Nov. 1969), 22–25.

United States, Department of Commerce. *Schedule B: Statistical Classification of Domestic and Foreign Commodities Exported from the United States, January 1, 1965*, with supplemental bulletins and insert pages. Washington, D.C.: GPO. Sold by subscription.

———, Department of Commerce, Domestic and International Business Administration. *A Basic Guide to Exporting*. Washington, D.C.: GPO, 1976.

———, Department of the Interior, Fish and Wildlife Service. *Museums and Federal Fish and Wildlife Laws*. Fact Sheet 16. Sept. 1976.

———, Department of the Treasury, Customs Service. *Customs Regulations of the United States*. Washington, D.C.: GPO, 1964. Sold by subscription.

———. *Exporting to the United States*. Washington, D.C.: GPO, 1977.

———. *Know before You Go: Customs Hints for Returning U.S. Residents*. Washington, D.C.: GPO, 1977.

———. *Marking of Country of Origin on U.S. Imports*. Washington, D.C.: GPO, 1976.

———. *Pets, Wildlife, Customs*. Washington, D.C.: GPO, 1978.

———. *Tariff Schedules of the United States (Annotated), 1978*, with supplements. Washington, D.C.: GPO. Sold by subscription.

———. *Trademark Information for Travelers*. Washington, D.C.: GPO, 1977.

———. *Treasury Decisions under Customs and Other Laws*. Published weekly; sold by subscription or by single copy.

———. *United States Import Requirements*. Washington, D.C.: GPO, 1965.

Insurance

Items listed below amplify the information in chapter 9.

An Approach to Museum Insurance. Information Sheet 23. London: Museums Association, 1978.

"Art Museum Insurance." *Museum News*, 52:6 (Mar. 1974), entire issue.

Association of Art Museum Directors. *Risk Management Manual*. 2 vols. New York: AAMD, 1974. Sold by subscription.

Block, Huntington T. "Insurance: An Integral Part of Your Security Dollar." *Museum News*, 50:5 (Jan. 1972), 26–29.

———. "Insurance in the Conservation Laboratory, Part 1." *Bulletin of the American Group—IIC* [now *Journal of the AIC*], 1:2 (Apr. 1961), 5–7.

DuBose, Beverly M., Jr. *Insuring against Loss*. AASLH Technical Leaflet 50. From *History News*, 24:5 (May 1969).

Pfeffer, Irving, and David R. Klock. *Perspectives on Insurance*. Englewood Cliffs, N.J.: Prentice-Hall, 1974.

Quandt, Eleanor S. "Insurance in the Conservation Laboratory, Part 2." *Bulletin of the American Group—IIC* [now *Journal of the AIC*], 1:2 (Apr. 1961), 7–9.

FORMS AND RECORDS

On the following pages are illustrated forms and records that expedite, standardize, and document work in museums. They were selected not as models, but as representative samples of the kinds of forms and records currently in use. Museums should analyze their specific information needs and consult legal counsel before following these examples, especially regarding new copyright laws.

The museum registrar is often responsible for devising and maintaining forms and records. In this work the registrar may be thought of as a kind of archivist, for under his or her supervision the official and legal records of the institution and of the objects in its custody are administered. It is therefore important that the registrar be conversant with modern methods of records management and with the materials and facilities that will best ensure the permanence of its documents. For this reason, acid-free, buffered stock is recommended for all forms and card records.

I. INTRAMUSEUM FORMS

A variety of forms are used among departments and offices within museums to make sure that the director, curators, registration staff, and shipping room personnel are aware of incoming and outgoing shipments, both expected and processed. See also forms III.A.

I.A. NOTICES TO THE REGISTRAR: One of the most common forms is the expect/collect/deliver form, which is sent by the director or a curator to the registration department. It alerts the registrar to incoming and/or outgoing shipments, specifies instructions for transportation and insurance, and provides whatever additional information may be required.

I.A.1. *Notice to the Registrar* (8½ by 11 in.), The Brooklyn Museum. This single sheet, designed so that information can be quickly checked off, is issued by the curator to advise the registrar of forthcoming shipments, required insurance, and transportation arrangements. A copy is retained in the curatorial department.

I.B. INCOMING REPORTS: In large museums, or in museums where the shipping office is not located near the registration department, the shipping custodian or building superintendent often sends the registrar formal notice of the arrival of material. See also the reports of incoming material issued by scientific departments, figures J.2 and K.1.

I.B.1. *Daily Report on Items Received* (8½ by 11 in.), The Museum of Modern Art. This form is completed every day and sent to the registrar by the supervisor of the shipping and receiving room, who is a member of the registrar's staff. The reports, filed chronologically in the registration department, serve as a record of incoming shipments. The museum also maintains a daily report form to record the movement of objects within the museum—to conservation, the frame shop, the photo lab, galleries, storage, and curatorial departments.

I.B.2. *Receiving Report* (8½ by 11 in.), National Museum of History and Technology, Smithsonian Institution. One copy is filled out for each shipment that leaves the shipping room and forwarded to the registration department. Another copy goes to the curatorial department, and a third is kept in the shipping room.

I.C. OUTGOING REPORTS: Various forms are used to inform the registrar, the shipping room, and the curatorial departments of the release and removal of museum objects. See also form III.E.1.

I.C.1. *Outgoing Report* (8½ by 11 in.), National Museum of History and Technology, Smithsonian Institution. One copy is filled out for each shipment that leaves the shipping room and forwarded to the registration department. Another copy goes to the curatorial department, and a third is kept by the shipping room.

I.C.2. *Registrar's six-page release, receipt, and pass form for outgoing material* (5½ by 8½ in.), The Museum of Modern Art. The registrar prepares the form and sends the top page (pass, bearing the registrar's original signature), second page (receipt, to be signed by whoever is authorized to remove the material), third page (release, the authorization for the material to be released), and fourth page (recipient's copy) with the outgoing material to the shipping custodian. The shipping custodian obtains a signature on the receipt from the carrier or messenger collecting the material and returns it to the registrar and gives the pass and recipient's copy to the carrier. The release is retained permanently in the shipping office. The pass is countersigned by the security guard at the exit and returned to the registrar. The fifth page (registrar's record) is held in the registrar's office until the signed receipt and pass are returned; then it is discarded. The sixth page (information copy) is sent to the curatorial department. The same serial number appears on all six pages.

I.C.3. *Out form* (5 by 8 in.), The University Museum, University of Pennsylvania. This shipping order is filled out in duplicate by the registrar. Both copies are sent to the shipping room, where they serve as a notice to pack and ship the object and as authorization for its release. If the object is mailed or shipped, all receipt numbers, insurance information, and/or postage are recorded. If the object is picked up, the messenger or agent must sign both forms. One form is then returned to the registration department, where it is permanently filed. The other copy is retained in the shipping room.

THE MUSEUM OF MODERN ART

Daily report on items received

TO: Registrar

Date: _____

Received from	Number or Mark	Title and Artist or Number of Items or Boxes	Remarks

Signed: _____

I.B.1.

THE BROOKLYN MUSEUM / NOTICE TO THE REGISTRAR

Date: ....

ALL INCOMING & OUTGOING OBJECTS:
- Name:
- Address:
- Phone:

PURPOSE:
- ☐ Gift   ☐ Examination   ☐ Other:
- ☐ Loan   ☐ Deposit
- ☐ Purchase   ☐ Special Exhibition

The following objects (or attach listing)
Loan No.   Descriptions $ Values (if insuring)

☐ Registrar to arrange transportation
☐ Curator to arrange transportation

METHOD OF TRANSPORTATION:
- ☐ Air Freight   ☐ Lender will deliver   ☐ Foreign Shipment
- ☐ Truck   ☐ Lender will collect   ☐ Other:
- ☐ Mail   ☐ Our messenger
                 ☐ Their messenger

Date and Time of Shipment:
Name of Carrier:
Packing & Shipping charges: ☐ Prepaid ☐ Collect ☐ Funds:
INSURED BY: ☐ Lender ☐ Brooklyn Museum ☐ None ☐ Other:
Objects are now located:
Special Instructions:

Signed: ....
(Curator)
Department: ....

(Do not type in this space)

TBMP 3M 76

I.A.1.

OUTGOING REPORT

OBJECTS PROCESSING FACILITY
OFFICE OF THE REGISTRAR
National Museum of History and Technology
Smithsonian Institution, Washington, D.C. 20560

Registrar No. _____

To: _____
From: curatorial unit _____
curator _____ ext. _____
by: _____ (OR staff)
CONDITION Inspection by ( ) Unit ( ) CAL ( ) OPF ( ) OR initials _____ date _____

Museum No.	Objects	Condition (report att'd)	Box #	Photo

continued on reverse.....

PREPARATION:
Packing: Materials used: _____ cost _____
Container: Materials used: _____ cost _____
Total man hours: _____ x rate _____ Total _____ cost _____
Bill to: _____

Box #1 _____ Size _____ Weight _____
Box #2 _____
Box #3 _____

PACKING LIST AND INSTRUCTIONS: attached ( ) in crate ( ) notes on reverse ( )
PREPARED BY: _____ date completed: _____
RELEASED TO: _____ date _____
TYPE OF TRANSACTION:
( ) outside loan   ( ) for examination   ( ) return from exam & rep.   ( ) deaccession
( ) return of loan ( ) for restoration   ( ) return from approval   ( ) transfer
( ) intramural loan ( ) for photography   ( ) exchange   ( ) other

LOGGED OUT BY: _____

SI-2888
3-24-76

I.C.1.

RECEIVING REPORT

OBJECTS PROCESSING FACILITY
OFFICE OF THE REGISTRAR
National Museum of History and Technology
Smithsonian Institution, Washington, D.C. 20560

Registrar No. _____
Date: _____

Received from _____
For: _____ ext. _____
Unit: _____ rm. _____
Via: _____
GBL #: _____
Number of crates/boxes: _____ SI 1711: [ ]no [ ]yes (# ____)

INSPECTION by [ ] Unit [ ] CAL [ ] OPF [ ] OR initials _____ date _____

Museum No.	Object(s)	Condition (report attached)	Box #	Photograph

continued on reverse.....

FUMIGATION: [ ] unnecessary [ ] fumigated location _____ dates _____
CUSTOMS INSPECTION, if applicable: [ ] in-house [ ] at port   date _____
CRATE DISPOSITION: [ ] stored for return   location _____
                   [ ] discarded
                   [ ] recycled

REPORT BY _____ date _____
OBJECTS RELEASED TO: _____ date _____
TYPE OF TRANSACTION:
[ ] loan   [ ] intramural loan   [ ] gift   [ ] restoration
[ ] on approval   [ ] loan return   [ ] transfer [ ] photography
[ ] exam. & report [ ] purchase   [ ] other

LOGGED BY: _____ Receipt No., if issued: _____

SI-2887
3-24-76

I.B.2.

I.C.2.

II. TEMPORARY DEPOSIT FORMS

Receipts acknowledge and document the arrival and return of objects placed in the temporary custody of the museum for study, examination, consideration for acquisition, or any other reason. Lenders of material covered by loan agreements, however, are generally given separate loan receipts, as the conditions governing loans are different from the conditions governing temporary deposits. Conditions are often printed on the reverse of receipts. See forms III.D and III.H.3 and figure L.1.

II.A. TEMPORARY DEPOSIT RECEIPTS: Whenever an object enters the temporary custody of a museum, a receipt acknowledging its entry must be issued to the depositor. The registrar's copy of the receipt usually serves as the object's official record of entry. In some museums, each object is assigned a temporary deposit number, which is recorded on the receipt, and the receipts are filed by number. In other museums, no number is assigned, and the receipts are filed by depositor's name. Many museums require that the depositor present and surrender his or her copy of the receipt when withdrawing the object from the museum, and thus the temporary deposit receipt serves also as a receipt of delivery.

II.A.1. *Temporary receipt* (5 by 7¾ in.), The Metropolitan Museum of Art. The original goes to the depositor, and the carbon is retained by the registration department, filed by curatorial department and then by donor's name. The depositor's copy of the receipt must be surrendered when the object is withdrawn. At that time the depositor must also sign a receipt of delivery (form II.B.1), which is retained in the registration department.

II.A.2. *Receipt* (8½ by 11 in.), Hirshhorn Museum and Sculpture Garden, Smithsonian Institution. The first copy is the depositor's receipt. The second copy (acknowledgement of disposition) is retained in the registration department until the disposition of the object has been determined. It is then sent to the depositor either, if the object is returned, as a receipt of delivery, or, if the object is acquired, as a notice to that effect. In both cases it must be countersigned and returned. The third copy is the registrar's copy; it is permanently filed in the registration department with the completed and returned acknowledgement of disposition. The fourth copy is sent to the curatorial department at the time the object is first deposited. The conditions of temporary deposit are shown on the reverse; use of the waiver under the first paragraph is optional.

II.B. RECEIPTS OF DELIVERY: When an object that has been on temporary deposit with a museum is returned to its depositor, a receipt of delivery must be signed and returned to the museum as an acknowledgment. In some museums, the temporary deposit receipt (or another copy of it) issued to the depositor when the object was placed in the museum's custody becomes the receipt of delivery; it must be signed and surrendered when the object is returned (see forms II.A.1 and II.A.2). In other museums, a separate receipt of delivery is issued at the time the object is returned. And in some museums the depositor must both surrender the temporary deposit receipt and sign a separate receipt of delivery. For additional forms that serve as receipts of delivery for material deposited temporarily with a museum, see forms III.H.1 and III.H.3 and figure J.3.

II.B.1. *Receipt of delivery* (5 by 8½ in.), The Metropolitan Museum of Art. Only one copy is made, which is signed by the depositor upon receipt of the object and returned to the museum for its files. This receipt is used for a variety of transactions; the purpose for which the object is delivered is specified under Remarks. The museum also has a formal, multicopy receipt, which is used for loans in addition to the receipt shown.

I.C.3.

II.A.1.

Hirshhorn Museum and Sculpture Garden

CONDITIONS

1. Unless otherwise agreed to below by the Depositor, the Hirshhorn Museum and Sculpture Garden, Smithsonian Institution (the "Museum") will exercise the same care with respect to the work(s) of art referred to on the face of this Receipt (the "work(s)") as it does in the safekeeping of comparable property of its own.

The Depositor hereby releases the Museum from all liability with respect to any loss or damage to the object(s) referred to on the face of this Receipt while in its possession or in transit and agrees that the Museum shall not cover such object(s) with insurance.

_____ _____
Depositor   Date

2. Attributions, dates and other information shown on the face of this Receipt are as given by the Depositor. Any valuations shown are those stated by the Depositor and are not to be considered as appraisals by the Museum. The fact that an object has been in Museum custody shall not be misused to indicate Museum endorsement.

3. Unless the Museum is notified in writing to the contrary, the work(s) may be photographed and reproduced for its private purposes. The Museum assumes the right, unless specifically denied by the Depositor, to examine the work(s) by all modern photographic means available, and it is understood and agreed that information thus gathered will remain confidential and will not be published without the written consent of the Depositor. It is understood that the Museum will not clean, restore, or otherwise alter the work(s) without the consent of the Depositor.

4. In receiving or surrendering deposits of imported objects the Museum requires that the Depositor comply with all government regulations. If the Depositor has knowledge of special conditions governing the work(s), such as copyrights, lien, etc., he should inform the Museum thereof.

5. The Museum may request the return of any property deposited with it by written notice directed to the Depositor. If the Museum, after making all reasonable efforts and through no fault of its own, shall be unable to return the work(s) within sixty days after such notice, then the Museum shall have the absolute right to place the work(s) in storage, to charge regular storage fees and the cost of insurance thereof, and to have and enforce a lien for such fees and cost. If, after five years, the work(s) shall not have been reclaimed, then, and in consideration for its storage, insurance and of safeguarding during such period, the work(s) shall be deemed an unrestricted gift to the Museum.

6. The work(s) will be returned only to the Depositor at the address stated on the reverse unless the Museum is notified by the Depositor in writing to the contrary. Any such notice must be accompanied by this Receipt or by written order of the Depositor, his duly authorized and accredited agent or local representative who shall submit proof of his authority.

7. If the legal ownership of the work(s) shall change during the pendency of this deposit, whether by reason of death, sale, insolvency, gift or otherwise, the new owner shall, prior to its return, be required to establish his legal right to receive the work(s) by proof satisfactory to the Museum.

8. In the event that any work(s) is (are) offered as a gift, it is understood that unless the Museum has been notified in writing to the contrary, the gift is outright and unconditional.

9. The Museum accepts this deposit on the understanding that the Depositor has full authority to make the same.

HIRSHHORN MUSEUM AND SCULPTURE GARDEN
SMITHSONIAN INSTITUTION
INDEPENDENCE AVENUE AT 8th STREET, S.W.
WASHINGTON, D.C. 20560 (202) 381-6512

RECEIPT

Receipt no. _____
Date received _____

The object(s) described below has (have) been received by the Hirshhorn Museum and Sculpture Garden subject to the conditions printed on the back of this receipt.

From:

for

_____
Registrar

Artist	Description	Owner's Valuation

Remarks

ACKNOWLEDGEMENT OF DISPOSITION

The object(s) described below, deposited with the Hirshhorn Museum and Sculpture Garden

by

for

has (have) been

_____
Registrar

Please sign and return this statement.

_____   _____
Depositor or his agent   Date

III. LOAN FORMS

Several types of forms are used by museums to verify and document the transactions whereby loans are made to and from collections.

III.A. LOAN REQUESTS: When a request for a loan is received by a museum, an intramuseum form is often circulated among the relevant departments to inform them of the request and to solicit information that will lead to the final approval or denial of the loan.

III.A.1. *Request for Loan* (8½ by 11 in.), Hirshhorn Museum and Sculpture Garden, Smithsonian Institution. This form is initiated by the curatorial department, circulated to the departments noted, and ultimately returned to the registrar with a copy of the reply to the institution that requested the loan.

III.B. LOAN AGREEMENTS (borrower to lender): After a loan request has been approved, the borrowing museum generally sends a loan agreement to the lender, to be completed, signed, and returned. The loan agreement states the conditions governing the loan, and clarifies such matters as insurance responsibility, credit and photograph information, and shipping details. The signed loan agreement constitutes a contract between lender and borrower, binding them to the loan and to the conditions of the loan. For additional loan agreements and conditions governing incoming loans, see form III.C.3 and figures G.6 and J.1.

III.B.1. *Loan Agreement* (8½ by 11 in.), The Museum of Modern Art. Two copies are sent to the lender for completion. The lender retains one copy and signs and returns the other. Note, in particular, the questions pertaining to copyright.

III.B.2. *Loan Agreement and Catalog Information Form* (8½ by 11 in.), The Newark Museum Association. This loan agreement, requiring two signatures, is usually sent after the lender has agreed to the loan, accompanied by a follow-up letter of thanks. Until new forms that take into account the recent copyright law are printed, this covering letter also includes the following questions: (1) If the work was created after January 1, 1978, do you own copyright in the work? (2) If not, do you know who does? (3) If not, who was the previous owner? Two copies of the loan agreement are signed by the Newark Museum and forwarded to the lender. One is countersigned and returned. A tissue copy is retained until the signed copy is returned.

III.C. LOAN AGREEMENTS (lender to borrower): In addition to the loan agreement sent by the borrower to the lender, some lending museums send their own loan agreements to the borrowing institution to verify the conditions under which the loan is being granted. These loan agreements, often requiring the signatures of both parties, are also binding contracts. For additional loan agreements and conditions governing outgoing loans, see forms III.H.1 and III.H.2 and figure G.8.

III.C.1. *Loan Agreement* (8½ by 11 in.), Chicago Historical Society. Both copies are sent to the institution requesting the loan, and a photocopy of the form is kept in the file until one signed copy is returned. Usually the second option for insurance—to pay pro-rata on the society's policy—is crossed out to eliminate any loss being charged against the society's policy.

III.C.2. *Loan Out Form* (8½ by 11 in.), The Newark Museum Association. This form serves as a contract of loan and defines the borrower's responsibilities and restrictions. Two copies are sent in advance of the loan to the borrower, one for the borrower's files and one to be signed on receipt of the loan and returned to the museum. A carbon is also kept by the museum.

```
┌─────────────────────────────────────────────┐
│                                             │
│                          April 6, 1977      │
│                                             │
│  RECEIVED FROM                              │
│         THE METROPOLITAN MUSEUM OF ART      │
│                                             │
│         Dressing table, American            │
│         XVIII c., mahogany                  │
│                                             │
│  RECEIVED BY                                │
│                 ─────────────────           │
│  DELIVERED BY  MMA jeep                     │
│       "    TO  Mr. John Doe                 │
│                123 East 45th St.            │
│                New York, N.Y. 10022         │
│  REMARKS:      return after examination     │
│                                             │
└─────────────────────────────────────────────┘
```

II.B.1.

III.C.3. *Loan Agreement* (8½ by 11 in.), The Minneapolis Institute of Arts. This loan agreement covers both incoming and outgoing loans. For incoming loans, three copies are prepared by the curatorial department, one as an interim copy, and the original and one copy to be sent to the lender. The lender keeps the copy and signs and returns the original. The curatorial department then photocopies the signed original and sends one copy to the registration department. For outgoing loans, the registration department prepares three copies, one for the curatorial department and two to be sent to the borrower. The borrower retains the copy and signs and returns the original, which is filed permanently in the registration department. Two separate sets of conditions—those governing the receipt of loans and those governing the granting of loans—are printed on the reverse of the original of the form.

III.D. INCOMING LOAN RECEIPTS: As soon as an object covered by a loan agreement arrives at a museum, a receipt acknowledging its arrival must be issued to the lender. This incoming loan receipt is often made in multiple copies, one for the lender, one to be retained by the borrowing museum for its records, one that will serve as the receipt of delivery when the loan is returned to the lender, and other copies as needed. The conditions governing the loan, which always appear on the loan agreement, are sometimes repeated on the incoming loan receipt. See also figure G.6.

III.D.1. *Loan Receipt* (8½ by 11 in.), The Museum of Modern Art. This loan receipt packet is a multicarbon set producing four copies. The original is issued to the lender when the loan arrives at the museum. The second copy is filed in the registration department, by exhibition and then by lender's name. The third copy is a receipt of delivery, sent to the lending museum when the loan is returned, for signature and return as an acknowledgment. The fourth copy is filed in the curatorial department. The conditions governing loans (see form III.B.1) are printed on the reverse of the first, second, and fourth copies.

III.D.2. *Loan Receipt* (8½ by 11 in.), The Solomon R. Guggenheim Museum. The loan receipt is made in packets of one original and five copies, all of which are self-carbonized. The design allows for the use of a window envelope, which reduces duplicate typing of names and addresses. The note concerning the conditions at the bottom of the page eliminates the need for routinely sending all lenders formal condition reports. The conditions governing loans do not appear on this form but appear on the reverse of the loan agreement. The original is sent to the lender at the time the loan arrives. Two copies are kept in the registration department—one filed with correspondence pertaining to the loan and the other as a record of insurance. Additional copies go to the photography department and the curatorial department. There is one extra copy.

III.E. RECEIPTS OF DELIVERY: When a loan is returned, the lending museum sends the borrowing museum a receipt of delivery, which is signed by the lender and returned to the borrower as acknowledgment of the safe return of the object. For additional forms that serve as receipts of delivery, see forms II.B.1, III.G, III.H.1, and III.H.3 and figure J.3.

III.E.1. *Receipt of Delivery* (8½ by 11 in.), The Solomon R. Guggenheim Museum. The receipt of delivery is similar in format to the loan receipt packet (form III.D.2), with the exception that it includes a release form. Six copies are typed at once, the bottom three constituting the release. Two of these are sent to the shipping room as notification that the loan is to be packed and shipped—one is signed by the agent who picks up the loan and returned to the registration department; the other is given to the agent. A third copy is kept by the registrar. When the loan has been released, the original is sent to the lender, to be signed and returned as an acknowledgment. The second and third copies are kept in the registration department—one filed with correspondence pertaining to the loan and one as an insurance record.

III.E.2. *Loan Receipt* (8½ by 11 in.), Chicago Historical Society. This form is used when any or all borrowed objects are returned to the lender after exclusion from an exhibit before installation, if materials are to be rotated or changed for conservation reasons, or at the close of an exhibition. Two copies are prepared. The original is sent to the lender, for signature and return, at the time the objects are released. The second copy is retained by the registration department until the original is returned.

III.F. OUTGOING LOAN RECEIPTS: When a museum ships an approved loan to a borrowing institution, it sends an outgoing loan receipt to the borrower for signature and return as an acknowledgment of the object's safe arrival. The conditions governing the loan are sometimes repeated on this receipt. For additional forms that serve as outgoing loan receipts, see forms III.H and figure J.3.

III.F.1. *Loan Receipt* (8½ by 11 in.), Chicago Historical Society. This loan receipt is sent at the time of shipment to the institution borrowing material, for signature and return. A second copy is retained by the registration department until the signed original is returned.

III.F.2. *Outgoing loan receipt* (8½ by 11 in.), The Museum of Modern Art. The first two copies of this multicarbon packet are sent to the borrowing museum at the time the object is shipped. The first copy is for the borrower's signature and return; the second is for the borrower's records. The third copy is retained for the registration department's records. The fourth copy is for the curator of the department from which the work is lent. The fifth copy is for the use of the accounting department in billing for handling and preparation charges.

III.G. GENERAL RECEIPTS: While some museums have receipts designed to document specific transactions—the return of material deposited with the museum temporarily (see forms II.B), the return of a loan (see forms III.E), or the forwarding of material approved for loan (see forms III.F), other institutions employ general receipts that serve to document all outgoing material. In addition to the general receipt that follows, see also forms II.B.1, III.H.1, and III.H.3 and figure J.3.

III.G.1. *General receipt* (8½ by 11 in.), The Art Institute of Chicago. This receipt is used with all outgoing material—outgoing loans, loans being returned, and the return of material temporarily deposited with the museum. Two copies are sent to the recipient, the original for signature and return and the second to be retained as a file copy. A third copy is held by the museum until the signed original is returned. The SO (Shipping Order) number refers to the museum's shipping order form, sent by the curator to the registrar and then on to the shipping room.

III.H. INVOICES OF SPECIMENS: Museums of natural history, which by their nature engage in more extensive borrowing and lending than other types of museums, generally employ a single receipt to document all transactions whereby material is shipped from the museum; some have a single receipt for both shipments and arrivals. The checking of appropriate boxes indicates whether the material is being shipped as an outgoing or a returned loan, has been received on loan or for examination, or whatever the nature of the transaction. The same form sometimes serves also as a loan agreement, with the conditions governing the loan outlined on it. The form is sent to the participating museum or individual at the time of the transaction, and requires a signature and return as an acknowledgment of the transaction. For another invoice of specimens, see figures J.3 and J.8.

III.H.1. *Invoice of Specimens* (8½ by 11 in.), The Cleveland Museum of Natural History. This form serves as both a receipt and a loan agreement. Three copies are prepared. An original and copy are sent to the borrower at the time the material is shipped, the copy for its files and the original for signature and return as an acknowledgment. The second copy is kept in the registrar's files in case the original is lost and/or not returned. The conditions governing loans from the museum's collections are printed on the reverse. The length of the loan is determined by the use for which the material is intended and is generally decided by the curator. Shipping charges are usually paid by the institution or individual requesting the loan. This form also serves as a receipt of delivery for material returned to lenders or depositors.

III.H.2. *Loan Agreement* (8½ by 11 in.), Denver Museum of Natural History. This form serves as both a receipt and a loan agreement. Two copies are sent to the borrowing institution or individual at the time the loan is shipped, while a third copy is retained by the museum. The borrower keeps one copy and returns the other as an acknowledgment that the loaned material has been received.

III.H.3. *Invoice of Specimens* (8½ by 11 in.), Field Museum of Natural History. This multipurpose form serves to document all incoming and outgoing transactions. Appropriate boxes are checked to indicate whether the transaction at hand is an incoming or outgoing shipment or loan. For incoming material, the second copy is sent to the lender, usually with the lender's invoice, or to the donor, as an acknowledgment of receipt. Then when (if) the material is returned, the original is sent to the lender for signature and return as a receipt of delivery. For outgoing material, the first and second copies are sent to the consignee, who signs and returns the original and retains the copy. The third and fifth copies are sent to the scientific department. The fourth copy is retained in the registration department until the signed original is returned. Originals are filed permanently in a master file.

III.A.1.

LOAN AGREEMENT

The Museum of Modern Art, 11 West 53 Street, New York, N.Y. 10019 (212) 956-6100
Cable: MODERNART NEW YORK Telex: Western Union International 62370

Exhibition: _____

Lender: _____ Phone: (Business) ( ) _____
Address: _____ (Home) ( ) _____

Exact form of lender's name/credit for exhibition label and catalog: _____

Name of Artist: _____
Title of Work: _____
Medium or Materials: _____ Where? _____
Is the work signed? _____ Where? _____
Is the work dated? _____

Dimensions: Painting, drawing, etc. (without frame or mat): Height _____ Width _____
Sculpture (without pedestal): Height _____ Width _____ Depth _____ Approx. Weight _____
Frame and/or pedestal: Height _____ Width _____ Depth _____ Approx. Weight _____
Style of frame: Decorative _____ Plain _____

Framing: Is the work framed? _____ May we substitute plexiglas for glass? _____
If necessary to ensure the safety of the work or to meet other requirements of the exhibition, may we reframe, remat or back your work? _____ (Your loan will be returned to you in its original frame and mat unless other arrangements are made with the Museum in writing.)

Copyright: If the work was created after January 1, 1978, do you own the copyright in the work? _____
If not, do you know who does? _____
If not, who was previous owner? _____

Catalog and Publicity: Do you authorize the work to be reproduced for:
Will you supply a photograph? _____ 1. Press and publicity purposes of the exhibition _____
Photograph/Negative Number _____ 2. Publications published or copublished by
If you do not have one, will you have one taken at our   the Museum _____
expense? _____   a. published by us _____
Do you authorize the loan to be photographed? _____   b. published under our supervision _____
 3. Postcards, slides or reproductions _____
 4. Film or television _____

Insurance: (See conditions on reverse of this loan agreement.)
Insurance value of work: _____ (U.S. dollars) (Insurance value cannot exceed selling price, if any.)
Do you elect to maintain your own insurance? _____
If so, what is estimated cost of insurance premium? _____ Selling price _____
Is the work for sale? _____
(See conditions regarding handling charges on reverse of this loan agreement.)

Shipping Instructions: _____

Address for pickup of work: _____

Address to which the work must be returned: _____

Signature: _____ Date: _____
Please return the completed green copy to The Museum of Modern Art and retain the white copy for your records.

MF 160 a - i

LOAN AGREEMENT

CONDITIONS GOVERNING LOANS

1. The Museum of Modern Art will exercise the same care with respect to loans as it does in the safekeeping of comparable property of its own.

2. Loans shall remain in the possession of The Museum of Modern Art and/or other museums participating in the exhibition in question for the time specified on the face of this receipt, but may be withdrawn from exhibition at any time by the director or trustees of any such museum.

Unless the Museum is notified in writing to the contrary, loans will be returned only to the owner at the address stated on the face of this agreement. If the legal ownership of the work should change during the period of this loan, whether by reason of death, sale, insolvency, gift or otherwise, the owner will, prior to its return, be required to establish his legal right to receive the work by proof satisfactory to the Museum. If the address of the new owner should be of much greater distance than the locality from which the loan was borrowed, the new owner will be required to pay any difference in the charges for the delivery of the work.

3. Unless the lender expressly elects to maintain his own insurance coverage, The Museum of Modern Art will insure this loan wall-to-wall under its fine-arts policy for the amount indicated on the face of this loan agreement against all risks of physical loss or damage from any external cause while in transit and on location during the period of the loan. The policy referred to contains the usual exclusions of loss or damage due to such causes as wear and tear, gradual deterioration, moths, vermin, inherent vice, war, hostilities, insurrection, nuclear reaction or radiation, and for damage resulting from any authorized repairing, restoration or retouching process.

If a work which has been industrially fabricated is damaged, and it can be repaired or replaced to the artist's specifications, the Museum's liability shall be limited to the cost of such replacement.

The lender agrees to U.S. Government Indemnity, if applicable to this loan, at U.S. dollar value as of the date of this loan agreement.

If the lender elects to maintain his own insurance, the Museum must be supplied with a certificate of insurance naming The Museum of Modern Art and each of the participating museums as an additional assured or waiving subrogation against the Museum and each of the participating museums. Otherwise, the loan agreement shall constitute a release of the Museum and each of the participating museums from any liability in connection with loaned property. The Museum can accept no responsibility for any error or deficiency in information furnished to the lender's insurers or for lapses in coverage.

4. If the loan listed on the face of this receipt is for sale, it is understood that the selling price shall include a Museum handling charge as follows:

On sales up to $10,000. 10%
On the next $15,000. 7½%
On everything over $25,000. 5%

The Museum waives its standard handling charge on sales of the work of living artists when the artist himself or his gallery is the seller.

CONDITIONS GOVERNING LOANS

LOAN PERIOD

1. Loaned objects shall remain in the possession of the Newark Museum for the time specified on the face of this loan agreement, but may be withdrawn from exhibition at any time by the Director. Loans will be returned only to the lender or his or her duly authorized agent or representative.

2. The Museum will give reasonable notice in writing if it desires to have any object taken back by the lender; and the Museum will make reasonable efforts to return the objects to the lender.

   If such efforts are unavailing for any reason, the right of the Museum to require the lender to withdraw such object shall accrue absolutely on the date of and by mailing a notice to the lender for any of the following reasons: it is declined by the Museum, the loan period has terminated or the Museum no longer desires the loan thereof. If the lender shall not withdraw such property within sixty (60) days from the date of such notice, then the Museum shall have the absolute right to dispose of such property in any manner it may elect, and if it stores such property to charge regular storage fees therefore and to have and enforce a lien for such fees. If after five years such property shall not have been withdrawn, and in consideration for its storage and safe-guarding during this period, it shall be deemed an unrestricted gift to the Museum.

3. Loans may be removed from the Museum by the lender or his or her duly authorized agent or successor in interest after reasonable notice and the delivery of the lender's written order.

   In the case of the death of a lender, the legal representative of the deceased is requested to notify the Museum giving his full name and address and enclosing a certified copy of his authority.

   In the event that an object, the ownership having meanwhile passed by sale, bequest or gift, is not to be returned to the original lender, the new owner must establish, in advance of such return, his authority to receive it.

COSTS

4. All costs of insurance, packing, crating, transportation and customs formalities will be borne by the Newark Museum.

5. If the loaned objects are to be returned, at the lender's request (without prior written agreement), to any address other than that from which they were collected, the Museum may ask the lender to pay any additional cost necessitated by such change.

INSURANCE

6. Unless the lender expressly elects to maintain his or her own insurance, the Newark Museum will insure this loan wall-to-wall under the terms of its fine-arts policy, for the amount indicated on the face of this loan agreement.

   If the lender elects to maintain his own insurance, the Newark Museum must be supplied with a certificate of insurance naming the borrower as additionally assured or waiving subrogation against the borrower. Otherwise, this loan agreement shall constitute a release of the borrower from any liability in connection with the loaned property. The Newark Museum can accept no responsibility for any error or deficiency in information furnished to the lender's insurers or for lapses in coverage.

   The lender agrees that in the event of loss or damage, recovery if any, shall be limited to such amount as may be paid by the insurer, hereby releasing the Museum, its officers, agents and employees from liability for any and all claims arising out of such loss or damage.

7. In respect to an object which has been industrially fabricated and can be replaced to the (living) artist's specifications, the Museum's liability shall be limited to the cost of such replacement.

CARE AND HANDLING AND CREDITS

8. The Newark Museum will exercise the same care in respect to loans as it does in the safekeeping of comparable property of its own.

9. If damage or deterioration is noted, the lender will be notified at once. Should damage occur in transit, the carrier will also be notified and all packing materials saved for inspection.

10. Loaned objects shall remain in the condition in which they are received. They shall not be unframed, unglazed or removed from mats, mounts or bases, cleaned, repaired or transported in damaged condition except:
    a. with the express permission of the lender to be confirmed in writing
    b. when the safety of the work makes such action imperative.

11. The loaned objects will be identified by the use of the information on the face of this form including the lender's identification as listed.

The signatures below indicate the conditions of this loan as stated above are accepted.

_____ _____
Borrower (representative of The Newark Museum)   Date

_____ _____
Lender (authorized representative)   Date

Enclosed are two copies of our L.A.F.; please sign and return one in the enclosed envelope.

THE NEWARK MUSEUM ASSOCIATION, 43-49 Washington Street, Newark, New Jersey 07101
Registrar's Phone: 201-733-6653

We should greatly appreciate your filling in this blank where checked.

LOAN AGREEMENT AND CATALOG INFORMATION FORM

Exhibition and Dates: _____

Lender: _____

Address: _____ Telephone: _____

Credit Line: _____
(To be used on label and/or in catalog)

Name of Artist (or Object): _____ Medium & Support: _____

Exact Title of Work: _____

Date and Location: _____
(If not dated, do you know evidence for attributed date?)

Signature (or Mark) & Location: _____

Size: Painting: Unframed, Height (inches) _____ (cm.) _____
                 Width (inches) _____ (cm.) _____
       Framed,   Height (inches) _____ (cm.) _____
                 Width (inches) _____ (cm.) _____

Object: Height _____ Width _____ Other _____

Insurance Value: $ _____ May we insure? _____ Do you wish to insure? _____
*If you elect to maintain your own insurance, see condition #6 on reverse.
If more than one object please itemize.*

Shipping Instructions: _____

LOAN SHOULD ARRIVE ON OR BEFORE _____
(Unless special arrangements are made with the borrower in writing before the receipt of the loan, the work will be returned to the lender's address given above. See condition #4 on reverse.

Photographs: How can we obtain them for catalog reproduction and publicity? _____

PHOTOGRAPHY AND REPRODUCTION: Unless we are notified in writing to the contrary, it is understood that this loan may be photographed and reproduced in the Museum's publications and for publicity purposes connected with this exhibition.

May amateur photographers take pictures of this work if they agree in writing not to use the pictures for commercial purposes? _____

Installation or Handling Requirements: _____
(Any special problems or requests?)

Do we have permission to make minor repairs to frame? _____

CATALOG INFORMATION: Provenance, Previous Exhibitions, Bibliographical references:
_____
_____
_____

III.B.2.

CONDITIONS FOR LOANS BY THE CHICAGO HISTORICAL SOCIETY

1. The Chicago Historical Society lends materials from its collections only to museums, historical societies, libraries, and other organizations which in the Society's judgment can comply with the conditions stated below. Loans will generally not be approved for extremely fragile materials, frequently used library holdings, or materials that will be used soon in forthcoming exhibits at the Society.

2. The borrower must pay all costs for matting, packing, crating, and shipping, including charges for hiring special packers when necessary. Objects shall be repacked in the lender's crate for return to the Society by the same manner of shipment as used by the lender unless otherwise mutually agreed upon by the lender and borrower. Damages, whether in transit or on the borrower's premises and regardless of responsibility, shall be reported immediately to the lender.

3. Insurance in the amount of the value determined by the Chicago Historical Society must be placed on all loans and carried in force from the time the objects are removed from the Society until the objects are returned in satisfactory condition. This must be an all risk, wall-to-wall policy subject to standard policy exclusions. The borrower may elect to (1) insure the loan under the borrower's policy, in which case a certificate of insurance must be forwarded to the Chicago Historical Society prior to the shipping date, (2) insure the loan under the Chicago Historical Society's policy, in which case the borrower must pay the pro-rata cost of the insurance, or (3) in the case of loans in which the total value of all objects loaned by the Chicago Historical Society for a specific exhibit is less than $1,000, the borrower may, in lieu of insurance, agree to assume liability for loss or damage.

4. Objects must be given special care to protect them against loss, breakage, or deterioration. Small objects (including books and other bound volumes) must be displayed in locked cases. Prints, maps, and other flat materials must be displayed in locked cases or in frames using glass or ultra-violet filtering plexiglass and acid-free matting materials. Large objects and costumes not displayed in cases or behind glass must have sufficient distance from the public to avoid touching. Exhibit areas must be under surveillance by guards or other staff when open to the public.

5. Objects must be protected against light damage by the use of (1) ultra-violet filters on fluorescent and incandescent lights or (2) ultra-violet filtering plexiglass in frames or cases. Cases must be designed so that the lighting element (or at least the ballast) is outside the enclosed area.

6. No restoration, repair, or cleaning of objects may be performed by the borrower without prior permission in writing. Such a request must state precisely what will be done to the object.

7. Objects may be photographed and the photographs may be reproduced for an exhibit catalog or publicity purposes connected with this exhibit. Written permission must be obtained from the Chicago Historical Society for all other uses.

8. Requests for loans must be made at least two months prior to the time objects are to leave the Society to allow time for photography, packing, and other arrangements.

9. The duration of the loan must be stated by the borrower at the time the request for a loan is made. Objects must be returned to the Chicago Historical Society at the end of the loan period unless an extension has previously been requested by the borrower and approved in writing by the Chicago Historical Society.

10. Objects shall bear labels indicating that they were loaned by the Chicago Historical Society. Labels will also include the name of the donor if requested in the loan agreement.

11. In the case of foreign loans, all packing, shipping, insurance, destination, and customs information must be clearly stated in writing before the loan will be approved. The borrower must give the name of the person at the borrowing institution who is in charge of coordinating the foreign loan and who will handle all communications concerning the loan.

12. The Chicago Historical Society is to receive a copy of any publication or catalog of the exhibit for which Society objects have been lent.

CHICAGO HISTORICAL SOCIETY
Clark Street at North Avenue

Area Code 312 MI2-4600
Chicago, Illinois 60614

LOAN AGREEMENT

The Chicago Historical Society agrees, subject to the conditions printed on the reverse of this sheet, to lend the objects described below for the purpose of exhibition to:

Institution: United States Marine Corps Historical Center

Address: Washington, D. C. 20380

for a period from March 31, 1977 to June 30, 1977

Title of Exhibition: THE MARINE CORPS AS SEEN THROUGH CONTEMPORANEOUS ART

Description of Objects   Condition   Value

1920.1502   American silver-mounted powder horn engraved with a map of the Hudson and Mohawk River Valleys. The silver base engraved as follows: "The Gift of James Coakley to Saml. Nicholas May 2d 1785."   Excellent $7500.00

Insurance (see Condition 3):

X   Borrower will insure loan under own policy and forward certificate of insurance to the Chicago Historical Society prior to shipping date

___ Borrower wishes to insure loan under Chicago Historical Society's policy, and will pay pro-rata cost of insurance

___ Borrower agrees to assume liability for loss or damage in lieu of insurance (option available only when total value of all objects loaned for a specific exhibit is less than $1,000)

Shipping instructions:
Name of individual to whom shipment should be sent and address if different from above:
U. S. Marine Corps Historical Center, Bldg. 58, Washington Navy Yard, Washington DC 20374

Date materials should be shipped: 1 April 1977

Method of shipment preferred (subject to approval by Chicago Historical Society):

The borrower acknowledges that he/she has read the conditions on the reverse of this sheet and that he/she accepts them.

Signature _[signed]_
Title Deputy Director
Date February 10, 1977

Loan approved for the Chicago Historical Society by:

Signature _Joseph B. Zywicki_
Title Chief Curator
Date February 23, 1977

Please sign above and return both copies. After the loan has been approved, we will send your copy.

For Chicago Historical Society use:
Objects sent _____ Staff Init. _____
Objects returned _____ Staff Init. _____

CONDITIONS GOVERNING LOANS OUT

By accepting the objects described on the face of this receipt the borrower agrees to the following conditions:

CARE AND HANDLING

1. Each object shall remain in the condition in which it is received.

2. No object shall be unframed, removed from mats, mounts or bases, cleaned, repaired, retouched or altered in any way whatsoever except with the express written permission of the Newark Museum.

3. Newark Museum numbers or tags must not be removed. Borrower's loan numbers should be carefully placed (with non-permanent materials) so as not to damage or alter the object in any way. Exhibition stickers for paintings may be placed on backing or frame.

4. Each object shall at all times be given special care to insure it against loss, damage or deterioration, and when necessary a suitable case shall be provided for exhibition and protection. The borrower shall provide suitable protection against theft, fire, and damage from any cause whatever at all times. Should loss, damage or deterioration be noted, whether in transit or on the borrower's premises and regardless of who may be responsible therefor, the Newark Museum shall be informed immediately and in detail. Should damage occur in transit all packing material should be saved for inspection.

5. Unless special permission is granted in writing for outdoor exhibition, objects shall be protected at all times against direct sunlight, rain, excessive humidity and excessively dry conditions. In addition all watercolors, drawings, prints, fabrics and photographs shall be properly protected from the damage of fading by exposure to direct or reflected sunlight and strong artificial light, flourescent light or proximity to heat sources.

6. No foreign materials (i.e. pins, nails, etc.) are to be used to fasten an object for exhibition purposes. When in doubt consult Newark Museum curator.

7. The Newark Museum will decide on the method of packing and shipping to and from the borrower. Objects should be returned carefully packed in the same manner as received and by a competent carrier of Newark Museum choice. The Newark Museum reserves the right to give binding instructions to borrowers as to these matters.

COSTS

8. All handling, packing, transportation and insurance costs incurred during the loan are to be paid by the borrowing institution.

INSURANCE

9. Each object shall be insured at the borrower's expense for the benefit of Newark Museum against all risks of physical loss or damage from any external cause while in transit and on location during the period of the loan. Required insurance shall be arranged by either the borrower or the Newark Museum and agreed to by the Newark Museum before any objects covered by this receipt may be removed from the Museum. If insured by the borrower, the objects shall be covered "wall-to-wall" by the amount set forth under the column "Insurance Value" opposite the description of said object overleaf, which amount shall be considered the actual value (whether market, intrinsic or otherwise) of said object for all purposes. If specifically requested, the borrower shall supply the Newark Museum, before shipment, a certificate of insurance in conformance with the foregoing terms.

LOAN PERIOD

10. If an extension of time is desired on this loan, application must be made in writing, within a reasonable time before the end of the period noted overleaf. Extensions, if granted, must be noted on this receipt. The Newark Museum reserves the right to recall any object for its own purpose upon reasonable notice to the borrower.

PHOTOGRAPHY AND TECHNICAL EXAMINATION

11. The borrower may photograph the objects only for record and publicity purposes. Photographs required for an exhibition catalog will be supplied by the Newark Museum. Paintings and drawings must not be removed from their frames for photography. Borrower may not reproduce such objects in any medium (including photographs) for purpose of sale, nor may such objects be subjected to technical examination of any type whatever without written permission of the Newark Museum.

MISCELLANEOUS

12. Information about the object used for catalogs, labels or for any other purpose shall conform to data furnished by the Newark Museum and shall always include a credit line to the Newark Museum.

13. If the Newark Museum has specifically advised the borrower of any applicable common-law or statutory copyright, borrower agrees that ownership of such copyright is reserved to the Newark Museum, that it will make no reproduction or other use of the copyrighted object which will or might impair such copyright, and that it will assign to the Newark Museum the copyright of any reproduction.

14. This document shall be signed by an authorized staff member of the borrower and shall be returned to the Newark Museum immediately after receipt of the object.

THE NEWARK MUSEUM ASSOCIATION
43-49 Washington Street, Newark, New Jersey 07101

LOAN OUT FORM

Date _____

The following objects are lent by The Newark Museum

to _____
   (Borrower)

   _____
   (Address)

for the purpose of _____

from _____ to _____
     (Date leaving Newark Museum)   *(Approximate return date)*

under the conditions printed overleaf.

To be insured in transit and
while on exhibition ("wall-to-wall") by _____

Approved _____   _____
          Director   *Registrar*

Newark Museum Registration Number	Description of Objects	Insurance Value

Received by institution _____ Date _____
per (signature and title)

When object has been received, please sign and return the original white copy to Newark Museum in enclosed envelope. Borrower may retain blue copy.

III.C.2.

LOAN RECEIPT
The Museum of Modern Art, 11 West 53 Street, New York, N.Y. 10019 (212) 956-6100
Cable: **MODERNART NEW YORK** Telex: **Western Union International 62370**

Date received ....

The object(s) described below has (have) been received by The Museum of Modern Art as loan(s) under the conditions noted on the back of this receipt.

from

for

.... Registrar

Museum Number	Description	Insurance Value

RECEIPT OF DELIVERY
The Museum of Modern Art, 11 West 53 Street, New York, N.Y. 10019 (212) 956-6100
Cable: **MODERNART NEW YORK** Telex: **Western Union International 62370**

Date received ....
Date returned ....

The following object(s) lent to the Museum of Modern Art:

by

for

has (have) been

.... Registrar

Please sign and return this Receipt of Delivery to confirm that you have received the above mentioned works of art and have found them to be in satisfactory condition.

Received by .... Date ....

III.D.1.

The Minneapolis Institute of Arts
2400 3rd Avenue South
Minneapolis, Minnesota 55404
Telephone 612-870-3046
Cable Minnart

Loan Agreement

Please complete, sign and return the original of this form. The copy is for your records.

EXHIBITION ....

DATES OF EXHIBITION ....

DATES OF LOAN ....

LENDER/LENT TO ....

ADDRESS AND TELEPHONE ....

Return shipment will be made to this address unless otherwise instructed

CREDIT ....
Lender's name as it should appear in the catalog and on gallery label

ARTIST ....

TITLE ....

MEDIUM .... Dimensions in inches: H............ W............ D............
Painting, drawing, print: without frame or mat. Sculpture: without base.

DATE .... Signature:............ How signed............ Where............

INSURANCE *Valuation:* ....
Coverage: Unless otherwise specified, the borrowing institution will insure in the amount specified above throughout the period of loan.

TRANSPORTATION To arrive no later than................ Shipping instructions will follow

PHOTOGRAPHS Are photographs available? Yes:........ No:........ If available, please send .... 8 x 10 glossies.
Permission to reproduce in the catalog, for publicity and for educational purposes, is assumed unless otherwise stated by lender.
Is color reproduction material available? Yes:........ No:........
If yes, please state type:............ plates............ color separations............ transparencies
May this work be photographed for television broadcasts in connection with the exhibition? Yes:........ No:........

CATALOG Previous collections, exhibitions, publications, bibliography. (Please indicate on separate sheet.)

CONDITIONS GOVERNING LOAN THIS LOAN IS SUBJECT TO THE CONDITIONS PRINTED ON THE REVERSE SIDE OF THIS FORM.

SIGNATURE OF LEGAL OWNER .... Date:............

SIGNATURE OF AUTHORIZED BORROWER .... Date:............

III.C.3.

GUGGENHEIM

Receipt of Delivery

THE SOLOMON R. GUGGENHEIM MUSEUM, 1071 FIFTH AVENUE, NEW YORK CITY 10028   (212) 860-1300

DATE   July 15, 1977

FOR   DISPERSAL - JANE DOE: A RETROSPECTIVE EXHIBITION

The following objects, which were lent to The Solomon R. Guggenheim Museum, have been returned

TO   Ms. Jane Doe
       1527 Fourth Avenue
       New York, New York 10001

VIA   JD truck

SHIPPING
BILLED TO   SRGM

MUSEUM NUMBER	DESCRIPTION - one wrapped painting:
723.77 Cat. #14	Jane Doe: UNTITLED. 1977 Oil on canvas, 25 x 35" frame: painted wood/plexi

Registrar   John Anthony

RECEIVED BY _____   DATE _____

Please sign this receipt and return to The Solomon R. Guggenheim Museum

III.E.1.

GUGGENHEIM

Loan Receipt

THE SOLOMON R. GUGGENHEIM MUSEUM, 1071 FIFTH AVENUE, NEW YORK CITY 10028   (212) 860-1300

DATE   March 9, 1977

FOR   JANE DOE: A RETROSPECTIVE EXHIBITION: April 1, 1977-July 1, 1977

The objects described below have been received by The Solomon R. Guggenheim Museum as loans

FROM   Ms. Jane Doe
       1527 Fourth Avenue
       New York, New York 10001

VIA   JD truck

Registrar   John Anthony

MUSEUM NUMBER	DESCRIPTION	Insurance Value
723.77 Cat. #14	Jane Doe: UNTITLED. 1977 Oil on canvas, 25 x 35" frame: painted wood/plexi COLLECTION OF THE ARTIST	$5,000=

A record has been made of the condition of each loan upon receipt by the Museum and can be furnished to the lender on request.

III.D.2.

III.E.1 continued.

GUGGENHEIM
THE SOLOMON R. GUGGENHEIM MUSEUM 1071 FIFTH AVENUE NEW YORK CITY 10028 (212) 860-1300

Receipt of Delivery
Copy

DATE July 15, 1977

FOR DISPERSAL – JANE DOE: A RETROSPECTIVE EXHIBITION

The Solomon R. Guggenheim Museum has delivered the following

TO Ms. Jane Doe
    1527 Fourth Avenue
    New York, New York 10001

VIA JD truck

ALL CHARGES BILLED TO SRGM

III.E.2.

CHICAGO HISTORICAL SOCIETY
Clark Street at North Avenue

Area Code 312 MI2-4600
Chicago, Illinois 60614

LOAN RECEIPT

I hereby acknowledge that I have examined the shipment of materials lent to the Chicago Historical Society in the agreement executed under date of July 20, 1976 and that the materials listed below have been returned.

Signature: *Sylvia Shields*
for: Newberry Library
Date: December 15, 1976

These materials represent X partial _____ complete shipment of materials lent.

1 page of draft manuscript with handwritten annotations. Anderson, Sherwood, "Chicago: An Impression — A Feeling."

GUGGENHEIM
THE SOLOMON R. GUGGENHEIM MUSEUM 1071 FIFTH AVENUE NEW YORK CITY 10028 (212) 860-1300

Release

DATE July 15, 1977

FOR DISPERSAL – JANE DOE: A RETROSPECTIVE EXHIBITION

Please release the following

TO Ms. Jane Doe
    1527 Fourth Avenue
    New York, New York 10001

VIA JD truck

ALL CHARGES BILLED TO SRGM

Special Instructions

III.F.1.

CHICAGO HISTORICAL SOCIETY
Clark Street at North Avenue

Area Code 312 MI2-4600
Chicago, Illinois 60614

LOAN RECEIPT

I hereby acknowledge that I have examined the shipment of materials loaned by the Chicago Historical Society to The Art Institute of Chicago for an exhibit on Art of the North American Indian and that all of the materials listed in the loan agreement have been received.

Signature _____
Title Curator of Primitive Art
Date _____

Please sign and return to the Chicago Historical Society in the enclosed envelope.

If any items are missing or damaged, contact the Chicago Historical Society immediately.

The Museum of Modern Art

All loans of objects from the Museum Collections are made subject to the borrower's agreement to the following conditions:

1. Each object is received in good condition unless otherwise noted.

2. Each object shall at all times be given due care to insure it against loss, damage or deterioration. Should loss, damage or deterioration be noted, The Museum of Modern Art shall be informed immediately and in detail. Should damage occur during transit, the Museum and the carrier shall be notified at once, and all packing materials shall be saved until the carrier or its agent has had an opportunity to inspect them. When Railway Express Agency is the carrier, a copy of the "Joint Inspection Report" shall be obtained.

3. Objects lent by The Museum of Modern Art shall remain in the condition in which they are received. They shall not be unframed or removed from mats, mounts or bases for any purpose whatsoever, or cleaned, repaired or transported in damaged condition except with the express permission of The Museum of Modern Art.

4. Unless special permission is granted in writing for outdoor exhibition of loans, objects shall be protected at all times against direct sunlight, rain, excessive humidity and excessively dry conditions. In addition, all watercolors, drawings, prints, posters, fabrics and photographs shall be protected against fading, scorching and cockling caused by direct or reflected sunlight, strong artificial light, fluorescent light or proximity to heat sources.

5. All packing, transportation and customs formalities shall be arranged by the borrower through firms acceptable to The Museum of Modern Art, and all costs thereof shall be paid in full by the borrower. The Museum of Modern Art may elect, however, to have loans packed on its own premises at the borrower's expense. The borrower shall reimburse The Museum of Modern Art for any special framing, glazing, etc. made necessary by the loan.

6. Each object shall be insured by the borrower for the amount specified on the face of our receipt. The insurance shall cover all risks from the time the object leaves The Museum of Modern Art until it is returned to it and shall guarantee payment of claims, for depreciation as well as restoration and related costs, in United States currency. When objects are lent outside the United States or Canada, the borrower may at the discretion of The Museum of Modern Art be required to purchase insurance under a special policy carried by The Museum of Modern Art.

7. Unless written notice to the contrary is given in advance, objects other than photographic prints may be photographed and reproduced for normal publicity and catalog purposes before and during the exhibition and for condition records; but special permission shall be obtained in writing for all other reproduction and for any reproduction whatsoever of photographic prints. Except for detail views, all reproductions for any purpose shall show an unobstructed view of the entire object without cropping or bleeding. If a detail is reproduced, this fact shall be clearly indicated in the caption. No reproduction of any kind may be tinted or otherwise distorted.

8. The borrower shall pay any fee of which he has been notified in advance as a condition of The Museum of Modern Art's agreement to lend the objects.

9. Information about the object used for catalogs, labels or for any other purpose shall conform to the catalog date furnished by The Museum of Modern Art and shall always include a credit line to The Museum of Modern Art, giving the name of the donor or purchase fund when specified.

10. Exhibitions in which works borrowed from The Museum of Modern Art are shown shall be open to the public without any restriction involving racial discrimination or segregation.

The Museum of Modern Art

11 West 53 Street, New York, N.Y. 10019 Telephone 956-6100

Date

The following objects are lent by The Museum of Modern Art

to

for _____ from _____ to

under the conditions printed on the back of this receipt.

Approved
Curator _____ Registrar _____

Number	Artist	Description	Insurance valuation

Received by _____ Date _____

Please sign this receipt and return to The Museum of Modern Art.
You will be billed under separate cover for the following:
$ _____ Handling charge
$ _____ Preparation cost
$ _____ Other (specify)
$ _____ Total

Memorandum to Accounts Receivable

Date

The objects listed below have been lent by The Museum of Modern Art

to

for _____ from _____ to

Registrar _____

Please bill the borrower for the total amount shown below and credit the receipts to account number 15.0.176

$ _____ Handling charge
$ _____ Preparation cost
$ _____ Other (specify)
$ _____ Total

III.F.2.

THE ART INSTITUTE OF CHICAGO
Michigan Avenue at Adams Street

Chicago, Illinois 60603   December 20, 1978

Name   Mr. Michelangelo Buonarotti
Address Rome, Italy

Dear Sir:

We herewith advise you we have today forwarded to you by air freight prepaid on SO ___ CR03 ___ the objects insurance $50. described below.

Yours very truly,

THE ART INSTITUTE OF CHICAGO

By _____
   Museum Registrar

Terracotta study for the Tomb of Julius II.

Submitted for consideration for purchase but declined and now returned to owner.

Please sign and return   Received the objects listed above in good condition

Date _____   Signed _____

III.G.1.

INVOICE OF SPECIMENS

CLEVELAND MUSEUM OF NATURAL HISTORY
Wade Oval, University Circle
Cleveland, Ohio 44106

Date 18 August 19 76

TO: Institution Department of Biological Sciences, Illinois State University
Normal, Illinois 61761

Attention: Mr. Tom Bunker

The following specimens have been forwarded to you as:
☒ Loan at your request for three (3) months (period of loan)
☐ Loan for examination at our request
☐ Exchange
☐ Return of material borrowed
☐ Return of material sent for identification
☐ Other _____ (specify)

Mode of Shipment United Parcel Service

Authorized by Lynda Howell, Registrar
              Jim Jamson, Staff Biologist

DESCRIPTION OF SPECIMENS

One specimen of Natrix kirtlandi with the following data:

Location: Ohio, Lucas Co., Toledo
Collector: Fletcher Reynolds
Date: 29 December 1940
CMNH Museum #ZF 143

Please sign the white acknowledgement copy and return it to the Museum.

Received ☐ in good condition
         ☐ as noted
For loans, conditions on reverse side shall apply.

Acknowledged _____
(Name of Institution)

BY _____
(Authorized Signatory)

Date _____

LOAN CONDITIONS

1. Loaned specimens will be maintained in good condition, protected from theft and mishandling and returned to the Museum at the expiration of the loan in the same condition as when they were loaned.
2. Preparation or casting of loaned specimens is permitted only with the written consent of the Cleveland Museum of Natural History.
3. Responsibility for specimens while on loan is to remain jointly with the person acknowledging the loan and the institution he represents. No assignment of this responsibility or transfer of specimens to another person or institution is permitted without the written consent of the Cleveland Museum of Natural History.
4. Lender shall advise the Museum of any taxonomic changes and publications dealing with the loaned specimens.
5. Other conditions:

III.H.1.

FIELD MUSEUM OF NATURAL HISTORY
CHICAGO, ILLINOIS 60605, U.S.A.
INVOICE OF SPECIMENS

INVOICE DATE _____ YOUR NO. _____ OUR INVOICE NO. _____

APPROVED _____ AUTHORIZED _____

☐ RECEIVED _____
☐ SHIPPED _____ DATE _____

RECEIVED FROM:
☐ SHIP TO:

☐ FIRST CLASS ☐ INSURED
☐ AIR MAIL ☐ REGISTERED
☐ PARCEL POST ☐ SPECIAL HANDLING
☐ FREIGHT ☐ LIBRARY RATE
☐ AIR FREIGHT ☐ PREPAID
☐ EXPRESS ☐ COLLECT

☐ PICKED UP PERSONALLY BY

CONTAINED IN

PACKED BY _____

THE MATERIAL LISTED BELOW,
CATEGORIZED AS NO. _____
HAS BEEN ☐ RECEIVED BY US
☐ SENT TO YOU

1. ☐ AS A GIFT
2. ☐ AS AN EXCHANGE
3. ☐ AS A LOAN AT YOUR REQUEST
4. ☐ FOR EXAMINATION AT OUR REQUEST
5. ☐ AS A RETURN OF MATERIAL BORROWED BY US
6. ☐ AS A RETURN OF MATERIAL SENT US FOR IDENTIFICATION
7. ☐ AS A LOAN TO US
8. ☐ FOR IDENTIFICATION
9. ☐

Signature _____ Date _____

PLEASE SIGN AND RETURN THIS COPY PROMPTLY TO:
FIELD MUSEUM OF NATURAL HISTORY
Roosevelt Road at Lake Shore Drive
CHICAGO, ILLINOIS 60605, U.S.A.

Received: in good condition ☐ except as noted ☐
Signature _____ Date _____

Received: in good condition ☐ except as noted ☐
Signature _____ Date _____

TO CONSIGNEE: KEEP THIS COPY FOR YOUR FILES

WEIGHT ___ LBS. ___ OZ. POSTAGE $ ___
VALUE $ ___ ☐ INSURANCE FEE $ ___
☐ REGISTERED FEE $ ___
TOTAL $ ___

INSURANCE NO. ___
REGISTERED NO. ___

THIS COPY FOR DEPARTMENTAL RECORDS

WEIGHT ___ LBS. ___ OZ. POSTAGE $ ___
VALUE $ ___ ☐ INSURANCE FEE $ ___
☐ REGISTERED FEE $ ___
TOTAL $ ___

INSURANCE NO. ___
REGISTERED NO. ___

USE ONLY WHEN WHITE AND YELLOW INVOICES ARE TO BE MAILED TO CONSIGNEE

EXTRA COPY

III.H.3.

DENVER MUSEUM OF NATURAL HISTORY
CITY PARK
DENVER, COLORADO 80205
LOAN AGREEMENT

DEPARTMENT Zoological Colls.

RECEIVED FROM:
SENT TO: Joseph P. Brady   575-9311
          1701 Colorado Boulevard
POSITION: researcher and artist
INSTITUTION: Independent

☐ FIRST CLASS   ☐ INSURED $
☐ LIBRARY RATE   ☐ REGISTERED
☐ AIR MAIL   ☐ SPECIAL HANDLING
☐ AIR FREIGHT   ☐ RETURN RECEIPT REQUEST
☐ UPS   ☐ OTHER
☒ IN HAND

Reference: This relates to letter of
inquiry/agreement of 1/2/78 date.

MUSEUM ACCESSION #

T270   Ovis ammon skin and skull

LOAN PROCESSING DATE January 8, 1978
AUTHORIZED BY Betsy Webb, Curator
PACKED BY BW
DURATION OF LOAN 2 months
RECEIVED/SENT 1/8/78   RETURNED 2/14/78
INSPECTION OK (BW)

MATERIAL LISTED BELOW IS:
☒ LOAN AT YOUR REQUEST   ☐ EXHIBITION LOAN
☐ LOAN AT OUR REQUEST   ☐ OTHER
☐ FOR IDENTIFICATION

DESCRIPTION OF LOAN MATERIAL WITH PRESENT CONDITION

excellent condition; chipped molar on skull

State fully the reason(s) for borrowing items: artistic reference and study
Publication X no ___ yes (when possible, please provide a copy for the Museum)

The borrower agrees that he will assume full responsibility for all materials on loan FROM the Museum in relation to loss or damage while they are under his care and, when requested, will provide the museum with adequate proof of insurance policy or insurance certificate to guarantee proper coverage. When borrowing materials, the Museum will exercise all due care in the handling of them, however, the Museum insurance covers only those objects which have been accessioned into Museum collections and, therefore, the Museum may not accept any liability on loan materials.

Signed Joseph P. Brady   Date January 8, 1978

Please complete the following information and RETURN THE WHITE COPY:
Received in good order by Joseph P. Brady   Date January 8, 1978

Form 3 (11/77) DMNH

III.H.2.

THE CHICAGO HISTORICAL SOCIETY

Deed of Gift to

from

Harvey G. Nelson
1456 West Chesterfield Avenue
Chicago, Illinois 60657

hereafter referred to as the "Owner" of the property described below, hereby gives, transfers, assigns, and delivers all of the Owner's right, title, and interest in and to the property described below, including any literary rights which the Owner may possess in and to said property, to the Chicago Historical Society as an unrestricted gift.

Dated this _____ day of _____, 19____:

_____
(Signature of donor)

_____
(Signature of donor)

Description of property:

1976.273ab   Pair of Remington New Model Army Revolvers, cal. 44, 6 shot, marked "Patented Sept. 14, 1858/ E. Remington & Son/ Ilion, New York, U.S.A." and "New Model"

Archives: Photograph of Willard Rufus White, maternal great-grandfather of the donor, who used the pistols during the Civil War.

The Chicago Historical Society hereby accepts the above property under the conditions specified above.

Dated this _____ day of _____, 19____:

CHICAGO HISTORICAL SOCIETY

By _____

Please sign both copies of the Deed of Gift form and return them to the Chicago Historical Society in the enclosed envelope. You will then receive a formal acknowledgement and your copy of the Deed of Gift signed by a representative of the Society.

IV.B.1.

THE CHICAGO HISTORICAL SOCIETY

gratefully acknowledges
A GIFT TO THE SOCIETY

from

Harvey G. Nelson
1456 West Chesterfield Avenue
Chicago, Illinois 60657

Description of property:

1976.273ab   Pair of Remington New Model Army Revolvers, cal. 44, 6 shot, marked "Patented Sept. 14, 1858/ E. Remington & Son/ Ilion, New York, U.S.A." and "New Model"

Archives: Photograph of Willard Rufus White, maternal great-grandfather of the donor, who used the pistols during the Civil War.

Date   December 12, 1976

Harold K. Skramstad, Jr.
Director

IV.A.1.

IV. GIFT FORMS

Gifts accepted by museums are formally acknowledged and legally documented.

IV.A. ACKNOWLEDGMENTS: The acknowledgment is the formal letter of thanks from the museum to the donor. Some museums write such letters individually; others employ a form. For another acknowledgment, see figure G.3.

IV.A.1. *Acknowledgment* (8½ by 11 in.), Chicago Historical Society. This form is designed to be typed simultaneously with the society's deed of gift (form IV.B.1). It is sent to the donor with the validated deed of gift.

IV.B. DEEDS OF GIFT: The deed of gift serves to transfer ownership of the object from the donor to the museum. Deeds of gift are an important part of the museum's legal records. For additional deeds of gift, see figures A.1, A.4, and G.4.

IV.B.1. *Deed of Gift* (8½ by 11 in.), Chicago Historical Society. After a donation has been accepted by the society, two copies of the deed of gift are typed simultaneously with the formal acknowledgment (form IV.A.1). Both copies are mailed to the donor for signature and return. One copy is then sent back to the donor, together with the acknowledgment. The second copy of the deed of gift becomes the museum's permanent record of acquisition. Photocopies are made for the donor's list, from which annual report information is taken, and for the registrar's office, where a checklist stamped on the form serves as an acquisitions procedure record.

V. RECORDS FOR PERMANENT ACCESSIONS

Museums keep a variety of formal records on permanent accessions. The number and kinds of these records depend on the activities and needs of the museum.

V.A. ACCESSION BOOKS: Some museums maintain, as part of their permanent records on accessions, a book or ledger in which each accession is recorded by accession number. For samples of pages from other accession books, see figures B.1–2, E.1, and G.1.

V.A.1. *Page from accession book* (8½ by 11 in., broadside), Arizona Historical Society. As each new accession is processed, it is recorded, by accession number, in the accession book. The accession book is a lock-post binder, so pages can easily be removed for typing and added as necessary.

V.B. WORK SHEETS: The registrar often prepares a work sheet on each newly accessioned object, gathering together the information that will be needed for the permanent record and checking off the various steps of the accessioning procedure as they are completed. For additional work sheets, see figures E.2–3, N.4, and P.2.

V.B.1. *Catalog Record* (8½ by 11 in.), Hirshhorn Museum and Sculpture Garden, Smithsonian Institution. After the work sheet is filled in by a cataloguer in the registration department, it is sent to the curatorial department for approval and the completion of certain information. The Hirshhorn's catalogue is computerized, and the numbers that precede the categories shown are code numbers for data processing. The information on the work sheet is typed into the museum's computer for the production of the permanent record. The original of the work sheet becomes a part of the museum collection archives.

V.B.2. *Work sheet* (8½ by 11 in.), Arizona Historical Society. The work sheet is the record of information on the museum's temporary deposit receipt as provided by the source of acquisition as well as the material gathered during the cataloguer's research. The bottom lines enable the registrar to check off various steps in the procedure as they are completed. The cataloguer then transfers the information from the work sheet to the subject card, the source card, and, when applicable, to the historical figure or place card (forms V.C.1, V.D.1, and V.F.1).

V.C. ACCESSION CARDS: One card, recording all pertinent information, is made for each permanent accession. In some museums these accession cards are then duplicated to form other files, such as source-of-acquisition files or location files (see forms V.D and V.E). For additional accession and catalogue cards and records, see figures A.3, D.3–6, E.2–4, G.5, I.1, J.4–5, K.1–4, L.1–2, P.5, and P.7.

V.C.1. *Subject card* (5 by 8 in.), Arizona Historical Society. One card is prepared for each accession from the information gathered on the work sheet (form V.B.2). A dated record of repair and fumigation and location is maintained on the subject card. Location information is maintained in pencil so that it can be changed as necessary. The storage location shown indicates closet 1, range 3, section A, shelf 7.

V.C.2. *Catalogue card* (4 by 6 in.), The Museum of Fine Arts, Boston. One card for each accession is typed on Library of Congress stock, and from it three photocopies are made. A photograph of the object is dry mounted on the card, and the photograph number is recorded in the column on the right. One card is retained by the registrar and filed in accession number order. Three cards go to the curatorial department holding the object, where they are filed by accession number, by category, and by location.

V.C.3. *Catalogue card* (4 by 6 in.), Philadelphia Museum of Art. The original card is prepared by the curatorial department. It is photocopied on 8-by-12-inch sheets of card stock perforated to produce four additional 4-by-6-inch cards. A photograph of the object is dry mounted on a blank card, which is attached to the accession card by cloth tape. Two cards are kept in the registration department, filed by accession number and by location. The location record is maintained on the back of the card. One to three cards are kept in the curatorial department, filed by style, artist, location, accession number, etc., depending on the department's needs.

V.C.4. *Accession Card and Historical File* (containing Catalogues of Collections; Letters and Memoranda concerning Specimens) (3½ by 9¼ in. card; 4 by 9¾ in. envelope), Field Museum of Natural History. The cards are color coded according to the four scientific departments in the museum. The department fills out a card for each accession (which may contain a great many specimens), and forwards a copy to the registration department, together with copies of all pertinent correspondence, notes, and other material. The departmental secretary assigns an accession number and uses the information on the card to maintain the donor file kept by the registration department. The card is then placed with all its supporting material in the historical file envelope, and the packet is filed by accession number in a permanent master file.

V.D. SOURCE-OF-ACQUISITION RECORDS: Most museums maintain a file that records the sources of permanent accessions—donors, lenders, vendors, bequests, expeditions, purchase funds, and others. In many museums, a duplicate of the accession or catalogue card is filed by source in a special source-of-acquisition file. In others, a separate card is made for each source, and gifts, purchases, and/or

187

loans are listed on it chronologically, together with the accession and/or loan numbers. For additional source-of-acquisition records, see figures D.5 and E.7 and form VI.B.1.

V.D.1. *Source card* (5 by 8 in.), Arizona Historical Society. One card is made for each source and filed alphabetically. On it are listed accessions, with accession numbers and dates.

V.E. LOCATION RECORDS: Location records show the exact location—in museum exhibition galleries, in storage, out on loan, or elsewhere—of every object in the museum's collection. Museums use various systems to maintain location records. Penciled notations or colored flags or tabs on accession cards may indicate location (see form V.C.1); or separate files may be maintained for each gallery or other location, and duplicate accession cards shifted from one file to another as objects are moved (see forms V.C.2 and V.C.3). Some museums maintain Flexoline files (see figure 3.11). Others maintain a separate file that shows storage locations and dates. For additional location records, see figures D.7, E.1, and H.1–2.

V.E.1. *Location card* (4 by 6 in.), The Museum of Modern Art. One card is maintained for each accession. It is filed by artist, then title, and each change in location is recorded on it, and continued on the reverse when necessary. The location system is supplemented by a collection history card (V.E.1a), which lists each time the object is exhibited. Collection history cards are filed by artist and then by title. Information is recorded on additional cards as needed.

V.F. SUBJECT RECORDS: A subject file is of particular use to researchers and the exhibit departments of some museums. Curatorial departments of paintings or drawings and prints, for example, sometimes maintain a file of the subjects depicted in their collections; see articles D and E and figures D.1–2 and E.8. History museums in particular often keep a historical association file that lists accessions relating to a specific person, event, or location important to the historic period that the museum interprets; see articles G and H, and figure G.2.

V.F.1. *Historical Figure or Place card* (5 by 8 in.), Arizona Historical Society. A card is made for each historical figure or place that is pertinent to the society's collections, and new accessions are recorded on the relevant cards as they are processed. Cards are filed alphabetically.

ACCESS. NUMBER	CATALOG NUMBER	DATE	DESCRIPTION AND REMARKS	SOURCE	TYPE OF ACQ.
75.1	75.1.1	1/9/75	1913 Arizona license plate	John Smith, 29 E. Second, Tucson, Az. 85704	Gift
75.2	75.2.1	1/10/75	Buttons, card mounted with 30 vegetable ivory buttons	Mrs. Ellen Orion, 4000 N. Stevens, Sparks, Nev. 89431	Gift
75.2	75.2.2	"	Buttons, card mounted with 42 metal buttons	"	"
75.2	75.2.3	"	Buttons, card mounted with 35 fabric buttons	"	"
75.3	75.3.1	1/14/75	Branding iron, short handle, a cross mounted on the back of a laying down C	Mrs. Max Freer, 1200 W. Calle Verde, Tucson, Az. 85716	Gift
75.3	75.3.2	"	Branding iron, short handle, an arrow head mounted on the center of a laying down S	"	"
75.3	75.3.3	"	Carbide mining lamp, made by Justrite	"	"
75.4	75.4.1	1/14/75	M1861 carbine sling, black leather	Craig Matson, 1307 N. Silver, Tucson, Az. 85719	Trade
75.5	75.5.1	1/16/75	Oil on canvas painting of St. John the Baptist blessing the Lamb, Spanish-Mexican	Stephen Clark, no address	AHS Pur.
75.6	75.6.1	1/16/75	Bullet, unfired, from a cartridge for 52 cal. Sharps carbine, 1859 or 1863, excavated	Ken Anderson, 9391 E. Broadway, Tucson, Az. 85719	Gift
75.6	75.6.2A–B	"	M1865 lance ferrule, excavated	"	"
75.7	75.7.1A–C	1/20/75	Plaster casts of the Abraham Lincoln life mask and hands, painted bronze	John Sparks, 3711 Cottage Rd., Prescott, Az. 86301	Gift
75.8	75.8.1A–B	1/23/75	Pr. of brass epaulettes, 1854 pattern	Annesley Doe, 5700 N. Camino Seco, Tucson, Az. 85718	Gift
75.9	L 75.9.1	1/27/75	M1876 Winchester rifle, cal. 45–60, lever action. (Replaces item stolen)	Arizona State Museum Univ. of Arizona, Tucson, Az. 85719	Ext. Loan
75.10	75.10.1A–C	1/16/75	3 piece charro buckskin suit, orange-brown w/ white trim	R.W. Johnson, P. O. Box 22, San Manuel, Az. 85631	Gift
75.11	75.11.1	1/22/75	M1833 suspenders, pr. of regulation, 1st Army issue	Allen Sparks, 27th E. 7th Stravenue, Tucson, Az. 85716	Gift
75.12	75.12.1	1/23/75	Cartridge belt, civilian, leather, VILLAESCUSA, TUCSON, A.T.	Paul Austin, 3000 S. Indiana, Tucson, Az. 85706	Trade

V.A.1.

HIRSHHORN MUSEUM AND SCULPTURE GARDEN * CATALOG RECORD

SI-2357
REV. 10-14-75

100. ACCESSION NUMBER: 105. PREVIOUS NUMBERS:

10. ARTIST: CROSS REFERENCE:
    ATTRIB/AFTER/PUB:
20. NATIONALITY: 25. SEX/ETHNIC GROUP:
30. LIFE DATES:
110. TITLE:
115. PREVIOUS TITLES:
120. DATE OF EXECUTION:
125. OBJECT CLASS:
130. MEDIUM/SUPPORT:
155. MEDIUM INDEX:
156. SUPPORT INDEX:
140. STATE:
150. EDITION:
160. DIMENSIONS: WEIGHT:
170. SIGNATURE: ☐ UNSIGNED
                  ☐ NO VISIBLE SIGNATURE
174. DATE: ☐ NOT DATED
                  ☐ NO VISIBLE DATE
175. ARTIST'S INSCRIPTIONS:

180. STYLE/PERIOD:
190. SUBJECT (GENERAL): ☐ ANIMAL ☐ FIGURE ☐ LANDSCAPE ☐ NONREPRESENTATIONAL ☐ STILL LIFE
                          ☐ ARCHITECTURE ☐ GROUP

SUBJECT (SPECIFIC):

REMARKS:

HMSG * CATALOG RECORD * PAGE TWO

ACCESSION NUMBER:
MOUNTING UNIT AT TIME OF CATALOGING:

CONDITION AT TIME OF CATALOGING:

SECONDARY INSCRIPTIONS:

200. ACQUISITION METHOD: ☐ GIFT OF ☐ BEQUEST OF ☐ PURCHASED FROM
                          ☐ JOSEPH H. HIRSHHORN (JH) ☐ JOSEPH H. HIRSHHORN FOUNDATION (F)
     ACQUISITION SOURCE:
205. ACQUISITION DATE:
210. CREDIT LINE:
220. CONFIDENTIAL:
225. RESTRICTION OF GIFT:
230. PROVENANCE METHOD: ☐ JH PURCHASED FROM ☐ GIFT TO JH FROM ☐ GIFT TO FOUNDATION FROM
     PROVENANCE SOURCE:
235. PROVENANCE DATE:
PRICE PAID:
INSURANCE VALUE ON ACQUISITION: DATE OF VALUATION:
CATALOGED BY: DATE: APPROVED BY: DATE:

V.B.1.

190

V.C.1.

ARIZONA HISTORICAL SOCIETY

Object: Spurs	Photo.: B & W ☐ Color ☐	Neg.: Slide	Catalog#: 76.12.2 AB
Date: 2/23/76			Access.#: 76.12

Source: Mabel F. Sourbee, 1353 E. Elm, Jerome, Az. 86301. Spurs were given to the donor by Tim Nolen on March 28, 1916, as a birthday gift. Donor lived in Oatman Flats on the John A. Sourbee homestead which was taken over by her father, Thomas W. Sourbee, in 1910.

Description: Pair of woman's spurs. Iron with silver overlay. Five point, star rowel. Silver sections are on the stud faces, on both sides and on the shank at the neck and at the rowel box. The silver is engraved with simple leaf motifs and the outside edge is bordered with simple, reciprocating fret patterns. The spurs are marked A and B. Spur A has half of the silver on one stud face missing. Spur B has one large piece of overlay partially detached. Both spurs show considerable wear. Good condition. Hist. Fig. or Place Card-Oatman Flats, Az.

Dimensions: 5 3/8" x 3 15/16" W, 13.7 x 10cm.

Circa: 3/28/1916

Cataloged By: MCA

Reference:

Accompanying Materials: See photograph of donor on her horse "Bird" in the AHS library collections.

Repair & Fumigation: Generalized pest control treatment—3/76.

Location: CLOSET 1 R3-A7

V.C.2.

17.1697	Painting	65B42.1
Chinese 1244 by Ch'en Jung, active c. 1235 — c. 1255	Southern Sung Dynasty (1127–1279) Nine Dragons Ink and slight color. Inscriptions and seals. Paper scroll, 0.463 x 10.964 meters	
	Francis Gardner Curtis Fund, June 14, 1917	

V.C.3.

1977-256-41a,b   OVERLAY GLASS   SNUFF BOTTLE
China
Ch'ing Dynasty (1644-1912)

SOURCE: Gift of Eugenia Fuller Atwood
SIZE: H. 2-3/4" (7 cm.) W. 2-1/8" (5.3 cm.)
CONDITION: One section of green glass chipped off at upper right on shoulder.
DESCRIPTION: Overlay glass body with milk-glass ground; dark-green cameo design of grapes with leaves and vines—squirrels eating grapes; fei tsui jade stopper with metal-bound lip/rim.
NOTE: See Document File for original notes on purchase of this bottle (No. 31) made by Mrs. Atwood's mother, who originally acquired the snuff bottles in this series.

CATALOGUERS: Solomon and Fischer.

V.B.2.

ARIZONA HISTORICAL SOCIETY
WORK SHEET

DATE: 2/23/76   CATALOG NO.: 76.12.2 AB
ACCESSION NO.: 76.12
NATURE OF ACCESSION: Gift
NAME & ADDRESS OF SOURCE: Mabel F. Sourbee, 1353 E. Elm, Jerome, Az. 86301
DATE COLLECTED BY DONOR, ETC.: Spurs given to the donor by Tim Nolen on her birthday, 3/28/16. She lived in Oatman Flats on the John A. Sourbee homestead which was taken over by her father, Thomas W. Sourbee, in 1910. Cattle & hay.
DESCRIPTION: Pair of woman's spurs. Iron w/ silver overlay. 5 point star rowel box. Silver sections are on the stud faces, on both sides and shank at neck and at rowel box. Silver is engraved w/ simple leaf motifs, the outside edge being bordered w/ a simple reciprocating fret pattern. Spurs A & B.

CONDITION: Good. Spur A has ½ of silver on one stud missing. Spur B has 1 large piece of overlay partially detached. Both show considerable wear.
REFERENCE:
DIMENSIONS: L-13.7, 5 3/8"; W-10, 3 15/16"
REPAIR, FUMIGATION, ETC.: 3/76
ACCOMPANYING MATERIALS & INFORMATION: See pic. of donor & horse "Bird" in AHS Lib. Collec.
ESTIMATED VALUE, APPRAISER:
OBJECT CARD: ✓   DONOR CARD: ✓   FIGURE/PLACE CARD: ✓   MARKED: ✓
PHOTO: 4/76   NEGATIVE: 4/76   GIFT ACK.: ✓   PROV. RECEIPT:
REGISTRAR:

V.D.1.

ARIZONA HISTORICAL SOCIETY

Source: Sourbee, Mabel F.   Mabel F. Sourbee, 1353 E. Elm, Jerome, Az. 86301.

Card # 1

Object	Catalog #	Date
Horsehair rope, brown, knot & tassel at one end Gift	76.12.1	2/23/76
Pair of woman's spurs, iron with silver overlay "	76.12.2 AB	"
Horse bridle, split ear style, nickeled brass spots on crown "	76.12.3	"

V.E.1.

ARTIST MATISSE, Henri   **TITLE AND MEDIUM** DANCE (First Version), oil   **MUSEUM NUMBER** 201.63   **LOCATION**

REMARKS

TAKEN BY OR SENT TO	DATE OUT	DATE RET'D
Main Lobby	5-69	—
Loan	1-66	3-69
Main Lobby	3-9-69	5-1-69
Storeroom C	5-15-69	
III, gal.	11-7-69	3-6-70
Outgoing loan - Paris	3-17-70	10-26-70
III - 8	10-27-70	11-10-72

V.E.1a.

History
Grafton Galleries, London, exh. "Second Post-Impressionist Exhibition", 1912, #185.
Berlin, exh. "Secession", 1912.
Pierre Matisse Gallery, New York, exh. "La Danse", 1936.
Boston Museum of Modern Art, Massachusetts, exh. "The Ballet", January 1938.
Arts Club of Chicago, Illinois, exh. "Henri Matisse 1896-1938", March-April 1939.
Exh. 85-91* (39.304).
Arts Club of Chicago, Illinois, exh. ("Origins of Modern Art", April 1940, #41.
The Virginia Museum of Fine Arts, Richmond, exh. "Collection of Walter P. Chrysler, Jr.", January 16-March 4, 1941, #117*.
Philadelphia Museum of Art, Pennsylvania, exh. "Collection of Walter P. Chrysler, Jr.", March 20-May 11, 1941, #117*.
Philadelphia Museum of Art, Pennsylvania, exh. "Henri Matisse Retrospective Exhibition of Paintings, Drawings and Sculpture", April 1-May 10, 1948, #20*. (Remained on loan to Museum until July 1955).

Matisse, Henri   Dance (first version)   201.63

V.C.4.

Accession Card Z No. 808-12

Date January 22, 1979

Field Museum of Natural History

GIFT, EXCHANGE, PURCHASE, COLLECTED, MUSEUM EXPEDITION

Credit to David Starr Jordan

Address: Dept. of Ichthyology, Calif. Academy of Sciences, Golden Gate Park, San Francisco, California 94118

Received from Dr. Seth Eugene Meek

Address (same as above)

Collector David Starr Jordan, Louis Agassiz

Date Collected Sept. 19, 1890

Locality Lake Michigan:Illinois:Chicago

Description

U.S.A.: ILLINOIS: COOK COUNTY: CHICAGO: LAKE MICHIGAN: 0.1 to 0.2 KM. EAST OF LOYOLA UNIVERSITY NORTH CAMPUS (ABOUT 7000 NORTH). DEPTH: 8-12 meters. TIME: 1930-2030. Depth of Capture: 3-4 meters. 16 foot semi-balloon trawl.

107517	Osmerus mordax	3 spec.
107518	Notropis hudsonius	16 spec.
107519	Rhinichthys cataractae	3 spec.
107520	Percopsis omiscomaycus	75 spec.
107521	Perca flavescens	13 spec.
107522	Etheostoma nigrum	1 spec.
107523	Cottus bairdi	1 spec.

Total Number of Specimens 112
Catalogue Numbers 107517 - 107523
Value of Material (estimated—actual) $23.00

Acknowledgment: ☐ Formal ☐ Letter ☒ Card
☐ None Sent ___ 19

Notes These specimens are being included in publication no. 2068 of Fieldiana: Zoology.

Signed M A Traylor / RKJ
       R K John   Chairman

Field Museum of Natural History

Date of Accession Jan. 22, 1979 No. 808-12

Department OF ZOOLOGY, DIVISION OF FISHES

HISTORICAL FILE

Catalogues of Collections
Letters and Memoranda concerning Specimens

Credit to David Starr Jordan

(Sender) Dr. Seth Eugene Meek

U.S.A.: ILLINOIS: COOK COUNTY: CHICAGO: LAKE MICHIGAN: 0.1 TO 0.2 KM. EAST OF LOYOLA UNIVERSITY NORTH CAMPUS (ABOUT 7000 NORTH). DEPTH: 8-12 METERS. TIME: 1930-2030. DEPTH OF CAPTURE: 3-4 METERS. 16 foot semi-balloon trawl.

7 species, 7 lots, 112 specimens

This packet may be taken for temporary use by officials of the Museum, and by them only. They must sign a receipt for it, and return within one month. If any paper is needed for permanent retention, a copy will be furnished upon application. When removed the receipt must be put in its place.

```
THE MUSEUM OF MODERN ART—LOAN RECORD SHEET    LENDER New York           MUS. NO. 76.621
                                                     (Cooper-Hewitt)    OLD NO.
EXHIBITION  THE NATURAL PARADISE: PAINTING IN
            AMERICA 1800-1950                 EXH. NO. 1148             LENDER NO.
ARTIST      Frederic Edwin Church             CAT. NO. 27*   p.18    PHOTO NO. lender
TITLE       Iceberg                 SIGNATURE   Not signed — if signed verso, not visible due to mat
MEDIUM      Pencil and oil on cardboard.  AND DATE                                     and backing
DATE        (1859)  Not dated
INSCRIPTIONS
SIZE
  Painting, drawing or print: Height: Sight 11 3/8" (28.7 cm)  Width: Sight 19" (47.8 cm)
  Sculpture:                  Height:                          Width:              Weight:
SHIPPING:
  Received: 8/11/76  via Hahn
  Box size:     Height: 24"    Width: 30"        Depth: 8"       Weight
  ✓Flat pack  ✓Wood, plywood top and bottom  Waterproof paper   Box may ride flat
  Slide box    Plywood          ✓Screws        Packed face up   Directional markings
  Tray box     Wood              Nails         Packed face down Special marking
  Internal braces               Wrapping glassine  Padding Ethafoam  Filling
  Special return instructions
  Returned: 12/8/76  via  Hahn
FRAME RECORD:
  Height 17 3/4"              Width 23 3/4"          Depth 1 1/8"
  Description & Condition:
  Reframing record:
  ✓Frame         Inner Fr.      Passpartout    ✓Mat          ✓Plexiglas       Glass
  Stretcher      Crossbars      Keys           Screweyes     Wire
  ✓Backing       Strainer       Label          Other:
                 Plates
  Corrugated cardboard
  REGISTRATION:
  ✓Loan Form     ✓Loan Rec.     ✓Custodian Bk.   ✓Lender Cd.    ✓Insur. Cancelled
  ✓Release 8257  ✓Rec. of Del.  ✓Conservation   ✓Lender Cd. Completed  ✓Rec. Bk.
  ✓Old Obj. Cd.  ✓Obj. Cd.      ✓Obj. Cd. Completed  ✓Cond. Photo
  REMARKS                                             CAT. BY TH    DATE: 8/11/76
  MF 714
```

VI.A.1.

```
ARIZONA HISTORICAL SOCIETY                                          Card # 1

Historical Figure or Place: Oatman Flats, Az.  Oatman Flats is located in
Maricopa County about 18 miles east of Agua Caliente.

Pertinent Cataloged Artifacts:
  Object & Description                                          Catalog #
  Pair of woman's spurs, iron with silver overlay. Used by Mabel F.   76.12.2 AB
  Sourbee while living on the John A. and Thomas W. Sourbee home-
  stead in Oatman Flats, 1916+.
  Split ear style horse bridle, nickeled brass spot trim. Same history 76.12.3
  as above.
```

V.F.1.

VI. LOAN RECORDS

In some museums, the lenders recorded in the source-of-acquisition file and copies of loan receipts are the only permanent records maintained for loans. In other museums more extensive records are maintained. See, for example, figures G.7, J.2, and K.1. The following records are maintained by the Museum of Modern Art.

VI.A.1. *Loan Record Sheet* (8½ by 11 in.). One form is prepared for each object borrowed by the museum. A copy is sent to the curatorial department, where it is used to prepare the exhibition catalogue. The original is retained in the registration department for use in making the two cards listed below. The form also provides a permanent record of packing and shipping information. A separate condition report is completed on each loan object.

VI.B.1. *Lender card* (4 by 6 in.). Each lender has a separate card, on which all loans are recorded. Information is continued on additional cards as needed.

VI.C.1. *Loan card* (5 by 8 in.). This permanent card is made for each loan and filed by artist, then title.

VII.A.1.

OBJECT RECORD
Department of Painting and Sculpture
HIRSHHORN MUSEUM AND SCULPTURE GARDEN
Smithsonian Institution

1 Artist:

2 Title of work:

3 Date: 4 Place executed:

5 Medium (as fully descriptive as possible):

6 If a cast or commercially fabricated work, please indicate foundry or factory:
number of this cast, total number in edition:
in what collections are other casts?

7 If the process of making this work is of special interest, the Museum would like a description:

8 Are there any special instructions for the installation or maintenance of this work?

9 If appropriate, please discuss title:

10 Is there any documentation you care to provide on the personal, social, or symbolic references in this work?

11 Are there any exceptional circumstances or incidents that relate to the making of this work or its subsequent history?

VII. MISCELLANEOUS FORMS AND RECORDS

Each museum maintains additional files and forms as required by its activities. See, for example, figures A.3, E1, E.5, H.3, P.8, and R.26-27. The Department of Painting and Sculpture at the Hirshhorn Museum and Sculpture Garden, Smithsonian Institution, which acquires works by living artists, finds the following form useful.

VII.A.1. *Object Record* (8½ by 11 in.). This form is sent out by the curatorial department at the time of cataloguing. Additional questions are listed on the reverse. The original becomes part of the museum collection archives.

ARTIST	EX'N. & CAT. NUMBERS	TITLE	MUSEUM NO.	DATE REC'D	DATE RET'D
Guimard	NY only 921	Tea cloth, embroidered/ embroidered silk.	70.104	2/5/70	5/11/70
"	NY only	Panel for wedding gown,/ linen.	70.105	"	5/11/70
Misc.	984	Exh.: Education of an Arch-/itect	71.604	11-71	1-72
Church	1148-26*	Iceberg, o/cardboard	76.620	8/11/76	12/8/76
"	-27*	Iceberg, pencil and oil/ cardboard	76.621	8/11/76	"
"	-24	Icebergs, o/cardboard	76.622	8/11/76	"
"	-25*	Icebergs, pencil and white/ gouache on paper	76.623	8/11/76	"
Moran	-104*	Cliffs of the Rio Virgin/ watercolor, gouache, pencil/paper	76.624	8/11/76	"
Crane		PEACOCK GARDEN, wallpaper.	76.954	10/8/76	12-1-76
Zen		Desk, wood, leather, inlaid/ stones.	76.955	1/8/76	" " "

NAME   NEW YORK CITY: Cooper-Hewitt Museum of Design, (Cooper Square.)   ADDRESS   9 East 90th Street, N.Y./ N.Y., 10028 2.

VI.B.1.

Artist CHURCH, Frederic Edwin   Title ICEBERG   Museum No. 76.621

Lent by Cooper-Hewitt Museum of Design

Cat. Acknowledgment Cooper-Hewitt Museum of Design, Smithsonian Institution, New York   Exhibition No. 1148   Catalog No. 27*

Date (1859)

Medium Pencil and oil on cardboard   ☐ Frame ☐ Mat
                                                     ☐ Inner Fr. ☐ Glass Plexiglas

Size Sight 11 3/8 x 19" (28.7 x 47.8 cm.)

Ins. Value   S.P. nfs   Signed ns

Remarks

Photo No.   Cooper-Hewitt Museum of Design

Reproduced   P.18

Condition (see over)   See Loan Record Sheet

VI.C.1.

VIII. SHIPPING DOCUMENTS

Airwaybills and bills of lading are the basic shipping documents. The forms that appear below and the explanations of them are adapted from articles in *Registrars' Report*, 1:3 (Oct. 1977), 6–7, and 1:5 (Dec. 1977), 8–10, respectively.

VIII.A. AIRWAYBILLS:
The airwaybill is the basic shipping document for air transport. As the object moves from origin to destination, responsible parties throughout the transit add data to the airwaybill. To read an airwaybill, one must understand the meaning and purpose of the various information areas. A sample bill (6¾ by 8½ in.) has been reproduced; the superimposed numerals correspond to the numbered descriptions that follow. The sections of the airwaybill are numbered in the order in which the form is filled out. Unexplained sections are not unimportant but are presumed to be clear without discussion.

VIII.A.1. *Airwaybill.*

1. "Non negotiable" means that the airwaybill cannot be exchanged for currency.
2. This number, known as the airwaybill number, is crucial, as it identifies the shipment for the air freight company.
3. The date that the airwaybill is made out is usually filled in by the shipper.
4. A "prepaid" shipment will be paid by the shipper either before or after completion of the transit.
5. A "collect" shipment will be paid by the consignee (person to whom the shipment is being sent). In most cases, the consignee will be billed and will not be required to pay the charges at the time of delivery.
6. This box is checked when the charges are to be billed to a third party, one who is neither the shipper nor the consignee (see number 9).
7. The origin point of the shipment must include the complete name and address, with zip code, of the shipper.
8. The destination point of the shipment must include the complete name and address, with zip code, of the consignee.
9. If a third party, neither the shipper nor the consignee, is to pay the charges (see number 6), the third party's complete name and address are entered here.
10. This figure is the actual number of boxes received and handled, not the number of pieces within.
11. The contents of a museum shipment should be described with the minimum of information required for the forwarder to apply the proper tariff code. Any special box numbers used for easy identification can also be noted here.
12. The weight of the box or boxes listed in number 11 is given here. In most cases, this is the total weight of the shipment. If diverse commodities are shipped together, weights of the individual boxes are given, but it is generally best to pack and ship diverse commodities separately.
13. The "declared value" is the value that the shipper assigns to the shipment; it is not necessarily the actual value of the item(s) being shipped. Many institutions have their own transit insurance, and to declare full value on the airwaybill would constitute purchase of double insurance (see number 25). In most cases, the value declared will be the total amount the shipper can expect to be reimbursed by the air freight company in the event of loss or damage. The museum's insurance company can advise what percentage of value should be declared, though in most cases a declaration of nominal value is made as a safe-handling precaution.
14. Special instructions are notations the shipper wishes to bring to the attention of the forwarder or consignee, e.g., deadlines or special arrangements like priority service or guaranteed air freight.
15. This number is usually the shipper's purchase order or identification number.
16. The airwaybill should be signed at the shipper's dock by the individual who is responsible for releasing freight to the air freight forwarder's driver.
17. The box checked indicates the point at which the forwarder assumes responsibility for the shipment, whether at the shipper's dock or at the forwarder's terminal. This information is used by the forwarder to calculate charges.
18. This space is for the signature of the driver making the pickup at the shipper's dock.
19. This space is completed when more than one shipment for a single customer is picked up from one shipper at any one time.
20. Dimensional weight is calculated by the air freight company for low-density shipments, i.e., shipments that occupy more cargo space than their actual weight would normally require. When greater than the actual weight, the dimensional weight is used as the basis for the cost of the shipment.
21. The forwarder fills in here the code for the destination airport, e.g., "SFO" for San Francisco.
22. The cost of air transport to be charged to the customer is entered here.
23. The cost of transit from the shipper's dock to the air freight terminal (the origin airport) is entered here.
24. The cost of transit from the destination airport terminal to the consignee's dock is entered here.
25. The "valuation charge" calculations are based upon the value declared by the shipper (number 13). The freight company assumes the cost of insurance for shipments up to a set nominal value; for amounts over this value, the customer will be billed for the additional insurance premium.
26 and 27. Origin and destination charges apply when the forwarder must contract out to an "over-the-road" trucker. In each metropolitan area, forwarders have transport rights up to a specific distance from the city. If a pickup or delivery must be made outside that circumference, another trucker must be used, thus incurring extra charges for origin or destination points.
28. Total charges due the forwarder by the payer are entered here.

VIII.A.1.

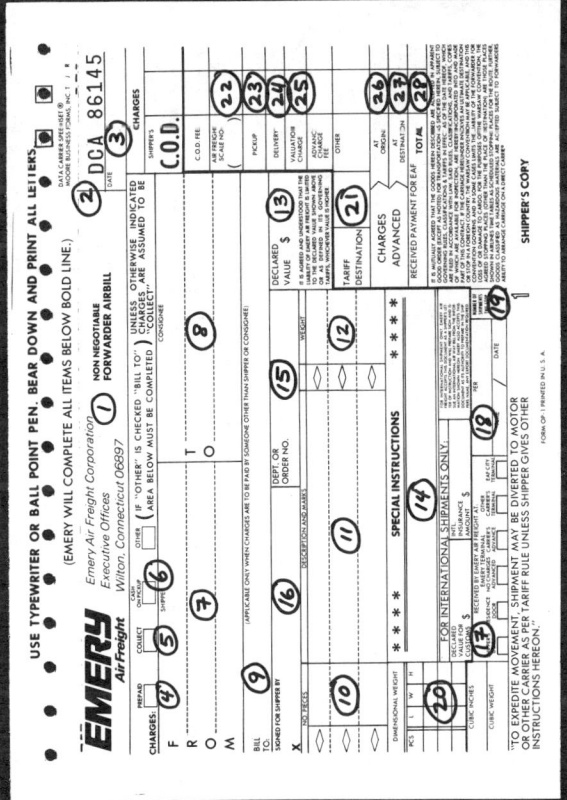

VIII.B.1.

VIII.B. BILLS OF LADING: The bill of lading is the basic document in the truck transport industry. The form is filled out by the carrier and is signed at shipment origin and destination. Contract terms and conditions are listed on the reverse. Three types of bills of lading (all 8½ by 11 in.) are reproduced here. The superimposed numerals correspond to the following numbered explanations. Unexplained sections are not unimportant but are presumed to be clear without discussion.

VIII.B.1. *Bill of lading for household goods shipped locally or intrastate.*

1. The bill or lading number identifies the intrastate shipment for the carrier.
2. The origin point of the shipment must be correct and complete.
3. The destination point of the shipment must be correct and complete.
4. The driver is required to enter start, finish, and specific activity times. The shipper should check these notations before signing the bill of lading.
5. The information filled in here is used for calculating charges for intrastate moves greater than 50 miles. For such moves, charges are based on the actual weight of the shipment or according to space reservation (the amount of space occupied in the van). Museum objects are usually shipped on a space reservation basis, not only because they generally weigh less than the same volume of household goods, but also to ensure that nothing is packed on top of the boxes or within the amount of space specified for the shipment.
6. Additional charges are entered in these boxes as applicable.
7. The information filled in here is used for calculating charges of intrastate

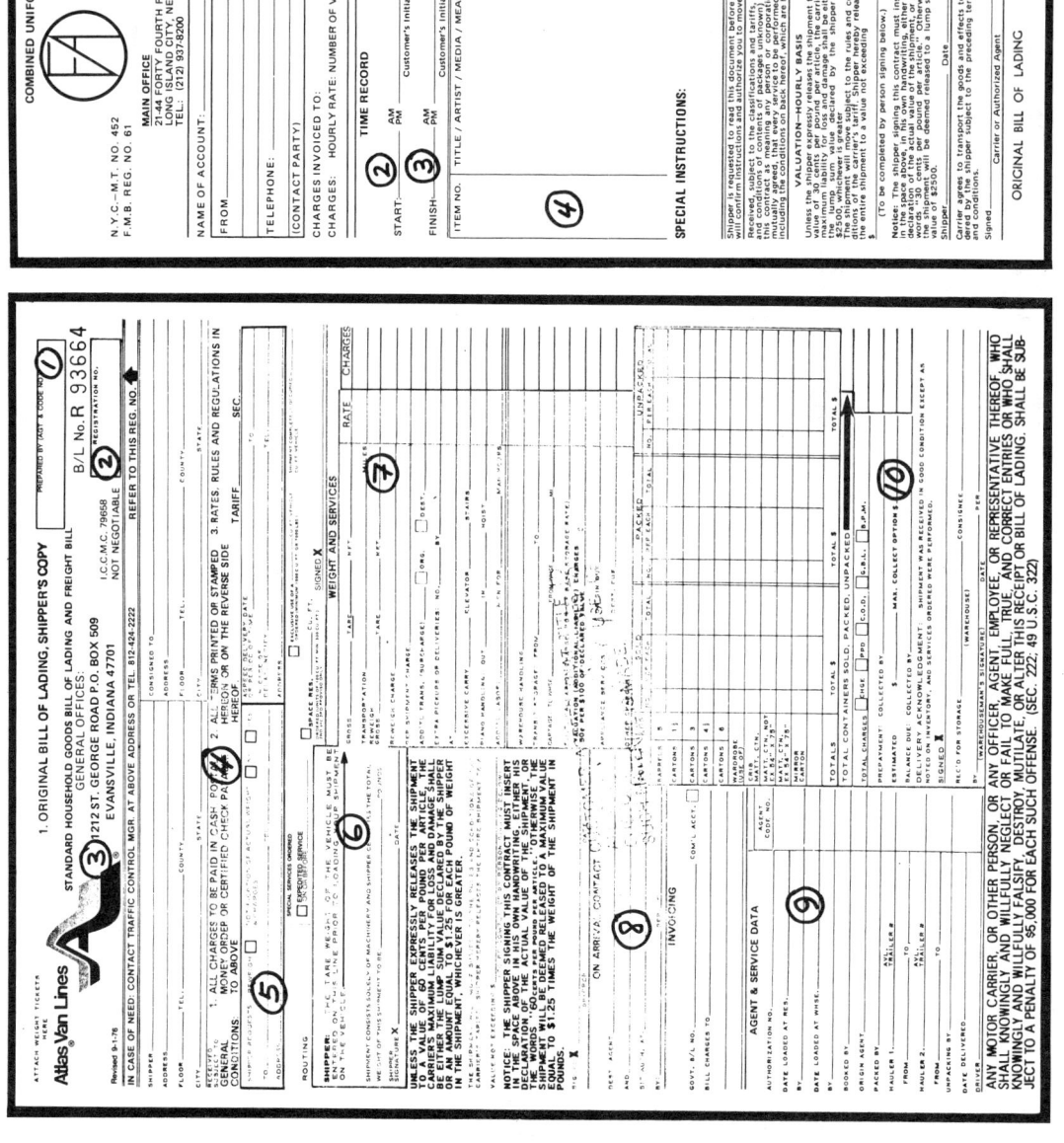

VIII.B.2.

VIII.B.3.

[Form image]

IX.A.1. *Declaration for Free Entry of Articles for Colleges, Religious Institutions, Etc.* (Customs Form 3321) (8 by 10½ in.), required for the duty-free entry of dutiable materials imported by cultural, scientific, and educational institutions.

moves under 50 miles. Complete moves within a 50-mile radius are charged by the hour.

8. For "declared value," see number 13 under airwaybills.

9. The representative of the institution releasing the shipment to the carrier signs here.

VIII.B.2. *Bill of lading for household goods shipped interstate.*

1. The bill of lading number is issued by the local agent. In the case of Atlas Van Lines, whose form is used for this example, this number is used only to keep track of bills issued and does not relate to dispatch or billing.

2. The registration number is used by the carrier for tracing and shipment identification.

3. Traffic control manager is another name for central dispatch.

4. The shipper can request a copy of the carrier's tariff to check the billing.

5. The information filled in here applies to actual weight shipments (as opposed to space reservation shipments). A reweigh, done after the van is loaded, provides the shipper with another means of checking billing accuracy. It must be requested in advance.

6. The tare weight here is the weight of the empty vehicle.

7. The mileage is not actual mileage, but is based on a specific mileage guide filed with the Interstate Commerce Commission.

8. If a shipment requires storage in transit prior to final delivery, the name of the warehouse authorized for storage is entered here.

9. The identification of the agent and carrier personnel involved with the shipment and dates of service performed are entered here.

10. This line pertains to the collection of charges for COD shipments. If the actual cost is greater than the estimated cost, the carrier may collect only a percentage of the excess upon delivery. The remainder must be billed to the payer.

VIII.B.3. *Bill of lading for museum objects shipped locally.*

1. The carrier reference number should appear on all correspondence relating to a specific shipment.

2. The time of the carrier's arrival at shipment origin is entered here.

3. The time of the carrier's departure from the shipment destination is entered here.

4. If the objects being collected are for a specific exhibition, the numbers entered here might correspond to catalogue numbers, or these may simply be numbers assigned consecutively by the carrier.

5. Under Exceptions, an object's condition and any special circumstances are noted.

IX. FORMS REQUIRED FOR IMPORTING AND EXPORTING

The following customs forms are samples of the kinds of documents required by U.S. Customs and the Department of Commerce for importing and exporting museum objects.

Customs Form 3325
DEPARTMENT OF THE TREASURY
10.31, 10.34, 10.49, 10.69, C. R.
(3-20-75)

DECLARATION ON ENTRY OF THEATRICAL EFFECTS FOR TEMPORARY USE OR OF WORKS OF ART, ETC., FOR TEMPORARY OR PERMANENT EXHIBITION

(Sec. 308 (11) and (12) and paragraph 1809, Tariff Act of 1930, as amended)

U.S. CUSTOMS SERVICE

DISTRICT No. .... PORT .... , ... (Date)

I, ... , declare that I am the ....
(Manager or proprietor)
of a theatrical exhibition arriving from abroad, and that the theatrical scenery, properties, and apparel covered by the annexed entry are imported for temporary use by me in theatrical exhibitions in the United States, and are not for any other person nor for sale.

I, ... , declare that I am not a resident of the United States; that
I am a .... arriving from abroad, and that the articles covered
(Professional artist, lecturer, or scientist)
by the annexed entry are brought by me to the United States for use by me for temporary exhibition and in illustration, promotion, and encouragement of art, science, or industry in the United States, and not for sale, nor for the account of any association or corporation engaged in or connected with business of a private or commercial character.

I, ... , declare that I am
(Name of institution) (Official use)
of .... and that said institution is established for the encouragement of the arts, sciences, agriculture, or education, and that the articles covered by the annexed entry are imported for exhibition by said institution at .... and not for any other
(Place of exhibition)
purpose nor for sale.

....
(Signature) (Capacity)

(Execute applicable declaration only) ....
(Address)

GPO 956-122

EXHIBITION BOND

(To be taken on entry of articles under the provisions of schedule 8, part 5B, Tariff Schedules of the United States)

Know All Men By These Presents, That*—

.... , as principal
of ....
and* .... of ....
and* ....
as sureties, are held and firmly bound unto the UNITED STATES OF AMERICA in the sum of
.... dollars ($..................................),
for the payment of which we bind ourselves, our heirs, executors, administrators, successors, and assigns, jointly and severally, firmly by these presents.
Witness our hands and seals this .... day of .... 19......
Whereas, the above-bounden principal imported at the port of .... filed at the port of .... dated ....
certain articles described below and in entry No. ....
Articles: ....

....

....

Now, Therefore, The Condition of This Obligation Is Such, That —

(1) If the said principal shall not sell, expose for sale, transfer, or use any of the said articles within 5 years after the date of entry contrary to schedule 8, part 5B, Tariff Schedules of the United States and the regulations issued thereunder; or in default thereof if the obligors shall pay to the District Director of Customs the full amount of duties imposed by law thereon;

(2) And if the above-bounden principal shall furnish the District Director of Customs all invoices, certificates, declarations, oaths, and other documents or proofs required by law and regulations in connection with this importation and entry thereof, in the form an .... within the time required by law and regulations, or any lawful extension thereof; or if in the event of failure to comply with any or all of the conditions of this section the obligors shall pay to the District Director of Customs such amounts as liquidated damages as may be demanded by him in accordance with the law and regulations, not exceeding the amount of this obligation;

Then this obligation shall be void; otherwise it shall remain in full force and effect.
Signed, sealed, and delivered in the presence of—

.... (SEAL)
(Address) (Principal)

.... (SEAL)
(Name) (Surety)
(Address)

.... (SEAL)
(Name) (Surety)
(Address)

(Name)

*If the principal or surety is a corporation, the name of the State in which incorporated should also be shown.

Department of the Treasury
United States Customs Service
10.49, 25.4, C.R.

Customs Form 7565 (3-20-75)

IX.B.1. *Declaration on Entry of Theatrical Effects for Temporary Use or of Works of Art, Etc. for Temporary or Permanent Exhibition* (Customs Form 3325) (8 by 10½ in.), required for duty-free entry under exhibition bond.

IX.C.1. *Exhibition Bond* (Customs Form 7565) (8½ by 11 in.), required for duty-free entry under permanent exhibition bond.

PART 2 SPECIFIC APPLICATIONS

Articles in part 2 offer special information on the work of the museum registrar. They not only amplify the procedures and techniques described in part 1, but they demonstrate how these procedures and techniques have been adapted to meet the needs of individual museums of various sizes and kinds.

The part begins with a discussion of a procedure for acquiring works of art and the special circumstances of partial gifts. A series of articles follows that describes aspects of the registrar's work at various kinds of museums, namely art, history, natural history, and science. Four articles on the computerization of registration records have been included in recognition of the growing interest in automated record processing. These are followed by guidelines for the handling and packing of museum objects generally, and finally by a discussion of the registrar's role in a museum building program.

It has not been possible to include articles on every aspect of a registrar's responsibilities in all museum situations. The selection here, however, does attempt to represent the variety of those responsibilities and to suggest ways in which the methods of part 1 can be tailored to a museum's specific needs.

Fig. A.1.
Form for a deed of gift (8½ by 11 in.), Museum of Modern Art.

Fig. A.2.
Museum label (3 by 4 in.), Museum of Modern Art.

Fig. A.3.
Card maintained on each work in which the museum has a remainder or fractional interest (4 by 6 in.), Museum of Modern Art.

A PROCEDURE FOR ACQUIRING OBJECTS, INCLUDING PARTIAL GIFTS, AT THE MUSEUM OF MODERN ART

BETSY B. JONES

The article that follows outlines briefly the steps through which each work passes on its way to becoming part of the painting and sculpture collection at the Museum of Modern Art. The procedures discussed are those of the Department of Painting and Sculpture, but other curatorial departments at the museum (except film, which, because of its special nature, has its own guidelines) also follow these or similar practices.

Basic Procedure

As is customary at most art museums, acquisitions by all collections at the Museum of Modern Art must receive formal approval from the Board of Trustees or a duly authorized committee of the board before they are accessioned as part of the permanent collections. Since the museum may acquire several thousand objects in a year, it is impossible for the trustees to see each one. This responsibility is therefore delegated to a system of committees, one for each curatorial department, chaired by a trustee and made up of trustees and other individuals who are experts in each collecting field or who are knowledgeable about or particularly interested in it. The committees have the professional advice of the curatorial staffs of each department.

Before being shown to such a committee, however, all works proposed for acquisition—whether by the staff or members of the public—are studied by the curatorial staff. The staff has discretionary power to select from the many gifts offered and purchases proposed those they feel are most relevant and valuable to the collection. The resulting selection may include works that do not have the unanimous approval of the staff. A member of the public who has proposed an acquisition the staff has decided not to recommend may, if he or she wishes, ask to have the committee review this decision.

The Committee on Painting and Sculpture meets at regular intervals during the year, normally the day before a meeting of the Board of Trustees so that decisions can be formally reported to the trustees promptly. At its meeting, the committee is given an agenda of topics for discussion or report, including a list of contributions to purchase funds received since the last meeting. In addition, members are provided with a list of all pertinent data—name of artist, title of work, date of execution, medium, source, and price where relevant—on works they will be considering. They are also given a list of current purchase fund balances so that they will know what money is available for any purchases they may be asked to vote on. All works to be discussed are present at the committee meeting unless for good reason that is not possible; for instance, the work may be on exhibition in another part of the city, country, or world, or it may be too large, too heavy, too fragile, or too unmanageable to be brought to the committee's meeting room or other available viewing space in the building. In such cases, the work is examined in slide or photograph, and the committee may elect to approve it tentatively or in principle only until it can actually be seen. In any case, when the work is finally visible at the museum, the committee is asked to view it.

Members of the curatorial staff discuss each work before the committee, giving the considerations that make the staff believe it is or is not a desirable acquisition, such as its quality, its relation to the whole collection, its historical importance, and its quality or value in relation to other works by the same artist or from the same period already in the collection. The committee then considers the proposal and votes whether to acquire the work.

In addition to its museum collection—the body of works included in its catalogues and exhibited in its galleries—the painting and sculpture collection also maintains a study collection, consisting of works acquired more for their historical relevance or value to students and scholars than for their aesthetic interest. Such works are not listed in published catalogues and are, in general, not exhibited in the museum galleries; however, they are reviewed by the committee periodically and may be shifted to the museum collection at a future time. A donor offering a work deemed appropriate for the study collection is so informed so that the gift may be withdrawn if the donor feels it would be more useful to another institution.

The Committee on Painting and Sculpture also sees all works in the collection that the staff feels should be disposed of, perhaps because similar but better works by the same artists have been acquired subsequently or because a work no longer seems appropriate to the collection. The disposal of a work that has once been part of the museum collection requires not only approval of the committee but also approval by formal action of the Board of Trustees, which must be shown the work when this approval is requested. It should be noted that the museum does not accept gifts if the donors stipulate that the works must be kept in perpetuity, since it does not feel it should bind future trustees with what may prove to be onerous limitations. (See figure A.1.) Instead, the donor is asked to provide the names of other museums to which the gift should be offered in the event that the museum no longer wishes to retain it. Another policy of the museum prohibits the sale of works by living American artists. However, exchanges instigated by living American artists or approved by them are undertaken on occasion. When a work is sold or exchanged, the proceeds of the sale or the new work acquired by exchange always bears the name of the donor of the work disposed of. For instance, the credit line of the new work might read "John Doe Fund" if it is a purchase, or "Gift of John Doe (by exchange)" if it is acquired through trading.

At the trustees meeting that follows the committee meeting, a report is made by the committee chairman, and some or all of the new acquisitions are shown to the trustees. The chairman sends a formal receipt of gift accompanied by a letter of thanks on behalf of the Board of Trustees to the donor of each gift that has been accepted. Members of the staff are responsible for acting on other decisions of the committee, such as those involving purchase negotiations or notification to a donor that his gift was accepted for the study collection or was not accepted.

Immediately after the trustees meeting an agenda that has been marked to show the decisions about each work considered is signed by the director of the Department of Painting and Sculpture and sent to the registrar, who then assigns accession numbers to all new acquisitions.

Minutes of the meeting are prepared by the staff and submitted to the committee chairman for approval before distribution. They are accompanied by a final acquisitions list reflecting all of the committee's decisions. This list constitutes the formal record of acquisition for the registrar. The minutes and the full acquisitions list are sent to committee members, the curatorial staff of the department concerned, the registrar, and various other staff members, including the director of the museum, who regularly attends the committee meetings. In a slightly abbreviated form, the list alone is sent to all trustees and to members of the staff not directly concerned but who should be kept informed of new acquisitions.

The acquisitions list contains the basic data about each work: accession number, name of artist, title of work, date of execution, medium, form for credit line, price paid if a purchase, and insurance value. Since this list is usually issued before each item has been fully studied, some information, such as date of execution, medium, or even credit line, is subject to change. Nevertheless, the list serves as the basis for fuller documentation and provides an immediate inventory of acquisitions with accession numbers, which is extremely helpful to the registrar as well as to the curators. In addition to acquisitions, the list records decisions on works that have been approved for elimination from the collection (these are listed again when they have actually been disposed of), extended (i.e., long-term) loans received or returned, works accepted in principle or tentatively, works considered but not approved for acquisition, and those on which decision was postponed.

The registrar next proceeds to record each acquisition as fully as possible on a work sheet, which is then sent to the Department of Painting and Sculpture. The curators are responsible for adding pertinent data not available to the Office of the Registrar and for returning the work sheets so that final records can be prepared.

Accessioning and Insuring Partial Gifts

Partial gifts are of two kinds: those in which the museum is given a remainder interest and the donor retains a life (or term) interest, and those in which the museum is given a present fractional interest and the donor retains the remaining partial interest. The immediate tax deductibility of remainder interest gifts was essentially discontinued under the Tax Reform Act of 1969, but the gift of a present fractional interest in a work of art is still deductible.

In accessioning such gifts, it has been the practice to assign an accession number upon receipt of the first deed of gift, even though the museum's share may be small. A museum label is attached to the stretcher or protective backing of a painting, or in any inconspicuous spot on a piece of sculpture. (See figure A.2.) If the work cannot be brought to the museum, the label is mailed to the donor with the request that it be attached to the work. The label identifies the work and its accession number and states what the museum's equity in it is at the date of accession. Filed in the museum's vault together with the original copy of the deed of gift is a photograph of each work to which the museum does not have full title, so that at the death of the donor there will be no question as to the identity of the work. The registrar maintains a separate card file of all the works in which the museum has a remainder or fractional interest. (See figure A.3.)

Fractional interests must be conveyed by a duly acknowledged deed or equivalent document, and each additional fraction given requires a new deed. In an optional paragraph of the deed, the donor may undertake to execute a codicil to his or her will bequeathing the museum any remaining fraction still owned by the donor at time of death. (See figure A.4.) The existence of such a codicil is a valuable guarantee, since without the codicil the museum may find itself involved in joint ownership—and possible controversy—with the donor's heirs, even though a fractional gift to a public institution would seem to imply an intention to give full title eventually. An institution receiving a fractional interest in a work of art must physically possess it for that part of each year proportionate to its ownership (e.g., for one-half interest, six months' possession) or the donor's tax deductibility will be jeopardized.

Insurance of works in which a museum has a partial interest will be handled differently, according to the policies of each museum and its insurance company. The Museum of Modern Art's insurance policy, which is nonreporting (see chapter 9), permits it to insure only its share of any such gifts (unless of course the work is temporarily in its possession, in which case the donor's share is automatically covered by the museum). This arrangement seems practical and reasonable. Since the museum has no physical control over a work in which the donor retains a life interest, it should not be responsible for insuring the life interest. In the case of a fractional gift, where both parties share outright ownership, the museum should of course be consulted about the use and treatment of the work in the same way that joint owners of any other kind of property would act in concert.

Fig. A.4.
Form for a deed of gift of a fractional interest in a work of art (8½ by 11 in.), Museum of Modern Art.

```
FORM FOR A DEED OF GIFT OF A FRACTIONAL INTEREST IN A WORK OF ART

KNOW ALL MEN BY THESE PRESENTS:

        That I, _____, of (city, county, state), desiring to further the pur-
poses of The Museum of Modern Art, New York, New York, do hereby, by way of gift,
transfer and assign to The Museum of Modern Art, its successors and assigns, an
undivided ____ percent ( %) present interest in my (painting, sculpture, etc.), by
_____, entitled, _____, and executed in (date), retaining to myself the
other ____ percent ( %) present interest.

        This Deed transfers to The Museum of Modern Art, its successors and
assigns, possession, dominion and control of said _____ for ____ percent ( %) of
every year hereafter, and creates a tenancy in common in said _____ between The
Museum of Modern Art and myself.

        I further undertake to provide in a Codicil to my Last Will and Testament
that if at the time of my death I have any proprietary interest in said _____
that I devise and bequeath such proprietary interest to The Museum of Modern Art
absolutely and forever.

        IN WITNESS WHEREOF, I have executed this Deed of Gift this ____ day of
_____, 19___.

                                                (signature) _____
STATE OF _____)
                    ) ss:
COUNTY OF _____)
        On this ____ day of _____, 19___, before me personally came
_____, known to me to be the person described in and who executed the
foregoing Deed of Gift, and duly acknowledged to me that he executed the same.

                                                (Notary Public) _____
```

A CLASSIFICATION SYSTEM FOR ART OBJECTS

WINIFRED KENNEDY

A situation occasionally presents itself in which a director or registrar is faced with the problem of recording a collection that has been built up over many years, possibly over a quarter of a century or more, but has never been catalogued. The records available may be so inadequate that long and patient research is required to ascertain the data prerequisite to registration. The usual method of assigning accession number by acquisition date may then prove impractical.

The Walters Art Gallery, housing a collection of over 20,000 objects bequeathed to the city of Baltimore by Henry Walters in 1931, presented such a dilemma. The system instituted at the Walters for the accessioning of this large and diversified collection may be of interest to those whose collections offer similar problems. It is not, of course, recommended in instances where the established practice of accessioning by acquisition date and running numbers is applicable.

The Walters Art Gallery based its system of accessioning objects of art on a method for classifying and cataloguing photographs of works of art initiated by the Metropolitan Museum of Art and subsequently adopted for the same purpose at the Fogg Art Museum. This method divides the arts by classes and further subdivides them geographically and chronologically. In the case of the Walters Art Gallery, the method originally applied to cataloguing photographs was simplified and adapted to serve as a system for accessioning and classifying the actual collections. Our revision of the system for works of art, as set forth below, employs a two-digit number to denote the class within which an object falls. Running numbers within each class—21.1, 21.2, 21.3, etc.—are used to identify the individual items. This method differs from the customary system of accession by date solely in that the class number is substituted for the year of acquisition. When no category designation is indicated, the space has been left to allow for new fields or media as required.

In addition to making it possible to proceed with the work of registration without first establishing acquisition dates for all objects, this method was found to have other advantages. It permitted us to retain as accession numbers the catalogue numbers long associated with our paintings. It automatically classified objects and records in a logical sequence that facilitated the task of marking and cataloguing—a task that, as a result, could be handled by several people without the risk of duplicating numbers—and made it easier to trace numbers that had been rubbed or obliterated in handling. Furthermore, during the early stages of cataloguing, the cards could be easily located for reference or for the addition of such new information as further bibliographic material, comments of visiting scholars, notes concerning restoration, and location changes. This

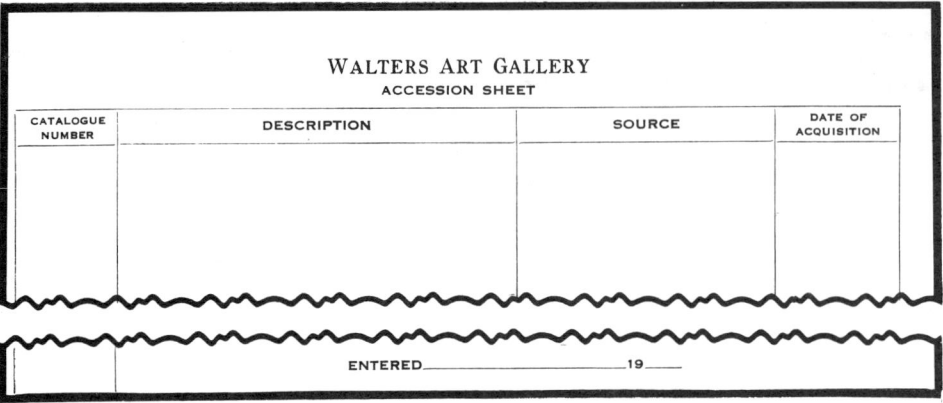

Fig. B.1.
Page from the accessions book, showing entries grouped by catalogue number (8½ by 11 in.), Walters Art Gallery.

method also enabled us to keep the registration numbers for many classes of objects down to five, or at most six, digits. Very small objects will not permit the use of more than three or four digits. The first two, being the same for all objects within a class, could be left off if necessary. A small gem, for example, need carry only its serial number, the 42 indicating its class being omitted. (See below.)

As set up at the Walters Art Gallery, the system calls for a minimum of three 4-by-6-inch catalogue cards, with photographs printed on the backs, for each object—one for the numerical index, another for the location chart, and the third for the classified index. It also calls for an accessions book (a Typofax loose-leaf record book, which can be permanently locked when all entries have been completed). The entries are listed in the book in the same order as in the numerical index, the number being placed at the left of the page. (See figure B.1.) This book constitutes a permanent record of the collection as it existed at the time of Mr. Walters's death. A second accessions book, in which to record objects acquired since the collection was taken over by the city in 1934, has also been established. In this book, additions to the collection are entered by acquisition date and the classification number is placed at the right of the page. (See figure B.2.)

Classification for Art Objects

10. MANUSCRIPTS
    11. Illuminated manuscripts
    15. Holograph manuscripts (letters, deeds, documents, etc.)
20. SCULPTURE
    21. Ancient Near East (Asia)
    22. Ancient Egypt
    23. Classical (Ancient in Europe)
    24. Near East (Muhammadan)
    25. Oriental (China, Japan, etc.)
    26. Africa and Oceania
    27. Post-classical in Europe
    28. America
    29. American Indian (includes Pre-Columbian, South America, etc.)
30. PAINTINGS AND DRAWINGS
    31. Ancient Near East (Asia)
    32. Ancient Egypt
    33. Classical (Ancient in Europe)
    34. Near East (Muhammadan)
    35. Oriental (China, Japan, etc.)
    36.
    37. Europe and America
    38. Miniatures
    39.
40. WORK IN MINERAL STUFFS
    41. Stone (includes alabaster, rock crystal, marble when not under no. 20)

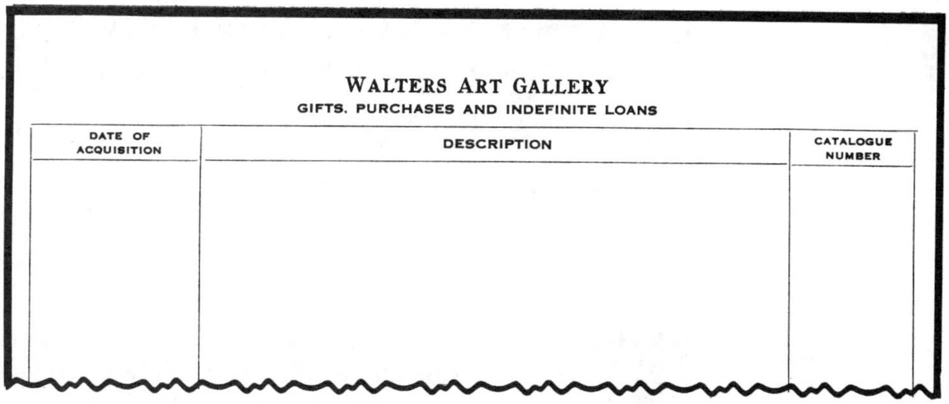

B: A CLASSIFICATION SYSTEM FOR ART OBJECTS

*Fig. B.2.
Page from the accessions book, showing entries grouped by date of acquisition (8½ by 11 in.), Walters Art Gallery.*

WALTERS ART GALLERY
GIFTS, PURCHASES AND INDEFINITE LOANS

DATE OF ACQUISITION	DESCRIPTION	CATALOGUE NUMBER

42. Gems (includes Oriental jades, Egyptian scarabs, seals, stamps, etc.)
43. Mosaics and Cosmati
44. Enamels (includes metalwork when decorated with enamel)
45. Niello
46. Glass (stained and painted)
47. Glass (cut and other)
48. Ceramics (all ceramics except as under no. 49)
49. Oriental ceramics

50. WORK IN METALS
    51. Arms and armor
    52. Iron and steel
    53. Brass and copper
    54. Bronze (includes ormolu)
    55. Pewter and lead
    56. Other metals
    57. Goldsmiths' and silversmiths' work (includes snuffboxes, jewelry, etc.)
    58. Timepieces (clocks and watches)
    59. Coins and medals

60. WORK IN WOOD
    61. Woodcarving (statuettes, altarpieces, etc.)
    62. Painted wood (mummy cases, coffins, etc.)
    63. Church furniture
    64. Wood, decorative (carved panels, ceilings, doors, etc.)
    65. Domestic furniture
    66. Vehicles
    67. Lacquer, inlay, boulle, marquetry, etc. (except when furniture)
    68. Gourds
    69. Baskets and wickerwork

70. WORK IN IVORY, LEATHER, ETC.
    71. Ivory and bone
    72. Tortoiseshell, mother-of-pearl, coral, horn, etc.
    73. Leather
    74. Amber
    75. Wax
    76. Composition
    77. Papier mâché and paper manufactures
    78. Stucco
    79. Mummies

80. TEXTILES AND LACES
    81. Carpets and rugs
    82. Tapestry
    83. Textiles
    84. Lace
    85.
    86. Costumes and accessories
    87.
    88.
    89.

90. PRINTS AND PRINTED BOOKS
    91. Incunabula
    92. Printed books after 1500
    93. Prints
    94.
    95. Japanese prints
    96.
    97.
    98.
    99.

CLASSIFYING PAINTINGS, DRAWINGS, AND PRINTS BY MEDIA, WITH A NOTE ON CLASSIFYING CONSTRUCTIONS

LAWRENCE J. MAJEWSKI

The descriptive terms involving media that are used in classifying objects of art can be of considerable value, particularly to the student interested in the creative process and to those responsible for maintaining the good health of the work of art.

"Medium" is a term used by artists in a variety of connotations. It is, variously, (1) the mode of expression or technique employed by an artist, e.g., etching, painting, sculpture; (2) the actual instrument or material used by an artist, e.g., oil paint, metal, chiseled stone; (3) the technique or method of application involved in using these materials (although almost synonymous with (1), this is rather a subdivision of it; for instance, painting might be subdivided into such techniques as palette knife, splatter, impressionism; it will not be discussed here); or (4) the binding agent of a paint, that is, a liquid in which pigments are suspended and which dries after application, and in this sense is practically synonymous with the term "vehicle." It is this latter meaning of the word that is emphasized here in classifying works of art.

Of the modes of expression employed by the artist, only painting, drawing, and the graphic arts are discussed in this article. The materials employed in any of these modes of expression all have the following in common: (1) the *support* is the paper, canvas, wood panel, plaster wall, sheet of metal, or other material that acts as a base upon which the expression is executed; (2) the *ground* (not always used in some expressions) is a preliminary coating given to the support to make a more desirable surface for rendering the expression, e.g., gesso, sizing, lead white; (3) the *design* layer consists of the pencil, chalk, ink, paint film, etc., applied to the ground and support to form a painting, drawing, or print.

In classifying an object by medium, therefore, one must include, first of all, the broad terms—painting, drawing, and the graphic arts—and be able to distinguish one from the other. Painting is characterized by the more or less manual application of pigments, ground or mixed in a medium, to a surface. Drawing is characterized by the application to a surface of pigments or coloring material, such as charcoal, pencil, or silverpoint, by friction or rubbing or by the use of pens and ink. Sometimes thin washes in a vehicle are used in drawings. There are, of course, borderline cases when a wash drawing might be called a painting and vice versa. Graphic arts are characterized by the fact that they are printed from another surface or through the use of stencils, plates, or other means of mechanical reproduction.

Paintings

A painting may be classified according to its design layer, ground, and support. In considering the design layer, the vehicle, or medium with which pigments are mixed, is the important factor, for it is the variable that determines characteristics of appearance, stability, and often procedures for exhibition, storage, and conservation.

C: CLASSIFYING PAINTINGS, DRAWINGS, AND PRINTS BY MEDIA

THE VEHICLE OR MEDIUM

The numerous vehicles or binding media available for the artist's use generally consist of one or more of the following:

SIZES: a term used more or less synonymously with the word "glue." The most common glues, or sizes, are gelatin, skin glue, and casein.

GUMS: a group of noncrystalline materials occurring in plants and forming viscous solutions or mucilages. They are soluble in water and form a clear solution. Gum arabic is the most common of the gums and is often used in the manufacture of watercolors.

WAXES: complex organic compounds (esters of monohydric alcohols) obtained principally from animal secretions and from hydrocarbons, e.g., beeswax, paraffin.

OILS: substances belonging to the class of chemicals known as esters. Certain oils, such as linseed oil, poppy-seed oil, and walnut oil, are of a drying type. They become a jelly or polymerize when heated or exposed to atmospheric oxygen, but when spread out in thin layers, they form a hard solid.

RESINS: secretions or excretions of certain plants, mostly living trees, although sometimes fossil trees. Natural resins form the basis for all natural varnishes and sometimes are used as a paint medium, either alone or mixed with oil or other media.

SYNTHETIC POLYMERS (ALSO CALLED SYNTHETIC RESINS): complex organic semisolids made from chemical reactions on a variety of raw materials; the chemical process is known as polymerization, which is the production of large or chain molecules by the union of molecules of the same kind. These artificial products have some of the physical properties of natural resins, but they also have certain distinct characteristics, such as ease of manipulation, controlled setting or drying time, and controlled gloss and transparency, that have made them popular with contemporary painters, both as paint media and as coating or varnish materials.

LIME WATER: used in fresco painting. It combines with carbon dioxide from the air to produce the carbonate of lime that binds the pigment to the plaster.

MIXTURES AND EMULSIONS: A mixture is a combination of two or more of the above elements, as in the mixture of linseed oil and a resin; an emulsion consists of drops of one liquid suspended in another liquid. Liquids that normally will not mix, such as oil and water, may be suspended in each other if the droplets of either the oil or the water are surrounded by an emulsifying agent. Egg yolk, for instance, is a natural oily emulsion in which the oil particles are suspended in a solution of albumen, and the lecithin in the egg acts as an emulsifying agent.

MEDIUM AND TECHNIQUE

In describing the final product of the artist, a list of terms that denote the technique employed as well as the medium used has been adopted. These include the following:

PASTEL: a chalk or crayon made from pigments and fillers held together in stick form by a weak gum medium. It is applied dry, usually to a support of paper, and may be fixed with a thin spray of film-forming material such as bleached shellac in alcohol or a synthetic resin in solution.

WATERCOLOR: used to describe a standard preparation of pigments ground in water-soluble gums. The typical transparent watercolor painting is executed with paint applied thinly and with a degree of transparency on a support, usually paper.

GOUACHE (ALSO CALLED DISTEMPER): actually a watercolor (or gum tempera) and a term synonymous with the terms "poster paint" and "opaque watercolor." The word is used more to describe the opacity obtained with such paints than to define a different material. Ordinarily it is applied on a paper support but with thicker layers than in a watercolor technique and is further distinguished by the use of mixed tints of white for the light colors instead of transparencies of color.

Tempera: Until the fifteenth century, it may have meant all painting media, but it generally refers to a medium prepared from egg. For specifications, a second term should be used, such as glue tempera, gum tempera, egg tempera, casein tempera.

- Glue Tempera and Gum Tempera: almost identical in appearance with and commonly called "gouache" paintings.

- Egg Tempera: in the traditional manner, generally painted on a wood support with a gesso ground. Egg yolk is mixed with pigments ground in water, and the mixture is applied to the smooth gesso surface in thin layers. Gesso is a mixture of chalk or gypsum and glue and is applied in several thin coats over a sized wood panel to produce a ground that is smooth and white. In making an egg tempera painting, a drawing is first made on the gesso with ink and brush. Frequently gold leaf and silver leaf are used, laid on where needed, before the layers of pigment mixed with egg yolk and water are applied. The water evaporates quickly, and the oil in the egg hardens slowly, producing a hard, strong paint film.

- Casein Tempera: Casein, usually referred to as a glue, is an organic protein compound generally made from the curds of milk. In casein tempera, the medium is made from skim milk and lime or from powdered casein dissolved with ammonia. Pigments are mixed with this medium and applied to a variety of supports including paper, canvas, plaster, and wood panels. It resembles gum tempera in application of paint to support and in final appearance; however, the distinguishing difference is that casein tempera dries to a very hard finish not soluble in water.

Oil: painting using a standard preparation of pigments ground in a drying oil, usually linseed oil. The oil dries first to a jelly and then to a hard film in the presence of oxygen in the air. Oil painting may be applied to a variety of supports including wood panels, Masonite, paper, glass, metals, and canvas. Oil paintings are usually varnished after a period of drying to increase the amount of light reflected by the pigments and to impart to the painting a greater luminosity as well as a somewhat glossy finish.

Encaustic: a method of painting with wax that was more or less common in ancient times. The word literally refers to the process of melting or burning the color mixed with wax into the surface on which it is applied. Generally, encaustic paintings are on an absorbent support or ground, such as a gesso panel, paper, or plaster wall.

Fresco: painting on plaster with lime water as a medium. There are two types: buon fresco or true fresco, and fresco secco or dry fresco. Both types are often finished in egg tempera.

- Buon Fresco (or true fresco): the method of applying pigments to a freshly laid coat of wet plaster before it has had time to absorb much, if any, carbonic acid from the air. In the process, a thick layer of fine plaster is laid over a section of a rougher plaster so as to cover only the area that an artist can paint in one day. The artist then mixes the pigments ground in water with lime water and applies this mixture to the wet plaster. The carbonate of lime binds the pigment to the wet plaster, producing a quite permanent colored plaster surface.

- Fresco Secco (or dry fresco): a process similar to buon fresco except that the plaster coat is allowed to dry. The plaster is then drenched with lime water the night before painting is to take place and again in the morning. The colors are mixed with a little lime water and/or with some other medium (gum, tempera, emulsion) and are applied as in buon fresco. Fresco secco is not so permanent or durable as buon fresco, but it is a faster method of decoration. The term "fresco secco" has also been used to describe buon fresco with egg tempera revisions. Egg tempera and casein tempera are sometimes done on plaster, but such paintings should be referred to as "egg tempera on plaster" or "casein tempera on plaster," and not "fresco" unless there is a fresco foundation.

ENAMELS: hard gloss paints varying somewhat in composition with the manufacturer. Generally the medium is a heat-treated oil combined with either natural or synthetic resins.

SYNTHETIC POLYMER PAINTS (OR SYNTHETIC POLYMERS USED FOR PAINTINGS): are thermoplastic (i.e., may be softened with heat) and are dissolved in a solvent when used as a medium for mixing with pigments. Polyvinyl acetate, polyvinyl alcohols, polyvinyl chlorides, polyesters, epoxies, and acrylic resins are among the synthetic polymers used by painters as media. Paints using acrylic resins have become especially popular because they have properties that modern artists find desirable. They may have thick or thin consistency; they are water insoluble after drying; they dry quickly and can be overpainted soon after the application of the initial tone; and they may be painted on a variety of supports including paper, canvas, and panels.

MEDIUM, GROUND, AND SUPPORT

In classifying paintings by media, then, it is most desirable to include the name of the technique employed, the material component of the support, and sometimes the ground, as, for example, egg tempera on gessoed wood panel; oil on canvas; gouache on paper; or casein tempera on plaster. Sometimes the artist employs different techniques and media in the same painting. These might be classified as mixed technique —egg tempera with oil glazes on paper; or mixed technique—casein tempera with oil glazes on canvas. If the support is of complex structure or has undergone a major change, this might be noted as follows: egg tempera transferred from wood panel to canvas; oil on paper attached to canvas.

It is often difficult to determine the exact technique that has been used, especially in modern experimental painting. In these cases it is most desirable, when possible, to obtain the exact process or technique from the artist himself. Such information is extremely valuable in determining the kind of treatment the painting should have to preserve it in the best manner.

In addition to the common media used in painting that have been discussed, there are sometimes unusual elements found in paintings, such as metal foils, metal paints, sand, small stones, jewels, wood chips, plastic strips, or strings. Generally these substances are used in connection with one or more of the above-mentioned techniques and might be classified as follows: egg tempera with gold leaf on gessoed wood panel; oil mixed with sand on canvas; casein tempera with brass filings, leather, and feathers on paper.

As a result of experimentation and scientific discovery, there are also new products appearing on the market that contemporary artists are employing in their paintings. Again, it is best to obtain from the artist information on the medium used. These might be classified, for example, as Duco enamel on paper; synthetic polymer paint—acrylic resin—on canvas; synthetic polymer paint with oil glazes on Masonite; synthetic polymers—Lucite 44 and polyvinyl acetate—on unsized cotton canvas, etc.

Drawings

The classification of drawings usually involves the type of material used as a pigment rather than a vehicle or medium with which pigments are mixed. There are, then, drawings in pencil, pen and ink, brush and ink, charcoal, crayons of colored wax, colored chalks, points of metals such as silver, gold, and lead, and sometimes paint. The classification of drawings might include the word "drawing" and the coloring material used as well as the support, e.g., drawing—graphite pencil on paper; drawing—silverpoint on paper; drawing—charcoal on paper.

Occasionally a drawing is complex enough that the result might be referred to as a painting, as in the case of pastel drawings by Degas and Lautrec. Technically, however, when a dry-pigment process is used, that is, when the coloring substance is rubbed into the ground or support, the result should be referred to as a drawing. The classification of works in pastel as drawings or paintings is more or less a matter of opinion. Thus, in this classification, pastel is listed as a type of painting as well as a drawing medium.

GRAPHITE PENCILS (COMMONLY CALLED LEAD PENCILS): consist of graphite (crystalline carbon) compressed with fine clay.

CHARCOAL: the residue from the dry distillation of wood made by heating sticks of wood in closed chambers or kilns.

CHALK: a natural form of calcium carbonate composed largely of the remains of minute sea organisms. It is often used on tinted surfaces for the light areas while charcoal is used for the dark. (Conté crayons are a variety of chalk.)

PASTELS (OR COLORED CHALKS): crayons made from pigments and fillers and held together in stick form by a weak gum medium. Some color pencils are of a pastel type but may be held together with a stronger gum.

WAX CRAYONS: made from pigments and fillers held together with wax and perhaps certain resins. Color pencils are often a type of hard wax crayon.

COLOR PENCILS: usually pigments in a stick held together by either a gum or a wax. Some gum pencil drawings may have been worked over with a brush and water to achieve something of a watercolor effect by redissolving the gum, and so gum pencils are sometimes called watercolor pencils. Wax pencil drawings and wax crayon drawings are sometimes heated, as by ironing, so that the wax melts; such a technique is really an encaustic technique and more properly belongs under the classification of paintings.

SILVERPOINT, LEADPOINT, AND GOLDPOINT: thin wires of lead, silver, and gold or other metals that are sharpened and drawn across paper that has been coated with a pigment, usually white (to provide a tooth). A small deposit of the metal is rubbed into the porous or granular surface of the coating. Of these drawings, referred to as silverpoint, leadpoint, goldpoint, etc., the silverpoint tends to darken as the silver tarnishes, and this is generally desirable.

INKS: made from dyes and from pigment suspensions. India ink is carbon black suspended in a water solution of a gum or suspended in a water solution of borax and shellac. Ink drawings may be made with pen or brush, and most inks may be diluted with water to give lighter shades or tints.

Painting materials also may be used in a sketching or drawing technique and should be referred to by noting the type of paint used (see pages 209–11), e.g., drawing—watercolor on paper; drawing—oil on paper; drawing—egg tempera on paper.

Any combination of the above media could exist in a single drawing. In such drawings the various media should be listed in the order of their importance in the design, e.g., drawing—wax crayon, pencil, and ink on cardboard; drawing—pen and ink and watercolor washes on paper.

Graphic Arts

The term "graphic arts" is in general use for designating all processes for the production of multiple-proof pictures on paper on a handmade basis, the work being done either wholly or for the most part by the original artist and the editions limited. The processes are also referred to as printmaking and the resulting pictures as prints.

In classifying prints it is important to know something about the various processes in use today, for the technique used is the important factor in the classification of the graphic arts. These processes may be grouped into four types based on the surface that holds the printing ink or coloring substance for the print. The four types are relief, intaglio, planographic, and stencil.

RELIEF PROCESSES

In the relief processes part of the surface of a flat block is cut away so that the design stands up to provide a printing surface. Woodcuts, wood engravings, and cuts of linoleum, Lucite, cardboard, chipboard, and composition board as well as plaster blocks are among the variations.

- WOODCUT: a block of wood cut plankwise is cut away with knives, gouges, and chisels to leave that part of the surface which is the design. The raised surface is then inked and the print made on soft paper. Several different woodblocks may be used for the same print and several colors may be used on these blocks, as in the case of Japanese woodcuts. Generally a woodcut is characterized by angular, direct, coarse lines and inked and uninked areas in sharp contrast. Linoleum cuts, Lucite cuts, and cuts of such materials as Masonite, plywood, etc., are variations of the woodcut process. The cellocut, also a variation of the woodcut process, is made by coating a smooth block or plate with coats of a plastic varnish composed of Celluloid dissolved in acetone; when this varnish has set, the resultant surface is worked as a woodcut.

- WOOD ENGRAVING: Crosscut sections of boxwood or similar fine-grained wood are glued together to form an absolutely smooth cutting surface. The design is cut using burins or gravers of various sizes. The burin is a very hard steel shaft with a V-shaped cutting edge and rounded wooden handle. Because the wood is crosscut, a skilled artist can achieve delicate lines of surgical precision and gray tones through cross-hatching. Wood engravings are printed on soft paper.

- PLASTER BLOCK PRINT: smooth blocks of plaster of Paris are obtained by casting the plaster in a frame on glass. The plaster block is engraved or worked and printed like a woodcut. Since the plaster is rather soft, a limited edition of only about thirty prints is possible.

INTAGLIO PROCESSES

The principle of the intaglio process is the exact opposite of that of the relief process. The printing line is a groove or furrow below the nonprinting surface of a metal plate. In other words, the lines that are etched or cut away from the plate carry the ink rather than the high-standing areas, as in the relief processes. Engravings, etchings, soft-ground etchings, aquatints, mezzotints, and cellocuts are examples of this process.

ENGRAVING: A steel, copper, or zinc plate is worked with the burin—the V-shaped hard steel graver. Sharp, clean-cut lines with tapering ends are characteristic. The engraved plate is inked so that the lines are filled, and the surface is wiped clean. The paper support for the engraving is then dampened, and the print is made under pressure in an etching press. The cellocut (see above) can be printed in the same manner, and thus is a variation of the engraving as well as of the woodcut.

ETCHING: In making an etching, a clean copper or zinc plate is covered with a varnish or other substance impervious to acid. Lines are then drawn with an etching needle to penetrate this substance and expose the copper or zinc. The plate is immersed in an acid bath, and the acid attacks the drawn lines of the bare copper or zinc. The length of time the plate remains in the acid determines the depth of the etched line. Etching lines are flowing and threadlike. The plate is printed in the same manner as an engraving, in an etching press under pressure on dampened paper.

SOFT-GROUND ETCHING: a process similar to etching except that a softer coating is used on the plate; paper is laid over this soft ground plate, and the drawing is done on the paper. Pressure from drawing on the paper picks up part of the ground and exposes the copper or zinc so that it can be etched with acids. The resulting lines are coarse, grainy, and pencil-like—no sharp lines are obtainable by this process.

AQUATINT: The plate is carefully and evenly covered with a powdered resin dust and heated, so that each particle of dust becomes crystallized and adheres firmly to the plate. The particles leave small exposed sections of the plate, which are then bitten by immersion in acids. Through a series of resin treatments delicate gradations of tone can be produced. The aquatint is characterized by a fine or coarse grainy texture of tones and no lines. It is printed like an etching.

MEZZOTINT: similar to an aquatint in appearance but the plate is prepared by scraping, tooling with special tools, and burnishing the metal surface until the desired gradations of tone are achieved. The mezzotint is characterized by a grainy, stippled texture with fine gradations of tone. It is printed like an etching.

DRYPOINT: made by applying a sharp tool or diamond-pointed needle directly to the copper plate. The needle tears into the smooth copper plate leaving a rough edge known as a "burr" along the side of the line. This burr gives a character of fuzziness to the drypoint line but quickly wears away in the etching press so that the first prints from a drypoint plate are most characteristic. It is printed under pressure on dampened paper as in an etching.

INKLESS INTAGLIO OR EMBOSSED PRINT: prints made from engraved or etched intaglio plates without ink. The design is created in relief through embossing the paper by running the dampened paper and plate through a press under pressure.

PLANOGRAPHIC PROCESSES

The planographic process includes lithography and zincography used on two materials—stone (lithos) and zinc.

LITHOGRAPH: a technique of surface printing achieved through a change in surface structure of the printing stone rather than through a change in the physical contours of the block or plate as in the relief and intaglio processes. In the lithograph the design is drawn directly on a smooth limestone slab with a grease crayon or with tusche, a liquid, oily ink. The design is fixed on the stone by a wash of acid gum arabic solution, so the grease crayon does not spread. When this solution is completely dry, the stone is washed with clear water and inked. The water wets that part of the stone where there is no grease crayon, and the greasy ink adheres to that part of the stone where there is no water. The stone is placed face up on the traveling bed of the lithographic press and printed on slightly dampened paper under pressure.

ZINCOGRAPH: the same process as used for lithographs but with a zinc plate substituted for a stone. This process is commonly but erroneously called lithography.

STENCIL PROCESSES

In the stencil processes ink or color is applied to the perforated or cutout sections of specially treated paper or other thin material so that the desired pattern comes through to the paper or surface below the stencil.

SERIGRAPH: Primarily a color technique, the serigraph is a fine silk-screen print. In simple terms, a stencil or series of stencils are placed on one or more screens of pure silk. A support (usually paper) is placed beneath the silk screen, and paint is forced through the silk in the design areas where the stencil is cut away. Through the use of several screens (as many as fifty or more although usually far fewer), different colors and gradations of tone may be achieved in the serigraph.

ALLIED PROCESSES

In addition to the four types of processes mentioned above, certain allied processes are often included in the category of the graphic arts.

MONOTYPE (OR MONOPRINT): a unique print made from a painted plate. Any smooth surface such as glass, metal plates, or plywood may be used as a support for the design, and the transfer is usually made to a sheet of paper with the aid of a press, a hot iron, or merely by rubbing the back surface of the paper as it is placed on the painted plate.

PLASTER-MOLD PRINT: a print on plaster made from an engraved or etched plate usually of bold design that is well inked and placed face upward on a sheet of glass. A frame ¾ inch deep, with a margin of a few inches, is placed around the plate, and plaster is poured over the plate to fill the frame. After the plaster has set, the plate of glass is removed and the etched or engraved plate is removed from the plaster by heating slightly. The resulting print has the smooth surface of polished marble, and the engraved or etched line stands in relief.

PHOTOMECHANICAL PROCESSES:

PHOTOGRAPHY: an act of producing a negative or positive image directly or indirectly on a sensitized surface by the action of light or other radiant energy.

COLLOTYPE: a process of printing from a hardened gelatin film. A sheet of heavy glass is coated with gelatin sensitized with dichromate of potassium or ammonium. During closely controlled drying, a finely reticulated, grained surface develops. It is so fine that the grain cannot be seen with the naked eye, but under magnification the fine reticulation of the gelatin printing surface can be seen. This is exposed to light through a positive transparency, and the gelatin is hardened in proportion to the amount of light transmitted. Unexposed areas are kept moist with water and glycerine, which repels the greasy ink applied to the hardened areas. Fine gradations of tone are produced by the collotype process.

PHOTOENGRAVING: Both etched-relief and intaglio-metal printing plates may be produced by this process. A metal plate is sensitized with a dichromated solution. This is exposed to light through a negative. The sensitized coating on the plate becomes hardened and insoluble wherever it is exposed to light. The soluble parts are washed away, and the hard coating acts as a resist during etching of the plate with appropriate acids. The plate is then printed like an etching or engraving plate. Often photomechanical reproductions are made of original prints and are difficult to distinguish from original etchings or engravings. The photomechanical engraving, however, tends to have an even thickness of the ink line and a loss of sharpness in fine lines. Photoengraving is being used as a fine arts form by many modern artists.

HALFTONE PRINTS: photomechanical prints made by placing a black gauze between the negative and light-sensitive plate coating. The result is an etching in tiny dots. Because of these dots, halftone prints can readily be identified under a magnifying glass.

HOLOGRAMS: a visually three-dimensional image recorded on a two-dimensional emulsion. The image appears to be a "true" image—it can be viewed from various angles. The image is formed in the emulsion by laser light reflected from the object along with a laser reference light. By passing a strong white light through the emulsion on the plate, the three-dimensional image is reconstructed. Some contemporary artists are making use of holograms for artistic expression.

The Classification of Constructions

During the twentieth century there has been a radical turn in art away from tradition and what may be termed studio painting, printmaking, and sculpting. Modern objects of art often present a collaboration with science and technology, embodying in their structures elements of the ready made, the accidental, the machine, light, motion, and the many products of new technology. The classification of these creations for purposes of cataloguing and communication is sometimes extremely difficult. While these modern objects are not readily considered paintings, sculpture, or art virtu, the classification "constructions" seems to apply to nearly all. Constructions may be almost flat, as in the case of collages, or they may be electronic devices in complex mechanical structures that move and emit sounds and even odors.

The following list suggests how at least some of these modern art constructions might be assigned a name and classification. This system for classification has been developed by this author and is intended to help the collector of such objects in cataloguing and categorizing various types of modern artistic expression. Since this is an experimental classification, it is of course subject to reorganization and revision by those who try to adopt it. The author would appreciate comments from anyone using this system.

CONSTRUCTIONS THAT ARE REASONABLY FLAT AND SOMEWHAT RESEMBLE PAINTINGS

COLLAGE: a composition of fragments of such materials as printed matter, textiles, string, photographs, wood chips, etc., pasted or glued on a picture surface. A collage may be used along with traditional painting media.

MONTAGE: a composition of several distinct pictures that may or may not appear to be made up of separate pictures or a composite picture made by combining fragments or whole pictures.

PHOTOMONTAGE: a montage in which photographic images are used. Infrared photographs as well as radiographs may be used in photomontage.

ASSEMBLAGE: a collection of particular things brought together and attached to some common support or to each other.

CONSTRUCTIONS RESEMBLING SCULPTURES

STABILES: constructions of abstract forms typically made of sheet metal, wire, and wood. The materials used in all types of stabiles should be specified.

    COMPRESSED STABILES: large objects compressed by mechanical or other forces to produce the aesthetic expression, e.g., an automobile, a plastic container, or a pile of trash compressed into a new form.

    EXPLODED STABILES: objects that have been expanded or deformed by an explosive force.

    STENCILED, PAINTED, AND STUFFED STABILES: objects made of textiles or other materials that may be decorated and then stuffed with a filling material. The filling material, such as feathers, wool, etc., may be included in the classification as well as the paint media.

    INFLATED STABILES: a construction that requires a gaseous filling. In classifying such items the gas should be specified, e.g., oxygen, air, helium, etc.

    STABILES WITH LIQUID COMPONENTS: devices where colored or clear liquids form a part of the aesthetic experience.

    STABILES WITH AUDIO COMPONENTS: Gongs, chimes, sirens, music boxes, musical instruments, radios, cassette tapes, etc., that emit sound are a part of the artist's expression.

    STABILES WITH ELECTRONIC COMPONENTS: These include visual tapes, slide projections, television components, contact microphones, contact illuminators, etc. In classifying, the electronic component(s) should be specified.

MOBILES: a construction that may be assembled of parts that are delicately balanced and may be set in motion by air currents or mechanical propulsion. Mobiles may also have liquid, audio, or electronic components and may be inflated wholly or in part.

    MOTOR-DRIVEN MOBILES: Electric or spring-driven motors may cause the movement.

    MOBILES WITH ELECTRONIC MOTIVATION: Timing devices or random electronic switches may control the movement in such mobiles, which may perform simple or complex programs of movement.

CONSTRUCTIONS WITH LIGHT:

    STATIC: constructions that depend primarily on lighting devices for their effect. The type of light used should be specified, such as incandescent light, ultraviolet light, fluorescent tubes, neon tubes, etc.

    KINETIC: These constructions have either programmed or random switching devices that produce flashes of light or project light patterns on a screen, ground glass, or other surfaces.

CONSTRUCTIONS WITH GAS: These artistic expressions may contain gasses of various colors that mingle and settle or that are introduced from compressed gas containers. They may also expel gasses to form smoke rings or other effects.

LIQUID CONSTRUCTIONS: These expressions may depend upon liquids primarily for their effect, either in containers or on surfaces. When possible, the liquids, such as oil on water, colored glycerine, liquid paraffin, etc., should be specified.

ELECTRONIC CONSTRUCTIONS: These are constructions that utilize electronic components including duplicating devices, computers, television sets, video tapes, etc. The components used and the programming intended by the artist should be specified.

BIOLOGICAL CONSTRUCTIONS: If plants or animals, either living or dead, are the most important part of the expression and the plants or animals may be recognized as such (as distinguished from a plant part such as wood or an animal part such as bone or ivory), the expression may be considered biological. The birds, insects, flowers, or other biological species may be identified to complete the classification.

GEOLOGICAL CONSTRUCTIONS: These include constructions made up of one or several geological specimens assembled to create the effect. The parts may be rocks, minerals, earth, or other natural nonliving material. Sand and earth constructions are an example.

ENVIRONMENTAL CONSTRUCTIONS: These include all constructions that create a new environment to be experienced. The anechoic chamber (soundless room), the plastic enclosed mounting, the audio-hydro-kinetic room (with mirrors, programmed sound, and lighting), and the computer-generated carpet that activates ceiling patterns are examples of environmental constructions. As part of the classification the materials of construction and electronic or other devices should be indicated.

Bibliography

Benthall, Jonathan. *Science and Technology in Art Today*. New York: Praeger, 1972.

Brett, Guy. *Kinetic Art*. New York: Reinhold, 1968.

Cennini, Cennino d'Andrea. *The Craftsman's Handbook*. Translated by Daniel V. Thompson, Jr. New York: Dover Publications, 1954.

Constable, William George. *The Painter's Workshop*. 1954. Rpt. Boston: Beacon Press, 1963.

Davis, Douglas M. *Art and the Future: A History/Prophecy of the Collaboration between Science, Technology, and Art*. New York: Praeger, 1973.

Feller, Robert L., Elizabeth H. Jones, and Nathan Stolow. *On Picture Varnishes and Their Solvents*. Rev. ed. Cleveland: Press of Case Western Reserve University, 1971.

Francke, Herbert W. *Computer Graphics; Computer Art*. London: Phaidon, 1971.

Gettens, Rutherford J., and George L. Stout. *Painting Materials: A Short Encyclopedia*. 1942. Rpt. New York: Dover Publications, 1966.

Hayter, Stanley William. *New Ways of Gravure*. Rev. ed. New York: Oxford University Press, 1969.

International Centre for the Study of the Preservation and the Restoration of Cultural Property. *Synthetic Materials Used in the Conservation of Cultural Property*. Rome: International Centre, 1963.

Ivins, William Mills. *How Prints Look: Photographs with a Commentary*. 1943. Rpt. Boston: Beacon Press, 1958.

Jensen, Lawrence N. *Synthetic Painting Media*. Englewood Cliffs, N.J.: Prentice-Hall, 1964.

Kaprow, Allan. *Assemblage, Environments & Happenings*. New York: H. N. Abrams, 1966.

Mayer, Ralph. *The Artist's Handbook of Materials and Techniques*. 3d ed. New York: Viking Press, 1970.

Peterdi, Gabor. *Printmaking: Methods Old and New*. Rev. ed. New York: Macmillan, 1971.

Pierce, John Robinson. *Science, Art, and Communication*. New York: C. N. Potter, 1968.

Seitz, William. *The Art of Assemblage*. New York: Museum of Modern Art, 1961.

Thompson, Daniel V. *The Practice of Tempera Painting*. 1936. Rpt. New York: Dover Publications, 1962.

Watrous, James. *The Craft of Old-Master Drawings*. Madison: University of Wisconsin Press, 1957.

CATALOGUING IN THE METROPOLITAN MUSEUM OF ART, WITH A NOTE ON ADAPTATIONS FOR SMALL MUSEUMS

MARCIA COTTIS HARTY
MARICA VILCEK
BRICE RHYNE

ecognition of the necessity of systematic accessioning, cataloguing, and photographing of museum collections dates from the beginning of this century. In 1906 the process of registering and accessioning works of art began at the Metropolitan Museum of Art. The central catalogue was initiated in 1910 by Margaret A. Gash under the supervision of Henry W. Kent. It was started as "an experiment," but its function has been maintained ever since. Miss Gash and her staff, with Mr. Kent as consultant, compiled the first cataloguing manual and developed a system that in format resembles a library card catalogue, with the important addition of a photograph of the object printed on a record card of the same size.

The central catalogue is essentially a card file record of information on each object in the Metropolitan, arranged in the order most useful within the museum. The card file system has the advantage of permitting continuous updating of information by the addition of new cards. Development of this cataloguing procedure has been considered an invaluable contribution of the Metropolitan to museum methods. Many museums throughout the country have used it as a model for their systems of recording works of art.

Cataloguing has generally been considered a curatorial function, but, in order to maintain uniformity in a museum with many curatorial departments, the central catalogue was first set up as a separate department, with cataloguers working under the supervision of the appropriate curators. In 1949 the central catalogue (a file arranged by classification) and the registrar's accession file (a numerical file) were brought under one department head, the registrar, but the procedures and forms used in cataloguing remained basically the same. Working procedures were made more efficient by this collaboration and by ready access to the objects in the registrar's storeroom, where all incoming objects remained until recorded. Although the central catalogue was again separated administratively from the Office of the Registrar in 1973, the two units continue to work in close cooperation.

In 1972 cataloguing of objects became the responsibility of the curatorial departments. It also became their responsibility to supply the central catalogue with complete sets of records for each object. At that time the original manual had to be revised for use by members of curatorial departments involved in cataloguing. But in spite of the updating of techniques over more than half a century, the cataloguing manual at the Metropolitan remains very close to Miss Gash's original description of basic procedures for cataloguing works of art.

The system of maintaining catalogue records on index cards is preferable to a book catalogue because of its versatility. The card catalogue reflects the various types of objects in the museum and can expand with the growth of the collections. It can also adapt to changes in classification and facilitate transfer of materials in the event of reorganization of curatorial departments.

The adaptability of the catalogue is counterbalanced by the permanence of the accession number. The accession number for an object should never change. If this number were based on classification, it, too, would be subject to revision, and there would be no fixed point of reference in the system. Furthermore, such a numbering system would necessitate partial cataloguing before the accession number could be assigned.

In contrast, an accession number based on the year and the sequence of transactions during that year does not depend on curatorial study and so can be assigned immediately after an object is accepted as part of the permanent collection. In the event that two large collections arrive at the same time, they can be worked on simultaneously, because the numbering of one is not dependent upon the completion of the numbering of the other. The accession number 53.19.2 signifies that the item was acquired in 1953, that it was part of the nineteenth transaction of the year, and was the second item in that particular transaction. When a single object is obtained from one vendor or donor, a two-part number is all that is necessary, e.g., 53.4. (See chapter 3.) In 1970, one hundred years after the first object was acquired by the museum, the first part of the accession number was augmented to avoid confusion. Accession numbers for objects acquired after 1970 incorporate all four digits of the year in question to distinguish them from objects acquired between 1870 and 1970; thus, 70.1 indicates an object acquired in 1870, while 1970.1 indicates one acquired in 1970.

Classification

The classification system is determined by the nature of the collection and the way the system is to be used. The large and diversified collection in the Metropolitan requires a complex classification system. Objects are classified first according to the civilization that produced them, and then, within the civilization, according to the materials of which they are made or by certain specialized categories. The primary breakdown is by civilization:

FAR EASTERN

EGYPTIAN

NEAR EASTERN

GREEK AND ROMAN

WESTERN ART (Western art was divided into European and American when the latter field was placed under a separate curatorial department)

PRIMITIVE ART

Classification within these divisions is by material, such as ceramics, textiles, and woodwork, with such specialized exceptions as arms and armor, coins, paintings, and sculpture. These are arranged alphabetically as follows:

ARMS AND ARMOR

CERAMICS (porcelain, pottery)

COINS

COSTUMES

DRAWINGS AND WATERCOLORS

D: CATALOGUING IN THE METROPOLITAN MUSEUM OF ART

Enamels
Fans
Glass
Horology
Ivories
Lacquers
Lapidary work
Leatherwork
Medals and plaquettes
Metalwork (brass, bronze, gold, silver, etc.)
Miniatures
Musical instruments
Natural substances (amber, straw, wax, etc.)
Paintings
Sculpture (sculpture, sculpture architectural, sculpture miniature)
Silhouettes
Textiles (embroideries, laces, tapestries, woven, etc.)
Wallpapers
Woodwork (architectural, furniture)

Not all departments require the same classifications, however, as classifications are determined by the nature of each civilization, and some departments have categories that are especially suited to their needs. The Ancient Near East Department, for example, has a special category for seals and sealings, and the Greek and Roman Department has one for vases. Where necessary, a classification may be subdivided. Arms and armor, for example, is divided into various categories based on use—armor for a man, armor for a horse, firearms, weapons.

In the catalogue the basic classification is shown by labels on the outside of the drawers, by guide cards within, and at the bottom of the first card in a set. All the cards for an individual object are tied together with a string through the bottom hole, so that classification information need appear only on the first card for any one object.

The Subject Index

A subject index presents facts about an object that are not apparent from the classification system. The subject index is prepared by the staff of the Catalogue Department and is maintained in a separate file. This file contains entries for artists and makers, subject matter, title, ex-collections, and provenance, arranged alphabetically. Each of these entries will lead the inquirer to the cards for the object in the main catalogue. At present, subject indexes in the Metropolitan Museum of Art are provided for European and American, Greek and Roman, and Egyptian objects, and for Islamic paintings.

As an example, Gauguin's painting *Ia Orana Maria* is indexed under the following subject headings:

Gauguin, Paul

Ia Orana Maria

Hail Mary

Virgin and Child

CHRIST CHILD AND VIRGIN (cross-reference)

MANZI, MICHEL (ex-collection)

LEWISOHN, ADOLPH (ex-collection)

LEWISOHN, SAMUEL A. (ex-collection)

The silver loving cup made by Jacob Hurd is indexed under:

HURD, JACOB

CUP   LOVING

HERALDRY   CAVE

HERALDRY   PETIT

Cards illustrating the various types of entries for these works are shown in figures D.1 and D.2.

Cataloguing Procedures

To register an object is to record the data necessary to identify it and to document the transaction by which it was acquired. To catalogue an object is to record the full scholarly information about it. Since the registration of objects has been described in chapter 3, only the records made for the catalogue will be discussed here. However, an adaptation of these methods for small institutions is discussed later in this article.

At the time of this writing, cataloguing at the Metropolitan Museum of Art is done by the curatorial staff. When each object arrives, it is carefully measured and examined; any visible damages and repairs are noted; and the accession number is assigned. The cataloguer then gathers and organizes all available information about the object in preparation for making a set of catalogue cards. This information comes from notes made by the cataloguer when examining the object for signatures, marks, colors, and technical details; from records of collections and exhibitions of which the object has been a part; and from publications in which it or related pieces have been described.

The final catalogue cards are typed, and additional sets are photocopied. The curatorial departments keep the original catalogue cards; the Catalogue Department keeps two sets of catalogue cards—one in the central catalogue file under the proper classification and the other in a file arranged solely by accession number. On the catalogue cards in this numerical file the following information is recorded: all duplicate sets of cards sent to various departments, the number and sizes of photographs supplied to the Photo Sales Department, and the subject index entries that have been made. Thus, when curatorial departments notify the Catalogue Department of subsequent changes in cataloguing information, or when an object is deaccessioned, all records can be easily located and updated.

The catalogue cards prepared by the curatorial staff form the scholarly records for all objects owned by the museum. The information on them should be as accurate as possible. Care in their preparation prevents confusion and misinformation later.

CATALOGUE CARDS

Cataloguing information is recorded on a standard library card, 7.5 by 12.5 centimeters. This information is arranged so that the most important facts usually appear on the first card. Basic information on this card includes: accession number, heading, material and measurements, source from which the object was acquired, classification,

Fig. D.3.
Catalogue cards for Gauguin's Ia Orana Maria *(7.5 by 12.5 cm.), Metropolitan Museum of Art. The cards, each with the accession number typed at the top left corner, are filed in the following order: artist and title, photograph, ex-collections, notes, exhibitions, references.*

```
51.112.2
    Gauguin, Paul                        1848-1903
       Ia Orana Maria

    Inscribed (lower left): IA ORANA MARIA
    Oil on canvas           H. 44-3/4, W. 34-1/2 in.
                                  (113.7 x 87.7 cm.)
    Signed and dated (lower right): P. Gauguin, 91.

    Bequest of Samuel A. Lewisohn, 1951


    Paintings                            French
```

Artist and title entry.

```
51.112.2
    Notes
       Gauguin wrote to his friend, de Monfreid, that Ia
    Orana Maria, or Hail Mary, was the first work of im-
    portance as distinct from sketches and studies which
    he executed after his arrival in Tahiti. He added
    that he was "rather pleased with it". (see Ref.
    Gauguin, Lettres à Georges-Daniel de Monfreid)

       The fruit at the feet of the Virgin is placed on
    a "fata", an altar of the type once used to make
    offerings to the Tahitian gods.
```

Notes.

Photograph.

```
51.112.2
    Exhibitions
       M.M.A. New York.  The Lewisohn collection, 1951, no.
          34 (lent by Mrs. Sam A. Lewisohn; Bequest of Sam
          A. Lewisohn to M.M.A.).
       M.M.A. New York.  Art treasures of the Metropolitan,
          1952-1953, check list no. 152.
       Art Institute of Chicago, and M.M.A.  Gauguin, 1959,
          p. 15 (ill. in color); p. 38, no. 28 (catalogued
          with additional bibliography; discussed; mentions
          several other works, for, after, and related to
          this painting).
```

Exhibitions.

```
51.112.2
    Ex collections
       Michel Manzi, Paris (purchased at the Durand-Ruel
       exhibition, Nov. 1893; sale, Galerie Manzi et
       Joyant, Paris, Mar. 13-14, 1919, no. 56, ill., for
       Fr. 58,000 to Knoedler); [Knoedler, New York
       (1919)] ; Adolph Lewisohn, New York (1919-1938);
       Samuel A. Lewisohn, New York (1938-1951).
```

Ex-collections, showing names and dates of ownership, with dealers' names in brackets.

```
51.112.2
    References
       M.M.A. Art treasures of the Metropolitan, 1952, p.
          159 (ill. in color), no. 152, p. 234 (described).
       Notes on the cover in M.M.A. Bulletin, N.S., vol. XV,
          1957 (Apr.) inside cover (identified), cover (ill.).
       M.M.A. French paintings, vol. III, XIX-XX centuries,
          1967, by Charles Sterling and Margaretta Salinger,
          p. 170 (ill., catalogued).
```

References (arranged by publication date), showing book entry, periodical entry, and museum publication. Additional cards of notes, exhibitions, and references are added as needed.

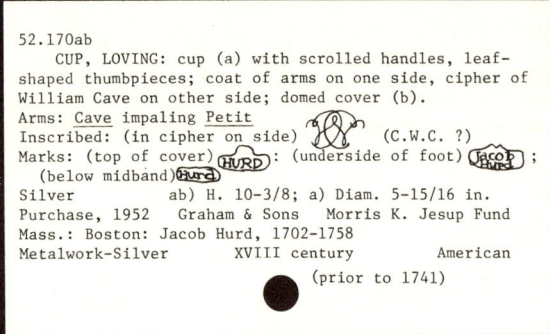
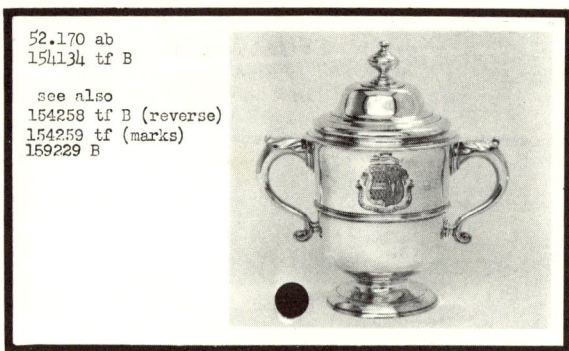

Fig. D.4.
Catalogue cards for Jacob Hurd's silver loving cup (7.5 by 12.5 cm.), Metropolitan Museum of Art. Descriptive heading entry, showing place and maker.   Photograph.

Fig. D.5.
Simplified accession card and donor-vendor card (3 by 5 in.).

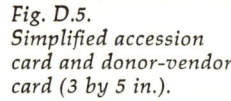

Fig. D.6.
Simplified catalogue card (3 by 5 in.).

Fig. D.7.
Simplified finding card and location card, with guide cards (3 by 5 in.).

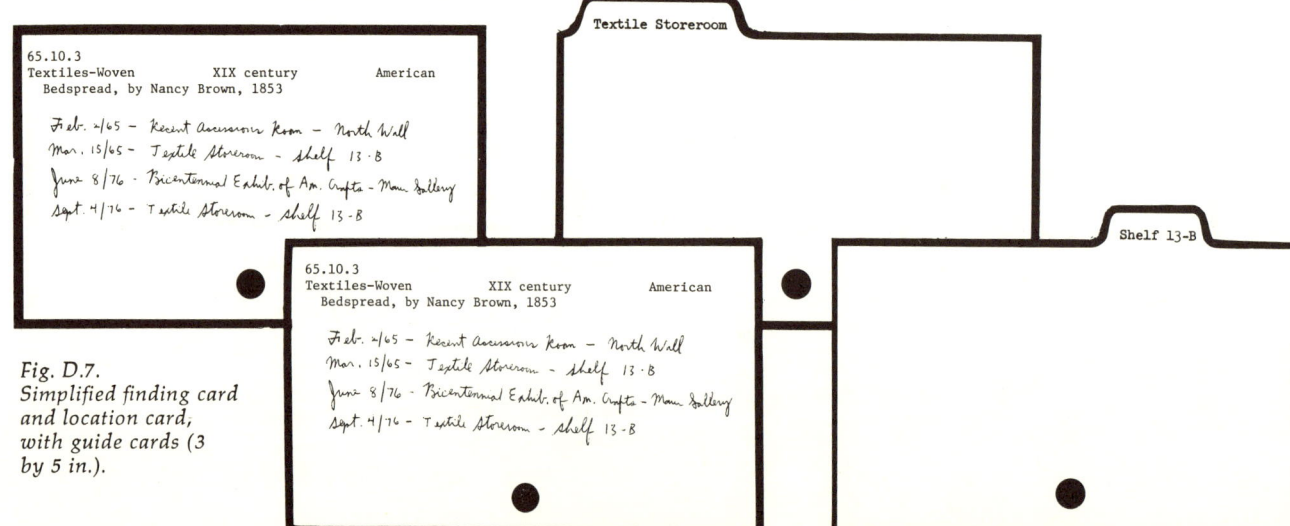

Cards for simplified records would include:

ACCESSION CARD: identifies each object by its accession number; filed numerically.

DONOR-VENDOR CARD: duplicate of accession card, with name of donor, bequest, or vendor underscored for quick identification and filing; filed alphabetically by name, then, within each name, by accession number. The donor-vendor file thus readily identifies all the objects acquired from each source. The accession and donor-vendor cards should be on different colored stock so that they cannot be confused. (See figure D.5.)

CATALOGUE CARD: records each object by its classification; filed with all other objects of the same class, such as furniture, glass, paintings, sculpture, etc.; then filed by country, century; then, where appropriate, by artist, school, maker, or descriptive title of object. (See figure D.6.)

FINDING CARD: gives present location for each object; each change should be recorded as soon as the object is moved; filed by accession number. In a small institution where all records are kept in one office, the finding card could be filed behind the accession card; otherwise it could be kept in the curatorial office in a separate numerical file.

LOCATION CARD: duplicate of finding card; identifies each object by the position it occupies; filed by gallery, storeroom, office, and specific location within that space. If an object seems to be missing, its last known location can be quickly determined. The finding and location cards should be on different colored stock so that they cannot be confused. (See figure D.7.)

PHOTOGRAPH: definitively identifies each object and its physical condition. The number of prints of the photograph will depend upon the use and location of the files. Ideally, there would be one for the accession file, one for the catalogue, and one for the public to see.

If the institution has a typewriter with interchangeable platens—a standard one for ordinary office use and a specially designed card-holding platen—the accession and donor-vendor cards can be typed in one operation by using carbon paper. The finding and location cards can likewise be typed simultaneously, thus considerably reducing the time and labor involved.

In a system with simplified records, curators might keep a file of folders, one for each object, to hold bibliographies, large photographs, lists of negative numbers, correspondence, work notes, and other material. If the museum is later able to expand the simplified records into a full catalogue, the additional cards can be made from information stored in the curators' files.

A catalogue open to the public as a central information service saves the curators time and is beneficial to the public as well. Each institution must determine the methods and procedures that best suit its particular needs.

Bibliography

American Library Association. *A.L.A. Cataloguing Rules for Author and Title Entries*. Edited by Clara Bettle. 2d ed. Chicago: ALA, 1949.

Chamberlin, Mary Walls. *Guide to Art Reference Books*. Chicago: ALA, 1959.

Glass, Elizabeth, comp. *A Subject Index for the Visual Arts*. London: Her Majesty's Stationery Office, 1969.

CATALOGUING PRINTS IN THE MUSEUM OF MODERN ART

DOROTHY L. LYTLE
RIVA CASTLEMAN

The basic system of cataloguing prints in the Museum of Modern Art was set up by Carl O. Schniewind, curator of prints and drawings at the Art Institute of Chicago, working in conjunction with the museum's registration department. Subsequent modifications have been made to facilitate the computer maintenance of the museum's catalogue. Though suited particularly to twentieth-century conventions in printmaking, this system can be altered to meet the requirements of museums with collections for earlier periods. Some museums, especially those whose print collection is not open to the public, may not need such extensive records.

The accession number is assigned by the registration department. It is marked by the print room staff on the lower left corner of the verso of the print. Prints at the Museum of Modern Art are placed in window mats of 100 percent rag board (Ivins) cut, whenever possible, to standard sizes (see page 233) and hinged so that the print may be lifted in the same direction as the top window portion of the mat. Vertical prints are hinged along the back of the left side; horizontal prints are hinged at the top.

The print collection is listed in its entirety by accession number in an inventory book. The registration department also maintains a numerical card file that lists the accession number, artist, title, and other information available at the time of a print's acquisition. However, the inventory book is the record-keeping device that is marked as each task in the processing of an acquisition is completed. The inventory book also serves as a location file, as the physical location of each print is recorded in it. (See figure E.1.)

Catalogue Records

Cataloguing is done by the print room staff. A carbon copy of the catalogue sheet is sent to the registration department, which takes from it such information as registration records require and then enters this data into computerized files.

In cataloguing a print, the following records are made:

CATALOGUE SHEET AND ARTIST'S SHEET (master records; filed in lock-post binders)

CATALOGUE CARD AND ARTIST'S CARD (for use by the public)

MAT LABEL

DONOR CARD

SUBJECT FILE

PHOTOGRAPH ALBUMS

A description with examples for each type of record follows.

E: CATALOGUING PRINTS IN THE MUSEUM OF MODERN ART

Fig. E.1.
Print cataloguing inventory sheet (8½ by 11 in.), Department of Prints and Illustrated Books, Museum of Modern Art.

Location	PHOTO No.	LEICA No.	Mat Size	Mat Label	Artist Rcd.	QUEST'N OBJ Sent	QUEST'N OBJ Ret'd	QUEST'N ART Sent	QUEST'N ART Ret'd	CARDS Donor	CARDS Subject	CARDS Artist	CARDS Object	CARDS Accession	WORK SHEET Written	WORK SHEET Approved	WORK SHEET Cc. to Reg.	Temp. Card	Numbered	DESCRIPTION	MUSEUM NUMBER

Fig. E.2.
Catalogue sheet for individual print (8½ by 11 in.), Department of Prints and Illustrated Books, Museum of Modern Art.

PRINT COLLECTION

Artist: JOHNS, Jasper

Accession N°: 291.68

Photo N°: Mathews 1354

Nationality and Dates: American, born 1930

Leica N°: 5395 E   **Mat:** IV

Title: Flags

Credit: Gift of The Celeste and Armand Bartos Foundation

Date and Place Executed: 1967-68, dated West Islip, L.I., New York

Source: Universal Limited Art Editions, West Islip, L.I., New York

Medium: Lithograph, printed in dark gray, light gray brown, vivid green, black, medium gray and vivid orange

Price Paid:

Purchase Order N°:

Paper: White, smooth, wove (East Indian)

Insurance: $1,000 (4/68)

Watermark/Trademark: None visible

Date Accepted: April 23, 1968

Dimensions:
Comp and Sheet (Irreg): 34 5/8 x 25 7/8" (87.9 x 65.7 cm)

Announced:

Definitive Catalogue: Field 70

Collections:

Signature: "J. Johns/'67-68" lower right corner, black ink

Bibliography:

Impression: "1/43" lower left corner, black ink, artist's hand

Condition:
Edges brittle and folded causing ink cracking
General rippling overall surface comp
Hinged all sides

Exhibition/History:
ICE-F-120-68 Jasper Johns Tour: June 17, 1968-September, 1970
MOMA Exhibition #951, Jasper Johns: Lithographs. December 22, 1970-May 3, 1971. Tour: July 15, 1971-June 25, 1972

Subject Headings: Objects

Remarks: Title: Universal Limited Art Editions, Information Sheet, 2/14/68

"[ULAE]" Publisher's embossed chop lower left comp

Catalogued by: CHN   **Date:** 8-24-72

Approved by: HDP   **Date:** 8-31-72

P&D - 8,2 (rev. 4/68)

*Fig. E.3.
Catalogue sheet for portfolio (8½ by 11 in.), Department of Prints and Illustrated Books, Museum of Modern Art.*

```
                              PRINT COLLECTION

      Artist:   CRUZ-DIEZ, Carlos          Accession N°:  37.68.1-5
                                           Photo N°:
      Nationality and Dates: Venezuelan, born 1923
                                           Leica N°:           Mat:  P (I)
      Title:    Transchromies, portfolio
                                           Credit:   Inter-American Fund

      Date and Place Executed: (1965), Paris
                                           Source:   Galeria Conkright,
                                                     Caracas, Venezuela
      Medium:   Serigraph, printed in color
                (see Individual)           Price Paid: $110

                                           Purchase Order N°: 19604
      Paper: (a) white, smooth, wove and
             (b) clear acetate             Insurance:   $110  (2/68)
      Watermark/Trademark:  None visible
                                           Date Accepted: February 5, 1968
      Dimensions: Comp. (sight): 7 7/16 x 7 7/16"
          (18.9 x 18.9 cm); Sheet (approx.): 10 1/2   Announced:
          x 11 1/2" (26.7 x 29.2 cm)
      Definitive Catalogue:                Collections:

      Signature:  None
                                           Bibliography:
      Impression: None

      Condition:    Portfolio: fingerprints upper   Exhibition/History:
         right cover; light dirt general verso

                    (see Individual)

      Subject Headings:
          Abstract composition; Portfolios

      Remarks:   "cruz-diez . transchromie . paris 1965" verso of each print's folder,
          printed in black; "C-D." justification page, blue-black ink, artist's hand


      Catalogued by:   LB               Date:  3/21/69
      Approved by:     RC               Date:  3/21/69
      P&D - 8,2 (rev. 4/68)
```

CATALOGUE SHEET

The forms shown in figures E.2 and E.3 are printed on white bond paper of 100 percent cotton stock, 8½ by 11 inches. Plain white bond second sheets are used. One copy of the form is used as a work sheet, and the information is later transferred to another copy, which is the permanent record. The following are notes concerning some items on the catalogue sheets that require further explanation:

DATE AND PLACE EXECUTED: A print is considered to have been dated by the artist if the date is either written by hand on the print or worked on the stone, plate, block, etc. The date is recorded in quotation marks exactly as it appears, with missing digits added in parentheses, e.g., "(19)'52." If the date appears in conjunction with the signature, its location and medium are shown under SIGNATURE. If the date appears,

```
CRUZ-DIEZ, Carlos                           37.68.1-5

Transchromies, portfolio

Remarks:        Published by Signals, London in Paris, 1965.
                Date: title page, and verso of each folder containing print.
                Edition:   205 (104) numbered and signed.
                           10 dedicated to collectors.
                Portfolio: heavy paper with title and artist's name printed
                           in black on top cover; top interlocking flaps
                           are vivid red and white; inner flaps are medium
                           gray and gray olive green.
                Contents:  10 sheets folded at the right side:
                           Title page; blank; blank; blank.
                           Notes in French; blank; blank; notes in English.
                           Notes in German; blank; blank; notes in Spanish.
                           Introductory sheet; blank; blank; blank.
                           5 2-part serigraphs, (a) on white paper tipped
                              onto folder, (b) on acetate, movable within
                              folder.
                           Justification page; blank; blank; blank.

37.68.1         Printed in (a) black, very light green blue and
                           (b) medium pink.
                Condition: folder: dented upper left corner; tiny spots
                           lower left margin; black ink left verso.

37.68.2         Printed in (a) dark gray, strong yellow pink, brilliant
                           yellow and (b) black.
                Condition: folder: dented upper left corner; ink smudge
                           left lower margin; ink upper center verso.

37.68.3         Printed in (a) black, and (b) light blue green.
                Condition: folder: blue green ink right upper margin;
                           dirt upper center, upper right and lower center
                           verso; blue green ink lower right verso.

37.68.4         Printed in (a) black, vivid orange, light green blue,
                           light yellow green, medium pink and
                           (b) dark gray.
                Condition: folder: abrasion and glue upper center and
                           right center verso; dirt lower right verso.

37.68.5         Printed in (a) light blue green, strong blue, gray red
                           orange, vivid green and (b) medium blue green.
                Condition: folder: dirt lower left margin; dirt right
                           center, right lower and lower left verso.
```

but not in conjunction with the signature, then this information is recorded under REMARKS. If the date is known but does not appear on the print, it is recorded under DATE AND PLACE EXECUTED in parentheses and is justified either by the proper numerical entry from a published definitive catalogue or, under REMARKS, by exact references—for example, verbal corroboration from artist or publisher, specific entry in published (but not definitive) catalogues, and so forth. Any available information about the workshop, city, and/or country where the artist made the print is recorded after the date and, again, justified under REMARKS.

MEDIUM: The print medium (etching, lithograph, etc.), or media, is specified, followed by the color or colors of ink used. For uniformity in designating colors of ink (not for tones that result from overprinting), the National Bureau of Standards's *ISCC-NBS Centroid Color Charts* (see bibliography) are consulted.

PAPER: The general type of paper (laid, wove, China, Japan, etc.) is given, together with its texture (rough or smooth) and its color. Shades of white and off-white running into buff are determined by the following standard, set up arbitrarily on the basis of Ivins matboard:
  white: lighter than Ivins matboard
  ivory: same as Ivins matboard
  cream: darker than Ivins matboard
  buff: considerably darker than Ivins matboard

WATERMARK/TRADEMARK: A watermark that consists of one or more words is recorded in quotation marks, as, for example, "Vollard." Where a portion of the watermark is cut off, the missing letters are recorded in parentheses, as, for example, "(Ar)ches." For watermarks that are monograms, a description or a sketch of the monogram is provided. If no watermark appears, "none" is specified. Trademarks are sometimes printed or embossed on the paper and are recorded in the same way as watermarks.

DIMENSIONS: Measurements of both the image (plate or composition) and sheet are given in inches to the nearest 1/16 of an inch and in centimeters to the nearest millimeter. For intaglio prints, such as etchings, engravings, aquatints, or drypoints, measurements of the plate marks are taken at the right edge and bottom, and include the outermost mark of the beveled edge, if any. So as to record the full size of the plate, particularly if the corners are rounded, measurements are made from a point about ¼ inch, or 0.5 centimeter, in from the corners. If there is no plate mark, the composition is measured. For planographic and relief prints, such as lithographs and woodcuts, measurements of the composition size are taken by lining up two transparent triangles, or two strips of Plexiglas, with the outermost points of the composition—at top and bottom for height and at its sides for width. If the composition is irregular (not square or rectangular), this fact is indicated. The sheet size is measured at the right and bottom edges at a point a little in from the corners. Again any irregularities in the sheet are indicated.

DEFINITIVE CATALOGUE: If a definitive catalogue of an artist's work has been made, the number and state, preceded by the key letters of the compiler's name, are recorded. If more than one definitive catalogue is listed, the key letter or letters of the catalogue according to which the sheets are filed are underlined. For example, for Ensor *Music in the rue de Flandre, Ostend*, "D.81, only state; C̲.83 I/II," indicates that Delteil describes only one state; Croquez describes two states, of which this impression is the first; the sheets are filed according to Croquez. Where a book is in general use as a catalogue, although it is not actually a definitive catalogue, the compiler's name and catalogue number are given in parentheses.

SIGNATURE: The signature is recorded in quotation marks exactly as shown on the print only if written in the artist's hand; otherwise it is specified as "not signed." A signature worked on the plate, stone, or block does not constitute a bona fide signature, and such a print is not considered signed unless signed by hand also. A location specified as "lower left," "center bottom," or "lower right" indicates that the signature appears in the usual place on the margin, just below the plate mark or composition. If the signature does not appear here, it is necessary to specify the location, e.g., "lower left on composition," or "lower left corner of margin." The medium of the signature is also given, e.g., pencil, red crayon, blue ink, or whatever.

IMPRESSION: The number within the edition or any other notation regarding the sequence of the printing of the print (trial proof, artist's proof, etc.) is cited in quotation marks exactly as given. "Artist's hand" is added if the handwriting is the same as the signature. Location and medium are designated in the same manner as the signature.

CONDITION: Holes, tears, creases, wrinkles, spots, stains, foxing, rippling, and so forth are described, and their locations are noted. Location must be specified as within the composition or printed area, or in the margin; "one ⅛-inch hole center left side one inch from edge," for example, might be in either. Information regarding later damages and repairs is added as necessary.

SUBJECT HEADINGS: These subject headings are an arbitrary group of subjects devised to aid public users of the print collection who are seeking illustrations of particular subjects. Examples of subject categories are "Cubist," "Nudes," "Portraits," and "Religion."

PHOTO NO.: Important prints and those needed for reproduction are photographed, and the negative number, or numbers, recorded here.

LEICA NO.: The negative number of the 35-mm photograph that appears on the catalogue card is recorded here. In recent months the 35-mm photograph has been assigned the print's accession number, so in the future there will be no need to record the negative number.

MAT: The size of the mat is noted here, according to the following designations:
- I: 16 by 22 inches
- II: 22 by 28 inches
- III: 25 by 32 inches
- IV: 30 by 40 inches, or odd sizes not exceeding this size in which one dimension is larger than size III
- O: oversize, or larger than 30 by 40 inches

These designations facilitate locating prints, for prints at the Museum of Modern Art are all matted and grouped according to size, then stored in cabinets. Sizes I and II are stored in Solander boxes in the cabinets.

CREDIT: The credit line provides the exact form in which the name of the donor or purchase fund is to be listed on the catalogue card and whenever the print is exhibited or published. Additional information that may be necessary for identification but should not be published appears in parentheses.

COLLECTIONS: Former collections are recorded, and whether and where their stamps appear on the print. If no information or marks are found, "no marks" is specified.

BIBLIOGRAPHY: The bibliography lists only those sources that refer to or illustrate the museum's impression of a particular print. References and illustrations of other impressions are not recorded.

EXHIBITION/HISTORY: The exhibition history lists each time the print has been on exhibition—within the museum, out on loan, or as a part of a traveling exhibition. Dates, title of the exhibition, and place are recorded in each instance. The exhibition history of the print prior to its acquisition is noted under either BIBLIOGRAPHY or REMARKS.

REMARKS: All information not included above is given under this heading. Other handwritten inscriptions, such as title and dedication, and inscriptions on plate, block, or stone, such as title and signature, may also be mentioned here. For illustrated books or portfolios, the entry should include the publisher; date and place of publication; size of edition; a description of the portfolio, case, or binding; contents; and a list of plates.

Catalogue sheets are filed in lock-post binders alphabetically by artist, then, if a definitive catalogue exists, by definitive catalogue number; if there is no definitive catalogue, then chronologically by date of execution.

ARTIST'S SHEET

Preceding the catalogue sheets of each artist's prints is an artist's sheet on colored, acid-free paper stock. This sheet contains the artist's full name, biographical information, and a listing of definitive catalogues that specifies the abbreviations of the compiler's name or initials used on the catalogue sheets. The biographical information is stated in the form that would be used in an exhibition catalogue or on a label: legal nationality, country of birth if not that of which the artist is a citizen, years of birth and death, and any country in which the artist may have done a considerable amount of work (e.g., "French, born Lithuania 1891. In USA since 1941."; or "Swiss, 1879–1940. Worked in Germany."). More detailed information may also be given, such as town of birth, dates of residence in foreign countries, or date of naturalization.

CATALOGUE CARD

For the use of the public, a catalogue card is prepared on a 4-by-6-inch white file card of acid-free stock. This is a printout from the computer catalogue and contains only selected data. (See figure E.4.) Basic information appears at the top and bottom of the card to accommodate both drawer and visible file systems. The catalogue card includes a 35-mm photograph, which does not appear on the catalogue sheet. Some portfolios and illustrated books require more than one photograph, and these are placed on separate cards. Because of the expense, only a selection of plates from a profusely illustrated book or large portfolio is photographed unless the importance of the book or portfolio warrants complete coverage.

ARTIST'S CARD

The artist's card, also for the use of the public, contains the same information as the artist's sheet. It is tabbed to serve as a guide card. (See figure E.5.)

MAT LABEL

Where the print collection is handled by the public, a mat label, on white bond, is pasted with library paste on the lower right corner of the inner matboard, below the print. The label includes the following: name of artist; biographical information; title (foreign title also given, if desired); date; medium; definitive catalogue number; portfolio or book in which published, if any; credit line; accession number; and name of institution. (See figure E.6.)

DONOR CARD

The donor card gives the name and address of the donor and lists the donor's gifts. The donor card is white, 4 by 6 inches, all rag stock. (See figure E.7.) A similar card is made for each purchase fund and is filed alphabetically with the donor cards. Red lines are drawn through the entry if the print or illustrated book is deaccessioned.

SUBJECT FILE

Information for the subject file is drawn from the catalogue sheet. The subject headings are recorded on blue guide cards with half-cut tabs for the main categories and fifth-cut tabs for the subheadings. A 3-by-5-inch card on white stock is made for each subject category to which a print pertains. This card includes the name of the artist

JOHNS, Jasper Print - United States 291.68
Field 70. O

FLAGS. 1967-68.
Lithograph, printed in dark gray, light gray brown, vivid green, black, medium gray and vivid orange,
Sheet and comp. 34 5/8 x 25 7/8" (87.9 65.7 cm.)(irreg.).
Gift of the Celeste and Armand Bartos Foundation.

Accepted 4-23-68. Leica 5395e.
Purchased by the donor from Universal Limited Art Editions, West Islip, L.I., New York. Mathews 1354.

Signed L.R. corner, black ink "J. Johns/'67-68".
Dated - see above.
Impression: "1/43" L.L. corner, black ink, artist's hand.

Paper: white, smooth, wove (East Indian).

Place executed: West Islip, L.I., New York.
MOMACTL2 3016 131215
JOHNS, Jasper FLAGS. (PR) 291.68

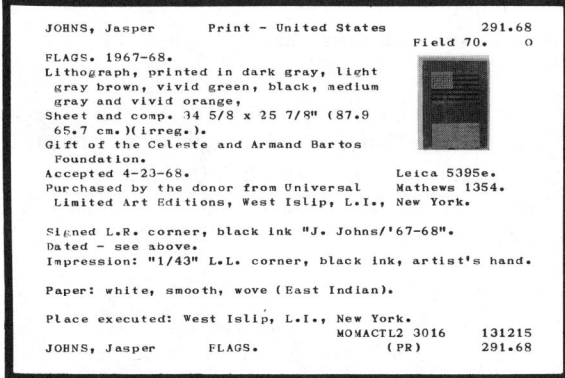

Fig. E.4.
Catalogue card (4 by 6 in.), Department of Prints and Illustrated Books, Museum of Modern Art.

KIRCHNER, E.L.

Kirchner, Ernst Ludwig German, 1880-1938

Born May 6, 1880, Aschaffenburg, Germany
Died June 15, 1938, Davos, Switzerland

Sch.: Schiefler, G., Die Graphic Ernst Ludwig Kirchners. Berlin, Euphorion, 1925 (Vol.I); 1926 (Vol.II)

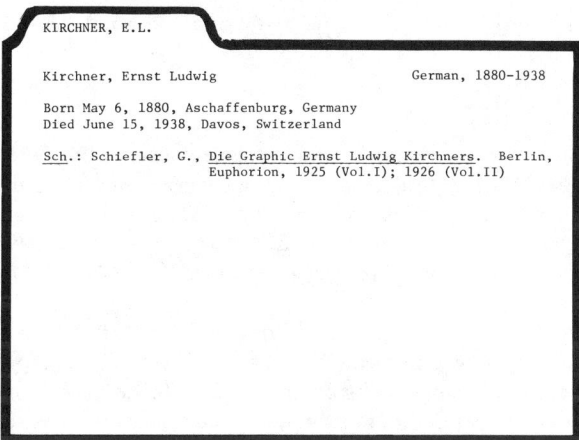

Fig. E.5.
Artist's card (4 by 6 in.), Department of Prints and Illustrated Books, Museum of Modern Art.

VUILLARD, Edouard French, 1868-1940

The Game of Checkers (La Partie de dames). (1899.)
Lithograph, printed in color, R.M.32 III/III
Plate I from portfolio Paysages et intérieurs, Paris, Ambroise Vollard, 1899.
Gift of Mrs. John D. Rockefeller, Jr. 599.40.2

Museum of Modern Art, New York

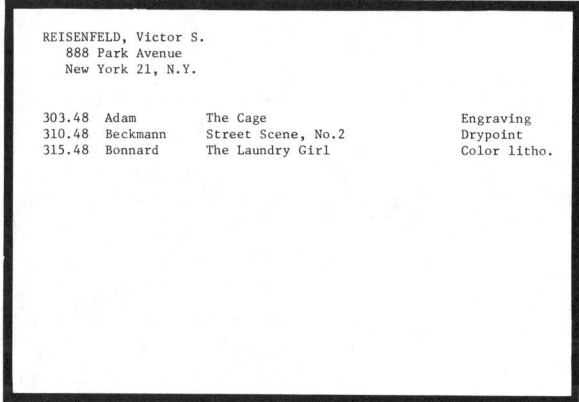

Fig. E.6.
Mat label, Department of Prints and Illustrated Books, Museum of Modern Art.

REISENFELD, Victor S.
888 Park Avenue
New York 21, N.Y.

303.48	Adam	The Cage	Engraving
310.48	Beckmann	Street Scene, No.2	Drypoint
315.48	Bonnard	The Laundry Girl	Color litho.

Fig. E.7.
Donor card (4 by 6 in.), Department of Prints and Illustrated Books, Museum of Modern Art.

FEININGER, LYONEL (American, 1871-1956) 151.45 II

Railroad Bridge. 1919. Woodcut

Architecture - bridges
See also: Transportation

Fig. E.8.
Subject file card (3 by 5 in.), Department of Prints and Illustrated Books, Museum of Modern Art.

and biographical information, accession number of the print, mat size, title, date, medium, subject file heading, and cross-references when applicable. (See figure E.8.)

PHOTOGRAPH ALBUMS

Important prints and those needed for reproduction are photographed and printed in 8-by-10-inch size. The photographs are labeled with catalogue information and the negative number, and mounted in loose-leaf binders alphabetically by artist. The negative numbers of these prints are also recorded on both the catalogue sheet and the catalogue card.

Charge-Out System

When prints are removed from their normal place of storage for conservation, framing, exhibition, or loan, the registration number and the artist are recorded in a charge-out ledger, and places to which the work is going and the date are listed as well. When a print is removed for exhibition or loan, a colored tab is placed on the catalogue card to indicate to the public that the work is not available. In addition, the staff member in charge of exhibitions and loans maintains an alphabetical list, by artist, that records the exact dates when the work will be away and the name of the exhibition or borrowing institution.

Bibliography

United States, Department of Commerce, National Bureau of Standards. *ISCC-NBS Centroid Color Charts.* SRM 2106. Washington, D.C.: GPO, measurements made in 1964. This series of color charts is available for purchase from the National Bureau of Standards, Standard Reference Materials, Washington, D.C. 20234, either separately or together with *Color: Universal Language and Dictionary of Names* (SP 440) (1977), as part of a *Color Kit* (SRM 2107).

Zigrosser, Carl, and Christa M. Gaehde. *A Guide to the Collecting and Care of Original Prints.* Sponsored by the Print Council of America. New York: Crown Publishers, 1965. Rpt. 1973. Contains a short list of publications on the history, techniques, and appreciation of prints; a glossary of terms relating to prints; and a chapter on the care and conservation of fine prints.

INSPECTING AND DESCRIBING THE CONDITION OF ART OBJECTS

RICHARD D. BUCK

Condition refers to the state of preservation of an object. That state is determined by three basic considerations: insecurity, damage, and disfigurement. An object may be insecure because of weakness of material or construction brought about by deterioration or mechanical stresses. It may be damaged because deterioration has become so advanced that there are actual losses or ruptures, or it may be damaged by mechanical or physical violence or chemical change. Finally, an object may be disfigured by dirt, stains, discolored coatings, poor restorations, or by damage. A comprehensive description of condition includes these three aspects.

The Registrar and Condition

The registrar should be familiar with condition examination and records because the registration department is a checkpoint in the traffic of museum objects, a place where all aspects of condition should be observed and understood, even if they are not all recorded. The full record of condition belongs in the curator's dossier and in the records of periodic inspections carried out by the conservator. These more detailed records should, however, be available to registrars, as the need for information on condition arises whenever objects are to be handled or arrangements made for their exhibition, storage, or shipment. For this reason insecurity is an aspect of condition that is of primary concern to a registrar. The registrar should also be able to recognize and describe recent or unrepaired damage. Old damage, hidden under restorations, and disfigurement are generally of less immediate importance to the registrar and are more properly the concern of the curatorial or conservation departments.

INSECURITY

Insecurity is often the most difficult aspect of condition to detect and describe. It is indicated by a wide range of symptoms, in the past largely ignored, that may be taken as omens of damage.

Insecurity may be the result of a natural weakening of the materials of which the object is made. Fabrics, paper, bone, leather, varnishes, and almost all organic materials tend to become weaker and more brittle in time, and tiny splits and breaks are signs of the beginnings of larger ruptures. Insecurity may also result from a weakness in construction. Joins and repairs should always be examined; repaired breaks are particularly vulnerable.

Mechanical stress, too, causes insecurity. Both wood and fabric expand and contract in response to seasonal changes. It is safer to permit some movement than to

*Fig. F.1.
A cradle is used to prevent the warping or splitting of a wood panel that has been used as the support of a painting. Strips of a hardwood such as mahogany or oak are glued to the back of the panel parallel to the wood grain. These strips are notched so that transverse strips can be fit under them against the panel running across the grain. The transverse strips are not glued to the panel but remain loose to allow the panel to expand and contract without warping.*

thwart it by nailing paintings into their frames or by using other rigid fastenings. Room for expansion is particularly important for panel paintings. The free members of a cradle might be tested to see that they are not locked; the looser they are, the better for the panel. (See figure F.1.) Metal clips or board backing should be props, not levers exerting great pressures against the painting. On the other hand, mountings should never be so loose that they are inadequate. The fit of the painting into the rabbet of the frame should be checked to see that there is no danger of the painting falling through the frame and that the thin step of the rabbet is not cracked or broken, threatening to give way.

Insecurity may be simply the result of an object's material or design. Objects made of glass, for example, are inevitably insecure; so, too, are ceramic pieces and objects with free-standing elements. Stone objects are often surprisingly insecure. Stone is usually heavier than commonly thought—a cubic foot of marble weighs about 175 pounds. A statue of several cubic feet in volume may seem easy to handle, particularly if there is an arm, head, or other projection to grasp, but these handles are almost always too weak to stand the stress of lifting. It is therefore suggested that, if possible, the weight of stone sculpture be recorded. Points of possible weakness in stone objects should by checked. The presence of real weakness is revealed by identifying hairline cracks.

Insecurity is normally described in detail by the curator and conservator. But, because of the registration department's service as a checkpoint in the traffic of museum objects, it is an aspect of condition with which the registrar should be thoroughly familiar.

F: INSPECTING AND DESCRIBING THE CONDITION OF ART OBJECTS

INSPECTING FOR CONDITION

To some extent the limits of the registrar's concern with condition are defined by the equipment available for inspections. A registrar should have a large table, over which are fitted at least two strong, cool beam lights. To reveal the necessary evidence of condition, the lights should be adjustable so that they are capable of both general illumination and cross-lighting. The table should be well padded, not only to protect frames, but also to protect paintings and drawings turned face down for a scrutiny of their backs and solid objects and ceramics upended for study. With this equipment and a hand lens it is possible to observe even small, inconspicuous defects, such as cleavage in paintings, checks or splits in the backs of wood panels (where they usually appear first, before breaking through to the front), scratches or dents in metals, stone, and ceramics, foxing on paper, and so forth, all of which may be signs of insecurity or new damage. (See figures F.2–3.)

It is the function of the registrar to inspect an object upon its arrival at the museum. This first inspection is important in view of possible insurance claims. Another inspection is advisable at the time an object leaves a museum. An object should have been carefully examined before its shipment was authorized, but the registrar makes the final check to see that an object is fit to travel, to be handled by another staff, to endure another climate, and to make a safe return.

Drawings should be inspected to see that frames are sound; that the backings are stiff enough to take a moderate accidental blow without bursting the glass; and that the back is sealed to exclude dust. Paintings should be checked to see that they are secure in their frames but not bound; that the stretcher keys are all present and firm and that none has fallen down behind the lower stretcher stick; and that, for larger paintings, a small wad of cotton is lightly taped between the canvas and the center of the middle stretcher cross-member to prevent vibration of the canvas during shipment. Occasionally a registrar may discover some evidence of insecurity not previously noticed. If so, special precautions must be taken in the handling of the object, or it may even be withheld from shipment.

Failure to perform the final check can have serious consequences, not only for the safety of the object in travel but also for the museum shipping the object, should damage occur. It is an insurance that gives protection not offered by any underwriter. After the final check, objects should be kept in a safe storage area until they are ready to be put into their packing cases, thus keeping them out of the shipping-room traffic as long as possible.

RECORDING CONDITION

The method of recording condition varies from museum to museum, but some general instructions are applicable to the content of the notes. There is a need for brevity and accuracy. Every attempt should be made to describe three attributes of any defect: its nature, its location, and its extent. As the nature of a defect is often the most difficult to describe, it will be considered last.

Location may be described a number of ways. A defect, like grime, may be generally distributed, in which case the word "general" will suffice. Occasionally stains or scars may be described as being "scattered generally." A defect appearing in a specific area only may be located in terms of the design—in the background, for example, or in or near a figure or other design feature. It may also be located in reference to the eye, arm, or leg of a figure. In locating a defect in terms of the design, the point of view must be clear. It is useful to adopt the heraldic terms "dexter" and "sinister" to designate the subject's right or left, respectively, as distinguished from the viewer's right or left.

For locating defects on paintings, either an approximate or an exact method can be used. In the approximate method the surface is divided into nine zones like those of a tic-tac-toe figure. The three horizontal positions are designated "left," "center," and "right"; the three vertical positions "top," "center," and "bottom." Thus any zone can be designated by capital letters such as TL, C, BR, etc. In the exact method the coordinates of the defect are measured in height (vertical distance above the bottom left corner) and width (horizontal distance from the same point), just as one would plot a point on a graph. The point of reference is always the bottom left corner of the stretcher or panel, unless otherwise specified.

The extent of a defect must be recorded according to its nature. A split, a tear, a hole, or a stain can be measured in length or area. But abrasion, grime, cleavage, weakness, brittleness, dullness, and so forth are not easily measured, and adjectives must be used. The following sequence of five adjectives that represent arbitrary degrees has been used with success: "negligible," "slight," "moderate," "marked," "extreme." Thus "slight," for example, has a fairly specific meaning because it refers to a defect more serious than "negligible" and less serious than "moderate."

The use of any routine terminology saves time in writing records and automatically increases accuracy. Such entries as "slight general dullness," "flaked loss of paint, size of a dime, H. 6½ in., W. 8¼ in.," or "disjoin at dexter elbow" all have reasonably clear meanings.

The nature of a defect should be described in a word or two with specific meanings. Much of the misunderstanding about condition is traceable to a casual use of terms for describing defects. The need for more accurate communication in art technology has brought about a gradual refinement of terminology over the past fifty years. The glossary offered here represents a step toward some standardization. The glossary of terms published in the first edition of *Museum Registration Methods* was revised for the second edition in light of suggestions offered by the Committee on Terminology, International Institute for Conservation—American Group. This third edition of the glossary includes some new terms and revisions of earlier definitions. It has been prepared with the assistance of George L. Stout, who, as editor of *Technical Studies in the Field of the Fine Arts*, introduced many terms now in common use. I acknowledge with many thanks Mr. Stout's extremely helpful suggestions. I assume responsibility for the selection of these terms from many others that might have been included and realize that there are gaps that may need to be filled.

Concise Glossary of Terms Used to Describe Condition of Works of Art

ABRASION (ALSO CALLED RUB, SCRAPE, WEAR): one type of EROSION; a surface loss assumed to be caused by friction on the varnish, paint, or ground in a painting, on the design material or the support of a drawing or print, on the finish of furniture, sculpture, or other objects.

ACCRETION (ALSO CALLED INCRUSTATION): an accumulation of extraneous material on the surface of an object that alters the original design.

AUXILIARY ATTACHMENTS: materials or constructions fastened to an artifact with the evident aim of contributing strength and stability: e.g., cradles on panels to restrain warp, linings on fabrics, dowels and splines in three-dimensional objects of wood or stone.

Figs. F.2–3. Registrars should have at least two strong lights available for inspecting objects for condition. The lights should be flexible to give both general illumination and crosslighting. The illustration at the left shows a detail of a fifteenth-century painting under general illumination. At the right, the same detail is shown under raking light. Examination by raking light can reveal irregularities and possible insecurities not otherwise apparent.

BLANCHING: irregular, obtrusive, pale, or milky areas in paint or varnish; not a superficial defect like BLOOM, but a scattering of light from microporosities or granulation in aged films.

BLEEDING: the suffusion of a color into adjacent materials, often caused by water or other solvents.

BLOOM: superficial surface cloudiness, white or blue white, caused by moisture penetrating a surface coating of varnish.

CHECK: a rupture in wood along the grain and less than the length of the piece, usually caused by the accelerated drying of wood at the exposed end grain (cf. SPLIT). In plywood and in wood that has been too rapidly dried, checks may appear anywhere along the grain as a result of surface shrinkage.

CHIP: see DENT.

CLEAVAGE: a parallel disruption occurring as separation between or in any of the laminae of a stratified construction, so called because it runs parallel to the surface. When marked, it is visible as an elevation of contour and audible as having a sonancy (the faint sound emitted upon contact) different from that of coherent structures in the same artifact.

OBSCURE, BLIND, OR FLAT CLEAVAGE: a cleavage not evident to the eye in surface examination, but sometimes revealed by sonancy.

BLISTER: one type of laminal disruption. It is rare but may be found in paintings, veneer, and engaged leather coverings, where it appears as an inflated, semiglobular bulge (i.e., convex in section) and is usually caused by excessive heat. In film it appears as an inflated pocket and is produced when the film is made plastic by the action of solvents, heat, or both.

BUCKLED CLEAVAGE OR BUCKLING (ALSO CALLED TENTING): one type of laminal disruption in which loosened layers take a conformation of gablelike ridges. These ridges may combine parallel and perpendicular disruption and may be caused by compressive forces underneath the laminae. They are recognized by contour and by sonancy.

CUPPED CLEAVAGE OR CUPPING: a type of laminal disruption in which FLAKES of paint are created with paint surfaces bent concavely into the shape of cups.

COAPTATION (ALSO CALLED REATTACHMENT, REJOINING, SETTING DOWN): a repair that involves fitting to each other parts that belonged together, such as broken pieces of sculpture and pottery; also recovery of altered shape. Evidence of such treatment may be clear.

COCKLING: a broad wrinkle or system of wrinkles without creasing, usually referring to the conformation of paper or parchment.

CORROSION (ALSO CALLED PATINA, ERUPTIVE PATINA, NOBLE PATINA): the chemical alteration of the surfaces of metals caused by agents in the environment or by reagents applied purposely. The color and texture of a metal surface may be changed without alteration of the form if there is no increase in the volume of the corrosion products, as in the gray green corrosion of Chinese bronzes. If the volume of corrosion products is increased, hard nodules or crusts are formed on metal surfaces. (Cf. EFFLORESCENCE.)

CRACK: a fracture or fissure in any surface, especially a paint film. No loss is implied.

CRACKLE: a perpendicular disruption of laminae. Crackle is common in old paintings and may also occur in lacquer, inlays, ceramic glazes, and other laminae. Two main types are recognized: the CREVICE, which usually has a narrow aperture and often penetrates more than one lamina; and the RIFT, which usually has a relatively wide aperture and penetrates only a single lamina. Description of crackle patterns requires a complex vocabulary.

TRACTION CRACKLE: an "alligator" pattern of crackle produced by shrinkage forces in a rapidly drying upper layer, lying over a slow drying plastic layer. The pattern of traction crackle is a characteristic complex branching, and the apertures are frequently wide and disfiguring.

DENT, DIG, GOUGE, CHIP: a defect in the surface, caused by a blow. A dent is a simple concavity; a dig implies that some material has been displaced; a gouge, that material has been scooped out; a chip, that material has been broken away.

DIG: See DENT.

DISCOLORATION: changes of hue, value, or chroma, often having uneven distribution and plainly detrimental to the prevailing tone relations.

DISHING: a defect in the stretcher caused by the torque of a drawn fabric. If the stretcher members are twisted out of a common plane, a shallow dihedral angle is formed at the corners. Dishing is a common cause of corner wrinkles in stretched canvases (cf. DRAW).

DISJOIN: a partial or complete separation of a join between two members of an object, as distinguished from a CRACK, TEAR, CHECK, or SPLIT.

DRAW: a wrinkle or system of wrinkles in stretched fabric, radiating from corners or edges, usually caused by uneven tension. Corner draws may also be caused by various stretcher defects, especially DISHING.

EFFLORESCENCE: Although efflorescence has a specific chemical meaning referring to the change from a crystalline salt to a powdery mass with loss of water, in recording condition the term is used more broadly to describe powdery or crystalline crusts resulting from other interactions on the surface of stone, plaster, ceramics, or metal. Efflorescence has been used to refer to crystalline accumulations on the surface of paint, a relatively rare phenomenon not yet fully investigated, which seems to involve certain ingredients in the paint interacting with each other or with agents in the environment. The bright green spots of powder sometimes found on bronzes and called "bronze disease" are an efflorescence caused by the transformation of cuprous chloride corrosion into cupric chloride. This reaction requires moisture and can be controlled by maintaining a dry environment, i.e., below 60 percent relative humidity. (Cf. CORROSION.)

EMBRITTLEMENT: a perceptible decline of firm, pliant, and supple organic material toward an amorphous or even pulverized state; easily observed in fabrics, paper, and leather.

EROSION: a degradation of the integument of an artifact with loss of outer portions in consequence of decay, EMBRITTLEMENT, ABRASION, or agitation of a weak bond.

FADING: a discoloration with loss of chroma and usually with change to a higher value; a change of hue may also occur. It is evident particularly in textiles where parts, such as seams, have been protected from light.

FLAKE (ALSO CALLED ISLAND): a portion of a lamina isolated and bound by fissures. Flakes may have profiles (sections) that are flat, rimmed, convex, or concave.

FLAKING, FLAKED LOSS: LACUNAE left by sloughing of laminal FLAKES through a combination of CLEAVAGE and CRACKING.

FOXING: yellow or brown spots on paper, or occasionally pale spots on toned paper, which follow the degradation of cellulose by mold. Similar brown spots are sometimes caused by the rusting of iron particles in the paper.

GOUGE: See DENT.

INSECT INVASION: signs of the working of insects, such as tunnels or "honeycombs" in wood or open gaps and holes in fabrics or paper. These are often clear upon careful inspection.

LACUNA: a void in the integument of an artifact where design material has been lost.

LINING: a repair that involves an auxiliary attachment applied to a planar artifact, such as textiles, paintings, and leatherwork. Linings can usually be noticed readily. (Cf. MOUNT.)

MOLD, MILDEW: a large group of small fungi, the vegetative structures of which invade many organic substances. Provided sufficient moisture is present, these structures or hyphae produce enzymes that dissolve or degrade the host material. This chemical action may leave wastes that stain the hosts, as, for example, FOXING marks on paper. On maturity, reproductive structures will appear on the surface of the host as visible and often colored, furry, or weblike excrescences. Until mature, mold or mildew may not be detectable except by the characteristic musty odor. Because mold requires moisture for growth, mold activity may usually be arrested by maintaining a dry environment, i.e., below 65 percent relative humidity.

MOUNT: a repair that involves an auxiliary attachment to weakened artifacts such as paper and textile fragments. With paper, attachment may have been by adhesion throughout. Textiles are usually sewn to their mounts. (Bases, pedestals, and removable frames are not considered to be mounts or parts of an artifact.)

PENTIMENTO: literally, repentance or a change of mind; in a painting, a visible evidence of an early design below a revised design. If the upper paint has become slightly translucent, either through an increase in the refractive index of an oil medium or other causes, a ghost of the earlier design may be seen. Evidence of the earlier design may also consist of brush marking in the surface conformation unrelated to the visible design.

SOIL: a general term denoting any material that dirties, sullies, or smirches an object.

    DUST: loose soil generally distributed on surfaces.

    GRIME: soil tenaciously held on surfaces.

    SMEAR, FINGERPRINT: types of local grime. FINGERMARK may refer to local BLOOM on varnish, or occasionally to an interruption in general varnish bloom.

    SPATTER, RUN, STREAM: dried droplets or splashes of foreign material.

    STAIN: a discoloration that usually darkens the substance of an artifact in streaks or spots. Its appearance depends on the contacting material.

SPLIT: a rupture running along the grain of a piece of wood from end to end, usually caused by exterior mechanical stress.

STRETCHER CREASE: a crease or line of CRACKS in the ground and paint layers of a painting on fabric, following the inside edges of stretcher members or the edges of cross-members. It is caused by the flexing of the fabric against the edges of these members.

TEAR: a break in fabric, paper, or other sheet material as a result of tension or torsion.

Bibliography

Buck, Richard D. "What Is Condition in a Work of Art?" *Bulletin of the American Group—IIC* [now *Journal of the AIC*], 12:1 (Oct. 1971), 63–67.

Stout, George L. "A Provisional Conspectus of Conservation in the Arts." In *Miscellanea in Memoriam Paul Coremans (1908–65), Bulletin de l'Institut royal du patrimoine artistique*, 15 (1975), 381–86.

———. "A Trial Outline of Conservation in the Arts." *Bulletin of the AIC* [now *Journal of the AIC*], 14:1 (Oct. 1973), 6–11.

REGISTRATION RECORDS IN A HISTORY MUSEUM

MARGOT PAGE PEARSALL
HOLLY B. ULSETH

The registration procedure of a history museum must take into account several distinctions from art or science museums. Whereas the acquisitions of an art museum may be relatively few during a given year, but of high monetary value, a historical museum is likely to process many acquisitions, though perhaps of small intrinsic worth individually. Unlike science museums, the history field has no universally accepted classification nomenclature for materials that would facilitate identification and description. (See article N.) For history museums, the context or associations of an artifact with people, places, or events may be as important to record as the object itself. Furthermore, the great variety of types of objects received by history museums may be as staggering as the quantity, and, thus, the keeping of records for every button, hatpin, hammer, or automobile may be complicated. This situation is all the more aggravated if the staff available to do the record keeping is limited.

The recording program of the Detroit Historical Museum is an example of one designed to handle the problems of large numbers of accessions and a limited staff. While the museum is interested primarily in local history, the collections touch on all phases of human activity—the houses, the industries and businesses, the governments, as well as the military and marine endeavors of the people who have made the Detroit area their home. The accessioning procedures were developed with this diversity in mind.

Accessioning

When the registrar is informed that an item is to be accessioned, he or she assigns it an accession number from a master list (to avoid duplications) and supervises the preparation of the accession records. New accessions are listed in order of their receipt. Other information on the master list includes simply the name of the donor, number of objects included in the accession, and a brief description.

The accession number is composed of two figures, one indicating the year of receipt and the other the number of the accession within the year, as described in chapter 3. In the case of permanent accessions, this number will become the catalogue number. The catalogue number is comprised of three parts—the year of receipt, the number of the accession, and the number of the item in that accession. For example, 78.63.4 represents an item received in 1978 as part of the sixty-third accession in that year and the fourth item catalogued in that accession. Even when only one item is in an accession, a three-part number is used to avoid possible confusion

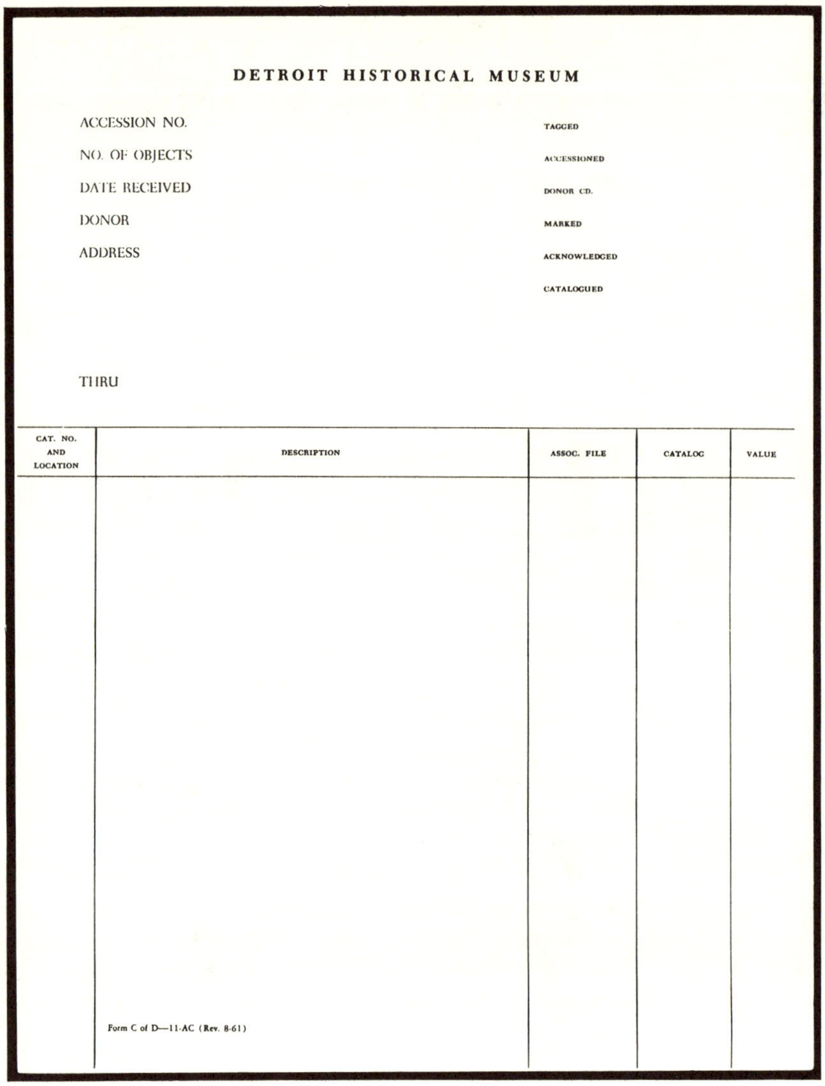

SPECIFIC APPLICATIONS

Fig. G.1.
Accession sheet (8½ by 11 in.), Detroit Historical Museum.

(for example, 78.64.1). Thus, at the Detroit Historical Museum, the catalogue number is based on year of accession and has nothing to do with classification. The catalogue number is an object's identification number and, once assigned, is never changed. It is marked on the object permanently.

Each curator is responsible for identifying and describing each artifact added to his or her collection. This information, along with the identification number, location of the item (in storage or on exhibit), catalogue designation, and insurance value, goes to the registrar, who prepares the permanent records using the curator's information.

The basic, permanent accession sheet (figure G.1) shows the name of the donor or donors, their addresses, telephone numbers if known, and the name of the interested person through whom the gift was obtained, if applicable. It further includes the date of receipt and the number of objects making up the accession and a place to note that the processes of acknowledgment to the donor, marking the objects, and preparation

```
CADILLAC, ANTOINE DE LA MOTHE                    (1)
                                           (1658-1730)
  b. March 5, 1658, St. Nicholas-le-Grave, France
  d. October 18, 1730

  m. Marie Therese Guyon (d. 1746), June 25, 1687, Quebec City
  13 children: (at least 6 born in Detroit) - Marie Therese,
      Francois, Joseph,

  1701, July 24 - founded Detroit
  1711 - appointed governor of Louisiana, all territory from
      Gulf of Mexico to the ridge of the Rockies
  1716 - returned to France; spent most of remaining years as
      governor of Castelserrasin, near his birthplace
```

```
------      Large collection of items associated with
              (in bio. folder)
------      Cadillac Coat-of-Arms
------      Original 3-dimensional water color of Languedoc
              costume
L.8.23      Watercolor of birthplace
29.56       Picture, Coat-of-Arms
29.61       Portrait of
30.58.6     Letter, agreement signed by, photo of original
30.74.2     Photo, Cadillac Bi-Centennial
30.128      Model of City Hall statue
33.9        Drawing of
35.63       Large plaque of
36.14       Photo, Cadillac Bi-Centennial
43.469      Pen sketch of
49.240.1    Model of Cadillac chair
51.298.1    Oil painting, landing of Cadillac, by
              John Coppin, c. 1951
51.299      Bronze bust of
54.144.1    Family documents of
54.144.2    ibid
```

Fig. G.2. Association card (4 by 6 in.), Detroit Historical Museum.

of the catalogue cards have been completed. The accession number is typed in the lower right-hand corner of the sheet as well as at the top for quick reference when the sheets are bound. Notes relating to the history of the donor, his or her association with the objects presented, and any other information that might be of future use are likewise made on the accession sheet. At the end of the year all typed accession sheets are placed in numerical order and bound. The bound volumes of accession records, one volume for each year, constitute the museum's permanent accession records and are filed in fireproof vaults.

Information pertaining to donors included on the accession sheet is summarized and transferred to a 4-by-6-inch donor card, filed alphabetically by donor name. This provides a record that briefly lists the objects received from a specific donor at a specific time.

The accession sheet also indicates whether any of the items should be listed in the association file. This file consists of 4 by-6-inch cards (figure G.2), arranged alphabetically within certain classifications, such as people, events, places, and institutions or major local businesses. The front of the association card lists the name of the subject, a brief history (or biography), and references for additional information. The reverse side carries a listing in numerical catalogue order of the objects in the museum's collection associated with that subject. The association file provides a quick reference to indicate whether the museum possesses any material or information pertaining to a specific person, event, or location. The file is especially useful for determining whether or not an exhibit on a particular subject can be based on the museum's own collection.

Deaccessioning takes place when an object is permanently removed from the museum's collection because of deterioration or transfer to another institution. In such cases, appropriate notes are made in red ink on the accession sheet, the donor card, the association file card, and the accessions record book; and the catalogue card is removed from the active file and destroyed. Such action occurs only on the recommendation of the curator and with the official permission of the governing board.

Acknowledgments

A formal printed acknowledgment (figure G.3), signed by the curator in whose department the material falls and by the director of the museum, is sent for each new accession. It lists the objects received and expresses appreciation for the gift. Each

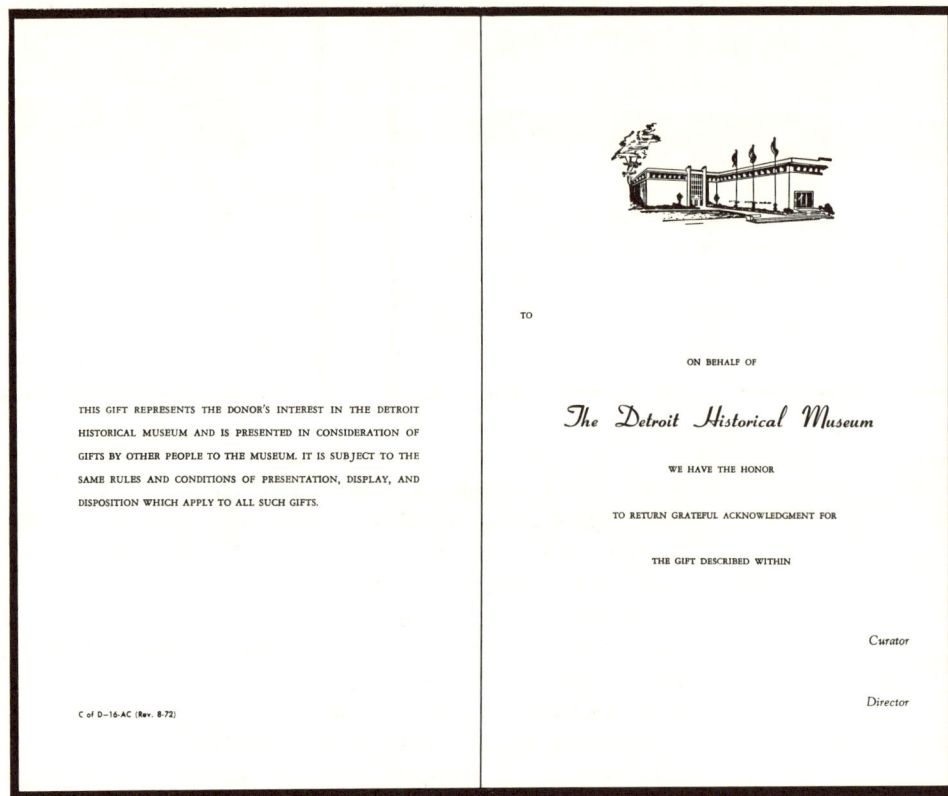

Fig. G.3.
Acknowledgment of gift form (5¼ by 8⅜ in., folded), Detroit Historical Museum.

acknowledgment also bears the accession number assigned to the gift so that if there is any question, the original records can be consulted.

The donor of any gift accepted by the museum must sign a "Certificate of Gift" card (figure G.4) waiving all rights of ownership or control of the objects given. This is a printed form authorized by the museum's governing board stating its policy that the museum will not accept a collection under the condition that it be kept intact, that it be exhibited permanently, or retained permanently. The accession number is typed on the card, which the registrar files in numerical order. If the form does not accompany the accession sheet when it is given to the registrar for processing, the card is sent to the donor at the time of acknowledgment. If the donor is unwilling to sign the donor card, the proposed gift is returned.

Cataloguing

The Detroit Historical Museum has six basic divisions—military, marine, social, industrial, urban, and architectural history—and collections are sorted and stored accordingly under the supervision of six curators. Artifacts are catalogued by specific subject groups, under the six major divisions, using subheadings wherever practical. For example, under "Tools, Carpenter's," there are such subheadings as "Chisels," "Planes," and "Hammers." The subject headings are determined by the curator and can be expanded or reduced as the composition of the collection changes. For instance, as the doll collection at the Detroit Historical Museum increased in size, more subheadings were added, based on the heights of the dolls. Earlier headings merely differentiated between completely china dolls, china head dolls, cloth dolls, bisque

Fig. G.4.
Certificate of gift card (3¼ by 5½ in.),
Detroit Historical Museum.

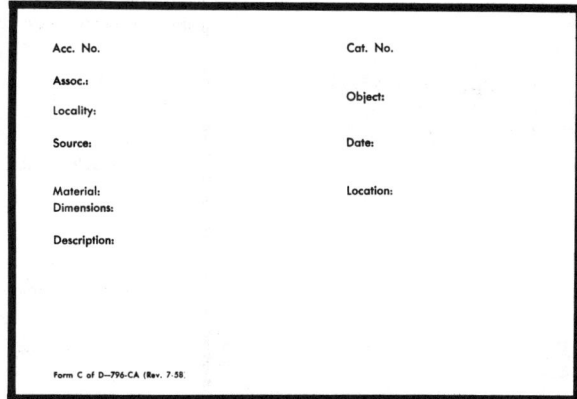

Fig. G.5.
Catalogue card (4 by 6 in.), Detroit Historical Museum.

head dolls, etc. The new catalogue breaks down each kind of doll into subheadings based on height—under 10 inches, 10–14 inches, 14–18 inches, and 18 inches and over. The new headings enable the curator to select quickly from the catalogue the exact item needed.

The 4-by-6-inch catalogue card (figure G.5) contains all known information pertaining to the object described; namely, the donor, address, association, and a complete description. A photograph of the object is attached to the reverse of the card when possible. If the amount of descriptive information exceeds the space available, additional cards are typed and marked with the appropriate catalogue number followed by "(2)," "(3)," etc. General information is never typed on the reverse of a catalogue card.

The registrar's office permanently maintains a complete set of catalogue cards. Each curator has a duplicate set of catalogue cards for his or her division. These duplicates serve as a working set of cards that can be used in the curator's office or taken to storage areas for checking locations and conducting inventories.

Loans

Loans to and from the museum are also recorded in the registrar's office. Loan policy is determined by the governing board, and under these guidelines loans are implemented by the curatorial staff. Each loan requires completion of a specific form that is filed in the registrar's office.

Loans to the museum are made when specific items needed for an exhibit are not available in the museum's collection. They are usually initiated by the director or curatorial staff, but all original copies of loan forms are retained by the registrar.

The "loan-to" form (figure G.6) requires that the loan be made for an established length of time. The items are listed on the form along with an appropriate replacement value for each item as determined by the lender. The lender signs the loan form twice, once to initiate the loan and again to record the return of the loaned material in satisfactory condition. The responsibilities of the museum for loaned items are printed on the reverse side of the loan form. The museum reserves the right to consider any item left in the museum's care for five years with no request for return or for renewal of the loan to be an unrestricted gift to the museum.

The registrar assigns loan numbers when the loan is received. Loan numbers consist of the letter "L" prefix and the reverse order of digits used for accessions. For

SPECIFIC APPLICATIONS

Fig. G.6.
Receipt for loans ("loan-to" form) (8½ by 11 in.), Detroit Historical Museum.

example, L13.76 indicates that the object is the thirteenth loan item in the year 1976. The loan number consists of two sets of digits only. Each loan is individually recorded in a bound ledger (figure G.7), and, when returned, an appropriate entry to the ledger is made in red ink. Forms for loans are kept in one of the following file folders: loans to the museum; loans to the museum/returned; loans from the museum; loans from the museum/returned. Forms for returned loans are pulled from the file at the end of each year so that files remain current.

Loans from the museum are made primarily at the discretion of the director or a curator, based on guidelines set up by the governing board. However, long-term loans of items of significant value must be specifically authorized by the director and governing board. As a public institution, the museum has an obligation to loan materials for educational purposes to schools and other organized groups, as well as to other museums.

Loans from the museum are recorded in duplicate on the appropriate form (figure

> **CONDITIONS GOVERNING THE RECEIPT OF ITEMS LOANED TO THE DETROIT HISTORICAL MUSEUM**
>
> 1. For the period of the loan the items may be displayed, stored or otherwise used by the Museum, at our discretion, subject, however, to our exercising the same care and decision in such display, use and storage as is customary in dealing with similar items owned by the Museum.
>
> 2. The Museum will insure each item against fire, theft and other casualty for the period of the loan and in the amounts shown on this receipt as the value of each item. It is agreed that the liability of the Museum for loss or damage thereby ceases and is replaced by the liability of the Insurance Company.
>
> 3. It is further agreed that each item will, while on display, be identified as the property of the lender.
>
> 4. After receiving reasonable notice, the Museum will return items loaned to the lender on presentation of this receipt.
>
> 5. Any item that has been left with the Museum as a loan for a period of five years from the date hereof, without a request having been made for its return, in consideration for its storage and safeguarding during said time, shall, after said five years, be deemed an unrestricted gift to the Detroit Historical Museum and shall thereupon become the property of the Museum.

G.8). One copy is signed by the borrower and maintained in the registrar's office. The second copy, signed by the curator, serves as the borrower's receipt acknowledging the legitimacy of the loan.

Long-term loans, both to and from the museum, are renewed on a yearly basis. Both parties know at the outset that the loan is for an extended period. The registrar sends out renewal notices at the first of each year. If one party desires to end the loan, objects are returned to the proper owner.

Once the registration system is established and its purposes are understood, the process becomes routine. Complete and careful records are necessary not only to maintain an inventory of the collections but to make these collections useful. Registration records of all types and the catalogue and association files help present and future curators of the institution to know and understand their collections and to serve the museum's public.

SPECIFIC APPLICATIONS

LOAN NO.	NAME AND ADDRESS	DATE REC'D.	DATE RET'D.	ITEMS	REMARKS
L.6.56	Harold Bowen, 818 Lawrence, Detroit	3-2-56	6-5-67	3-Books	
L.7.67	Dr. Alfred Whittaker, 1407 E. Jeff.	3-3-67	5-4-67	1-collection of pictures	

Fig. G.7.
Page from loan ledger (8½ by 11 in.), Detroit Historical Museum.

LOAN FROM

DETROIT HISTORICAL MUSEUM
WOODWARD AND KIRBY
DETROIT, MICHIGAN 48202

321-1701

TO:
ADDRESS:

DATE:
TO BE RETURNED:
RETURNED:
CONDITION:
CLEANING CHARGE:

FOR:
ITEMS:

NOTE: Materials from the Museum's Collection require special handling and cleaning. The sum quoted above should not be construed as a rental fee. It is made to help defray the expense of cleaning and laundering the items included in this loan. The amount is payable upon return of loan (checks should be made out to the Detroit Historical Society).

AUTHORIZED BY:

N.B. Recipient of loan is responsible for items in above list. The utmost caution must be exercised in their use. They must be returned in the same condition in which they were loaned.

SIGNED:

Form C of D—111-LO-A

Fig. G.8.
Loan form ("loan-from" form) (8½ by 11 in.), Detroit Historical Museum.

REGISTRATION IN A HISTORIC HOUSE MUSEUM

DIANE GREENE TAYLOR

Special Concerns for the Historic House Registrar

The basic methods for recording and keeping track of objects in any museum collection have been set forth in earlier chapters of this book, but the very specialized concerns of a museum collection in a historic building deserve particular attention, both because the collection relates so specifically to the structure being used to house it and because, in most cases, the material in the collection achieves its relevance as part of local or community history. These factors affect artifact documentation and storage, and they predicate specialized files. Further, because so many historic house museums are the projects of local historical societies, with small and untrained staffs, registration work must be arranged to make the most of any help at hand, be it professional or amateur, paid or volunteer. Registration duties in a museum of this sort must be understood by everyone on the staff. For a staff coming after workers who have not understood or appreciated the purpose of registration, correcting past errors and omissions in historic house records can be difficult and time consuming. The registrar of the historic house museum needs to know not only the special requirements of historical collections but also methods for developing and expanding the museum's files and for enlarging upon existing information.

The registrar will be confronted by four classes of objects on the historic site: (1) material that was acquired by previous owners and that has remained on the site, either above or below ground, into the period of operation as a museum; (2) material allegedly from the site and returned to it for use by the museum; (3) material acquired by the museum for display at the site when research suggests objects like these would have been used at the building during the time being interpreted by the museum; and (4) "nonartifacts," or reproductions for use in period rooms or craft demonstrations.

At Mount Vernon, for example, the key to the Bastille had remained in the house from the time Lafayette presented it to George Washington, and it was acquired by the Mount Vernon Ladies' Association when it acquired the property. Artifacts like Washington's bed and Nellie Custis's piano, which had been in the house when Washington lived there but had been removed by heirs, were returned to the building when it became a museum. Furnishings such as books in the library, which appeared on Washington's inventories but which had been sold from the house, had to be filled in by the purchase of duplicates. Finally, in the outbuildings, reproduced objects, as varied as tack for the stables and hams for the smokehouse, were fabricated for display. Only if careful documentation exists can the researcher or the general public determine which of the objects are native to the site, which though purported to be native have had a history away from the site before being returned to it, and which period artifacts were never part of Washington's surroundings at all.

Careful records of reproductions are equally important. While museum copies may be readily detected by the expert when still new, the more use they get and the more wear and tear they undergo while on exhibit, the more these objects take on the contours and surface textures of the genuine "antique." The registrar's records are the key to distinguishing among the different classes of artifacts. Conveying these distinctions to the public and to researchers is essential to the museum's honesty as an educational institution. Maintaining the records to support these distinctions is the primary responsibility of the registrar at the historic site.

If the registrar hopes to maintain high standards of documentation for a historical collection, he or she must have a firm appreciation of how much an artifact can tell someone who wants to learn from it. Traditions, letters, interviews, and the like, contribute to the history of an artifact and indicate the web of associations that originally surrounded it. This kind of information generally cannot be read from the artifact alone, and unless the registrar makes the effort to preserve these facts, valuable, intangible aspects of the artifact can be lost forever. Preserving information on the background of objects can also give significance to artifacts that have little intrinsic value but whose history of use in a particular community can raise and even answer unexpected questions and give new insights into the life of the community. There is no predicting which objects will yield important information, so it is the registrar's responsibility to retrieve and preserve every shred of information about even the humblest, simplest artifacts in the collection.

If, for example, three identical apple corers made by the same company under the same patent have been donated or collected from the community, the registrar must consider each of them a unique part of the collection. All three objects can be "read" in the same way and tell the same things about what forces in the society caused the raw materials in the gadget to be assembled, transported, and probably even marketed in the community. Only one can be used in the kitchen of the historic house. What, then, makes the other two worth the space in storage and the time and effort in adding to the documentation in the files? One may have been the first of its kind to be seen or used in the community, with a dated letter accompanying it describing how the original owner saw and purchased it at a trade fair in Chicago. Another may have been repaired by a local blacksmith and may bear the marks and show the special finishing techniques of that particular artisan. If the museum had business records or books from the blacksmith shop in its archives, the apple corer would be a part of the material that tells about an important business in the community. If the third apple corer descended through generations of a family forced to leave the community and migrate to another area, the subsequent travels of the artifact and family before the return of the object to the historic site can tell much about the demographic history of the community's population.

In each case, the registrar's files provide the information that will help unite material culture and traditional history. Because documentation of each artifact is so crucial and can be so ephemeral, the registrar must develop a sensitivity to spotting and collecting clues about the artifact's original context.

This sensitivity to context is most important when an artifact arrives to be accessioned. By maintaining an awareness that the object performed a specific duty in a real society, the registrar achieves a more unified and apt technical examination and description of the object. Knowing how evidence of use or adaptation of an object can tell something about its functions helps the examiner to be more attentive to detail. Understanding that objects found in association with an artifact may tell something unexpected about the history of the artifact at some later date justifies the extra time, effort, and space required for retrieving and storing bits and pieces of information. For instance, flowers pressed between the pages of a book with a history of use in a historic house may give clues to early landscaping and may affect the interpretation of the site. Scraps of molding, old rusty nails, and lumps of glue found in a cabinetmaker's toolbox may enable a furniture specialist to attribute unsigned furniture to that maker. It is even possible that bits of lint and cottonseed found in a cotton wagon from a particular community may show an agricultural historian what variety and quality of cotton was grown in the vicinity and might even provide a historic farm with the seed for starting a field of the very crop that was grown there years ago.

DETERMINING THE NEEDED FILES

Sensitivity to context extends also to analyzing just what files the particular collection of the historic house may require and how best to arrange them. At the time of accession and even before, documentation can come to the museum office in the form of plans, notes, tapes, photographs, archival materials, and even motion picture reels. A researcher may have visited the location of the object to be accessioned and photographed it where it was being kept, or filmed it as it was being used. The researcher may have collected documents relating to the object and interviewed the donor or other informants on tape. All this information must then be stored in a single place where it will be available as needed. If all of this documentation will not fit comfortably into a standard file folder or if some of it requires archival care and must be stored in another place, the registrar should maintain a list of all the files where information on the subject is stored. This list should be kept in the accession file, along with the accession forms, correspondence, and other primary documentation on the object.

Since every collection has its own peculiarities, specialties, and gaps, files should be adapted to perform the duties required for a given site, and the information should be arranged in a manner that makes it easy to find. Like other kinds of museums, the historic house should keep a card file on accessions, arranged by accession number, but the additional files the registrar keeps in a historic house can be modified to achieve the specialized aims of this kind of museum. For instance, unlike other types of collections, which might be categorized by material, epoch, or geographic origin, historical artifacts can be sorted most logically by *use*.

Catalogue designations of artifacts on a historic site should reflect the original use of the objects, and, presumably, the way the historic site museum uses the artifacts in its exhibits. In an exhibition of a kitchen, a cabinetmaker's shop, or a stable, for instance, the objects have been arranged to show how they operated in the society and, in a larger sense, how the piece of society in which they had their place related to the whole. A catalogue that recognizes this and sorts objects by use will best serve the aims and purposes of both curatorial and exhibit departments of the historic site museum.

The entire collection should be indexed, and each entry should be cross-referenced to point to all related entries. The historic house collection is usually so specialized and so small that headings can include, at the very least, owners and makers of objects, names of communities, towns, streets, farms, buildings, and—in deference to the site's involvement in historic preservation—architectural styles of buildings.

If the index includes headings for visual material such as subject matter of photographs or portraits, the index card(s) should make it clear that the material is representational, not three dimensional. If there is a great deal of representational material for a given index heading, it may be useful to list the representational material on a separate card, filed behind the card for three-dimensional artifacts under the same index heading. Photographs and paintings have a wider range of associations than do three-dimensional objects related to the index category in which they are placed. A researcher may seek the representational information, such as the subject of a portrait or the objects in a photo, as well as the information about the specific painting or photo, such as the artist or photographer. The registrar should be aware of the variety of information researchers may seek and should make it as easy as possible for them to find representations of indexed topics within the general file.

The usefulness of including local history information in historic house files increases when the cross-indexed files are examined together. For instance, when the donor file, cross-indexed, can be integrated into the general index of the collection, it reveals family ties and interconnections within the community, and the descent of artifacts through these families can be traced and understood.

Location files for a historic site serve the same purposes as location files in other museums. Unlike catalogue designations, however, the location designations at the historic site should not refer to use. Terms like "upstairs bedroom" or "butchering shed" will be confusing if later research turns up information that the bedroom was actually an upstairs parlor and the room is reinterpreted as such, or if the accession of cigar-making equipment turns the abatoir temporarily into a tobacco-curing shed in connection with cigar-making demonstrations. Architects' measured drawings of historic buildings designate rooms by numbers, much like rooms in an American hotel, starting with 101 on the first floor, 201 on the second, and so on. The registrar should follow these designations for both location files for the artifacts and room-by-room exhibit files for the site. If no room numbers have been assigned to the outbuildings, specific architectural terms or designations by the name of a person or place should be employed—"transverse crib barn," "single pen log structure," "Schoenemann building," "Fredericksburg cabin"—rather than designations by use, such as "storage shed," "garage," "outside kitchen."

An effort should be made to keep location files to a minimum in order to reduce the number of places where the registrar must make notations when an object is moved. For instance, the historic house museum should avoid placing a looseleaf notebook or other form of exhibit list in each period room. While this is frequently done to give new docents a reassuring crutch when they are not certain of their touring scripts, such lists are difficult to keep up to date. The historic house may seem to be a static kind of exhibit, but a look at a room list compiled for docents only a few months earlier will show just how mobile artifacts in these collections can be and how quickly extraneous location files can fall out of date.

The likelihood of keeping any location file current—and consequently of being able to retrieve objects immediately—depends upon keeping the records simple and easy to maintain. In a small house museum, the location files can simply be a log for recording the transfer of an artifact at the time it is moved, and a location card file showing the objects by accession and catalogue number, which is kept up to date from the log. Both the log and card files are necessary. The log (figure H.1) enables the person who transfers an artifact to note the move easily and immediately; the card file (figure H.2) enables someone to find quickly the location of any object without perusing the entire log. Another important advantage of the card file is that it provides a dated record of the artifact's use in the museum. This can be helpful in tracking down the causes of conservation problems and in evaluating the object's importance to the collection when considering loaning or even deaccessioning the item. Neither catalogue nor accession cards themselves should contain space for location notations, for they would have to be changed whenever an artifact is moved. As with the room file notebooks, these extra location notes can cause the registrar to fall behind in all location record keeping, or, at the very least, waste time in duplicated effort.

The registrar of a historic house museum may be responsible for maintaining files other than those for artifacts and exhibits. Housekeeping and maintenance records, for example, may be kept in the registrar's office if the museum is too small to have a maintenance division. Some of these files, such as records of what kinds of chemicals an exterminator used on baseboards that retain original paint or graining, what kinds of cleaners and wiping rags the janitorial staff employs on artifacts, and what fluctuations of temperature and humidity occur within the building, have great bearing on the objects in the collection. If files on these operations are not maintained by the registrar, he or she should know where they are kept or, in the event they do not exist, see that they are established.

Similarly, records on the restoration of the building require special filing space. This documentation should include the title information on the property; the restoration architect's daily journal; measured drawings of each building and outbuilding; a map showing the grid of the site; plans of restoration work, wiring, plumbing, and fire and burglar alarm systems on the entire site; identification of original plant material and planting on the site; and old and new photographs that document the original state of the buildings and the progress of their restoration. These can be important in the future. For instance, if the site has exterior lighting and the electrical wires are buried, accurate plans are imperative, so that maintenance workers or demonstrators digging or plowing will know to avoid them. Contractors and even architects sometimes fail to recognize the public nature of the historic buildings they are rebuilding. They should be reminded of the need to deposit all plans and related papers with the museum. As in the case of maintenance records, the absence from the restoration file of plans of such things as electrical or plumbing lines on the site could mean that the plans are not in the museum's possession at all. If so, the registrar should try to secure copies for the site's files.

When the museum maintains a good file on its own site restoration, people in the community who have material on other historic structures in the area may want to contribute these to the museum to develop an archive of information on the architectural history of the locality. Maps, plans, or manuscripts relating to such buildings may go into the archives or a curatorial research file, but some other kinds of information may become part of the main museum collection. Old photographs of buildings, for example, could be integrated into the museum's collection of historical photographs. The registrar should see to it that the documentation of the photographs is

258 SPECIFIC APPLICATIONS

*Fig. H.1.
Page from artifact transfer log (8½ by 11 in.), Winedale Museum. At the front of the book used as a log of artifact transfer there are room plans showing exhibit and storage areas. Storage rooms and shelves are numbered, and abbreviations used to identify the locations. For instance, "Wagner 9:4e" refers to the Wagner building, room "9," storage compartment "4," and shelf or table space "e." The ledger is used to keep a record of the movement of objects within or out of the museum. The person who moves an object for any reason is responsible for recording the move in the book at the time of the move. The registrar's staff then records the location changes in other files on a weekly basis.*

5–16 Sept. 77 :

Date	Object & No.	To	From	Loc. change noted in card file	By
5 Sept. 77	toy horse & wagon W76.10.1	Spiess 1:3	L02:1d	12 Sept	DgT
5 Sept. 77	toy cowboy W76.10.4	Spiess 1:3	L02:1d	12 Sept	DgT
6 Sept. 77	photo: P159	Photographer: Austin 2300 Windsor Rd.	L02:1A	12 Sept.	RLH
6 Sept. 77	plow point: W74.3.25	L02A	Wagner 9:5A	12 Sept.	VW
7 Sept. 77	plow point: W74.3.25	Log barn 3.4c	L02A	12 Sept.	LWT
7 Sept. 77	candlesticks WL74.35.15+16	Lauderdale kitchen for cleaning	McGregor 4.closet	12 Sept.	RLH + VW
7 Sept. 77	"	McGregor 4 closet	Lauderdale	12 Sept.	RLH
15 Sept. 77	plane WL70.21	Wagner 9:4e	Log Barn	18 Sept.	RLH
15 Sept. 77	plane WL70.13.16 A-C	Wagner 9:4e	Log Barn	18 Sept.	RLH
15 Sept. 77	shucks mattress W75.12.1	Lewis 205	L03 textile storage	18 Sept.	RK
16 Sept. 77	" "	Lewis upstairs porch to air	Lewis 205	18 Sept.	RLH
16 Sept. 77	" "	Lewis 205	Lewis porch	18 Sept.	LJ

*Fig. H.2.
Location card (3 by 5 in.), Winedale Museum.*

```
Winedale Museum: Location File    Acc. No.:_____
Catalogue No.:_____    Other No.:_____
Building          Room        Date Moved into Room
```

complete, that rights have been properly conveyed to the museum, that negatives have been made and properly stored, and that the subject headings for the museum's index of visual material are expanded to accommodate the new architectural data.

Original architectural photographs that come into the museum as a result of its involvement in historic preservation should be copied and stored. Copies can be made from the museum's negatives for use in exhibits, survey notebooks, publications, or other uses, but the originals should remain undisturbed. Other artifacts from the locality, such as architectural remnants from outbuildings unrelated to the museum site, should be accessioned and stored in regular fashion if the museum chooses to accept them.

ARRANGING STORAGE AREAS

The registrar of a historic house or site must also adopt a special approach to museum storage. Objects native to the site should be stored separately from similar objects that are not native to the site but are acquired for display purposes. Such a distinction is not likely to exist in the collections of other types of history museums. To the historic house or site museum, native objects are infinitely more important to the collection than the others, and having the material makeup of the site readily viewable in one area is of great help to the curator considering room changes or additional exhibits, to the architectural historian planning restoration, or to the student of material culture attempting to interpret the history of that site. Therefore, regular shelf storage should contain separate native and nonnative artifact storage areas, each arranged as far as possible in the order in which the cards are filed in the museum's catalogue. Thus, a researcher studying a group of objects, such as baskets or bottles, can distinguish at a glance those that are native to the site from all other baskets or bottles. In specialized storage areas, such as painting, paper, or textile storage, this same distinction between native and nonnative artifacts should be maintained.

DEALING WITH ARCHAEOLOGICAL FINDS

Within the native artifact storage areas there should also be space provided for architectural remnants removed during restoration of the building and for archaeological fragments either discovered as chance surface finds or retrieved during archaeological investigation. If the site underwent archaeological investigation prior to restoration, it will already have been put on a grid, and artifacts from the dig may have been returned to the museum. In this case, objects that have been reconstructed from fragments can be catalogued and added to the collection of native artifacts. Other pieces of artifacts will have been documented and illustrated in the archaeological report of the dig. They will be returned to the museum boxed and arranged according to grid location and should be allowed to remain in that order. Archaeological artifacts from each subsequent dig should be kept separately, shelved in clearly marked boxes beside those from the first dig. Chance surface finds should be arranged according to the grid location of their discovery. The space allotted to archaeological material may become the largest and most important storage area in the historic house museum.

On a historic site, archaeology affects the registrar's role directly. If the site is on the National Register of Historic Places or the National Register of Engineering Monuments, government permission is required for any modification in the structure or disturbance of the soil, even plowing up an area for a garden or burying a power line. In such cases, archaeology may have to be performed before the work begins, or, at the very least, an archaeologist will have to be on hand as an observer in order to document the location and evaluate the importance of any data retrieved. In the case of a dig, artifacts will probably be removed from the site for processing and will be returned after the archaeological report is complete. The registrar will want to make a note of where the artifacts are being taken and who is in charge of them. A written agreement should clarify the ownership of the objects before the dig begins. If the archaeologist is present only as an observer and the objects will not be removed from the site, there will have to be day-to-day accessioning, cleaning, and storage in the museum as the excavation proceeds.

Further, archaeological artifacts do not arrive simply by planned accession or scheduled excavation at the historic site. The planting of a tree, the installation of a water faucet, even a hard rain on an exposed foundation can bring to the surface objects that may tell a great deal about earlier times on the site. For such occasions, the registrar should maintain a copy of the measured drawings of the buildings and a site grid. Should such chance discoveries occur, the registrar should mark the location of the find as a part of the accessioning process. If the site has not already been put on a grid, a pipe or rod should be set at the location of an outdoor find to mark the spot until a grid can be laid out. Accession records should contain careful and close documentation of the location and depth of these archaeological finds, with as precise a description as possible, especially if there is no grid or bench mark for reference. Though surface finds seldom prove to be valuable artifacts in themselves, repeated recovery of objects from one spot on the site may indicate the location of earlier foundations or dumps. By documenting the location of these surface finds, the registrar pinpoints likely locations for future archaeological work, thereby saving much time and expense when a dig on the site is finally possible.

DEALING WITH NONARTIFACTS

The registrar at the historic site faces another problem not common to other types of museums—that of nonartifacts: reproductions in period rooms, tools for craft demonstrations, and props that may be necessary for living history interpretation in order not to jeopardize the safety of the museum's artifacts. Because nonartifacts are often used in exhibits and demonstrations, documentation and storage of these objects must be carried out scrupulously. As a rule, such objects either are placed in a historical exhibit next to genuine artifacts or are the sort of objects that demonstrators tend to leave in museum exhibit areas when not working with them. To avoid confusion with genuine artifacts, reproductions of all kinds should be given permanent numbers. Indeed, because such objects often receive heavy use, the number should be engraved or branded on all removable parts of the object at places that are least affected by wear and tear.

In larger museums the interpretation or education department may be responsible for numbering and tagging tools and costumes used by demonstrators, but in the small museum, this is often the registrar's responsibility. When demonstrations are given, whether regularly or on special occasions, careful attention should be paid to the demonstrators' tools, so that no museum property is mislaid. The registrar should provide a place for storing the museum's demonstration equipment and insist that demonstrators return items to storage when not using them. If these items cannot be stored in an area apart from collection storage, care should of course be taken not to confuse them with actual artifacts. Reproduction tools or furniture that remain in a museum display should be recorded as such in the room files.

If demonstrators bring their own equipment, they should be advised to mark the objects as their own before bringing them into the museum. Though such objects may not seem valuable, both registrar and demonstrator may be surprised to discover how costly and difficult it can be to replace specialized tools. Consequently, whenever a demonstrator prefers to deposit tools, spinning equipment, or the like for more than a day, the registrar should obtain a written temporary deposit agreement. (See figure H.3.) These objects should be treated just like artifacts brought into the museum for study and authentication, and the agreement should state that the objects are not a part of the museum collection. Also, the museum should waive responsibility for taking special security precautions while housing the objects and should obtain a hold-harmless agreement from the owner.

The temporary deposit agreement should be adequate to cover most kinds of objects used in interpreting a historic site. However, in the case of livestock brought onto the museum grounds for use in demonstrations, the museum should be aware of the kind of liability the institution and the individual may have to assume should the animals kick, gore, bite, or otherwise inflict themselves on museum visitors or staff. These special considerations should be addressed by the director or the security or legal officers of the museum.

Correcting Inadequate Registration

Beyond the daily tasks of documenting current accessions and keeping track of the movement of objects through the museum, many registrars face an enormous backlog of poorly documented objects. Traditions about the provenance of the artifacts recede further and further into the realm of forklore with every passing generation of donors, lenders, and staff members. At historic site museums, poor documentation of the collection is often the case from the very beginning. Too often the expense and planning go into the restoration of the building, and the furnishings are a mere afterthought. Even in some of the most professionally managed restorations, collection and documentation of artifacts seem subsidiary to the more immediate business of preserving and shoring up the historic building. As a result, records of the preservation process may be in much better order than even the ownership records for the artifacts.

When the University of Texas accepted the donation of the farm buildings and land at the Winedale Museum in 1967, the gift was accompanied by an architect's detailed daybook documenting the restoration, photographs of the original condition of the buildings and of the restoration work as it proceeded, and numerous measured drawings and plans. However, only the sketchiest description of the collection, and no written conveyance of the artifacts, was received. Similarly, the deed that transferred the Sam Rayburn House to the custody of the Texas Historical Commission neglected, by accident, to include the furniture and other memorabilia left in the building at Rayburn's death. The absence of the necessary documents was noted and steps were taken to remedy these situations, but instances of omissions like these are more common in house museums than might be supposed. In grassroots preservation in this country, money and effort seem to go first for the purchase and preservation of the building. The decision to make the building into a museum often comes at the last moment, when alternative uses cannot be found. By the time a collections curator appears on the scene with a furnishing plan, nervous preservationists may have already moved in a houseful of artifacts to fill up the building. More often than not, there are no documents to show the sources of the objects or whether they were meant as gifts or loans.

It cannot be overstated that, regardless of the apparent insignificance of an object or the casual nature of a gift or loan, some signed statement as to the ownership of each accession that enters the museum must be on file in the museum's records. When these records are not obtained at the time a historic house museum is established, a registrar years later may have the difficult task of trying to determine what the source and conditions of the gift or loan were.

CONDUCTING AN INVENTORY

The first step the registrar must take toward establishing control of a poorly documented collection is to perform an inventory to determine the exact nature, number, and location of all the artifacts presently in the museum. This information forms the basis for planning and budgeting any collection-related project as well as for checking the adequacy of collection records. The basic goal of an inventory is to obtain a dated list of objects by location and by identifying number. If permanent numbers are already affixed to the objects, the inventory taker needs only to proceed room by room, writing down the name of each object and its number.

Inevitably, however, a thorough survey of the collection will turn up artifacts that have never been numbered or whose numbers have rubbed off. The registrar should be ready to assign a special inventory prefix to such objects for the survey. Unnumbered objects can then be marked quickly with this prefix and a simple number (A–1, A–2, A–3). Later, research may turn up the correct accession number assigned, but in the meantime a reference number will be on the object and on the records for use during the days or months it may take to complete the research. If the museum collection is completely unregistered, assigning and placing an inventory number on the object will be the only way to establish a permanent reference number for the artifact until the museum's accession information is organized—and that process could take years. When no accession information can be located, the date of the inventory becomes the date at which accession records begin.

The inventory procedure should be designed, just like merchandising inventories, to be completed as quickly as possible. At least two persons should make up an inventory team, one person to locate the objects and read the number and one person to do the recording. A single individual attempting both to locate and to record, moving back and forth from object to notebook, runs a risk of overlooking or omitting artifacts. A third person on the team can be an added help, especially when a great deal of object numbering is involved or when the survey includes storerooms in which some objects must be moved out of the way in order to reach others.

The inventory team should work straight through the collection, proceeding room by room, building by building. Once a rhythm is established, as many as five hundred objects can easily be covered in a day. If several coordinated teams work together, even a much larger assemblage of objects can be surveyed simultaneously. The registrar should determine which rooms or buildings each team will survey and which inventory numbers each team may assign, and should otherwise coordinate and supervise the groups.

The inventory list that is compiled should be photocopied rather than copied by hand to ensure that no omissions or errors are introduced when duplicating the list. The complete and accurate inventory list that emerges from this project will be invaluable to the registrar. When compared with earlier files or inventories, the list can

```
WINEDALE INN PROPERTIES TEMPORARY DEPOSIT NO. _____

object _____    location _____
object _____    location _____
object _____    location _____
object _____    location _____
object _____    location _____

                    CONDITIONS OF THIS LOAN:

1. These objects were brought into the museum for _____
   and are in no way part of the museum collection.

2. These objects will be given the same care as objects in the collection
   but they will not be placed in high security museum storage nor will
   they be covered by museum insurance.

3. Owner hereby releases and holds museum harmless from any and all claims
   demands, suits, causes and/or causes of action for any loss or damage
   due to any cause except the gross negligence of the museum.

4. Owner hereby grants museum permission to clean or fumigate the objects
   if museum deems it necessary.

5. These objects are to remain in the museum no longer than _____.

6. The receipt below must be retained by Owner and presented along with
   sufficient identification in order to reclaim the objects.

I agree to the above conditions:

_____            _____
(Owner's signature)                (Registrar's signature)

                                   DATE: _____
_____
(Address)

_____            DATE RETURNED: _____
-------------------------------------------------------------
                            RECEIPT

WINEDALE INN PROPERTIES TEMPORARY DEPOSIT NO. _____

OWNER: _____     DATE: _____
object _____     RECEIVED: _____
object _____     Date: _____
object _____
object _____     For: _____
object _____
```

Fig. H.3. Temporary deposit agreement for demonstrators' tools and equipment (8½ by 11 in.), Winedale Museum. This form is merely a model. Local law varies, and a museum should consult its own attorney before drawing up a temporary deposit agreement for this purpose.

indicate what artifacts have been added to the collection or lost from it. Even more important, the inventory can show what objects the museum has in its possession without documentation or title. A concerted effort can then be made to acquire these objects properly, or, if they are of no value to the museum, to return them to their respective donors, lenders, or heirs.

If documentation can be found to show the ownership of objects that the museum has in custody but for which it does not have title, the museum may still be able to trade on the goodwill that brought about the deposit of the artifacts in the museum in the first place. Donors or heirs may be willing to cooperate by signing documents of transfer, even years after the actual donation of the artifact. If the appeal to the donor shows that the museum is undergoing a major improvement in organizing its collection and that the donor's cooperation is a step toward a collection of which the whole community can be proud, the donor will probably be willing to help. If not, it is high time the museum knew about the donor's feelings and returned the object.

For objects that have no documentation of ownership, or if the museum prefers not to contact each donor or lender individually, the museum should consult its counsel regarding the procedures to be followed in its state for adverse claims to objects, as laws dealing with these procedures differ markedly from state to state. In most states, the museum may publish an adverse claim to the objects, usually in the local newspaper. The announcement should include a description of the objects, an indication, if possible, of when and by whom they were deposited with the museum, and a statement that the museum claims these objects as its own. Failure of the owner or heirs to claim their personal property within the statute of limitations—two years from the date of adverse claim in most states—establishes the museum's ownership of the objects. In states that do not admit adverse claim to personalty, the museum may attempt to prove abandonment of property in the courts. However, if the property is determined not to have been abandoned but merely mislaid, the museum will be charged to keep the object until the owner shall claim it. When mislaid personalty remains with the museum longer than the state's statute of limitations, the owner can no longer remove it from the museum, even though the museum cannot obtain legal title to the object. Obviously a specific agreement with the donor or heirs is preferable.

Aside from helping to assess just how well documented a collection may be, the inventory list allows the museum staff to have a good overview of the variety of objects in the collection and the success with which the museum catalogue sorts and describes the objects. It may become apparent that a disproportionate part of the collection falls into one or another category. Revising the catalogue is a curatorial responsibility. It may require nothing more than breaking up existing categories into smaller, more detailed ones, so that, for instance, a particular china platter can be found without scanning the museum's entire collection of tableware. If, however, a large part of the collection, including everything from eyeglasses and figurines to books, is classified under "Decorative Items," then a major revision of the catalogue will be needed. Once the curator has established the new catalogue designations, and if reorganization does not involve the renumbering of objects, the registrar can implement the project much more quickly than might be supposed. A collection of six thousand objects, for instance, with catalogue classification or number recorded only on accession and catalogue files, can be adjusted in a few weeks.

Finding and Using Assistance

Because documenting artifacts in the museum and maintaining control of the collection depends so much on a registrar's one-to-one relationship with the artifacts in the collection, he or she not only must direct the work flow of the office into logical and efficient channels but also must enlist assistance in keeping up with normal collection activity. In the small historic house musem, one person serving as both curator and registrar is likely to fall behind in registration responsibilities unless help can be found to enable the normal business of planning exhibits and collecting materials to continue uninterrupted. As long as adequate supervision can be maintained, the more individuals who are involved in registration projects in a museum, the more efficiently the registrar's office can operate.

Given the limited staff and limited budget that handicap most small museums, the registrar may want to seek registration helpers among people who are already familiar with the collection. Janitorial staff members, for instance, who have worked around the objects for a good while and are interested in working even more closely with them, can often make excellent additions to a registrar's team. Likewise, craft demonstrators who have interest and expertise with a particular group of artifacts in the museum can do a sensitive job of documenting these artifacts while at the same time expanding their own understanding of the scope and purposes of the entire museum collection.

When the historic house museum has to rely on volunteers for registration work, only people who are genuinely interested in working with the collection should be enlisted. Furthermore, the registrar must recognize that inexperienced workers, regardless of whether they are paid or volunteer, must have careful supervision if allowed to work with the collection. A job description, listing duties and responsibilities, should be given to the worker, and it may be wise also to have a written contract drawn up and signed to impress upon the prospective worker the seriousness of the responsibility that he or she is undertaking. Even a volunteer assistant must understand from the outset that work in a registration department of a museum demands the commitment of at least two or three days a week. It is unrealistic to assume that one person working one day per week could complete a registration project. Neither a volunteer nor a professional person is likely to keep up enough momentum to see a project to the end by working only one day a week, and the majority of registration projects mean nothing if they are started and left incomplete.

Volunteers or part-time workers who will be assisting the registrar should be given a table or desk of their own and their own copies of the office work-flow chart and all written procedural guidelines to be followed in dealing with the artifacts. These should be clearly explained during training sessions. New assistants should also be shown where the files are kept and how they work.

A good first project for new part-time people on the registration staff is a team activity that will familiarize them with the entire collection—doing an inventory, for example, or recording the dimensions of a backlog of unmeasured objects. An ongoing activity, such as typing and filing new accession information, might help to acquaint a newly hired member of the full-time staff with the collection and the functions of the registration office. The work of the new person should be checked carefully, however, to see that it is correct and that he or she clearly understands any errors, so as not to repeat them.

When there is a special registration project to be assigned, whether to a volunteer, a part-time paid employee, or a regular member of the registration staff, the registrar must have a clear idea of exactly what is to be done and exactly how and in what order it should be carried out. Registration projects, or parts of larger projects, are best set up in six- to eight-week blocks, with a readily perceivable beginning, middle, and end. This enables a conscientious assistant who takes on the project to master it and have the satisfaction of completing it in a reasonable length of time.

With an efficiently organized registration office at the historic site, projects can be successfully mounted to gain possession of objects improperly or incompletely accessioned in the past or to document collections hastily brought together as an afterthought to the restoration of the building. Artifacts native to the site can be sorted and displayed to give the most information about the site, and nonartifacts can be properly logged and kept track of. Sensitive documentation can be carried out on a day-to-day basis in order to preserve as much information as possible about the three-dimensional history of the area's past.

SPECIFIC APPLICATIONS

The interests of a historic house museum may seem very specific and very local. However, historians are coming to realize that carefully preserved information about simple, specific, unextraordinary communities is a key to understanding our nation's past. By being sensitive to the enormous number of details that historic buildings and artifacts can tell, the registrar of a historic site plays an important role in broadening the museum's interpretation and the historian's understanding of the society from which our present culture springs.

Bibliography

Butler, Patrick H., III. Introd. to *Material Culture As a Resource in Local History: A Bibliography*. Newberry Papers in Family and Community History 77–2. Chicago: Newberry Library, 1977.

Chambers, J. Henry. *Cyclical Maintenance for Historic Buildings*. Washington, D.C.: National Park Service, Office of Archaeology and Historic Preservation, 1976.

Hester, Thomas R., Robert F. Heizer, and John A. Graham. *Field Methods in Archaeology*. 6th ed. Palo Alto, Calif.: Mayfield Publishing Company, 1975.

Kubler, George. *The Shape of Time: Remarks on the History of Things*. New Haven: Yale University Press, 1962.

Mount Vernon Ladies' Association of the Union. *Minutes of the Grand Council Meeting, 1854–1898*. 2 vols. Mt. Vernon, Va.: MVLAU, n.d.

Noël Hume, Ivor. *Historical Archaeology*. New York: Alfred A. Knopf, 1969.

Reibel, Daniel B. *Registration Methods for the Small Museum: A Guide for Historical Collections*. Nashville: AASLH, 1978.

Schuyler, Robert L., ed. *Historical Archaeology: A Guide to Substantive and Theoretical Contributions*. Farmingdale, N.Y.: Baywood Publishing Company, 1978.

A STANDARD TERMINOLOGY FOR DESCRIBING OBJECTS IN A MUSEUM OF ANTHROPOLOGY

GERALDINE BRUCKNER

The University Museum's collections include the archaeology of Europe and the Mediterranean area, Egypt, the Near East, and North, Middle, and South America; the material culture of the native peoples of Africa, Australia, the islands of the Pacific, southeastern Asia, and the Eskimo and American Indian; a Chinese, an Indian, and an Islamic collection. There are no examples of Western European civilization after about the fall of Rome.

The museum uses the same type of catalogue card for all of these collections. (See figure I.1.) The catalogue card includes the accession number, name of the object, locality, culture or date or people, physical description of the object, photographic negative number, field number or former owner's number, dimensions, how and when collected and acquired and by whom, and the initials of the cataloguer and date of cataloguing. Of these items, the name of the object and its physical description are the most difficult to state briefly and clearly. This is especially true because of the varied cultures represented in the museum's collections.

A standard terminology had to be adopted that was basically uniform and at the same time flexible enough to include the specialized terms peculiar to any one area or people. That terminology is presented in this article as a recommended system for describing and naming anthropological collections.

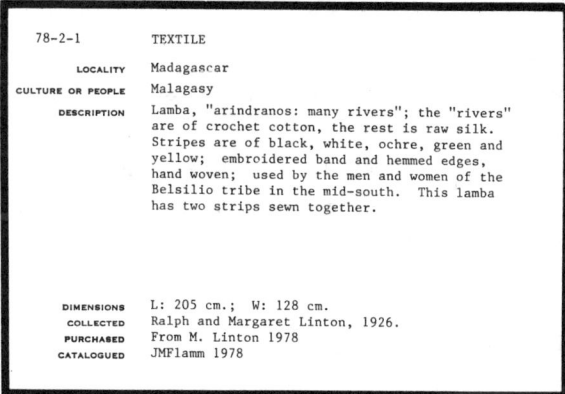

Fig. I.1.
Catalogue card used for all collections (4 by 6 in.), University Museum, University of Pennsylvania. The accession number and the name of the object are typed at the top of each card. Material is the first item recorded under Description. Other information recorded in this space includes publications, negative number if the object has been photographed, and conservation number if it has received conservation treatment.

Describing the Object

Correct identification of the materials and accurate, precise statements of the dimensions, decoration, and condition of an object are essential to its description.

MATERIALS

The same materials are used for such a variety of objects that identifying the material is a good place to begin the description. For this, some knowledge of mineralogy, metals, botany, zoology, ceramics, and textiles is necessary. The registrar can hardly be expected to be an expert in all these fields, but he or she should, if at all possible, examine other collections and discuss each type of material with an expert (even if only briefly), perhaps have a small sample collection for comparison, and always have a good unabridged dictionary. It is relatively easy to determine into what large category the material falls, but if the particular material is not recognized, its physical properties should be described, e.g., "hard, dark green stone, highly polished," "porous, gray stone," "soft wood," "very hard, close-grained wood." With a little practice, however, more definite descriptions can be given.

Stone

Of the igneous rocks, those most frequently found in archaeological collections are basalt, diorite, and pumice; of the sedimentary rocks, shale, sandstone, and limestone are most common; and of the metamorphic rocks, gneiss, schist, quartzite, slate, marble, and serpentine. The appearance of some of these varies considerably with the locality; for example, Chinese limestone and Northwest Coast slate differ markedly from the limestone and slate encountered elsewhere. On the other hand, quite different stones sometimes look very much alike, and identification must be made by one of the recognized tests for relative hardness, type of fracture, specific gravity, or chemical content. Hardness is determined according to the Mohs scale, ranging from 1 for very soft to 10 for the hardest known. Any material can be scratched by a harder material; for example, 6 will scratch 5 but will be scratched by 7. The fingernail will scratch up to a hardness of 2.5; a copper coin up to 3; a knife blade up to 5.5. It is important in testing by scratching to distinguish between an actual scratch and a chalk mark that is powder from the softer material. In the following list, the first material is always that given in the Mohs scale and the others are materials the museum worker frequently encounters:

1. Talc: steatite (soapstone)
2. Gypsum: alabaster; amber, which is a fossil resin (both 2.5)
3. Calcite: marble; limestone
4. Fluorite: malachite (3.5 to 4); serpentine (2.5 to 4)
5. Apatite: lazurite, usually called lapis lazuli; glass; and obsidian, which is volcanic glass (all 5 to 5.5)
6. Feldspar: turquoise; hematite (5.5 to 6.5)
7. Quartz: agate; amethyst; carnelian; chalcedony; chert; flint; jade; jasper; onyx; rock crystal (5.5 to 7)
8. Topaz
9. Corundum: sapphire; ruby
10. Diamond

Precise identification is sometimes difficult. For instance, relative hardness alone may not be enough to distinguish among various rock materials. The terms "flints" and "flint implements," for example, are used even though the substance may really be jasper. Actually, flint is translucent and is usually gray, black, or smoky brown in color; jasper is opaque and is usually red, yellow, or gray; chert has a hornlike appearance, but the name is also used for impure flints and jaspers. Both jadeite and nephrite are called "jade," but the name is also used loosely for the very hard, opaque, white to green stone found in Middle America, and for the hard, usually translucent, dark green stone found in Alaska and British Columbia and in New Caledonia and New Zealand, though sometimes this is called "greenstone."

Much of what used to be called "alabaster" in ancient Egypt is really limestone; true alabaster is not found in Egyptian collections, but it is found in quantity in Iraq, Iran, and Arabia. There is a very simple chemical test to make the distinction: alabaster and gypsum are calcium sulphates, while limestone, marble, calcite, and chalk are calcium carbonates. The latter will effervesce with any acid, such as hydrochloric, while alabaster and gypsum will not. Hematite can also be determined by a simple test: if used as a pencil, hematite will leave a red or reddish brown mark.

Descriptions of stone objects should explain not only material but also how the stone was shaped—by chipping, flaking, grinding—and whether the surface is polished.

Pottery

Pottery, terra-cotta, and brick are basically clay that has been baked. Pottery ranges from a lump of clay pressed into shape and slightly baked to the most exquisite vessels and sculpture. In describing pottery, the following should be noted: the color and texture of the ware (called by ceramists the "biscuit"); whether there is a slip or a glaze; how it was made, whether built up with coils of clay or shaped from a lump of clay either by hand or with the potter's wheel; how well it is baked; and whether there is any decoration.

Terra-cotta means, simply, "cooked earth." The term is used to describe the material of which architectural adornments such as antefixes are made. It is also used as a general term for any small figure of baked clay, whether god or human, animal or bird, miniature bed or chair, or other. These are known collectively as terra-cottas, even though in descriptions the individual piece is treated as pottery. Terra-cottas are either modeled or made in a mold. Occasionally both techniques are used—one for the head, the other for the body of a figure. Other small objects such as spindle whorls or game pieces, if well baked, are usually called "terra-cotta"; if not so well baked, "clay."

Brick is really the name of an object rather than a material. It is clay that has been formed into a comparatively small rectangular slab and dried in the sun or fired in a kiln for use in building. Depending on the degree and method of baking, it is termed "sun-dried brick" or "brick." Either may be inscribed.

Glass

Glass is another material frequently encountered in anthropological collections. Glass is a substance that results from the fusion of a combination of silica (rarely boric acid) with various bases. It may be built up from coils or blown. The beautiful iridescence of Roman glass is actually a breakdown of the surface due to the action of minerals in the soil in which it has been buried.

Archaeological faience has about the same chemical content as glass but is not so completely fused; it has a very grainy texture, and there is usually a thin glaze that tends to wear off. In other words, it is a glazed frit. The color varies from white through blue and green to a quite deep turquoise. The faience of Egypt and the Near East is completely different from the glazed pottery made in France and Italy and named for Faenza in Italy.

Metal

Metal objects may be hammered into shape, modeled from sheet metal, or cast. Most metals are easily recognizable and should be described by their common names. Bronze is the exception. The formula for bronze is copper with up to 10 percent tin added to harden it; but in Old World archaeology, unless there is a specific reason for distinguishing between copper and bronze, all of this metal is called "bronze" and objects made of it are spoken of collectively as "bronzes." In American archaeology the practice has generally been reversed; all is called "copper" unless proven by analysis to be bronze. Why there should have arisen such a difference in terminology is not clear. Chemical analysis is required to distinguish between copper and bronze, and since in many places a certain amount of tin occurs naturally in copper, it is difficult to know whether the presence of tin was intentional or accidental. Metallurgists have been working on the problem of when tin was first deliberately added to copper to make bronze. Many archaeologists are now using "Cu/bronze" to describe this metal.

Others

Ivory, bone, antler, horn, wood, shell, and coral are all well enough known to need little explanation. However, a few characteristics of each should be noted here. Ivory is of various kinds. The most common sources of ivory are elephant tusks, walrus tusks, and whale teeth. Ivory is more uniform throughout and therefore heavier than bone, which is porous inside or even hollow. Antler is solid and rather like wood in appearance. Horn is hollow where it joins the animal's head but solid towards the tip; it has a rather oily feel and, when cut into a very thin sheet, is translucent, but otherwise can easily be mistaken for wood. Baleen, the material our grandmothers called "whalebone," is the horny material that comes from the fringelike strainer in the mouth of certain whales; whalebone in anthropological collections means any bone of the whale. Shell, particularly the shell of the large tridacna clam, sometimes looks like stone; the distinguishing characteristics are that the outer surface is always slightly curved and that both inner surface and cross-section show its construction of many curved layers. Shell is very fine grained and takes a high polish. Pearl shell and mother-of-pearl are usually thought to be light in color, but abalone is a darker iridescent blue to green. Coral, which is the skeleton of a tiny marine animal, contains principally calcium carbonate and is always white to red in color; it has a hardness of 3.5 and will take a high polish.

To identify the material of which textiles are made takes an expert's knowledge, but with a very strong magnifying glass wool, linen, cotton, and silk can be distinguished relatively easily. Wool threads are scaled and curly; linen threads are almost straight; cotton has a twisted, ribbonlike structure; and silk has an even, fuzzy outline and is lustrous.

The expert will also be needed to make precise identification of the many different animal and vegetable products—tusks, teeth, bones, claws, feathers, skins, reeds, gourds, seeds, berries, etc.—that may be encountered, especially in an ethnological collection.

DIMENSIONS

Dimensions are an important part of the description of an object, and are always the maximum unless otherwise noted. The dimensions for anthropological objects are given in the following order: height, length, width; or length, width, thickness. Diameter may be substituted for length and width. Sometimes the dimension is given for a part of an object, such as the mouth diameter of a jar as well as the maximum diameter, or the length and width of the blade as well as the length of the whole knife. Separate dimensions are always given for objects composed of several parts, as an arrow or spear. If part of an object is missing, it is noted that the dimension is incomplete, or an estimated complete dimension may be given (e.g., for a two-handled jar missing one handle and part of the neck and body: "Existing height, 21 cm.; estimated total height, 24 cm. Existing width, 13 cm.; estimated total width, 20 cm."; "present height" and "present width" may be used instead of "existing height" and "existing width").

DECORATION

An explanation of the ways of decorating a surface, such as by painting or engraving, is not included here, but it should be noted that negative painting means painting the background rather than the decorative motif itself; that pottery as well as stone can be carved; and that finger impressions, gouging, and punctates (punctured dots) are included among the decorative techniques.

Decorative motifs may be in abstract or natural forms. The former may be rectilinear or curvilinear and may include any combination of straight, angled, curved, or wavy lines, as well as geometric forms such as squares, diamonds, circles, hexagons, or triangles. Some motifs are named, such as hatching, cross-hatching, chevron, ladder, stepped, net, meander, scroll, rosette, star. Natural forms, whether human, animal, or vegetable, may be realistic, stylized, or conventionalized; the conventionalization is sometimes so great that the original form is barely recognizable. There have been some attempts at a uniform nomenclature for design elements, but, for the most part, these have been limited to single areas or fields.

CONDITION

Unlike the collections in an art museum, archaeological and ethnological pieces in absolutely perfect condition are relatively rare; so, except for an especially fine piece, minor cracks and chips are not noted. However, serious damage and completely missing parts are noted, and, in measuring, a distinction is made between complete and incomplete. A specimen may have been broken and mended in antiquity or a piece may have been broken and refinished. If so, that is always noted. Any change in the material such as the corrosion of metal or the charring of wood or ivory is noted. Archaeological bronzes, however, which always display the characteristic green patina that is the result of corrosion, are an exception; a note is made if they have been cleaned. "Patina" denotes any change in the surface, and while most often the term is used in connection with metals, it can be applied to any materials. Sometimes patina is very beautiful, sometimes destructive.

Naming the Object

In naming many archaeological and ethnological objects, everyday usage is followed, as for example, in speaking of a hat, dress, shoe, bow and arrow, sword, axe, chisel, knife, basket, or box. Frequently in addition to the English name, the native name is known and may either be substituted for or added to the usual name. The blouse worn by the Indian women of Guatemala today is called a "huipil"; an Eskimo woman's knife is an "ulu." Using these names saves considerable description, for each has a very definite meaning. Care must be taken, however, not to carry such names over into any other area simply because the objects from the two areas have a superficial resemblance.

Often the use to which a thing is put is indicated by the name, such as a sewing basket, a tool chest, a blacksmith's knife. However, there are many other things that, although they fit into one of the common categories, are peculiar to a certain area and have a particular name. A long, carved wooden box with a handle at each end and an inset lid, made by the Maori of New Zealand, is a "feather box" because in it are kept the feathers worn by the men. In those parts of the world where betel or coca mixed with lime (which is usually finely powdered shell) is chewed, "lime gourds" and "lime spatulas" are used, the latter usually made of bone or wood. The piece of rawhide folded and painted and used as a carrying case by the Plains Indians is a "parfleche," while the small netted bag carried by the Australian native is a "dilly bag." The list could be extended indefinitely. While these terms, if known, are helpful to use, a simple description will generally suffice for object identification. But, again, great care must be taken not to imply a use that is not really known; therefore, "figurine" is usually a better term than "doll" or "idol," and "miniature vessel" is better than "model" or "toy." It is even more important not to suggest cultural traits that do not exist; a nonagricultural people would not have a hoe or spade; a people with no knowledge of textiles would not have a spindle whorl or a loom weight.

CATEGORIES OF OBJECTS

Vessels

The names used for vessel forms are an important exception to the use of the everyday name for an object. Because vessels (archaeologically principally of pottery with some stone and metal and ethnologically of a variety of materials) form such a large and important part of the collections in a museum of anthropology, and because there is no consistency in the common usage, a nomenclature has been established in which the names of the basic shapes are determined by the relation of the mouth diameter to the overall size of the vessel. The basic shapes are plate, bowl, pot, jar, bottle, and a high, wide-mouthed vessel for which there is no completely satisfactory name. There are particular names for certain groups of objects of which extensive studies have been made, such as Attic vases and Chinese bronzes, but these should be used only in their original meaning unless the name has been generally accepted in other areas.

The following names are applied to specific vessel shapes:

Plates

PLATE: an extremely shallow vessel, the diameter at least eight times the height.

SAUCER: a small plate.

PLATTER: a very large plate, usually longer than wide.

Bowls

BOWL: a vessel with open mouth, the height never greater than the diameter and usually much less. If the height is less than one-third the diameter, it is a SHALLOW BOWL; if as great as the diameter, it is a DEEP BOWL. It may have any number of handles, but a bowl with a very long handle is a LADLE or SCOOP.

STRAINER BOWL OR SIEVE: a bowl, usually rather shallow, with many pierced holes in the bottom.

GRATER BOWL: a bowl, usually rather shallow, the bottom interior deeply striated.

MORTAR: a bowl with extremely thick walls; for use with a pestle.

BOX: a bowl, usually deep, and usually with a cover, more often rectangular than round; nearly always with vertical sides.

CUP: a small bowl, sometimes with one handle; occasionally used for a vessel with vertical sides and wide mouth, but if height is in excess of that proper for one of the bowl category, the vessel should probably be called a TUMBLER.

GOBLET: a cup on a high foot.

MUG: a deep cup, usually with flat base and straight vertical sides; with one handle.

Pots

POT: a vessel with a slightly constricted mouth; the height and the maximum diameter are about the same, and the mouth diameter is at least half the maximum diameter; it may have any number of handles.

COOKING POT: a crude, poorly made pot meant to be used over the fire.

KOHL POT OR COSMETIC POT: a name used mostly in Egyptian archaeology for a small pot, usually with high shoulder; it has a cover and, between the pot and the cover, frequently a flat ring.

Jars

JAR: a vessel whose apparent height is usually but not always greater than its diameter; the mouth is much more constricted than that of a pot; usually with a neck, which may be quite high, but may have only a spout opening directly from the body of the vessel; does not necessarily have handles but may have two or more (a jar with one handle is a JUG).

STORAGE JAR: any very large jar.

OLLA: a term used most often for the archaeological and recent pottery from the southwestern United States; an olla has a very low neck, and the body diameter is never less and sometimes considerably more than the height.

SEED JAR: this name is also used in the Southwest; it is a squat, globular vessel with small hole-mouth.

HOLE-MOUTH JAR: usually cylindrical in form; top nearly flat, with an opening in its center.

GINGER JAR: a Chinese porcelain shape; it is a jar with a rather high, flat, or very slightly rounded shoulder and a small hole-mouth with a very slight rim, just pronounced enough to hold the cover, which is a small, inverted, straight-sided cup.

STIRRUP JAR: in Mediterranean archaeology, a small vessel, usually spherical, with a closed, flat top, open only at the base of a very small spout; beside the spout and also set on top of the vessel is a strap handle supported in its middle and at both ends. In South American archaeology, a vessel with the neck at the top of a hollow handle, which is stirrup shaped and set on top of the vessel.

Jar with Double Spout: a vessel found archaeologically in South America, usually more or less spherical, whose only openings are two spouts set at opposite sides of the top; it may have a strap handle connecting the spouts.

Jar with Spout and Bridge to Head: also found archaeologically in South America; it differs from the jar with double spout in that one of the spouts is replaced by a head or figure (human, bird, animal), and this head or figure is always connected with the spout by a strap handle.

Whistling Jar: two jars, each complete in itself but with the bodies joined and with a handle connecting the vessels at the top; occasionally more than two vessels may be so joined.

Jug: a jar with a single handle at one side; sometimes has a pouring lip but this is not essential.

Pitcher: a jug with pouring lip; term not used for archaeological specimens.

Juglet: a small jug with rounded or pointed base, meant to be carried; a term used almost exclusively in Palestinian archaeology.

Ewer: a jug of sophisticated shape with long spout.

Bottles

Bottle: a vessel with a very narrow mouth; usually, but not always, with a high, narrow neck.

Flask: a bottle meant to be carried, usually small and somewhat flat so the dimensions of the body are width and thickness rather than diameter; small neck and mouth; usually with some provision for the attachment of a carrying strap.

Aryballos: One of the Greek vase forms; as such, it is a globular bottle having a small neck with wide overhanging rim; in South American archaeology the name is used for a jar or bottle with pointed base and two small handles placed very low on the body; such jars were carried on the back, the handles holding the tumpline in place.

High, Wide-mouthed Vessels

Beaker: a vessel with nearly vertical or flaring sides; may be convex near the base and either straight or recurved to the open mouth; the bell beaker of Neolithic Central Europe and the quero of South American archaeology are two variations.

Tumbler: a small but relatively high vessel with open mouth; usually an inverted cone with small base (see Cup).

Cylinder Jar or Cylinder Vase: a high cylinder with flat base; the term is used particularly for the beautiful painted vessels, sometimes also called picture vases, made by the Maya.

Names Applied to More Than One Vessel Shape

Footed Vessel or Vessel with Foot: any vessel with a base or foot that is not an integral part of the container itself; it is best to be definite: footed bowl, footed jar, etc., or bowl with foot, jar with foot; a vessel with three feet is a TRIPOD; with four, a TETRAPOD.

Effigy Vessel: a vessel made in human, animal, or plant form; again, it is best to be definite: effigy bowl, effigy bottle, etc.; such vessels are described as are figures; the position of the vessel mouth and whether or not there is a handle are also noted.

Lamp: in its simplest form, a saucer with a lip into which the wick is laid; but lamps are made in a variety of forms, sometimes quite elaborate; the ROMAN LAMP is a low, circular or oval pot with a rather small mouth and a horizontally projecting nozzle having a hole for the wick; sometimes a horizontal or vertical handle is on the side opposite the nozzle; sometimes there are several nozzles.

LANTERN: may be of any form, usually has some provision for the attachment of a candle or small lamp to the base interior; must have openings of some kind to allow the air to enter and the light to shine out.

INCENSE BURNER: any vessel designed for the burning of incense.

CENSER: an incense burner to be carried.

MINIATURE VESSEL: any tiny vessel; it is best to be definite: miniature jar, miniature jug.

VASE: in a particular sense, any vessel, usually ornamental rather than useful, which cannot be fitted into a definite category; in a general sense, any group of more or less decorative vessels.

LID OR COVER: anything used to cover the mouth of a vessel; it varies from a simple disk or slab to another vessel, inverted.

SHERD: potsherd; a fragment of a vessel, usually of pottery but occasionally of stone; sherds are described as RIM SHERD, BODY SHERD, etc., of a particular type of vessel; sometimes it is possible only to name the ware of which the sherd is made; frequently it is possible to determine from it the exact shape and size of the whole vessel.

While the name of a vessel gives a general idea of its shape, it is necessary to add further description. Sometimes the description can be very simple, such as "hemispherical" or "truncated conical"; frequently it is very detailed. This description should follow a definite order, beginning at either the bottom or the top of the vessel (the former is usually more convenient) and at the conclusion mentioning such added parts as lid, handles, spout, etc.

The base is described as flat, flattened, rounded, ring; or having a foot or feet, which are described as hollow or solid, rattling, ball, slablike, effigy, or a high ring.

The body is described as spherical, hemispherical, squat (spherical with top and bottom compressed), or lentoid in section; or, if no simple term applies, the sides are described as rounded or straight, as expanding to the shoulder, which may be high, wide, flat (on top), convex (on top); or perhaps expanding to the maximum diameter, which is below the middle of the vessel, and then contracting to the mouth or neck. The term "carination" is used for the more or less sharp angle formed when the sides, which have expanded from the base, contract to the mouth.

The neck is described as wide, narrow (remembering that by definition the widest neck of a bottle is narrower than any jar neck), high, low.

The mouth is the vessel opening; the rim is the edge of the mouth. The rim may be wide or narrow, inturned, outturned, flaring, rolled, vertical, overhanging, or with pouring lip; and may have a crenellated or a serrated edge. The term "spout" is sometimes used instead of "pouring lip," but is preferably used only for one added to the vessel proper.

Handles may be "loop" (attached at both ends) and may be set on the shoulder, or vertically as from neck to shoulder or side of body, or horizontally; they may also be "strap" (a flat loop), "bail" (a loop handle over the top of a vessel, a bucket handle), or "ledge" (flat and projecting, usually horizontally); a "lug" is a small projection, sometimes pierced for the insertion of a carrying cord or for the attachment of a lid.

Implements, Tools, and Weapons

Whether to classify implements, tools, and weapons by form or by function, or to use a combination of the two, presents a problem. In the classification by form, the flints of the Stone Age, which were made by chipping and flaking, are divided into two large categories: (1) those made from the flint core, as the fist or hand axe and the chopper; and (2) those made from a flake struck from a core, these flake tools being further subdivided into those struck from a prepared core.

For Stone Age material this objective approach seems ideal; but, in fact, for European flints a whole French terminology has developed, with a somewhat different English counterpart, and quite a different one has developed for American stone tools. For example, the European blade is a long, narrow flake struck from a prepared core; by secondary flaking and chipping it can be made into a knife, scraper, burin, or saw. The American blade is a flint with a cutting edge; it may be of any shape. The French burin (English graver) is a small thin tool, with small sharp edge, used for cutting fine lines, i.e., an engraving tool. Its working edge has been formed through the removal of an additional small flake by the characteristic burin technique. It is only from recent excavations that scientists have learned that there were burins in America before the coming of Europeans. The term graver has been used in America, but to refer to a flake with one or more projecting points (also an engraving tool); and when there are at least two points, the edge between them is always concave.

Efforts to establish a uniform terminology for European and American Stone Age material have thus far been unsuccessful. Until such a terminology has been worked out, the local custom in terminology should be followed. Since the use of later archaeological objects (such as those found in collections from the Near East) is frequently but not always known from representations on sculpture or from written evidence, a compromise in classification leaning toward the functional is most satisfactory. Classification by function is also best for ethnological specimens, since the use is usually known.

With the Bronze Age, metal as well as stone began to be used, and ethnologically there are a variety of ethnological materials. The following names of implements, tools, and weapons are used:

Blade: a tool used for cutting; it may be complete in itself, or it may have a haft; if it has a serrated edge, it is a saw.

Scraper: a tool, usually with one flat surface, the edges of which are used for scraping; it has many forms and uses, some of which have specific names, as flesher or hide scraper.

Awl: sometimes called a perforator, a tool for punching holes; it is circular or rectangular in section and tapered to the point, which is the working part.

Drill: an implement similar to the awl but thinner and of more uniform circumference and with a tiny point; sometimes used with a bow.

Axe and Adze: the difference between an axe and an adze is in the use, and that depends on the manner of hafting. An axe is used vertically to the surface to be cut, whereas an adze is used horizontally to the surface and working toward the user. The term "axe" or "adze" should always be used to refer to the complete tool; without the haft, it is "axe blade" or "adze blade." Sometimes these can be distinguished—an axe blade is bifacial, an adze blade has a sharp bevel on one face to the edge—but the distinction is not always clear and there is the further complication that the Eskimo use the same blade for both, converting it from one to the other by a quarter-turn change in the hafting. In describing an axe or adze blade, the shape should be noted, and whether the sides are parallel, triangular, or oval in section; whether the faces are rounded or beveled to the edge; and whether there is a groove near the butt end for hafting. Although it has been applied quite generally to such a tool, CELT is one of those indefinite terms that is best to avoid; a celt may be, but usually is not, hafted; if it is hafted, it is called a HAFTED CELT.

CHISEL: has one flat face that rests on the surface to be chipped; the end of the upper face is rounded or beveled to the working edge, which is away from the user; the term "chisel" is used whether or not the tool is hafted.

HAMMER OR POUNDING STONE: what the names imply; may be of any shape.

GRINDING STONE: also what the name implies; it is usually rather flat.

PESTLE: a pounding or grinding stone used in a mortar; it is usually long, circular in section, with a small working surface.

KNIFE: may be either a tool or a weapon; it is used for cutting or slashing; it may be hafted, in which case the working part is called a BLADE. In describing a knife, it is important to give the shape of the blade, whether the faces are flat, convex, or concave, and whether they are grooved, the position of the cutting edge, and what provision has been made for hafting. The long, spikelike projection for insertion in the handle is called a TANG. The general category of knives includes all the highly specialized forms, as the KRIS and the BARONG, as well as the better-known SWORD and DAGGER.

SWORD: a large, flat-bladed knife, always used as a weapon.

DAGGER: a long narrow knife, always a weapon.

THROWING KNIFE: a knife, frequently with several subsidiary blades, thrown either in hunting or in warfare.

BOW: may be used with an arrow when it is a weapon; but it may also be used as the driving force for the drill in fire making and in drilling holes. In describing a bow, it is important to indicate whether or not it is composite, i.e., made of one or more materials, and what string is used.

POINT OR HEAD: the effective end of an arrow or any similar weapon; it is described as to shape (triangular, long triangular, lanceolate); whether the base is straight, convex, or cancave, or is tanged; whether there are barbs, and their position.

ARROW: a long, thin weapon meant to be used with a bow; it may be of one piece with a sharpened end; or it may consist of a point, a foreshaft (not always present), and a shaft. It is described as to each part, whether the shaft is feathered and what has been used for the feathering, and how the parts fit together.

SPEAR: a thrusting or throwing weapon; it is much larger and heavier than an arrow and is described in the same way.

SPEAR THROWER, THROWING BOARD, ATLATL: used to give additional leverage and power in throwing a spear; may be long and narrow with a groove in which the spear rests, or may be flat and wider; has a hook at the farther end (from the hand) to engage the spear.

HARPOON: a spear with long detachable head connected to the shaft by a long cord.

DART: a small, very thin, lightweight weapon meant to be thrown; used with blow gun; frequently poisoned.

BLOW GUN: an extremely long narrow tube (perhaps ten feet long, with a diameter of little more than an inch) through which darts are expelled.

CLUB: a weapon of a variety of shapes, whose efficacy depends on the force of the blow; the shape is described; but it is to be noted that in some areas the names of clubs are as carefully differentiated as are knives in other areas.

MISSILE CLUB OR THROWING CLUB: any club meant to be thrown.

BOOMERANG: a long, thin, curved throwing club. In spite of the name, few are returning; those that do return (ones having a very sharp curve, sometimes an angle) must be noted.

BOLA: a throwing weapon composed of two or more balls, each attached to a thong.

MACE: originally a club with ball head; frequently used as a symbol of authority.

SCULPTURE

For architectural sculpture the accepted architectural terms are used: "column," "capital," "lintel," "antefix," etc. The description includes the material, the shape, and the type of decoration and what it represents.

STELA: a term peculiar to archaeology; a free-standing upright slab of stone (rarely of pottery), decorated on at least one face, sometimes on both faces and both edges, and of any size from a few inches to many feet. A stela may be set on a pedestal or base, as also may a statue.

PEDESTAL: may be of any shape and size and may be elaborately decorated; the essential characteristic is that it is a support for something else.

PLAQUE: a slab, not free standing, either with one decorated face or used as a background for a figure.

FIGURE AND STATUE: The distinction between the two is in the material, a statue being made of stone or metal, a figure of wood or clay. Occasionally a large important figure is called a statue and a small piece meant to be hung from a necklace or belt is a pendant figurine, no matter what the material.

FIGURINE AND STATUETTE: The distinction between figure and figurine, statue and statuette is one of size; using the human figure as a guide, a representation less than approximately one-fourth life size is a figurine or statuette. For all these, it is important to note who or what is represented; the position (standing, seated, etc.); how dressed; any attributes or attendant figures; and whether the figure is in full round or forms part of a stela or plaque.

CEREMONIAL OBJECTS

The very large category of ceremonial objects includes everything to do with a religion or a cult: dance paraphernalia (costumes, masks, musical instruments, wands); totemic objects; votive objects; amulets; fetishes and the tools of the medicine man. Each of these should be given its own proper name and described by use, as though it had no religious significance. The use of the term "ceremonial object" as the designation for an individual piece is permissible only in the rare case of an object for which there is no better identification. Following are some of the types of ceremonial objects:

AMULET OR CHARM: any object, usually small, that because of its form (as the figure of a god or sacred object), or because of its association, or because of some formula of blessing or cursing said over it, is thought to have power to protect or destroy.

SCARAB: an Egyptian amulet in the form of a beetle; the base is frequently inscribed with the owner's name or cartouche and the scarab may then be used as a seal.

FETISH: an object also thought to have protective or destructive power; applied particularly to the African figures with a cavity in the head or the abdomen to contain "medicine," which imparts the power.

TOTEM: an object peculiar to a group or an individual, frequently in the form of an animal that is associated with the group or individual's history or character. An elaborated form is the totem pole of Alaska and British Columbia. The conical headdress with totemic bird or animal on top, worn by the Tlingit Indians of Alaska, is called a CREST.

CHURINGA: an Australian totemic object; a slab of stone or wood, usually long and narrow but occasionally nearly round, inscribed with totemic symbols.

BULLROARER: a wooden churinga pierced at one end for the insertion of a string by which it is twirled rapidly to make a loud, whirring noise.

KACHINA: a painted wooden figurine made by the Pueblo Indians of New Mexico and Arizona, representing the gods and other personages associated with the corn-growing and other ceremonies.

SHAWABTI: a figurine, usually of faience but may be of stone or wood, in mummy form, placed in an Egyptian tomb.

MISCELLANEOUS

Among miscellaneous objects not fitting into the above categories are the following:

PAPYRUS: actually the older form of paper made from the papyrus plant, but the term is used for any document written on papyrus.

CUNEIFORM TABLET: a Babylonian document in the form of a rather thick, rectangular (occasionally circular) piece of clay, inscribed with a triangular stylus, and baked; it may have an envelope, also of clay and inscribed.

BULLA: a clay or metal ball with inscription or seal impression; used as a tag.

SEAL: There are two forms, stamp and cylinder, the impression of the latter being made by rolling the seal over the surface to be marked. The designs on seals are the contemporary record of physical type and material culture as well as of myths and beliefs and worship. They must, therefore, be described in detail. Cylinder seals are particularly plentiful in Near Eastern archaeological collections.

SEAL IMPRESSION OR JAR SEALING: a lump of clay that has been placed over the mouth of a jar (usually over a cloth or reed cover) and stamped, usually many times, with the owner's seal; peculiar to Near Eastern archaeology.

QUIPU: a mnemonic device used archaeologically in Peru for recording information; it consists of cords of various lengths and colors, knotted.

CAT'S CRADLES: string figures made on the fingers in recognized patterns.

BARK CLOTH: frequently called TAPA; a cloth made by pounding the inner bark of certain trees, most frequently the paper mulberry, the breadfruit, and the fig; frequently painted and sometimes waterproofed.

BEADS: The most common shapes are: ring, short tubular, tubular, disk, ball, barrel shaped, cylindrical (i.e., long narrow, slightly tapering to the ends), biconical, and irregular. Most of these can be faceted or fluted. The term STRING OF BEADS is used rather than NECKLACE unless it is definitely known that the beads were worn about the neck.

PENDANTS: When spoken of in connection with beads, pendants are beads with the suspension hole at the top rather than through the middle.

GORGET: a pendant, usually flat, worn on the breast.

BANNERSTONE: an object found archaeologically in the eastern United States; rather flat, more or less rectangular with a greater width than height, the center section vertically pierced and flanked by two wings; was almost certainly used as an atlatl weight.

BIRD STONE: also found archaeologically in the eastern United States and may be an atlatl thumb rest; long and narrow with flat base and somewhat resembling a resting bird.

New Techniques

Technological advances in recent years have resulted in improved methods of determining both age and authenticity of museum objects and the steps to be taken for their care and preservation. To make this information more accessible, the University Museum has established an Applied Science Center for Archaeology. In addition to its own scientific work, the center publishes a newsletter, *MASCA*, containing notes, reports, and articles concerning new techniques applicable to archaeology.

The application of the computer has also brought about changes in the recording of anthropological collections. It has been used in the field, notably by the University Museum's Akhenaten Temple Project, which has photographed and codified some 25,000 blocks from the structures that were erected by Akhenaten at Karnak in the fourteenth century B.C. and systematically destroyed shortly after his death. Many of the blocks were used as fill in the monumental pylons erected by later pharaohs. With the aid of the computer, these incised and painted blocks are being assembled (at least on paper) into the scenes that covered the walls of Akhenaten's buildings, thus providing much important information about that period of Egyptian history. As use of the computer becomes more widespread among museums, the standardization of terminology for describing objects will become increasingly necessary.

Bibliography

Buck, Sir Peter (Te Rangi Hiroa). *Arts and Crafts of Hawaii.* Honolulu: Bishop Museum Press, 1957.

Churchill, William. *Club Types of Nuclear Polynesia.* Washington, D.C.: Carnegie Institution of Washington, 1917.

Edge-Partington, James. *An Album of the Weapons, Tools, Ornaments, Articles of Dress, etc., of the Natives of the Pacific Islands.* Manchester, England: Privately printed, 1890–98.

Foster, Kenneth E. *A Handbook of Ancient Chinese Bronzes.* Rev. ed. Claremont, Calif.: Viola Minor Westergaard Foundation, 1949.

Frankfort, Henri. *Cylinder Seals: A Documentary Essay on the Art and Religion of the Ancient Near East.* London: Macmillan and Co., 1939.

Gardner, Helen. *Art through the Ages.* 4th ed. New York: Harcourt, Brace, 1959.

Griffin, James B., ed. *Archaeology of Eastern United States.* Chicago: University of Chicago Press, 1952.

Hodge, Frederick W., ed. *Handbook of American Indians North of Mexico.* Bureau of American Ethnology Bulletin 30. Washington, D.C.: Smithsonian Institution, 1907–10.

Lucas, Alfred. *Ancient Egyptian Materials and Industries.* London: E. Arnold, 1948.

———. *Antiques, Their Restoration and Preservation.* 2d ed. London: E. Arnold, 1932.

Newberry, Percy E. *Scarabs: An Introduction to the Study of Egyptian Seals and Signet Rings.* London: A. Constable, 1906.

Paul, Frances. *Spruce Root Basketry of the Alaska Tlingit.* Bureau of Indian Affairs, Indian Handcrafts 8. Lawrence, Kans.: Haskell Institute, for the Department of the Interior, 1944.

Richter, Gisela M. A. *Attic Red-figured Vases: A Survey.* New Haven: Yale University Press, 1946.

———, and Marjorie J. Milne. *Shapes and Names of Athenian Vases.* New York: Plantin Press, 1935.

Shorter, Alan W. *The Egyptian Gods: A Handbook.* London: K. Paul, Trench, Trubner, 1937.

Steward, Julian H., ed. *Handbook of South American Indians.* Bureau of American Ethnology Bulletin 143. Washington, D.C.: Smithsonian Institution, 1946.

Stone, George Cameron. *A Glossary of the Construction, Decoration, and Use of Arms and Armor.* Portland, Maine: Southworth Press, 1934.

Underhill, Ruth. *Indians of the Pacific Northwest.* Bureau of Indian Affairs, Indian Life and Customs 5. Riverside, Calif.: Sherman Institute Press, for the Department of the Interior, 1945.

———. *Pueblo Crafts.* Bureau of Indian Affairs, Indian Handcrafts 7. Lawrence, Kans.: Haskell Institute, for the Department of the Interior, 1944.

Wormington, Hannah Marie. *Ancient Man in North America.* 5th ed. Denver: Denver Museum of Natural History, 1964.

A REGISTRAR'S ROLE IN A NATURAL HISTORY MUSEUM

ANITA MANNING

The position of registrar is relatively new in many natural history museums. Traditionally, many of the duties described in *Museum Registration Methods* as the registrar's have been carried out in natural history museums by curators or under curatorial supervision. Alternatively, museums employed curators of collections to supervise accessions and loans, see to the physical needs of the collections as a whole, and curate those collections that did not have an active curatorial staff.

As museums grew in size and complexity, however, and the need for legal documentation became of increasing administrative concern, some natural history museums established the position of registrar. Occasionally the positions of curator of collections and registrar exist in the same museum. In such cases, the curator of collections retains overall collection responsibility, while the registrar assumes responsibility for legal documentation. In other museums, the position of registrar may be established without a curator of collections.

Because the position is so new, the duties assigned to the natural history registrar are not well defined in the profession. The suggested duties outlined in this article are presented in the form of a job description that draws on the experience of the Bernice Pauahi Bishop Museum but utilizes policies and practices of other museums as well. The citations given in parentheses throughout the text are not intended as footnotes but refer to items in the bibliography that provide a resource or an in-depth discussion of the topic. Since the discussion of a registrar's duties in this article is only an attempt to outline some of the problems of natural history museum registration, the reader is encouraged to consult the resources listed in the bibliography for a more thorough treatment of the topics discussed here.

The job description itself is written as though for a specific registrar in a specific museum. It states what the registrar is expected to do on the job. It is intended, however, as an example, not as a model or standard. Following the job description is a discussion of special problems and concerns that will, it is hoped, demonstrate how the duties described might be adapted to meet a particular museum's needs.

The registrar's duties as described in the following pages have two central aims. The first aim is administrative: to provide the museum with a centrally housed and indexed permanent file documenting the legal ownership of collections in the musem. Such a system can alleviate several problems. For instance, there is the problem of the curator who leaves the staff and takes along personal correspondence that may also include information about the collections. In the museum without a registrar, the curator's correspondence may contain the only record of donations, exchanges, and loans. Central registration may also be necessary to provide proof that collections were acquired by both collector and donor in a manner that complies with state, federal, and foreign laws and regulations regarding national patrimony or restricted species of plants or animals. Central registration may also assist where museums feel a need for increased documentation of collections in response to public inquiry into the administration of museums or in response to descendants of donors questioning a museum's title to collections.

The second aim of the duties described here is personnel oriented: to provide curatorial staff more time for research and curatorial care of the collections. This may be accomplished by relieving curatorial staff of much of the clerical and filing duties associated with registration records.

Fig. J.1
Loan agreement form (8½ by 11 in.), Bernice P. Bishop Museum. The conditions are listed on the reverse.

BERNICE P. BISHOP MUSEUM
P.O. Box 6037, Honolulu, Hawaii 96818 • Telephone 847-3511

TL- 1977.00

LOAN AGREEMENT   EL-_____

The below described object(s) has(have) been offered as a loan to the Bishop Museum by:

Name: Joyce Lani Kaaihue
Address: 1355 Kalihi Street
Honolulu, Hawaii 96819

Daytime Telephone: 847-3511

and has(have) been accepted by the Bishop Museum subject to the conditions on the reverse side of this page.

Description:
One copy of the newspaper "Ka Nupepa Ku'oko'a"
October 1861, Buke I, Helu 1

PLEASE SIGN ON REVERSE - remove carbons before signing; sign all copies in ink. Original to Lender, first carbon to Registrar, second carbon remains with material in Museum.

BPBM Reg form #106 JL75

Job Description

The registrar's primary function is the storage and retrieval of information concerning the legal ownership of collections in the museum. This is an administrative activity, and the registrar is immediately responsible to the director.

1. The registrar is responsible for the accumulation, retrieval, storage, and preservation of the museum's accession, exchange, gift, and loan records on an administrative level.

    a. The registrar develops and administers systems for the accumulation and storage of registration information relating to material entering or leaving the museum.

    b. The registrar establishes and maintains systems for the retrieval of registration information regarding material entering or leaving the museum.

    c. The registrar provides a proper physical environment for the museum's registration records. The registrar uses and encourages museum-wide use of archival

---

LOAN AGREEMENT CONDITIONS

1. The described property offered to the Bishop Museum will receive the same care given the Museum's regular collections.

2. Unless this loan agreement indicates that the described property is loaned for a specified period of time it may be removed from the Bishop Museum by the lender or his duly authorized agent or legal representative after not less than ten days written notice to the Bishop Museum and upon surrender of the lender's copy of this agreement or the delivery of the lender's written order.

3. The Bishop Museum may request removal of the described property by sending written notice by certified mail to the lender at the address shown on the face of this agreement or the last change of address sent by the lender. Failure of the lender to remove the property within thirty days after the termination of the specified period of the loan or within thirty days after the mailing of the notice requesting removal by the lender will constitute authorization to the Bishop Museum to return the described property to the lender by express collect, or to deliver it to any warehouse company to be stored for the lender's account, or to otherwise store it in any manner the Bishop Museum may elect at the lender's expense, or to continue to retain the described property for Museum purposes.

4. Unless the receipt indicates that the property is loaned for a specified period of time, the term of this loan shall not exceed three years. After the period of the loan has expired and the Bishop Museum has sent the notice requesting removal of the property, as set forth in paragraph 3 above, then the Museum may retain the property for Museum purposes.

    If after Bishop Museum retains the property for one year and the described property shall not have been withdrawn by the lender, it is hereby agreed by the lender and the Bishop Museum that the described property shall be the unrestricted property of the Bishop Museum.

5. If the legal ownership of the described property shall change during the pendency of this loan, whether by reason of death, sale, insolvency, gift or otherwise, it is the responsibility of the new owner(s) and the lender to notify the Bishop Museum giving full name and address in writing. The new owner(s) may be requested to establish his (their) legal right to receive the described property by proof satisfactory to the Bishop Museum.

6. The Museum assumes no liability for loss or damage by theft, fire or other causes to the described property. Insurance is the responsibility of the owner.

7. All damage to the property upon receipt should be indicated in the description. The absence of notation as to condition of the property at the time it was received shall not mean it was in good condition at the time it was received.

8. Acceptance of this loan indicates that the described property may be available at the Bishop Museum to scholars and researchers, but does not imply that the property listed will be on extended public display in the Bishop Museum.

9. If any of the conditions to this loan are to be altered, changed, waived or otherwise affected, this must be done in writing on this agreement or by separate subsequent agreement with the Bishop Museum.

10. In signing this agreement the lender(s) certifies that he (they) is (are) the legal owner(s) or authorized agent(s) of the legal owner of the described property in question.

It is specifically understood by the undersigned that this loan is subject to the conditions listed above and that subject thereto the loan can become a gift. I have read the conditions above and accept them.

Offered by .... Date ....

Received by .... Date ....
(for the Bishop Museum)

```
incoming material loaned to B.P. Bishop Museum

Loaned to BPBM by:                                          TL- 1976.12
National Museum of Natural History, Smithsonian
Dr. Joseph Rosewater, Curator Mollusca                      EL-
Washington D.C.  20560


Quantity      Name of Specimen        Origin          ID or Cat. #

   1          Partula milleri Solem   New Hebrides    USNM
              USNM 619738             Espiritu Santo  619738

                                                      Registrar
                                                      321876
                                                      Invoice
                                                      4468
                                                      Shipping
                                                      227630


date received:              received by (name & department):
  10th May 1976               Yoshio Kondo, Malacology
condition when received:    comments:
  Excellent                   Loan to January 1st 1981 - 5 years

MAKE TWO COPIES, SEND BOTH TO THE REGISTRAR, ONE WILL BE RETURNED

BPBM Reg. Form No. 102  Sept 72
```

Fig. J.2.
Report form for incoming material received on loan (8½ by 11 in.), Bernice P. Bishop Museum.

quality supplies for collections records. When necessary, the registrar arranges for competent conservation of the records.

2. The registrar aids the curators in implementing the museum's policy on ethics of acquisition.

3. The registrar in concert with the curatorial staff conducts research to augment the accession records of poorly documented collections.

4. The registrar is custodian for inactive administrative and curatorial files.

5. The registrar provides temporary and secure storage for incoming and outgoing materials when necessary.

6. The registrar assists in determining the type and amount of insurance needed by the museum for its collections, and, when necessary, assists in processing insurance claims.

7. The registrar drafts guideline procedures for shipping, importing, and exporting specimens, may assist in the importing, exporting, and domestic shipping of specimens, and helps curators keep informed on federal and state laws and regulations involving collecting and transporting specimens.

8. The registrar maintains records of the catalogue number and location of materials exhibited by the museum. The registrar makes periodic inspections of the exhibits and reports on their condition to the respective curatorial staff.

9. The registrar is responsible for permit application, distribution, and report filing for ethyl alcohol, isopropyl alcohol, naphthalene, and other preservatives and fumigants. The registrar aids in choosing a fumigant and in the fumigation of specimens.

Explanation of Duties

RECORDS OF INCOMING AND OUTGOING MATERIAL

The registrar in a large, multidisciplinary natural history museum cannot possibly oversee each incoming shipment or unpack each box. Nor is this advisable, as handling each kind of material varies and often requires special training. In addition, botanical and zoological material is frequently staff collected and may not enter the museum through a shipping and receiving room. Thus, in any large science museum the registrar is highly dependent on information reported by the curators through the completion of accession sheets, shipping invoices, and other forms. This dependence means that a part of the registrar's work is tactfully cajoling, entreating, and enticing curators and staff in general into following rules and procedures set down by trustees, directors, and registrars.

The diversity of collections in a natural history museum affects the administration of registration procedures. Although it is necessary to have one set of rules for all departments, the method of observing the rules may differ from one department to another. For instance, procedures may require all disciplines (anthropology, entomology, history, ornithology, etc.) to report incoming loans, but there may be more than one form for reporting loans. In some cases, such as loans received in the history department from the general public, a form will include specific wording to limit the museum's liability and protect it from loans that are never retrieved by their owners. (See figure J.1.) In other cases, such as loans that are received by the botany and zoology departments from universities or other museums, a simpler form suffices to tell the registrar the material is on the museum premises. (See figure J.2.)

Even when there is only one form by which to record a registration procedure, flexibility is necessary. For example, it may be the policy to have all materials leaving the museum accompanied by a signed shipping invoice. The manner of describing the items shipped and the detail of the description may vary from department to department and still provide adequate information. (See figure J.3.)

The registrar is generally responsible for the format and administration of registration forms for museum-wide use. Forms should be brief and to the point; duplication of information and unnecessary questions should be avoided and unneeded forms eliminated. Abbreviated instructions for use should be printed on each form. Remembering that the registration system is highly dependent on information volunteered by curatorial staff through the completion of these forms, the registrar should strive to keep paper work to a minimum. The less paper work the registrar asks curatorial staff to do, the greater chance it will be done. When new forms are designed or old forms revised, the wise registrar solicits input from all the staff—guards, reception-

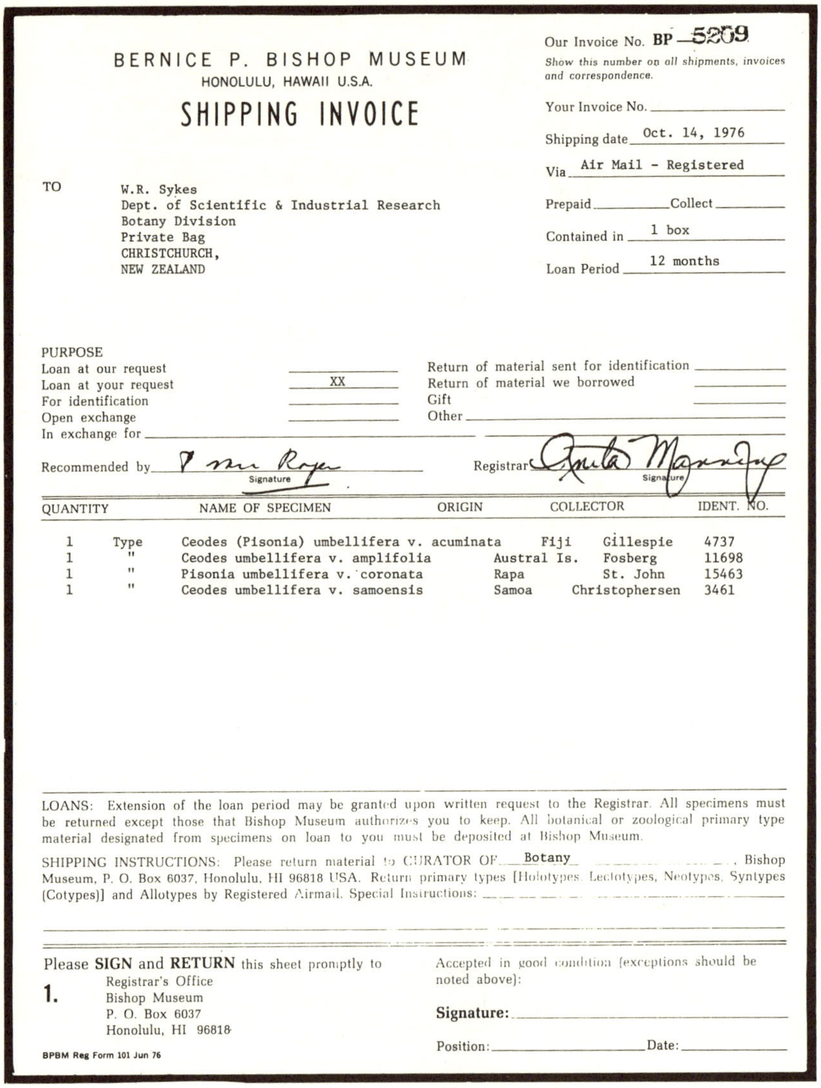

*Fig. J.3.
Shipping invoices from the Department of Botany and the Department of Entomology (8½ by 11 in.), Bernice P. Bishop Museum.*

ists, curators—involved in their use. (United States, General Services Administration, 1960a and 1960b.)

To design forms and systems for the accumulation and storage of information relating to registration needs, the registrar must understand some curatorial functions and activities. He or she should be familiar with the scope and orientation of each department's collections as well as the standards of documentation necessary in each discipline. In particular, the registrar in a natural history museum ought to be cognizant of the special kinds of loans, exchanges, and accessions common in the botanical and zoological sciences. Some of these special procedures are discussed below.

Loans of scientific specimens are generally made only to recognized researchers under the auspices of organizations where standards for care and handling are equal to those of the home institution. Students usually receive loans only when ultimate responsibility is assumed by a senior professor. Some institutions maintain a separate

```
                    BERNICE P. BISHOP MUSEUM          Our Invoice No. BP-5208
                        HONOLULU, HAWAII U.S.A.       Show this number on all shipments, invoices
                                                      and correspondence.
                         SHIPPING INVOICE             Your Invoice No. _____
                                                      Shipping date  2 July 1976
                                                      Via            Surface
          TO    Dr. C.H.C. Lyal
                Hemiptera Section                     Prepaid    X    Collect _____
                Department of Entomology
                British Museum (Natural History)      Contained in   12 cartons
                Cromwell Road
                London SW7 5BD                        Loan Period    3 years
                ENGLAND


          PURPOSE
          Loan at our request        _____          Return of material sent for identification ____
          Loan at your request          X             Return of material we borrowed            ____
          For identification         _____          Gift                                      ____
          Open exchange              _____          Other                                     ____
          In exchange for _____

          Recommended by _____         Registrar _____
                              Signature                                Signature
                           G.M. Nishida
          QUANTITY        NAME OF SPECIMEN         ORIGIN        COLLECTOR       IDENT. NO.

                    HEMIPTERA: SCUTELLARIDAE

          4,999 specimens on pins.  From the following localities:
                    Philippines       390    China        512
                    Australia         111    Laos         714
                    New Hebrides      290    Java          30
                    New Guinea      1,637    Borneo        65
                    New Caledonia     158    Malaysia       2
                    Fiji              133    Cambodia       2
                    Micronesia          6    Hong Kong     30
                    Solomons          446    Nepal          1
                    Society I.          3    India        198
                    Samoa             123    Taiwan        41
                    Japan              51
                    Viet Nam           27
                    Thailand           28    Total      4,999
```

LOANS: Extension of the loan period may be granted upon written request to the Registrar. All specimens must be returned except those that Bishop Museum authorizes you to keep. All botanical or zoological primary type material designated from specimens on loan to you must be deposited at Bishop Museum.

SHIPPING INSTRUCTIONS: Please return material to CURATOR OF **ENTOMOLOGY**, Bishop Museum, P. O. Box 6037, Honolulu, HI 96818 USA. Return primary types [Holotypes, Lectotypes, Neotypes, Syntypes (Cotypes)] and Allotypes by Registered Airmail. Special Instructions: _____

Please **SIGN** and **RETURN** this sheet promptly to   Accepted in good condition (exceptions should be
        Registrar's Office   noted above):
   1.   Bishop Museum
        P. O. Box 6037   Signature: _____
        Honolulu, HI 96818
                                                          Position: _____ Date: _____

collection for use by students below the graduate level. (Black, 1975; Force, 1975.)

Loan and exchange programs for botanical and zoological collections are determined in part by the frequent occurrence of duplicate specimens in material collected in the field. Natural history specimens of one species collected at the same time and place may be termed duplicates. One form of botanical duplicate occurs when an entire plant is collected and divided into several specimens. In entomological fieldwork, a large number of insects of the same species, sex, and age taken at one place and time are considered duplicates.

A common practice in loan programs is the retention of representative duplicate material by collaborators who identify undetermined specimens.[1] This practice of retention of duplicates comes about in the following way. A researcher at another

---

1. An undetermined specimen is one that has not been authoritatively named and described.

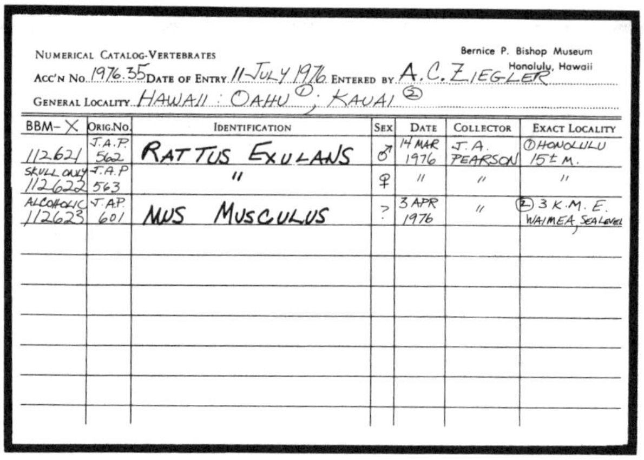

NUMERICAL CATALOG-VERTEBRATES

Bernice P. Bishop Museum
Honolulu, Hawaii

ACC'N NO. 1976.35 DATE OF ENTRY 11-JULY 1976 ENTERED BY A. C. ZIEGLER

GENERAL LOCALITY HAWAII : OAHU ①; KAUAI ②

BBM-X	ORIG.NO.	IDENTIFICATION	SEX	DATE	COLLECTOR	EXACT LOCALITY
112621	J.A.P. 562	RATTUS EXULANS	♂	14 MAR 1976	J. A. PEARSON	① HONOLULU 15± M.
SKULL ONLY 112622	J.A.P 563	"	♀	"	"	"
ALCOHOLIC 112623	J.A.P. 601	MUS MUSCULUS	?	3 APR 1976	"	② 3 K.M. E. WAIMEA, SEA LEVEL

Fig. J.4.
Catalogue card (4 by 6 in.), Division of Vertebrate Zoology, Bernice P. Bishop Museum.

institution may be an expert in an area for which the lending museum has no staff member. The museum, through its curator, sends undetermined material in that specialty to the collaborator, who then identifies and returns the majority of the material, including primary types[2] of any new species. Any retained duplicates, as authorized by the lending institution, are added to the collection of the museum for which the identifying scientist works. This system serves several functions in that it provides for: (1) the identification of the material because no one museum can maintain a staff adequate to identify all specimens received; (2) compensation for the labor of identification in lieu of cash payment; and (3) the distribution of duplicate material to other suitable systematics collections for future reference by researchers and as a reserve in the event of damage to the first series. Since a curator may close a loan even though all material sent has not been returned, the loan system should allow for this possibility.

A customary method of acquisition in botany and zoology departments is the open exchange agreement. Usually upon the recommendation of the curator to the director and trustees, two institutions enter into an agreement that defines mutual responsibilities and the class of specimens to be exchanged. In one version of the open exchange, the museums agree to send duplicates to each other. While exchanging institutions generally receive as much as they send, it is not necessary for the museum receiving a shipment to reciprocate immediately. Open exchange agreements have several benefits: (1) the exchanging museums do not duplicate their efforts by sending collectors to the same locality; (2) the collections grow without large expense; (3) representative material is housed in several locations for reference and as a reserve in the event of the destruction of specimens at the originating institution; and (4) the curator does not need to obtain special permission from the trustees for each shipment, and only the regular invoices are needed. (Nicholson, 1975.) The registrar should keep on file a list of organizations and/or letters of agreement, which will serve as authorization for the open exchange. In addition, the registrar may be asked to keep a tally that will enable departments to monitor the status of materials sent and received in each open exchange.

Whatever the method whereby materials enter the museum, registration procedures are under the control of the registrar. Accession numbers are assigned according to

2. "A type specimen is the single specimen or any one of a series of specimens from which a species is described" (de la Torre-Bueno, 1962). As such it is invaluable for comparison and study by researchers.

Fig. J.5.
Catalogue information, typed on a label (4 by 4¾ in.), Bernice P. Bishop Museum, is attached to each herbarium sheet.

the system described in part 1 of this book. However, cataloguing—the recording and numbering of individual specimens by artifact type, country of origin, species, etc.—is strictly a curatorial function. In order to design registration forms that take into consideration the documentation needs of all disciplines, the registrar will want to be familiar, at least on a cursory level, with the cataloguing procedures of each department as well as with the aim of its loan and exchange programs. The form of the catalogue card, the vocabulary, and the numbering system may vary from department to department within a museum. For example, at the Bishop Museum, the Department of Anthropology describes each specimen in detail in a manner similar to that outlined in article I, while the Vertebrate Zoology Division describes each specimen with a minimum of information. (See figure J.4.) In the Department of Entomology, only type specimens are individually numbered and described. The majority of this collection, totaling over ten million specimens, is stored phylogenetically and geographically for study purposes and ease of retrieval. In the Herbarium, each specimen is numbered, but no catalogue is kept. Instead, the descriptive information is attached to the herbarium sheet. (See figures J.5–6). For details on the standards for catalogue data in the various disciplines, the reader is referred to the following sources listed in the bibliography: Anderson and Choate, 1974 (mammals); Black, 1975 (botany and zoology); Fosberg and Sachet, 1965 (botany); Fritts, 1976 (botany and zoology); Hall, 1962 (vertebrates); Knudsen, 1972 (botany and zoology); Manning, R. B., 1969b (marine invertebrates); Oceanographic Sorting Center, n.d. (botany, marine specimens); Shetler, 1973 (botany); Wake, 1975 (herpetology); Zusi, 1969 (ornithology); Zweifel, 1966 (herpetology).

RETRIEVAL OF REGISTRATION INFORMATION

The registrar is also responsible for establishing and maintaining systems for the retrieval of registration information regarding material entering or leaving the museum. A well-designed index or other retrieval system serves administrative needs and assists the curatorial staff. When designing or redesigning data retrieval systems the registrar should get input from all departments in order both to see the system through the eyes of others and to learn the major collections-oriented questions to which curators need answers. In addition to responding to administrative and curatorial questions, the retrieval system may be designed to meet a variety of other needs. It may, for example, provide information for grant applications or progress reports: how many loans were made last year? how many exchanges? how many of the transactions were with foreign, how many with domestic organizations?

In natural history museums having a very active accession, loan, and exchange program, the registrar can profitably employ mechanical or electronic data retrieval systems. Data retrieval equipment may be easily available to organizations affiliated with a university or funded by city or state. Private museums, on the other hand, often assume that lack of funds will frustrate their attempts to attain automated data retrieval services. Actually data processing equipment may be available in the museum itself. Accounting and membership association offices often possess mechanical data retrieval equipment that might also be useful to the registrar or curator. For five and a half years the Bishop Museum's accounting department's punch card and printing machine doubled to index and review the registrar's files of incoming and outgoing loans and exchanges. (See figure J.7.) Sharing equipment is not the most convenient method of acquiring automated data retrieval capability, but it can be a beginning. Much can be accomplished with this type of data retrieval equipment, which is less sophisticated than a computer. (Manning, A., 1975.)

However, electronic data retrieval is regarded by many as the most practical method for handling registration and catalogue information on collections that may contain millions of specimens and for other collection management applications, as well as for managing research data and generating publications. Attempts are being made to standardize terms and types of data to make such systems even more effective. (Articles M–P; Beschel and Soper, 1970; Black, 1975; Chenhall, 1971, 1974, and 1975; Creighton and Packard, 1974; Edwards and Grotta, 1976b; Hale, 1970; Humphrey and Clausen, 1977; Manning, R. B., 1969a and 1969b; Neff and Chaffee, 1977; Shetler, 1973; Sutton and Black, 1976; Van Devender, 1976.)

The study of botanical and zoological material involves scientific institutions in large-scale borrowing and lending of specimens. An important component of such a loan program is invoicing of outgoing loans and recording of incoming loans. (See chapters 2 and 6.) In a museum where the volume of loans is large, a retrieval system can be designed to provide for periodic review of loan status. The system should allow for regular reports to the curatorial staff of overdue loans made by their departments. The curator then determines whether an inquiry should be sent to the borrowers regarding the status of such loans. The registrar should also provide the curatorial

Fig. J.6.
Herbarium storage cabinet provides for folders containing several specimens of the same species. Guides to location and finding aids for easy retrieval are attached or close to the storage area.

staff with a chance to review incoming loans on a regular basis. Such a review ensures that loans are not forgotten by staff or lender. Periodic review of loans also offers the registrar and curatorial staff a chance to reconcile discrepancies, such as unreported returns of loans. At the Bishop Museum curators find it useful for the retrieval system to provide, in addition to names, invoice or form numbers, and due dates, an alphabetical list of borrowers or lenders arranged by department as well as a museum-wide alphabetical list of consignees who have returned loans. With the experience and data base gained from the use of the accounting department's punch card and printing machine, the loan and exchange indexes are now being computerized. A few additional columns of information, plus the increased capabilities of the computer, should make it possible for the same records to help curators with reports and surveys, which now needlessly consume valuable time.

Loaning botany and zoology specimens creates some special problems for the retrieval system. In the process of studying a group of insects, for instance, a researcher will borrow a large number of specimens from several organizations over a period of years. Also, several loans may be made by each of these institutions. As the researcher finishes identifying the insects and describing each new species within the group, the specimens that are no longer needed are repacked and returned to the lending organization. The problem arises in identifying which insects belong to which loan when parts of several loans are returned simultaneously. Perhaps the insects were loaned as specimens preserved in alcohol but have been remounted on slides: the outgoing loan invoice lists "twelve vials" sent, but twenty slides are returned. Confusion can be reduced by asking borrowers to return the packing copy of the shipping invoice with the specimens. (See figure J.8.) It is also important that the retrieval system allow for partial returns. Furthermore, it might be designed to provide recall not only by borrower's name, but also by scientific name of the specimens or other key factors that could help in correctly crediting returned specimens to the proper invoice.

Another valuable service of an information retrieval system is the provision of a donor index, which is particularly important in museums with anthropology and/or history collections. The majority of these collections are received from private donors rather than through staff collection. With the growth of interest in family history and cultural origins throughout the United States, museums are visited more frequently by donors or donors' relatives, and often these visitors come unannounced. Perhaps they are in town for only a few days or hours. They may not know exactly what was donated or when, or even the exact name of the donor. Prompt answers to family inquiries often result in further donations or, at the least, in the forestalling of demands for the return of past donations. Thus, an effective registration system can be a part of good public relations for the museum. (See figure J.9.)

PHYSICAL CARE OF RECORDS

The registrar usually has responsibility for providing a proper physical environment for the museum's registration records. Records should be given care equivalent to that provided the collections, for without this record the value of museum collections, particularly historical or anthropological specimens, is greatly diminished. Certainly all registrars should provide the records in their care with an environment that is dust and insect free and temperature and humidity controlled. Registrars can learn to care for their records by reading some of the conservation literature written for librarians and archivists. (Barrow, 1972; Clapp, 1974; Cunha and Cunha, 1971–72; Winger and Smith, 1970.)

Archival supplies, such as acid-free folders, papers, and envelopes, are now readily available and should be used for registration records. The most important forms and records, for instance the accession sheets, should be printed on an acid-free paper such as Permalife. Although the registrar cannot control the quality of paper on which such accession documentation as correspondence and memoranda are written, the use of acid-free supplies will contribute to the general preservation of the records. The accession sheet or file folder of acid-free paper, for instance, acts as a buffer preventing acid migration from a newsclipping to the sheets on either side of it.

In older museums, the earliest records may need treatment by a paper conservator. If such professional help is not available, the registrar can take some simple precautions. When any record becomes fragile, it should be copied and removed from active use, so that the original will not deteriorate further through handling but will be available for reference should the clarity or accuracy of the copy be challenged. Ideally, as an added protection, the registrar should arrange for microfilming all registration and department catalogue records. At least one microfilm copy should be deposited outside the museum as a safeguard should the originals be destroyed.

ETHICS OF ACQUISITION

The registrar can contribute to the implementation of the museum's ethics-of-acquisition policy by maintaining a file of current export laws for countries within the scope of the museum's collections. This file helps curatorial staff in preparing for fieldwork and in determining if an item offered for sale or donation was properly collected and exported from the country of origin. (Chapter 8; Anonymous, 1970 and 1976b; Burnham, 1974; Nicholson, 1974a and 1975.)

RESEARCHING DOCUMENTATION

In many museums, documentation standards are higher today than half a century ago. Registrars may find that early registration records lack the completeness now demanded for proof of ownership. Yet information for completing the records may be found in annual reports, accounting records, correspondence files, minutes of committee meetings, court records, and newspaper articles. Research into such sources may be necessary to establish a clearer and more complete registration record for museum accessions. This is an important goal in an era when the descendants of donors are confidently asking for the return of donations made years ago. Such research could have many spin-off benefits, as well, to aid curatorial work. For instance, exhibit labels can be more interesting with a bit of history added, or doubtful attributions can be supported or disproved. Occasionally the documentation found in support of an accession will be important in its own right, for instance, a letter of donation signed by a leading citizen of the turn of the century. (Article H; Force, 1975; Manning, A., 1977; Nason, Hopkins, and Medicine, 1973.)

INACTIVE FILES

Most museums are documenting the history of the items in their care, but few are doing anything to document their own institutional history. While museum archivists are busily collecting the business and administrative records of their community, they and other museum workers may be failing to retain their own records. An in-house archival program should be established. The collection that was not accepted and the proposed field trip that did not become reality have no accession record, but not un-

Fig. J.7.
Registration systems should provide for a periodic review of the status of incoming and outgoing loans by curator and registrar. Data processing equipment can greatly facilitate this work.

commonly such events raise questions years later. The grant-supported expedition will generate extensive correspondence that may not be in the accession file but that can later be of administrative as well as curatorial interest. Or a particular discipline or branch of science may no longer be under active study at the museum. The registrar may provide the repository for these and other kinds of inactive administrative and curatorial files and records in museums lacking an archivist.

STORAGE FOR INCOMING AND OUTGOING MATERIALS

In some natural history museums storage is an infrequent responsibility and is not an important consideration when designing the registrar's office and work area. Incoming materials may actually pass through the registrar's office only on rare occasions. In such cases, the curatorial staff may report to the registrar by completing accession sheets or other forms so that the need for a large handling area is reduced. In other museums, the registrar actually does receive the materials and must provide for their safekeeping while in the custody of the registration department. (Article T.)

INSURANCE

A natural history museum registrar may be concerned with buying insurance only at infrequent intervals. Botanical and zoological specimens in transit rarely need special insurance. Anthropology and history specimens, on the other hand, do need to be insured, especially when loaned for exhibit. Whether or not the registrar is directly involved in selecting and purchasing the insurance, he or she should be completely familiar with the coverage held by the museum, exceptions to that coverage, and the claim procedures. (Chapter 9; ALI-ABA, 1973.)

IMPORTING AND EXPORTING AND SHIPPING

The registrar provides a standard for invoices, shipping labels, and addressing of shipments. Each discipline has particular packing practices designed to ensure the safe handling and preservation of specimens, and the actual packing and unpacking are carried out in each department. Descriptions of packing and shipping techniques in the various disciplines are found in Fosberg and Sachet, 1965 (botany); Hall, 1962 (vertebrates); Knudsen, 1972 (botany and zoology); Mason, 1974 (entomology); Oceanographic Sorting Center, n.d. (botany and marine specimens); Pisani, 1973 (herpetology); Sabrosky, 1971 (entomology); Wake, 1975 (herpetology); Zweifel, 1966 (herpetology).

Even though it may be the policy for each department to arrange for the shipment of its own specimens, the registrar may be asked to assist in choosing a carrier. The most common method of shipping zoological and botanical specimens is through the mail. Domestic shipments of common specimens usually make use of the U.S. Postal Service's inexpensive library rate. Type specimens, however, should be sent by registered air mail because of their importance. Shipments of large specimens or large lots may be by freight or by one of the other methods described in chapter 7. (United States, Postal Service, a and b.)

Shipments to and from foreign countries require special attention. In addition to U.S. Customs entry requirements (see chapter 8), imported botanical and zoological specimens must face inspection by representatives of federal and state departments of agriculture and wildlife. The registrar can speed clearance by anticipating the inspectors who are required for a particular shipment and arranging for them to be present at one inspection.

The registrar should keep on file the museum's federal and state permits relating to specimen importation and collection and should make periodic renewal applications. Registrar and curator alike should keep informed on proposed and newly implemented laws and regulations affecting the collecting and shipping of biological materials. The *Association of Systematics Collections Newsletter* is a good source for up-to-date information. (Aldrich, 1975; Czajka and Nickerson, 1975; Edwards and Grotta, 1976a; Genoways and Choate, 1976; McGaugh and Genoways, 1976.)

LOCATION AND EXHIBIT RECORDS AND INSPECTIONS

Maintaining exhibit records and inspecting exhibits are common duties for registrars, although in some larger museums record keeping and inspection of exhibit cases are the responsibilities of a separate exhibits department. Large museums may operate several branch exhibits, and periodic inspection can be a burdensome travel problem. In such cases, the routine inspection of exhibits may be shared with personnel at each site.

Exhibit records generally include specific information on the collections displayed (accession number, title or name, etc.) and their location in the exhibit halls. If the museum does not have an exhibits department, the registrar may also file information necessary for the upkeep of the exhibit cases (paint color, light bulb type, location of locks or entry panels, etc.). (Article H.)

In making an inspection of exhibit areas the registrar should review for conservation, pest, and maintenance problems in the exhibit cases. In addition, the registrar should look for potential fire or public safety hazards and make note of general appearance and upkeep in the exhibit halls. Exhibit inspection should also include provi-

BERNICE P. BISHOP MUSEUM
HONOLULU, HAWAII U.S.A.

SHIPPING INVOICE

Our Invoice No. BP— 201
Show this number on all shipments, invoices and correspondence.

Your Invoice No. ____________

Shipping date ____________

Via ____________

Prepaid ________ Collect ________

Contained in ____________

Loan Period ____________

TO

PURPOSE
Loan at our request ________ Return of material sent for identification ________
Loan at your request ________ Return of material we borrowed ________
For identification ________ Gift ________
Open exchange ________ Other ________
In exchange for ____________

Recommended by ____________ (Signature) Registrar ____________ (Signature)

QUANTITY	NAME OF SPECIMEN	ORIGIN	COLLECTOR	IDENT. NO.

LOANS: Extension of the loan period may be granted upon written request to the Registrar. All specimens must be returned except those that Bishop Museum authorizes you to keep. All botanical or zoological primary type material designated from specimens on loan to you must be deposited at Bishop Museum.

SHIPPING INSTRUCTIONS: Please return material to CURATOR OF ____________, Bishop Museum, P. O. Box 6037, Honolulu, HI 96818 USA. Return primary types [Holotypes, Lectotypes, Neotypes, Syntypes (Cotypes)] and Allotypes by Registered Airmail. Special Instructions: ____________

PACKING COPY Shipping Room: Before sealing carton, place this copy on top of contents. If more than one carton, place in Carton 1.
2.

CONSIGNEE: Please sign and return the white original of this Invoice, sent you on shipping date shown above. Loans: Please enclose this copy when returning specimens to insure material is credited to proper loan. All other consignments: Keep this copy for your files.

BPBM Reg-Form 101 Jun 76

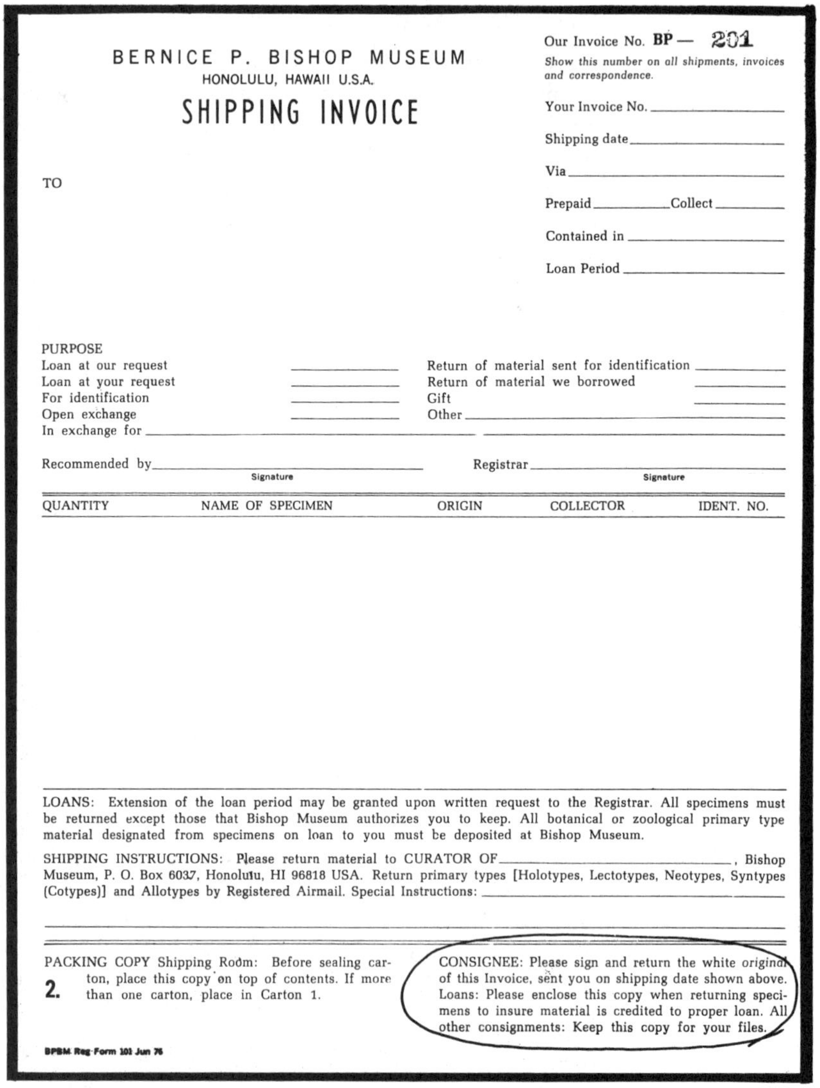

Fig. J.8.
Shipping invoice, packing copy (8½ by 11 in.), Bernice P. Bishop Museum. Note that the consignee is asked to return this sheet when returning loan material to ensure proper crediting of specimens.

Fig. J.9.
The index to donors' names can be an important public relations tool, especially for history and/or anthropology collections. Such an index can help the staff readily retrieve objects in response to queries from former donors or their descendants.

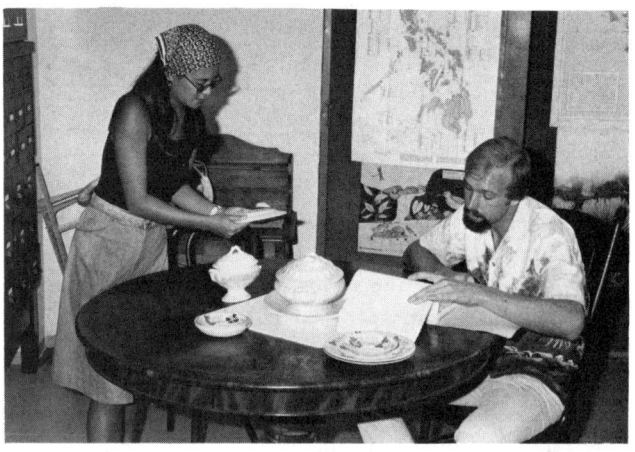

sion for routine trial of the museum's security devices (alarms, barriers, locks, etc.). It may be useful to use a checklist or report form during the inspection to ensure that all items of concern are reviewed in each tour of the exhibits. Copies of the report can serve as a notice to curatorial, janitorial, or maintenance staff of problems. Prompt attention to problems in these areas not only results in the reduction of potential harm to the collection but also enhances the visitor's impression of the museum. (Article T.)

PRESERVATIVES AND FUMIGANTS

The registrar may be designated by the director as a central agent for ordering and controlling chemicals needed by all departments. The registrar should file permit applications and necessary reports[3] promptly, and should keep a record of all chemicals dispensed. In some museums the registrar may also be actively involved in the actual fumigation of incoming specimens. These activities carry considerable responsibility for the safety and health of staff and collections. The registrar must be aware of the hazards and precautions for each substance, and must make safety information concerning each chemical available to the staff involved. Many of these materials are controlled by federal, state, or local laws and regulations, with which the registrar will need to be familiar. (Anonymous, 1976a; United States, Department of the Treasury, 1972; Pisani, 1973; Quay, 1974; Wake, 1975; Zweifel, 1966.)

3. Application and Withdrawal Permit to Procure Spirits Free of Tax, U.S. Department of the Treasury, Bureau of Alcohol, Tobacco and Firearms Form 1450; Report of Tax-Free Alcohol User, U.S. Department of the Treasury, Internal Revenue Service Form 1451.

Bibliography

Aldrich, John W., chairman
    1975   "Report of the American Ornithologists' Union ad hoc Committee on Scientific and Educational Use of Wild Birds." *Auk*, 92:3, supp.

American Law Institute–American Bar Association (ALI–ABA)
    1973–   *Courses of Study: Legal Problems of Museum Administration* (syllabus
    annual   and transcripts). ALI–ABA, Philadelphia.

Anderson, Sydney, and Jerry R. Choate, eds.
    1974   *Report and Recommendations of the Advisory Committee for Systematic Resources in Mammalogy*. American Society of Mammalogists, Stillwater, Okla. 30 pp.

Anonymous
    1970   "Responsibility in Biological Fieldwork and Guidelines for Biological Field Studies." *Taxon*, 19:6, pp. 950–51.
    1976a   "Fumigants—Procedures, Precautions and Institutional Responsibility for Their Safe Use. *ASC Newsletter*, 4:1, pp. 5–6.
    1976b   "Caution Advised in Transport of Pre-Columbian Materials." *Aviso*, no. 1 (Jan.), p. 1.
    1977   "Simpson Reversal: Good and Bad." *Aviso*, no. 3 (Mar.), p. 1.

Barrow, William J.
    1972   *Manuscripts and Documents: Their Deterioration and Restoration*. 2d ed. University Press of Virginia, Charlottesville. 84 pp.

Beschel, R. E., and J. H. Soper
    1970   "The Automation and Standardization of Certain Herbarium Procedures." *Canadian Journal of Botany*, 48:3, pp. 547–54.

Black, Craig C., chairman
  1975 "Report of the ASC Council on Standards for Systematics Collections." *ASC Newsletter*, 3:3, insert.

Burnham, Bonnie, comp.
  1974 *The Protection of Cultural Property: Handbook of National Legislations.* Ceres Productions, for ICOM, Tunisia. 204 pp.

Chenhall, Robert G.
  1971 *Computers in Anthropology and Archeology.* IBM Corporation publication GE-20-0384.
  1974 "The Mythical Magic Black Box." *Museum News*, 53:1, pp. 30–33.
  1975 *Museum Cataloging in the Computer Age.* AASLH, Nashville. 261 pp.

Clapp, Anne F.
  1974 *Curatorial Care of Works of Art on Paper.* 2d ed. rev. Intermuseum Laboratory, Oberlin, Ohio. 107 pp.

Creighton, Reginald, and Penelope Packard
  1974 *Computer Assisted Information Management: Getting Oriented.* Procedures in Computer Sciences 1:2. Smithsonian Institution, Washington, D.C. 28 pp.

Cunha, George Martin, and Dorothy Grant Cunha
  1971–72 *Conservation of Library Materials: A Manual and Bibliography on the Care, Repair, and Restoration of Library Materials.* 2d ed. 2 vols. Scarecrow Press, Metuchen, N.J. 414 pp. and 406 pp.

Czajka, Adrian F., and Max A. Nickerson
  1975 *State Regulations for Collecting Reptiles and Amphibians in the Fifty United States.* Special Publications in Biology and Geology 1. Milwaukee Public Museum, Milwaukee, Wis.

de la Torre-Bueno, J. R.
  1962 *A Glossary of Entomology.* Brooklyn Entomological Society, Brooklyn, N.Y. 372 pp.

Edwards, Stephen R., and Leonard D. Grotta, eds.
  1976a *Systematics Collections and the Law.* The Proceedings of a Symposium held in conjunction with the 3rd Annual Meeting of the ASC. Lawrence, Kans. 29 pp.
  1976b *Systematics '75: A Report on a Workshop Assessing the Current Status of Systematics Collections.* ASC, Lawrence, Kans. 77 pp.

Force, Roland W.
  1975 "Museum Collections—Access, Use, and Control." *Curator*, 18:4, pp. 249–55.

Fosberg, F. Raymond, and Marie-Hiléne Sachet
  1965 "Manual for Tropical Herbaria." *Regnum Vegetabile*, 39, pp. 1–132.

Fritts, Thomas H.
  1976 "Criteria for Accession—One Solution to the Problem of Collection Growth." *ASC Newsletter*, 4:4, pp. 54–55.

Genoways, Hugh H., and Jerry R. Choate
  1976 "Federal Regulations Pertaining to Collection, Import, Export, and Transport of Scientific Specimens of Mammals." *Journal of Mammalogy*, 57:2, supp. 9 pp.

Hale, Mason E., and Reginald Creighton
    1970   "An Automated System for Recording Exchanges." *Flora North America Report*, 32, pp. 1–9. American Society of Plant Taxonomists.

Hall, Eugene Raymond
    1962   *Collecting and Preparing Study Specimens of Vertebrates.* Miscellaneous Publication 30. University of Kansas, Museum of Natural History, Lawrence, Kans. 46 pp.

Humphrey, Philip S., and Ann C. Clausen.
    1977   *Automated Cataloging for Museum Collections: A Model for Decision and a Guide to Implementation.* ASC, Lawrence, Kans. 79 pp.

Knudsen, Jens W.
    1972   *Collecting and Preserving Plants and Animals.* Harper and Row, New York. 320 pp.

McGaugh, M. Houston, and Hugh H. Genoways
    1976   "State Laws As They Pertain to Scientific Collecting Permits." *Museology* 2. Texas Tech Press, Lubbock.

Manning, Anita
    1975   *Data Retrieval without a Computer.* AASLH Technical Leaflet 85. *History News*, 30:9, insert. 8 pp.
    1977   *Converting Loans to Gifts: One Solution to "Permanent" Loans.* AASLH Technical Leaflet 94. *History News*, 32:4, insert. 12 pp.

Manning, Raymond B.
    1969a   "Automation in Museum Collections." *Proceedings of the Biological Society of Washington*, 82, pp. 671–86.
    1969b   "A Computer-Generated Catalog of Types: A By-Product of Data Processing in Museums." *Curator*, 12:2, pp. 134–38.

Mason, W. R. M.
    1974   "Shipping Alcohol Collections in Plastic Bags." *Proceedings of the Entomological Society of Washington*, 76:2, pp. 229–30.

Nason, James D., Kenneth R. Hopkins, and Bea Medicine
    1973   "Finders Keepers?" *Museum News*, 51:7, pp. 20–26.

Neff, Jeffrey M., and Holly M. Chaffee
    1977   "REGIS—A Computerized Museum Registration System." *Curator*, 20:1, pp. 32–41.

Nicholson, Thomas D.
    1974   "The Publication of a Statement of Guidelines for the Management of Collections." *Curator*, 17:2, pp. 83–90.
    1975   "The Australian Museum and the Field Museum Adopt Policy Statements Regarding Collections." *Curator*, 18:4, pp. 296–314.

Oceanographic Sorting Center
    n.d.   *Draft Bibliography of Specimen Handling Techniques.* Smithsonian Institution, Washington, D.C. 356 pp.

Pisani, George R.
    1973   *A Guide to Preservation Techniques for Amphibians and Reptiles.* Society for the Study of Amphibians and Reptiles, Lawrence, Kans. 22 pp.

Quay, W. B.
    1974   "Bird and Mammal Specimens in Fluid—Objectives and Methods." *Curator*, 17:2, pp. 91–104.

Sabrosky, Curtis W.
  1971 "Packing and Shipping Pinned Insects." *Bulletin of Entomological Society of America*, 17:1, pp. 6–8.

Schneider, Mary Jane, ed.
  1970 "A Guide to Inventorying Ethnological Collections" (unpublished but circulated). University of Missouri—Columbia, Museum of Anthropology.

Shetler, Stanwyn G., et al.
  1973 *An Introduction to the Botanical Type Specimen Register*. Smithsonian Contributions to Botany 12. Smithsonian Institution Press, Washington, D.C. 186 pp.

Sutton, John F., and Craig C. Black
  1976 "Data in Systematics Collections." *ASC Newsletter*, 4:4, pp. 48–50. Also as Museum Data Bank Research Report 6.

United States, Department of the Treasury, Bureau of Alcohol, Tobacco and Firearms
  1972 *Distribution and Use of Tax-Free Alcohol*. Part 213 of Title 26 Code of Federal Regulations, GPO, Washington, D.C. 35 pp.

——, General Services Administration
  1960a *Forms Analysis*. National Archives and Records Service, Office of Records Management, GPO, Washington, D.C. 62 pp.
  1960b *Forms Design*. National Archives and Records Service, Office of Records Management, GPO, Washington, D.C. 88 pp.

——, Postal Service
  current (a) *Instructions for Mailers*. Publication 8. GPO, Washington, D.C. Loose leaf, paging varies.
  current (b) *International Mail*. Publication 42. GPO, Washington, D.C. Loose leaf, paging varies.

Van Devender, R. Wayne
  1976 "Michigan Studies Computer Costs." *ASC Newsletter*, 4:6, pp. 72–73.

Wake, David B., chairman
  1975 "Recommendations for the Management of Herpetological Museum Collections." Committee on Resources in Herpetology. *Herpetological Review*, 6:2, pp. 34–36.

Winger, Howard W., and Richard Daniel Smith, eds.
  1970 *Deterioration and Preservation of Library Materials: The Thirty-Fourth Annual Conference of the Graduate Library School, August 4–6, 1969*. University of Chicago Press, Chicago. 200 pp.

Zusi, Richard L.
  1969 "The Role of Museum Collections in Ornithological Research." *Proceedings of the Biological Society of Washington*, 82, pp. 651–61.

Zweifel, Richard G.
  1966 "Guidelines for the Care of a Herpetological Collection." *Curator*, 9:1, pp. 24–35.

ACCESSIONING, MARKING, AND STORING SCIENTIFIC COLLECTIONS

WILLIAM A. BURNS
JEROME G. ROZEN, JR.

At the American Museum of Natural History each scientific department records and numbers its own specimens and maintains its own files. A report of accessions, however, is made, in duplicate, on the accession record form (see figure K.1) and forwarded to the Central Files Department for recording and filing in the museum's central accessions file.

On the accession record form are noted a description of the specimen or specimens; the date of receipt; the name and address of the donor or the name of the collector; the locality where collected; the number and condition of the specimen or specimens; the estimated value; and whether the accession is a gift, purchase, exchange, transfer, or acquired as a result of an expedition. The scientific department's catalogue number and its file or accession number, if assigned, are also reported on this form.

A central accession record number, which differs from the file or accession number used in the various scientific departments, is then assigned by the accessions clerk. The numbering system used in assigning this central accession number is simply consecutive; at the time of this writing, accession number 57,856 was assigned. The accession number is entered in a ledger, together with a description of the accession and how it was acquired, the name of the department receiving it, and so forth. The number is also recorded on the accession record form. The first copy of this form (white) is kept in the Central Files Department. From it two cards are made, each containing full accession information; one is filed by subject matter and the other by donor or other source of acquisition. The second copy of the accession record form (pink) is returned to the scientific department. If the accession has been received as a gift, a formal acknowledgment is prepared by the Archives Department and sent to the donor.

Specimens received as loans are also reported, in duplicate, on the accession record form, together with the purpose of the loan. The loan is registered in the Central Files Department, and the pink copy of the accession record form is returned to the scientific department, where it is filed under "open loans." When the loan is returned, the pink copy is marked "returned," dated, and signed by a staff member, and then sent to the Central Files Department so that the loan may be closed in its files. The Central Files Department retains this signed copy and returns the white copy to the scientific department, where it is filed in the "closed loans" file.

Each scientific department has developed a method of marking and storing based on methods standard for all museums of natural history but modified to meet its individual needs and those of this institution. In this article, the departments of anthropology, entomology, herpetology, mammalogy, ornithology, and vertebrate paleontology are used as examples. All the methods described are subject to local modification, depending upon the needs and the resources of each institution. Air conditioning and humidity control are desirable but expensive, and neither is absolutely essential for the climate in which the American Museum is located.

Anthropology

Collections in the Department of Anthropology fall into three categories: ethnology, archaeology, and physical anthropology.

When a collection is received, an abbreviated notebook record is made listing the name of the donor (or vendor, collector, or expedition, depending upon the circumstances), the type of collection, provenance, number of objects, and estimated value or actual cost. A museum accession record form is also completed and sent to the Central Files Department. Each acquisition in the Department of Anthropology's system is numbered sequentially for each calendar year (1978-1, 1978-2, 1978-3, etc.). All correspondence, photographs, final catalogue numbers, and notes concerning a given accession are kept in an envelope filed in an annual accession file under this accession number. A donor file giving name, accession number, locality, and catalogue numbers of the collection furnishes easy access to these original data.

After a collection has been accessioned, it is catalogued. Since the collections fall into the three major categories noted above, a series of area or subject catalogues, each with an index number (arbitrarily assigned), is maintained. For example, North American ethnology bears the index number 50, which becomes the numerator for the sequence number of a specific object, assigned chronologically, according to the order in which it is catalogued. Thus, a specimen catalogued in 50 would bear a number like 50-6742 (which may also be written $\frac{50}{6742}$ or 50/6742); the next specimen catalogued would be number 50-6743. When 50-9999 is reached, the numerator for North American ethnology changes to 50.0, then to 50.1, and so on. Other designations in this system of subject and area catalogues include North American archaeology, 20; Middle American archaeology, 30; African ethnology, 90; and physical anthropology, 99. The actual catalogue records are in manuscript volumes designated by catalogue number. Duplicate typed copies of these are bound in loose-leaf binders for laboratory and office use. The cataloguing system, although dating from the organization of the department, is still very practical.

Archaeological and ethnographic specimens (except textiles) are marked with the catalogue number according to the color of the specimen: dark-colored specimens are marked with white India ink, and light ones with black India ink. Both inks are shellacked when dry. Marks are located on the reverse side or on the base of objects (e.g., pottery) so that the numbers will not be apparent when the specimen is exhibited. Skeletal material is marked with India ink on each bone. Where possible, the catalogue number is also written on a metal-rim tag attached with string to the specimen. Textiles are marked by sewing to one corner of the fabric a cotton tape label on which the catalogue number has been typed.

The department is currently planning and executing new storage facilities for the collections. Artifacts are being consolidated and stored according to geographical provenance, with particular attention to the special climatic and other requirements of the different materials of the specimens. For instance, a new, climate-controlled facility for the storage of all ethnographic textiles has been constructed. Here the textiles are stored flat on acid-free tissue in large, shallow wooden trays inside air-

DEPARTMENT
File or Accession Number.......... Accession Number..........

THE AMERICAN MUSEUM OF NATURAL HISTORY

ACCESSION RECORD

New York, N. Y. ....
DATE OF RECEIPT OF SPECIMEN

Received from..........

Address..........

Description of Material..........

....

....

....

....

Locality.......... No. of Specimens..........

Collector.......... Estimated Value $..........

How Acquired:
- GIFT ☐ ....
- *PURCHASE ☐ PRICE $..........
- *EXPEDITION ☐ ....
- EXCHANGE ☐ ....
- TRANSFER ☐ ....

Condition:
- GOOD ☐
- FAIR ☐
- POOR ☐

Loans received for:
- EXAMINATION ☐
- DEPOSIT ☐
- STUDY ☐
- IDENTIFICATION ☐
- VIEW TO PURCHASE ☐
- EXHIBITION ☐
- USE IN LECTURE ☐

PLEASE SEND FORMAL ACKNOWLEDGMENT ☐

Department Catalog No..........

Number and nature of specimens given in exchange, or other information..........

....

....

Loan Returned on.......... 19..........

SEND TO ACCESSIONS FILE–OFFICE SERVICES Signed..........

*INSERT NAME OF EXPEDITION OR FUND Dept. of..........

Fig. K.1.
Accession record form (8½ by 11 in.), American Museum of Natural History. This form is completed in duplicate by the scientific departments and forwarded to the Central Files Department, where the first copy is retained. After the accession is recorded and the accession number assigned, the second copy is returned to the originating scientific department.

tight metal storage units. (A card catalogue with analysis of these textiles is being maintained: one card for each textile, containing full information, is filed by provenance, and a cross-index, arranged by weaving technique, makes reference to these cards.) The entire North American archaeological collection has been placed in wooden trays in metal storage cabinets. Any cabinet containing materials requiring fumigation is so marked.

Within the storage areas not yet modified, objects are stored in trays in wooden or metal cabinets. Some large and/or perishable specimens are kept in enclosed, room-size storage vaults where they may be placed in trays, on open shelves, or on wall and ceiling racks. These vaults are regularly fumigated.

Skeletal material is stored as a separate unit. Crania are stored in cardboard boxes on open shelves. Postcranial material is kept in wooden or metal trays inside wooden or metal storage cabinets.

Entomology

In the Department of Entomology, accessions are recorded on the accession record forms, which are sent to the Central Files Department. Most of the information on specimens of the Department of Entomology is contained on the label that accompanies the specimen. This includes the date of collection, the collector's name, the exact locality where found, and any other information that would assist in the study of the specimen. Field notebooks may contain additional habitat or biological data that are keyed to the specimens by numbers. No department accession or catalogue number is assigned, however, and, as the specimens are stored by families in easily accessible drawers, there is no need for a card catalogue file.

The collecting data on pinned insects are written with India ink on small labels of good quality paper. The label is then put on the pin directly below the specimen. Its position on the pin is kept uniform by the use of a pinning block. Pinned insects are kept in glass-topped insect drawers in insect-proof, fireproof cabinets. A low percentage of humidity is desirable; light is excluded as far as possible; and constant protection is given by fumigation.

Arachnids, myriapods, and insects in a liquid preservative are marked by inserting India ink or soft-penciled labels in the jar or vial. Labels marked with an alcohol-proof typewriter ribbon are also suitable. Specimens are stored in ethyl alcohol in vials or jars of various standard sizes. The jars or vials are kept in standard metal cabinets and are periodically inspected to make sure that the alcohol has not evaporated.

Herpetology

When a collection or individual specimen is received, it is accessioned. Duplicate copies of the accession record form are sent to the Central Files Department, which retains one and returns the other to the Department of Herpetology. The method of acquisition (e.g., gift, purchase, expedition, exchange), general nature of the material, and donor are noted on the accession record form.

Specimens are catalogued after accessioning. Minimum catalogue data include number, taxon, collector, date, and locality. Each specimen receives an alcohol-resistant fiber tag bearing the catalogue number; tags are tied with carpet thread to a hind leg or, in the case of limbless forms, around the anterior body. The alcohol-filled jars are arranged taxonomically in wooden trays that fit movable shelves in metal cases. Jars, trays, and cases have labels indicating their contents. Jar labels are typed and placed inside the jars. The storage area is air-conditioned, and the specimens are protected from heat and light.

Skeletal specimens are marked with fiber tags attached to the larger parts, and in many instances have the catalogue number written in India ink on one or more bones. They are stored in boxes with typed labels permanently affixed. Boxes are stored in trays inside metal cases.

Mammalogy

In the Department of Mammalogy specimens are given catalogue numbers and are entered, by number, in a catalogue book. Catalogue cards are also made (see figure K.2), and information is entered into a punch-card retrieval system.

Small mammal skins are marked with carbon-based ink on a label attached to the right hind foot of the specimen. Small skins are stored in trays and kept in slide-tight, lightproof, dustproof, and insect-proof cases. The storage areas must be relatively dry and be fumigated twice a year with paradichlorobenzene. Large mammal skins are marked with perforations made with a three-cornered awl in the middle of

CHIRODERMA VILLOSUM

BRAZIL: TERR. RONDONIA; COSTA MARQUES

209575	♂	10 OCT. 1964	S. ANDERSON	5776	SKELETON ONLY

Fig. K.2. Catalogue card (3 by 5 in.), Department of Mammalogy, American Museum of Natural History.

the lower back and are also labeled in the same fashion as small skins. The skins are stored in a dry area and are hung by the head.

Both small and large skulls are degreased and marked with carbon-based ink on the cranium and mandible. Small skulls are kept in glass vials or in pasteboard boxes in the same tray as their skins. Large skulls are kept in boxes or in trays and are stored in slide-tight cases. Large mammal skulls with antlers are hung from metal racks on the wall. Skeletons are kept in boxes or in trays, with the catalogue number written in carbon-based ink on the shaft of each bone. Stored materials should be protected from light, dust, and insects. A relative humidity of 55 percent is desirable, as is air conditioning.

Mammals preserved in spirits are marked by attaching a paper or parchment label, written in carbon-based ink or soft pencil, to the right hind foot of the specimen. A sized cloth label should not be used.

Ornithology

Material in the Department of Ornithology is recorded by number in a ledger kept in the department and reported on the accession record form.

Bird skins are tagged with a label cut from heavy, strong paper, on which the catalogue number is marked in waterproof ink. The label is tied to the feet of the specimen with good linen or nylon thread. The study skins are stored in special metal cabinets with plastic-bottomed trays. Cases with rubber strips exclude dust. In this climate, no special humidity and temperature arrangements are absolutely essential. Insect repellents are introduced into the cases as a precautionary measure.

A label may be tied to the feet on mounted specimens. If this is objectionable or if the bird is to be displayed, the label may be pasted to the bottom of the stand or perch. Mounted birds are stored in the same manner as bird skins.

Whole bird specimens, preserved in fluid, are also marked with a label, written in ink or crayon, placed in the jar or crock with the specimen. A second label may be pasted to the outside of the container. The problem in storing jars with Formalin or alcohol is to prevent breakage. Jars are stored in the same type of metal cabinet used for bird skins and skeletons.

For bird skeletons, the catalogue number is written in ink on the larger bones. A label is also pasted on the box in which the specimen is kept. Skeletons in boxes need little attention and may be stored in any convenient dust-free area.

Vertebrate Paleontology

The Department of Vertebrate Paleontology lists all information known about a specimen on the catalogue cards. (See figures K.3–4.) All recently collected specimens are catalogued in this manner.

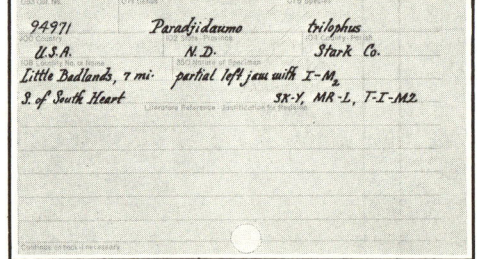

Figs. K.3–4. Catalogue cards, Department of Vertebrate Paleontology, American Museum of Natural History. The smaller cards (3 by 5 in.), provide an index to the collection. Catalogue numbers refer the user to the numerical file where larger cards (4 by 6 in.) contain more detailed information.

Specimens, including all parts of one individual, are assigned one catalogue number. Two cards of all-rag stock are filled out for each specimen. The cards are designed to record in a minimum of space the pertinent information about the specimen along with its geographic and geologic occurrence. The larger cards, 4 by 6 inches, are filed numerically. If the number of a specimen is known, the data concerning it can be found immediately in the numerical file. The smaller cards, 3 by 5 inches, constitute a systematics catalogue, which provides an index to the collection. The catalogue number of this card will allow the user to refer to the numerical catalogue card for more detailed information. If the department wishes to know whether a specific taxon is in the collection or how many specimens of a particular taxon are available, the information is quickly available in the systematics catalogue.

The catalogue card format and data entries follow the recommendations of the Society of Vertebrate Paleontology and conform with the curating and data-capturing procedures used by the Department of Paleobiology of the National Museum of Natural History, Smithsonian Institution. These permanent catalogue reference cards will someday serve as data capture sheets for electronic data processing. Eventually the information on the catalogue cards will be stored in a national data bank.

The catalogue number for each fossil vertebrate specimen is marked directly on the specimen with India ink. Vertebrate fossils are stored, depending upon their size, in vials or cardboard and plastic trays, which in turn are placed in wooden drawers and stored in metal storage cans. Large specimens are stored on shelves or on open racks.

REGISTRATION METHODS IN A MUSEUM OF SCIENCE AND INDUSTRY

STERLING H. RUSTON

The registration of exhibits in a museum of technology presents a variety of problems different from those encountered in recording material for an art, history, or natural history museum. Unlike an art object, historical artifact, or natural history specimen, the scientific apparatus, machinery, and operating models that constitute a museum of technology's collection do not qualify, by virtue of uniqueness, authorship, or intrinsic value, as "museum pieces." Their value is rather in their ability to demonstrate a technological process. Maintenance and rebuilding of a machine or a model may result, over the years, in an exhibit different in appearance and in component parts from the one originally received and recorded by the registrar. Furthermore, exhibits on a particular subject may contain hundreds of units or pieces that may or may not be used continuously; some may be discarded, some interchanged with other exhibits, and some stored for future exhibits.

So, while there are broad exhibit categories such as "physics" or "chemistry," any system of identification based on a coded classification would be useless in a museum of technology. The quarter-horsepower, split-phase induction motor used to activate a demonstration of some law of physics might burn out and be rebuilt, removed, or used to replace a similar motor in the chemical section. It must, therefore, have an identifiable and permanent status in the museum's records, one that is separate from the exhibit of which it is a part.

The system of registration used at the Museum of Science and Industry in Chicago deals with the special problems of a museum of technology. Like the registration system outlined in part 1 of this book, it makes use of a series of numbers. The simplicity of the system works well for a museum where constant change in physical condition, content, or purpose of a special exhibit or an item in an exhibit precludes the use of categorical identifications or catalogue classifications.

An exhibit may be received as a donation, loan, or purchase, or it may have been made in the museum shop; it is seldom received for examination only. It may consist of a single item, such as a motor, or hundreds of items, as in a large industrial exhibit like General Motors's "Story of the Automobile." Regardless of the nature of the exhibit and the number of items involved, exhibits received from any one source, at any one time, are issued a single receipt (see figure L.1), and a single entry is made in a control number book, which determines the number of the receipt. The receipt number is called the registration number. Numbers run consecutively from the time the first such receipts were made. Number 1, issued when the museum first began in 1929, was assigned to a telephone receiver, while the last one issued at this writing,

(Temporary Receipt)

Museum of Science and Industry
Founded by Julius Rosenwald
Chicago 37, Illinois

RECEIPT Nº 3998

DATE__________

RECEIVED FROM:

The objects described below,

For the President:__________
Registrar

DESCRIPTION

(Temporary Receipt)

Museum of Science and Industry
Founded by Julius Rosenwald
Chicago 37, Illinois

RECEIPT Nº 3998

DATE__________

RECEIVED FROM:

The objects described below,

For the President:__________
Registrar

DESCRIPTION	Accession No.	Value	

REGISTRAR'S COPY

R Form 1

Fig. L.1.
Receipt for exhibits received (8½ by 11 in.), Museum of Science and Industry. Each exhibit (and all constituent parts) received from a single source at the same time is covered by a single receipt and issued a single receipt (or registration) number. Three copies of this receipt are made. The copies that will be retained by the museum contain spaces for entering the accession number that will be assigned to each item in the exhibit, and the value.

number 3981, was assigned to a 1934 Rolls Royce.

Three copies of the receipt are prepared, one to be sent to the source of acquisition, one for the files, and one for the exhibits department. All correspondence and contracts pertaining to the exhibit, together with the copy of the receipt, and photographs and other papers, are placed in a folder marked with the registration number. These folders are filed chronologically (numerically) in the accessions files and are cross-indexed as necessary.

Because an exhibit in a museum of technology is not likely to remain intact permanently, especially as individual parts wear out and are replaced, each item in an exhibit must have an independent and permanent status. This is achieved by assigning each item an accession number prefixed by the last two digits of the year of acquisition, as in the system described in part 1 of the text. The telephone receiver acquired in 1929 was assigned accession number 29.1; the last number assigned as of this writing, 78.16, was issued to the sixteenth item acquired in 1978, a reproduction of a prehistoric coal forest that is part of a coal energy exhibit.

The accession number is entered on a Kardex visible record. (See figure L.2.) One Kardex record, containing an abstract of pertinent facts from the folders in the

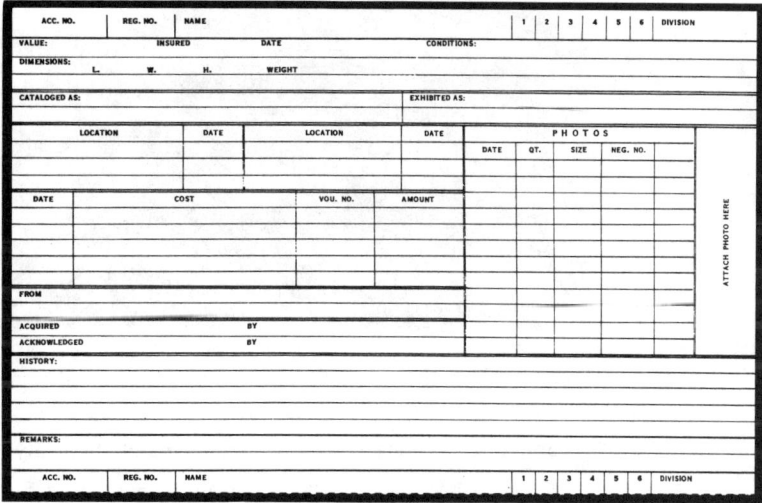

Fig. L.2.
Kardex record prepared for each item in an exhibit (5 by 8 in.), Museum of Science and Industry. Each item in an exhibit is given a permanent status in the museum's records by being assigned an accession number. The entry for the registration number serves as a cross-reference to the documentation on the exhibit of which the item is a part.

accession files, is made for each accession. The Kardex record provides space for the registration number in addition to the accession number, to provide a cross-reference to the accession files. In addition, the Kardex record shows complete name identification of the accession, value and insurance data, dimensions and weights, current location (on display or in storage), cost data, date acquired, source of acquisition (whether a donation, loan, purchase, or made in the museum shop), any qualifications on its status, and a brief history and related facts. The source of acquisition is further distinguished in the Kardex record by color of card: white cards are used for donations, salmon cards for loans, blue cards for purchases, and buff cards for products of the museum shop. Colored signal tabs are attached to the cards to indicate items that are on loan or have been returned to owners or otherwise disposed of. The cards are filed

Fig. L.3. *Color-coded record cards for each accession of the Museum of Science and Industry are filed in a Kardex visible index file cabinet.*

in a visible index cabinet and are updated as necessary. (See figure L.3.) Supporting the Kardex record are four card files:

SOURCE OF EXHIBIT MATERIAL, arranged alphabetically

SOURCE OF EXHIBIT MATERIAL, arranged according to the museum's technical divisions

NAME OF EXHIBIT OR EXHIBIT MATERIAL, arranged alphabetically

NAME OF EXHIBIT OR EXHIBIT MATERIAL, arranged according to the museum's technical divisions

These records are made on 3-by-5-inch cards that carry out the same color scheme used in the Kardex record.

An annual report is made to the museum's accounting department of all exhibits acquired during the year, classified as to whether they were obtained as donations, loans, or purchases, or were made in the museum shop. The report also lists exhibits returned or disposed of, and their sources and valuations.

Since the museum's opening, more than fifteen thousand separate acquisitions, ranging in size from a single radio tube to a full-size submarine, have been registered by this method.

COMPUTERS AND REGISTRATION: A DEFINITION OF TERMS

DAVID VANCE

When the second edition of *Museum Registration Methods* appeared in 1968, there was great excitement among registrars at the prospect of a machine able to store and look up data, sort records, and copy without effort or error. Planning and experiment were already under way. The Museum Computer Network had recently been formed. The great conference on "Computers and Their Potential Applications in Museums" was about to take place. However, there was no body of working experience and almost no literature.

Today's view is more sober but far more substantial. Real applications are so numerous and varied that they can no longer be counted. Some abandoned efforts already stand as warnings that no machine is magical. Three of the more successful and advanced applications, differing greatly in their goals, subject materials, and methods, are described in the following articles. This one will introduce basic computer terminology and concepts and will present a very selective bibliography of the most useful and readily available publications.

Hardware

The word "hardware" means tangible equipment. A computer installation consists of a cluster of interconnected machines. The main component is the computer itself, called the "central processing unit" or "CPU." Attached to it, either adjacent or remote, are input devices, storage units, and output devices. Input and output terminals may be at any place, however distant, served by telephone or other communication lines. Most installations are so designed that devices can be added or replaced as needed, and often the CPU itself can be enlarged by the attachment of additional internal storage capacity.

INPUT

An input device is any machine capable of bringing new information (data) or instructions (program) into the system. It usually does so by scanning tape, punched cards, or pages of machine-readable type, which pass through the machine physically. The most direct method, however, employs a typewriter communication terminal, with a more or less standard keyboard, on which messages are typed directly into the system. The typist sees what has been typed, either on paper in the typewriter or on a screen, and can correct or cancel an erroneous message immediately or at any time during the working session. This is the input technique used by the REGIS system, discussed in article O.

Input devices transform a coded pattern, such as that of holes punched in a card or magnetized dots on a magnetic surface, into a series of electrical impulses that flow into the computer. The computer, in turn, emits patterned electrical impulses that flow either to storage devices, where they leave traces of themselves on a magnetic surface, or to output devices, where they activate printing or other visual display.

STORAGE

There are important differences among storage units in cost and speed of access: the faster the access, the more costly. "High-speed storage," formerly called "core storage," has no moving parts and is therefore fastest of all, but it is also the most expensive. Data in high-speed storage is not permanently stored: it won't keep when the machine is turned off. This kind of storage is used inside the computer to hold the program being executed and the data being processed.

Programs and data that ordinarily reside in other storage units may be transferred temporarily to high-speed storage during any operation for which they are needed. A master program called the "operating system" is always in high-speed storage. One of its functions is to keep track of where all other data and programs are stored so they may be called in as needed.

"Drum storage" is another fast but expensive storage unit. However, it has relatively small capacity, and, if used at all, it is primarily for programs rather than data. Large masses of information and programs for occasional use are more often kept on disks or, less often, on data cells. A disk "pack" is a demountable unit, occupying a little more than a cubic foot. A typical present-day pack has a storage capacity of up to 200 million characters, and any one character is accessible in less than a hundredth of a second.

The above are "random access" storage devices. This means that any item of information in them can be found directly, without scanning from end to end. The computer opens them to the required "record" as a person opens a book to a page. "Sequential" storage devices, such as magnetic tape storage, are relatively less expensive than the random access devices, but the computer must search for information from the beginning, as a person reads a scroll. This latter type is excellent for "back-up" storage, to preserve information that might be lost if the primary disk copy were damaged.

OUTPUT

An output device is any machine designed to pass information from the system to its human users. This may be done by displaying characters or graphs on a screen or typing, printing, or drawing maps or diagrams on paper or on microfilm. The device best suited to production of catalogue listings is the "high-speed printer." A typewriter terminal may be used for output as well as input, but, at fifteen to thirty characters per second, it is relatively slow.

CPU

The central processing unit consists of a vast array of electronic switches through which impulses representing numbers and letters flow. The data these characters embody may move unaltered from input to storage or from storage to output, or they may be "processed"—i.e., rearranged—by opening and closing combinations of switches. These specific combinations, arranged to perform specific transformations, are "programs."

Software

Software is the intangible part of a computing system, the programs. Today, the word "software" is often reserved for programs supplied by the manufacturer, such as the operating system, while other programs are called "application programs."

Input to a machine is of two distinct kinds: data and programs. Both enter the system in the same ways and are transformed into the same kinds of electrical impulses. The difference is in how the system treats these impulses. The system knows by context whether it is receiving program or data. Program information is arranged in high-speed storage as a logical chain, each unit representing an instruction to be executed. Data for processing is stored where specified by the program and remains there until some program instruction causes it to be changed, moved, erased, or sent out. Data may be in plain English, in numerical form, or in any code, but programs must be in a rigorously formal program "language."

The program that is actually executed must be in absolute machine language, which differs from one make of machine to another. Because machine languages, which consist of nothing but thousands of numbers, are almost impossible for a person to read or write, higher-level languages, among them APL, FORTRAN, COBOL, ALGOL, and PL/1, have been invented. As written, these look like a mixture of English and algebra, but while their syntax is as rigorous as that of machine language, they can be learned by a person and used without great difficulty. The text of a program in a high-level language enters a computer system as data. There it is processed by a program called a "compiler," which is supplied by the manufacturer. The compiler destroys the high-level code and replaces it in high-speed storage with an equivalent machine language program. This program may then be executed, or it may be stored for future use.

Above the high-level languages and written in one (or several) of them are "data management systems." These are integrated sets of programs designed to perform record-keeping functions such as organizing catalogue files, making corrections, building indexes to the data, analyzing vocabulary, checking for exceptions such as missing data fields, retrieving required data, and printing such output as selective catalogue lists, file cards, copy for reproduction, graphs, tables, maps, and diagrams, all based upon stored data. Some of the data management systems used by American museums are GIPSY, GRIPHOS, MARK IV, SELGEM, and STIRS (a descendant of TAXIR). For a description of most of these systems, see *Museum Cataloging in the Computer Age* by Robert G. Chenhall.

Each data management system has rules of its own for entering, altering, indexing, retrieving, and formatting data. These rules constitute ultra-high-level languages and are the only languages that need concern a museum user. Normally a system has at least an input language, a correction language, a query language, and a format description language. These are easy to learn because they are merely formal rules for doing familiar work.

DATA

Data are simply facts or, speaking more strictly, the representation of facts. A data base is the sum total of all data available for use by a given program system. Within a data base all data are stored in a code and format that will fit into the programs designed to process that data base, and all words, numbers, and codes have consistent meaning. Data foreign to the data base either will not fit into the programs or, if they do, will produce nonsense.

A data base consists of one or more datasets. A dataset is an organized collection of data. It has certain permanent characteristics that are necessary for processing. Among these are a unique name by which the dataset is found when wanted, a consistent internal code (meaning, for example, that the letter "A" is always represented by the same sequence of bits), and uniform lengths for physical subdivisions, such as records, fields, etc. There are subtle distinctions between the terms "dataset" and "file," but they may be used interchangeably except in highly technical discussions.

Datasets within a data base may be of many kinds, but two are of special importance in museum work. One is a catalogue file, a dataset in which each record contains the unique identification (e.g., accession number) of something described plus all the recorded data about that something. The subject may be an accession, an object, a publication, a person, a site, a taxon, or anything whatever that a museum may wish to catalogue. The second type of file that is important in museums is an inverted index file, similar to a book index. The subject of each record is an index term (e.g., MATERIAL: ivory), while its content is a list of the serial numbers of all catalogue records containing that index term. A catalogue record names something and lists its attributes. Conversely, an inverted record names an attribute and lists all the things that share it. Both are examples of what we call "logical records."

A dataset is subdivided into "records," records into "fields," and fields into "words." These terms cause confusion because each is used in two or more different ways, and data processing personnel often overlook the distinctions. There are "physical" records, fields, and words, and there are also "logical" records, fields, and words. We, the users, have no concern whatever for the physical entities, yet we must know about them to avoid misunderstanding.

To locate specified information in the vastness of a dataset, the computer needs some guideposts. They are provided by marking out uniform areas before information is recorded. These large units may be called "records" or "blocks" or "regions." They relate to the dataset as pages relate to a book. These are physical spaces, uniform in size and numbered.

These units may be further subdivided into smaller physical units comparable to the lines on a page. These may be called "records" or "fields." Still smaller units are physical "words." All the physical units are merely *places* that may be found by number. They are independent of what may be written into them.

In the early history of computing, most data were numbers, and it was convenient to fit each number into exactly one record or field. This led to speaking as if the space were the same as its content. The same terms came to be used for both physical and logical units.

They are not the same. A logical record relates to a physical one as a paragraph relates to a page. One paragraph may occupy many pages, or a page may contain many paragraphs. The only connection is that a paragraph can be found by the number of the page on which it begins.

Figure P.4 in article P is an example of a logical catalogue record. Its content is divided into logical fields. Like the sentences in a paragraph, they are variable in length and number. A logical word, as in a book, is anything found between two blanks. A physical one is a fixed number of characters regardless of blanks.

The logical fields in systems used by museums are almost always divided into two main parts. One is called the "tag," which corresponds to the printed entry Artist, Object, Genus, etc., that may appear on a catalogue card and identifies the data category. Computer specialists call the tag an "attribute," but that word means something else to museums, so we use "tag." The other main part of the field is called "value" or "content" or "descriptor." It corresponds to what we write in the blank space following the tag, i.e., the name of the artist, the object, or the genus.

INPUT LANGUAGE

Information enters a data base as an "input stream." It is called a stream simply because one character follows another in single file. A system's input language is the set of rules for dividing this stream into segments corresponding to logical records, logical fields, tags, and values.

Dividing the stream into segments is usually accomplished by either "delimiters" or position. A delimiter is a character or a short sequence of characters inserted into the stream to mark the end of something. Punctuation marks are the delimiters of natural language. Of course, a given delimiter must be used in only one way. For example, the delimiter "0 = =" may be used in GRIPHOS to mark the end of a logical record. In positional notation, on the other hand, the input stream is read in units of some fixed length, usually eighty characters at a time (corresponding to the length of a standard computer card), and each distinct part begins in a certain position. For example, in the SELGEM input stream, a tag is always found in positions ten through twelve of an eighty-character unit.

Most if not all input languages impose some length limitations, but these are usually too high to be a nuisance. For example, a SELGEM tag is three numerals. A GRIPHOS tag is one to seven characters. A GRIPHOS value is one to five thousand characters.

The input stream may be ordered or unordered. In unordered input streams, any field can follow another. This is not the case for ordered input. Rules for ordered input may stipulate, for example, that every record consist of a set sequence of data categories. In this extreme case, tags are unnecessary since the first field is always the first data category, the second field the second category, and so on. Ordered input requires that all predetermined categories be included in each record and no unforeseen categories be used. The SELGEM input language operates less stringently; fields are entered in ascending numerical order by tag number, but every field need not be present in every record.

An input language may allow insertion of "escape" codes into the input stream that change the interpretation of something that follows. For example, in GRIPHOS, the escape code ¢, if followed by two numerals, places a diacritical mark over the following character: ¢02E is interpreted as é. If ¢ is not followed by two numerals, it remains a cent sign. Escape codes greatly extend our ability to record information, for they allow us literally to escape the limitations of the keyboard in use.

Interactive systems, such as REGIS, actively assist the user in building an input stream. Rather than passively reading the input stream, these systems send messages to the user's terminal, asking a programmed series of questions. The user's responses become the input stream. The user's answer to one question may determine what the next will be. REGIS is also an example of a "system interface," for one of the functions of REGIS is to pass information to the SELGEM data management system in that system's input language. A flow of information from REGIS to SELGEM is possible because one of REGIS's output formats is identical with the SELGEM input language. This matching of input and output languages constitutes the interface.

Conclusion

The preceding introduction should enable the reader to follow the discussion in the next three articles. It will also help in understanding the following comments on the thorny topic of costs.

Some museum computer applications have proved surprisingly inexpensive (see Sarasan et al. in the bibliography). Others have come to grief because of unforeseen expenses. No really satisfactory formula has been found for cost projection. The best attempt to date will be found in Humphrey and Clausen. (See bibliography.) The soundest single piece of advice is from Robert G. Chenhall: "Searching a large computer file costs more than searching a small computer file."[1]

To illustrate, let us assume that a museum decides, for the sake of appearance, that ten categories of information in its files should end with a period. This might add 100,000 characters to the length of a dataset. Each character is recognized in the computer by examining the on or off positions of a number of electronic switches, eight switches per character in most systems. An active file may be copied once a week and processed in part even more often. The cost of checking a single switch may be vanishingly small, but the 800,000 switches representing those periods are clearly going to cost money as the years go by. It also costs something to record them in the first place—a typing key stroke has an identifiable price.

Much museum information can be found well enough in manual files. If a period is expensive, consider the cost of maintaining a descriptive paragraph. The projects that have been most cost effective have generally been those that use the computer as an index to collections, have carefully selected those categories of information that serve to classify objects, and have eliminated comment. What those categories may be depends, of course, upon the nature of the collections and the reasons that led to their formation and justify their continued existence.

The cost of computing (not the human labor but the running of machines) has declined dramatically throughout the short history of electronic data processing. The cost of storing a character in magnetic form declined by a factor of about 300 between 1963 and 1976, with no end in sight. There is speculation that the introduction of superconductor technology in perhaps fifteen years will increase processing speed by up to 10,000 times (i.e., 1 million percent) over present speeds, already measured in billionths of a second. One might conclude, even without taking such speculation at face value, that computing will soon be virtually free. That would be the wrong conclusion. However fast machines become, the price of data processing must cover the cost of manufacture, electricity, the buildings in which machines are housed, the personnel who operate and program them, and a fair return on the $100 billion or so that has been invested in developing hardware and software. Processing costs will not vanish.

On the other hand, it is reasonable to conclude that the *proportion* of costs attributable to electronic processing will continue the historic decline relative to the proportion attributable to increasingly expensive human labor. It makes sense to surrender

1. Robert G. Chenhall, *Museum Cataloging in the Computer Age* (Nashville: AASLH, 1975), p. 12.

to the machines those repetitive, boring, and mechanical tasks to which they are better suited than we.

Bibliography

The following list is very selective. It is limited not only to particularly useful, current works but also to those that are readily available from the publisher or published in periodicals normally found in museum libraries. It is further limited to works in English. Most works listed contain citations for further reading. Those having extensive bibliographies are marked with the abbreviation "bibl." IBM publications must be ordered by the identification codes shown at the end of the entry.

Bergengren, Göran. "Automatic Data Processing in the Registration of Museum Collections in Sweden." *Museum*, 23:1 (1970–71), 53–58.

Brill, R. C. *The TAXIR Primer.* 2d ed. Ann Arbor: University of Michigan Computing Center, 1975. 151 pp.

Chenhall, Robert G. *Museum Cataloging in the Computer Age.* Nashville: AASLH, 1975. 261 pp.

———. *Nomenclature for Museum Cataloging: A System for Classifying Man-Made Objects.* Nashville: AASLH, 1978. 512 pp.

Humphrey, Philip S., and Ann C. Clausen. *Automated Cataloging for Museum Collections: A Model for Decision and a Guide to Implementation.* Lawrence, Kans.: ASC, 1977.

International Business Machines Corporation. *Computers in Anthropology and Archeology.* White Plains, N.Y.: IBM Corporation, 1971. 71 pp., bibl. Text by Robert G. Chenhall. GE-20-0384.

———. *Computers in the Museum.* White Plains, N.Y.: IBM Corporation, 1973. 69 pp., bibl. Text by David Vance (in part). GE-20-0406.

———. *Introduction to Computers in the Humanities.* White Plains, N.Y.: IBM Corporation, 1971. 76 pp., bibl. GE-20-0382.

Manning, Anita. *Data Retrieval without a Computer.* AASLH Technical Leaflet 85. From *History News*, 30:9 (Sept. 1975). 8 pp.

Metropolitan Museum of Art. *Computers and Their Potential Applications in Museums.* New York: Arno Press, for the Metropolitan Museum of Art, 1968. xx, 402 pp. A conference sponsored by the Metropolitan Museum of Art, April 15–17, 1968.

Museum Computer Network. *Manual for Museum Computer Network Data Preparation.* Stony Brook, N.Y.: MCN, 1975. Pt. I, text, 30 pp.; pt. 2, definition of data categories and index, ix, 76 pp.

———. *GRIPHOS Users' Guide.* Stony Brook, N.Y.: MCN, 1979. iv, 110 pp.

Museum Data Bank Committee. Museum Data Bank Research Reports. Rochester: MDBC. Each report separately bound.

1. Vance, David. *What Are Data?* 1974. 10 pp.
2. Scholtz, Sandra. *Data Structure and Computerized Museum Catalogs.* 1974. 8 pp.
3. Heller, Jack. *On Logical Data Organization, Card Catalogs, and the GRIPHOS Management Information System.* 1974. 21 pp.
4. Shetler, Stanwyn G. *The Flora North America Generalized System for Describing Morphology of Organisms.* 1975. 18 pp.
5. Chenhall, Robert G. *Museum Information Networks.* 1975. 19 pp.
6. Sutton, John F., and Craig C. Black. *Data in Systematics Collections.* 1975. 6 pp.
7. Scott, David. *The Yogi and the Registrar.* 1976. 13 pp.

8. Swinney, H. J. *Characteristics of History Museum Activity and Their Influence on Potential Electronic Cataloging.* 1976. 8 pp.
9. Mello, James F. *Computerization of Synonymy Data from Biological Collections.* 1977. 20 pp.
10. Chenhall, Robert G. *The Onomastic Octopus.* 1977. 15 pp.
11. Scholtz, Sandra. *A Management Information System Design for a General Museum.* 1976. 15 pp.

Neff, Jeffrey M., and Holly M. Chaffee. "REGIS—A Computerized Museum Registration System." *Curator*, 20:1 (1977), 32–41.

Neuner, A. M. *SELGEM Manual.* Lawrence, Kans.: ASC, 1976. vii, 104 pp.

———. *SELGEM Workbook.* Lawrence, Kans.: ASC, 1976. viii, 50 pp.

Sarasan, Lenore, Marilyn J. Miller, and members of the [Field Museum] Department of Anthropology. "Cannibals, Catalogs & Computers: The AIMS Computerization Project at the Field Museum." *Field Museum of Natural History Bulletin*, 48:8 (Sept. 1977), 10–13.

Vance, David. *GRIPHOS.* Stony Brook, N.Y.: State University of New York, Center for Contemporary Arts and Letters, 1977. v, 55 pp., 54 text figures, bibl.

———. "Museum Computer Network: Progress Report." *Museologist*, no. 135 (Dec. 1975), 3–10.

———. "Museum Data Banks." *Information Storage and Retrieval*, 5:4 (Feb. 1970), 203–11.

———, and Jack Heller. "Structure and Content of a Museum Data Bank." *Computers and the Humanities*, 6:2 (Nov. 1971), 67–84.

Van Devender, R. Wayne. "Michigan Studies Computer Costs." *ASC Newsletter*, 4:6 (Dec. 1976), 72–73.

COMPUTERS AND REGISTRATION: PRINCIPLES OF INFORMATION MANAGEMENT

CAROLE E. RUSH
ROBERT G. CHENHALL

The application of computer technology to museum registration and cataloguing requires a thorough examination of present and future museum activities, the demands made upon the museum's record system, the current state of the museum's records, and the goals the museum has for its proposed record system. The use of computer techniques will usually necessitate an improvement—in some cases, a major improvement—in the consistency of the museum's cataloguing methods. Such an examination of information and record-keeping needs is worthwhile, however, whether or not there are plans to implement a computerized system in the near future. The principles of information management outlined here will help in analyzing a museum's needs, and they are applicable to both manual and automated systems.

This article explores the impact of computer technology on record-keeping practices of museums and describes the analyses that are necessary prerequisites to a satisfactory use of computers. It is especially applicable to history museums, which have lagged behind other types of museums in the application of computer technology to meet their record-keeping and data-organizing needs. The progress has been more rapid in museum fields where the use of a computer has shown immediate advantages. For example, science museums have the advantage of a defined terminology (e.g., the Linnaean system of nomenclature) that facilitates consistent communication about specimens; art museums, whose objects are usually identified by artist and title, have been spurred on by the need to locate appropriate art objects in other museums for exhibit purposes; and archaeology museums have needed computers to facilitate management of information about large numbers of objects and sites. History museums, however, have not had as much specific need to communicate in a structured way with other history museums; and they have suffered from the lack of both a consistent terminology for man-made objects and a well-defined methodology for cataloguing information about the objects.[1]

Beyond communication among history museums, computer technology can have significant value within history museums, and, in fact, within all museums, whether general or specialized. This article concerns the integration of internal record-keeping systems and draws upon the experience of the Margaret Woodbury Strong Museum in Rochester, New York, which is developing a computerized record system. The

---

1. For elaboration on this idea, see H. J. Swinney, *Characteristics of History Museum Activity and Their Influence on Potential Electronic Cataloging*, Museum Data Bank Research Report 8 (Rochester: Museum Data Bank Committee, 1976).

Strong Museum is now in the formative stages. When it opens to the public in the early 1980s, it will be a museum depicting the social and cultural development of northeastern America during the postindustrial era, roughly 1820 to 1930.

The analyses required in designing an integrated record-keeping system and the steps required in implementing such a system are important in any evaluation of a museum's information management needs. The two basic stages are an *analysis phase*, which includes an examination of (1) the management philosophy essential to the creation of a museum-wide record system; (2) the activities within a museum that require written records and the various data files that are desirable to support these activities; (3) the process of identifying, defining, and controlling data categories that must appear in the museum's files; and (4) the design of interrelated files; and an *application phase*, which includes an examination of (1) the design of forms for recording data; (2) the creation and specification of rules to control the flow of information and the museum-wide management of the record system; (3) the selection of a computer system if one is to be used; and (4) the design of a versatile report system to facilitate the actual use of the data records.

The process of creating a record-keeping system requires systematically organizing and recording all observations that are pertinent for a thorough description of a group of people, places, things, events, or ideas—the entities that are the focus of any given description. Definitions of some of the terms used in this article will help in clarifying the concepts involved in such a process. A "data category" (which computer specialists sometimes call a "data element") is defined as a standardized frame within which is expressed an observation about or classification of an object (or other entity) according to an attribute that is distinct from every other attribute. The "content" of a data category is the actual descriptive information. A "record" is an organized collection of observations, recorded in data categories, presumably containing all pertinent information necessary to describe the entity. A "file" is a collection of related records. A "pointer" is a logical connector between separate records, which may be in the same or different files. An "integrated record-keeping system" is an information system with interrelated data files, either manual or computerized, in which each file contains records using (1) a well-defined and delimited set of data categories that are pertinent to that particular file, and (2) carefully controlled pointers to data in other files.

For example, the focus of an accessions file is information concerning the accession of new objects into the museum's collection. The file encompasses data on all accessions; each record describes one accession; and each data category covers one descriptive attribute of a single accession. A separate file might encompass all of the museum's collections data with each record as a description for one object in the collection. Depending upon the museum's decisions concerning what data to record in what file, a pointer from an object record to an accessions record and vice versa might be constructed either from the object registration number or from an accession number (if the museum assigns such a number as distinct from a specific registration number). Thus, the accessions file and object collections file would be part of an "integrated system."

Analysis Phase

MANAGEMENT COMMITMENT

A fundamental requirement for success in the creation of a controlled museum record system—either from the onset (as is the case of the Strong Museum) or as a revision of an existing record system—is a firm commitment on the part of the director and the trustees to take whatever steps are necessary to bring the project to successful completion. The analysis necessary to structure the museum records with the required precision demands a commitment of both time and resources. In addition, there must be a willingness to be innovative and, perhaps, nontraditional in terms of record-keeping techniques.

Time is an absolute requirement for the creation of an integrated record-keeping system. Time is needed not only for thorough planning and precision work but also for reflection and revision. The museum's overall objectives and needs must be thoroughly examined in order to define the records that must be created and the elements of information that must be entered into each record. Each segment of descriptive information in each file must be defined, and rules for recording that segment must be developed. The process also requires defining record system rules, testing the rules, revising the rules to meet more accurately the specified requirements, and testing again until each information file meets the specifications. This is a slow process because it usually calls for changes in old methods of record keeping and, more important, changes in old ways of thinking. It demands long-term support, and it demands patience and a willingness on the part of each person involved (the director, the curators, the registrar, the data system analyst, the data entry clerk, the users of the files) to make every effort to be precise and accurate in every aspect of the work. Thus, there must be continual cooperation, flexibility, and compromise.

The Strong Museum began in 1972 with a personal collection of more than 300,000 undocumented objects, largely in the decorative arts of the nineteenth century, which were left for museum purposes by the late Margaret Woodbury Strong. The need for systematic records has been evident from the beginning, and the director of the museum has had a firm commitment to use the most advanced technology to create an integrated, museum-wide record system. Funds were available to enable the museum management to consider seriously the use of a computer in the creation and control of records, and all personnel have come to the organization with a commitment to utilize modern computer methods for the creation of a well-organized record system.

ANALYSIS OF MUSEUM ACTIVITIES

The first step in designing an integrated record system is to analyze the activities of the museum and the needs that exist for various record files. While this article examines only activities that are related to collections management, other activities such as accounting, payroll, personnel, and security subsystems could and should be examined in the same way.

There are three principal categories of activities involving museum collections.[2] While subactivities within each of these categories will differ among museums, the three major categories seem generally applicable.

INITIAL ACTIVITIES: When an artifact or specimen is first acquired, a number of things happen. The object must be accessioned; various registration files must be completed; the object must be catalogued and, possibly, restored. In some museums a photograph is also made as a routine part of these initial activities.

2. Adapted from Robert G. Chenhall, *The Onomastic Octopus*, Museum Data Bank Research Report 10 (Rochester: Museum Data Bank Committee, 1977).

ONGOING ACTIVITIES: Once the first surge of activities has been completed, most museum objects remain in storage until they are needed for research or for exhibition, either at home or while on loan to some other museum, or until deterioration in the object's condition requires some conservation effort. Ongoing collections management activities also include inventory control and evaluation. These ongoing activities are the essential business of a museum. The purpose of all of the initial activities is simply to make the ongoing activities possible.

TERMINAL ACTIVITY: The terminal activity of deaccessioning must be included in order to make the cycle complete, and to allow for times when a museum decides to dispose of an object for one reason or another. However, the ongoing activities of the museum are the most important.

When each subsystem and the key activities that constitute it have been defined, the next step in the analysis of an information system is to develop a clear and precise statement of what is needed in order for those activities to be performed most efficiently. "What is needed" always boils down to having all of the information required for each defined activity available at the right time and place for the person who is to perform the activity, and accomplishing this as economically as possible.

SPECIFICATION OF REQUIRED FILES

After examining the activities of the museum, it is possible to define various data files that are required in order to meet the ongoing needs of the museum. These files can be any combination of manual and computerized files. Everyone involved in the analysis must understand how the various files relate to each other and how access to each file might be gained. Files that can be useful in a history museum might include:

ACCESSIONS FILE: legal acquisition information about newly acquired objects

OBJECT CATALOGUE FILE: descriptive data about objects in the museum's collections

SOURCE FILE: information about each donor, vendor, or lender of museum objects

LOANS/EXHIBITS FILE: records concerning specific objects on loan or on exhibit

COLLECTION PHOTOGRAPH FILE: a photographic record of each object, together with basic data concerning the photograph

INVENTORY FILE: financial and location data on each object

CONSERVATION FILE: conservation data on each object

RESEARCH FILE: research records and/or historical photographs organized by theme

LIBRARY FILE: a library catalogue organized by subject

DISPOSITION FILE: data about the deaccessioning of objects

These are only suggestions of the types of files that might be applicable. A museum might have an entirely different configuration of files, or within this sample list, several files might be combined into one, or larger files separated into smaller segments.

Figure N.1 shows an initial diagram of a record system. Later, as museum needs are more closely defined, and as data elements necessary for each file are specified, the connections among the files will be indicated. Once the interrelationships among the files are specified, it is possible to visualize how various files might be used together or even combined.

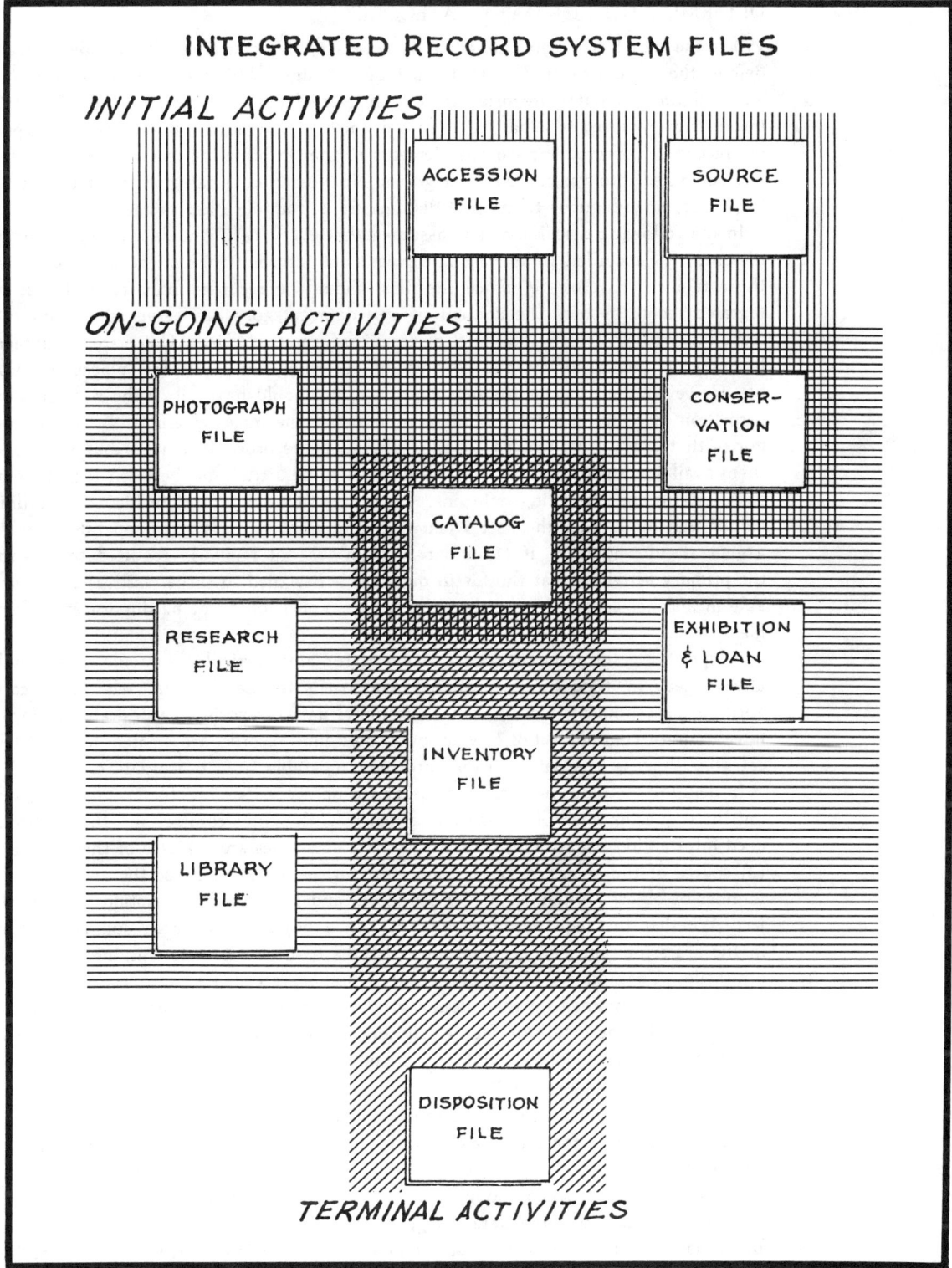

Fig. N.1.
Preliminary diagram for an integrated record system before the interconnections among files have been determined.

DETERMINATION OF DATA CATEGORIES

When the files have been defined, it is necessary to determine (i.e., to identify and define) the categories of data that must be contained within each file. *Identification* and *definition* of data categories are closely related but separate processes. First, the information required in a particular record must be determined, based on the purpose the record is to serve. The various elements of that information can then be identified and separated into various data categories. Next, each data category must be defined in precise, unambiguous terms that distinguish it from all other categories.

In the following discussion it is assumed that every pertinent data category for all files must be recorded in at least one place; but informational categories, other than those required to cross-reference the files, should be recorded only once. In an integrated record system, the content of any data category can serve as a pointer to some other file in which additional pertinent information exists. There are advantages in terms of time, accuracy, and economy in recording data in as few places as possible. However, the users of the museum's records should have all of the necessary information at hand to meet the ongoing needs of the museum efficiently. Data categories that are always needed together should be recorded in a way that will make them available together. Often there will have to be a trade off between the economy of recording and correcting data only once in the most appropriate file and the difficulties that might face the user when trying to combine data from separate files. As a general rule, however, if (1) a data category is not regularly required to perform the primary activities that the file in question is designed to serve, and (2) it is available in another accessible file, then the information should not be duplicated in both files.

In specifying the data categories required for any particular data file, one should always keep in mind these questions: who needs to use this file? what data categories are essential in this file? what additional data categories are desirable to facilitate accurate communication? what other museum records are related to this data category? how is this data category uniquely separable from other data categories?

In defining the data categories necessary for an accessions file, for example, answering these questions is not difficult. The registrar, the chief curator, and the controller need information from the file. Necessary data categories are (1) date of the accession, (2) source of the accession (e.g., donor, vendor, etc.), (3) value of the accession, (4) number of objects contained in the accession, and (5) a brief description of each object. Whether the registration number for each object in the accession is recorded in the accessions file will be determined by the ease of access to this information in other files. The address of the source need not be recorded in the accessions file if records are maintained on each donor/vendor in a separate file that is readily available. Similarly, the extent of the description of the accession is dictated by the availability of access to the object catalogue and other records.

The most complex file pertaining to collections is the object catalogue file. All classes of objects in the museum must be considered in determining the data categories that should be available for the cataloguing of man-made objects. To catalogue different subcollections of objects accurately, different subsets of the available data categories (i.e., combinations of some, though not necessarily all, of the data categories) are often required. For example, the data category TITLE is necessary for the curator of art but usually meaningless to the curator of dolls. At the later stage of data recording, cataloguers should be encouraged to use only those data categories that are necessary to describe the particular subcollection of objects in hand. But the person initially creating the system must ask: what data are required to meet each of the ongoing activities of the museum for all types of objects? are the required data available? how can each data category be separated from all other categories? and, perhaps, how might the interpretation of each data category vary from one subcollection to another?

The type of object collections and the needs of the museum are the important factors in determining the data categories to be used for the object catalogue. For example, a hypothetical museum, after examining its needs for its object catalogue file, might determine that the following information is necessary:

1. for object identification: REGISTRATION NUMBER, CLASSIFICATION, and OBJECT NAME;

2. for recording an object's physical description: STYLE, MATERIAL/TECHNIQUE, INSCRIPTION, GENERAL DESCRIPTION, DIMENSIONS, and CONDITION;

3. for recording the history of the object: MANUFACTURER, ARTIST, EARLIEST DATE, LATEST DATE, PERIOD, EXHIBITION HISTORY, PROVENANCE, IDENTIFICATION SOURCE, ASSOCIATIONS, and COUNTRY OF ORIGIN;

4. for identifying objects for exhibits or loan: THEME REPRESENTED and SUBJECT REPRESENTED;

5. for object inventory control: ACCESSION IDENTIFICATION, VALUE, LOCATION, and GENERAL STATUS.

Once the necessary data categories have been identified, the analyst can make final determination of the definitions of each category. Precision of definition is extremely important; both the people who record the data and those who use the data must understand exactly what attributes of information are included within a given data category. For example, does SUBJECT REPRESENTED encompass every element pictured in a painting, or does it include only an actual person or place? Any variations in interpretation of a data category from one subcollection to another should also be considered. Data categories should represent completely distinct data attributes so that both the name assigned to a particular data category and the content of that data category will communicate information: i.e., the name of the category should alert the user to what attribute of information is being described, and the content is the specific information recorded.

CONTROL OF DATA CATEGORIES

Two processes closely related to defining the meaning of each data category are (1) establishing the format for the data content, and (2) delimiting the actual content words. "Format," as used here, means the structure and rules used for data recording: the order of words, the number of characters that are required or will be allowed, the division of segments, the use of upper- or lower-case letters, the use of singular or plural, the meaning of special characters, etc. For example, one possible format for a date is the specific structure to be used for recording a date—such as year-month-day, with a four-digit year, a two-digit month, a two-digit day, and a slash to separate each segment (e.g., 1892/03/30).

Delimiting the content that can be recorded within each data category is governed by the question: is this data category to be used as a descriptor term for indexing (or sorting), or will free-text be acceptable? Free-text data categories are used to complete the description of an object but are not used for indexing. The content of free-text categories does not need to be controlled except in a general way. On the other hand, for descriptor data categories to be used for indexing, the process is more complex.

With descriptor categories, it is often necessary to work from an "authority file," which is a controlled list of acceptable words. The authority file must always be used when recording data in that particular data category. Also, if the final file is to be created on a computer, the order of multiword phrases is quite important. The computer does not have any intelligent means of sorting words and cannot make all the decisions that people make when searching a manual file. For example, a computer would index "Mechanical toy" and "MECHANICAL TOY" and "Toy, Mechanical" in completely separate locations, whereas a person would probably decide that records for all three items could be filed in the same place.

For some data categories, the authority file may be quite easy to develop. The number of style names that apply to furniture, for example, is relatively limited and identifiable. Similarly, a controlled list of terms to use for material/technique can be developed by curators of works of art.

For many data categories, however, the development of an authority file is more difficult. The lack of an authority file for the classification and naming of man-made artifacts has been a serious problem for history museums. In the English language there are often many different words that are considered acceptable names for the same object. The names given to objects in a museum catalogue are usually what the person doing the cataloguing considers most appropriate at a given time. This leads to inconsistencies in the words used for naming objects, even within one file in a single museum. For example, one cataloguer might use "sofa," another "couch," another "davenport," and a fourth "settee" to name the same object. The data retrieval becomes complicated and uncertain, no matter whether the file is managed manually or in a computer. Consistency in the use of our inherently inconsistent language is an extremely difficult problem.

From the outset, the management of the Strong Museum recognized the need for an authority file for the classification and naming of objects in the museum collections. With support from the National Endowment for the Arts and with the generous help of experts in other specialized history museums, an authority file or lexicon has been developed at the Strong Museum and has been published by the American Association for State and Local History.[3] The book includes a rationale for the categorization and classification of man-made objects and also a lexicon of object names.

The process of accurately defining each data category for a given file is a vitally important step in the design of the record system for a museum, regardless of whether the file under consideration is to be a manual or a computer file. The determination and then the defining of the data categories always lead to more accurate communication within the museum. Users of the files are better able to understand the record content and to rely upon consistent data.

DESIGN OF FILE RELATIONS

The analysis of the entire system should lead to answers to such questions as: what data files are needed? how should the files be separated? which files are used together

---

3. The new publication *Nomenclature for Museum Cataloging: A System for Classifying Man-Made Objects* by Robert G. Chenhall (Mar. 1978) is available from the American Association for State and Local History, 1400 Eighth Ave., So., Nashville, Tenn. 37203.

frequently so that they could be integrated? which files must be interrelated, and what data categories could be used to relate them? In an integrated record system there must be some pointer from the records in one file to the records in another file. This is true for any combination of manual and computerized files. Quite often the pointer will be derived from the content of a specific data category. For example, one common data category in the object catalogue file is the REGISTRATION NUMBER. From any record where it exists, this number can be used as an entry point into any other file that is indexed by the same number: e.g., from the photographic file, arranged by subject, into a master catalogue file indexed by registration number. Similarly, the content of the data category THEME might be an appropriate entry into a library or a research file sorted by subject. (See figure N.2 for an example of one possible integrated system design.)

DOCUMENTATION

The final part of the analysis phase is to document the decisions that have been made and the information that has been gathered thus far. The documentation should include a description of the museum activities under consideration, the people involved in each activity, and the data requirements to support those activities; the files that are needed to meet the museum's needs; the data categories needed for each file along with their definitions and formats; the authority files to be used for various data categories; the relationships among various files; and specifications for data pointers to connect the files. The documentation that relates to specific data categories within a file should be combined into a documentation manual for that file. This manual will be expanded to include application procedures determined during the next phase of the system development. Documentation should be in written rather than verbal form and should communicate as accurately and precisely as possible.

SYSTEM RE-EVALUATION

One word of warning at this point: it would be ideal to be able, all at one time, to examine all museum record-keeping needs, specify necessary files, determine what data are needed, define the data categories precisely, specify authority files for the control of data categories, document the system completely, and, furthermore, make no mistakes in the process. This, however, rarely happens. The steps in the process always overlap, and it is impossible to suspend all museum operations until the analysis is complete and the rules immutable. There will necessarily be some back stepping and revamping of the system. Users of the records, whether the museum management, the curators, or the public, will provide valuable input concerning how well the system actually meets their needs. Often it will be necessary to redesign various aspects of the system. Though frustrating, this re-evaluation process is a desirable and necessary part of the development of a workable information system in a museum. We learn more quickly from our mistakes than we do from instant success.

During a re-evaluation process at the Strong Museum, for instance, we have gradually developed an authority file for a data category we call THEME. THEME began as a data category called SUBJECT, which rapidly became a catchall for every possible generic subject, as well as for proper noun subjects depicted on an object. For example, "nature," "bumblebee," and "George Washington" could have been listed as subjects of a portrait of Washington having a nature scene as background. It soon be-

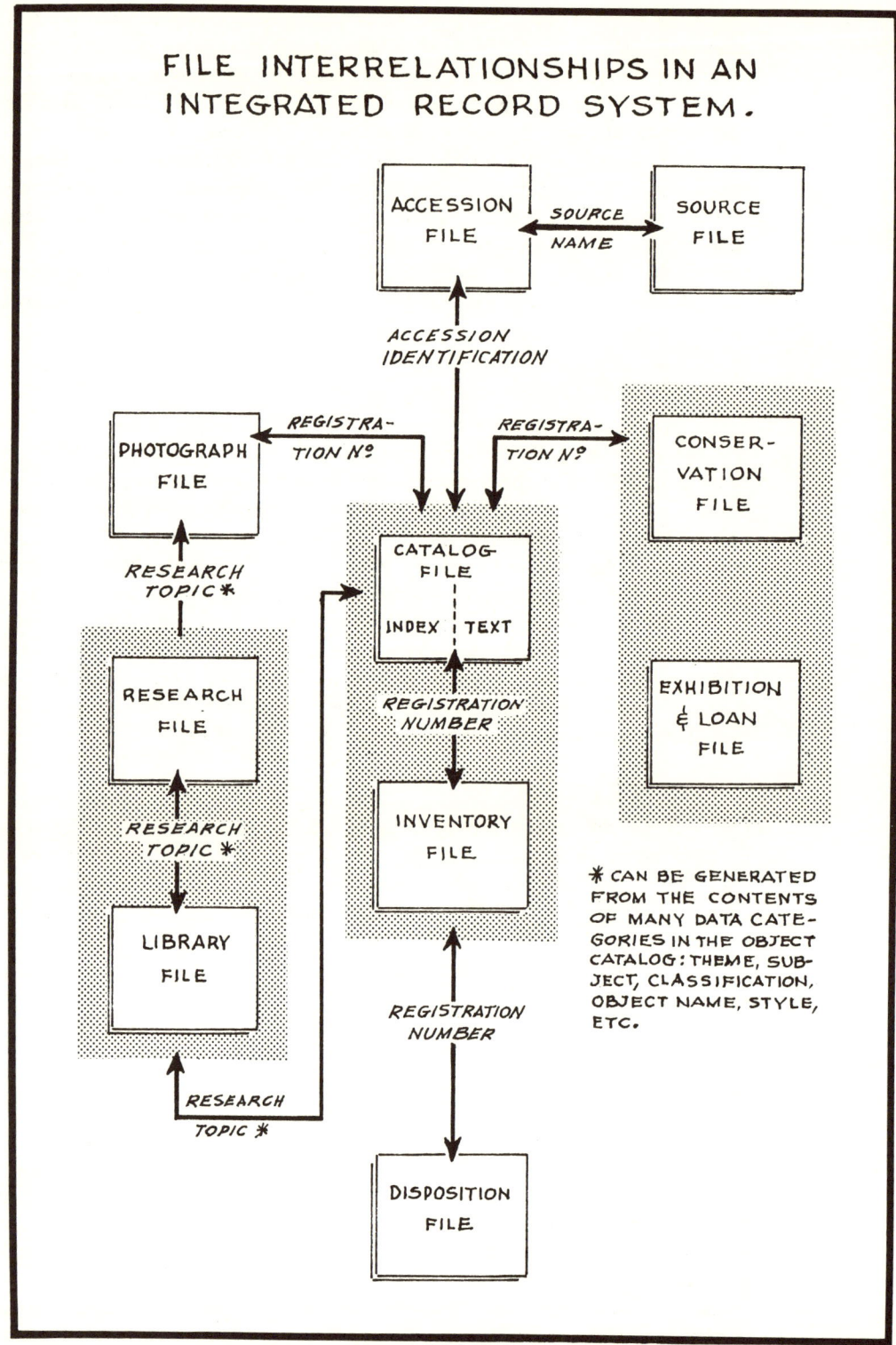

Fig. N.2.
Diagram showing one possible integrated record system.

Fig. N.3. General recording rules, Margaret Woodbury Strong Museum.

```
              The MWSM Cataloging Commandments

    1.  General rules:

          • Be brief

          • Be consistent (i.e., use terms consistently)

          • On every catalog sheet enter
              - a classification term
              - an object name
              - an accession number (a registration number)
              - a Parke-Bernet number (exception:  new acquisitions)*
              - an acquisition code (see MWSM 2.21)*
              - the date cataloged
              - your last name and initials (as cataloger)

          • Other data categories are optional; use them only if needed

          • With sets of related items, prepare one catalog sheet for the set;
            if space permits, record individual items on the reverse side

          • Except for sets, prepare one catalog sheet for every artifact
            (Suggestion:  for duplicate artifacts, make a Xerox copy before
            recording accession number and condition)

    2.  With descriptor categories (used for searching):

          • Enter only the exact words you would probably use to search for
            that record; avoid words which merely describe the object

          • Separate multiple entries within one data category with a triple
            slash ("///"); do not use any other symbol for this purpose

          • Avoid connective words or symbols (e.g., "and") and articles ("a,"
            "an," "the")

          • Avoid entering the same phrase in more than one data category

    3.  With free-text categories:

          • Do not repeat information recorded in a descriptor category

          • Record information in short phrases, not complete sentences (We do
            not give extra credit for literary style)

                      TO REPEAT - BE BRIEF AND CONSISTENT

    * (of internal significance only to the Strong Museum)
```

---

came apparent that SUBJECT was inadequately defined, could not be controlled, and had little utility as it was being used in our catalogue record. Consequently, this data category was divided into two separate data categories: SUBJECT and THEME. During the redesign, the curatorial staff discussed what was really needed from these two data categories. In the process of developing an authority file for THEME, we had to expand our ideas so that we could view the needs of the museum as a whole rather than merely considering a group of separate and unrelated collections. We also had to confront questions such as: how detailed should the catalogue records be? how can we unify diverse subcollections in a way valuable to the entire museum? The list of themes still occasionally requires revision, but it has become a very useful authority file for the Strong Museum. The redefinition process illustrated to all of us the need for cooperation and compromise in order to achieve an acceptable and useful solution to a problem.

Application Phase

Once the analysis phase necessary to create an information system has been completed, the ideas and plans can be converted into concrete results. Again, some important questions must be answered: how will the actual information needed for museum operations be gathered? who will gather what information? how will the in-

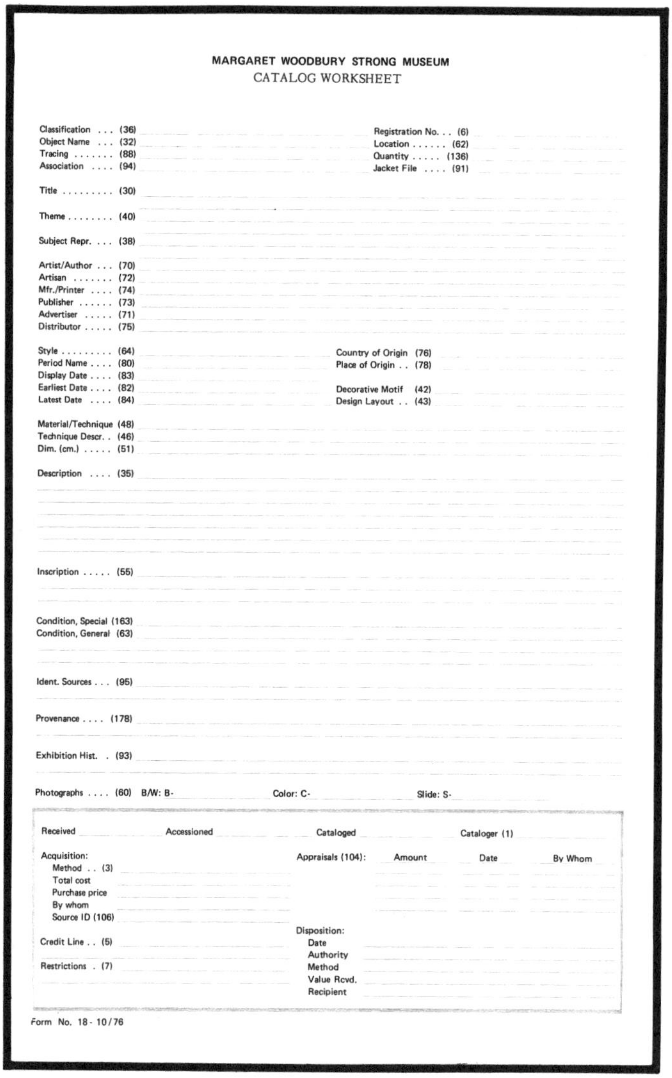

MARGARET WOODBURY STRONG MUSEUM
CATALOG WORKSHEET

Classification . . . (36)
Object Name . . . (32)
Tracing . . . . (88)
Association . . . . (94)

Registration No. . . (6)
Location . . . . . . (62)
Quantity . . . . . (136)
Jacket File . . . . (91)

Title . . . . (30)

Theme . . . . (40)

Subject Repr. . . . (38)

Artist/Author . . . (70)
Artisan . . . . (72)
Mfr./Printer . . . . (74)
Publisher . . . . . . (73)
Advertiser . . . . . (71)
Distributor . . . . . (75)

Style . . . . (64)
Period Name . . . . (80)
Display Date . . . . (83)
Earliest Date . . . . (82)
Latest Date . . . . (84)

Country of Origin (76)
Place of Origin . . (78)

Decorative Motif (42)
Design Layout . . (43)

Material/Technique (48)
Technique Descr. . (46)
Dim. (cm.) . . . . . (51)

Description . . . . (35)

Inscription . . . . . (55)

Condition, Special (163)
Condition, General (63)

Ident. Sources . . . (95)

Provenance . . . . (178)

Exhibition Hist. . (93)

Photographs . . . . (60) B/W: B- Color: C- Slide: S-

Received Accessioned Cataloged Cataloger (1)

Acquisition:
Method . . (3)
Total cost
Purchase price
By whom
Source ID (106)

Appraisals (104): Amount Date By Whom

Credit Line . . (5)

Restrictions . (7)

Disposition:
Date
Authority
Method
Value Rcvd.
Recipient

Form No. 18 - 10/76

Fig. N.4. Catalogue work sheet (8½ by 14 in.), Margaret Woodbury Strong Museum. There are additional lines on the reverse of the sheet for continuation of information that does not fit into space provided for the data category on the front.

formation be recorded? how many steps are there in the recording process? what tools can be designed to aid in the process? and will the final form of each file be manual or computerized?

DESIGN OF INPUT FORMS

When the data categories necessary for an object description have been determined, they must be organized on an input form or record. The design of the form will be affected by the answers to such questions as: what special recording rules must be followed? how will data be transferred to the final catalogue record? what data categories relate closely to each other? should the form cover data categories for only one file or for several? how can the data be corrected at some later time? what will be the ultimate disposition of the initial input form?

Whether the file will finally be manual or computerized will influence some of the design decisions. For example, the decision to create a computer file usually leads to a recording rule of brevity and the avoidance of repeating information in more than one data category. At the Strong Museum we discovered this to be one of the most difficult recording rules to follow. Curators sometimes feel the request for brevity takes away their poetic license. Figure N.3 shows some general recording rules for the Strong Museum. Figure N.4 shows a catalogue work sheet that groups the most common descriptor data categories together and in close proximity to the free-text DESCRIPTION category. This organization of the work sheets helps eliminate concerns the curators had about not repeating information. These may be good procedures to follow even if input forms will not be computerized. Once adjusted to the system, all curators at the Strong Museum have seen the benefit of being able to rely upon specified authority files for particular data categories. An enthusiastic attitude can lead to a helpful interchange of ideas among all people involved in the design process.

INFORMATION FLOW

By specifying the paths along which information forms will travel, the systems analyst attempts to control the various stages in the cataloguing process. At the Strong Museum, the curators record the information on the catalogue work sheet, which then goes to a data entry clerk for creation of a computer record. After it is recorded, the catalogue work sheet is returned to the curator who proofreads the typed computer record. The initial catalogue work sheet is ultimately bound and stored by the registrar, but during the interim stages of data entry, the curators prefer to keep the catalogue work sheets until they are replaced by completely acceptable computer output. If the initial catalogue work sheets are to be the final hard-copy records, penmanship must be good and rules for recording corrections have to be stringently enforced. Furthermore, it is important to record or log the transfer of catalogue work sheets from one person to another. Very clear rules for the flow of information should be specified and adhered to if a recording system is to proceed smoothly.

Up to this point in the system analysis the actual form of the final file—manual or computerized—has been of relatively minor importance. Possibly only descriptor categories will be entered into a computer file that will serve as a master index. In this case all free-text data categories could be stored in another file that is indexed by registration number; or a computer index could provide entry to a master file of all catalogue information stored on microfiche and indexed by registration number. Regardless of the actual storage media used, the analysis of the data needs and relationships will remain valid if it has been adequately carried out. Therefore, changing the form of the files at some future date from computer to manual or vice versa will not require reanalysis of the needs or rerecording of the data.

The analysis and application phases for manual files should result in the creation of a final catalogue file that can be duplicated, sorted, and stored in as many ways as required for usable indexes. The remainder of this article will deal primarily with the integrated record system that has at least some computerized files. The important aspects of the remaining phases of analysis are the selection of a computer system, the design of files for daily operational use, and the design of a report system.

SELECTION OF A COMPUTER SYSTEM

In selecting a computer system to implement the computerized segments of the record-keeping system that has been designed, it is important to keep in mind how the museum wants to use the computer file. Other important considerations are (1) what connections between computer files and what pointers to manual files will be needed, and (2) whether the computer system allows for later expansion of files and connections of files that have not been originally designed together. The museum should investigate nearby computing facilities, such as a local university as well as local consulting groups, and should also examine available data management computer systems and advanced software packages. Using well-designed prepackaged systems will almost always be less expensive than creating a new system. Whether consulting support will be available on a given system is another point to be considered. The degree of consulting support needed will depend upon whether there is someone on the museum staff who will be in charge of the actual computer work or whether it will all be done outside the museum.

In-house mini-computers are becoming viable alternatives to use of a large computing facility. Rapidly growing technology promises increased software facilities and larger data storage capacity at less cost in the near future. For example, a manufacturer recently introduced a desk-top computer that sells for $6,200 and has random access storage of 180,000 data characters. There must, of course, be a trade off between the more advanced capabilities of large data management systems at relatively high cost and the less sophisticated in-house facilities at a fixed cost. In actual current practice, a mini-computer system is usually integrated with a larger, more powerful computing facility, but the potential of the mini-computer should not be overlooked.

The most important considerations in selecting a computer system are: the complexity of the museum's needs, the alternative systems available, the funds allocated to create the computerized file, and the personnel available to monitor the work. A system can usually be found that can be specifically tailored to meet the museum's requirements.[4]

The computer system that is selected must be capable of meeting the daily needs of the museum. Whether the convenience of using an on-line computer index (one available for use at a computer terminal at any time) justifies its cost must be evaluated carefully after considering the types of daily demands that will be made on the system. Often the generation of a usable set of reports concerning the collection and various subcollections will be of much greater benefit than an on-line catalogue. If it is possible to receive computer output quickly, batch use of a computer system (using a computer without user interaction during the processing of data) is always more economical and is usually satisfactory for most needs. The system designer should weigh these factors and answers to such questions as: how often do we need the answer to a question right now rather than in several hours? are there any standard manual indexes that we could use easily in our daily jobs or is a computer query necessary? what parts of the catalogue record are really necessary in every instance?

The psychology of the user is a factor that must not be overlooked in making the

---

4. The Strong Museum has available the computing facilities at the University of Rochester Computing Center. Data entry is made into computer files by means of a remote terminal connected through an acoustic coupler and using a text editor program called WYLBUR. The data management system called INQUIRE (a proprietary software package of Infodata Systems, Inc.) has been selected for the creation of the master catalogue file. INQUIRE can be used in a batch or an on-line mode, and consulting support for INQUIRE is available at the Computing Center of the University of Rochester and through the Infodata office in Washington, D.C.

decisions about a computer system. A computer is a powerful tool that people can use to make their daily work more productive, and sometimes even more interesting. It should not be viewed as a tool that controls the people. Therefore, removing barriers between the museum user and the computer is an important process. One way this can be accomplished is to combine on-line terminal usage of a system with well-designed and meaningful reports and manual indexes. The users of a record system must be satisfied or even enthusiastic about the results in order to be cooperative. Unless that cooperation is achieved, the computer system will be of no long-term benefit.

REPORT SYSTEM DESIGN

Determining what information the computer will sort out, how, and in what form is the final step in the system design process. The analyst must be willing to consider the different needs of the separate subcollections in determining the report system. For example, for the doll curator at the Strong Museum, a report sorted by OBJECT NAME (i.e., merely "Doll") would be virtually meaningless, but a report sorted by MANUFACTURER is essential, as is one sorted by doll STYLE NAME. On the other hand, the curator of the Oriental collection needs a report sorted by OBJECT NAME. In addition, each curator of a special subcollection will probably need complete catalogue information about objects in that subcollection arranged by registration number or in whatever way provides the best access to the information.

Every museum should have a readily available master file of all museum objects arranged by registration number. Even in a computerized system there should be at least one "hard-copy" (paper or microfiche) master file. A hard-copy file is always available, whereas a computer sometimes is not, and people still like and often need to use hard-copy files. With the advances in microphotography, microfiche files will be even more useful and economical in the future for the creation of such a master.

Summary

The experiences of the Strong Museum illustrate some of the problems and potentials of a computer project. The evolving nature of the project has been difficult, for we have developed some of the authority files and rules as cataloguing has proceeded, rather than being able to begin with a completely designed and rule-bound system. It has taken time. Furthermore, the diversity of subcollections at the Strong Museum requires special rules or authority files for each subcollection and also special reports for each.

At first, the curators felt that they were duty bound to fill in every blank space on the catalogue work sheet. They also disliked the need for brevity and worried about the need for consistency. These initial concerns have been alleviated as they have gradually realized that only pertinent information is required. Patterns for each subcollection have emerged, and rules are being defined and recorded. Cataloguing has actually become easier. Curators also feared that they might lose control over their subcollections in a centralized and less-individualized system. Actually, a computer system should provide curators with additional tools for the management of their special subcollections. Such fears could have been allayed if the report phase of the computer system had been completed very early in the project. Now that reports are beginning to come back, however, those who once were apprehensive about computerization are thinking of ways a computer system can simplify their tasks by eliminating some of the tedium and freeing time for research.

The more familiar we become with computers, the more new ways we think of for using the computer system. In addition to creating a master index for the object catalogue on a computer, we are planning to develop subject and theme links to a computerized library file and also to our historical research files, which may eventually be computerized. The museum's registrar has obvious needs for the computer files in order to control our large number of loans, and we hope that carefully designed links between the object catalogue, the accessions file, and the source file will eliminate the redundant recording of information. The controller needs inventory information for audit records, for insurance purposes, for security, and for possible object disposition. The exhibits department hopes to use the computer files for control and development of exhibits and also for generating thousands of labels as well as reports to be used in the open study collections of the museum. The curators need standard reports for their daily work and for their special research projects. While it is not likely that a curator will need daily access to the entire object catalogue, this would be possible if microfiche records were used for the object catalogue, the library catalogue, and possibly for special research files. The clerical advantage of maintaining only one master catalogue file, which can be corrected simply and in one location, can be indexed on a number of data categories, and can be used for a variety of purposes, is obvious.

A museum's decision to develop a computerized object catalogue should lead to the design of an integrated and consistent record-keeping system with defined procedural rules for achieving the museum's overall objective. The steps discussed here are necessary if the project is to be successful, and its success can in turn result in accurate and meaningful communication of historical information internally and to the museum public.

COMPUTERS AND REGISTRATION: A CASE STUDY

HOLLY M. CHAFFEE
JEFFREY M. NEFF

REGIS (the Arizona State Museum's Interactive REGIStration System) is an example of the application of computer technology to the registration tasks of accessioning, receipt preparation, loan processing, and report generation. The REGIS system was developed specifically for the Arizona State Museum at the University of Arizona, and to our knowledge it is the first use of computer technology in registration work other than cataloguing. While the system would have to be revised to be used by another museum, it is likely that the underlying principles of its development would be applicable to any museum operation. It requires, however, access to a powerful computing facility. The Arizona State Museum utilizes the facility of the University of Arizona.

The Arizona State Museum is primarily an anthropological museum with an emphasis on the Greater Southwest. It houses more than 300,000 catalogued specimens, which include archaeological, ethnological, historical, osteological, photographic, library, and archival materials. The museum was founded in 1893. Formal cataloguing began in 1917, and catalogue files were first integrated with accession files in 1938. Other aspects of registration were largely ignored until 1950, when loan forms were introduced. In 1960 a multipurpose registration form came into use for all formal transactions, incoming or outgoing, temporary or permanent, and each transaction was called a "registration." Thus, the "registration numbers" mentioned hereafter are transaction numbers and should not be confused with accession, loan, or catalogue numbers.

Until recently the museum has struggled with documentary deficiencies that are all too typical of museums in general. In the past decade, however, this museum has been a pioneer in the use of computers for collection management, and in 1975 REGIS began operating.

Planning for REGIS

It is important to note that the logic used in designing this registration system is not unique to a computer system. It is equally applicable to a manual system, for information content is the principal concern, not the method of data entry or manipulation.

The major advantage of a computer system is its information retrieval capabilities. In a computer system, if a change in information is called for, the correction or addition need be made only in the master file in order to show up in all subsequent indexes and reports. This greatly reduces the chance of error in changing multiple records. Furthermore, while a registrar using a manual system can identify and record all the required categories of registration information, it is not feasible to index manually under more than a few headings. Producing a large number of cross-index cards manually would be difficult enough; making individual additions or corrections to them would be endless.

The Arizona State Museum had used computers to produce cross-indexes of the museum's ethnological collections since 1968. When it became apparent that the old registration system was inadequate and a new system needed, it was natural to want to take advantage of the recording and indexing capabilities of the University of Arizona Computer Center's CDC Cyber 175 and DECsystem–10 computers. Planning focused on how the information was to be entered into the computer.

Catalogue information for the museum's ethnology collection had been entered by "batch processing"; that is, computer cards were punched and read into the computer. The information was stored on magnetic tape and cross-indexes of the collection produced. The batch method of entry was considered but rejected because it would have involved the use of keypunchers and programmers for each addition or change to the registration file. A systems analysis approach was required to design a system that would produce the kinds of information needed in the desired formats.

The entire registration system was examined, not only to determine how registration was being handled but also to identify areas where it was failing to answer information needs. A team of three—the registrar, Holly Chaffee; a computer programmer, James Cushing; and a systems analyst, Jeffrey Neff—worked together in designing the system. The registrar initiated the project and was responsible for determining what reports and indexes were needed and, consequently, what questions were to be asked during registration. The computer programmer was responsible for designing a system of programs capable of accepting and storing the information that the registrar wanted recorded and also of producing the desired reports and indexes. The systems analyst was responsible for developing the overall plan, supervising the project, and ensuring that it was compatible with other computer systems that the museum was using. A prime consideration was to design a system that could be *used and controlled by the registrar*.

A registration system is only as good as the information it records. This information is fairly easily obtained if the right questions are asked at the time of registration. The registration staff must answer questions about gifts made by a particular donor, institutions where material has been placed on loan, or the whereabouts of material loaned to the registrar's institution. Also, statistical information is needed for annual reports. No registration system will supply the answers to these questions if the proper information has not been recorded.

In analyzing registration needs, it is essential not only to consider present information needs, but, where possible, to anticipate future needs. There are several ways of going about this. The most obvious is to examine the reports and indexes produced in the past and to evaluate their usefulness. Information categories that have been useful should be retained, and areas where information needs have not been met should be identified. Correspondence that asks for registration information should be examined to determine the kinds of information requested in the past. The needs of other museum departments should also be considered. Careful planning can help to answer most questions about registration information needs.

It was decided early in the planning stage that REGIS should record only information obtainable during registration. Questions would focus on the accession as a whole and would necessarily be objective. The gathering of information specific to the individual objects in an accessioned lot, except for a listing of the objects included, would be left to the cataloguing staff and handled through a different computer process.

Two types of registration information were identified: information that should be recorded for each registration transaction, and information that is specific to a particular type of registration. For example, registration number and registration date apply to every registration; a donor name and accession number apply only to permanent accessions; a date to be returned applies only to incoming and outgoing loans. Ultimately, a list of thirty-one categories of information applicable to one or all types of registration were identified. These categories, once entered into the computer, would constitute the registration data base, which would in turn be used to produce the desired reports and indexes.

For the registrar to have control over the entering and editing of information and the generating of reports, the computer system had to be designed to be interactive, operating by asking the terminal operator a programmed series of questions. Registration skills, not computer training, are necessary to operate REGIS. The registration staff need know only how to turn the terminal on, initiate the REGIS program, respond to its queries, and ask for desired reports. Once the system is operative, assistance of a computer programmer is not necessary.

REGIS Operation

The REGIS system queries on and records thirty-one categories of registration information. Each of these categories is identified by a category number, a tag. Not all categories apply to every registration. The registrar is asked to indicate at the beginning of a registration session whether an accession or a disposition is being entered and whether the transaction is a temporary or a permanent one. Once this information has been entered, the particular REGIS program that asks the proper questions for that type of registration will be activated. This eliminates the need to consider questions that do not apply to the registration being entered.

To assure that certain information is always entered, some categories have been made obligatory, so that the program will not proceed to the next query until the question is answered. One of these obligatory categories is REGISTRATION NUMBER, which must be assigned to each transaction that involves bringing material into the museum or sending it out. Other categories of information for which responses are obligatory are SOURCE, DONOR, PURPOSE, DATE TO BE RETURNED, DEPOSITOR, RECIPIENT, TRANSACTION DATE, and DESCRIPTION.

An accession number is assigned to all material that is brought into the museum to be registered as a permanent addition to the collections. The accession number can be automatically assigned by the computer. It is not an obligatory category, however, for old registrations do not necessarily have accession numbers and REGIS is designed to accommodate both old and new registrations.

Other categories of information can be automatically assigned. For instance, the queries REGISTERED BY and TRANSACTION DATE can be answered by typing in the required information or by having the computer check for the name of the person using REGIS and/or that day's date and automatically assign that information to those categories.

REGIS is also designed to produce registration receipts. Categories of information appropriate to the receipt being generated are selected and printed on a teletype terminal. In addition to the registration information, the receipt has a place for the signature of both the registrar and the donor, depositor, or recipient. This signed receipt is filed in the registration documents file.

An activity summary is automatically produced at the end of each registration session. It contains information about the number and type of transactions entered, the number of loan reports or receipts generated, and the number of records eliminated from the active registration file.

Active registrations, such as loans that are outstanding and accessions that have not been completely processed, are kept on disk because the information recorded for these types of transactions must be available for quick retrieval and editing. However, once a loan is returned or material from an accession has been catalogued and stored, the registration information is transferred from disk to an inactive "archive" file on magnetic tape. This information is still available for producing reports.

REGIS Reports

REGIS interfaces with the SELGEM system to produce reports. Both REGIS and SELGEM are written in COBOL (COmmon Business-Oriented Language). SELGEM (SELf-GEnerating Master), which was developed at the Smithsonian Institution, has been used extensively at the Arizona State Museum. It is a collection of general purpose computer programs that have six basic functions to manipulate data: updating, listing, editing, sorting, retrieval, and report writing. A series of simple commands, typed at the terminal, initiate production of reports. The reports are printed at the computer center and delivered to the computer services offices at the museum. Each time a registration is entered into the computer it is assigned an identifying serial number and written into a master file. It is from this combined file that most REGIS reports and indexes are produced.

A variety of useful reports can be produced by REGIS. For instance, if a listing of outstanding loans is desired, the registrar indicates the beginning and ending dates of the period the report is to cover. The report that is produced lists the loans by date due and gives the serial number, name of depositor or recipient, registration number, and a description of the material included. For reports of donors, depositors, or recipients, the printout includes the serial number, registration number, accession number (if there is one), transaction date, source or purpose, and a brief description of the registration. If more information about the registration is needed, the master file and the registration document files can be examined. REGIS will also produce an authority list. This list includes the names of all donors, depositors, or recipients that are in the registration file and the serial numbers associated with those names. Registration information can be retrieved by searching for the desired name and then checking the information in the master file under each serial number. This list is also used to standardize names entering the registration file.

Another report generated by REGIS lists archaeological projects by site number and includes the site name, accession number, serial number, type of archaeological project, and a brief description of the contents of the accession and the catalogue numbers assigned. Other reports that can be produced include a listing of the registration file in order by accession number; a listing of the number of times material has left the museum for exhibit, research, or teaching; a listing of the number of accessions that have been received as gifts, purchases, exchanges, or through archaeological or ethnological projects; and a listing of the number, type, and value of objects that have come into the museum.

Conclusion

REGIS has streamlined registration at the Arizona State Museum. In addition to making the registration process more efficient, REGIS provides a simple way of handling the filing of registration documents. Documents such as receipts, correspondence, deeds of gifts, gift reports, and appraisals, which were once filed alphabetically by type of registration, are now filed by their automatically assigned serial number. Indexes and reports that allow access to the information in the computer file also serve as indexes to the registration documents.

All the objectives sought in the design of REGIS are being met: the registrar has control of the system; the categories of information to be entered have been defined; access to the registration information is efficient; and the system successfully absorbs all previous registration systems.

REGIS was designed to relieve the registrar of some of the routine paper work associated with registration. While its on-line capability is the major feature of REGIS, the registrar is not a slave to that method. Information can be entered as soon as it is available or it can be recorded on special preregistration work sheets and entered when convenient for the registrar. Receipts can be produced by the computer or, if preferred, typed in the registrar's office on the museum's own forms. REGIS has proved to be a versatile tool for registration at the Arizona State Museum.

COMPUTERS AND REGISTRATION: PRACTICAL APPLICATIONS

THERESE VARVERIS

Computers are useful to museums for the same reasons they are useful to businesses: they perform repetitive tasks quickly and accurately. For this reason they are particularly helpful to a record-keeping department such as that headed by the registrar. Once information has been recorded accurately with the use of a computer, it does not ever have to be retyped again. Computer programs select, sort, format, and print it according to various specifications. And they can do this at incredible speeds. Cards for half a year's acquisitions, for example, can be produced in a matter of minutes. Hundreds of corrections can be made at a time. Lists of thousands of records can be printed in a few hours.

The registrar's department of the Museum of Modern Art supplies cards for up to seven cross-reference and curatorial files. These are now printed by computer, thereby relieving us of a tremendous burden. Furthermore, it is no longer necessary to have a typist working solely on new and corrected records. We have been able to produce, experimentally, complete listings of the entire museum collection and of each curatorial department. Although our current budget does not yet allow us to do this on a regular basis, we have the facility to print a complete catalogue of the entire museum collection within hours.

The main justification for computerizing, therefore, is the ability to relieve the burden of repetitive work, whether it entails preparing cards of the same records or lists in varying formats.

Selecting the Programming System

The Museum of Modern Art seriously investigated the possibility of maintaining its catalogue records by computer in 1967. A sound and highly reliable system of registration had long been established, and although we were interested in the benefits of computerization, we were prepared to wait until we found a system that could meet our specifications for the present and allow unlimited growth in the future. We discovered that an extremely flexible system for use in the humanities had been designed by Professor J. Heller, presently at the State University of New York at Stony Brook. The name given to this system was GRIPHOS (General Retrieval and Information Processor for Humanities Oriented Studies).

In addition to GRIPHOS there are several other data processing systems that have been designed specifically for museum catalogue records. (See figure P.1.) The Museum Data Bank Coordinating Committee was formed in 1972 to assemble objec-

© Copyright Therese Varveris, 1979.

General Information Systems Currently Used in Museum-Related Activities			
Acronym	System Name	Developer	Types of Museum Data * That Have Been Processed Using the System
GIPSY	General Information Processing SYstem	James Sweeney Georgia Tech	Ethnographic museum specimens
GIS	General Information System	IBM Corporation	Flora North America, a large-scale centralized data bank, designed to collect, analyze, maintain and disseminate diverse kinds of information about the plants of North America
GRIPHOS	General Retrieval and Information Processing for Humanities Oriented Studies	Jack Heller SUNY at Stony Brook	Museum Computer Network, an organization of 15-20 museums and related organizations, primarily to record art objects and archaeological data
SELGEM	SELf-GEnerating Master	Information Systems Division Smithsonian	Specimen inventories in the biological sciences (mammals, conodont types, foraminifera, nematodes, crustacea), art museums, zoos
TAXIR	TAXonomic Information Retrieval	David J. Rogers Univ. of Colorado	Biological specimen data

* Several of the systems described here have also been used for the storage and retrieval of other types of data.

*Fig. P.1.
Data processing systems designed for museum catalogue records. From Robert G. Chenhall, "Sharing the Wealth,"* Museum News, *51:8 (Apr. 1973), 22.*

tive information about these systems to enable museums to study the characteristics and advantages of the available systems before selecting one.

Many museums associated with or near universities have also found they can use the university facilities and programs at greatly reduced cost. However, like all data processing possibilities, these should be evaluated carefully. Frequently the programs offered, which may have been designed for library or other types of catalogue data, can be altered to include the characteristics desired by the museum to make them more flexible in manipulating museum records, and to make them as compatible as possible with systems used by other museums.

Although the basic principles of data processing are the same in all systems and systems with like characteristics are largely compatible with one another, once a commitment is made to one system and input has begun, a change to another system is unlikely. Therefore, it is very important that the museum considering computerization fully understand what each system offers, clarify museum needs from the outset, and be prepared to wait for improvements if they can be made.

The following are some of the features the Museum of Modern Art was looking for when it selected GRIPHOS. They are examples of the kind of capabilities a museum might want from a computer system. Although only a few of these features were available in GRIPHOS at the time, we were assured that they were included in the basic system design and would be implemented in the future, as they have been. In considering the future potential and plans for a computer package as part of our criteria for selection, we sought a package that would:

1. allow for upper- and lower-case letters, permit up to fifteen diacritics, and accept non-Roman script (such as Cyrillic). The Museum of Modern Art needs all of these features for its published catalogues, which we hope will be prepared by computer in the future.

2. impose no limit on the number of characters that can be included in one unit of information (such as title), no limit on the number of units of information that can be included in one record, and no limit on the size of any one record. This is important in order to allow curators complete freedom to record all the pertinent information about an object.

3. have a hierarchical facility that permits the recording of a whole work (such as a portfolio) and its subparts (such as the prints in it). The subparts can be treated as separate entities or as parts of the whole.

4. have a joining facility that permits both separate files for different types of information (such as an object record, a biographical record, and an exhibition record) and a linking or cross-referencing of them when desired.

5. permit sorting on other than the first character or on certain specified characters within a larger number of characters without affecting the proper format for publication. (For example, "The House" can be sorted by "H" and not "T.")

Examples and illustrations used in this article are from the GRIPHOS system of the Museum Computer Network (which operates on IBM and IBM-compatible computers) and the SELGEM system developed by the Smithsonian Institution (which was first implemented on a Honeywell computer and has now been recorded for machines of all major manufacturers).

Converting the Records

Once a system is selected, the museum's records must be converted to machine-readable form. Inside the computer all characters are recognized by codes made up of ones and zeros. In an IBM computer, for example, each character is denoted by a unique combination of eight ones and zeros. Therefore, before catalogue information can be read by the computer it must be transferred to a medium that records the characters in the codes the computer can recognize. This medium can be punch cards, magnetic tape, paper tape, or disk.

In addition to the code requirements, each logical category must be assigned a code number. For example, in the Smithsonian system using SELGEM, an artist is code number 010; a title is code number 110. In the Museum Computer Network system using GRIPHOS, an artist is 70; a title is 30. Thus, converting catalogue records to machine-readable form involves retyping the entire catalogue onto one of the media mentioned above and adding the system code number to each logical category. Before this is begun, several critical decisions must be made.

INFORMATION CATEGORIES

Both SELGEM and GRIPHOS were designed to accommodate a great variety of information from many disciplines. In order to be able to handle all the different types of data that might be of interest to a museum, a library, an archaeologist, a zoologist, an architect, a musicologist, etc., it was decided to set aside a great many code numbers, but it never was expected that any individual user would need or want to use very many of them. For example, at the Museum of Modern Art, fully catalogued works quite often have extensive references, history, and condition information. It would be prohibitively expensive and not very useful to include all the material that is only referred to occasionally. We continue to maintain these records manually.

The choice of how many and what categories of information to use depends entirely on each museum's needs. It is a museum decision, not a computer one, and should be made by museum personnel responsible for basic decisions about the museum's record-keeping systems.

If a museum does not have a highly organized and dependable catalogue system, it may wish to work extensively on its records before converting them to machine-readable form. However, there is a great difference of opinion about the advisability of this for two reasons: it could delay the use of computers indefinitely, and once the records are in machine-readable form, the computer itself can help in discovering and correcting errors. Again, this is an individual museum decision.

Of course any decisions about the amount of information to include can be changed. There are no technical bars to this, but since changes usually affect the budget, this flexibility should not be abused.

A selection of perhaps twenty or thirty of the most commonly used categories of information should be made. Below is a short listing for illustration of some of the categories used by the Museum of Modern Art, and these can be typed in any order.[1]

ACCESSION OR INVENTORY NUMBER (unique category number assigned to each user)
70. ARTIST
30. TITLE
83. DATE
82. EARLIEST POSSIBLE DATE
84. LATEST POSSIBLE DATE
47. MEDIUM
48. INDIVIDUAL MATERIAL OR TECHNIQUE
51. DIMENSIONS
59. FRAME, MAT, OR PEDESTAL DESCRIPTION
5. CREDIT LINE
61. PHOTO SOURCES
91. HISTORY OF OWNERSHIP
90. EX-COLLECTION
35. ADDITIONAL INFORMATION ABOUT HOW THE OBJECT WAS MADE
7. LEGAL RESTRICTIONS
76. COUNTRY OF ORIGIN OF THE OBJECT (the Museum of Modern Art assigns the artist's nationality)
78. PLACE EXECUTED
36. ADMINISTRATIVE CATEGORY
3. ACQUISITION INFORMATION
12. DONOR
14. VENDOR
99. RELATED WORK
10. STATUS IN THE COLLECTION
9. CONFIDENTIAL INFORMATION
72. COLLABORATING ARTIST
74. MAKER OTHER THAN ARTIST
75. EDITION INFORMATION
105. HOMAGE

The number preceding each logical category is the code number assigned by the Museum Computer Network. In all catalogue data processing systems, each logical category is assigned its own separate code number. The museum can thus not only select

---

1. For a more extensive description, see the Museum Computer Network's *Manual for Museum Computer Network Data Preparation* (Stony Brook, N.Y.: Museum Computer Network, 1975).

the categories it needs, but it can retrieve its catalogue data in the combination it wants, sorted by whatever category of information it chooses.

Certain types of information are entered into the computer twice, once in display form (as it might be used in a published catalogue) and once in an index form. Display forms typically have a good deal of text that is irrelevant for indexing purposes. The index form enables the computer to locate desired information more efficiently, just as the index of a book enables the researcher to find the desired information without reading from cover to cover. SELGEM has a similar capacity for indexing. In the Museum Computer Network, odd numbers are assigned to categories that contain information in display form and even numbers are given to categories containing index terms.

Following is an example of a medium in its display form (47) and its index forms (48). The == sign tells the computer the numbers preceding it are code numbers.

Drypoint, printed in black, colored with watercolor in red-orange, yellow-orange, yellow, green, blue, and red-violet. 47==

drypoint 48== paper 48== watercolor 48==

Following is an example of a credit line (5) and the index forms for donor (12) and name of person in whose honor a gift has been made (105).

Gift of Philip Johnson in memory of Rene d'Harnoncourt. 5==
Johnson, Philip 12==d'Harnoncourt, Rene 105==

WORK SHEETS

Once a decision has been made regarding what information to include in the computerized catalogue, the tendency is to design a data sheet that will have space for both display and index terms. For most museums, this is a good approach, but it is not the only one. For example, at the Museum of Modern Art, because cataloguing the object and entering the information about it into the computer are considered part of one process, we did not feel this was necessary.

Formerly the work sheets at the Museum of Modern Art corresponded to the layout of the final catalogue card to make typing the cards easier. Now that the cards are printed under computer control, however, we have been free to reorganize the items to correspond to the flow of work. (See figure P.2.) The face of the work sheet is divided into four basic sections, separated by a double line. Section 1 includes photographic sources and information generally available from the curatorial departments or from the museum's existing records at the time of acquisition. Section 2 is filled out during the physical examination of the work. Section 3 contains information that the curatorial departments often cannot provide immediately but that can usually be completed when the official acquisitions lists are issued. Section 4 contains information that usually requires further research. Computer code numbers were added, where they applied, to the work sheet to facilitate coding when typing into the computer. But no effort was made to fit in or allow extra space for computer index terms, as a trained cataloguer extracts the index terms from the display terms while typing at the computer terminal.

The reverse of the work sheet is for recording condition, secondary inscriptions, and other information that the Museum of Modern Art does not enter into the computer. The work sheet is printed on all rag stock, in duplicate, with snap-out carbons, so that a copy can be sent to the curatorial departments for further research and a copy can be retained in the registration department.

FORMAT CONVENTIONS

Most museums consider the appearance of the catalogue listings or cards the computer will print out to be important. The format for cards and lists must be designed and existing records edited accordingly. A museum may follow established formats or design a new format suitable for both catalogue cards and published catalogue listings. Although inconsistencies can be corrected at a later time, such changes are costly in time and money.

The format conventions can be stated simply in a notebook or 3-by-5-inch card file. Here are a few examples:

70. ARTIST: Type last name first in capital letters, followed by a comma, followed by first name in lower case.

   Examples: BECKMANN, Max
   NEWMAN, Barnett

30. TITLE: Type in capital letters, followed by a period.

   Example: HIDE AND SEEK.
   SELF-PORTRAIT.

   If there is a prefix to the main title, type the prefix in lower case and the main title in upper case, followed by a period.

   Example: Study for__HIDE AND SEEK.

   NOTE: The underscore in front of HIDE AND SEEK is a programming convention that directs alphabetical sorting to take place at this point, instead of with the first character in the title. In this case, the title would sort under "HIDE AND SEEK" instead of "Study for." The underscore does not show when this category is printed.

THE WORK ITSELF

Who will do the actual work of converting the museum catalogue into machine-readable form and entering it into the computer? It is difficult to know the best answer to this question, because there is still too little experience on which to base a decision. The following are some points to consider: (1) Who will be in charge of the project, make the day-to-day decisions, plan and supervise the work, keep track of the budget, and coordinate the museum work with the work schedules at the computer installations? (2) Who will do the data conversion or actual typing? There is a distinction. Trained museum cataloguers can transfer the information to a coded data sheet and then hand it to someone who will type the coded data into the computer. (See figures P.3–5.) But this means every record will have to be typed twice, once by a cataloguer on the data sheet and once by a typist into the computer. The alternative is to train either a cataloguer or other museum staff member to code and type the information simultaneously directly into the computer. This is more difficult. It takes an average of two months' training to become fairly competent at data conversion; but the work then proceeds quickly and accurately and one whole step is saved. (3) Who will proofread the coded information? Ideally, the curator and/or the registrar of the collection and the person in charge of the computer project should do the proofreading, because these people will be most familiar with the data, the goals of the project, the desired format, and the proper use of the annotation categories and conventions. If at all possible, at least two people should be assigned to proofreading.

SPECIFIC APPLICATIONS

```
Master Card PAINTING & SCULPTURE COLLECTION WORKSHEET      66. Museum no: 201.63
 70. Artist: MATISSE, Henri                                106. TR no:
                                                                         Leica 3682d.
                                                                Leica no: Pollitzer 6012;
                                                            61. Neg. nos: Pollitzer 6006 (instal-
 30. Title: THE DANCE (First version)                      lation photo, 1st floor). MMA 1288
                                                            10. Study coll:
                                                                Sale or exch:
     Date accepted: 4-9-63                                   9. Price paid:
     Date confirmed if accepted by letter:                      Ins. Val:
  3. Source & method of purchase: Sidney Janis Gallery, New York   P.O. no:
                                                            36. Category: Painting
     Fractions or restrictions of gift:                     76. Nationality: France
                                                                Dates: 1869-1954
 83. Date of work: (early 1909)
 47. Medium: Oil on canvas.

     Size: 102 3/8 x 152 3/4" (259.7 x 387.8 cm.).
 51.

     Weight of sculpture:
 55. Primary inscriptions (Sig. & date): Not signed. Not dated.


  5. Credit: Gift of Nelson A. Rockefeller in honor of Alfred H. Barr, Jr.


112. Anonymous donor:
114. Anonymous vendor:
 33. Alternate titles:

 99. Related works:

 35. Remarks about the object: Study for mural commissioned by Sergei I. Shchukin, Moscow.
                               Smaller version painted for Albert Barnes, Merion, Pa.
     Cross references:


 91. Ex-Collections: Pierre Matisse, Walter D. Chrysler, Jr., 1936, Artist.
```

Fig. P.2. Work sheet for Matisse's Dance *(first version) (8½ by 11 in.), Museum of Modern Art. The work sheet is designed to be filled in according to the flow of work.*

The whole project can be turned over to an agency that will do all the work for a fixed fee. A museum that had to enter very large amounts of data in a short period of time chose this method as a matter of expediency and found it satisfactory. The only problems were due to the speed with which the work was done. One museum hired an experienced systems analyst to be in charge of its project and then trained college students to do the data conversion and proofreading. This worked quite well and seems to be the method other museums are considering.

The registration staff of the Museum of Modern Art was itself very interested in computers. We thought that it would be better for us to study data processing than to teach registration to systems analysts. We hired an extra cataloguer to make up for the total time being spent on the computer terminal by others, and four people took turns doing data conversion on an hourly or half-day basis. This, too, worked out successfully, and the project of converting 26,000 records was completed in 1970. We

```
Card Two         PTG. & SC. WORKSHEET—Page 2    66. Museum no:  201.63
Mounting unit (on acq.):   stretcher

Mounting unit (permanent):

Former MoMA nos:

57. Secondary inscriptions:
ON STRETCHER:

Minneapolis Art Institute              HISTORY
No. L56.1672                           Exh. 85 -91*
Lent by Los Angeles County Museum      Exh. 492 -20*

112

Chrysler-Art Museum of Provincetown
Provincetown, Mass.
The Controversial Century
   1850-1950
Matisse, Henri
   LA DANSE

Philadelphia Museum of Art
Parkway at 26 Street, Philadelphia

Artist: Matisse
Title: La Danse, 1910
Owner's value for insurance _____
Lender:  Walter P. Chrysler
Address of lender:  Fifth Avenue, New York

Warehouse labels:
Day & Meyer & Murray & Young Corp.
W.P. Chrysler
10624
3043

Day & Meyer ... Corp.
W.P. Chrysler
10624
Condition Card     Date of condition photo:           Date examined: 4-2-63
Condition on acquisition:    Slightly slack; flaked losses along old creases throughout;
several areas of paint crudely inpainted; vertical scratch with losses in figure's
head below C.; vertical crackling center figure's hair and shoulders; scratch
extreme UL corner; puncture near T L. of C.; water stain top C.




Cataloged by:                          Date sent to curator:
Approved by:                           Date approved:
```

learned not to expect one person to type data input all day long. It is a very concentrated, tiring job, and very few people can manage more than two or three hours at a time without losing efficiency.

SELECTING EQUIPMENT

The SELGEM system is flexible enough to run on most computer equipment. The GRIPHOS system, on the other hand, at present can be run only on IBM and IBM-compatible computers, although a project to remove this limitation is under way. If there are several computer installations from which to choose, it is best to select one that has as many resources above the minimum requirements as possible, particularly in storage capacity. The personnel at the selected installation should be given as much information about the museum's data processing needs as possible to determine that their computer system can fulfill the museum's requirements.

The equipment for typing the catalogue information will also have to be selected. Before it can be input to the GRIPHOS, SELGEM, or any other computer system, catalogue information must be entered into computer code-recording machines. Many different manufacturers have developed special machines for this process. A few used by Museum Computer Network members are described here.

In the pilot projects of the original members of the Museum Computer Network, catalogue information was recorded on data sheets by the museums and then turned over to a keypunch service to be transferred to punch cards. Although keypunching is still used for recording data and generally is considered satisfactory, we were not pleased with the results. Punch cards are bulky and clumsy and are easily mixed up. Furthermore, they are hard to proofread and correct. Since a keypunch does not have upper- and lower-case letters, still more special codes are necessary to create them.

An alternative used by two museums is the IBM 2741 Communications Terminal, which was installed in the registrars' offices. As its name implies, it is not an independent piece of machinery but a terminal connected to a computer. It looks like an ordinary office typewriter, but, through a special telephone, it can connect to a time-sharing, text-editing computer center. Many different users from remote locations can dial into this type of center and share the use of the computer, each paying only for the actual time and services used. A text-editing program permits each user to edit and correct information typed while connected to the computer. The information can be typed back at the terminal for proofreading, or printed out and mailed to the user. When the user is satisfied, the data is recorded on magnetic tape for input to the GRIPHOS system, which is usually run at another computer center with different specifications.

The IBM Mag-Card Terminal is a variation of this process. Like the Communications Terminal, it can connect to a computer center by telephone, but it can also function as an independent machine. Information can be typed, recorded, proofread, corrected, and stored temporarily on special magnetic cards. At the end of the day, or at any other time, the user can dial into the computer center and have all the corrected data on the magnetic cards transmitted to the computer and stored there. The magnetic cards can then be reused for new data. Periodically, the accumulated data in the computer is placed on magnetic tape and input to the data base. The Mag-Card Terminal is convenient for users who have only limited telephone access to a computer center.

Another type of machine, the IBM Magnetic Tape Selectric Typewriter (MTST) is completely independent. Data is recorded on its own tapes as it is typed. It also can be corrected and re-stored on the same tapes. Later it is transferred onto standard magnetic tapes and read into a computer.

Many manufacturers are producing devices for recording data, and new equipment is constantly being developed. The operating difficulties, training problems, and costs differ greatly. A museum's choice probably will be determined largely by the type of computing facilities available locally.

BUDGETING

The main factors determining the budget for computerizing records are, of course, the size of the input and the amount of time and staff it will take to complete the project. An estimate of the size of the records involved can be made by first establishing the average number of characters per record, then adding to this figure the

```
MATISSE, Henri 70==Painting 36==France 76==201.63 66==DANCE (first version). 30==(1909, early). 83==
+1909 82.84==Leica 3682d.///MMA 1288.///Pollitzer 6006.///Pollitzer 6012. 61==Oil on canvas, 47==
oil 48==canvas 48==102 3/8 x 152 3/4" (259.7 x 387.8 cm.). 51==Gift of Nelson A. Rockefeller in honor of Alfred H. Barr, Jr. 5==
Rockefeller, Nelson A. 12==Barr, Alfred H. Jr. 105==Accepted 4-9-63. 3==
Ex-Collections: Pierre Matisse, Walter P. Chrysler, Jr., donor. 91==Rockefeller, Nelson A. 90==
Matisse, Pierre 90==Chrysler, Walter P. Jr. 90==Study for mural commissioned by Sergei I. Shchukin, Moscow.
 Smaller version painted for Albert Barnes, Merion, Pa. 99== 0==
```

Fig. P.3.
Record for Matisse's Dance (first version), as it looks when typed with codes for input into the computer, Museum of Modern Art.

```
 21847 - - - - - - - - - - - - - - -   21848 - - - - - - - - - - - - - - - - -   314 - - - - - - - - - - -
 0 70         MATISSE, Henri
 0 36         Painting
 0 76         France
 0 66         201.63
              1963  0201
 0 30         DANCE (first version).
 0 83         (1909, early).
 0 82 84      +1909
 0 61         Leica 3682d.///MMA 1288.///Pollitzer 6006.///Pollitzer 6012.
 0 47         Oil on canvas,
 0 48         oil
 0 48         canvas
 0 51         102 3/8 x 152 3/4" (259.7 x 387.8 cm.).
 0 5          Gift of Nelson A. Rockefeller in honor of Alfred H. Barr, Jr.
 0 12         Rockefeller, Nelson A.
 0 105        Barr, Alfred H. Jr.
 0 3          Accepted 4-9-63.
 0 91         Ex-Collections: Pierre Matisse, Walter P. Chrysler, Jr., donor.
 0 90         Rockefeller, Nelson A.
 0 90         Matisse, Pierre
 0 90         Chrysler, Walter P. Jr.
 0 99         Study for mural commissioned by Sergei I. Shchukin, Moscow. Smaller version painted for Albert Barnes, Merion, Pa.
 0 2          The Museum of Modern Art
              museum of modern art the
```

Fig. P.4.
Record for Matisse's Dance (first version), after it has been processed by the GRIPHOS system, Museum of Modern Art.

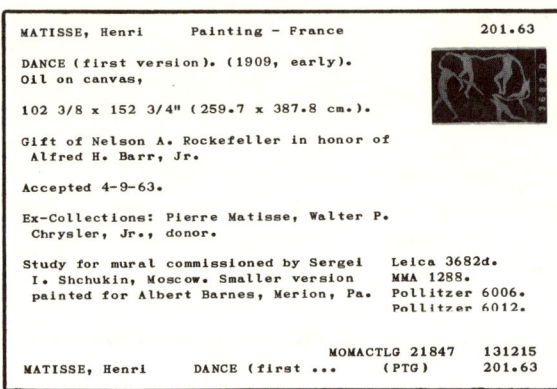

Fig. P.5.
Resulting computer card for Matisse's Dance (first version), printed under computer control (4 by 6 in.), Museum of Modern Art.

number of characters required for the index categories. It should be taken into account that records for works that have been fully catalogued will be two or three times the length of those that have only been accessioned. To estimate the time it will take to convert the records, determine the number of records that can be input in any given period of time. At the Museum of Modern Art we found that 25 records, averaging 350 characters each, could be input per hour, including the time required for proofreading and correcting. If possible, it is a good idea to run a small test project to verify the estimates before making up a final budget.

Then, when it is determined what staff will be available to work on the project, it will be possible to calculate how long completion of the project will take and the personnel costs. Equipment costs will be determined by the fixed monthly rental charge for the equipment selected for typing catalogue information and the length of time it will be needed. The budget for processing will depend upon the charges of local computer centers, and the cost of running the programs should be worked out with someone from the selected installation. This should include the costs of running diagnostic, correction, and index, as well as input programs.

If the museum plans to reprint its entire card catalogue by computer, the cost of the card stock, printing, and filing of cards should be included in this initial budget. However, the continuing work of adding new acquisitions and making corrections to the catalogue can be absorbed in the annual operating budgets since it is part of the regular work of the registrar. Data processing is simply a new way of doing it.

LOCATING AND CORRECTING ERRORS

Manual work on existing and new records should continue well after the computer input has been completed, because, at first, the computer records cannot be considered completely reliable.

In spite of careful proofreading and correcting during input, at least three types of common problems occur: simple typing errors, leaving out fields within records, and skipping of entire records. Many of these errors can and should be found and corrected before the computer is completely relied upon. Depending on the size of the data base and the staff, several months immediately after initial input has been completed should be devoted exclusively to checking the new computerized records against the originals. After the initial conversion of existing records, future input and corrections can be kept up as part of the registration department's day-to-day work.

The main diagnostic tool of the GRIPHOS system is the frequency dictionary program. This is a generalized program that will work on whatever and as many categories of information as the user specifies. It scans through the data base, selecting, sorting, and listing each entry in the categories specified, the number of times the entry appears, and the location of the records in which it can be found. The listing makes it possible for the staff to find possible errors quickly and correct them.

For example, to check the entries under artist (category 70), the program will locate all the category 70s, sort them, and list the location of each occurrence. The listing would look like this:

10	BECKMANN, Max	204 309 445 694 709 720 725 830 1178 3333
1	BEFORE THE MIRROR	3336
1	BICKMANN, Max	3336

This example shows that the artist entry, "BECKMANN, Max," appears ten times in the data base in records to be found at the locations shown at the right. Also listed as an artist are "BEFORE THE MIRROR" and "BICKMANN, Max," both of which appear once and in the same record. It is obvious that "BECKMANN, Max" is a correct entry (the only possible mistake is that he is not the artist of the work) and that "BICKMANN, Max" has a typing error in it. "BEFORE THE MIRROR" looks like a title (category 30), so it probably had a typing error in the category number. The entire record at location 3336 should be printed and the suspected errors confirmed and marked for correction. Once the entries are reasonably correct, the figures at the left provide useful statistics on the collection.

Since the information available on each work varies from record to record, it is difficult to discover omissions. Generally, certain categories of minimum information should always be included in each record, even if the correct entry is still unknown. These obligatory categories might be ACCESSION NUMBER, ARTIST, TITLE, DATE, ADMINISTRATIVE CATEGORY, and CREDIT LINE. Usually these categories will appear only once in each record. The Museum of Modern Art has a small program to check on one category at a time that scans the entire data base and prints out the locations of records that either have no entry or have more than one entry for the category being checked. The pertinent records are then printed in full. The missing information is added, and any duplicate information is deleted.

Once it is certain each record has one accession number in it, an accession number list should be printed out by the frequency dictionary program and proofread very carefully. In this way it is possible to find simple typing errors and to determine what, if any, records were skipped over entirely during input. The missing records can be input, and the entire accession number sequence rechecked until it is confirmed that the data base is complete.

When corrections are needed, the appropriate one of four simple GRIPHOS commands can be used:

1. DPH deletes an entire record from the data base. This is a very powerful command and is rarely needed. Since it can erase a great deal of work very quickly, it should be used only by the person in charge of the project.

2. ADD adds a new unit of information to a record.

3. DUN deletes a unit of information from a record.

4. CHA changes an existing unit of information in a record.

A unit of information consists of the data and its associated code number(s).

In the record shown in figure P.6, CHA is used to correct the typing error in the artist's name by changing unit 70 from "BICKMANN, Max" to "BECKMANN, Max." The DUN command is used to delete "BEFORE THE MIRROR," which was incorrectly entered with the category of 70, and the ADD command adds it to the record as a new unit with the correct code number for title, which is 30. A new card of the corrected record can then be printed simply by giving the print program its location (3336). (See figure P.7.)

It is also possible that the same error will appear throughout the entire data base. For example, a credit line may have been typed in as "Gift of William Jones"; later the donor requests that the credit line read "Gift of Mr. and Mrs. William F. Jones, Jr." If the donors have given the museum several hundred items, finding the records and making the changes individually would be indeed tedious. Therefore, GRIPHOS, SELGEM, and most systems have a program for mass changes or corrections. The program is given the credit line code number 5 and the information "William Jones" to search for. It scans the data base, and whenever it finds the information, will substitute "Mr. and Mrs. William F. Jones, Jr." New cards of the corrected records can then be printed and filed. If there were no other reason to maintain a catalogue by computer, this facility alone would make it worthwhile.

CRITERIA FOR RETRIEVAL

GRIPHOS has a set of extremely flexible generalized programs called permuted-index programs that retrieve records on the basis of criteria provided by the user. The user can specify the units by which he or she wants the retrieved records sorted, the units he or she would like printed, and the order and positions on the page of the units. Criteria to be matched are usually given with the appropriate logical operators *and*, *or*, and *not*.

For example, at the Museum of Modern Art, each curatorial department is assigned certain administrative categories for its collection. To produce a listing of the collection of the Department of Architecture and Design, the permuted-index program is asked to scan the data base for the administrative category code 36 and then to look for "architecture" *or* "design" *or* "poster." It is told to sort the selected records first by artist (70) and second by title (30). Once the records are in the right alphabetical order, the units to be printed and their positions on the line (expressed by column numbers) are given. The program, if asked, will also print headings and skip a line after each record to make it easier to read. (See figure P.8.)

In another, more complicated retrieval example, all three logical operators are used. To produce a list of works of art on paper in the regular collection of the Department of Painting and Sculpture, it is necessary to test three categories of information: ADMINISTRATIVE CATEGORY (36), MATERIAL (48), and STATUS IN THE COLLECTION (10). The permuted-index program scans the data base for the administrative category code 36 and then matches for "painting" *or* "sculpture" *or* "watercolor" *or* "collage" *and* the material code 48 for "paper" but *not* to retrieve any record with the status code 10 if it matches with "study collection" *or* "canceled" *or* "for sale or exchange." Sorting and printing are the same as for the architecture and design listing. When the object files are joined to other files, such as biographical or reference files, there are permuted-index programs that will also retrieve from them, according to criteria supplied by the user.

P: COMPUTERS AND REGISTRATION: PRACTICAL APPLICATIONS

```
    3336 - - - - - - - - - - - - - - 3337 - - - - - - - - - - - - - - 143 - - - - - - - - - -
                   E
  0 (70) CHA    BECKMANN, Max
  0  36         Print
  0  76         Germany
  0  66         259.40
                1940  0259
  0 (70) DUN    BEFORE THE MIRROR.
  0  83         (1923).
  0  82         +1923
  0  84         +1923
  0  47         Drypoint, printed in black,
  0  48         paper
  0  48         drypoint
  0  51         Plate 19 7/8 x 8 9/16" (27.5 x 21.7 cm.).
  0   5         Gift of Abby Aldrich Rockefeller.
  0  12         Rockefeller, Abby Aldrich
  0   3         Accepted 4-5-40.
  0  55         Signed L.R. in pencil "Beckmann".///Impression: "18/60" L.L. in pencil.
  0  49         Paper: laid, white.
  0  61         Leica 1342a.
  0  95         Not in B.G. 244.
  0  59         I
  0   2         The Museum of Modern Art
                museum of modern art the
     30         BEFORE THE MIRROR.
```

Fig. P.6.
A computer listing of an incorrect record indicating corrections to be made, Museum of Modern Art.

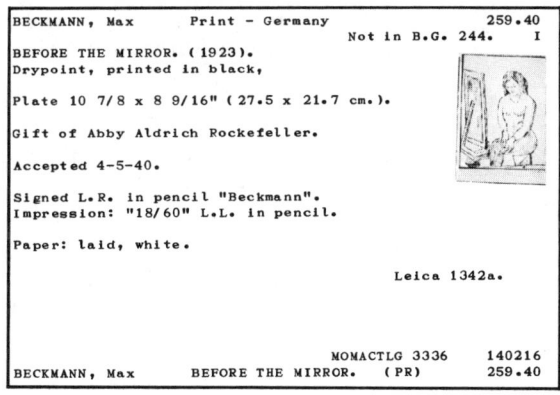

Fig. P.7.
Card printed under computer control as a result of the corrected record shown in figure P.6, Museum of Modern Art.

```
                                  439
                                          The MUSEUM of MODERN ART                                                      06/12/71
                                       Department of Architecture and Design
                                            Confidential: for Staff Use

         Artist                 Title                         Date                    Category
                                Credit                        Photo Source
                                Size                          Signature                                    Accession #
                                Medium                        Remarks


         TIFFANY, Louis         WINE GOBLET.                                           Design              MOMACTLG   17452
         Comfort
                                Gift of Joseph H. Heil.       Barrows 3295/45.                             304.60
                                5" h. (12.7 cm.).             Markings: L.C.T.
                                Glass,                        Flaring rim. Pale gold iridescence inside and outside of bowl with
                                                              horizontal swirl pattern around outside. Base, stem and bottom of
                                                              bowl clear amber, cut and polished.
         - - - - - - - - - - - - - - - - - - - - - - - - - - - - - - - - - - - - - - - - - - - - - - - - - - - - - - - - - -
                "               "                             "                        "                   MOMACTLG   20633
                                "                             Barrows 3295/52.                             560.60
                                8 7/8" h. (22.5 cm.).         Markings: L.C.T. Favrile.
                                Favrile glass,                Circular foot, elaborate baluster stem in clear yellow glass, light
                                                              gold iridescence inside of top baluster. Flat bottomed bowl with
                                                              straight side flaring out on top, pink glass with light white
                                                              overlays outside. "Venetian style".
         - - - - - - - - - - - - - - - - - - - - - - - - - - - - - - - - - - - - - - - - - - - - - - - - - - - - - - - - - -
         TINGUELY, Jean         ALEXANDRE IOLAS MILANO 1966.  (1966).                  Poster              MOMACTL2    2254
                                Gift of Mr. and Mrs. Leo Farland.                                          2273.67
                                27 1/2 x 19" (69.8 x 48.2 cm.).
                                Poster,
         - - - - - - - - - - - - - - - - - - - - - - - - - - - - - - - - - - - - - - - - - - - - - - - - - - - - - - - - - -
         TOMASZEWSKI, Henryk    THE CHARM OF SATAN.           (1954).                  Poster              MOMACTLG   20645
                                Given anonymously.            Leica 3105a.                                 86.61
                                22 1/2 x 33 1/4" (57.1 x 84.4 cm.).
                                Poster
         - - - - - - - - - - - - - - - - - - - - - - - - - - - - - - - - - - - - - - - - - - - - - - - - - - - - - - - - - -
         TONTSERE               TREBALLA PER ALS QUE UNITEN U G T.                     Poster              MOMACTLG     807
                                Gift of Christian Zervos.                                                  218.36
                                Sheet 27 1/2 x 39".
                                Poster,
         - - - - - - - - - - - - - - - - - - - - - - - - - - - - - - - - - - - - - - - - - - - - - - - - - - - - - - - - - -
         TOOROP, Jan            DELFTSCHE SLAOLIE.            (1895).                  Poster              MOMACTLG   27586
                                                              Leica 5072d.                                 684.66
                                36 1/4 x 24 3/8".
                                Poster,
         - - - - - - - - - - - - - - - - - - - - - - - - - - - - - - - - - - - - - - - - - - - - - - - - - - - - - - - - - -
         TOWNSEND               WAR RACES IN EUROPE.                                   Poster              MOMACTLG    8878
                                Gift of Mrs. Harry Townsend.                                               27.45

                                Poster,
         - - - - - - - - - - - - - - - - - - - - - - - - - - - - - - - - - - - - - - - - - - - - - - - - - - - - - - - - - -
         TRACE & WARNER         TEAKETTLE.                    (1939).                  Design              MOMACTLG    8793
                                Gift of the manufacturer.     Schiff 9032-3-M.                             228.44
                                                              Barrows 3201-54.
                                4 3/4"h. x 10"w. (bottom).
                                Cast aluminum,
         - - - - - - - - - - - - - - - - - - - - - - - - - - - - - - - - - - - - - - - - - - - - - - - - - - - - - - - - - -
```

Fig. P.8.
A page from a listing of the collection of the Department of Architecture and Design, printed under computer control, Museum of Modern Art.

    Up to now the computer has been used to make the traditional work of the registrar more economical, more efficient, and more productive. This is what justifies the cost of the project. But gradually, as we begin to explore related benefits to be obtained from the computer's speed and accuracy in manipulating records, we realize what a powerful tool we have.

RULES FOR HANDLING WORKS OF ART

ERIC B. ROWLISON

A set of rules for handling works of art is only one of the ingredients necessary to ensure their safe movement within the museum. Demonstrations of correct techniques (preferably demonstrations in which staff can participate) are absolutely essential supplements to the printed word. Good equipment, in good working order, is another must. All the care in the world will not make a truck with a sticky wheel into a safe vehicle for the transport of paintings. Another necessity is a supervisory staff capable of adapting rules to unusual circumstances and of adjusting to emergencies of every sort. The most important requirement of all is a handling crew that work well together, are totally familiar with the correct procedures, and possess the ability to work in a careful and methodical manner. This is, perhaps, a tall order, but one deserving of the best efforts of all responsible institutions.

The moving of extremely large or heavy sculpture with cranes or rigging (see figures Q.1–2) falls outside the realm of these rules. Such works present difficulties that the museum professional is not equipped to cope with: finding the correct balance point, attaching the ropes in such a way that they will neither slide off nor place undue strain on delicate projections, anticipating the movement of the ropes so as to cushion against abrasion, and so forth. Such efforts must be undertaken by specialists. The dangers involved in moving heavy sculpture (not only to the works themselves but to those handling them) turn the expense of hiring good riggers into an investment in safety.

In a similar way, the safe handling of works of art of any kind pays off in their increased well-being and in reduced premiums for the insurance that covers them. The following rules for handlers and supervisors and for the handling of specific kinds of museum objects are the product of observation and experience in art museums, but they should be useful for those responsible for moving many other kinds of valuable museum objects as well.

Rules for Handlers and Supervisors

HANDLERS

Only one person directs any operation. Be sure you know who the supervisor is. Do not give directions unless you are in charge. Accept directions only from the supervisor, and address suggestions and comments only to that person.

Look for existing damages before moving a work of art, and point them out to the supervisor. This protects you from blame and can save the object from further harm.

© Copyright Eric B. Rowlison, 1973, Adelaide.

Understand exactly where and how an object is to be moved before you move it. Be aware of any idiosyncrasies of the material involved. Ask questions freely.

Ascertain whether a work contains loose or easily moving parts before handling it. If such parts are designed to be separated from the object (such as the pendulums of most clocks or heads of some marble sculptures), remove and transport them separately. If they are intended to remain attached to the object (such as portions of many modern sculptures and constructions or leaves of tables), secure them in such a way that they will not be harmed or cause damage during the move.

Unless one person can easily and without hesitation manage both the size and weight of the object, two people must handle it. Never be reluctant to say that an object is too large or heavy for you to manage.

Do not make any sudden or unnecessary movements while in the vicinity of works of art.

Never walk backwards in the vicinity of works of art. Always be aware of what is behind you and how close you are to it.

Do not smoke while handling works of art or while in the same room with them.

Use clean cotton gloves to handle works of art at all times except when the objects you are moving are too smooth to grip safely through gloves. Keep your hands clean, even when using gloves; dirt and oil from fingers can cause serious damage.

Handle only one object at a time, no matter how small. Use both hands in carrying.

Handle works of art as little and as infrequently as possible. Carry them no farther than necessary; bring the vehicle to the works rather than the works to the vehicle.

Never drag works of art.

Take your time. Move slowly while carrying objects or pushing vehicles containing them.

Never leave works of art sitting directly on the floor.

Safely pad, pack, or otherwise secure every object before moving it in a vehicle.

Never put dissimilar works (such as sculpture and watercolors or ceramics and paintings) on the same vehicle. Never move objects of the same general type but of vastly different sizes, weights, or materials together.

Fig. Q.1.
An adjustable, wheeled, A-framed gantry can be used to lift and move large, heavy sculpture.

Never overload any vehicle.

Never discard packing materials before searching them thoroughly for fragments that may have dropped off in transit.

Report all damages or possible damages to the supervisor immediately. Save all fragments. Remember that damages caused by careless handling frequently do not become visible for a considerable time. If the surface of a painting is bumped, it may be months or years before cracking and lifting of the paint surface appear.

Make no distinctions as to supposed value or artistic merit. Treat every work of art as if it were the most important item in the collection.

SUPERVISORS

Only those totally familiar with correct handling should supervise an operation or train a new person.

Supervisors who are not themselves conservators should consult with a conservator before undertaking moves of particularly fragile or unusual material. The supervisor should immediately report to the conservator any damage and should make a written record of the circumstances under which it occurred.

Be sure it is clear to everyone who the supervisor is.

No person but the supervisor, whether a member of the work crew or an observer, must be allowed to issue instructions to the crew. See to it that all comments are directed to the supervisor.

Check condition and note any special features of the material involved before making the move. If a work suffers from damage that may worsen in transit (such as lifting paint or a serious crack in a vase), ask a conservator to be present during the move.

Always plan a move fully, transmit instructions to the crew clearly, and, once you have made a plan, follow it through. Be sure the crew understands precisely what is to be done.

Refuse to undertake any move if you feel that you have too few handlers or that other considerations make the operation unduly hazardous. A good supervisor, however, can often devise an alternative method that can be safely undertaken with the existing group of handlers.

Remember that too many hands are as dangerous as too few. It is up to the supervisor to ensure that objects are moved by the appropriate number of handlers.

The rules for handlers given above apply to everyone. Infractions are permitted *only* when the special nature of the material being moved dictates an exception. Only the supervisor can decide if such a situation exists. Should a supervisor break a rule for some reason, he should be sure to point out to the others involved why he has done so.

When correcting someone for breaking a rule, always point out the reason for the rule. People are more inclined to do something right if it makes sense.

Do not base cautionary instruction on value. In handling works of art, all are of equal value. The physical requirements of each object and the safety of the handlers must be the only considerations.

Do not act nervous, no matter how delicate a handling operation may be. Do not make irrelevant comments or conversation during a move.

Never urge haste.

Fig. Q.2. The services of professional riggers and crane operators may be required to assure the safe moving of large and heavy sculpture.

Rules for Handling Various Kinds of Works of Art

PAINTINGS AND FRAMED WORKS

Handling Paintings and Framed Works

Before picking up a painting, be sure it is secure in its frame.

Do not touch the front or back of a painting. Never allow *any* object to rest, however lightly, against either surface.

Never apply tape or adhesive to either the front or the back of a painting or to the visible parts of its frame.

Do not carry paintings by one side. Grip the painting with one hand beneath and one hand on the side of the frame, or with one hand on either side, whichever seems more stable.

Hold paintings at points where the frame is strong, never on fragile gesso decoration.

Never insert your fingers between the stretcher bar and the back of the canvas. This can do serious damage to the paint surface.

Carry unframed paintings by grasping only the inner and outer *edges* of the stretcher bar, not the broader sides parallel to the canvas. Your fingers must not touch the front or back of the painting or wrap around the stretcher bar.

Always move paintings with their surfaces vertical unless instructed to the contrary by the supervisor.

If you need to carry a painting through a closed door, be sure an extra handler is along to open *and hold* the door for you.

Carry large paintings as close to the floor as possible without striking door sills or placing yourself in a clumsy position.

Carry wrapped paintings with extra care. It is frequently impossible to recognize the problems of works that are covered, and often very hard to obtain a firm grip through the wrappings. Wrapped paintings should be moved on trucks or dollies whenever possible.

Do not set paintings down balanced by one corner on the floor and one in your hand. Either hold the painting correctly or set it down completely.

Always store paintings with their surfaces vertical unless instructed to the contrary by the supervisor. Works framed under glass should not be stored flat. Works whose paint is lifting or flaking, however, should be stored flat, paint surface up.

Before hanging a painting, be sure its hanging devices are firm.

Never hang paintings with their frames overlapping. Even in closely packed storage, allow enough room on all sides of the frame to grip and remove the painting without touching neighboring works.

Stacking Paintings and Framed Works

Avoid stacking whenever possible. Paintings and framed works are frequently stacked, however, on painting trucks, and many of the rules given here apply to stacking both on trucks (see below) and in storage.

Never stack unframed works or works whose frames do not extend beyond the surface of the painting.

Never stack works with protruding hanging devices.

Always stack on a nonskid surface such as rubber or cloth, never on tile or polished wood.

Stack works of a similar size together. Put the largest work at the back tapering to the smallest at the front.

Stand the inside work in as vertical a position as possible; it should hold easily without falling forward. Stand all succeeding works flush with this one. The natural tendency is to stack at too great an angle. This creates pressure harmful to works on the inside and may cause the stack to slide forward from the bottom. (See figure Q.3.)

Crisscross the works back to back and face to face so that they lie alternately vertically and horizontally. (See figure Q.4.) This eliminates the danger of one frame slipping off another into the work next to it and protects the faces of the works from protruding objects on the backs of adjacent frames. Adjacent works must be large enough to crisscross each other completely.

Keep stacks as shallow as possible. The weight of works at the front of a deep stack can damage frames at the back.

Do not stack extremely large or heavy works directly against each other. Support each such work (or, in some cases, every other work) with a 2-by-4-inch beam angled out from the wall. (See figure Q.5.) Keep such stacks very shallow; access to any work can be gained only by moving everything in front of it, and it is easy to damage the paintings in shifting the beams. Furthermore, because the beams all

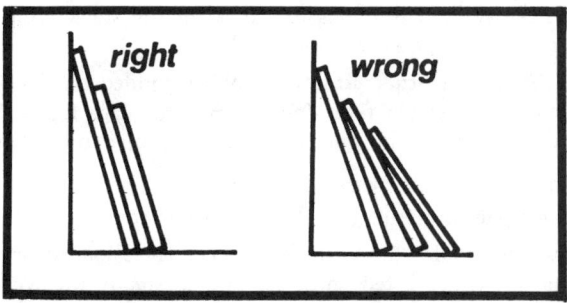

Fig. Q.3.
Right and wrong way to stack paintings and other framed works.

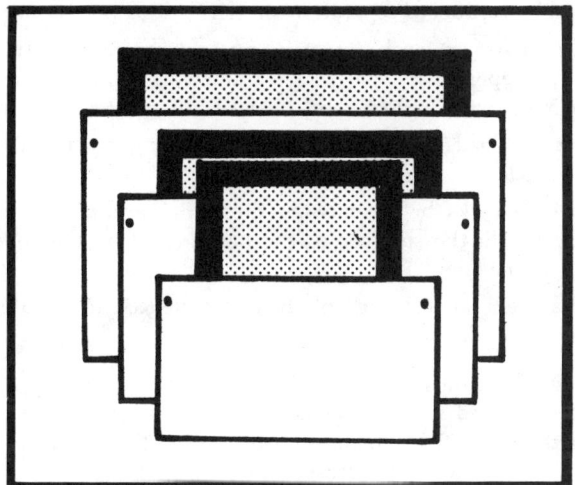

Fig. Q.4.
In stacking, crisscross framed works back to back and face to face, vertically and horizontally.

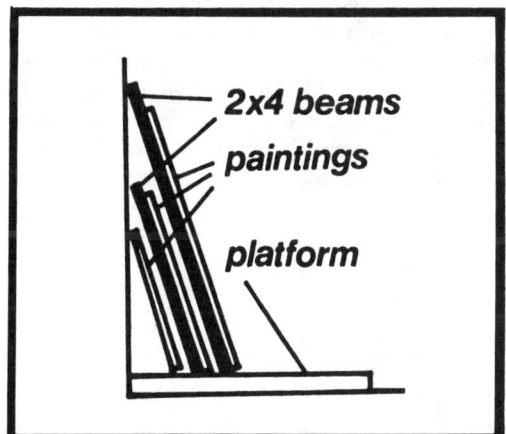

Fig. Q.5.
When stacking large or heavy works, insert 2-by-4-inch beams for support.

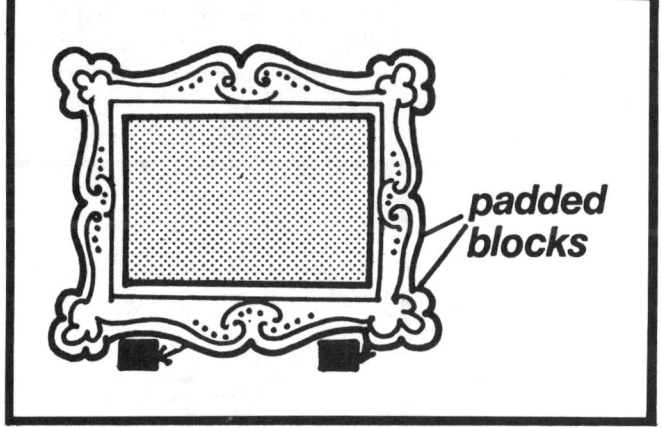

Fig. Q.6.
Stack works with ornate frames on padded blocks.

touch the wall, it is impossible to keep the stack lying flat, and after a few layers it begins to assume a dangerous angle.

Stack works with ornate frames only on padded blocks, which will spare fragile, extended corners from receiving the weight. (See figure Q.6.) Place a sheet of cardboard larger than the outermost frame projection between each of the works.

Moving Paintings on Painting Trucks

In loading painting trucks, follow the rules for stacking given above.

One handler should stay with the truck as it is loaded or unloaded to prevent its rolling as works are lifted on or off and to steady the works remaining on it.

Do not allow the inside paintings on opposite sides of the truck to rest against each other above the truck's framework.

Place unframed works on the outside of painting trucks, unless the works are protected by cardboard separation sheets.

Do not load on a truck any painting so large that its frame or stretcher will not be firmly supported by the truck's framework. There must be no chance of a painting slipping from this framework. For handling oversize paintings, see below.

Do not overload trucks. The outside painting must not extend beyond the sides of the vehicle.

Tie loaded trucks before moving them. Be careful that the rope does not come into contact with the surfaces of the paintings. Coil the rope neatly; do not allow it to drag on the floor.

Two handlers, at least one of them experienced in handling works of art, should accompany each loaded truck.

Oversize Paintings

Handles screwed to the stretcher or frame of an extremely large or heavy work give a better grip. Extra handlers can steady the center of the painting by means of handles attached to the crossbars of the stretcher.

When carrying a very tall painting, the handler at each end should hold the sides only (rather than a side and the bottom). Lifting from underneath could raise the center of gravity sufficiently to make the painting topple.

Works too large for painting trucks can often be moved on sculpture dollies. This is hazardous but, if done carefully, less dangerous than carrying. At least three handlers are necessary. One handler supports each end of the painting. If the work is fairly light, these two can lift its edge onto the dolly, which is steadied by the third handler. If the work is heavy, one handler can raise the corner while the third handler slips the dolly under the center of the work and holds it flush to the edge

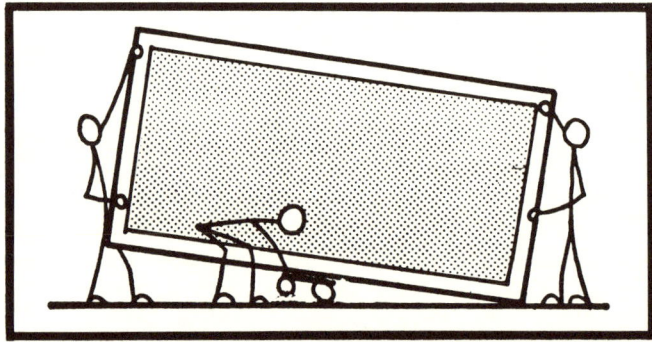

Fig. Q.7.
When placing a large painting on a dolly for transport, lift the dolly to the edge of the painting and lower the two together.

of the painting. (See figure Q.7.) The painting and the dolly are then brought to the horizontal together and lowered to the floor. (If a heavy painting is angled onto a dolly set flat on the floor, the dolly might kick out when the painting is lowered.) The third handler steadies the dolly until the painting is securely set. Keep the painting *absolutely vertical* while it is being moved, as dollies have no fixed wheels and can kick out to one side if the painting is tilted. The third handler should steady the dolly over door sills and rough spots.

TAPING GLASS ON WORKS OF ART

Taping glass on works of art before packing them for travel affords protection against damage should the glass break during transit. Fragments of broken glass will adhere to the tape rather than fall onto the surface of the work. Never tape Plexiglas, as it is impossible to remove the adhesive marks from it.

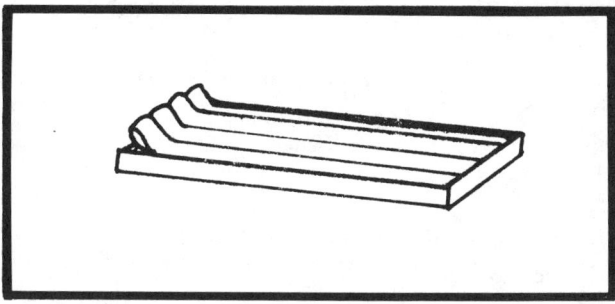

Fig. Q.8.
When taping glass on works of art for protection during transit, double one end of the tape over against itself for ease in removing.

Use masking tape or a similar pressure-sensitive paper tape.

Apply tape in parallel strips that overlap slightly or are at most ¼ inch apart.

Do not allow the tape to touch any part of the frame.

Double the tape over against itself at one edge of each strip. (See figure Q.8.) This makes the tape easier to remove. It is particularly advisable if the frame is gilt or has any surface susceptible to damage from adhesive.

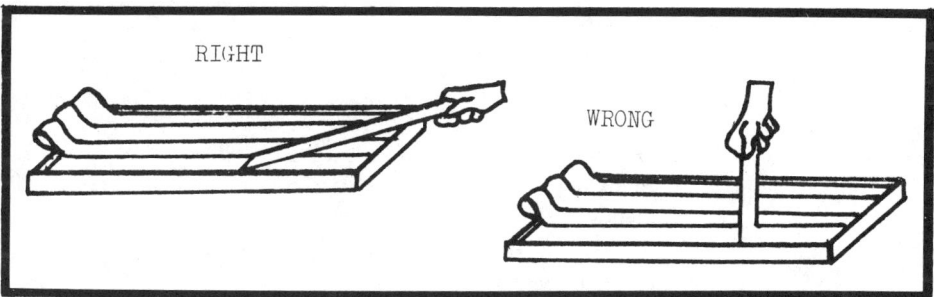

Fig. Q.9.
Right and wrong way to remove tape from glass.

To remove the tape, pull each strip back slowly along its own length. Do not pull it at right angles to the surface, as the strain can break the glass. (See figure Q.9.)

To remove traces of adhesive from the glass, dampen a cloth and wipe with benzene if available, or with Windex, turpentine, or rubbing alcohol. Do not pour the cleaning fluid directly on the glass. Do not allow the cleaning fluid to touch the frame or seep under the rabbet of the frame. Remove stubborn bits of adhesive with a razor blade.

UNFRAMED WORKS ON PAPER

Handling Mounted Works

Handle mounted works only by the mount; never touch the work of art itself.

Keep mounts flat, face up.

Handling Unmounted Works

Lift sheets by the upper corners so that they hang free without buckling. But do not carry them any distance in this manner, as air currents can cause creases.

For carrying, lay unmounted sheets on clean cardboard. Keep works flat, face up.

Lay works only on a clean, absolutely level surface.

If rolling is unavoidable, roll the sheet face out with separation sheets lining the entire surface.

Carry works that are on thin paper in a portfolio or Solander box or between sheets of cardboard.

Take great care with charcoal, pencil, and other easily smudged media. Carry each pastel separately, by itself, in a Solander box.

Piling Mounted Works

Pile works face up.

Pile only works of the same or similar sizes together, the largest at the bottom and the smallest at the top. If two adjacent edges of a pile are lined up, no mat opening should be visible.

Keep piles shallow.

Cover each pile with a large separation sheet to keep out dust.

Do not rest objects on top of piles, not even weights to hold them down.

Do not disturb piles. Shuffling through can cause creases and introduce dirt. If you must find something in a pile, search by creating a new pile.

Move piles of mounted works on a tray truck or a flatbed truck.

Piling Unmounted Works

Piling unmounted works is a *very* bad practice, but it is sometimes unavoidable. The following rules represent recognition of the existence of the custom, not an endorsement of it.

Never pile works of easily smudged media. There is *no excuse* for piling pastel or chalk drawings.

Place a separation sheet between each work. If the works are small, place each within a separation sheet folded in half. This helps to prevent the sheets and drawings from sliding apart.

As with piling mounted works, keep the piles shallow, cover them with separation sheets, do not rest objects on top of them, and do not disturb them by shuffling through.

Do not move piles of mounted works, unless the pile is contained in a Solander box, which will protect it from slipping or blowing apart. Keep the Solander box absolutely level while moving it.

Do not allow piles to exist for longer than necessary.

SCULPTURE

GENERAL

Never handle or lift sculpture by a projecting member such as an arm or head.

Move and store sculpture in its most stable position. Some pieces are too top-heavy to stand upright without reinforcement; others can be damaged if laid flat. See, especially, the rules for marble and stone sculpture, below.

Protect sculpture in transit with clean blankets, pads, or cushions. Pad all ropes used to tie the sculpture to the vehicle on which it is to be moved. Never allow sculpture to touch anything except padding, especially another work of art.

METAL SCULPTURE

Do not touch metal sculpture with bare hands, as fingerprints can leave dirt and oils that will eat into the metal. Touch metal sculpture only with gloves or soft cloth.

MARBLE AND OTHER STONE SCULPTURE

Touch stone sculpture only with clean hands, as stone is porous and absorbs dirt and oil readily. Even better, wear gloves when handling stone sculpture.

Support all protruding members of the sculpture with pads. Support all areas that do not rest on the body of the vehicle in a similar manner. Be sure the weight is distributed evenly; overpadding is as dangerous as inadequate padding.

Move and store stone sculpture in the position in which it is installed unless this is not possible. Often the weight of a piece causes dangerous stresses if it lies at an unaccustomed angle. Stone can actually break under its own weight.

SMALL SCULPTURE

Always use two hands in carrying small pieces. Support the work with one hand under the base and steady the body of the piece with the other.

Be sure a sculpture is firmly attached to its base before setting it down.

LARGE OR HEAVY SCULPTURE

Moving heavy sculpture is a specialized field. Refuse to move any such work unless someone well versed in the subject is present and approves all arrangements. Each move is a unique problem. Do not assume you know everything about moving heavy sculpture; no one does.

Do not carry heavy sculpture. Always transport it on properly padded trucks or dollies.

Do not drag sculpture. Lift it onto the vehicle that will transport it.

If a sculpture must be tilted to be placed on the dolly, one handler should lift the dolly and hold it flat against the underside of the work. Then tilt both the dolly and the sculpture back to the horizontal and lower them to the floor at the same time. This method offers maximum leverage and diminishes the danger of the dolly kicking out.

Tie heavy sculpture down for transit, or otherwise completely secure it in position.

Move even more slowly with heavy sculpture than with other material. These works can be dangerous and can seriously injure those handling them.

Institutions that own hydraulic lift trucks can store and move heavy sculpture on skids or pallets, thus eliminating the need for physical contact with the work of art in transit.

When circumstances warrant (for instance, when a heavy piece must be moved a short distance within an exhibition gallery), a work may be tilted onto a rug and the rug dragged slowly to the new location.

Do not store heavy sculpture on the floor. This is the most difficult surface from which to pick it up, for there is no way to get under the piece. Store heavy sculpture on platforms or skids.

DECORATIVE ARTS

SMALL OBJECTS

Wear gloves when handling metal objects and unglazed ceramics, or handle them with tissue paper. Slippery items (such as highly glazed ceramics) and objects whose surfaces are likely to catch on the threads of gloves (such as porcelain figures and some enamels) should be carried with *clean* bare hands.

Lift objects by sliding one hand underneath and steadying the body of the object with the other. Never lift by handles or edges; these are often the weakest parts, even if they were originally designed for carrying.

Stand objects on their most stable surface for moving. Many bowls, for instance, are wider at the brim than the foot and should be transported in an inverted position.

Always rest decorative art objects, especially glass and ceramics, on padded surfaces. Take care, however, that the surface is not so deeply cushioned that the objects cannot stand firmly.

Pack objects in such a way that they cannot shift position in transit.

Insofar as possible, move only objects of the same size together. Never move objects of different materials together.

Do not overcrowd any vehicle. Objects should never be allowed to come into contact with each other or to protrude beyond the edge of the vehicle.

FURNITURE

Remove marble or glass tops and similar material before handling furniture; transport these tops vertically.

Tie down drawers, leaves, and other loose or hinged parts of furniture with soft cord.

Never drag furniture; always lift it. Lift from a point of structural strength; do not lift by arms or other protrusions. Lift chairs by the seat rail.

Keep furniture in its intended position, never upside down or on its side.

Bibliography

Burnham, Elizabeth L., and Eric B. Rowlison. *Handling Works of Art*. Film. 20 minutes, 16 mm; videotape, ¾ in. New York: Downtown Community Television Center, 1975. Order from the Museum of Modern Art.

Clapp, Anne F. *Curatorial Care of Works of Art on Paper*. 2d ed. rev. Oberlin, Ohio: Intermuseum Laboratory, 1974.

Dolloff, Francis W., and Roy L. Perkinson. *How to Care for Works of Art on Paper*. Boston: Museum of Fine Arts, 1971.

Fall, Frieda Kay. *Art Objects, Their Care and Preservation: A Handbook for Museums and Collectors*. La Jolla, Calif.: Lawrence McGilvery, 1973.

Keck, Caroline K. *A Handbook on the Care of Paintings, for Historical Agencies and Small Museums*. Nashville: AASLH, 1965.

Sugden, Robert P. *Care and Handling of Art Objects*. New York: Metropolitan Museum of Art, 1946.

PREPARING ART EXHIBITIONS FOR TRAVEL

VIRGINIA PEARSON
ELIZABETH L. BURNHAM

Traveling exhibitions are handled by many people. It is, therefore, essential that the objects themselves be made as safe as possible and that all instructions accompanying them be concise and clear. Both the institution that originates the exhibition and the receiving institution share responsibility for the well-being of the traveling exhibition. The originating institution must pack the objects in such a way as to assure their safety in transit and must prepare instructions, packing diagrams, condition reports, and whatever else may be necessary to ensure the same care in unpacking, handling, and repacking by the borrowers. The receiving institution must carefully follow all these instructions.

The procedures for preparing art exhibitions for travel outlined below are based on the experience of the Museum of Modern Art in New York. They have been satisfactory for preparing and packing both single works of art and entire exhibitions, and they amplify the instructions for packing recommended in chapter 7.

Preparation

TWO-DIMENSIONAL WORKS: PAINTINGS, WATERCOLORS, DRAWINGS, PRINTS, PHOTOGRAPHS

The frames of all paintings, watercolors, and other works of art on paper that are to travel should be simple moldings made of wood or metal, or Plexiglas wraparound frames. Carved plaster frames should never travel; they are too easily broken, and pieces that loosen in transit may cause damage to the work of art. Special traveling frames should be made to replace all fragile or plaster moldings. Removable handling frames can be designed for paintings that must be exhibited unframed. However, these frames require very special construction, must be accompanied by unframing and reframing instructions, and should be handled only by very experienced museum personnel.

For the protection of paintings, frames should project ½ inch beyond the greatest thickness of the painted surface. The stretcher and frame are checked to make certain that the stretcher keys are in place and tight, that metal plates or straps fasten the frame of the painting to the stretcher on all four sides, and that the screws attaching them do not go through either the frame or the stretcher. A heavy (not corrugated) cardboard backing is then fastened to the back of the stretcher with screws. Tacks and/or staples are not used, because they may loosen and be a hazard to the painting. (See figure R.1.) Large paintings can be backed with polypropylene board such as HXC Board, which comes in sheets 48 by 84 inches. Large paintings that are irreg-

Fig. R.1.
Before a painting or other framed work is packed, the stretcher and the frame must
be checked and secured for travel. Note here the dense cardboard (not corrugated) backing
fastened to the stretcher with screws and washers, and the metal plates attaching the
frame to the stretcher. Both will provide added strength during the stress of travel. A museum
collection label with catalogue information is attached to the backing. The painting's
museum number also appears on the backing and the frame.

ular in shape can be backed with plastic-coated screening such as Electro Glass, which comes in rolls 48 inches wide by 100 feet long. Both materials are strong but lightweight. The screening can be easily cut with sturdy scissors to conform to an irregular shape and can be attached to the back of the stretcher and stretcher bars with heavy-duty staples. Strips of strong industrial tape should be placed over the staples to prevent their loosening, and strips of masking tape should be folded over the raw, cut edges of the screening to prevent injuries to handlers.

For watercolors and other works of art on paper, the matted work and the backing board are held in the frame by brads driven into the frame parallel to the backing board. The brads and the edge of the frame are then covered with paper tape backed by water-soluble adhesive. Tape applied in this way is preferred to covering the backing board with paper, for with the tape there is less danger of the brads loosening and causing damage by working between the frame and the glass.

For both paintings and works of art on paper, projecting nameplates and screw eyes for hanging are removed. If it is necessary to provide a hanging device, a flat metal plate with a hole or hinged loop may be screwed to the frame. At the Museum of Modern Art, works that are to travel are usually equipped with a double set of hanging devices, one set with wires for hanging on the wall and another set, without wires, for hanging from a picture rail or molding. For works that are to be packed in slide boxes, the latter set must be placed on the frame or stretcher so as not to interfere with the groove or track of the slide box. The double set of hanging devices provides the borrowing institution with alternatives and, therefore, discourages any changes. However, a sticker that cautions against removing or altering the wire, hanging devices, or frame should still be attached to the backing. (See figure R.2.) The sticker should be placed half on the backing and half on the frame so that any changes to the backing or the frame will be signaled by a torn sticker.

To protect paintings and works of art on paper covered with glass, strips of 2- or 3-inch masking tape are laid on the glass not more than ¼ inch apart across the longest measurement. Tape with water-soluble adhesive should never be used here,

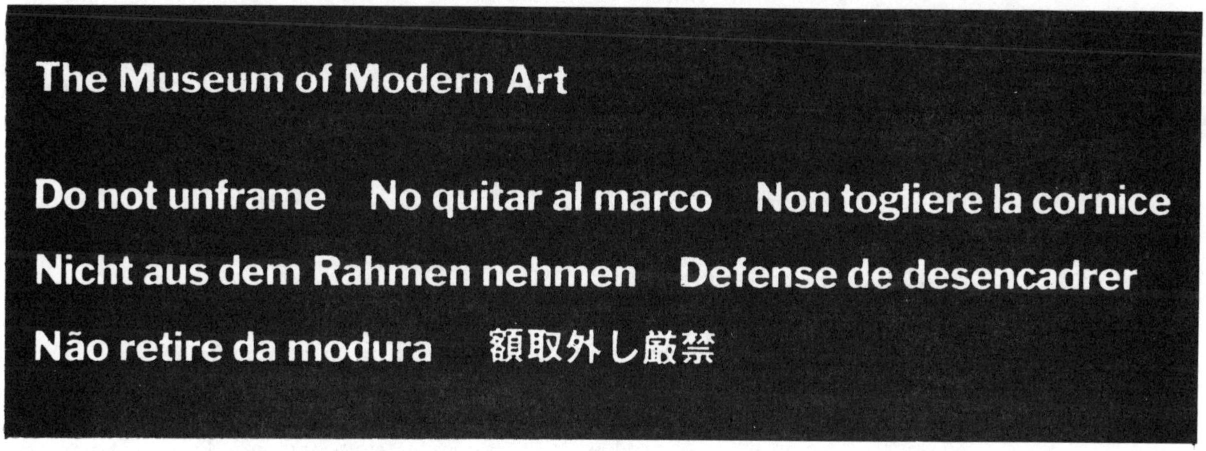

Fig. R.2.
A "Do not unframe" sticker is attached to the backs of paintings loaned from the Museum of Modern Art.

The Museum of Modern Art

Do not unframe   No quitar al marco   Non togliere la cornice

Nicht aus dem Rahmen nehmen   Defense de desencadrer

Não retire da modura   額取外し厳禁

*Fig. R.3.
Masking tape applied to protect the glass on a glazed work during travel must be removed carefully. It should be pulled back parallel to the picture plane to avoid straining the glass.*

for water running to the edge of the glass and penetrating beneath can cause serious damage to the work. Top and bottom edges of each strip of masking tape are turned back against themselves to prevent the tape from adhering to the frames and causing damage, especially to gilt frames, and to provide small tabs to grasp when removing the tape. The tape should be removed by slowly pulling it back parallel (not vertical) to the picture plane, so as to avoid straining and cracking the glass. (See figure R.3.)

For works larger than 25 by 30 inches, it is best to replace the glass with Plexiglas. If this is not practical, the glass should be removed, covered with masking tape, and packed between corrugated cardboard sheets in a separate compartment in the box. Plexiglas should never be used on pastels or charcoals, however, as the static electricity it generates can do serious damage to the surface of these and other works done in friable media. For a work of this nature, the glass can be removed and packed in the manner described above. The work itself should then be protected by a wrapping of nonelectrostatic material, such as glassine paper. The advice of a conservator should be sought on such occasions.

THREE-DIMENSIONAL WORKS: SCULPTURE, CERAMICS, SMALL FRAGILE OBJECTS

Each sculpture, ceramic piece, or other small fragile object must be treated as a special case. The size, weight, and fragility must all be considered. In general, the shipping of fragile pieces, particularly plaster pieces and those with thin, projecting parts, should be avoided.

Unless they are to be packed in the contour method described below, small objects must be completely wrapped with tissue or soft cloth and tied. Projecting parts are padded and wrapped separately, and then the entire object is wrapped to make a large, soft package that will be fully protected against shock. Projecting parts of large sculptures are also wrapped, unless, again, they are to be packed in a braced box, described below.

Packing

BOXES AND PACKING MATERIALS

At the Museum of Modern Art boxes are made of seasoned wood, such as number 2 pine shelving, ¾ to 1 inch thick and free of knots and cross grain. Open crates are never used. In order to allow for proper cushioning, each box must be at least 2¼ inches larger in each dimension than the object it will contain. Coated nails, which have greater resistance to withdrawing, are used in constructing the box, but not for attaching the lid. If the box is to be used for shipment to one place and return, the lid may be screwed into place, using washers to protect the wood. If the box will be used for more than one round trip, the lid should be bolted into place, preferably with 1½-inch bolts and with protective metal plates on the lid and edge of the box. (See figure R.4.) Boxes are lined with waterproof paper, and, for purposes of identification and inventory, each box in a traveling exhibition is numbered and sometimes painted with the same color.

Boxes for domestic or Canadian shipments are stenciled or otherwise marked with the name and address of the originating shipper and of the consignee. (See chapter 8 for the identifying marks to be stenciled on boxes for foreign shipments.) In addition, the following outside markings may be added: "Fragile" and/or the broken wine glass indicating fragility; "This Side Up" and/or arrows indicating the direction in which the box should ride; an umbrella, indicating that protection from the elements is required; "Open This Side"; and the box number. For security reasons, boxes should not be marked "Works of Art," nor should any indication be given of valuable contents.

All loose packing materials—pads, separation boards, braces, battens, etc.—are marked with the box number and the museum number of the work of art for which

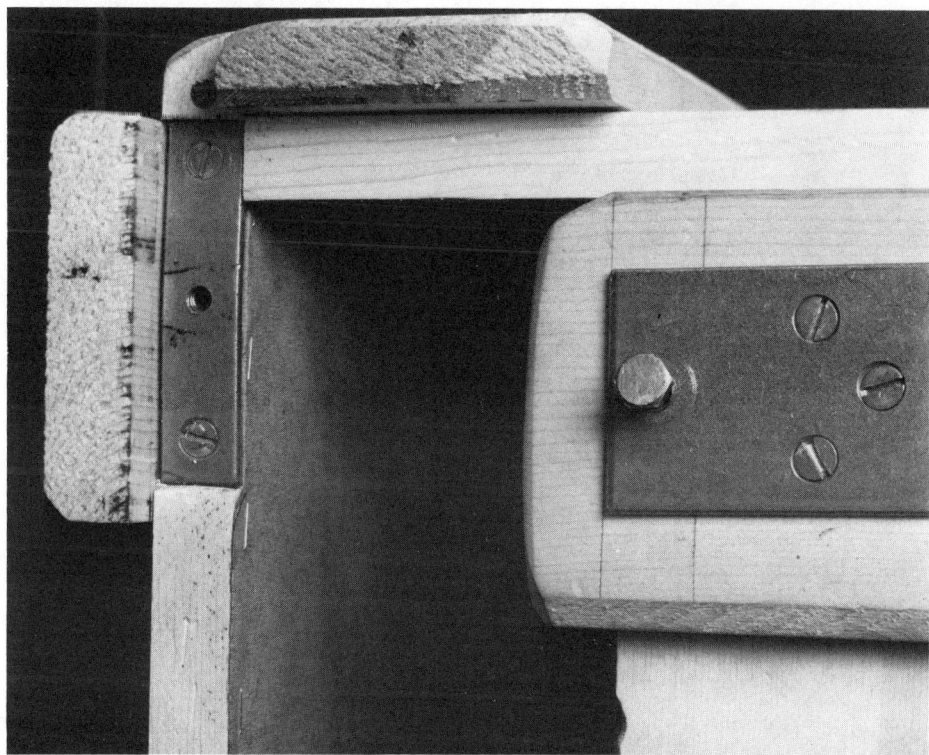

Fig. R.4.
Bolts with protective metal plates are used for securing the lids of boxes that must serve for more than one round trip.

they are designed. Special instructions for unpacking and repacking (e.g., "remove brace A first," "remove bolt A first," etc.) are also marked on the packing materials and on the interior of the box itself. Additional instructions are attached inside the box lid, and a copy is included among the documents accompanying the exhibition. For exhibitions traveling abroad, all instructions must be written in the appropriate foreign language or languages as well as in English. The receiving institution must save all boxes and packing materials for use in repacking. Any worn packing materials should be replaced with new material of the same kind and size and marked appropriately.

TWO-DIMENSIONAL WORKS: PAINTINGS, WATERCOLORS, DRAWINGS, PRINTS, PHOTOGRAPHS

One method for packing a single painting is known as flat packing. In flat packing, pads fitted on the corners of the frame provide a cushion that helps to absorb shock. The pads are fitted diagonally across the corners of the frame and stapled (never tacked) to the back of the frame. These corner pads are made of two layers of ½-inch-thick compressed paper or cellulose wadding or plastic bubble wrap. Polyurethane corner pads can also be used and do not require stapling. (See figure R.5.) Paper-covered excelsior is sometimes used, but it is not generally recommended as it often escapes from the paper wrapping (even when the open ends of the pads are folded back and stapled) and is dusty and dirty. In addition, stray shavings can easily hide in hard-to-see places, where their hygroscopic qualities can cause damage. A strand of excelsior, for example, lodged between the stretcher and canvas of an unbacked painting exerts subtle but definite pressure on the painted surface. Removing such a strand is a delicate operation.

The museum number of the painting and the box number appear on each pad and piece of loose packing material. The box itself is padded at the corners with a cushioning material such as polyurethane or Ethafoam. The museum number of the painting is marked in the bottom of the box, as are directions for placing the painting face up or face down. Paintings are generally placed face down, but there are enough exceptions, usually on account of the frame, to warrant such an indication. After the painting is placed in the box, compressed paper or cellulose wadding or plastic bubble wrap is fitted between the outside edge of the frame and the inside of the box for further cushioning to absorb shocks in transit and protect the frame. Finally, on top of the painting is placed a separation sheet of corrugated cardboard, Fome-Cor board, or Masonite. If there is space between the box lid and the separation sheet, a wood batten, cleated at the ends, is gently pressed into contact with the separation sheet and nailed to the box from the inside. These nails are not driven in completely; the nail heads are left slightly raised to make the removal of the battens easier when the box is unpacked. The box lid is then screwed or bolted into place. (See figure R.6.)

The flat-packing method can also be used for packing two or more paintings in one box, providing the paintings are of a similar size. A separation sheet is placed between each painting. These sheets and all loose packing materials are marked with the museum number of the painting for which they are designed, with the box number, and with any special packing instructions. Not more than five paintings should be packed in one box. (See figure 7.2.)

A more elaborate method for packing a single painting, and one particularly recommended for paintings traveling long distances or as part of an overseas shipment,

*Fig. R.5.
Frames of works that are to travel must be protected by corner pads, such as the convenient fitted polyurethane pads shown here.*

involves the use of a box padded with hard rubber. For this method, hard rubber strips about 5 inches wide, covered with canton flannel, are firmly attached diagonally across the bottom corners of the box and then up the sides. For a large painting, additional pads may be attached along the sides and bottom of the box. The bottom of the box, again, shows the museum number of the painting and instructions for placing it face down. After the painting is placed in the box, battens, padded with hard rubber and cleated at the ends, are laid across the narrow dimension of the box, with the pads resting across the back of the painting to hold it firmly in place. By this method, the painting is completely floated, and no additional pads are needed. (See figures R.7–8.) Or canton-flannel-covered hard rubber strips may be firmly attached across the narrow dimension of the inside of the box lid. This method is preferable, for not only is the painting held firmly in place when the lid is secured, but there are no loose packing materials of any kind.

Paintings of varying sizes may be packed in a single box by using the tray-packing method. The corners of the frame of each painting are padded as described above. The largest work is packed face down in the bottom of the box, and a sheet of corrugated cardboard, Fome-Cor board, or Masonite is placed on top of it. The wooden tray unit is attached to supporting battens that are cut to fit the inside of the box. The smaller painting is then packed in the tray in the same manner. (See figure R.9.) The same

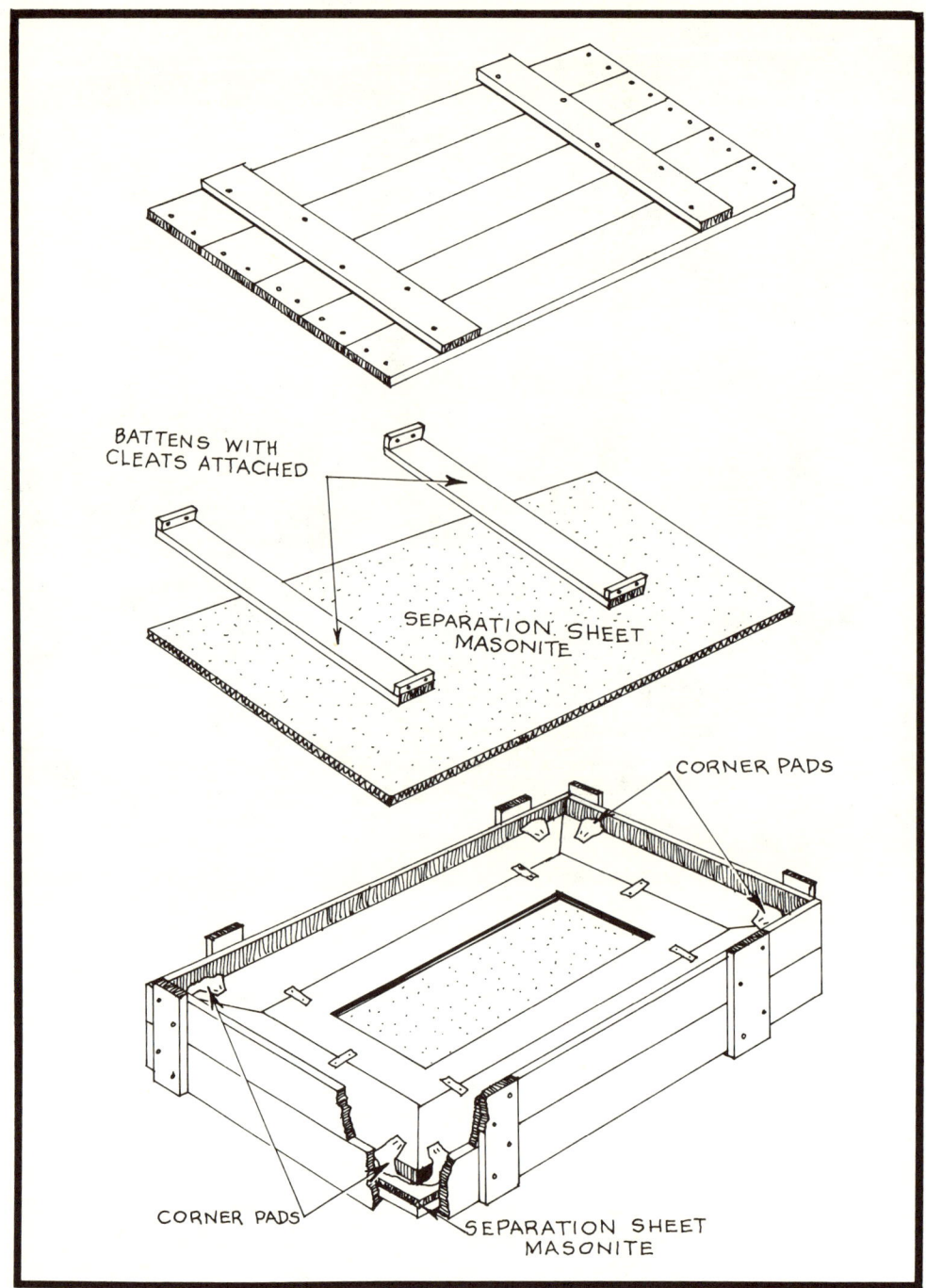

Fig. R.6.
This diagram from the Museum of Modern Art shows one way to pack a single painting with a simple frame in a flat pack. Each corner of the frame is padded, and the painting itself is protected, front and back, by separation sheets of Masonite or heavy cardboard. For ornate and/or heavy frames, additional cushioning should be placed between the frame and the edge of the box.

Figs. R.7–8.
A box padded with hard rubber strips affords the best protection to a single painting traveling long distances or overseas. The painting is held firmly in place by pads attached to the bottom and sides of the box and to battens secured after the painting is in place.

basic tray method can be used with the pads permanently fastened to the box and tray, as described in the previous paragraph for packing a single painting. (See figures R.10–13.) Two paintings of similar size can be packed in one box by using padded battens to separate them. (See figures R.14–17.)

The slide (sometimes called groove) method of packing is by far the best method for packing several paintings, or a single large painting, in one box, for it requires the least amount of handling and gives the greatest amount of protection to the works of art. The floor of the box is mounted on a layer of hard rubber that acts as a shock mount. Then individual wooden grooves (also called tracks), padded with carpeting or heavy felt, are constructed to fit the frames of individual paintings and firmly attached to the top and bottom of the box. Each work will thus slide into its own compartment and fit snugly—tight enough to prevent vibration but not so tight as to put undue strain on the frame or stretcher. The closed end of the groove at the back of the box should also be padded with carpet or felt-covered hard rubber. The end of the groove that remains open is clearly marked with the museum number of the painting for which it is designed and with an indication of the direction the painting should face in the box. Pads of hard rubber covered with canton flannel are attached to the lid or door of the box so they touch the outside edges of all the frames in the box. The paintings are thus completely cushioned against jarring in transit. (See figure R.18.) To assure that the paintings ride on edge when traveling, arrows and directions such as "This Side Up" should be clearly marked on the outside of the box.

The slide method for packing paintings may be used for packing watercolors or other works of art on paper. Or, if small enough and of similar size, these works can be packed in a double- or triple-decker slide box. (See figure R.19.) Note that the upper deck has a shock mount exactly like the lower deck. If the frames have delicate surfaces (such as Plexiglas wraparound frames), the felt-lined grooves may be covered with polyethylene sheeting to prevent abrasion.

Another method for packing works of art on paper again involves the use of a box padded with hard rubber. Hard rubber strips are attached across the bottom and sides of the box. These are covered with a liner of fiberboard, preferably Masonite, which makes it possible for a group of pictures to ride on one surface with their weight distributed evenly. The works of art are either individually wrapped in cardboard slipcases or separated by sheets of corrugated cardboard or Fome-Cor board. Or, up to five works of a similar size may be wrapped in heavy paper and the package sealed with tape. An Upson board or Homasote separation board, marked with the appropriate box and museum numbers, is then inserted between each package as it is placed on the Masonite. If pictures of various sizes are packed in one case, all empty spaces at the sides and top of the box are filled with compressed paper or cellulose wadding or plastic bubble wrap to prevent shifting. (See figure R.20.)

THREE-DIMENSIONAL WORKS: SCULPTURE, CERAMICS, SMALL FRAGILE OBJECTS

Each three-dimensional work presents its own problems, but certain general methods of packing are used.

Small solid objects, wrapped in tissue or soft cloth, can be nested or floated in thick layers of expanded polystyrene pellets in a wooden box. (See figures R.21 and 7.4.) Small fragile objects, wrapped and packed in a wooden box as above, should be floated

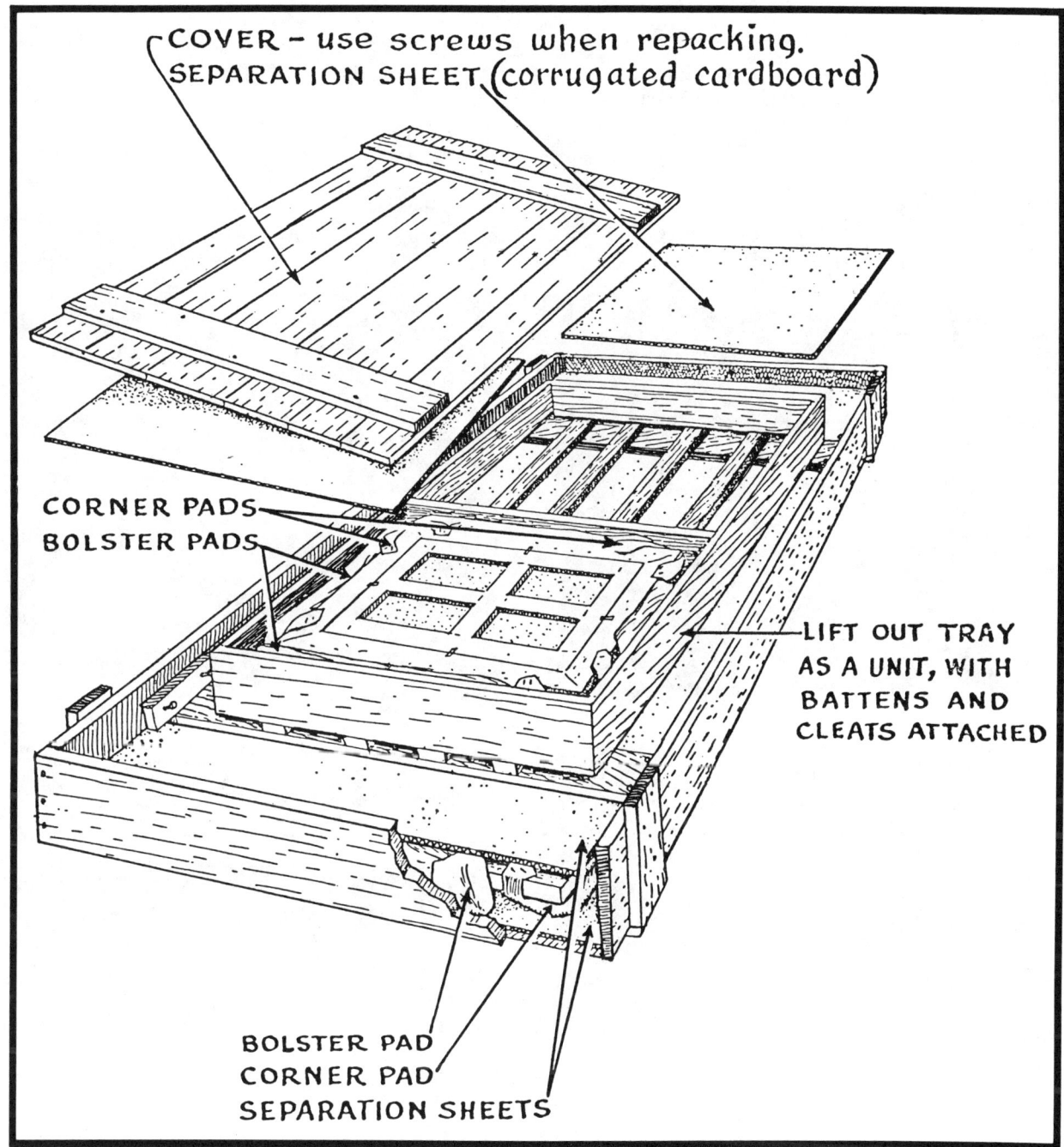

Fig. R.9.
The tray-packing method is used for packing paintings of various sizes. The largest painting is placed on the bottom, and smaller paintings are fixed in trays attached to supporting battens. The frame of each painting is protected with corner and bolster pads and separation sheets front and back. From Robert P. Sugden, Packing Instructions for Paintings: For Supervisors and for Packers *(New York: Metropolitan Museum of Art, n.d.).*

378 SPECIFIC APPLICATIONS

Figs. R.10–13.
The tray-packing method can also be adapted to a
box padded with hard rubber strips. Pads attached to
the bottom and sides of the box and to the inside
of each tray unit as well as to all supporting interior
battens hold each painting securely in place.

Figs. R.14–17.
Two paintings of a similar size can be packed in one box by using padded battens. The pads in this box are made of Ethafoam. Note that the paintings here are wrapped first in glassine and then loosely in plastic, though the plastic is not essential, since the box is lined with waterproof paper.

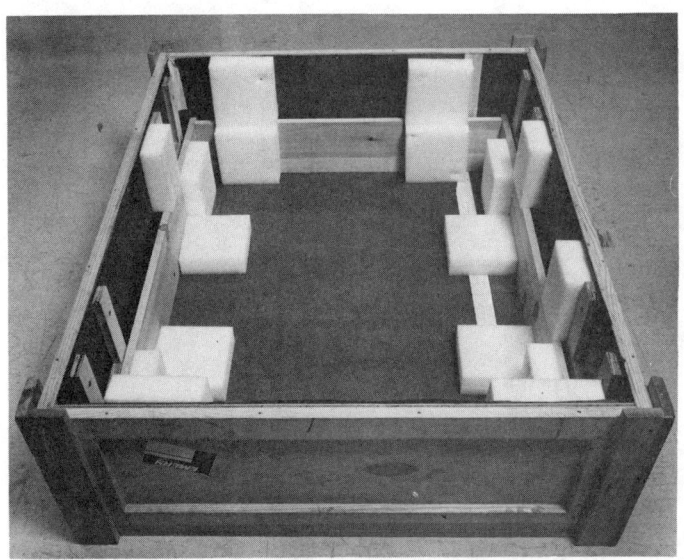

Fig. R.18.
The slide box is an excellent method for packing several paintings. Note the rubber shock mount framing the entire box. Each painting slides into its own padded, clearly marked groove.

Fig. R.19.
A double-decker slide box may be used for shipping framed works of the same size. Again note the shock mounts, the individually marked padded grooves, and the padding on the lid that will hold the works in place when the lid is secured.

Fig. R.20. Watercolors, drawings, and prints may be packed in a box lined with hard rubber strips. The works are protected either by individual slip cases or by heavy paper wrappings.

in an additional, outer wooden box packed firmly with expanded polystyrene pellets. Peanut-shaped pellets are preferred to flakes, strands, or beads, as they have a better locking action and are, therefore, less apt to settle and cause shifting within the box. The lid of the inner container is marked to indicate the contents, the museum number, and any special instructions regarding the piece.

More satisfactory, however, is the contour method. For small solid objects, sections of hard rubber, sometimes in combination with foam rubber and plastic foams, are constructed to fit the shape and size of the work, then covered with canton flannel and permanently attached to the sides, bottom, and lid of the box. The object is completely floated, and there are no loose packing materials. For small fragile objects, trays are made of wood and permanently fitted with layers of Ethafoam into which the shapes of the individual objects are cut. It may be necessary to cover the Ethafoam with canton flannel to protect objects with delicate surfaces. Lids, hinged to the trays, are packed on the inside with bonded foam covered with canton flannel. On the outside of the lids are diagrams, photographs, and museum numbers of the objects that show what each tray contains and how to repack it. Again, the objects are completely floated,

*Fig. R.21.
A ceramic bowl may be wrapped in tissue paper and floated in expanded polystyrene flakes.*

and there are no loose packing materials. The trays slide into an outer box. (See figure R.22.)

Large pieces of sculpture must stand on their bases in their packing boxes, in the position in which they are exhibited. The bottom of the box is fitted with a shock mount as described for slide boxes. Then contoured braces are constructed to hold the objects firmly in place. The back part of each brace is permanently fixed in the back of the box. The front part slides out between tracks, which are attached to the sides of the box; it is held in position when the lid is attached. Each removable brace is marked with the museum number of the sculpture, the box number, and special instructions for removing and replacing it. Parallel lines, for example, running across the end of the brace and the edge of the box, might show where and how each brace is fitted. The edges of the braces that are in contact with the sculpture are padded with carpeting, heavy felt, hard rubber, or bonded foam covered with canton flannel, depending upon the individual sculpture. (See figure R.23.) In order to keep the sculpture upright on its base, the outside of the packing box should be clearly marked with arrows and "This Side Up."

R: PREPARING ART EXHIBITIONS FOR TRAVEL

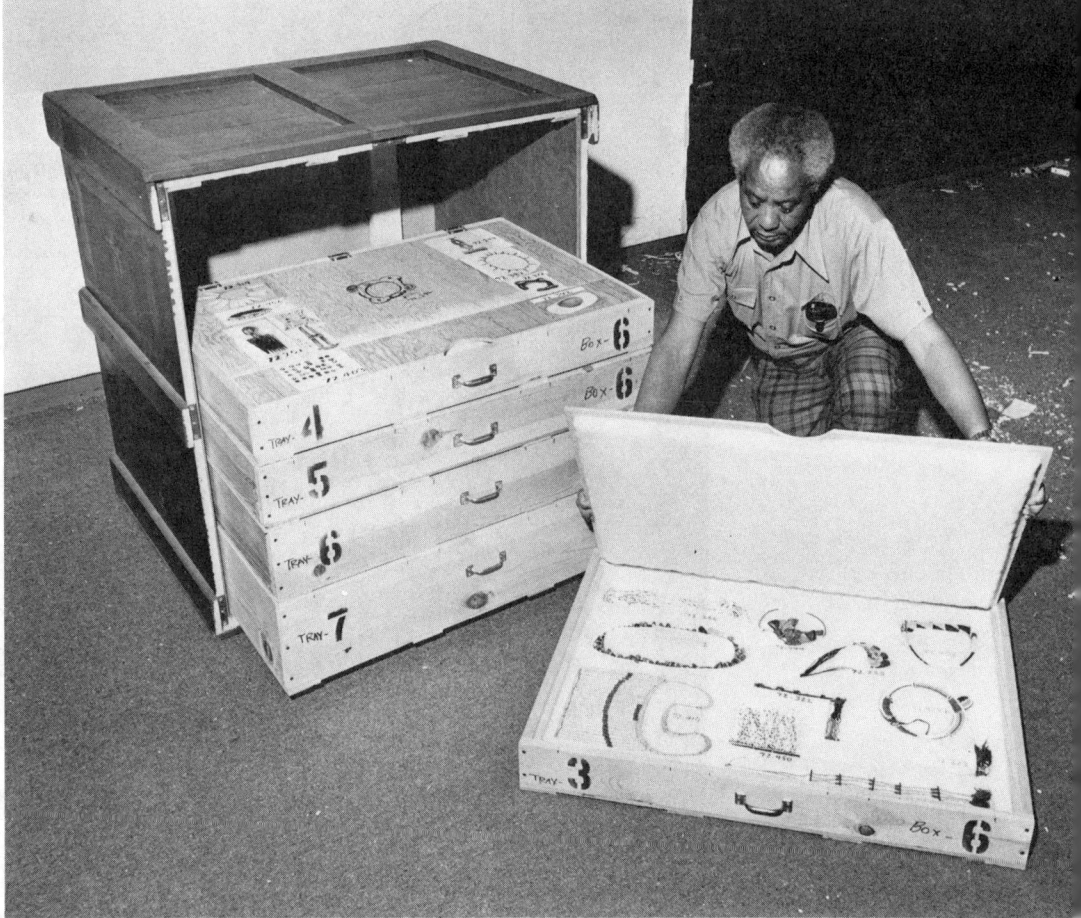

Fig. R.22. The contour-tray method of packing provides excellent protection for small, fragile objects. Each piece is fitted securely into a space cut to its shape in a layer of Ethafoam. Note the photographs and museum numbers of the objects marked on the top of the tray lid.

Documents

For each traveling exhibition, the originating institution prepares unpacking and repacking instructions including special instructions regarding glass, a checklist, a box list, condition records, condition diagrams and/or photographs, and special information regarding installation. Even single works of art require the preparation of this information. For exhibitions traveling abroad, a box list serves as an invoice for customs and must include, in addition to the number and contents of each box, individual and total values and the dimensions and net and gross weight of the box. All documents and instructions must be in the appropriate foreign language, or languages, as well as English, and dimensions noted in centimeters and kilograms as well as inches and pounds. (See chapter 8 for information on additional documents required by U.S. Customs.)

UNPACKING AND PACKING INSTRUCTIONS

If the shipment is small, most of the instructions for unpacking and repacking may be incorporated with the markings inside the box. For larger shipments, however, or unusual and complicated packing, instructions are prepared for each box and copies

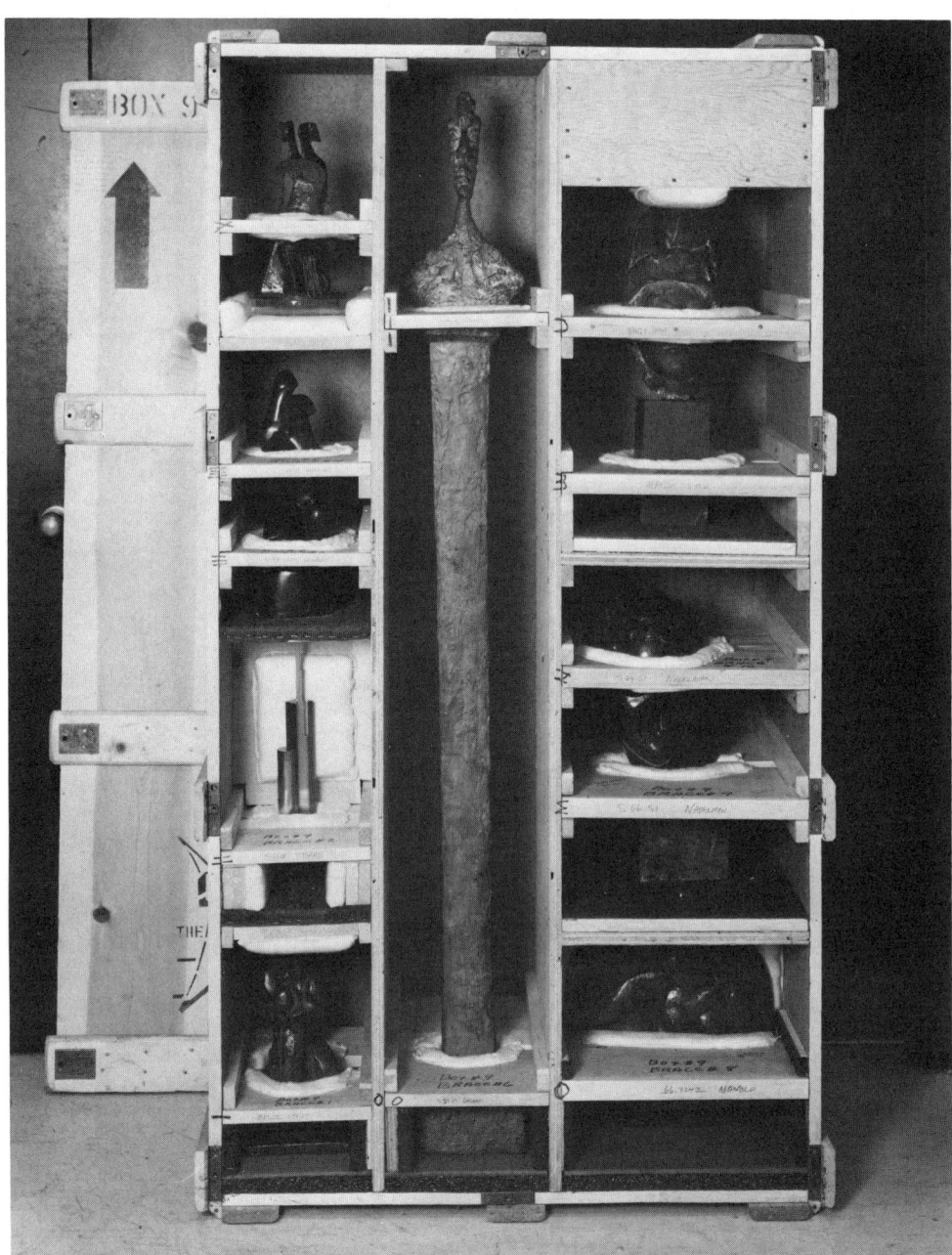

Fig. R.23.
Sculpture of various sizes and shapes may be packed in individual compartments within a larger box. A layer of medium-density foam rubber serves as a shock mount at the bottom of the box. The surfaces on which the pieces rest are padded with carpeting or cotton-covered foam; heavy pieces rest on Masonite. The front halves of the braces slide out between tracks fastened to the sides of the compartments. Each removable brace is marked with the museum number and the name of the artist of the sculpture for which it was designed. The contoured edges of all braces, where they fit against the sculpture, are padded with cotton-covered foam. Large, heavy sculpture should be packed in individual boxes using this method of packing.

```
AMERICAN ART SINCE 1945        R-33                      1975-76

An exhibition circulated by the Museum of Modern Art, New York, New York.
_____

UNPACKING INSTRUCTIONS:  Box # 15

1. Carefully remove braces "A" and "B" releasing LIPTON 550.54.  (see illustration)

2. Carefully remove STANKIEWICZ 11.61 from bottom slot.

3. Return braces "A" and "B" into their slots, close lid and save all
   box bolts for repacking.
_____

PACKING INSTRUCTIONS:  Box 15

1. Carefully insert LIPTON 550.54 into position in slot.  The point of the
   work should be placed towards the back of box and below rear brace "B"
   as illustrated.

2. Secure LIPTON sculpture 550.54 with braces "A" and "B".  When inserting
   brace "B" adjust star shaped appendage in middle of sculpture so that
   it rests on tongue of brace "B".  This will avoid vibration of piece
   during transport.  (see illustration).

3. Return STANKIEWICZ 11.61 into its cushioned slot.

4. Close outer lid and bolt securely.
_____

INCLUDED IN BOX # 15

550.54       LIPTON
11.61        STANKIEWICZ
_____

WGHT:        N-187
             G-440

SIZE:        L-34" x H-46" x W-41"
```

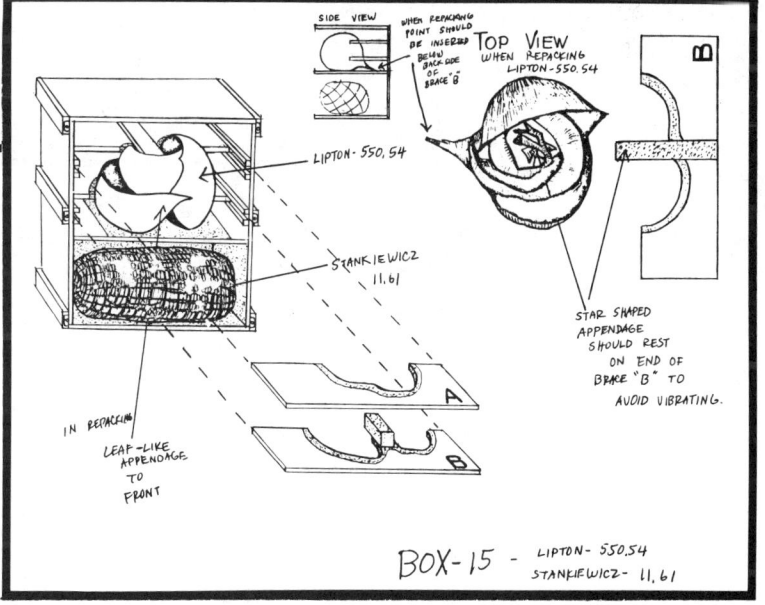

Figs. R.24–25.
Unpacking and packing instructions are part of the documents accompanying a traveling exhibition. They should include sizes and weights of the box and may be supplemented by diagrams, if needed, as in this set of packing instructions for Box 15 of "American Art since 1945," an exhibition circulated by the Museum of Modern Art.

SPECIFIC APPLICATIONS

The Museum of Modern Art

11 West 53 Street, New York, N.Y. 10019 Tel. 956-6100 Cable: Modernart

AMERICAN ART SINCE 1945, Selected From the Collection of The Museum of Modern Art

An exhibition organized by The Museum of Modern Art, New York, New York

CHECKLIST:

- 45 Paintings
- 13 Sculpture
- 1 Relief in 2 parts
- 2 Lithographs
- 1 Sculpture maquette

All works are in the Collection of The Museum of Modern Art or promised gifts.

MUSEUM NUMBER	ARTIST	TITLE/DATE/MEDIUM CREDIT/PHOTO CREDIT	FRAME DIMENSIONS Unframed/Framed H x W	BOX NO.
664.67	ALBERS, Josef	Homage to the Square: Broad Call. 1967. Oil on composition board. The Sidney and Harriet Janis Collection. Photo credit: Mathews-483	48 x 48"	23
495.69 a-c	BAER, Jo	Primary Light Group: Red, Green, Blue. 1964-65. Oil and synthetic polymer paint on 3 canvases. Philip Johnson Fund. Photo credit: Mathews-3684	60 3/8 x 60 1/4"(.a-red) 60 3/8 x 60 3/8"(.b-green) 60 1/4 x 60 1/8"(.c-blue)	19
386.70	BAILEY, Malcolm	Hold, Separate but Equal. (1969). Synthetic polymer paint, presstype, watercolor and enamel on composition board. Mr. and Mrs. John R. Jakobson Fund. Photo credit: Mathews-4780	84 x 48"	11
1075.69	BANNARD, Walter Darby	Mandragora Number 3. (1969). Oil on canvas. Given anonymously. Photo credit: Mathews-4200	66 1/8 x 99 1/8"	10
153.62	BOURGEOIS, Louise	Sleeping Figure, II. (1959). Bronze (variant of the wood sculpture of 1950). Purchase. Photo credit: Sunami-17.812	75 1/4 x 17 1/2 x 12 1/8"	24

Fig. R.26. Checklists are also part of the documents accompanying a traveling exhibition. This first page of the checklist for the Museum of Modern Art's "American Art since 1945" includes, for each object, the museum number, artist, title, date, medium, credit, photo credit, framed size or height and weight, and box number.

attached to the inside of each lid. These instructions include as separate items information regarding the handling of glazed paintings and pictures and the use of masking tape on glass. Copies of these instructions should be included with other documents accompanying the exhibition. (See figures R.24–25.)

CHECKLISTS AND CONDITION RECORDS

Checklists are prepared for all shipments containing several works of art. The checklist includes the artist, title, date, and medium of each work, and it is helpful to add the museum number, lender, and box number, particularly if the exhibition is being sent to a number of institutions. A checklist used for the Museum of Modern Art circulating exhibitions includes the museum number, artist, title, date, medium, credit, photo credit, framed size (for two-dimensional works), height and weight (for three-dimensional works), and box number. (See figure R.26.)

R: PREPARING ART EXHIBITIONS FOR TRAVEL

The Museum of Modern Art
11 West 53 Street, New York, N.Y. 10019 Tel. 956-6100 Cable: Modernart

REPORT ON THE CONDITION OF THE CIRCULATING EXHIBITION:_____

upon its receipt in _____ for booking _____

      IMPORTANT: This report must be returned at once to the above address
      as soon as the exhibition has been unpacked and checked.

Please answer each of the following (use additional paper when necessary):

1. Are any cases damaged?_____ Can you fix?_____
   How many bolts are missing?_____

2. When received, was exhibition packed according to packing instructions on inside of cover?_____

3. According to check list, _____ items are missing.

4. Are any frames damaged?_____

5. When Condition Record Sheets have been provided, compare them to the respective works and note any change in condition on the Condition Record Sheet as well as on verso of this report. List all damages.

   If you believe damage occured in transit, please wire us immediately. Contact carrier and forward the necessary joint inspection report to us.

   NOTE: Before hanging, check hanging devices and secure any which are weak.

PERSON IN CHARGE (print):_____
SIGNATURE:_____ TITLE:_____
ORGANIZATION:_____ TEL:_____
ADDRESS:_____

1/70

Fig. R.27. Condition records are also included in the documents accompanying a traveling exhibition. This form (8½ by 11 in.) is used for all exhibitions circulated by the Museum of Modern Art.

The checklist may include space for the receiving institution to indicate the condition of each piece upon its receipt and departure. Sometimes the institution originating the exhibition includes on the checklist a brief description of condition. However, it is better to prepare a complete condition record for each work. The Museum of Modern Art checklist includes a diagram showing the location of all marks, spots, and damages as they appear at the time the work leaves the museum. A good photocopy of a photograph often makes an excellent diagram on which to note these conditions. In addition, for paintings and sculpture, an album of condition photographs taken before the works leave the Museum of Modern Art travels with the exhibition. Each exhibitor is requested to check the condition of the works upon arrival and departure against the original condition and to report any changes. (See figure R.27.) This running record greatly facilitates the processing of insurance claims should any damages occur. Whether or not a checklist includes space for condition records, it is important that obvious changes in condition be reported to the originating museum immediately. If the material in the exhibition is available for sale, instructions for handling the sales can be attached to the checklist.

Bibliography

United Nations Educational, Scientific and Cultural Organization. *Temporary and Travelling Exhibitions.* Museums and Monuments 10. Paris: UNESCO, 1963.

THE IDEAL CONTAINER FOR TRAVEL OF HUMIDITY-SENSITIVE COLLECTIONS

NATHAN STOLOW

If a work of art is acclimatized to a fixed relative humidity and temperature in a museum and is then shipped to another museum, for reasons of preservation it is important to maintain the same environmental conditions. The transit stage for a work of art often may be lengthy, as in international exhibitions, and cases of works may be exposed to unusual weather conditions and unsatisfactory warehousing. The effects of variations of relative humidity and external temperature upon internal conditions in a sealed case containing humidity-sensitive works of art have been studied (see the bibliography), and, fortunately, there are now means and methods for maintaining constant conditions during transit.

The specifications described below are for the transport of the most valuable collections of works of art, where cost is secondary to maximum preservation. In more ordinary situations, some of the conditions may be modified for reasons of economy. In such instances, the use of silica gel, recording instruments, and accompanying personnel may be omitted (items 6, 8, part of 11 concerning escort, 15, and 17 below).

Specifications and Procedures

1. Records should be available indicating environmental conditions (relative humidity and temperature) to which the works of art have been initially exposed in the museum. The same conditions should be specified for exhibition in the borrowing institution. The system of packing and the mode of transportation must be adjusted to maintain the specified relative humidity (R.H.) and temperature in transit.

2. All container materials must be preconditioned (seasoned) to the same level of R.H. and temperature as for the works of art to be transported. Thus, if the R.H. and temperature are 50 percent and 20° C. (68° F.) respectively, then the wood, plywood, insulating boards, and papers should likewise be kept in such an environment for two to three weeks or longer prior to use. (See figure S.1.)

3. The case should be constructed of plywood (water-impervious adhesives) of ¼ inch to ½ inch thickness, reinforced on the exterior with sufficient pine wood battens to provide rigidity. The lid should close down firmly against rubber gaskets by means of screws, bolts, or other positive locking devices. The case should be made as airtight as possible. The exterior should be painted with a waterproof paint, and labels should be stenciled on, rather than fixed with staples.

4. The shape of the case should be as "cubical" as possible to conform to desirable temperature-retaining properties, i.e., to have a minimum external surface for a given total weight. (See note 1.)

Fig. S.1. Effect of R.H. on moisture content (EMC = equilibrium moisture content) of typical packing materials. Data for curves 2, 5, 6, 7, 8, 9, 10, 11 from author's laboratory. Legend: 1. wood; 2. Ten-test (compressed fiberboard of soft wood fibers, no binders, 0.5 in. thick, density 0.28 gm./c.c., manufactured by Canadian International Paper Company, Gatineau, Quebec, Canada); 3. kraft paper; 4. newsprint paper; 5. two-ply kraft paper with bitumen sandwich, thickness 0.018 cm., density 0.75 gm./c.c.; 6. British Columbia fir plywood, three-ply, synthetic glue binder; 7. Homasote board, compressed paper fibers, 0.5 in. thick, density 0.43 gm./c.c.; 8. Masonite board, a dense compressed fiberboard; 9. cotton; 10. linen; 11. Styrofoam, an expanded polystyrene insulating board of 2 in. thickness, density 0.02 gm./c.c.

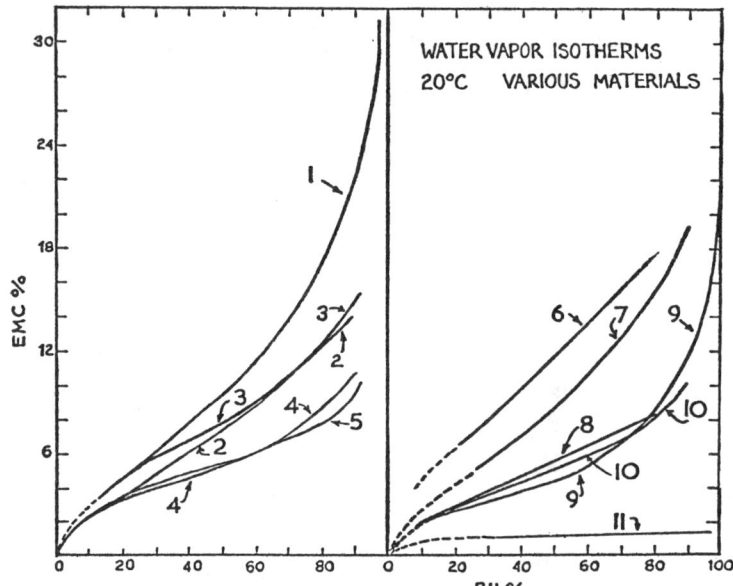

5. The immediate inside surfaces of the case should be lined with heavy-gauge polyethylene film to act as a water and vapor barrier. Any seams should be either heat sealed or taped—but not stapled.

6. Silica gel system: The inside of the case should be lined with an expanded foamed plastic, e.g., polystyrene foam (or polyvinyl chloride foam) of at least 2 inches (5 cm.) thickness on all six interior faces. If these boards of plastic are carefully cut, they will hold snugly in position. Two screened silica gel panels should be mounted on the two largest vertical interior surfaces, next to the foamed plastic. To buffer the humidity changes that may occur, as much silica gel as possible should be used. (See note 2 and figure S.2.) Trays and packing devices should be placed inside the case so as to permit continuous free circulation of air between the exposed silica gel surfaces and the supported works of art. The latter should *not* be wrapped in polyethylene, wax paper, or other moisture-impeding films. Prior to packing the works, the silica gel, trays, and packing devices (if they are of wood) should be preconditioned for, say, three weeks to the desired level of R.H. and temperature (e.g., 50 percent R.H. and 20° C. [68° F.]). The conditioning of the silica gel is most important; at 50 percent R.H., it should contain 30 percent by weight of moisture (dry weight basis).

7. Fiberboard system: If it is desired, the cases may be lined with preconditioned fiberboard (Cellotex, Ten-test, Homasote, etc.) instead of foamed plastic, in which case the silica gel may be omitted. The fiberboard itself acts as a humidity buffer. However, the application of silica gel panels as in item 6 above does give better humidity control. To be effective as a thermal barrier (heat insulator), the fiberboard should be at least double thickness, 2.5 cm. or greater.

8. Provision should be made for installing within the case a recording hygrothermograph with a seven- or eight-day movement (or longer) that has been recently calibrated to read R.H. and temperature accurately. It may be feasible to introduce small strips of

*Fig. S.2.
Schematic drawing of plywood case containing Styrofoam insulators and screened silica gel panels. These panels are made of ¼-inch plywood and covered with polyethylene sheeting prior to fixing the ¼-inch plywood dividers. The chambers (also ¼ inch deep) are filled with preconditioned silica gel. Aluminum or fiber glass screening is then stapled over to retain the gel in position. To precondition the silica gel, which is initially dry, it must be exposed for approximately two weeks in shallow pans to the required environment, e.g., 50 percent R.H. and 20° C. (68° F.). It will gain approximately 30 percent by weight. This, then, will be the preconditioned silica gel. The silica gel, 3 to 8 mesh size—grade 308—may be obtained from Grace & Company, Davison Chemical Division, Baltimore, Md. 21203.*

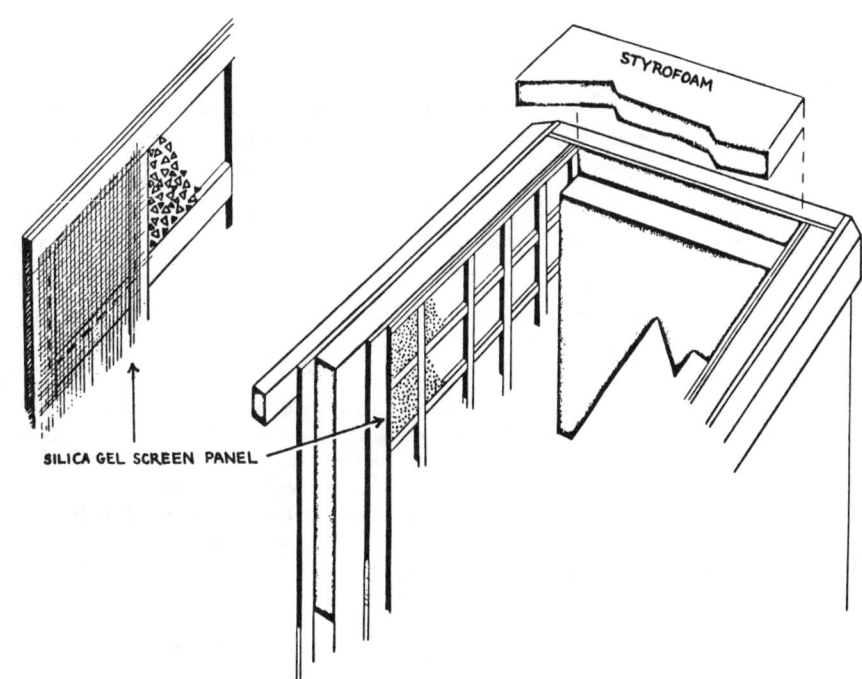

cobalt salt indicator papers to indicate R.H., although they do not give a time record of the events within the case.

9. The paintings or other objects should be packed in the case at the level of R.H. and temperature previously decided upon for conditioning.

10. The cases so packed should be handled by experienced, trusted personnel.

11. The external temperatures at all points (truck, train, railroad station, airplane, ship, etc.) should be specified and maintained at 20° C. ± 3° (68° F. ± 5°). It may prove useful to escort the shipment and to monitor the external conditions with a portable hygrothermograph.

12. In the event of air travel, the cabin must be *pressurized* as well as temperature controlled. Ambient R.H.'s in aircraft are often dangerously low, and this may cause replacement of air within the case when the external pressure changes.

13. Excessive vibration and shocks should be avoided. If necessary, blankets, foam rubber pads, or corrugated cardboard may be placed around or near the cases.

14. If through misadventure the cases have suffered a change in temperature on arrival beyond the range of 20° C. ± 3°, then it should be specified that the cases remain unopened for at least twenty-four hours at the destination (where the R.H. is also 50 percent and the temperature 20° C.). If this is not done, condensation or thermal or humidity "shock" may be experienced. In any event, it is prudent to specify that the cases remain unopened for twenty-four hours on arrival at the destination of the exhibiting center to allow for temperature equilibrium.

15. The opened cases, packing materials, etc., should be stored under the same conditions, 50 percent R.H. and 20° C. (68° F.), and not removed to a totally different environment (e.g., a warehouse or basement). The silica gel panels should be taken out of their cases and directly exposed to the environment so that their moisture content may be restored if necessary.

16. The return shipment should be followed through in the same manner as above.

17. The R.H. records for the transit should be incorporated into the condition reports and other documentation pertaining to the traveling exhibition.

18. Loan contracts and agreements should clearly specify methods of packing, control, and transportation. Provision should be made for consultation regarding alternative methods of packing, transportation, and care in transit. (See chapters 6, 7, and 8.)

Notes:

1. The assessment of thermal properties may be obtained from the relationship

$$t_{0.5} = \frac{0.69 \, Hl}{KA}$$

where K = thermal conductivity of case in calories meters/hr. m.^{2} °C.,
H = thermal (heat) capacity of case and contents in kg. calories/°C.,
A = average surface area of case in square meters,
l = thickness of case walls in meters,
$t_{0.5}$ = time in hours for the case to reach half of the total temperature change.

Therefore, to increase the half-time factor ($t_{0.5}$) as much as possible, one must strive for low values of K, low surface areas, and thick case walls. Some typical data are given below (tables 1 and 2).

TABLE 1

Thermal Conductivity, Specific Heats, and Densities of Typical Packaging Materials Used for Works of Art
(under standard conditions*)

Material	Density gm./cm.^{3}	Thermal Conductivity K† Btu in hr. ft.^{2} °F.	kg. cal. m. hr. m^2 °C.	Specific Heat Φ Btu lb. °F.	kg. cal. kg. °C.
White pine (across grain)	0.45	0.78	0.097	0.33	0.33
Plywood (Douglas fir)	0.57	0.80	0.099	0.35	0.40
Oak (and hardwoods)	0.51	1.02	0.127	0.57	0.57
Corkboard (no binder)	0.10	0.26	0.031	0.43	0.43
Ten-test (aspen fibers)‡	0.28	0.35	0.043	0.25	0.35
Cellotex (vegetable fibers)§	0.28	0.33	0.041	0.25	0.25
Homasote (paper pulp)‖	0.43	0.40	0.050	—	—
Masonite (dense wood fibers)#	1.02	0.33	0.041	0.34	0.34
Styrofoam (expanded polystyrene)**	0.019	0.25	0.031	0.27	0.27
Klegecell (expanded polyvinyl chloride)††	0.040	0.21	0.026	—	—
Silica gel	1.69	0.59	0.073	0.19	0.19

* The "standard conditions" referred to are generally 65 percent R.H. and 20° C.

† 1 Btu in./hr. ft.^{2} °F. = 0.124 kg. cal. m./hr. m.^{2} °C. The values of K and Φ have been obtained from various sources including W. H. Severns and J. R. Fellows, *Air Conditioning and Refrigeration* (New York, 1958); and D. F. Miner and J. B. Seastone, eds., *Handbook of Engineering Materials* (New York, 1955). The specific heat for plywood is estimated at 0.35 and that of silica gel at 0.19.

‡ Ten-test: a compressed fiberboard of soft wood fibers, 0.5 inch thick, marketed in Canada.

§ Cellotex: a fiberboard product marketed in the United States; in sheets 4 feet by 8 feet by 0.5 inch and composed essentially of matted vegetable fibers; quite similar to Ten-test.

‖ Homasote: a compressed pulpboard product marketed in the United States; in sheet form of sizes 4 feet by 8 feet and larger, and of thicknesses 0.5 inch and greater.

Masonite: a compressed fiberboard of high density; composed of "exploded" wood fibers.

** Styrofoam: an expanded polystyrene board marketed in the United States.

†† Klegecell: a type of expanded polyvinyl chloride foam of French manufacture.

TABLE 2

Calculation of Effective Thermal Conductivity K at Half-Time for Cooling Cycles 21° C. to 4° C.

Description	A m.^{2}	l m.	H* kg. cal./°C.	$t_{0.5}$ hrs.	K kg. cal. m. hr. m.^{2} °C.
Plywood case (empty)	2.8	0.015	9.7	0.5	0.072
Plywood case with two layers Ten-test (2.5 cm.)	2.6	0.04	15.6	2.0	0.082
Plywood case with two layers Ten-test (2.5 cm.) with two silica gel panels	2.5	0.05	21.0	3.5	0.075
Plywood case with 5.1 cm. Styrofoam with two silica gel panels	2.4	0.075	15.6	4.0	0.084
Pine case with two layers Ten-test (2.5 cm.)	1.8	0.05	11.8	3.0	0.075

* Included in each experiment is the thermal capacity of the Fuess recorder calculated to be approximately 0.3 kg. cal./°C.

2. The amount of silica gel required for a compactly packed case may be roughly gauged from this equation:

$$R_2 = R_1 + \frac{0.063 [T_2 - T_1]}{0.18W + 0.6S}$$

where R_1, T_1 = initial case relative humidity and temperature (°C.), respectively,
W = weight (dry basis) of wood (canvas, etc.) (gms.),
S = weight of silica gel (dry basis) (gms.),
T_2 = the external temperature to which the case is subjected,
R_2 = the final internal R.H. after time taken for equalization of case and contents (usually after many hours).

Therefore, to minimize the difference between R_2 and R_1, i.e., to stabilize the R.H., it is necessary to have appreciable quantities of silica gel. For a case of 255 liters volume approximately 6 kilograms of preconditioned silica gel are required.

Bibliography

Beale, Arthur. "Materials and Methods for the Packing and Handling of Ancient Metal Objects." Paper presented at the tenth annual meeting of IIC—American Group, Los Angeles, 1969. In *IIC—American Group Technical Papers from 1968 through 1970.* New York: IIC—American Group, 1970. Pp. 89–95.

Brown, Kenneth. *Package Design Engineering.* New York: Wiley, 1959.

Feller, R. L. "Transportation of a Panel Painting by Courier in Winter." Paper presented at the tenth annual meeting of IIC—American Group, Los Angeles, 1969. In *IIC—American Group Technical Papers from 1968 through 1970.* New York: ICC—American Group, 1970. Pp. 101–02.

Gordon, James B. "Packing of Michelangelo's 'Pieta.'" *Studies in Conservation,* 12:2 (May 1967), 57–69.

Hours, Madeleine. "Rapport sommaire sur la construction et l'utilisation d'un container spécial destiné au transport de la Joconde (Mona Lisa)." *Bulletin du Laboratoire du Musée du Louvre* (Paris), no. 8 (1963), 45–51.

Lefève, R., and D. Thomas-Goorieckx. "Le transport de la châsse de St. Remacle de Stavelot à l'Exposition de Montréal." *Bulletin de l'Institut royal du patrimoine artistique,* 10 (1967–68), 183–88.

Marconi, B. L. "Technical Conditions in the Transport of Polish National Treasures from Canada to Poland." *Ochrona Zabytkow* (Warsaw), 14:1–2 (1961), 33–38 [in Polish, with French summary].

Stolow, Nathan. *Controlled Environment for Works of Art in Transit.* London: Butterworths, for the International Centre for the Study of the Preservation and the Restoration of Cultural Property, 1966.

———. *Fundamental Case Design for Humidity Sensitive Museum Collections.* Reprint from *Museum News,* 44:6 (Feb. 1966).

———. *Report of the Working Group on the Care of Works of Art in Transit.* ICOM Committee for Conservation Meeting, Amsterdam, September 15–19, 1969. Ottawa: ICOM, 1970. Articles by Richard D. Buck, Bo F. D. Wennberg, Kenzo Toishi, and B. L. Marconi.

———. "Some Studies on the Protection of Works of Art during Travel." In *Recent Advances in Conservation: Contributions to the IIC Rome Conference, 1961.* Edited by Garry Thomson. London: Butterworths, 1963. Pp. 9–12.

———. "The Technical Organization of an International Art Exhibition." *Museum,* 21:3 (1968), 182–240.

———, Bo Wennberg, and Peter Cannon-Brookes. *Report of the Working Group on the Care of Works of Art in Transit.* ICOM Committee for Conservation Meeting, Madrid, October 1–8, 1972. Ottawa: ICOM, 1972.

Thomson, Garry. "Relative Humidity—Variation with Temperature in a Case Containing Wood." *Studies in Conservation,* 9 (1964), 153–69.

Toishi, Kenzo. "Humidity Control in a Closed Package." *Studies in Conservation,* 4 (1959), 81–87.

PLANNING AHEAD: THE REGISTRAR'S ROLE IN A BUILDING PROGRAM

DAVID VANCE

Museum buildings are used differently now than in the past. Suddenly (within the last few decades) we are faced with hordes of visitors, fabulous values, temporary installations, traveling shows, and a vogue for museum burglarizing. Today's museum buildings, like factories, must provide for safe, efficient movement of goods. They needn't be any the less beautiful for that.

Why should an article on building programs appear in a book about museum registration methods? Because in many museums the registrar, together with the building superintendent, security chief, conservators, and curators, has to understand the physical operation of the plant. The registrar can be of no greater service to a museum than by helping to plan, design, and supervise a building program, or even a slight remodeling of museum facilities. This is the only time for neat, lasting solutions to handling and security problems. The registrar has a special stake in the design of new facilities since it will determine the physical framework of registration operations and will determine how well the registrar's staff and their successors will be able to do their jobs.

For convenience this article is written as if all handling of exhibition material were the registrar's responsibility. In most museums this is not the case, and the headaches are shared with other departments. In a sense this article is not meant only for registrars and is really addressed "to whom it may concern." It could not have been written without the benefit of years of informal discussion with many different conservators, engineers, architects, building managers, and registrars, all of whom have been generous with their time and knowledge. While this is written with special reference to a registrar's needs in a large art museum, the fundamentals apply as well to smaller institutions and museums of other kinds.

The First Steps

A registrar who does not take the initiative and insist upon being heard may never be consulted about such vitals as loading docks, air-handling systems, and elevators. As the building program gets under way the registrar should learn the chains of command: who are the architects, the contractors, sub- and sub-subcontractors? who is responsible for what? who takes orders from whom? and who knows what? This may be difficult to find out. Become acquainted with key personnel in each organization. Obtain plans of the whole project and keep them up to date. Never take it for granted that drawings are current just because nobody has mentioned that they aren't. **For areas of** particular interest, get hold of shop drawings and learn to read them. Incidentally, this is one of the best ways to cultivate the technicians, who appreciate intelligent interest in their special fields. Their respect and confidence are important. Furthermore, they can help you understand the usually (though not always) compelling reasons for seemingly nonsensical arrangements that will be found in every set of plans.

Merely keeping abreast of the plans is not enough, however. If at all possible, you should keep an eye on the job itself. The organizational web on even a simple project can be so intricate that changes often occur without the knowledge of interested parties. Mistakes happen, too. Sometimes one has to take the responsibility for ordering the work stopped until the boss can be located. It's a great help if the foremen and supervisors know you and respect your judgment.

Storage during a Building Program

To go or to stay? This is one of the worst of many tough choices facing a museum when it remodels. There are risks in moving a museum collection and dangers in leaving it under the same roof with construction work. Special factors in each case determine which is the more to be dreaded. The registrar's recommendations may tip the balance.

Other things being equal, it is probably wiser to move. The hazards in that are well known, while those of staying are easy to underestimate and may come as a rude surprise.

PERMANENT STOREROOMS

If only part of the museum is affected by reconstruction, it may be safe to leave some collections in their regular storage places, somehow crowding in the material that would ordinarily be on exhibition. Often this is the answer. The trouble is that it looks safer than it is. The greatest dangers are fire and unauthorized entry, either of which may precipitate the other. Construction crews cannot be screened by the museum. Theft and vandalism on their part are not unknown. Then, too, the building trades take people into unlikely places—hollow walls, ceiling spaces, and air ducts—in pursuit of pipes and conduits. Breaking through a wall to reach some fixture is commonplace and usually innocent behavior. But the other side of the wall may be your storeroom. Always keep at least two fireproof barriers between any storeroom and the nearest demolition or construction. And inspect the storeroom often.

Local flooding from broken pipes is fairly common during construction, so it is even more important than usual to keep everything in the storeroom well off the floor. The dirt problem is also aggravated, and plaster dust is an especially vicious kind. **Tape the** cracks around doors; put cheesecloth over ventilators; and keep museum objects covered.

Safety and security throughout the museum depend upon electric lights, alarm systems, telephones, heating and cooling devices, etc. All these things are likely to fail in a building under construction.

TEMPORARY STOREROOMS

Each temporary storeroom raises problems of its own, but some standard precautions will always be necessary. In the first place, locks must be changed and security established. Windows and doors must be tightly sealed against dust and opened as seldom as possible. If the room receives direct sunlight, fluctuations in temperature can be minimized by hanging fiberglass insulation material against the window glass. Some degree of humidity control can be achieved with portable humidifiers or dehumidifiers, or both, with hygrostatic switches. Depending upon the local humidity condition, it may be advisable to keep the temporary storeroom below the usual temperature, or not to heat it at all. All the dangers cited with regard to permanent storerooms exist to at least the same degree in temporary ones.

EVACUATION

One objection to moving is that it takes a lot of time. Since most of the work may have to be done while the museum is closed but not actually under construction, evacuation tends to lengthen the closed interval. Another objection is the cost. Storage space at least as safe as the collection's old quarters is usually quite expensive.

Rooms under consideration should be examined personally by competent staff members and by representatives of the underwriters. In fact, the whole move should be worked out in cooperation with the insurers. Moving plans will be complicated by the need for prudent dispersal of the objects. Avoid huge concentrations of value (economic, historical, or aesthetic) in one place or vehicle. Don't put all the capital works of one master on one truck, even if the total insured value is within your limit.

When a storeroom is emptied, it is important to remove any equipment that will be needed again. This includes lifts, dollies, ladders, tables, chairs, and the storage units themselves. Anything left behind must be written off.

Reopening of the museum is usually timed to take advantage of a busy season or to coincide with some event that cannot be postponed. There is a deadline. Construction, however, usually takes longer than anyone would have thought possible. Time pressure mounts, and so does sentiment for moving in before the place is quite ready. The registrar and others concerned with safety of the collections may have all they can do to delay the return until conditions are tolerable, and then to accomplish it quickly and safely in a hostile environment.

In unfinished spaces, all the usual hazards are intensified. Security is shaky because construction crews are used to going where they please and resent interference. The guard force may be understrength and undertrained, especially if the museum has been closed for a long time or has been greatly enlarged. Once exhibition material enters a room, that room must be off limits to all outsiders, unless they are accompanied by a competent staff member.

Elementary registration procedure, on a grand scale, can accomplish miracles on moving day. Lists are the essence of it—precise lists of objects or of sealed containers of items from each room. Take one area at a time according to a working schedule; deliver all the material on the list and check it off; inspect each unpackaged item for condition; protect it against dust; seal the room and move on to the next. You will not only have moved the collection but also have made a complete inventory and condition check, all in a relatively short time.

Of course, the ideal would be to move at leisure into a finished and furnished museum, where the air-conditioning has been running for at least six months to get the kinks out.

Planning Work Space and Placing Equipment

Other chapters (see chapters 1 and 5) discuss various types of storage equipment. These units and heavy equipment, such as examining tables and supply cabinets, must be selected or designed for specific locations. Open spaces have to be reserved for handling, stacking boxes, and parking trucks and dollies. None of this can be worked out until you have an exact idea of the space available.

To plan work space for the registration department you need the following: (1) final architectural drawings, (2) reflected ceiling plans of suspended plumbing, and (3) reflected ceiling plans showing duct work, air vents, and humidifiers in and around the ducts. (Reflected plans are drawn as the room might be seen from above, looking down through a transparent ceiling. They should indicate the clearance under each pipe, duct, or other feature.) After the work space has been allocated and the equipment decided upon, and only then, the wiring and lighting plan should be drawn up.

You know the functions the rooms must serve and the desired capacity. The puzzle is how to fit in all the necessary objects without infringing upon the fire or building codes; interfering with planned circulation of air; allowing any vulnerable object to come under a humidifier, cold pipe, or air vent, or within range of any other source of dirt, water, or wind; inviting congestion; or blocking anything that has to be serviced.

You must pay special attention to local fire regulations; otherwise the museum may be denied a certificate of occupancy. Some of these rules are very tricky and may prohibit an otherwise suitable room from being used as planned. For example, the fire code may prohibit any use of space within two feet of the ceiling, a rule that drastically reduces storage capacity.

If circumstances force your museum to use storage space under a lot of pipes and ducts, give each unit a little roof of its own. One simple method is to place a sheet of cardboard or hardboard on top of the storage unit so that it projects a little from every side. Cover this with a single sheet of plastic large enough to hang slightly over the edges.

Examining tables should never be placed under anything that could leak. Liquids other than water may fall. Machinery will drip oil. In a new building, the "cutting compound" may ooze from joints in the plumbing. The transformers of fluorescent light fixtures have been known to lose their "ballast," a corrosive substance that looks like tar. Of course fluorescents should not be used at all in a well-designed museum, but just in case. . . .

When there just isn't enough room for everything to have its own place, some storage units, tables, or other heavy equipment may have to be put on casters—with brakes. This can greatly increase the usefulness of space. In addition, movable equipment doesn't show on plans and therefore isn't subject to building codes and fire regulations. In fact, there is great temptation to recommend that all museum equipment be mounted on casters and be designed to go through doorways. But such mobility has its own risks—someday someone may park something with a work of art on it under some leak—just for a second.

The Zone of Safety

The normal path of an object entering a museum leads through the loading dock, receiving room, examination room, photography studio, storeroom, and exhibition hall—in that order. (See figure T.1.) There may be side trips to the conservation laboratory, the frame shop, and curatorial offices. If the object is a temporary loan, it retraces the same path on the way out, probably skipping photography but making an excursion to the carpenter shop for packing. Each location is separated from the preceding one by a door, often a corridor, and sometimes an elevator. (If there are stairs, it's not a well-planned museum.) All these areas, together with the connecting passages, constitute what I call the "zone of safety." An object anywhere in this territory is entitled to protection against all the dangers described in the next section of this article.

If the first consideration within this zone is preservation, efficiency is a close second, at least in an active museum. Exhibition material moves along this path. Any obstacle is a double menace: its very existence increases the risk of damage, but it also wastes time and leads to dangerous haste.

The design of this zone of the building must take into account the techniques for handling exhibition material. One major consideration is that the material moves almost exclusively on wheeled vehicles. Another is that the handling of museum objects can never be rushed. No matter how pressing the deadline, the handlers must not be allowed to sense the slightest urgency. It is inadvisable to supplement the labor force with untrained help; and overtime, even if permitted by the budget, must be used sparingly to avoid the possibility of accidents resulting from fatigue.

VERTICAL COMMUNICATION

Elevators are the curse of the museum profession; yet they are preferable to stairs or ramps. As building sites grow smaller, museums taller, and the population denser, we shall need more and more of them. Consideration of the following suggestions may avoid a lot of problems:

1. Have the fewest possible levels in the museum building and group consecutive processes on the same level. Vertical transportation is far more dangerous and time consuming than movement on a level.

2. If you must have elevators, have plenty right from the start. They are expensive in new construction but enormously more so as an afterthought.

3. Don't mix passengers with freight, or either with art.

4. Make at least one elevator big enough (especially long enough) to handle the largest works you will ever want to take upstairs. And pay particular attention to the approaches on all floors; a sharp corner or low header can waste the size of the car.

5. Freight elevators usually open on two sides. Three open sides may be possible, but four are out of the question because of the counterweights. In a two-door elevator, opposite openings are better than adjacent ones, which may force one to negotiate a turn inside the elevator.

6. The whole side of a freight elevator should open. Its capacity for volume is determined by the size of the door.

THE LOADING DOCK

Loading and unloading out of doors is risky. It subjects museum objects to wind and rain, heat and humidity, traffic, children, and pigeons. The loading dock should be large enough for any truck that may arrive, and it must not be pre-empted by office supplies, books, groceries, lumber, or trash. If possible, separate facilities should be provided for other deliveries. Otherwise, all deliveries may have to be scheduled in advance, and that is difficult.

How big? The width of highway vehicles is standard, but remember that trucks have to get in and out. The narrower the street and the deeper your dock, the more width must be allowed for maneuvering. Truck length is limited by law in most places. Find out the local maximum and plan the dock to accommodate at least that length. Height is hardest to anticipate. Trucks seem to get taller every year. At present, a dock with a clearance of less than 14 feet is almost useless.

The platform, if any, should allow for end loading and side loading, at least on the right. No matter what platform height you select, it will usually be wrong. Better too low than too high. Some docks have no raised platform at all but rely on movable ramps and hydraulic lifts, movable or built-in, for raising heavy weights to the level of a truck bed or lowering them to the floor. An overhead crane running on an "I" beam will, on rare occasions, be a tremendous help.

Modern "container" ships, 747 transport planes, railroad cars, and trucks are increasingly designed to handle large shipments in standard containers measuring 8 by 8 by 10, 20, or 40 feet: the height and width of containers are fixed, but the length varies in multiples of ten. Such containers may be the best solution for moving "packaged" exhibitions, provided there is no excessive concentration of value. The single case with inner containers can provide maximum protection against damage, while the compact shape is ideal for insulation against climatic change. With such packing, pilferage is difficult, and scattering of an exhibition on route impossible. If and when international door-to-door delivery becomes available, the problem of dockside customs examination may disappear. Unfortunately, few existing museum buildings can accommodate containers of this size. It would be wonderful if all large and medium-size art museums built from now on were designed to receive and ship exhibitions in the standard containers.

Hazards To Be Avoided

CONSTRICTED SPACES

Registrars spend a major portion of their working lives, tape in hand, looking for an ingenious way to get some large object in or out. Too often the solution involves dismantling either the work of art or some part of the museum. The problem is not that the object is too large to display gracefully in the galleries; it just won't come through the door.

Bottlenecks take many forms—low doorways or headers, sharp turns, pipes, ducts, conduits and lighting fixtures hung below the slab, small or slow or weak elevators, and narrow doors. You may be told that it is impossible to take into account all possible works of art, past and future. In a sense, that is true and obvious. But the size and shape of museum exhibition galleries always impose certain restrictions upon the dimensions of works to be displayed in them. It is a simple matter to tailor the entrance and preparation areas to works on the same scale.

The possibility of rolling or folding paintings or tilting sculpture should never be relied upon. These are dangerous, destructive procedures—measures of desperation. Always design or select picture trucks, dollies, lifts, skids, and so forth, before building plans solidify. Once the wheelbase and turning circle of each conveyance are known, you can make sure it will go wherever needed.

Nothing is more dangerous than congestion. Because of the variety of materials to be exhibited, no ideal ratio of "staging" to exhibition space can be given. However, if the total staging area (receiving and unpacking plus recording and temporary storage) equals the largest single space devoted to one exhibition, and if only one exhibition is

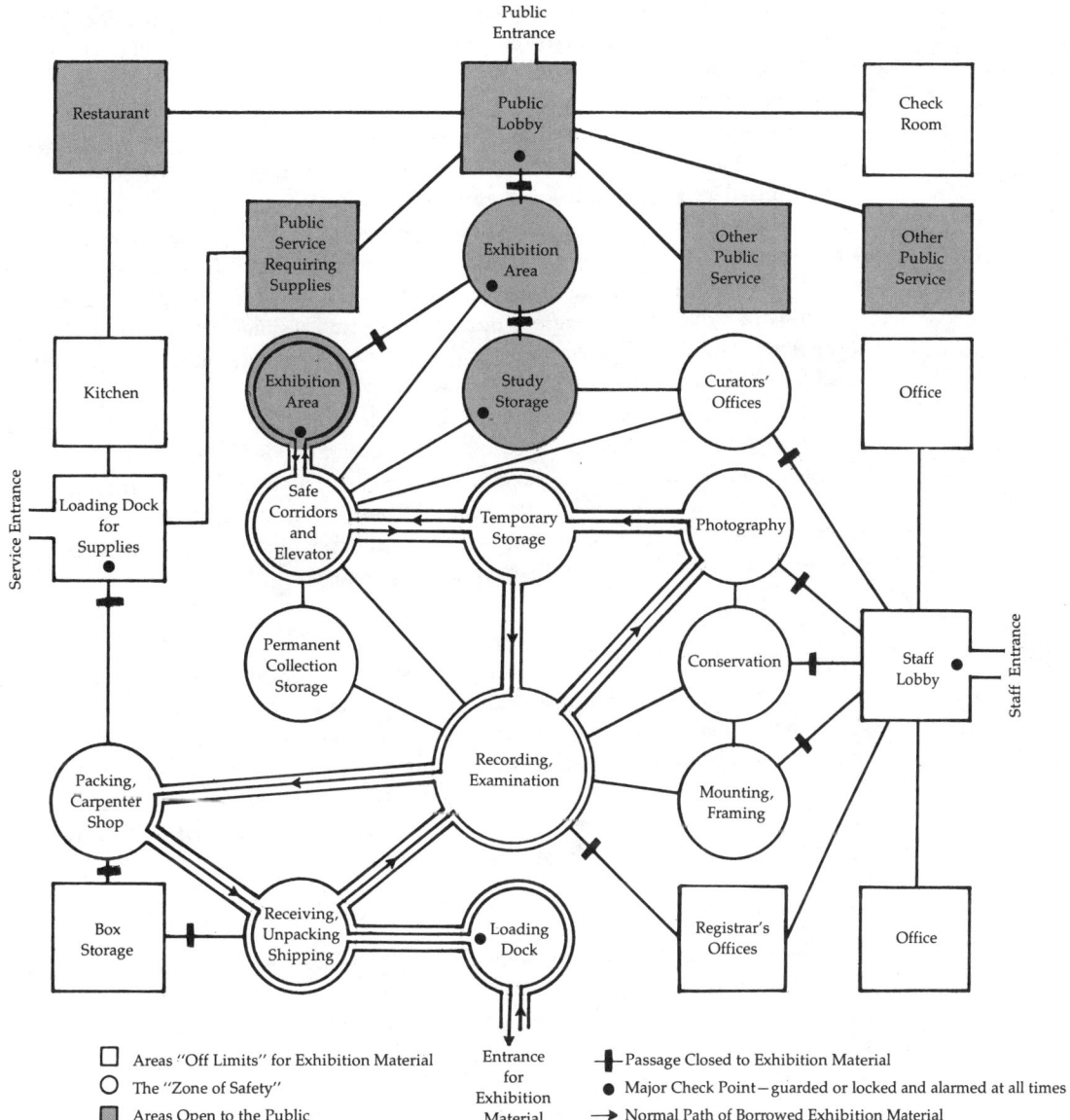

Fig. T.1.
Zone of Safety: recommended proximity and connection of areas in a large museum, with special reference to facilities for the preparation of exhibitions. Connections shown do not necessarily represent doorways but only the possibility of going from one area to another without passing through a third. For example, the Recording and Examination Room has nine connections, but one door might do for all. The absence of a connection on the chart means there should be no direct communication. For example, nothing should move from Permanent Collection Storage to the Carpenter Shop without being examined in the Recording Room. Separate connections to each Exhibition Area show that each can be installed or dismantled without moving material through the other. Exhibition material and the public meet only in the galleries and Study Storage.

changed at a time, there will always be enough room for safe handling. If this ratio is halved, the staging area will almost certainly jam up. In institutions where the exhibition program is leisurely and the installations are simple, some of the staging can be done right in the galleries.

The importance of regularly shaped rooms cannot be exaggerated. Regularity in space is equivalent to extra space. This rule applies to overhead clearance as well as to floor plan. Subgrade (cellar) spaces are especially congested and irregular. They are often utilized as staging areas but cannot be recommended for it. In addition to difficulty of access and the risk of flooding, basements are often a snarl of branching water, steam, electric, telephone, and gas lines, and they often house machinery as well. Spaces that seem large, high, and clear on the architect's early plans later shrink and fill with bulky, hot, dangerous apparatus. Rooms assume odd shapes, and headroom disappears. Lighting is inadequate, and chances for leakage multiply. In addition the need for servicing equipment threatens security.

Building and fire codes create further problems in the use of underground space. Fire codes often require subdivision of large spaces to allow for fire stairs and passages. The size and placement of storage units may also be restricted. Security may be impaired by required fire exits. If none of these specific objections applies to your museum, there is nothing wrong with using basement space as such. Some older museums, built on a grand scale, have good basement staging areas.

OBSTRUCTIONS

Anything projecting into work or storage space is a menace. Pipes, ducts, conduits, and fixtures have been mentioned. Nails partly sunk into walls are very treacherous. Even thermostats may be troublesome on a stacking wall. Worst of all are moving objects—mainly hinged doors and especially self-closing doors. A door with a will of its own poses a real threat when one person has to get through with a truckload of paintings. Sliding doors are harmless if they move inside the wall. Even when hung against the wall, they are safer than hinged doors.

IRREGULAR FOOTING

Irregularities under foot include steps and ramps as well as thresholds, edges of carpets and other surfacing, gaps at the entrance to elevators, and so forth. Minor irregularities are more dangerous than those that are bound to be noticed. Anything that can jar a moving truck or dolly is a hazard. Some kinds of flooring have a relief pattern to increase traction, but such a pattern sets up vibration in a vehicle moving over it.

The softer the floor surface, the harder you have to push anything on wheels; and the harder you push, the greater the risk of accident. So, thick carpets should be avoided. The surface must provide good traction even when wet. On the other hand, very hard floor materials tend to increase the risk of breakage when there is an accident. Besides, dollies may roll too easily, and many floors have an unplanned, imperceptible slope. The best compromise for any given space depends upon the work to be done there and the kinds of material to be handled. At the soft end of the spectrum, a heavy-duty cork linoleum is good. Where heavier loads are expected, ordinary vinyl-asbestos tile will do very well. The tile may become permanently indented if a large weight remains for long in one place, but this is a minor problem. Tiles that will not take dents are expensive. For very rugged use there is no substitute for concrete with a heavy-duty surface film. Asphaltlike "traffic toppings" are unacceptable; small wheels under heavy loads become mired.

DARKNESS

Good illumination is very important in preventing accidents. Plan lighting throughout the zone of safety after you know the layout of bins and other equipment, taking account of suspended pipes and ducts and making sure that intersecting shadows will not develop into blind spots. Floor, ceiling, walls, and furniture should be white, or as light as possible, to promote even distribution of light. (If it shows dirt, so much the better; you'll know when and where to clean.) Pitch darkness is less hazardous than the slight gloom of areas that seem well lighted but aren't. Never settle for less than twenty footcandles of illumination anywhere. Automatic battery-powered emergency lights are essential in any windowless space where works of art will be handled. Imagine yourself suddenly in the dark with an unframed Rembrandt in your hands!

LIGHT

The choice of a light source is unimportant in passageways where exposure is brief; but where works of art are to be kept for any length of time, it is a major consideration. All light, indeed all radiation, is somewhat destructive. It breaks materials down, one molecule at a time; and each molecule lost is lost forever. Objects allowed to rest in darkness stop deteriorating from the effects of light, but they do not recover. When exposure to light resumes, deterioration continues.

Assuming the quality of light to be constant, the number of molecules destroyed in a given time is proportional to the intensity of light. In other words, one footcandle for five hours does exactly the same damage as five footcandles for one hour. It follows, therefore, that all light not needed for viewing or safe handling should be eliminated from the museum environment and that storerooms should be dark. Where lights are required, only incandescent light should be used. If fluorescents cannot be eliminated, they should be shielded; but the shields are only partially effective and tend to deteriorate in use. Daylight is the most destructive light source of all.

Of course, some materials such as metal contain so many molecules of such stability that the destructive effect of ordinary light levels can be ignored. But many kinds of museum objects are exceedingly vulnerable. Among these are certain watercolor paintings, in which the color depends upon a relatively small number of pigment molecules dispersed in a very thin layer of transparent material (the medium). The color fades as the molecules are destroyed. Its life is fixed from the start in terms of footcandle hours! Other sensitive materials include paper, fabric, leather, and anything dyed. Conservators should always be consulted before it is assumed that material other than metal or stone can safely be exposed to unlimited light.

In areas that cannot be kept dark, such as exhibition galleries, light intensity should be monitored. Nearly all photographic light meters can be used for this, but not without a degree of understanding. Meters of the incident type are used differently from the more common reflected variety. Moreover, all photographic meters are geared to the wavelengths used in photography, i.e., to visible light. They tell nothing of light quality and may even fail to register dangerous ultraviolet rays from the sky or a fluorescent source.

DIRT

There is a tendency to think of dirt as merely unsightly, damaging to museum objects because it affects their appearance or, indirectly, because of the risks that must be taken in removing it. This is the least of the problem. Real damage is caused by corrosive and hygroscopic substances, which either attack materials directly or attract moisture to the surface. A dirty surface or material in which dirt has become ingrained may, in effect, be much wetter than the ambient atmosphere. Excess moisture promotes chemical, photochemical, and biological deterioration.

Cleaning is damaging to a work of art, so the trick is to keep dirt out in the first place. This can be accomplished, in part, through the air circulation system. It is usual to combine more than one kind of filter in a high-efficiency system. Mechanical filters are strainers designed to stop particles above a given size. Activated charcoal or curtains of water may be used to absorb gaseous pollutants. Charcoal also absorbs some of the stench that goes with modern civilization. In effect, the building wears a gas mask. Electronic precipitators remove very fine particles from the air through the attractive force of electrically charged elements. However, this system is seldom used in museums because it may generate intolerable concentrations of ozone. Water washes, too, seem unpopular, although the National Gallery in London has reported excellent results with such a system. The best available system now seems to consist of a combination of coarse mechanical filters followed by very fine mechanical filters followed by charcoal. This system is the most expensive to maintain, but is most recommended, at least in areas where the atmosphere contains sulfur compounds. Recirculating air should pass through the filters every time around, for it picks up dirt even in the museum.

Many objects can be kept reasonably clean simply by being covered. There are differences of opinion as to whether circulating air is necessary to keep organic materials in good condition. Some conservators say that organic materials must "breathe." Others now feel that, except in special cases, air circulation is unnecessary or slightly harmful. However, in the absence of circulation, the temperature in any enclosed air space must be kept fairly constant because a drop in temperature means a rise in relative humidity and a rise in temperature a drop in relative humidity. In extreme cases, water may actually condense on the inside of plastic wrapping or other vapor seal. Furthermore, where there are permanent sources of heat or moisture—a radiator, a sunny window, a moist wall, or the like—pockets of moisture or dryness may build up unless the air is kept in motion.

The wooden cabinets frequently used to store prints, drawings, or photographs keep dirt out and stabilize interior conditions without setting up an impenetrable moisture barrier. Beware, however, that the proximity of wood may have a slightly adverse chemical effect upon paper. Paper or cardboard coverings serve the same purpose as the wood but should not come into direct contact with the materials to be preserved, since all but the purest papers contain traces of the acids used in their manufacture.

FLUCTUATIONS OF TEMPERATURE AND RELATIVE HUMIDITY

It is often argued that, since objects borrowed from private collections rather than other museums spend most of their time in uncontrolled atmospheres and may be subjected to extremes while in transit, it is not necessary to keep them under controlled conditions for their few weeks in the museum. That contention may be valid enough but misses the main point—the permanent collection. Objects of a very high order usually reach public collections eventually. By the time they do, a great deal of deterioration may have taken place. It has to be arrested, and that is impossible unless the relative humidity, at least, is constant.

Atmospheric shocks received in transit from one institution to another are being reduced by better packaging, and there is increasing reluctance to lend where a controlled environment cannot be guaranteed. Excellent work is being done, especially in Canada, to develop insulated boxes in which works of art can travel great distances in unfavorable weather with little deviation from the ideal conditions under which they were packed. (See article S.) For the preservation of both traveling and permanent collections, a constant environment is important.

A lot has been written about the most desirable conditions for preserving museum collections. (See, especially, chapter 5.) Basically, relative humidity is far more important than temperature; it should never exceed 60 percent or fall short of 45 percent; within these limits it should fluctuate as little as possible, preferably within a total annual range of 5 percent or less. Temperature should be held as constant as possible, and the lower the better. Conditions throughout the zone of safety should be uniform.

The machinery for regulating temperature and relative humidity in the museum must be carefully selected. When a new building is planned it is most important that the exact conditions the machinery is expected to provide be set forth in a way that will be legally binding on all concerned. The museum should not accept any equipment until its own independent observations show that the conditions specified are being maintained. Buy performance, not hardware.

Independent measurements can be made easily with a sling psychrometer. However, to be sure an area is getting twenty-four-hour protection you need the rather costly hygrothermograph, in which pens trace a continuous record of temperature and relative humidity on a moving chart. These machines, driven by clockwork, may be used anywhere and are independent of the central system and its controls. It is important that they be managed by someone primarily concerned with preserving the collection; a conflict of interest can arise if the people responsible for running the air-handling system monitor its performance. Surveillance of the system must be continuous, not just during the months or years it may take to balance out a new system.

WATER

Condensation of moisture on windows and other cold surfaces gets to be a problem in cold weather if the relative humidity is kept as high as it should be. Mist on the windowpanes is a minor housekeeping problem, but when water runs down a glass wall and spreads over the floor, a real hazard exists. There are several solutions: double and triple thermopanes, drafts of hot air sweeping the inner surface, or gutters along the base of the window. Not having glass is the simplest.

Cold pipes are also dangerous. Drains and soil pipes as well as cold water lines may get cold enough to condense moisture. To prevent this possibility, these pipes should be insulated just as steam pipes are covered.

Condensation is a minor matter compared to leakage. Modern buildings are not immune to leaking roofs, seepage in the cellar, backed-up drains, and burst pipes. Broken mains outside the building can cause serious flooding. Minor floods, perhaps from a toilet or kitchen overhead, can find their way into a storeroom or gallery, sometimes penetrating several concrete floors along the way.

If water damage is to be avoided, spaces directly under the roofs or terraces should not be used for storage. The registrar must always know exactly what is over the rooms under his or her care, and must prepare for the worst if there is any possible source of water.

FIRE

The museum profession has traditionally ruled out automatic sprinklers on the grounds that they do more harm than a fire. Anyone who has been through a museum fire will doubt this. A painting protected in front by varnish or glass and behind by cardboard has some defense against water. If soaked, it will be damaged and require immediate conservation, but the substance is there and can be solidified. If fire gets to the same painting, there will be nothing left to fix. And each painting that burns may spread the flames to the next. Sprinklers, on the other hand, tend to limit the disaster area; and a sprinkler's discharge of twenty gallons per minute is very gentle treatment compared to tons of water under high pressure from a fire hose.

The chief worry with sprinklers is accidental discharge, where resulting damage cannot be balanced against the probability of much greater fire loss. Such discharge is very rare; but as a safeguard, museums should use only preaction sprinkler systems. The pipes leading to such sprinklers remain dry until an electronic smoke detector is activated. There can be no discharge until the smoke detector is activated and the air temperature has reached 165° F. (74° C.), the temperature needed to activate most sprinkler heads.

Sprinklers are the last line of defense against fire. Isolation in fireproof surroundings should be the first. Two fire barriers should separate works of art from works of construction, destruction, or house painting. Machinery and transformers should be separated from the art collections by a fire- and smoke-proof barrier. A smoky fire elsewhere in the building may force a museum to clean its entire painting collection since even an invisible smoke deposit will cause corrosion of the paintings' surfaces.

The carbon dioxide fire extinguishers that are often recommended may not be as completely harmless as is supposed. The expanding gas becomes so cold that it may condense moisture and cause water damage. In addition, extinguishers, like any other apparatus, are useless unless personnel are trained and practiced in their operation.

It is not clear whether metal or wooden storage cabinets provide better fire protection. Metal cannot possibly feed the flames, but it transmits heat rapidly and may collapse in less time than it would take a standard ⅝-inch board to burn through. (See chapter 5.) If plastic coverings are used for storage, choose a material that is nonflammable or self-extinguishing. Try to burn a sample before putting any in the storerooms.

PEOPLE

The greatest threat of all, people, has been saved for last because the subject is immense and it introduces the whole problem of museum security.

Security

The registrar makes his or her main contribution to security through records, periodic inventories, and control of entry and exit. However, we are concerned here with physical defenses; and these are built around the lock on the storeroom door.

This is no place to economize. The first edition of this article stated that the keys to certain expensive locks could be duplicated only by the lock manufacturer. Experience has shown that this is not true. Nevertheless, it is wise to render duplication as difficult as possible by seeking out the most sophisticated lock system available. Some museums employ a staff locksmith so that no outsider will ever have access to keys or locks.

A rigid key policy is essential. Here, security and convenience are in direct opposition to one another. It would be most convenient (assuming that doors be locked at all) to have one key for all locks and let each staff member carry one. On the other hand, maximum security requires that every lock be unique, recognizing one key only (no master); that no more than two copies of the key exist; and that each be signed out from and returned to the security office whenever it is used. Each museum must work out its own compromise.

Whatever key policy a museum settles upon, a record should be kept of every key and its possessor. All affected locks should be changed whenever a key is missing. All locks in a building that has been under construction should be changed as a precaution against keys having been stolen or copied.

Doors must be strong, fireproof, and opaque: a thief's job is simplified if he can see where his objective is, or isn't. Wire mesh makes a flimsy, transparent barrier. Devices as primitive as bars and throw bolts still have a place in the storerooms of a modern museum building, especially on doors that are meant for emergency exit only. Walls, of course, have to be at least as tough as the doors and so do ceilings and floors. Anyone with simple tools can get through a light partition (studs and Sheetrock, for example) quickly and easily. One who knows how can penetrate a block wall just as fast, though not without making a racket.

Pay attention to the various access panels, so familiar in modern buildings that we never see them. They lead to large ducts, hollow walls, and spaces above hung ceilings, where equipment may need to be serviced. Most are dead ends, but each should be checked carefully to be sure. Insofar as possible, fuse boxes and anything else requiring attention by service personnel should be eliminated from security areas.

Some museums use closed-circuit television to cover entrances to the building and other sensitive areas, and many electrical monitors are on the market. The major problem with this form of security is that the screens have to be monitored by a person, and it is a soporific show at best. Other systems may be roughly classified as peripheral protection or space protection. The former consists of contact point alarms and electric eyes covering every conceivable access to the area. Space protection is based upon sonic, ultrasonic, or infrared sensing devices detecting, respectively, noise within the protected area, movement within the area, or a heat source such as the human body. A sonic system, by listening only to overtones, can distinguish between sounds originating within the protected space and those from the outside. It can also be rigged to disregard the creaking of the building, functioning of the air conditioning, ticking of a clock, or any other routine sound. All electrical systems go into a state of alarm when tampered with.

Two reservations must always be borne in mind. First, any kind of automatic system is worse than useless unless it functions. The second and even more important reservation is that all security rests ultimately on manpower. The function of doors, walls, and locks is to delay the enemy until the troops arrive. Automatic alarms can only call for help.

In general, it is inadvisable for a watchman to enter the art storerooms, but there may be exceptions. Sometimes, for instance, a special hazard exists—something that may leak or overheat—and it has to be watched. Such situations are temporary, however, since either the danger or the art will have to be removed.

Vandalism and carelessness on the part of the general public afflict the exhibition halls as a rule, not the regions behind the scenes, where the registrar is concerned. Exceptions occur where public and staging areas overlap, as when people and pictures ride the same elevators, when storerooms have no entrance except through exhibition halls, and when works of art are carried in or out via the public entrance. There is no excuse for such conditions in a well-planned modern building.

GLOSSARY

Compiled by Patricia Nauert

This is a glossary of general terms that pertain to registration and other aspects of museum work. More specific glossaries and definitions of terms are found elsewhere in the book: on insurance terms, at the end of chapter 9; on classifying paintings, drawings, prints, and constructions, in article C; on terms for describing condition in a work of art, in article F; on terms for describing anthropological objects, in article I; and on computer terms, in article M.

Accession: (1) an object acquired by a museum as part of its Permanent Collection; (2) the act of recording/processing an addition to the permanent collection.

Accession Card: a card recording/containing primary information about an object in the Permanent Collection. Accession cards, filed in numerical order by Accession Number, constitute the Accessions File.

Accession Number: a control number, unique to an object, whose purpose is identification, not description. It is part of the numbering system encompassing the Permanent Collection of an institution and records the transaction whereby an object enters the collection. As described in this book, the accession number is based on order of acceptance as part of the permanent collection (not on Class of the object) and consists of the year of accession and the serial number within that year. See also Catalogue Number.

Accessions File: a file comprised of Accession Cards, one card for each object in the Permanent Collection.

Acid Migration: the transfer of an acid from a more acidic material to a less acidic material with which it is in contact. Since acid can cause certain materials, such as paper, to deteriorate, acid migration is one of the factors to be considered in planning the storage of museum records and artifacts.

Air Suspension System: a suspension system, found on some larger vans and trucks, that utilizes a cushion of air to absorb road shocks and soften the ride. For transport of Museum Objects, it is superior to a spring suspension system.

Airbill: see Airwaybill.

Airwaybill: the basic shipping document in air freight; it is both the contract of carriage between the shipper and carrier and the receipt for the shipment.

Antique: for U.S. Customs purposes, an object made at least one hundred years prior to date of entry.

BAILEE: one to whom the property of another (the BAILOR) is entrusted for a limited period; the museum that has assumed temporary custody of an object.

BAILOR: one who entrusts his or her property to another (the BAILEE) for a limited period; the individual from whom a MUSEUM OBJECT is received, that is, the owner of the object, also called the lender or depositor.

BATTEN: a strip of wood affixed to the exterior of a packing box to provide additional structural rigidity. A "riding batten" is a batten attached to the bottom of the box to provide added strength to areas upon which weight rests during transit and to keep the bottom of the box itself off the ground.

BILL OF LADING: the basic document in van, truck, or ocean shipping; it is both the contract of carriage between the shipper and carrier and the receipt for the shipment. See also AIRWAYBILL.

BOND: for customs purposes, a surety that, if duty is charged, it will be paid and that proper customs procedures will be followed. See also PERMANENT EXHIBITION BOND. For insurance purposes, a written agreement of obligation between the insurance company and the museum (or named insured), indemnifying the museum for dishonest acts of all officers and employees.

BUFFER: a substance that restrains the ACID MIGRATION of a material. Acid-free, buffered paper is often recommended for use in wrapping and storing MUSEUM OBJECTS.

CALIPERS: a measuring device consisting of a pair of movable, curved legs fastened at one end with a screw or rivet, used to measure the DIAMETER or thickness of an object.

CAMPHOR FLAKES: a solid, slow-vaporizing fumigant for moths or larvae, often used with objects that can be stored in a closed room or an airtight cabinet.

CARRIER: an individual or firm in the business of transporting people, objects, or materials; also called common carrier.

CATALOGUE: (1) a file comprised of CATALOGUE CARDS, one (or more) for each object in the PERMANENT COLLECTION; (2) a publication listing and describing objects in a SPECIAL EXHIBITION or collection; (3) the act of classifying objects methodically, and usually with descriptive detail; often a curatorial responsibility.

CATALOGUE CARD: a card recording/containing extensive information about an object in the PERMANENT COLLECTION. Catalogue cards are duplicated and filed as a CATALOGUE to the permanent collection and in other files according to the museum's needs.

CATALOGUE NUMBER: a term used in a variety of ways in museums: (1) in some museums, a catalogue number is assigned to an object or specimen based on its CLASS; its purpose is description; (2) in some museums, the number described in this book as an ACCESSION NUMBER is called a catalogue number, in which case its purpose is identification; (3) the number assigned to an object in a printed publication or CATALOGUE of a SPECIAL EXHIBITION or collection. See also ACCESSION NUMBER.

CATALOGUE PHOTOGRAPH: (1) a photograph used for object identification purposes, usually attached directly to the CATALOGUE CARD or record; also called a descriptive photograph; (2) a high-quality photograph taken for publication or publicity purposes, especially for use in a published CATALOGUE of a SPECIAL EXHIBITION or collection.

CERTIFICATE OF INSURANCE: a document, signed by the insurance company or its agent, that is written evidence of insurance in force at the time of issuance. Museums or lenders often require certificates of insurance from one another before releasing objects on loan.

CLASS: a number of objects that have been grouped together because of common characteristics. In natural history, a group of animals or plants having a common basic structure and ranking below a phylum and above an order.

CLIMATE CONTROL: the ability to adjust and regulate the TEMPERATURE and RELATIVE HUMIDITY in a particular environment.

CLIMATE-CONTROLLED VAN: a van in which the TEMPERATURE and RELATIVE HUMIDITY can be adjusted and regulated within certain limits.

COMMERCIAL MOVER: an individual or firm in the business of transporting objects or materials, usually by van or truck.

COMPOSITION: the area of the SHEET in which the design appears in a drawing or print. When the composition is limited to a distinct area of the sheet, its measurements are recorded in addition to the measurements of the overall sheet.

CONDENSATION: water that turns from vapor in the air to liquid on the surface of objects when the air becomes saturated with water vapor because of cooling or the addition of more moisture. CLIMATE CONTROL during exhibition, storage, and shipping can help prevent such condensation from damaging MUSEUM OBJECTS.

CONDITION: (1) the physical state of an object; (2) a contract provision or stipulation.

CONDITION PHOTOGRAPH: a photograph or series of photographs that clearly documents all defects, flaws, and physical condition of an object.

CONSERVATION: the application of science to the examination and treatment of MUSEUM OBJECTS and to the study of the environment in which they are placed.

CONSERVATOR: one who applies science to the technical study, preservation, and treatment of MUSEUM OBJECTS.

CONSIGNEE: the party to whom a shipment is sent.

CONSIGNOR: the party that assigns a shipment to a particular agent or CARRIER.

CONTAINER: a large receptacle, usually provided by the CARRIER, for consolidating (containerizing) a number of boxes for transport by rail, truck, ship, and/or plane.

COURIER: an individual, usually a representative of the owner of an object, who accompanies the object in transit to assure its safety and security.

CREDIT LINE: the wording with which a lender or donor wishes acknowledgment to appear on a gallery label or in a publication.

CURATOR: one who has responsibility for the care, research, exhibition, and increase or improvement of a museum collection.

CUSTOMS BROKER: an individual or firm that arranges customs clearance of objects traveling between countries; frequently employed also as a FREIGHT-FORWARDING AGENT for international shipments.

CUSTOMS ENTRY: the formal procedure whereby documentary, inspection, and other requirements of customs are met for a particular shipment and the shipment is granted entry into a country.

CUSTOMS INSPECTOR: an official whose duty is to enforce the laws and regulations that pertain to import and export shipments.

CUSTOMS POWER OF ATTORNEY: an authorization given by an importer or exporter to a CUSTOMS BROKER to sign shipping and customs documents on his or her behalf.

CUSTOMS SEAL: a warning tag or label affixed to a shipping box by a customs official at the original PORT-OF-ENTRY. It is a guarantee to the customs official who makes the inspection at the ultimate destination that the contents have not been tampered with.

DEACCESSION: (1) an object that has been removed permanently from the museum collection, usually through sale or exchange; (2) the process of removing an object permanently from the collection.

DECLARATION OF ORIGINALITY: for customs purposes, a document verifying that the art objects being imported are not copies or facsimiles and therefore not subject to duty.

DEED OF GIFT: a contract that transfers ownership of an object or objects from a donor to an institution. It should include all conditions of the gift.

DEPRECIATION: for insurance purposes, the difference in the value of an object before and after damage and any subsequent restoration.

DESCRIPTIVE PHOTOGRAPH: a photograph used for object identification purposes only, usually attached directly to the CATALOGUE CARD or record; also called a CATALOGUE PHOTOGRAPH.

DIAMETER: the measurement taken across an object or along a straight line passing through the center of a circle, sphere, etc., from one side to the other, perpendicular to the HEIGHT.

DOLLY: a low, two- or four-wheeled, flat cart or platform used to move objects.

DOMESTIC SHIPMENT: the shipment of objects within one country.

ENTRY RECORDS: the initial records created on an object upon its arrival at an institution. Entry records should identify the object and serve as a basis for later cataloguing.

EXAMINATION: the study and noting/recording of the physical characteristics of an object.

EXPORT LICENSE: permission, usually granted by a governmental agency, to ship a native cultural object out of the country.

EXPORT SHIPMENT: the shipment of an object or a group of objects out of the country.

EXTENDED LOAN: an object loaned to a museum for long-term, sometimes indefinite, use. In terms of record keeping, extended loans are often treated as a part of the PERMANENT COLLECTION.

EXTENDED LOAN NUMBER: see LOAN NUMBER.

FORKLIFT: a motorized truck, available in several sizes, used for moving objects and boxes weighing as much as 12,000 pounds.

FORWARDING AGENT: see FREIGHT-FORWARDING AGENT.

FOXING: a discoloration of paper caused by the action of mold on iron salts, which are present in most paper; usually the result of high RELATIVE HUMIDITY.

FRACTIONAL INTEREST GIFT: see PARTIAL GIFT.

FREIGHT-FORWARDING AGENT: an individual or firm that arranges and coordinates shipments, utilizing the services of commercial CARRIERS.

FUMIGATION: the chemical treatment of an object, group of objects, or structure for elimination of pests or mold.

GLASSINE: a thin, dense, slick-surfaced, translucent paper resistant to the passage of air and dirt; used as a wrapping material or for separation sheets.

GROSS WEIGHT: for shipping purposes, the combined weight of the objects to be shipped, the packing materials, and the packing box. See also NET WEIGHT; TARE WEIGHT.

HEAT SENSOR: a fire-alert device that sounds an alarm when the TEMPERATURE reaches a designated level.

HEIGHT: the measurement taken from the bottom to the top of an object, perpendicular to the LENGTH and WIDTH.

HYGROSCOPIC MATERIAL: a material capable of absorbing moisture.

HYGROTHERMOGRAPH: an instrument that measures and records TEMPERATURE and RELATIVE HUMIDITY changes.

IDENTIFYING NUMBER: a number, from the ACCESSION, TEMPORARY DEPOSIT, or LOAN NUMBER series, that is unique to a particular object in its relation to the museum.

IMPORT SHIPMENT: the shipment of an object or a group of objects into the country.

INCOMING LOAN: an object borrowed by an institution. It is an incoming loan from the perspective of the borrowing institution; such a loan would of course be an OUTGOING LOAN to the lending institution.

INCOMING LOAN RECEIPT: a document prepared by the borrowing institution to acknowledge receipt of a loan object, sent to the lender upon receipt of the object.

INSURANCE CLAIM: a formal, written demand to an insurance company for reimbursement for loss of or damage to an insured object.

INSURANCE VALUE: for insurance purposes, the estimated replacement cost, or the fair market value, of an object, usually established by the owner of the object and accepted by the insurer.

INVENTORY: (1) an itemized listing of objects, usually of objects for which the museum has assumed responsibility through either ACCESSION or LOAN; (2) the act of physically locating all or a random selection of the items for which the museum is responsible. See also SPOT INVENTORY.

JAPANESE MENDING TISSUE: a very thin, strong, transparent tissue paper used to strengthen old or worn paper or to mend tears in paper.

LENGTH: the measurement taken from one end of an object to the other, perpendicular to the WIDTH and HEIGHT.

LOAN: see EXTENDED LOAN; INCOMING LOAN; OUTGOING LOAN; TEMPORARY LOAN.

LOAN AGREEMENT: a contract between a lender and a borrower of an object or objects, specifying the object(s) and outlining the conditions of loan and the respective responsibilities of each party.

LOAN NUMBER: a control number, unique to an object, whose purpose is identification. It is part of the numbering system encompassing the objects on loan to an institution. In some museums the numbers assigned to TEMPORARY LOANS are distinguished from those assigned to EXTENDED LOANS.

LOCATION RECORD: a file or portion of a file noting the exact and current location of all objects in the museum's collection or for which the museum has assumed responsibility.

MUSEUM OBJECT: an object in a museum collection, or deemed worthy of study by or loan to a museum.

NAPHTHALENE: a toxic, crystalline material used as a fumigant for moths or larvae.

NET WEIGHT: for shipping purposes, the weight of the object being shipped, exclusive of the weight of the box or packing materials. See also GROSS WEIGHT; TARE WEIGHT.

NONACIDIC PAPER: paper made without acidic contaminants such as wood, wood pulp, or fillers. To prevent ACID MIGRATION, nonacidic paper is preferred both for museum records and for use in conjunction with MUSEUM OBJECTS.

OUTGOING LOAN: an object loaned by a museum to another institution. It is an outgoing loan from the perspective of the lending institution; such a loan would of course be an INCOMING LOAN to the borrowing institution.

OUTGOING LOAN RECEIPT: a document prepared by the lending institution, providing for a signed acknowledgment of the arrival of a loan; usually the receipt is sent by the lender to the borrower for signature and return to the lender.

PADDED TRAY: a flat receptacle with low sides and cushioned interior, used for holding or carrying objects.

PALLET: a low, portable platform, usually of wood or metal, on which a heavy or bulky object is placed for storage, transport, or shipment.

PARADICHLOROBENZENE: a crystalline compound used as a fumigant for moths and larvae.

PARTIAL GIFT: a donation of an object or collection of objects to which the museum does not receive full title. Partial gifts are of two kinds. A fractional interest gift is one in which the museum is given a present fractional interest and the donor retains the remaining fractional interest. In these cases the museum is entitled to possession of the object for that portion of each calendar year equal to its fractional interest in the property. A remainder gift is one in which the museum is given a remainder interest and the donor retains a life (or term) interest.

PERMANENT ACCESSION: an object acquired by a museum as part of its PERMANENT COLLECTION.

PERMANENT COLLECTION: those objects that are owned by the museum.

PERMANENT EXHIBITION BOND: a bond allowing qualifying importers to import into the United States dutiable items duty free for exhibition purposes, with the guarantee that the duty will be paid should the conditions of the bond not be kept.

PLATFORM TRUCK: a flat-bedded, four-wheeled truck or cart designed for the manual transport of MUSEUM OBJECTS such as sculptures and framed works.

PORT-OF-ENTRY: one of the cities designated by customs as a port of arrival for IMPORT SHIPMENTS and CUSTOMS ENTRY.

PROVENANCE: for works of art and historical objects, the background and history of ownership. The more common term for anthropological collections is "provenience," which defines an object in terms of the specific geographic location of origin. In scientific collections, the term "locality," meaning specific geographic point of origin, is more acceptable.

PSYCHROMETRIC TABLE: a chart used in conjunction with a SLING PSYCHROMETER to determine RELATIVE HUMIDITY.

RECEIPT: a written acknowledgment that an object or objects have been received. See INCOMING LOAN RECEIPT; OUTGOING LOAN RECEIPT; RECEIPT OF DELIVERY; TEMPORARY DEPOSIT RECEIPT.

RECEIPT OF DELIVERY: a written acknowledgment from a depositor or lender indicating that an object has been returned; often the receipt is prepared by the borrower and issued when the object is released, for signature and return.

RECEIVING ROOM: a room designed for the admittance and EXAMINATION of MUSEUM OBJECTS entering a museum.

RECORD: the act of processing the entry of an object into the museum.

REGISTRAR: an individual with broad responsibilities in the development and enforcement of policies and procedures pertaining to the acquisition, management, and disposition of collections. Records pertaining to the objects for which the institution has assumed responsibility are maintained by the registrar. Usually, the registrar also handles arrangements for accessions, loans, packing, shipping, storage, customs, and insurance as it relates to museum material.

GLOSSARY

REGISTRATION: the process of developing and maintaining an immediate, brief, and permanent means of identifying an object for which the institution has permanently or temporarily assumed responsibility.

RELATIVE HUMIDITY: the proportion of actual moisture in the air to the maximum amount possible at a specified TEMPERATURE. Fluctuation in relative humidity can damage MUSEUM OBJECTS.

RELEASE FORM: a security form, usually signed by the REGISTRAR, that authorizes removal of an object or group of objects from the museum.

REMAINDER GIFT: see PARTIAL GIFT.

SHEET: for works of art on paper, the complete piece of paper (or support) on which the work appears. See also COMPOSITION.

SHIPPING ROOM: a room designed for the packing and release of MUSEUM OBJECTS leaving a museum.

SIGHT MEASUREMENT: an approximate measurement of an object, usually a painting or a work of art on paper, taken when the full extremities of the piece are inaccessible.

SILICA GEL: a granular substance that has high moisture-absorbing and -emitting properties and is used as a moisture stabilizer in packing and storing humidity-sensitive objects.

SLING PSYCHROMETER: an instrument used in conjunction with a PSYCHROMETRIC TABLE to determine RELATIVE HUMIDITY. It consists of a wet- and dry-bulb thermometer, with the difference between their readings constituting the measure of the moisture in the air.

SMOKE DETECTOR: a fire-alert device activated by smoke.

SOLANDER BOX: a ready-made box of acid-free board; frequently used for the storage of documents, unframed works on paper, and so forth.

SOURCE-OF-ACQUISITION RECORD: a file of donors, bequestors, and vendors of objects to the museum as well as expeditions, purchase funds, and other sources of acquisition.

SPECIAL EXHIBITION: a gathering of MUSEUM OBJECTS, usually with a particular purpose or theme, for public display.

SPOT INVENTORY: an organized location search for a random selection of items for which the museum is responsible (as opposed to an accounting of all objects).

STORAGE: the place/space for the safekeeping of MUSEUM OBJECTS not currently on exhibition.

STRETCHER: wooden bars, usually made of pine, that constitute a frame over which the canvas of a painting is stretched. The size of a stretcher can be changed slightly through the adjustment of small wedges (keys) or expansion bolts at the four corners.

TARE WEIGHT: for shipping purposes, the weight of the packing box, including packing materials, without the object it was built to contain. The term can also be used to indicate the weight of an empty vehicle. See also GROSS WEIGHT; NET WEIGHT.

TEMPERATURE: the degree of hotness or coldness. Fluctuation in temperature, particularly a drop in temperature that leads to CONDENSATION, can damage MUSEUM OBJECTS.

TEMPORARY DEPOSIT NUMBER: a control number whose purpose is identification, unique to an object or a group of objects received at the same time from a single source, usually assigned to objects placed on temporary deposit with the museum for purposes of examination or study or when final disposition is not known at time of deposit.

TEMPORARY DEPOSIT RECEIPT: a formal acknowledgment prepared by a museum to confirm receipt of objects placed in its custody that are not covered by LOAN AGREEMENTS.

Temporary Loan: a short-term loan of an object, usually for a Special Exhibition or installation.

Temporary Loan Number: see Loan Number.

Thymol: a general fungicide in common use in museums, especially for the treatment of mold growth.

Ultraviolet Filter: a filter that can be placed over windows, skylights, and fluorescent light tubes, between the light source and Museum Object, to remove or reduce harmful ultraviolet rays in the light.

Valuation: see Insurance Value.

Waterproof Paper: a treated paper or combination of papers used in lining a shipping box to protect the contents from the effects of water.

Width: the measurement taken from one side of an object to the other, perpendicular to the Length and Height.

Work Sheet: an informal document used to record basic Catalogue information pertaining to an object. From this form, Catalogue Cards can be prepared.

CONTRIBUTORS

HUNTINGTON T. BLOCK is president of Huntington T. Block Insurance, a Washington, D.C., firm that specializes in fine arts insurance. He is a chartered property casualty underwriter and a past president of the Metropolitan Washington Association of Insurance Agents. Mr. Block has lectured extensively on various aspects of insurance.

GERALDINE BRUCKNER has been on the staff of the University Museum, University of Pennsylvania, Philadelphia, since 1921. She first worked in the administrative office, and, in 1929, became the museum's first registrar. Although retired, she continues to serve as associate editor of *Expedition*, the museum's quarterly magazine.

RICHARD D. BUCK was director of the Balboa Art Conservation Center, San Diego, California, at the time of his death in 1977. One of the profession's distinguished conservators, he served for many years as the chief conservator in the Department of Conservation at the Fogg Art Museum, Harvard University, Cambridge, Massachusetts, and as director of the Intermuseum Conservation Association, Oberlin, Ohio. Mr. Buck was a fellow and officer of IIC, an honorary member of AIC, and the author of numerous publications on conservation in the arts.

ELIZABETH L. BURNHAM is registrar of the Cooper-Hewitt Museum, the Smithsonian Institution's National Museum of Design, New York. She was formerly registrar of the Yale University Art Gallery, and associate registrar at the Museum of Modern Art, New York, where she worked for Dorothy H. Dudley. Ms. Burnham's contributions to the profession include co-authoring/directing *Handling Works of Art*, a videotape cassette and film sponsored by the Museum of Modern Art.

WILLIAM A. BURNS is director of the Florence Museum, Florence, South Carolina. He was formerly director of the San Diego Natural History Museum and of the Witte Memorial Museum, San Antonio, Texas, and assistant to the director of the American Museum of Natural History, New York. Dr. Burns is the author of many publications and has served on several committees of the AAM as well as on the Cultural Heritage Committee of California and the Governor's Historical Commission of South Carolina.

RIVA CASTLEMAN is director of the Department of Prints and Illustrated Books at the Museum of Modern Art, New York. She was formerly curator of the California Historical Society and on the staff of the Art Institute of Chicago. Ms. Castleman has been active here and abroad in the exhibition of contemporary prints, and is the author of several books on modern prints and of numerous articles in domestic and foreign periodicals.

HOLLY M. CHAFFEE is computerization coordinator at the Museum of New Mexico, Santa Fe. She was formerly curator of collections at the Arizona State Museum at the University of Arizona, Tucson. She has written, with others, several articles describing the computerization of the Arizona State Museum collections. She is currently an officer of the AAM's Curators Committee.

ROBERT G. CHENHALL is director of Data Services of the Margaret Woodbury Strong Museum, Rochester, New York. He was chairman of the Museum Data Bank Committee for five years, and is now chairman of the AAM's Documentation Committee and a member of the ICOM Documentation Committee. Dr. Chenhall has lectured and written extensively on the subjects of computer data banks and museum systems.

DOROTHY H. DUDLEY began her career in 1925 at the Newark Museum, Newark, New Jersey, as a member of John Cotton Dana's first apprentice class in museum work. After ten years as assistant in charge of exhibitions in the Newark Museum's branch museums, she became registrar at the Museum of Modern Art, New York, a position she held for thirty-three years. During this time she served on several AAM committees, was instrumental in the liberalization of tariff laws for works of art, and co-authored *Museum Registration Methods*. After her retirement in 1969 she received a John D. Rockefeller, III Travel Grant to survey museum registration procedures in several Asian countries. She is currently the volunteer registrar/curator of the Biddeford Historical Society, Biddeford, Maine.

MARCIA COTTIS HARTY was supervisor of the catalogue in the Office of the Registrar at the Metropolitan Museum of Art, New York, where she trained under Irma Bezold Wilkinson. She also served on the staff of the Buffalo Public Library. She is now retired.

BETSY B. JONES is associate director and curator of painting at the Smith College Museum of Art, Northampton, Massachusetts. She was formerly curator in the Department of Painting and Sculpture at the Museum of Modern Art, New York, and was also on the staff of the Portland Art Museum, Portland, Oregon.

WINIFRED KENNEDY is archivist at the Walters Art Gallery, Baltimore, Maryland. From 1934 to 1972 she served as the museum's registrar. She was also registrar at the Fogg Art Museum, Harvard University, Cambridge, Massachusetts, where she initially studied museum work.

JOHN B. LAWTON is a fine arts consultant for Huntington T. Block Insurance, Washington, D.C. He was formerly an underwriting superintendent for Aetna Insurance Company.

DOROTHY L. LYTLE is serving, during her retirement, as a part-time volunteer in the Department of Primitive Art at the Metropolitan Museum of Art, New York. She was formerly the registrar at the Museum of Primitive Art, New York, and associate curator of prints and assistant to the registrar at the Museum of Modern Art, New York. She also served on the staff of the Newark Museum, Newark, New Jersey.

LAWRENCE J. MAJEWSKI is professor of conservation and chairman of the Conservation Center of the Institute of Fine Arts, New York University. Since 1964 he has served as chief conservator of the archaeological expedition to Sardis, Turkey. He has traveled extensively and provided conservation services in India, Poland, Italy, and elsewhere. Mr. Majewski is a fellow and former officer of IIC and the author of numerous articles on conservation, especially of archaeological materials. In 1972–73 he authored the conservation column for *Museum News*.

ANITA MANNING is registrar at the Bernice P. Bishop Museum, Honolulu, Hawaii. She is a graduate of the Williamsburg Seminar and the author of two technical leaflets published by the American Association for State and Local History.

PATRICIA NAUERT is registrar at the Los Angeles County Museum of Art, Los Angeles, California. She was formerly assistant to the registrar at the Museum of Modern Art,

New York, where she trained with Dorothy H. Dudley. Ms. Nauert is the author of *Reg Tech* and the founder/editor of *Registrars' Report*, the first periodical directed to registrars.

JEFFREY M. NEFF practices law in Tucson, Arizona. He was formerly systems analyst at the Arizona State Museum at the University of Arizona, Tucson. He has written articles on computer applications in museums and in the field of anthropology.

MARGOT PAGE PEARSALL was assistant director of the Detroit Historical Museum, Detroit, Michigan, where she worked for over thirty years. She was active in a great many civic organizations in Detroit and an honorary member of the Detroit Historical Society, to whose bulletin she was a frequent contributor. She is now retired.

VIRGINIA PEARSON was circulation manager of the Department of Circulating Exhibitions at the Museum of Modern Art, New York, from 1944 until 1962. She died in 1964. She had attended the apprentice class in museum work at the Newark Museum, Newark, New Jersey, and worked in the children's section there before joining the staff at the Museum of Modern Art.

BRICE RHYNE is reference assistant in the Catalogue Department of the Metropolitan Museum of Art, New York. He was formerly on the staff of the Phillips Collection, Washington, D.C.

DOUGLAS J. ROBINSON is registrar at the Hirshhorn Museum and Sculpture Garden, Smithsonian Institution, Washington, D.C. He was formerly a cataloguer in the Office of the Registrar at the Museum of Modern Art, New York, where he worked under Dorothy H. Dudley. Mr. Robinson served as an adviser for the third edition of *Museum Registration Methods*, overseeing revisions throughout the book.

ERIC B. ROWLISON is director of the National Gallery of Victoria, Melbourne, Australia. He was formerly registrar at the Museum of Modern Art, New York, where he had worked in the Office of the Registrar under Dorothy H. Dudley, and at the Art Gallery of New South Wales, Sydney. Mr. Rowlison is the author of several papers and articles on registration and the co-author/director of *Handling Works of Art*, a videotape cassette and film sponsored by the Museum of Modern Art.

JEROME G. ROZEN, JR. is deputy director for research and curator of hymenoptera at the American Museum of Natural History, New York, and an adjunct professor at the City University of New York. He has directed numerous field expeditions to study the biology, immature states, and evolutionary relationships of bees, and has published on these subjects. He has served on committees of the Entomological Society of America and as editor of its miscellaneous publications.

CAROLE E. RUSH is registrar/systems analyst at the Margaret Woodbury Strong Museum, Rochester, New York. She was formerly a senior programmer at the University of Rochester Computing Center and was the systems design liaison for a computer publication on the toxicology of commercial products.

STERLING H. RUSTON is registrar at the Museum of Science and Industry, Chicago, Illinois. He began work at the museum in 1938 as an accountant, and in 1946 became the museum's second registrar.

MARYELL SEMAL is assistant director of the Japan House Gallery, New York. She was formerly registrar at the Asia House Gallery, New York, and at the Metropolitan Museum of Art, New York, where, as a member of the Registrar-Cataloguing Department staff, she was trained under Irma Bezold Wilkinson. Ms. Semal was an adviser for the third edition of *Museum Registration Methods* and, in particular, revised the chapter on importing and exporting.

NATHAN STOLOW is special adviser for conservation for the National Museums of Canada. He was the founder and first director of the Canadian Conservation Institute. Dr. Stolow is the author of numerous articles on conservation, a fellow of IIC and AIC, and recipient of the Canada Centennial Medal and the Queen's Jubilee Medal.

DIANE GREENE TAYLOR is currently working on a survey of textiles made and used in the state of Texas. From 1971 to 1977 she was registrar at the University of Texas at Austin Winedale Museum, Round Top, Texas. Ms. Taylor has presented several papers on registration and historic preservation.

HOLLY B. ULSETH is administrative assistant to the director of interpretation at the Pioneer Arizona Living History Museum, Phoenix, Arizona. She was formerly curator of social history at the Detroit Historical Museum, Detroit, Michigan.

DAVID VANCE is president of the Museum Computer Network, Inc. and visiting associate professor at the State University of New York at Stony Brook. He was formerly registrar at the Museum of Modern Art, New York, where he had worked for many years in the Office of the Registrar under Dorothy H. Dudley. He is a member of the ICOM Documentation Committee and the author of numerous publications on the use of computers in museums.

THERESE VARVERIS is adviser to the Catalogue and Information Retrieval Committee of the Australian Gallery Director's Council and technical consultant to the Department of Film at the Museum of Modern Art, New York. She was formerly associate registrar at the Museum of Modern Art, where she trained under Dorothy H. Dudley. Ms. Varveris is the author of publications and papers on cataloguing and computers.

MARICA VILCEK is associate curator and head of the Catalogue Department at the Metropolitan Museum of Art, New York. She was formerly assistant curator of the Department of Prints and Drawings of the National Gallery, Bratislava, Czechoslovakia, and adjunct assistant professor at the Academy of Arts, Comenius University, Bratislava.

IRMA BEZOLD WILKINSON began her career in 1929 at the Metropolitan Museum of Art, New York, where she studied under Henry W. Kent and Margaret A. Gash. After working in the Photograph and Slide Library, she was transferred to the Central Catalogue of the museum's collections and was made head of that department in 1942. In 1949 she was also named registrar, and held both positions until her retirement in 1963. During her years as registrar she assisted in setting up a system of record keeping for the United Nations and co-authored *Museum Registration Methods*. Since her retirement she has done consulting work for the Frick Collection, the Huntington Hartford Collection, the Brooklyn Museum, the Oriental Institute in Chicago, and for several historical societies in Connecticut.

ACKNOWLEDGMENTS

THE FOLLOWING INSTITUTIONS AND FIRMS generously supplied photographs, sample forms, information for the supplements to chapters 4 and 5, or other assistance:

Ace World-Wide Moving and Storage Company, Los Angeles, Calif.
The Alaska State Museum, Juneau, Alaska
American Association for State and Local History, Nashville, Tenn.
The American Institute of Architects Foundation/The Octagon, Washington, D.C.
The American Museum of Natural History, New York, N.Y.
American Swedish Historical Foundation-Museum, Philadelphia, Pa.
Arizona Historical Society, Tucson, Ariz.
The Art Institute of Chicago, Chicago, Ill.
Atlas Van Lines, Evansville, Ind.
The Baltimore Museum of Art, Baltimore, Md.
Bernice P. Bishop Museum, Honolulu, Hawaii
Block, Huntington T., Insurance, Washington, D.C.
The Brooklyn Museum, Brooklyn, N.Y.
Buffalo Museum of Science, Buffalo, N.Y.
California Academy of Sciences, San Francisco, Calif.
Chicago Historical Society, Chicago, Ill.
Children's Museum, Indianapolis, Ind.
The Cleveland Museum of Art, Cleveland, Ohio
The Cleveland Museum of Natural History, Cleveland, Ohio
Colorado Historical Society, Denver, Colo.
Connor, John S., Inc., Washington, D.C.
The Corning Museum of Glass, Corning, N.Y.
Denver Museum of Natural History, Denver, Colo.
Detroit Historical Museum, Detroit, Mich.
Emery Air Freight Corporation, Wilton, Conn.
Field Museum of Natural History, Chicago, Ill.
Fort Worth Museum of Science and History, Forth Worth, Tex.
Idaho State Historical Society, Boise, Idaho
Intermuseum Laboratory, Oberlin, Ohio
Japan Air Lines, New York, N.Y.
Japan House Gallery, New York, N.Y.
Kansas State Historical Society, Topeka, Kans.
Keating, W. R., and Company, New York, N.Y.
Los Angeles County Museum of Art, Los Angeles, Calif.
Maine State Museum, Augusta, Maine
The Margaret Woodbury Strong Museum, Rochester, N.Y.
Merrimack Valley Textile Museum, North Andover, Mass.
The Metropolitan Museum of Art, New York, N.Y.
The Minneapolis Institute of Arts, Minneapolis, Minn.
The Montreal Museum of Fine Arts, Montreal, Quebec, Canada
Museum of the American Indian, Heye Foundation, New York, N.Y.

The Museum of Fine Arts, Boston, Mass.
Museum of International Folk Art, Santa Fe, N. Mex.
The Museum of Modern Art, New York, N.Y.
Museum of Science and Industry, Chicago, Ill.
National Fire Protection Association, Boston, Mass.
National Gallery of Art, Washington, D.C.
National Trust for Historic Preservation, Washington, D.C.
The New Jersey Historical Society, Newark, N.J.
New York Department of State, Albany, N.Y.
New York State Historical Association, Cooperstown, N.Y.
New York State Museum, Albany, N.Y.
The Newark Museum Association, Newark, N.J.
The Oakland Museum, Oakland, Calif.
Ollendorff Fine Arts, New York, N.Y.
Oregon Historical Society, Portland, Oreg.
Peabody Museum of Archaeology and Ethnology, Cambridge, Mass.
Pennsylvania Academy of the Fine Arts, Philadelphia, Pa.
Philadelphia Museum of Art, Philadelphia, Pa.
Rochester Museum and Science Center, Rochester, N.Y.
The Seven Santini Brothers, New York, N.Y.
Smith College Museum of Art, Northampton, Mass.
Smithsonian Institution
  Conservation Analytical Laboratory, Washington, D.C.
  Cooper-Hewitt Museum, The Smithsonian Institution's National Museum of Design, New York, N.Y.
  Hirshhorn Museum and Sculpture Garden, Washington, D.C.
  National Museum of History and Technology, Washington, D.C.
  National Museum of Natural History, Washington, D.C.
  Office of the Registrar, Washington, D.C.
The Solomon R. Guggenheim Museum, New York, N.Y.
The Textile Museum, Washington, D.C.
United States, Department of the Treasury, Customs Service, Washington, D.C.
The University Museum, University of Pennsylvania, Philadelphia, Pa.
University of Texas at Austin Winedale Historical Center, Round Top, Tex.
Walters Art Gallery, Baltimore, Md.

In addition to the contributing institutions and individuals mentioned above, the following individuals served as reviewers for portions of this third edition or otherwise gave assistance:

Ruth Bowman	Ronald J. Kley	Katherine Paris
Thomas K. Bush	Eleanor McMillan	Agnes Peters
Roberta Faul	Mary Means Melbourne	Daniel B. Reibel
Jane Glaser	Martha Morris	George L. Stout
Charles W. Hart, Jr.	Suzanne D. Murphy	H. J. Swinney
Laurence Hoffman	Robert M. Organ	Stephen E. Weil

ACKNOWLEDGMENTS

The extensive editing of the third edition was done by editorial consultants Paula A. Degen and Ann Hofstra Grogg, with the assistance of Douglas J. Robinson and Maryell Semal. The staff of the American Association of Museums participating in the project include Migs Grove, Ellen C. Hicks, Richard McLanathan, Gwendolyn J. Owens, Maureen Robinson, and Pauline Schreiber. The typing was done by Barbara J. Baker. The index was compiled by Toni Warner. The book's design is by Bookmark Studio, Washington, D.C.

Photo credits for the third edition of *Museum Registration Methods* are as follows:

The American Institute of Architects Foundation/The Octagon: Kevin Green, Figs. 4.4, 6.2.
Arizona Historical Society: Bob Herskovitz, Figs. 3.2, 3.3, 3.4, 3.5, 3.6, 3.7, 3.8.
The Baltimore Museum of Art: Fig. 3.11.
Bernice P. Bishop Museum: Ben Patnoi, Figs. 1.4, J.5, J.6, J.7, J.9.
The Cleveland Museum of Art: Fig. 5.10.
Denver Museum of Natural History: Rhonda M. Barlow, Fig. 5.8; Dudley T. Smith, Jr., Fig. 2.1.
Hirshhorn Museum and Sculpture Garden, Smithsonian Institution: Peter Harholdt: Figs. 4.2, 5.1; John Tennant, Figs. 1.1, 1.5, 1.6, 1.7, 5.2, 5.5, 7.3, F.1, Q.1, Q.2, R.1, R.3, R.4, R.14, R.15, R.16, R.17, R.23.
Intermuseum Laboratory: Figs. F.2, F.3.
Japan Air Lines: Fig. 7.11.
Los Angeles County Museum of Art: Figs. R.21, R.22 (box prepared by The Museum of Modern Art).
Maine State Museum: Greg Hart, Figs. 2.3, 4.3.
The Metropolitan Museum of Art: Costume Institute, Figs. 5.6, 5.7; Rolf Petersen, Fig. 4.5.
The Montreal Museum of Fine Arts: Marilyn Aitken, Fig. 9.3.
The Museum of Modern Art: Fig. R.19; Alexandre Georges, frontispiece; Kate Keller, Figs. R.7, R.8, R.10, R.11, R.12, R.13; Rolf Petersen, Figs. 2.4, 7.4, 7.9, R.5; Soichi Sunami, Fig. R.20.
Museum of Science and Industry: Photo Ideas, Inc., Chicago, Fig. L.3.
National Gallery of Art: Figs. 3.1, 6.3, 8.2.
National Museum of Natural History, Smithsonian Institution: Figs. 4.1, 5.3, 5.4.
New York Department of State: George Proper, Figs. 6.1, 9.1, 9.2, 9.4.
Oregon Historical Society: Maurice Hodge, Fig. 2.2.
Pennsylvania Academy of the Fine Arts: cover.
Philadelphia Museum of Art: Eric Mitchell, Figs. 1.2, 1.3.
The Seven Santini Brothers: Figs. 7.5, 7.6, 7.7, 7.8; Si Drabkin Studios, Inc., New York, Figs. 7.1, R.18.
Smith College Museum of Art: Helga Photo Studio, New York, Fig. 5.9.
United States, Department of the Treasury, Customs Service: Figs. 8.1, 8.3, 8.4.

The authors also acknowledge the following individuals and institutions that assisted in the previous two editions of *Museum Registration Methods:*

N. Carl Barefoot, Jr.	William M. Milliken
Caroline Birenbaum	Paul Mills
Margaret F. Bush	George Montgomery
California Palace of the Legion of Honor, San Francisco, Calif.	Chester H. Newkirk
	Hugh G. O'Neill
Katherine Coffey	Charles Parkhurst
Laurence Vail Coleman	Murray Pease
Sal Costabile	Charles M. Richards
Cranbrook Institute of Science, Bloomfield Hills, Mich.	Monawee Allen Richards
	John Rogers and Associates
William D. Crockett	San Francisco Museum of Art, San Francisco, Calif.
James Delihas	
René d'Harnoncourt	Louis Santini
Helen M. Franc	Henrietta M. Schumm
Marianne Gannon	Dorothy Simmons
Robert T. Hatt	Alan Solomon
Elizabeth Heck	Emily Stark
A. G. Heim	Pauline H. Swayze
George Hulme	Gertrude Toomey
Caroline K. Keck	Ruth Osgood Trovato
Lillian M. Kern	Charlotte Trowbridge
Richard H. Koch	Robert W. G. Vail
Barbara LaSalle	Osmund L. Varela
John S. Lea	Jean Volkmer
Alicia Legg	Sarah Weiner
David B. Little	Warren L. Wittry
Sara Mazo	

To all of the above, the authors give their sincere thanks for contributing in many varied and important ways through over twenty years and three editions of the book. The authors are gratified that the first two editions have proved to be so useful and sincerely hope that this updated third edition will be equally helpful to museum staffs and students.

DOROTHY H. DUDLEY
IRMA BEZOLD WILKINSON

INDEX

Accessioning
  accession numbers, 21, 22, 24, 26–27, 31, 66, 203, 205–06, 220, 228, 245–46, 262, 288–89, 301, 309, 337, 343, 409; fig. 3.7
  accession records, fig. 3.10
    accession books, 30–31, 187, 206, 246–47; figs. B.1–2, G.1; forms V.A
    accession cards, 30–33, 187, 227, 409; figs. D.5, L.2–3; forms V.C
    accession files, 3, 27, 30–31, 219, 228, 255, 302, 309, 320, 322, 324, 333, 334, 409; figs. N.1–2
    other accession records, 29–30, 246–47, 255, 293, 301, 302, 338; figs. G.1, K.1. *See also* Cataloguing, work sheets
  computer applications, 31, 337, 338, 340, 342–45
  defined, 22, 409, 414
  partial interest gifts, 203–04
  poorly documented collections, 205–07, 261–62, 265
  procedures, 21–24, 26–27, 29–31, 203, 205–06, 219, 228, 245–47, 288–89, 301, 302, 304, 309–10, 337–38
  See also Acquisitions; Cataloguing; Deaccessioning; Records, types of; *types of museums and objects*
Acid migration, 71, 72, 74–87 passim, 293, 409, 410; fig. 1.4. *See also* Paper, acid-free
Acknowledgments (for gifts), 34, 187, 202, 247–48; figs. 3.10, G.3; forms IV.A
Acquisitions
  annual reports, 19, 310
  approval, 201–02
  ethics, 284, 293
  lists, 203, 338
  open exchange agreements, 288
  restrictions on, 34, 89, 202

  See also Accessioning; Gifts; Source-of-acquisition records
Acrylic paints
  for marking objects, 48–49, 56, 57–63 passim
Air circulation systems, 69, 404. *See also* Climate control
Air shipments, 108–09, 400
  courier escort, 113, 118, 124, 136–37
  importing and exporting by, 123–24, 136–37
  See also Airwaybills
Air suspension system, 409. *See also* Motor van shipments
Airwaybills, 106, 108, 122, 123, 125, 127, 133–34, 194, 409; forms VIII.A. *See also* Air shipments
Alabaster, 269
Amphibians. *See* Reptiles and amphibians
Anatomy specimens
  importing, 130
  storage, 74
Animal specimens
  marking, 48
  measuring, 42
  See also Animals; Endangered species; *types of specimens*
Animals
  at historic sites, 261
  importing, 131, 135
  marking, 63
  See also Animal specimens; Endangered species
Anthropology collections
  accessioning, 302, 337–38
  cataloguing, 267–80, 289, 302–03, 337–38
  classifying, 267–79
  computer applications, 280, 335–39
  condition, 271–72
  insurance, 294
  marking, 302
  measuring, 271

registering, 335–39
source-of-acquisition records, fig. J.9
storage, 302–03
terminology for describing, 267, 272–79, 280
See also Archaeological specimens; Ethnological specimens; *types of museums and objects*
Antiques, 409
  importing, 119, 122, 128
  See also Furniture; Reproductions
Antler
  classifying, 270
Aquatints, 214
  measuring, 232
Archaeological specimens
  accessioning, 22, 24, 259–60
  cataloguing, 302
  computer applications, 319, 338
  condition, 271–72
  at historic sites, 259–60
  importing, 131–32
  marking, 302
  on-site registration, fig. 2.3
  storage, 74, 82, 86, 260, 303
  weighing, fig. 4.3
  See also Anthropology collections; Ethnological specimens
Archives, 293–94, 338. *See also* Inactive files
Arms and armor
  marking, 48, 57
  storage, 74
  See also Firearms; Weapons
Art museums
  accessioning in, 203, 205–07, 220
  acquisitions procedure in, 201–03
  cataloguing in, 203, 205–07, 208–18, 219–27, 228–36, 340, 342–45
  computer applications, 319, 340–54
  registration in, 3, 205–06, 219, 228, 340
Art objects
  accessioning, 203, 205–07, 219, 228
  cataloguing, 203, 205–07, 208–18, 219–27, 228–36, 340, 342–45
  classifying, 205–07, 208–18, 220–22
  computer applications, 319, 340–54
  condition, 237–44
  handling, 67–68, 355–66
  importing, 118–19, 129–30, 412, 413
  insurance, 91, 140–42, 143–44, 204
  measuring, 42–44
  packing, 95–96, 98–100, 105, 118, 367, 371–82, 389–94
  preparing for travel, 367–70
  See also types of art objects
Assemblages, 217
Association files. *See* Subject records
Atmospheric conditions. *See* Climate control

Audiovisual material
  importing, 120, 130–31
Authority files, 326

Bailees and bailors, 18, 144, 151, 410
Baleen, 270
Bark cloth and containers, 279
  storage, 75
Baskets
  importing, 120, 122
  marking, 58
  measuring, fig. 3.5
  storage, 75
Bequests. *See* Gifts; Partial interest gifts
Bills of lading, 106, 110, 122, 125, 127, 133–34, 194, 195, 197, 410; forms VIII.B. *See also* Motor van shipments
Biological materials
  importing, 135
  See also types of specimens
Birds
  accessioning, 305
  fumigation, 72–73
  marking, 58, 305
  measuring, fig. 4.1
  storage, 75, 305
Boats
  storage, 75
Bond
  customs bond, 122, 123, 410
  employee bond, 144, 151, 152, 410
  permanent exhibition bond, 89, 120, 122, 130, 132, 134, 414
Bone
  condition, 237
  classifying, 270–71
  importing, 121
  marking, 48, 304, 305
  See also Anatomy specimens; Birds; Fishes; Mammals; Reptiles and amphibians; Skeletal material
Books
  classifying, 207
  importing, 121, 130, 135
  marking, 48, 49, 58
  storage, 75
  See also Manuscripts and documents; Printed matter
Botanical specimens
  cataloguing, 289; fig. J.5
  fumigation, 72–73
  importing, 131–32, 295
  insurance, 294
  loans and exchanges, 286–88, 290, 292
  marking, 58; fig. J.5
  shipping, 111, 295
  storage, 75; fig. J.6
  See also Plant material

Bottles
  classifying, 274
Bowls
  handling, 366
  classifying, 273
  See also Ceramic objects
Brick, 269
Bronzes
  care of, 74, 82
  identifying, 270
  marking, 58, 61
  patina, 271–72
  storage, 75, 82, 85
Buffer, 410. *See also* Acid migration
Building planning, 395–408
  avoiding hazards, 400–06
  elevators, 399
  lighting, 8, 67, 403; figs. 1.7, 5.2, F.2–3
  loading docks, 399–400; figs. 1.2–3
  registrar's role in, 395–408; fig. T.1
  work space, 6–8, 239, 398–99; figs. 1.1, 1.7, 5.2, F.2–3
  zone of safety, 398–99; fig. T.1
  See also Storage

Calipers, 41, 410
Camphor flakes, 72, 74–87 passim, 410
Carriers, 106–07, 111–12, 195, 197, 410
  certificates, 127
  liability, 19, 91, 106, 110, 144, 146, 148
  selecting, 106, 108–09, 111, 295; fig. 7.10
  See also Shipments, types of; Shipping
Cataloguing
  catalogue numbers, 27, 31, 205–06, 245–46, 289, 301, 302, 304, 305, 306, 410; figs. K.3–4
  catalogue (descriptive) photographs, 34, 187, 203, 206, 224, 227, 233, 234, 249, 410, 412; figs. 3.7, E.4, P.5, P.7; forms V.C.2–3
  catalogue records
    catalogue cards, 31, 187, 205–06, 219–20, 222–24, 227, 234, 248–49, 267, 289, 303, 304, 305–06, 314, 333, 334, 342–45, 410; figs. 3.6, 3.10, D.3–4, D.6, E.4, G.5, I.1, J.4, K.2–4, P.5, P.7; forms V.C
    catalogue files, 219, 224, 227, 255–56, 314, 322, 324–25, 334; figs. N.1–2
    other catalogue records, 228, 230–34, 236, 289–90, 302, 304, 305, 322, 324–25; figs. E.1–3, J.5. *See also* work sheets

computer applications, 228, 234, 290,
314, 319–34, 336, 340–54;
figs. E.4, N.4, P.2, P.5, P.7
defined, 21, 222, 289, 410
poorly documented collections, 205,
264
procedures, 27, 31–32, 203, 205–06,
219–22, 224, 228, 230–34,
246–47, 267, 289, 302, 304,
305–06, 324–26, 342–47;
fig. N.3
standard terminology, 158, 208–18,
231–32, 239–44, 267–80, 319,
333
work sheets, 31–32, 187, 203, 228,
230–33, 331, 333, 344, 416;
figs. 3.4, 3.6, 3.10, E.2–3,
N.4, P.2; forms V.B
See also Accessioning; Classifying
objects; Records, types of;
*types of museums and
objects*
Ceramic objects
condition, 238, 239
handling, 67, 365–66
marking, 48, 52, 58; figs. 4.4–5
packing, 100, 376, 382; fig. R.21
preparing for travel, 370; fig. R.21
storage, 70–71, 75–76
See also Potsherds; Pottery; Terra-
cotta; *types of ceramic
objects*
Ceremonial objects
classifying, 278–79
Chalk, 212
Charcoal drawings, 212
preparing for travel, 100, 370
China
accessioning sets of, 26–27
marking, 49, 52, 58
Class, 27, 205–07, 411
Classifying objects
by civilization (geographical area),
24, 220, 221, 302
by class, 27, 205–07
by form, 276
by material, 24, 220–21, 268–71
by media, 208–18
by provenance, 24
in science (natural history)
museums, 27
in science and technology
museums, 307
by subject, 248–49
by use, 24, 221, 255, 272–79
See also *types of objects*
Climate control, 404–05, 411
in packing and shipping, 96, 99, 109,
110, 118, 389–94, 405, 411
for records and files, 292
in storage areas, 8, 68–69, 74–87
passim, 302, 304, 404–05
See also Condensation; Humidity,
relative; hygrothermographs;

Sling psychrometers; Tem-
perature
Cloth
museum objects. See Costumes;
Textiles
for protecting objects, 67, 71, 74–87
passim, 100, 370, 376, 381
Clothing. See Costumes
Coins
marking, 58
storage, 70, 76
Collages, 216
importing, 118–19, 129
Collotypes, 215
Color pencils, 212
Computerization
accessioning by, 31, 335, 337, 338,
340, 342–45
applications, 280, 311, 319, 334, 338,
340
cataloguing by, 228, 234, 290, 314,
319–34, 336, 340–54; figs.
E.4, N.4, P.2, P.5, P.7
converting records, 332–33, 342–54
correcting errors, 350–52; figs. P.6–7
costs, 312, 316–17, 332, 340, 348–50.
See also time sharing
designing a record system, 290, 319–
29, 336–37, 340–45
equipment, 311–13, 332, 347–48
information
categories, 320, 324–26, 336–38,
342–44
indexes, 314, 316, 331, 336–37, 344
input, 311, 313, 315, 349
retrieval, 333, 335, 338, 353
storage, 312, 348
maintaining loan records by, 290,
338; fig. J.7
programs, 313, 352
registration by, 290, 319, 335–39
staff for, 4, 6, 321, 336, 345–47
systems, 313, 315–16, 336, 338, 340–
42; fig. P.1
selecting, 320, 331–33, 340–44,
347–48
terminology, 311–16, 320
time sharing, 290, 332, 336, 341
work sheets, 331, 333, 344; figs. N.4,
P.2
See also Data processing
Condensation, 68, 405–06, 411. See also
Climate control; Humidity,
relative; Temperature
Condition
defined, 237, 411
examining for, 15, 16, 237, 239, 359,
412; figs. F.2–3
incoming materials (including
loans), 15, 16, 37–39, 93, 237,
239; figs. 2.4, 6.3
outgoing materials (including
loans), 18–19, 89, 92–93, 95,
237, 239

insecurity, 237–38, 239
photographs, 16, 18–19, 34, 37, 39,
92, 95, 148, 227, 383, 387,
411; figs. 3.10, F.2–3
records and reports, 34, 38, 39, 92,
143, 197, 237, 239–44, 383,
387–88, 392; figs. 2.4, R.27.
See also photographs
Conservation, 322, 404, 411; fig. I.1.
See also Conservators
Conservation records, 322; figs. I.1,
N.1–2
Conservators, 16, 19, 37, 48, 69, 73, 74,
95, 96, 149, 237, 238, 293,
357, 359, 403, 411
Consignees and consignors, 19, 108,
124–25, 126–27, 194, 411. See
also Shipments, types of;
Shipping
Constructions
classifying, 216–18
Containerization, 106, 111–12, 137,
400, 411; figs. 7.11, 8.1
Copper
identifying, 270
storage, 81–82
Coral
classifying, 270
Correspondence records, 36, 187, 227,
281–82, 302, 309, 339
Costumes
marking, 49–50, 53, 58–59
measuring, 45–46
storage, 71, 76, 78; figs. 5.6–7
Couriers, 113, 118, 124, 136–37, 411
Credit line, 36, 202, 411
Curators, 3, 16, 19, 34, 37, 42, 53, 73,
74, 89–90, 93, 95, 117, 201–
03, 219, 222, 237, 238, 246,
249, 281–82, 287, 288, 289,
290, 297, 333, 334, 411;
fig. 4.1
Customs, 115, 117
bonds, 122, 123, 410. See also
Permanent exhibition bond
brokers, 12, 19, 107–08, 110, 112,
115, 117, 122–24, 126, 137,
411
documents, 19, 118, 119, 120, 122–
24, 126, 127–34, 197–98;
figs. 8.1, 8.4; forms IX
entry, 122–24, 411; figs. 8.1, 8.4
inspectors, 123, 411; figs. 8.1, 8.4
offices, 136
power of attorney, 117, 122, 411
seals, 123, 124, 411
U.S. provisions
for exporting, 126, 133–34
for importing, 118–22, 127–33,
134–36
See also Exporting; Importing

Damage, 237, 239; figs. 9.1, 9.3–4
  inspecting for, 16, 237, 239
  reporting, 16, 93, 148–50, 357, 387–88
  See also Building planning; Condition; Handling; Insurance; Packing; Water damage
Data processing
  categories, 324–26, 327, 329, 342–44
  data base, 313–14
  information flow, 312, 320, 331
  input, 311–13, 315–16, 330–31
  integrated systems, 256, 313, 315–16, 320–22, 324, 326–27, 331; figs. N.1–2
  retrieval systems, 290, 292, 338; fig. J.7
  systems analysis and design, 319–20, 321–22, 324–27, 333, 335–37, 340–41; figs. N.1–2
  See also Computerization; Record keeping
Deaccessioning
  defined, 412
  procedures, 35–36, 202–03, 224, 247, 322
  records, 35–36, 224, 247, 322; figs. N.1–2
Decoration
  describing, 271
Decorative arts objects (including small, fragile objects)
  classifying, 206, 207, 264, 271
  handling, 8, 67–68, 365–66; fig. 1.6
  marking, 48, 206
  packing, 96, 100, 105, 137, 376, 381–82; figs. R.21–22
  preparing for travel, 100, 370
  shipping, 137
  storage, 70–71, 74; figs. 5.3–4
  See also types of materials and objects
Deeds of gift, 34, 187, 203, 248, 261–62, 264, 339, 412; figs. A.1, A.4, G.4; forms IV.B. *See also* Ownership
Deposits. *See* Temporary deposits
Depreciation, 140, 148, 151, 412
Dirt
  preventing, 67, 404
  terms for describing, 244
Disposition files. *See* Deaccessioning, records
Documents. *See* Manuscripts
Dollies, 8, 67, 362–63, 365, 397, 398, 402–03, 412; fig. Q.7. *See also* Handling, equipment
Dolls
  cataloguing, 248–49, 333
  marking, 59
  storage, 78
Domestic shipments, 412
  arrangements, 11–12
  marking boxes for, 124
  packing for, 105–06

Donors, 202
  correspondence with, 202, 247–48, 301
  records of. *See* Source-of-acquisition records
Drawings
  classifying, 206, 208, 212–13
  condition, 239
  handling, 359, 360–64
  importing, 119, 129
  marking, 59
  measuring, 42, 43–44
  packing, 372–73, 376; figs. 7.10, R.20
  preparing for travel, 100, 367, 369–70
  storage, 78, 84, 404; fig. 5.2
  See also Framed works; Paper objects and works of art on; Unframed works
Drypoint, 214
  measuring, 232

Eggs
  storage, 75, 78, 85
  See also Birds; Reptiles and amphibians
Embossed prints. *See* Intaglio prints
Embroideries
  marking, 59, 63
  storage, 78, 87
Enamel paints, 211
Enamels
  handling, 365–66
  marking, 58, 59
  storage, 78
Encaustic, 210
Endangered species
  importing, 121, 129, 135, 282, 293, 295
  state regulations regarding, 282, 285, 295
Engravings, 214
  importing, 130–31
  measuring, 232
Entomology collections. *See* Insects
Etchings, 214
  importing, 130–31
  measuring, 232
Ethnological specimens
  cataloguing, 302
  computer applications, 336, 338
  condition, 271–72
  fumigation, 72–73, 78
  importing, 118, 119, 128–29
  marking, 302
  storage, 74, 78, 302–03
  See also Anthropology collections; Archaeological specimens
Exhibits
  inspecting, 285, 295, 297
  records, 256–57, 285, 295, 297
Exhibition catalogues, 36–37, 410
  importing, 121, 130, 135

Exhibition (or collection) history records, 93, 188, 233; form V.E.1
Exhibitions. *See* Loans; Special exhibitions; Traveling exhibitions
Exporting
  arrangements, 12, 19, 107–08, 111, 126–27, 136–37, 295
  documents, 126, 133–34
  duty-free return, 122, 132–33
  licenses, 117, 121, 126, 134, 412
  packing, 100, 124–25, 372; figs. 8.2, R.7–8
  shipping, 111, 124–25, 412
  U.S. provisions, 126, 133–34
  See also Customs; Packing; Shipping
Extended loans
  authorization for outgoing extended loans, 250
  defined, 11, 412
  marking, 48
  numbering, 21, 29, 412, 413
  records, 29–30, 33, 412; fig. 3.10
  renewal notices, 251
  return of, 30; fig. 3.10

Fabric objects. *See* Costumes; Textiles
Faience, 270
Fans
  marking, 59
  storage, 78
Feathers
  classifying, 271
  fumigation, 72–73
  importing, 121
  marking, 59
Files. *See* Records
Film
  importing, 131
  storage, 78
  See also Photographs
Fire, figs. 9.1, 9.4
  local regulations, 398, 402
  protection against, 67, 74–87 passim, 406
  See also Heat sensors; Insurance; Smoke detectors
Firearms
  importing, 135
  marking, 59
  measuring, 42, 46
  storage, 78–79
  See also Arms and armor; Weapons
Fishes
  marking, 59
  storage, 79
Flints
  classifying, 269
Foreign shipments, 412
  arrangements, 12, 19, 107–08, 111, 126–27, 136–37, 295
  marking boxes, 124–25, 372

packing for, 100, 124–25, 372; figs. 8.2, R.7–8
See also Couriers; Customs, brokers; Exporting; Importing
Forklifts, 8, 85, 365, 397, 412. *See also* Handling, equipment
Forms, 8–9, 167–98
  designing, 285–86, 330–31
  for gifts, 186–87
    acknowledgments, 34, 187, 202, 247–48; figs. 3.10, G.3; forms IV.A
    deeds of gift, 34, 187, 203, 248, 261–62, 264, 339, 412; figs. A.1, A.4, G.4; forms IV.B
  importing and exporting forms, 118, 119, 120, 122–24, 126, 127–34, 197–98; figs. 8.1, 8.4; forms IX
  intramuseum forms, 168–71
    incoming reports, 11, 19, 167, 285, 294, 301; figs. J.2, K.1; forms I.B
    notices to the registrar, 11, 89–90, 167; forms I.A, III.A
    outgoing reports (including releases), 11, 18, 19, 92, 167, 415; forms I.C, III.E.1
  for loans, 174–85
    general receipts, 174, 337–38; figs. 3.10, J.3; forms II.B.1, III.G, III.H.1, III.H.3
    incoming loan receipts, 13, 34, 37–39, 174, 249–50, 413; figs. 2.2, 3.10, G.6; forms III.D
    invoices of specimens, 174–75, 285, 292; figs. J.3, J.8; forms III.H
    loan agreements
      borrower to lender, 36–37, 89–90, 127, 174, 413; figs. 3.10, J.1; forms III.B, III.C.3
      lender to borrower, 90, 127, 174, 250–51, 413; fig. 3.10; forms III.C, III.H.1–2
    loan requests, 36, 89, 174; forms III.A
    outgoing loan receipts, 93, 174, 414; figs. J.3, J.8; forms III.F, III.H
    receipts of delivery, 13, 18, 30, 39, 93, 171, 174, 414; figs. 3.10, J.3; forms II.B, III.E, III.G, III.H.1, III.H.3
    release forms, 11, 18, 92, 167, 415; forms I.C, III.E.1. *See also* intramuseum forms, outgoing reports
    work sheets, 37, 192; fig. 3.10; forms VI.A
  shipping forms, 194–97
    airwaybills, 106, 108, 122, 123, 125, 127, 133–34, 194, 409; forms VIII.A
    bills of lading, 106, 110, 122, 125, 127, 133–34, 194, 195, 197, 410; forms VIII.B
  for temporary deposits, 171
    agreements for demonstrators' tools, 261; fig. H.3
    general receipts, 171, 337–38; figs. 3.10, J.3; forms II.B.1, III.G, III.H.1, III.H.3
    receipts of delivery, 13, 18, 171, 414; fig. J.3; forms II.B, III.H.1, III.H.3
    temporary deposit receipts, 13, 15, 34, 171, 307, 309, 415; figs. 2.2, 3.2, 3.10, L.1; forms II.A, III.H.3
Fossils
  cataloguing, 305–06
  importing, 130
  marking, 59, 306
  storage, 79, 306
Foxing, 84, 232, 239, 243, 412
Fragile objects. *See* Decorative arts objects
Framed works
  condition, 237–38, 239
  handling, 105–06, 359–60, 362–63, 386; figs. 1.5, Q.3–7
  importing and exporting, 126, 129
  marking, 51
  measuring, 41–42
  packing, 106, 372–73, 376; figs. 7.2, 7.9–10, R.6–20
  preparing for travel, 92–93, 95, 100, 105–06, 239, 367, 369–70, 386; figs. 7.9, Q.8–9, R.1–3, R.5
  shipping, figs. 7.9–10
  storage, 360; fig. 5.2
  See also Drawings; Paintings; Paper objects and works of art on; Pastels; Photographs; Prints; Unframed works; Watercolors
Freight-forwarding agents, 12, 19, 107–08, 112, 113, 116, 117–18, 122, 126, 127, 137, 412. *See also* Shipments, types of; Shipping
Fresco, 210–11
Fumigation
  of museum objects and specimens, 72–73, 74–87 passim, 285, 297, 303, 304, 305, 412; fig. 3.3
  permits and reports, 285, 297
  of quarantined imports, 122
  See also types of fumigants
Furniture
  handling, 67, 366
  marking, 60
  preparing for travel, 105
  storage, 71, 79
  See also Antiques

Furs
  fumigation, 72–73
  importing, 135
  storage, 79

Gems
  marking, 60, 61, 206
  storage, 70, 79, 82
Gifts
  acknowledgments, 34, 187, 202, 247–48; fig. G.3; forms IV.A
  deeds of gift, 34, 187, 203, 248, 261–62, 264, 339, 412; figs. A.1, A.4, G.4; forms IV.B
  partial interest, 33, 203–04, 414; figs. A.3–4
  restrictions on, 18, 34, 89, 202
  See also Acquisitions; Donors; Source-of-acquisition records
Glass objects, 269–70
  condition, 238
  handling, 67, 366
  marking, 48, 49, 52–53, 60
  measuring, 42
  packing, 100
  storage, 79
Glassine, 8, 74–87 passim, 100, 370, 412
Glossaries
  classifying paintings, drawings, prints, constructions, 208–18
  computer terms, 311–16
  describing anthropological objects, 272–79
  describing condition, 240–44
  general, 409–16
  insurance terms, 151–54
Gold
  marking, 60, 61
  storage, 81–82
Goldpoint, 212
Gouaches, 209–10
  measuring, 42
Gourds
  classifying, 271
  marking, 60
Graphic arts objects, 208
  classifying, 213–16
    allied processes, 215–16
      photomechanical processes, 215–16
    intaglio processes, 213–14
    planographic processes, 214–15
    relief processes, 213
    stencil processes, 215
  marking, 54
  See also Prints
Graphite pencils, 212
Gums, 209

Halftone prints, 216
Handling of objects
   crew, 11–12, 355, 357, 359
   equipment, 8, 67, 106, 355, 357–66 passim, 397, 398, 400, 402–03; figs. 1.5–6, 3.1, Q.1–2.
      See also types of equipment
   guidelines for, 67–68, 355–66, 399; fig. Q.7
   See also types of objects
Heat sensors, 67, 74–87 passim, 406, 412
Hematite, 269
Herpetology collections. *See* Reptiles and amphibians
Highway transportation. *See* Motor van shipments
Historic artifacts
   accessioning, 245–47
   cataloguing, 246–49, 253–59, 324–31, 333–34
   classifying, 245, 255
   computer applications, 319–34
   documentation, 245, 253–56, 261–62, 327
   insurance, 294
   marking, fig. 4.4
   reproductions, 254, 260–61
   source-of-acquisition records, fig. J.9
   storage, 74, 259–60
   See also types of museums and objects
Historic house museums
   archaeological finds at, 259–60
   correcting inadequate registration, 261–65
   craft demonstrations, 260–61
   location records, 256–57; figs. H.1–2
   maintenance records, 257
   registration in, 253–66
   restoration records, 257–59
   staff, 264–65
   storage, 259–60
History museums
   accessioning in, 245–47
   cataloguing in, 246–49, 324–31, 333–34
   computer applications, 319–34
   registration in, 3, 245–47, 249–51, 253–66
Holograms, 216
Horn
   classifying, 270
   importing, 121
Humidity, relative
   control during packing and shipping, 96, 99, 118, 389–94, 405, 411
   control for records and files, 292
   control in storage areas, 68–69, 71, 74–87 passim, 302, 404–05
   defined, 68, 415
   measuring, 68–69

   See also Climate control; Condensation; Hygrothermographs; Sling psychrometers; Temperature; *types of materials and objects*
Hygroscopic materials, 413
Hygrothermographs, 8, 68–69, 390, 405, 413

Identifying numbers, 413. *See* Numbering systems
Illuminations
   storage, 79, 84
Impervious materials
   marking, 52–53
Implements. *See* Tools
Importing, 117–24, 295, 413
   arrangements, 12, 117–18
   documents, 119–20, 127–33, 197–98; forms IX
   duty-free return of exported material, 122, 132–33
   licenses, 121, 135
   permanent exhibition bond, 89, 120, 122, 130, 132, 134, 198, 414; forms IX.B.1, IX.C.1
   restrictions, 120–21, 134–36
   U.S. provisions, 118–22, 127–33, 134–36
   See also Customs; Packing; Shipping
Inactive files, 31, 293–94, 338
Incoming loans. *See* Loans, incoming
Incoming material, 11–16, 239, 406, 414; figs. 2.1–3, 3.2
   conditions governing, 13, 37, 39, 171, 174, 249, 285; figs. G.6, J.1; forms II.A, II.B, III.B
   examining for condition, 15, 16, 237, 239; figs. 2.4, 6.3
   insurance, 19
   loans for special exhibitions, 15, 27, 29, 36–39, 46, 48, 174, 249–50, 413
   notices to the registrar, 11, 89–90, 167; forms I.A
   records, 4, 13, 15, 285, 301, 412
   reports, 11, 19, 167, 285, 294, 301; figs. J.2, K.1; forms I.B
   temporary deposit receipts, 13, 15, 34, 171, 307, 309, 415; figs. 2.2, 3.2, 3.10, L.1; forms II.A, III.H.3
   storage, 16, 65, 294
   See also Loans
Information management. *See* Data processing
Inkless intaglio. *See* Intaglio prints
Inks
   as art medium, 212
   for marking objects, 48, 49, 52–53, 56, 57–63 passim

Insects
   cataloguing, 289, 304
   fumigation, 72–73
   loans and exchanges, 286–88, 292
   marking, 60, 304
   storage, 79, 304; fig. 5.8
Insecurity, 237–38, 239
Insurance, 139–54
   Arts and Artifacts Indemnity Act, 150
   brokers and agents, 142, 152
   with carriers and packers, 19, 91, 106, 110, 144–45, 146, 148
   certificates, 90, 146, 151, 410
   claims, 16, 35, 93, 239, 148–50, 387–88, 413
   coverage, 19, 140–42
   employee bond, 144, 151, 152, 410
   fine arts, 91, 140–42, 143
   floater policies, 140–41, 142, 152
   glossary of terms, 151–54
   for incoming and outgoing material, 19
   for loans, 19, 39, 89, 90–91, 93, 126, 140–42, 143
   for objects imported under permanent exhibition bond, 120
   for partial interest gifts, 204
   purchase of, 142–45
   reports, 19, 35, 145–46
   subrogation clauses, 147, 154
   valuation records, 35, 139, 154, 302, 324, 413, 416; fig. 3.10
Intaglio prints, 213–14
   inkless, 214
   measuring, 232
Inventories, 67, 249, 322, 334, 397, 407, 413, 415
   numbers, 262
   of poorly documented collections, 262–64
   records, 228, 262–64, 322; figs. E.1, N.1–2. *See also* Location records
Invertebrates, lower. *See* Lower invertebrates
Invoices for importing and exporting, 122, 125, 127–28, 134
Invoices of specimens, 174–75, 285, 292; figs. J.3, J.8; forms III.H
Ivories
   classifying, 207, 270
   importing, 121; fig. 8.3
   marking, 58, 60
   storage, 79

Jade
   classifying, 269
Japanese mending tissue, 8, 413
Jars
   classifying, 273–74

INDEX

Jewelry
  marking, 60
  storage, 81

Kinetic art objects
  classifying, 217
  handling, 16
  importing, 119

Labels and tags, 7, 29
  location of, 50–51, 54–55, 57–63 passim
  mat labels, 234; fig. E.6
  in storage areas, 48, 54, 66–67; fig. 5.1
  types of, 48, 49–52, 53–54, 57, 203; fig. A.2
  See also Marking museum objects
Lace
  classifying, 207
  marking, 50, 60
  storage, 81, 87
Lacquer
  marking, 52–53
  removing marks on, 49, 52
  storage, 81
Leadpoint, 212
Leather
  classifying, 207
  condition, 237
  marking, 48, 53, 60–61
  storage, 69, 81, 403; fig. 3.8
  See also Organic materials
Lenders
  correspondence with, 36, 288
  records of, 39, 192, 288; figs. 3.10, G.7; forms VI.B. *See also* Source-of-acquisition records
Library files. *See* Subject records
Lighting
  damage to museum objects, 8, 67, 403
  exhibition areas, 403
  passageways, 403
  storerooms, 67, 403; fig. 5.2
  work space, 8, 239; figs. 1.7, 5.2, F.2–3
Lime water, 209
Linens
  marking, 61, 63
  See also Textiles
Lithographs, 214–15
  importing, 130–31
  measuring, 232
Loading docks, 399–400; figs. 1.2–3.
  See also Receiving room; Shipping room
Loans
  agreement forms, 392; fig. 3.10
    borrower to lender, 36–37, 89–90, 127, 174, 413; fig. J.1; forms III.B, III.C.3

  lender to borrower, 90, 174, 250–51, 413; forms III.C, III.H.1–2
  conditions governing, 37, 39, 174, 249, 285; figs. G.6, J.1; forms III.B, III.C, III.H.1–2
  exchanges of specimens, 286–90, 292
  extended loans
    authorization for outgoing loans, 250
    defined, 11, 412
    marking, 48
    numbering, 21, 29, 412, 413
    records, 29–30, 33, 412; fig. 3.10
    renewal notices, 251
    return of, 30; fig. 3.10
  incoming loans, 15, 27, 29, 36–39, 46, 48, 174, 249–50, 285, 301, 413, 416
    examining for condition, 15, 16, 37–39; fig. 6.3
    marking, 29, 46, 48, 51–52
    notices to the registrar, 11, 167; forms I.A
    numbering, 13, 15, 21, 27, 29, 34, 36, 37, 249–50, 413
    receipts, 13, 34, 36, 37–39, 174, 249–50, 413; figs. 2.2, 3.10, G.6; forms III.D
    receipts of delivery, 13, 18, 30, 36, 39, 174, 414; figs. 3.10, J.3; forms III.E, III.G, III.H.1, III.H.3
    records, 36–39, 192, 249–50, 285–89, 301; figs. 3.10, G.7, J.2, J.7, K.1; forms VI. *See also* Lenders, records of
    renewal notices, 251
    return of, 18, 36, 39, 126, 127, 249, 251, 301
    review of status, 251, 288, 290, 292
    work sheets, 37, 192; fig. 3.10; forms VI.A
    See also exchanges of specimens; extended loans
  insurance, 19, 39, 89, 90–91, 93, 126, 140–42, 143
  numbers, 13, 15, 21, 27, 29, 34, 36, 37, 249–50, 413
  outgoing loans, 89–93, 250–51, 286–90, 292, 413
    authorization, 89, 250
    bills to borrowers, 90–91, 93, 174; forms I.C.1, III.F.2
    examining for condition, 89, 92–93
    notices to the registrar, 89–90, 167; forms I.A, III.A
    receipts, 93, 174, 414; figs. J.3, J.8; forms III.F, III.H
    records, 18, 93, 236, 250–51, 290, 292, 322, 334, 338; figs. J.7, N.1–2. *See also* Exhibition (or collection) history records

    return of, 93, 122, 126, 251
    review of status, 93, 236, 251, 288, 290, 292, 338
    See also exchanges of specimens; extended loans
    requests, 36, 89, 174; forms III.A
    See also Exporting; Importing
Location records, 33, 67, 93, 187, 188, 227, 228, 236, 256–57, 295, 297, 413; figs. 3.10–11, D.7, E.1, H.1–2; forms V.C.1–3, V.E. *See also* Inventory records
Logs, 29; figs. 3.9–10
Lower invertebrates
  marking, 61
  storage, 81

Mail shipments, 111, 295
  importing and exporting by, 124, 128, 134, 295
  insurance, 144
Maintenance records, 257, 295, 297
Mammals
  cataloguing, 304; fig. K.2
  marking, 61, 304–05
  storage, 81, 304–05
Manuscript albums
  marking, 58, 61
Manuscripts and documents
  classifying, 206
  marking, 49, 61
  See also Books; Printed matter
Marking museum objects, 46–63, 206, 260–61, 302–06; figs. 2.3, 4.4, 4.5, A.2
  accessions, 29, 48–51, 52–53, 57–63
  colors, 48–49, 52, 55, 56–57, 57–63 passim
  guidelines for, 51–55
  loans, 29, 46, 48, 51–52
  location of marks, 48, 49, 50–51, 54, 57–63 passim; fig. 4.4
  partial interest gifts, 203; fig. A.2
  removal of marks, 29, 46, 48, 49
  reproductions, 260
  supplies and tools, 7, 48–50, 56–57
  techniques, 49–50
  temporary deposits, 29, 46, 51–52
  unacceptable methods, 53–54
  See also types of materials and objects
Marking packing boxes, 19, 99–100, 371–72, 382; fig. 7.3
  for domestic shipments, 124
  for foreign shipments, 124–25, 372
Masks
  marking, 61
  storage, 81
Mats
  sizes, 233
  labels, 234; fig. E.6

Matting
  storage, 81
Medium, 208, 231
  classifying by, 208–18
Measuring museum objects, 41–46; figs. 3.5, 4.1–2
  dimensions defined, 412, 413, 416
  guidelines for, 42, 44–46
  by sight, 41–42, 415
  See also types of objects
Meats, livestock, poultry, and by-products
  importing, 135
Metal objects
  classifying, 206–07, 270
  condition, 239, 271–72
  handling, 68, 365
  marking, 48, 52–53, 54, 61
  packing, 100
  storage, 81–82
  See also types of metals and objects
Metal storage units, 70, 74–87 passim, 304, 305, 306, 406; figs. 5.2, 5.6–7
Mezzotints, 214
Minerals
  classifying, 206–07
  importing, 131–32
  marking, 61
  storage, 82
Miniatures
  storage, 82, 83
Mixtures and emulsions, 209
Mobiles
  classifying, 217
  measuring, 44
Models
  importing, 120, 131
Mohs scale, 268
Monotype (monoprint), 215
Montage, 216
Mosaics
  importing, 119, 129
Motor van shipments, 11–12, 109–10, 400, 409, 411
  packing for, 96, 105–06; fig. 7.9
  See also Bills of lading
Mounted works. See Unframed works
Music boxes
  storage, 82
Musical instruments
  storage, 82

Naphthalene, 72, 74–87 passim, 413
Narcotics and dangerous drugs
  importing, 135
Natural history museums
  accessioning in, 288–90, 301–02
  cataloguing in, 27, 288–90, 302–06
  computer applications, 319
  loans and exchange practices, 286–90, 292
  registration in, 3, 281–97, 301–02

Natural history specimens
  duplicates, 287–88
  fumigation, 72–73
  importing, 131–32, 285, 295
  insurance, 294
  loans and exchanges, 286–90, 292
  marking, 48
  measuring, 42; fig. 4.1
  shipping, 111, 295
  See also Endangered species; types of specimens
Nonacidic paper. See Paper, acid-free
Numbering systems
  accession numbers, 21, 22, 24, 26–27, 31, 66, 203, 205–06, 220, 228, 245–46, 262, 288–89, 301, 309, 337, 343, 409; fig. 3.7
  catalogue numbers, 27, 31, 205–06, 245–46, 289, 301, 302, 304, 305, 306, 410; figs. K.3–4
  compound numbers, 24, 26–27, 220, 244–45, 309
  inventory numbers, 262
  loan numbers, 13, 15, 21, 27, 29, 34, 36, 37, 249–50, 412, 413
  temporary deposit numbers, 13, 15, 21, 34, 415; fig. 3.9

Ocean transportation. See Shipping, types of, by ship
Oil paints
  as art medium, 209, 210
  for marking objects, 48–49, 56
Organic materials
  classifying, 270–71
  condition, 237
  storage, 69, 404
  See also types of objects
Ornithology collections. See Birds
Outgoing loans. See Loans, outgoing
Outgoing material, 18–19, 89–93, 286–88, 406
  authorization, 18, 89
  conditions governing, 90, 174; fig. G.8; forms III.C, III.H.1–2
  examining for condition, 18–19, 95, 237, 239
  insurance, 19
  loans, 89–93, 250–51, 286–90, 292, 413
  packing, 90, 92–93; fig. 7.1
  receipts of delivery, 13, 18, 30, 39, 93, 171, 174, 414; figs. 3.10, J.3; forms II.B, III.E, III.G, III.H.1, III.H.3
  records, 4, 18, 19
  reports (including releases), 11, 18, 19, 92, 167, 415; forms I.C, III.E.1
  storage, 16, 65, 239, 294
  See also Loans

Ownership
  death of owner, 18
  documentation, 34, 248, 261–64, 281–82, 293
  See also Deeds of gift

Packing, 19, 90, 92–93, 95–106, 295, 367–88, 389–94
  boxes, 12, 16, 95–96, 98–100, 106, 371–73, 376, 381–82, 389–94; figs. 7.1–9, 9.3, R.4, R.6–23, S.2
  charges billed to borrowers, 90, 93, 174; forms I.C.1, III.F.2
  climate control within boxes, 96, 99, 389–94, 405
  for domestic (and local) shipments, 96, 105–06; fig. 7.9. See also marking boxes
  for foreign shipments, 100, 124–25, 372; figs. 8.2, R.7–8. See also marking boxes
  guidelines for, 95–96, 98–100, 105, 389–92
  instructions to packers and unpackers, 90, 92, 95, 372, 381, 383, 386, 392; figs. R.24–25. See also photographs and diagrams
  insurance, 144–45
  lists, 128, 134, 383, 386–87; fig. R.26
  marking boxes, 99–100, 124–25, 371–72, 382; fig. 7.3
  materials, 12, 16, 67, 100, 105, 371–73, 376, 381–82
  thermal conductivity, 392–93
  methods
    contour-tray, 381–82; fig. R.22
    fiberboard system, 390
    flat packing, 372–73; figs. 7.2, 7.10, R.6–8
    silica gel system, 390; fig. S.2
    slide box, 376; figs. 7.5, 7.10, R.18–19
    tray packing, 373, 376, 390; figs. R.9–17
  photographs and diagrams, 12, 95, 381; fig. R.25. See also instructions to packers and unpackers
  preparing objects for, 92–93, 95, 100, 239, 367, 369–70. See also types of objects
  protection within boxes, 100, 105, 371–73, 376, 381–82, 390–91
  weights and measurements, 99, 125, 194, 197, 412, 413; figs. 7.3, 7.10
  See also Containerization; Shipments, types of; Shipping; types of objects
Padded trays, 8, 414. See also Handling, equipment

Paintings
  cataloguing, 256, 327, 329
  classifying, 206, 208–11
    medium, ground, and support, 211
    medium and technique, 209–11
    vehicle or medium, 209
  condition, 237–38, 239
  handling, 67–68, 359–60, 362–63; figs. 1.5, Q.3–7
  importing, 119, 129
  marking, 51, 62, 203; fig. A.2
  measuring, 41–42, 43–44; fig. 4.2
  packing, 96, 100, 106, 372–73, 376, 389–94; figs. 7.2, 7.5, 7.9–10, R.6–19, S.1–2
  preparing for travel, 92–93, 100, 105–06, 363, 367, 369–70; figs. 7.9, Q.8–9, R.1–3, R.5
  storage, 68, 83, 259, 360; fig. 5.9
  See also Framed works; Unframed works
Paleontology collections. See Fossils
Pallets, 106, 137, 365, 414. See also Handling, equipment
Panel paintings
  condition, 238, 239; fig. F.1
  storage, 84
Paper
  acid-free, 9, 72, 74–87 passim, 100, 167, 413; fig. 1.4
  classifying types used for prints, 231–32
  for protecting objects, 8, 72, 74–87 passim, 100, 370, 376, 404, 410, 412. See also Glassine
  for records, 9, 167, 292–93; fig. 1.4
  watermarks and trademarks, 232
  waterproof, 72, 99, 371, 416
  See also Acid migration
Paper objects and works of art on
  composition and sheet, 42, 44, 232, 411, 415
  condition, 237, 239. See also Foxing
  fumigation, 73, 84
  handling, 359, 360–64
  marking, 48, 49, 53, 54, 62
  measuring, 42, 43–44
  storage, 68, 70, 84, 259, 403; fig. 5.9
  See also Drawings; Framed Works; Pastels; Photographs; Prints; Unframed works; Watercolors
Papyrus
  storage, 84
Paradichlorobenzene (PDB), 72, 74–87 passim, 304, 414. See also Fumigation
Parchment
  storage, 84
Partial interest gifts, 414
  accessioning, 203–04
  deeds of gift, 203; fig. A.4
  insurance, 204
  records, 33, 203; figs. A.3–4

Pastels, 209, 212
  importing, 119, 129
  preparing for travel, 100, 370
Patina, 271–72
PDB. See Paradichlorobenzene
Permanent collection, 414. See Accessioning; Deaccessioning
Permanent exhibition bond, 89, 120, 122, 130, 132, 134, 414
  customs forms, 122, 132, 198; forms IX.B.1, IX.C.1
  exporting objects under, 120, 134
  insurance, 120
  records, 120
Pest control. See Fumigation
Photoengraving, 215–16
Photographic records
  architectural photographs, 257–59
  collection photographs (rights and reproductions), 34, 227, 236, 322; figs. N.1–2
  condition photographs, 16, 18–19, 34, 37, 39, 92, 95, 148, 227, 383, 387, 411; figs. 3.10, F.2–3
  of damage, 16
  descriptive (or catalogue) photographs, 34, 187, 203, 206, 224, 227, 233, 234, 249, 410, 412; figs. 3.7, E.4, P.5, P.7; forms V.C.2–3
  negative numbers, 34, 224, 227, 233, 236
  of packing, 12, 95, 381
  of partial interest gifts, 203
Photographs
  cataloguing, 256, 257–59, 322
  importing, 130–31
  marking, 53, 62
  packing, 372–73, 376
  preparing for travel, 367, 369–70
  storage, 84, 404
  See also Film; Framed works; Paper objects and works of art on; Unframed works
Photography, 215
Photomontage, 216
Planographic prints, 214–15
  measuring, 232
Plant material
  importing, 120, 122, 129, 131–32, 135
  See also Botanical specimens
Plaster block print, 213
Plaster-mold print, 215
Plaster objects
  storage, 84
Plastic
  for protecting objects, 72, 74–87 passim, 369, 406; figs. R.14–17
  storage units, 70
Plastic objects
  marking, 48, 49, 53

Plates
  accessioning sets, 26–27
  classifying, 272–73
  See also Ceramic objects
Platform trucks, 8, 414. See also Handling, equipment
Porcelain
  handling, 365–66
  marking, 58, 62
  storage, 75–76, 84
Porous materials
  marking, 53
Portfolios
  accessioning, 26
  marking, 58, 62
  See also Prints
Ports of entry, 119, 123, 414
Pots
  classifying, 273
Potsherds, 275
  accessioning, 24
  marking, 58, 62
  measuring, 42
  storage, 74, 75–76, 84
  See also Ceramic objects; Pottery; Terra-cotta
Pottery
  classifying, 269, 272–75
  marking, 52–53, 58, 62
  storage, 75–76, 84
  See also Ceramic objects; Potsherds; Terra-cotta; types of pottery objects
Pre-Columbian art
  importing, 117, 121, 129
Preservatives, 74–87 passim
  permits and reports, 285, 297
Printed matter
  importing, 119, 130
  See also Books; Manuscripts and documents
Prints
  accessioning, 228
  cataloguing, 228–36
  classifying, 207, 213–16, 231
  condition, 232–33
  handling, 359, 360–64
  importing, 118, 119, 129, 130–31
  marking, 49, 54, 62, 228, 234; fig. E.6
  matting, 228, 233
  measuring, 42, 44, 232
  packing, 107, 372–73, 376; figs. 7.10, R.20
  preparing for travel, 100, 367, 369–70
  storage, 70, 84, 233, 404; figs. 5.2, 5.5
  See also Framed works; Graphic arts objects; Paper objects and works of art on; Portfolios; Unframed works
Provenance, 31, 224, 302, 303, 414

Psychrometers, sling. *See* Sling psychrometers
Psychrometric tables, 414

Rail shipments, 110, 400
Receipts
    computer preparation, 337–38
    See also Receipts, types of
Receipts, types of
    acknowledgments of gifts, 34, 187, 202, 247–48; figs. 3.10, G.3; forms IV.A
    general, 174, 337–38; figs. 3.10, J.3; forms II.B.1, III.G, III.H.1, III.H.3
    incoming loan receipts, 13, 34, 36, 37–39, 174, 249–50, 413; figs. 2.2, 3.10, G.6; forms III.D
    outgoing loan receipts, 93, 174, 414; figs. J.3, J.8; forms III.F, III.H
    receipts of delivery, 13, 18, 30, 36, 39, 93, 171, 174, 414; figs. 3.10, J.3; forms II.B, III.E, III.G, III.H.1, III.H.3
    temporary deposit receipts, 13, 15, 34, 171, 307, 309, 415; figs. 2.2, 3.2, 3.10, L.1; forms II.A, III.H.3
Receipts of delivery, 13, 18, 30, 36, 39, 93, 171, 174, 414; figs. 3.10, J.3; forms II.B, III.E, III.G, III.H.1, III.H.3
Receiving room, 7, 398, 414; fig. 1.7. *See also* Loading dock; Shipping room
Record keeping
    analyzing information needs, 3, 33, 254–59, 320–29, 335–37, 342–43
    computerization, 4, 6, 30–31, 32, 290, 314–15, 319–34, 335–39, 340–54
    confidential information, 32
    cross-references, 27, 221, 222, 224, 234, 255, 256, 301, 303, 306, 309, 320, 326–27, 331, 334, 336, 340, 352, 354; figs. N.1–2
    duplicate records
        for additional files, 8, 30, 32, 222, 224, 227, 249, 333, 340
        for security copies, 31, 293; fig. 9.4
    management of records, 3, 6, 285–86
    preservation and maintenance of records, 8–9, 167, 292–93; fig. 1.4
    standard terminology, 32, 158, 208–18, 231–32, 239–44, 267–80, 319, 325–26, 333. *See also* Authority files

    storage and retrieval, 19, 290, 292, 333, 334, 338, 352
    See also Data processing; Forms; Records, types of
Records, types of
    accession, 3, 27, 29–33, 187, 206, 219, 227, 228, 246–47, 255, 293, 301, 302, 309, 320, 322, 324, 333, 334, 338, 409; figs. 3.10, B.1–2, D.5, G.1, K.1, L.2–3; forms V.A, V.C
    authority files, 326
    catalogue, 31–32, 187, 205–06, 219–20, 222–24, 227, 228, 230–34, 236, 248–49, 255–56, 267–80, 289–90, 302–06, 314, 322, 324–25, 333, 334, 342–45, 410; figs. 3.6, 3.10, D.3–4, D.6, E.1–4, G.5, I.1, J.4–5, K.2–4, N.1–2, N.4, P.2, P.5, P.7; forms V.B, V.C
    condition, 34, 38, 92, 143, 237, 239–44, 383, 387–88; figs. 2.4, R.27. *See also* photograph, condition
    conservation, 322; figs. I.1, N.1–2
    correspondence, 36, 187, 227, 281–82, 302, 309, 339
    deaccession, 35–36, 224, 247, 322; figs. N.1–2. *See also* inactive
    exhibit, 256–57, 285, 295, 297
    exhibition (or collection) history, 93, 188, 233; form V.E.1
    extended loans, 29–30, 33, 412; fig. 3.10
    gift
        deeds of, 34, 187, 203, 248, 261–62, 264, 339, 412; figs. A.1, A.4, G.4; forms IV.B
        partial interest, 33, 203; figs. A.3–4
    inactive, 31, 293–94, 338. *See also* deaccession
    incoming material, 4, 13, 15, 285, 301, 412. *See also* loan, incoming
    insurance and valuation, 35, 139, 154, 302, 324, 413, 416; fig. 3.10
    inventory, 228, 262–64, 322; figs. E.1, N.1–2. *See also* location
    loan
        extended, 29–30, 33, 412; fig. 3.10
        incoming, 36–39, 192, 249–50, 285–89, 301; figs. 3.10, G.7, J.2, J.7, K.1; forms VI. *See also* lenders
        lenders, 39, 192, 288; figs. 3.10, G.7; forms VI.B
        outgoing, 18, 93, 236, 250–51, 290, 292, 322, 334, 338; figs. J.7, N.1–2. *See also* exhibition (or collection) history
    location, 33, 67, 93, 187, 188, 227,

228, 236, 256–57, 295, 297, 413; figs. 3.10–11, D.7, E.1, H.1–2; forms V.C.1–3, V.E. *See also* inventory
    maintenance, 257, 295, 297
    outgoing material, 4, 18. *See also* loan, outgoing
    partial interest gifts. *See* gift
    photograph
        architectural, 257–59
        collection photographs (rights and reproductions), 34, 227, 236, 322; figs. N.1–2
        condition photographs, 16, 18–19, 34, 37, 39, 92, 95, 148, 227, 383, 387, 411; figs. 3.10, F.2–3
        of damage, 16
        descriptive (or catalogue) photographs, 34, 187, 203, 206, 224, 227, 233, 234, 249, 410, 412; figs. 3.7, E.4, P.5, P.7; forms V.C.2–3
        packing photographs, 12, 95, 381
        partial interest gifts, 203
        of reproductions, 254, 260
    restoration, 257
    source-of-acquisition, 32–33, 35–36, 187–88, 227, 234, 247, 256, 292, 301, 302, 309, 322, 324, 334, 338, 415; figs. 3.10, D.5, E.7, J.9, N.1–2; forms V.D. *See also* loan, lenders
    subject, 33, 188, 221–22, 224, 233, 234–36, 247, 255–56, 257, 258, 302, 314, 322, 327, 329, 334, 352; figs. D.1–2, E.8, G.2, N.1–2
    temporary deposit, 13, 15, 171
Registrar
    duties, 414
        building planning, 395–408
        examining objects for condition, 16, 18–19, 37–39, 92–93, 237, 239; figs. 2.4, 6.3, F.2–3
        importing and exporting, 115, 117, 122–23, 126, 285, 293, 295
        incoming and outgoing material, 11–19, 219, 283, 284, 294; figs. 2.1–4, J.7. *See also* loans
        insurance, 19, 139, 142–43, 146, 148, 284, 294
        loans, 36–39, 89–93, 249–51, 286–88, 290, 292, 301; figs. 6.3, J.7
        marking objects, 29, 41, 42, 45, 46, 48, 51, 260–61; figs. 2.3, 3.5, 4.2–5
        measuring objects, 41–42, 45; figs. 3.5, 4.2
        packing and unpacking, 4, 12, 15, 19, 95; figs. 7.1, 8.2
        records and reports, 3–4, 6, 8–9, 13, 15, 18, 19, 21, 29, 31–36,

120, 167, 203, 205–06, 219, 228, 245–47, 249, 253–59, 260, 261–64, 281–82, 283–86, 288–89, 290, 292–93, 293–94, 295–97, 301, 337–39, 340; figs. 2.1–2, 3.1–2, 3.4, 3.6–7
  shipping, 4, 11–12, 18–19, 106, 115, 117, 295
  storing and caring for objects, 4, 7, 16, 65, 219, 239, 259–60, 294, 355, 396–97; figs. 3.3, 3.8, 5.1–10
  working with museum staff and volunteers, 4, 6, 264–65, 285, 336, 345–47
  job description, 283–85
  training, 4, 6
Registration
  analyzing information needs, 3, 33, 254–59, 320–29, 335–37, 342–43
  computer applications, 290, 319, 335–39
  correcting inadequacies, 261–64
  defined, 21, 222, 415
  numbers, 205–06, 307, 309, 335, 337, 339. *See also* Numbering systems
  on site, 11; figs. 2.1, 2.3
  procedures, 3, 13–15, 18, 19, 21–39, 41–55, 93, 203, 205–06, 245–47, 249–51, 261–65, 285–92, 307–10, 335–39; figs. 3.1–8
  purpose of, 4, 21, 222, 245, 251, 281–82
  staff, 4, 6, 245, 264–65, 321, 336, 345–47; fig. 3.9
  work space, supplies, and equipment, 6–9, 41, 48–50, 56–57, 239, 292–93, 398–400; figs. 1.1–7, L.3
  See also Record keeping; Records, types of; Registration; *types of collections and museums*
Registration, types of museums and collections
  for anthropology collections, 335–39
  in art museums, 3, 205–06, 219, 228, 340
  in history museums (including historic house museums), 3, 245–47, 249–51, 253–66
  in natural history museums, 3, 281–97, 301–02
  in science and technology museums, 3, 307–10
Relative humidity. *See* Humidity, relative
Release forms, 11, 18, 92, 167, 415; forms I.C, III.E.1
Relief prints, 213
  importing, 130
  measuring, 232

Reproductions, 253
  marking, 260
  records, 254, 260
Reptiles and amphibians
  accessioning, 304
  cataloguing, 304
  marking, 62, 304
  storage, 85, 304
Research files. *See* Subject records
Resins, 209
Restoration records, 257
Rocks
  marking, 61, 62
  storage, 82, 85
Rugs
  fumigation, 72–73
  marking, 49–50, 51, 62
  storage, 85

Science materials
  importing, 119, 130
Science and technology museums
  accessioning in, 309–10
  cataloguing in, 307
  registration in, 3, 307–10
Scientific instruments
  importing, 120, 131
  marking, 62
  storage, 85
Scientific specimens
  importing, 120, 131–32
  loans and exchanges, 286–88
  storage, 66
  See also Endangered species; *types of specimens*
Scrapbooks
  marking, 58, 62
Screens, oriental
  storage, 85
Scroll paintings
  marking, 62
  storage, 85
Sculpture
  classifying, 206, 278
  handling, 67, 106, 238, 355, 357, 364–65; figs. Q.1–2
  importing, 118, 119, 120, 121, 129, 131
  marking, 62, 203; fig. A.2
  measuring, 42, 44
  packing, 99, 100, 101, 376, 381–82; figs. 7.1, 7.4, 7.7–8, 7.10, R.23
  preparing for travel, 370
  shipping, 106
  storage, 85, 365; figs. 5.1, 5.10
  weighing, 42, 238
  See also Constructions
Security and safety measures, 297, 406, 407, 408; fig. 9.2
  in building planning, 398–99, 408
  during construction, 396–97

fire and smoke alert devices, 67, 74–87 passim, 406, 412, 415
  in storerooms, 67–68, 400–08
Serigraph, 215
Shells
  classifying, 270
  marking, 62
  storage, 85
Shields
  storage, 86
Shipments, types of
  by air, 108–09, 400
    couriers, 113, 118, 124, 136–37
    importing and exporting, 123–24, 136–37
    See also Airwaybills
  by mail, 11, 295
    importing and exporting, 124, 128, 134, 295
    insurance, 144
  by motor van, 11–12, 109–10, 400, 409, 411
    packing for, 96, 105–06; fig. 7.9
    See also Bills of lading
  by rail, 110, 400
  by ship, 110, 122, 400
  See also Shipping
Shipping, 106–13
  agents, 12, 19, 107–08, 112, 113, 116, 117–18, 122, 126, 127, 137, 412
  arrangements for, 19, 90–91, 106–08, 295
  charges billed to borrowers, 91, 93
  climate control in, 109, 110, 118, 392, 405, 411
  containerization, 106, 111–12, 137, 400, 411; figs. 7.11, 8.1
  courier escort, 113, 118, 124, 136–37, 411
  documents, 106, 113, 123–24, 125, 137. *See also* Airwaybills; Bills of lading
  domestic shipments, 12, 105–06, 412. *See also* local shipments; marking boxes
  estimating costs, fig. 7.10
  foreign shipments, 12, 19, 107–08, 111, 136–37, 295, 412. *See also* marking boxes
  insurance, 19, 91, 106, 144, 146, 148
  local shipments, 11–12, 105–06
  marking boxes, 99–100, 124–25, 371–72, 382; fig. 7.3
  See also Carriers; Consignees and consignors; Exporting; Importing; Packing; Shipments, types of
Shipping room, 11, 92, 167, 239, 415; figs. 1.2–3. *See also* Loading docks; Receiving room
Silica gel, 390, 393, 415; fig. S.2

Silver
  handling, 68
  marking, 49, 61, 63
  storage, 81–82, 86
Silverpoint, 212
Sizes, 209
Skeletal material
  importing, 130
  See also Anatomy specimens; Birds; Bone; Fishes; Mammals; Reptiles and amphibians
Sketchbooks
  marking, 58, 63
Skins
  importing, 121
  See also Birds; Furs; Leather; Mammals; Reptiles and amphibians
Sling psychrometers, 8, 69, 405, 415
Small objects. See Decorative arts objects
Smoke detectors, 67, 406, 415
Soft-ground etching, 214
Solander boxes, 70, 74–87 passim, 233, 364, 415; figs. 5.2, 5.5
Source-of-acquisition records, 32–33, 35–36, 187–88, 227, 234, 247, 256, 292, 301, 302, 309, 310, 322, 324, 334, 338, 415; figs. 3.10, D.5, E.7, J.9, N.1–2; forms V.D. See also Donors; Lenders
Special exhibitions, 18, 35, 36–39, 46, 48, 126, 415; figs. 6.1–3. See also Loans; Traveling exhibitions
Stabiles, 217
Staff
  for computerization, 4, 6, 321, 336, 345–47
  crews for handling, 11–12, 355, 357, 359
  registration department, 4, 6, 245, 264–65, 321, 336, 345–47; fig. 3.9
  volunteers and part-time workers, 264–65
Stamps
  marking, 63
  storage, 70, 86
Stencil prints, 215
  importing, 130
Stone objects
  classifying, 268–69
  condition, 238, 239
  handling, 238, 365
  marking, 52–53
  storage, 74, 86
  See also Archaeological specimens; Sculpture
Storage, 415
  access, 67, 406–08
  arrangement in, 65–67, 74, 259–60, 301–02, 306; fig. 5.2

climate control, 8, 68–69, 74–87 passim, 302, 304, 404–05
during construction, 396–97
fumigation, 72–73, 74–87 passim, 303, 304, 305
labeling objects in, 48, 54, 66–67; fig. 5.1
materials, 70–72, 302–06, 404; figs. 5.2, 5.4
of packing materials and boxes, 12, 16
planning in building programs, 398–408
safety measures, 67–68, 400–08
temporary (registration department), 7, 16, 65, 239, 294, 396–97
units, 69–70, 74–87 passim, 302–06 passim, 398, 404, 406; figs. 5.1–10
work space, 67, 398–99; fig. 5.2
See also Building planning; Handling; Location records; types of museums and objects
Stretchers, 415
Study collections, 202; figs. 5.6–7
Subject records, 33, 188, 221–22, 224, 233, 234–36, 247, 255–56, 257, 258, 302, 314, 322, 327, 329, 334, 352; figs. D.1–2, E.8, G.2, N.1–2
Synthetic polymers, 209, 211

Tags and tape. See Labels; Marking museum objects
Tapestries
  importing, 118–19, 129–30
  marking, 49–50, 62, 63
  storage, 86–87
Tariff regulations. See Customs, U.S. provisions
Tempera, 210
Temperature, 415
  control during packing and shipping, 96, 99, 109, 118, 389–94, 405, 411
  control for records and files, 292
  control in storage areas, 68–69, 404–05
  See also Climate control; Condensation; Humidity, relative; Hygrothermographs
Temporary deposits
  forms, 171
  agreements for demonstrators' tools, 261; fig. H.3
  general receipts, 171, 337–38; figs. 3.10, J.3; forms II.B.1, III.G, III.H.1, III.H.3
  receipts of delivery, 13, 18, 171, 414; fig. J.3; forms II.B, III.H.1, III.H.3

temporary deposit receipts, 13, 15, 34, 171, 307, 309, 415; figs. 2.2, 3.2, 3.10, L.1; forms II.A, III.H.3
  marking, 29, 46, 51–52
  numbers, 13, 15, 21, 34, 415; fig. 3.9
  records, 13, 15, 171
  review of status, 15
Terra-cotta objects
  classifying, 269
  marking, 53, 63
  storage, 87
  See also Ceramic objects; Pottery; types of terra-cotta objects
Textiles
  cataloguing, 303
  classifying, 207, 270, 303
  fumigation, 72–73
  importing, 135
  marking, 48, 49–50, 53, 63, 302
  storage, 69, 71, 74, 87, 259, 302–03, 403
  See also Rugs; Tapestries
Thymol, 73, 74–87 passim, 416. See also Fumigation
Tools (museum objects)
  classifying, 248, 276–78
  measuring, 42
Tools, demonstrators'
  at historic sites, 253
  marking, 260
  records, 254, 260–61; fig. H.3
  storage, 260
Toys
  storage, 82
  See also Dolls
Trademarked articles
  importing, 121, 135–36
Transportation. See Shipments, types of; Shipping
Traveling exhibitions
  documents accompanying, 383, 386–87, 392; figs. R.24–27
  preparation of, 367
  shipping, 400
Truck shipments. See Motor van shipments

Ultraviolet filter, 8, 67, 416
Unframed works
  handling, 8, 364
  importing and exporting, 126
  storage, figs. 5.2, 5.5
  See also Drawings; Framed works; Paintings; Paper objects and works of art on; Pastels; Photographs; Prints; Watercolors
Unmounted works. See Unframed works
Unpacking, 12; fig. 8.2

instructions, 12, 95, 372, 383, 386; figs. R.24–25
See also Packing

Valuation records, 35, 139, 154, 302, 324, 413, 416; fig. 3.10
Vapona, 72, 74–87 passim. See also Fumigation
Vertebrate paleontology collections. See Fossils
Vessels
　classifying, 272–75
　See also Ceramic objects; *types of materials*

Water damage
　condensation, 68, 405–06, 411
　leaks, 396, 398, 405–06
　from sprinklers, 406
Watercolors, 209
　light vulnerability, 403
　marking, 59, 63
　measuring, 42, 44
　packing, 372–73, 376; figs. 7.10, R.20
　preparing for travel, 367, 369–70
　storage, 84, 87
　See also Framed works; Paper objects and works of art on; Unframed works
Waterproof paper, 72, 99, 371, 416
Wax crayons, 212
Waxes, 209
Weapons
　classifying, 276–78
　marking, 63
　measuring, 46
　storage, 87
　See also Arms and armor; Firearms
Weighing museum objects, 42, 238; fig. 4.3
Weighing shipments, 99, 125, 194, 197; figs. 7.3, 7.10
　gross weight, 99, 125, 412
　legal weight, 125
　net weight, 125, 413
　tare weight, 125, 197, 415
Wood engraving, 213
Woodcuts, 213
　measuring, 232
　importing, 130–31
Wooden objects
　classifying, 207, 270
　condition, 237
　marking, 48, 53, 54, 63
　storage, 87
　See also Panel paintings
Wooden storage units, 69, 74–87 passim, 303, 306, 404, 406
Work sheets
　for cataloguing, 31–32, 187, 203, 228, 230–33, 331, 333, 344, 416; figs. 3.4, 3.6, 3.10, E.2–3, N.4, P.2; forms V.B
　for cataloguing by computer, 331, 333, 344; figs. N.4, P.2
　for loans, 37, 192; fig. 3.10, forms VI.A
Work space
　registration department, 6–8, 239, 398; figs. 1.1, 1.7, F.2–3
　shipping and receiving area, 11, 92, 167, 399–400, 415; figs. 1.2–3
　in storerooms, 69–70, 400–08; figs. 5.1–2
　See also Building planning

Zincograph, 215
Zoological specimens
　cataloguing, 289
　fumigation, 72–73
　importing, 131–32, 295
　insurance, 294
　loans and exchanges, 286–88, 290, 292
　marking, 63
　shipping, 111, 295
　See also Animals; Endangered species; *types of specimens*